Investment Analysis for Real Estate Decisions

2nd Edition

Gaylon E. Greer

Morris S. Fogelman
Chair of Excellence in Real Estate,
Professor of Finance
Memphis State University

Michael D. Farrell

Adjunct Assistant Professor of Finance
DePaul University

Longman Financial Services Publishing
a division of Longman Financial Services Institute, Inc.

© 1988 by Longman Group USA Inc.
Published by Longman Financial Services Publishing, Inc.,
a division of Longman Financial Services Institute, Inc.

Printed in the United States of America.

88 89 90 10 9 8 7 6 5 4 3 2 1

Executive Editor: Richard Hagle
Project Editor: Carole Bilina
Cover and Interior Design: Edwin Harris
Manager, Composition Services: Gayle Sperando
Copy Editor: Chris Benton
Proofreader: Maija Balagot
Indexer: Karen Schenkenfelder
Typesetting: Graphic World

Library of Congress Cataloging-in-Publication Data

Greer, Gaylon E.
    Investment analysis for real estate decisions.

    Includes bibliographies and index.
    1. Real estate investment—Decision making.
2. Investment analysis. I. Farrell, Michael D.
II. Title.
HD1382.5.G74   1988   333.63'24   87-36657
ISBN 0-88462-017-4

Contents

Preface

Uniform praise for the first edition of *Investment Analysis for Real Estate Decisions* made us reluctant to tinker further. Critics applauded the book for coherently integrating the diverse elements of economics, law, finance and taxation that are at the core of real estate investment analysis, and for being at the same time readable and intelligently challenging.

However, even the best book can be improved. Moreover, new income tax law and evolving market structures have largely outdated texts with pre-1987 copyrights. This new edition incorporates the latest tax provisions and includes discussion and analysis of the most recent innovations in market instruments and structures.

Determined that the second edition should be more than a mere reshuffling and updating of old components, we asked for advice from prominent real estate professors in the nation's top programs. With their help we have produced a book that gives students a competitive edge in today's sophisticated real estate investment arena.

READABILITY

Style is the ability to write with clarity, efficiency and grace, precisely what needs to be written; no more, no less. Pursuing this goal mercilessly, we eradicated jargon, condensed background material and simplified explanations wherever possible. Moreover, prose economy has enabled us to accommodate diverse learning goals in a single book.

A COMPREHENSIVE FRAMEWORK

Each chapter opens with an introduction that sets the tone for chapter coverage. Chapter subjects are expanded and elaborated through copious examples, exercises and case-like presentations that bridge the gap between theory and practice. Each chapter ends with a summary of key points and two kinds of questions—review questions that reinforce important chapter concepts and discussion questions that encourage consideration of ideas that go beyond the text's immediate scope. Lists of suggested readings point students toward additional information sources.

Chapters are organized into eight parts, each of which begins with its own introduction and ends with a short case problem that shows the operation of principles as they occur in the real world—integrated rather than isolated. Part case problems are coordinated so that they can be treated as a continuing case problem throughout the text.

This modular organization enables students to draw the logical connections between and among central concepts of real estate investment analysis and to understand their application in real-life situations.

A BOOK OF MANY TEACHING PATHS

One professor's textual irrelevancy is another's necessity. Some emphasize theory; others stress institutions. Some like case analysis; others abhor it. Instructional preferences are often conditioned by the academic department that houses the subject—market research is important here, capital budgeting there; one school accentuates real estate economics, another the federal income tax.

Investment Analysis for Real Estate Decisions resolves this dilemma by combining a wide range of material into a comprehensive analytical framework. It offers an accommodating reading path for every instructional preference. For example:

- For a theoretical emphasis, omit Parts Seven and Eight.
- To stress application, omit Chapters 3, 4, 5, 15, 16 and 19.
- Chapter 10 provides sufficient income tax information for most courses; yet, reading all of Part Four will instill a deeper insight into tax law.

To simplify selection of reading assignments, the teaching manual maps several alternative paths. Actual choices will depend on what is to be stressed and on the number of classroom contact hours available. In all cases, the text's organization will prove refreshingly adaptive and the teaching manual surprisingly helpful.

RATIONAL ORGANIZATION

Each part of the text covers a subject fundamental to informed investment decision making. To guide students in their study, each part begins with a brief explanation of purpose:

- Part One sets the stage by explaining fundamental terms and concepts used throughout the text. It describes a widely accepted analytical framework and introduces relevant basic economic ideas.
- Part Two emphasizes the essential nature of market research and introduces key marketing concepts.
- Part Three shows how market research is used to estimate future benefits from ownership and provides essential information about mortgage financing.

- Part Four is a protracted discussion of the income tax as it applies to real estate investment decisions.
- Part Five explains ratio analysis and presents an extended lesson on compound interest and discount. It includes an appendix on financial calculations and a separate chapter on computerized analysis.
- Part Six introduces traditional and modern risk analysis. The chapters permit selective degrees of immersion in this complex yet essential subject.
- Part Seven illustrates discounted cash-flow analysis to help make investment decisions regarding several major categories of real estate.
- Part Eight is a unique section on real estate as a security. A reviewer describes this as the most thoroughly researched presentation of the subject that he has seen.

A COMPREHENSIVE TEACHING PACKAGE

To make life a little easier, a complementary package of teaching aids is available. It includes:

- a comprehensive instructor's manual with detailed lecture notes,
- answers for end-of-chapter review questions,
- notes on utilizing the open-ended discussion questions at the end of each chapter,
- solutions for end-of-part case problems,
- transparency masters for all text illustrations and
- an extensive test bank.

ACKNOWLEDGMENTS

A veritable who's who of real estate educators collaborated to assure the quality and usefulness of *Investment Analysis for Real Estate Decisions*. The first edition was reviewed by Joseph Albert, then at North Texas State University; James H. Boykin, Virginia Commonwealth University; Roger Cannaday, University of Illinois, Urbana-Champaign; William Goolsby, University of Tennessee; Robert Mendelson, Southern Illinois University, Edwardsville; Wade Ragas, University of New Orleans; and James Vernor, Georgia State University. Reviewers for the second edition were Jaime R. Alvayay, *North Texas State University;* Roger E. Cannaday, *University of Illinois at Urbana-Champaign;* Charles P. Edmonds III, *Auburn University;* Charles F. Floyd, *University of Georgia;* Hans R. Isakson, *University of Texas at Arlington;* and Leonard Zumpano, *University of Alabama*. Their comments were thoughtful, incisive and valuable.

Financial assistance from the family of Morris S. Fogelman enabled the authors to spend additional time refining this revised edition. The text's quality is due in substantial part to this extra attention; we gratefully acknowledge the Fogelman family's role in its success.

PART ONE

Basic Issues in Real Estate Investment Analysis

Investors who consider including real estate assets in their portfolios face a bewildering array of alternatives. They must select from among myriad combinations of opportunities that differ not only in the amount and timing of expected investment benefits but also in the degree of confidence with which investors hold their expectations.

Rational decision making under such circumstances taxes even the most educated and experienced investment analysts. Approaches range from snap judgments based on little more than hunches or "hot tips" to carefully calculated decisions backed by research and sophisticated analysis. These first three chapters lay the groundwork for the latter approach. The nature of the investment decision, the market environment in which decisions must be made and basic considerations incorporated into rational investment analysis are all addressed in Part One.

CHAPTER 1

The Real Estate Investment Decision

INTRODUCTION

A successful medical doctor buys a $100,000 interest in a limited partnership formed to develop shopping centers; a college professor puts $10,000 into a real estate investment trust; a real estate broker buys a $500,000 apartment building; a manufacturing firm invests millions in a new plant; the U.S. government spends billions to create a dam and reservoir system. All these represent real estate investment decisions. As diverse as they appear, they all have a common element. Each represents sacrifice of something now for the prospect of later benefits. The sacrifice is immediate and certain; anticipated rewards will be received in the future, if at all. Moreover, both the timing and the magnitude of the benefit usually cannot be predicted with absolute certainty.

In these and all other investment decisions, estimates of total costs and benefits must be coupled with forecasts of the timing of disbursements and receipts. Rational decisions are then possible, based upon comparison of expected amounts and timing of receipts and expenditures and upon the degree of certainty with which expectations are held.

The problem of choosing between certain present benefits and uncertain future receipts is frequently compounded by the investor's need to select from a variety of opportunities. Several options might be sufficiently attractive to justify sacrifice of immediate gratification in order to magnify future potential, yet economic resources might not permit exploiting all these provisionally acceptable alternatives. Rational investors need a methodology for consistently ranking investment opportunities in order to pick among alternatives that, in the aggregate, exceed available resources.

STATE OF THE INVESTMENT ANALYSIS ART

Great strides have been made in real estate investment analysis techniques during recent years. Decision making has been enhanced by adapting analytical tools and techniques pioneered by economists and corporate financial analysts. As recently as 1970 this was not the case. Richard U. Ratcliff and Bernhard Schwab, writing that year in the *Appraisal Journal,* noted that terms such as *probability, utility function* and *time value of money,* used extensively in modern investment decision theory, were virtually absent from real estate appraisal and investment literature.[1]

Since Ratcliff and Schwab's seminal article there has been a steady stream of literature seeking to graft modern decision theory onto more traditional real estate investment techniques. Investors, however, have been slow to incorporate these new analytical tools into their decision making. In a 1976 survey conducted by Robert J. Wiley, almost one-half of a group of large institutional investors stated that they ignore income tax considerations in their investment decisions. More than one-half claimed to rely primarily upon the relationship between their initial cash outlay and the first year's projected cash receipts. Less than one-third of survey respondents reported adjusting expected cash receipts to account for differences in timing, a relatively simple technique widely employed in other investment analysis fields.[2]

Yet progress has been made. A similar survey involving institutional investors was conducted in 1981 by E. J. Farragher. Among the 354 respondent firms, an overwhelming majority reported that they employ feasibility analysis and long-run cash flow analysis on some or all of their projects. Sixty-two percent said they do adjust for differences in the timing of expected cash flows. Farragher found little or no indication of reliance upon rules of thumb, which dominated real estate investment decision making for so long.[3]

Individual investors and real estate consultants serving their needs are also moving toward modern investment analysis. A recent survey of members of the American Association of Individual Investors indicates that, among those that include real estate in their portfolios, approximately 40 percent adjust for differences in the timing of expected cash flows.[4]

There is virtually no end to the elaboration possible in modern decision models. Expenditure of sufficient time and economic resources can almost always generate additional information. The value of each increment of information or elaboration, however, must always be weighed against its cost. When additional cost approaches the additional value expected to be derived, the analytical model has reached its maximum level of cost-effectiveness. This simple proposition is evidently recognized by sophisticated investment analysts:

Respondents to the Farragher survey generally employed analytical techniques comparable to those used by the nation's 1,000 largest corporations, but the more sophisticated techniques were not used on all projects.[5]

REAL ESTATE ASSETS AND REAL ESTATE SERVICES

Real estate investors form a link in a complex chain of economic relationships designed to provide a good that incorporates both *shelter* and *locational benefits*. The shelter element is self-evident; the question of locational benefit is more subtle. The combination of shelter and locational benefits provided by the right to occupy a three-dimensional space for a specified time period is frequently referred to as *real estate service*. Thus defined, real estate services are not to be confused with personal services that may be somehow related to real estate, such as brokerage, appraisal or property management.

Relationships among activities at various sites require movement of people, goods and information. These relationships are called *linkages,* and they give rise to the costs (in terms of time, stress and dollar outlays) of overcoming the problem of distance between linked sites. Desire to secure a site that minimizes such costs, called *transfer costs,* creates competition among would-be users. This competition is evidenced by the rent that users are willing to pay and is a reflection of variation in the locational advantages various sites bestow.

Locational benefits are unique to the activity carried on at a particular site and are related to the functional needs of the activity. The very concept of locational benefit, therefore, is meaningless outside the context of a specific proposed use. James A. Graaskamp expresses this fact by noting that locational value is in the mind of the user rather than inherent in a site.[6]

The combination of shelter and locational benefit afforded by a site is secured by acquiring the right to occupy a premises for some specified time period. This period might be for as little as a stipulated number of hours, or it may extend into perpetuity. In each instance, *time* is a dimension that must be associated with the dimensions of length, width and height when describing the end product of real estate processes. Units of real estate service might be measured, for example, as cubic feet of warehouse space per annum or square feet of apartment space per month.

Real estate investors acquire interests in real estate that permit them to offer real estate service to ultimate users. The service (shelter and location) might be purchased by users as a *consumer good* (something desired as an end in itself) or as a *factor of production* (something to be utilized in producing other goods or services). In either case, the real estate from which the service is vended is a *capital good* whose value is a function of the market value of the service itself. Analysts contemplating the advisability of acquiring specific real property therefore must address the question of the market value of service the real estate will generate.

REAL ESTATE AS AN INVESTMENT

Real estate investors, either directly or indirectly, purchase a stream of anticipated future cash receipts that are expected to be generated by real estate. These cash receipts may result from rental operations, from refinancing the real property interest, from cash savings through offsetting otherwise taxable income with tax-deductible losses from the real property interest or from net profits upon resale of the property interest. The price an investor is prepared to pay for a defined property interest depends in part upon the amount and timing of these anticipated receipts and upon the degree of confidence with which expectations are held. It also depends upon the investor's tolerance for bearing risk and upon the relative attractiveness of alternative opportunities.

Passive and Active Investors

Many investors, called *active investors*, acquire direct title to real property in which they invest. They either oversee the property themselves or hire professional management firms to handle day-to-day management chores. Others, called *passive investors*, place assets with professional money managers who in turn acquire interests in real property. Passive investors also frequently acquire shares in corporations or partnerships that hold extensive real property interests. In all these instances the investor holds an interest in an enterprise whose products include real estate services and whose activities can be analyzed in much the same manner as any other enterprise that requires capital expenditures. The ultimate desirability of the investment depends upon the relationship between the assets the investor places at risk and the amount and timing of cash receipts therefrom.

Equity Investors and Mortgage Lenders

A distinction is usually made between investment in *real assets* such as land and buildings and investment in *financial assets* such as mortgage-backed promissory notes. Many authorities claim the distinction is purely semantic. It does, however, serve a very practical pedagogical function. Although investors in each instance are giving up certain and immediate liquid assets for uncertain expectations of future gain, analytical techniques employed in analyzing opportunities in one category are not necessarily directly applicable to the other. In this text we define *real estate investment* as acquiring an ownership or a leasehold interest in real property.

To illustrate the distinction, consider the typical arrangement associated with an apartment building. The apartments themselves are real assets (land, bricks, mortar and so forth). Some of the financial resources necessary to gain control over the asset will usually come from direct investment—by a wealthy professional seeking portfolio diversification, perhaps. The majority of the funds for such a project, however, are usually provided by an institutional lender in exchange for mortgage-secured promissory notes with repayment promised in fixed amounts on a specified schedule over many years. In a strict sense, both the institutional lender and the individual who contributes personal resources are investors. But as a matter of analytical convenience, we will exclude the mortgage lender from our discussion of investment analysis and decision making.

Assets that constitute a direct equity claim to real assets, however, do fit our definition of investments. Shares of stock in a corporation or partnership shares in a *syndication,* which in turn takes a direct equity or leasehold position in real property, represent indirect investment in the real property. Such investment ventures are amenable to *fundamental analysis,* the type of analysis discussed in this text, and therefore fit well into our analytical framework. Fundamental analysis, a term used by investment analysts, is the investigation of the underlying business undertaken by the firm whose securities are being considered. This distinguishes the approach from the alternative of simply investigating the market behavior of the shares themselves, an approach often called *technical analysis.*

Investment and Speculation

A distinction is sometimes made between *investment* and *speculation.* This distinction is too tenuous to be useful for our purposes, however, and no such dichotomy is drawn. *Webster's New Collegiate Dictionary* defines *speculation* as the assumption of business risk in hope of gain; more specifically, purchase or sale in hope of benefiting from market fluctuations. It defines *investment* as the commitment of money in hopes of financial gain. These definitions are sufficiently similar to merit classification as a single genre.

REAL ESTATE INVESTMENT PERFORMANCE

Comparison of real estate investment outcomes with consequences of investment in alternative assets has been difficult due to a dearth of reliable information about real estate yields. Yet major efforts by research scholars have generated useful data. These efforts have been abetted to no small extent by a pronounced trend toward holding real property in securities form.

Early Efforts to Evaluate Real Estate

During the 1960s a number of highly respected researchers attempted to assess the performance of real estate investments. The most common objective of these studies was to compare real estate portfolios with those comprised of stocks and bonds. Findings varied widely, due to the different premises employed by researchers. Stephen E. Roulac performed yeoman's service for the profession by summarizing these findings in an excellent article published in the *Journal of Portfolio Management.* He concluded that only limited generalizations can be drawn from the studies.[7]

Major shortcomings of past research efforts, as reported by Roulac,[8] include:

1. Unspecified or noncomparable investment strategies and time periods;
2. Naive and misleading measures of return;
3. Insufficient and unreliable information concerning actual outcomes from which conclusions were drawn; data sometimes assumed or unverified;
4. Conclusions drawn from unrepresentative data.

Even though early researchers disagreed about expected returns from real estate investment, they consistently found real estate investment returns to be more predictable and less volatile than returns to common stocks. Thus, a rather extensive body of research supports the thesis that real estate investment is generally less risky than investment in the stock market.[9] *Risk,* as discussed at length in Part Six, is generally defined as variability of returns. Roulac concludes that over an extended period real estate tends to generate returns roughly comparable to those available from common stocks, while offering significantly greater predictability of returns.[10]

More Recent Evidence

A recent surge of interest in real estate assets on the part of institutional investors and a phenomenal growth in public offerings of securities by real estate investment firms have produced data that permit much more precise comparisons of real estate returns with those available from investment alternatives. Research results, however, are heavily influenced by the period from which data are drawn.

Data from a 13-year period prior to the mid-1970s, for example, led Dennis G. Kelleher to conclude that a geographically diversified portfolio of multitenant rental property would have outperformed the Standard & Poor's composite index of 500 widely held common stocks throughout most of the period. Performance differentials were modest, however, and are rendered doubtful by techniques used to estimate real estate values at the end of each year of the measuring period.[11] Nonetheless, Kelleher's findings are supported by data reported by James Webb and C. F. Sirmans for the same general period.[12]

In contrast, Stephen Roulac and Robert Hatheway report that equal sums invested in each of eight publicly offered real estate limited partnership ventures that bought properties between December 1970 and August 1973 and sold all the properties by early 1983 would have yielded before-tax rates of return in excess of 12 percent per annum.[13] This compares more than favorably with a portfolio of common stocks drawn proportionally from the Standard & Poor's stock index, which would have yielded less than 5.5 percent per annum (before taxes) during the same period.

Yet data from the 1980s show equally dramatic results favoring common stocks over real estate. From 1982 through 1987 the stock market surged while real estate values stumbled. Early research conclusions are that publicly offered real estate syndications, on average, will produce after-tax yields roughly comparable with those available from Treasury bills.[14]

SUMMARY

Real estate investors make an immediate and certain sacrifice of current purchasing power for the prospect of future economic benefit. Investment proposals are evulated by comparing the magnitude of the sacrifice with the quantity and timing of expected benefits, and by considering the level of certainty with which expectations are held. Adjusting for time and uncertainty permits comparison between various alternative proposals.

The adoption of modern decision theory and analytical techniques by real estate investment analysts is a relatively recent phenomenon. Survey results indicate that investors seldom used time-adjusted measures of return or considered income tax consequences as recently as 1975. More recent survey data reveal that at least institutional investors are using modern analytical techniques.

The ultimate product of real estate processes is real estate service, shelter and locational benefits stemming from the right to occupy defined three-dimensional space for specified time periods.

Attempts to measure and compare real estate investment returns with returns on other investments have been inconclusive. Outcomes are heavily influenced by the dates over which performance is measured.

NOTES

1. Richard U. Ratcliff and Bernhard Schwab, "Contemporary Decision Theory and Real Estate Investment," *Appraisal Journal* (April 1970). (Reprinted in *Readings in Real Estate Investment Analysis,* vol. 1, p. 95. Cambridge, MA: Ballinger Pub. Co., 1977.)

2. Robert J. Wiley, "Real Estate Investment Analysis: An Empirical Study," *Appraisal Journal* 44 (October 1976): 586–92.

3. Edward J. Farragher, "Investment Decision-Making Practices of Equity Investors in Real Estate," *Real Estate Appraiser and Analyst* 48 (Summer 1982): 36–41.

4. Gaylon Greer and Michael Farrell, "Who Invests in Real Estate," research paper presented to the American Real Estate Society, Orlando, FL, April 1987.

5. Farragher, op. cit., 38.

6. James A. Graaskamp, *Fundamentals of Real Estate Development* (Washington, DC: The Urban Land Institute, 1980), 5.

7. Stephen E. Roulac, "Can Real Estate Returns Outperform Common Stocks?" *Journal of Portfolio Management* (Winter 1976): 26–43.

8. Ibid., 27.

9. Ibid., 31.

10. Ibid., 38.

11. Dennis G. Kelleher, "How Real Estate Stacks Up to the S & P 500," *Real Estate Review* (Summer 1976): 60–65.

12. James R. Webb and C. F. Sirmans, "Yields for Selected Types of Real Property vs. the Money and Capital Markets," *The Appraisal Journal* (April 1982): 228–42.

13. Stephen E. Roulac and Robert Hatheway, "Investment Returns to Limited Partners of Public Real Estate Programs," *Real Estate Securities Journal* (Summer 1982): 7–17.

14. See for example, Ronald C. Rodgers and James E. Owers, "The Investment Performance of Real Estate Limited Partnerships," *AREUEA Journal* 13 (1985): 153–66. Also see Steven D. Kaplin and Arthur L. Schwartz, Jr., "Investing in Real Estate Limited Partnerships," *AAII Journal* (September 1986): 8–12.

RECOMMENDED READINGS

Creedy, Judith, and Norbert F. Wall. *Real Estate Investment by Objective*. New York: McGraw-Hill, 1979.

Greer, Gaylon E. *The Real Estate Investment Decision*. Lexington, MA: Lexington Books, 1979, pp. 1–90.

Greer, Gaylon E., and Michael D. Farrell. *Contemporary Real Estate: Theory and Practice*. Hinsdale, IL: The Dryden Press, 1983, p. 257.

Jaffe, Austin J., and C.F. Sirmans, *Fundamentals of Real Estate Investment*. Englewood Cliffs, NJ: Prentice-Hall, 1986, pp. 1–20.

Ratcliff, Richard U. *Modern Real Estate Valuation*. Madison, WI: Democrat Press, 1965, pp. 8–35.

——— . *Real Estate Analysis*. New York: McGraw-Hill, 1961, pp. 1–12.

Seldin, Maury. *Real Estate Investment for Profit Through Appreciation*. Reston, VA: Reston Publishing Company, Inc., pp. 1–25.

REVIEW QUESTIONS

1. What are the major benefits provided by real estate assets?
2. Discuss the concept of linkages in real estate.
3. Discuss real estate as an investment. What are investors really purchasing when they invest in real estate?
4. Describe the differences between passive and active investors.
5. Discuss the concepts of fundamental analysis and technical analysis. Which is appropriate in real estate investment analysis?

DISCUSSION QUESTIONS

1. What difficulties might a researcher face when trying to compare the long-term investment performance of real estate and securities portfolios?

2. Real estate and mortgage markets are closely intertwined: Most new properties are financed in part with a mortgage-secured note, and there is an active secondary market for both mortgage notes and real property. Under what circumstances would you expect the value of these assets in the secondary market to move in the same direction? Under what circumstances would they most likely move in opposite directions?

CHAPTER 2

Risk, Return and Investment Value

INTRODUCTION

Investment analysis and decision making is at best a burdensome task, requiring consideration of a wide range of disparate yet interwoven elements. The analytical chore is greatly simplified when reduced to a consistently applied system. This book presents such a system, often called a *decision model*, which is widely used for evaluating real estate investment proposals. The model is not unique to real estate, however. In spite of its complexity, real estate investment analysis is not fundamentally different from decision making in other investment areas. Whatever the exact nature of the investment vehicle, for those schooled in modern financial analysis the investment decision process does not vary.

- *Step One*. Estimate the stream of expected benefits. Investment assets are desired only for the benefits ownership is expected to bestow. Investors in effect purchase a set of assumptions about the ability of a property to produce income over the proposed ownership period. Because different investors may make varying assumptions, there will not be general agreement about the investment merits of most properties.
- *Step Two*. Adjust for timing differences among expected streams of benefits flowing from investment alternatives. As a general rule, benefits are the more highly prized the sooner they are expected to be received. This general preference for more immediate receipt, often called *time preference for money,* requires that deferred benefits be adjusted by a process called *discounting*.
- *Step Three*. Adjust for differences in perceived risk associated with investment alternatives. Just as investors are not indifferent to the timing of expected

benefits, neither are they indifferent to the degree of certainty with which expectations are held. Risk is commonly interpreted as the possibility of variation between a set of assumptions about future benefits and the benefits actually received.

- *Step Four*. Rank alternatives in terms of relative desirability of the perceived risk-return combinations they embody. Attitudes toward risk differ, but rational investors seek financial return as a reward for bearing the risk associated with investment ventures. Most investors are averse to risk and will therefore insist upon additional expected benefits for every additional increment of perceived risk associated with an investment alternative. Because they differ in their degree of risk aversion, investors will not agree upon the required trade-off between risk and expected return.

The investment analysis system explained in this book represents an application of this four-step process. It is an adaptation of capital-budgeting techniques long employed among corporate financial analysts. It includes explicit recognition of the probabilistic nature of the forecast benefit stream and incorporates an adjustment for differences in timing of expected cash inflows and outflows. Techniques you will learn here are applicable regardless of the nature of the investment vehicle.

FUNDAMENTAL CONCEPTS

The investment perspective requires a slightly different view of real estate from that to which many are accustomed. An investor must develop a perception of the worth of a property as an addition to his or her personal portfolio and compare this with an estimate of the probable price at which the asset can be acquired. Neither the worth to the individual investor nor the price at which the property can be acquired can be determined with certainty. Investors must work with ranges within which they expect these values to lie. To facilitate discussion of this issue, several terms and concepts are introduced.

Transaction Price.   The price at which a transaction has actually taken place, the *transaction price,* is an indisputable historical fact. In the absence of interference with normal market relationships, a transaction price is the outcome of the bargaining process between a buyer and a seller. Transaction prices form the basis for most estimates of prices at which future transactions are likely to occur.

Most Probable Selling Price.   *Most probable selling price* is a probabilistic estimate of the price at which a future transaction will occur. It is a prediction of the transaction price that will emerge if a property is offered for sale under current market conditions for a reasonable time at terms of sale that currently predominate for such properties.

Market Value.   As the term is generally employed by appraisers, *market value* refers to the most probable price a property will bring in a competitive and open market under all conditions requisite to a fair sale. The prevailing definition presumes both that buyer and seller act prudently and knowledgeably and that the price is not affected by undue stimuli experienced by either party.

Whereas the market value concept assumes equal bargaining strength between buyer and seller, most probable selling price recognizes differences in the relative bargaining strength of the parties to a transaction. Market value is based on the "prudent investor" concept and places the parties to a transaction in equal bargaining positions. Most probable selling price recognizes that buyer and seller are frequently unequal in knowledge and bargaining strength and that "undue stimulus" frequently exists.

Subjective Value.   The value of a property to the present or a prospective owner, frequently called *subjective value,* is unique to the individual and need not be closely related to market value or most probable selling price. Subjective value represents the worth to the individual of assumed future benefits of ownership. Since there will not be precise agreement on the amount of these future benefits or upon the appropriate adjustment for waiting and for uncertainty, subjective value is necessarily unique for each individual.

Investment Value.   The subjective value of an investment property to a particular investor is frequently referred to as *investment value*. It reflects the investor's assumptions about the future ability of the property to produce revenue, about the likely holding period, selling price, tax consequences, risk, available financing and all other factors that affect expected net benefits of ownership.

Transaction Range.   Investment value from the present owner's perspective sets the lower end of the range of possible transaction prices. Investment value from the perspective of the most likely buyer determines the upper end of the range. The owner will not take less than the property's investment value to him or her, and the prospective buyer will not pay more than his or her perception of the property's investment value. The actual transaction price will fall somewhere in between these extremes.

Investment value from the owner–prospective seller's point of view is the minimum price he or she will be willing to take in exchange for the property, based upon assumptions about the remaining future benefits of ownership. To be motivated to sell, the present owner must conclude that the most probable selling price (V_p in Figure 2.1) is greater than investment value (V_s in Figure 2.1).

From the prospective buyer's point of view, investment value is the maximum amount he or she is justified in paying for the property, based on assumptions about the future benefits of ownership. To be motivated to buy, the prospective purchaser must conclude that investment value (V_b in Figure 2.2) is greater than the most probable selling price (V_p in Figure 2.2). Note that

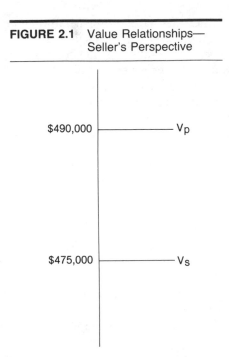

FIGURE 2.1 Value Relationships—
Seller's Perspective

buyer and seller need not agree on the most probable selling price. In our example the seller estimates the most probable selling price to be $490,000 (Figure 2.1), whereas the prospective buyer estimates it to be $480,000 (Figure 2.2).

For a transaction to be possible, investment value from the prospective buyer's perspective must be greater than from the prospective seller's point of view. Whereas the prospective buyer forms an opinion concerning the highest price he or she is justified in paying, the prospective seller arrives at a conclusion concerning the lowest price he or she is justified in accepting. These conclusions form the extremities of a range of possible transaction prices. Each party knows only the value at one end of the range and will try (usually unsuccessfully) to get the other party to reveal the opposite extreme. The actual transaction price will fall somewhere within this range, as depicted in Figure 2.3. The exact price within this range will depend upon the relative bargaining strengths and skills of the participants in the transaction.

ESTIMATING INVESTMENT VALUE: AN OVERVIEW

An investor who buys a particular property is in effect buying a set of assumptions about the ability of the property to generate cash flows over the period and the likely market value of the property at the end of the proposed holding

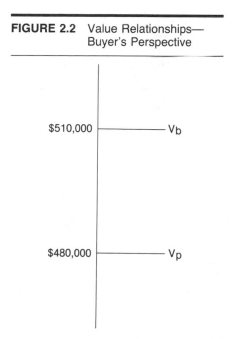

FIGURE 2.2 Value Relationships—
Buyer's Perspective

period. That the physical structure is tangential to the investment decision is sometimes difficult for students to grasp. But soundness of construction, distinguished architecture and harmonious surroundings are relevant to the investment decision only to the extent these factors affect the flow of benefits from ownership or control.

Of course, a prospective investor is interested in more than the amount of anticipated benefits. Of equally vital concern are when the benefits might be received and the certainty with which expectations are held. These three concerns—*amount, timing* and *certainty of receipt*—determine the relative value of all investment alternatives.

Benefits expected to be received in the far distant future add less to a property's investment value than do those whose anticipated receipt is more imminent. In general, the further in the future expected receipts lie, the less is their value today. The exact nature of the trade-off will differ among investors, depending upon each individual's time preference for money.

Expected benefits that are viewed with a greater degree of certainty will be more highly valued, other things being equal, than will those considered problematical. The exact trade-off between expectations and uncertainty varies with each individual investor, depending upon his or her degree of risk aversion.

Financial analysts have long recognized that the value of a business enterprise is the sum of the value of the outstanding debt plus the value of the equity. Real estate valuation theory also recognizes value of an investment property as the sum of the debt and equity positions. This is evidenced in valuation (ap-

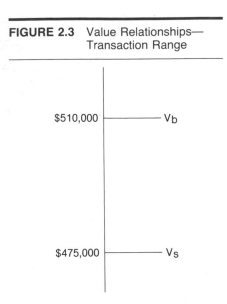

FIGURE 2.3   Value Relationships—
Transaction Range

praisal) techniques in which market value is estimated by capitalizing the property's expected net operating income by an estimate of the weighted average cost of debt and equity capital.

Investment value can, therefore, be expressed as the *present value of the equity position plus the present value of the debt position*. Present value of debt is the amount of available mortgage financing or the outstanding mortgage loan balance. Present value of the equity position is the value today of the anticipated after-tax cash flow during a prospective ownership period and of the anticipated proceeds from disposal. Investment value can be expressed algebraically as follows:

$$P_e = CF_1/(1 + r) + CF_2/(1 + r)^2 + \ldots +$$
$$CF_n/(1 + r)^n + CF_d/(1 + r)^n$$
$$P_v = P_e + P_d$$

where:

P_e = Present value of the equity position
P_d = Present value of debt
P_v = Present value of total investment position
CF = After-tax cash flows to the equity investor occurring in year t ($t = 1$, 2, 3, . . . n)
CF_d = After-tax cash flow to the equity investor from property disposal at the end of year n
r = Discount rate

Estimating present value of the equity position requires assumptions about income, operating expenses, amount and terms of financing, sales price and income tax. It also depends upon the investor's *opportunity cost of capital,* that is, the yield available on equally risky alternative opportunities.

If a prospective purchaser places a higher investment value on a property than he or she will have to pay for it, acquisition will increase his or her net worth. In like manner, selling a property that has a higher market value than investment value enhances the investor's total wealth position. Alternative investment strategies relative to the same property can also be evaluated using the investment value model. Holding financing constant, the investor varies other investment criteria (such as alternative income tax treatments as discussed in Part Four) and chooses the strategy that produces the highest investment value. Financing alternatives can be evaluated by holding all other factors constant and determining the effect of each financing plan on the value of the equity position. The investor accepts the alternative that produces the highest value of equity per dollar of required equity investment, provided each alternative is perceived as entailing equal risk.

If all the considerations we have previewed are incorporated appropriately, shouldn't every investor arrive at the same estimate of investment value? This question must be answered with a resounding, "No!" Investment value is unique to each individual, and any agreement among market participants will be largely coincidental. Investment value estimates differ because of differences in perception of expected future operating results, different income tax positions, variation in willingness to defer consumption and differing attitudes toward risk.

We all interpret information according to our own frames of reference, which result from our unique sets of past experiences. For this reason, individuals reviewing the same information will usually draw different conclusions. There will likely be disagreement about the future stream of rental revenue and operating expenses associated with a property. Individuals will also differ in the degree of certainty with which they hold their expectations; they will perceive differing levels of risk associated with expected outcomes.

Investors in high marginal income tax brackets benefit more from tax-deductible losses, which can be used to offset otherwise taxable income from other sources. Those in lower marginal tax brackets have more cash flow remaining after deducting income taxes when the property generates a stream of taxable income. Because income tax situations are seldom exactly comparable, most investors will anticipate different after-tax cash-flow streams even when they are in general agreement about the before-tax cash flow and the taxable income or tax-deductible loss a property is expected to generate. Part Four addresses income tax considerations in greater detail.

People also differ in their willingness to defer immediate consumption in the interests of even greater benefits in future years. Those with a high preference for present consumption will require a greater incentive to defer after-tax cash flows. Investment value for such investors will be relatively high for investments with a short-term payoff and relatively low for those requiring greater patience. This subject is pursued at length in Part Five.

We do not all have the same tolerance for risk. Those who are less bothered by the possibility of variance between expected and actual investment outcomes will be inclined to place a greater investment value on risky ventures than will those who prefer to face a more precisely determinable future. Other things being equal, almost all investors will prefer less risk to more risk. They differ greatly regarding the risk premium they attach to proposed investment ventures (that is, the reduction in investment value due to possible variations between expected and actual after-tax cash flows).

INVESTOR OBJECTIVES AND RISK

Any attempt to discuss investor objectives quickly runs afoul of the nebulous term *investor*. Like Humpty-Dumpty, we choose to let the expression mean just what we choose it to mean, and we mean it to include any person or entity that takes an equity position in real estate. This is sufficiently broad to encompass individuals, corporations, partnerships, trusts, pension funds and so forth. *Investor* could mean something entirely different—and frequently does when used elsewhere. Our definition is not to be applied universally, nor is it intended to be taken as exclusive. It is rather an operational definition that enables us to use *investor* as a convenient shorthand term.

Given the diverse entities included in this definition, there can be no doubt that investors will have varied objectives. Some (for example, real estate investment trusts, pension funds, commercial banks) are constrained by law and regulatory agencies. Others, because of their relatively high income tax obligations, seek tax-shelter situations. Others seek fixed incomes. Some look for speculative situations to yield spectacular capital appreciation, while others might consider real estate their inventory in a basic merchandising sense.

There are, however, certain basic traits most investors hold in common, regardless of their motivations or personal objectives. All rational investors seek financial return as a reward for committing resources and as compensation for bearing risk. The amount of expected compensation and the degree of risk borne depend on specific investor objectives and individual attitudes toward risk.

Attitude Toward Risk

Emotional temperament plays a large role in an investor's attitude toward risk. Some people are risk takers by nature; they not only accept it but go out of their way to incur it. These are people who gamble even when they know the game favors the house. They seem to revel in defying the odds. The long shot is worth courting almost certain failure.

Other people avoid risk at almost any price. They sacrifice expected returns to hedge their bets, even where the cost of hedging is disproportionate to the relatively small associated risk. As investors, these people favor fixed-income securities carrying a high degree of safety of principal, such as government bonds or certificates of deposit at large commercial banks.

FIGURE 2.4   Relationship Between Perceived Risk and
Expected Return for a Risk–Averse Invester

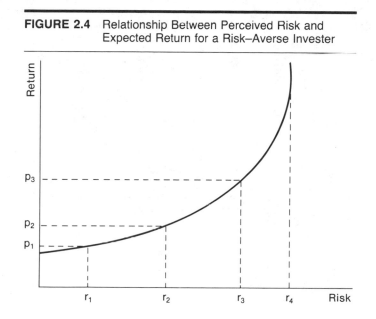

Most investors probably fall somewhere in between these extremes. They tend to minimize risk exposure, preferring the relatively low-return certainty to the higher-return long shot. Moreover, they tend to become progressively more risk-averse as their total wealth increases. These propositions about investor behavior have been explored at length in the economic and financial literature and are not generally a matter of serious dispute.

Authorities generally agree that, to the extent they are motivated by rational financial considerations, most investors have the attitude toward risk and expected return depicted in Figure 2.4. They prefer a higher return for a given perceived risk, they prefer less risk for a given expected return, and they accept additional perceived risk only if accompanied by additional expected return.

An additional investor characteristic demonstrated in Figure 2.4 is the tendency to become increasingly averse to additional risk as total perceived risk increases. Thus the investor whose attitude is depicted in Figure 2.4 can be induced to accept the additional risk indicated by the distance r_1 to r_2 by the promise of an increase in total reward indicated by the distance p_1 to p_2. But to be induced to accept an identical additional risk increment (from r_2 to r_3), he or she must be able to anticipate a substantially greater reward increment (from p_2 to p_3). In addition, as indicated in the illustration, there is some level of perceived risk (r_4) beyond which the investor cannot be induced to venture, regardless of the possible benefits.

Of course, the exact shape and location of the curve depicted in Figure 2.4 depends on an investor's personal attitude toward risk. A more risk-averse attitude would be depicted by a much more steeply inclined curve, while a less risk-averse attitude would be depicted by a shallower curve. Someone who

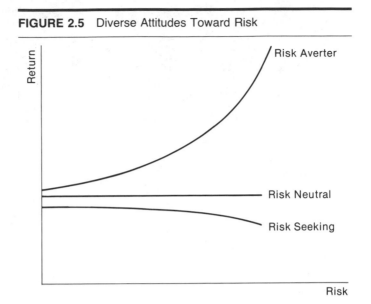

FIGURE 2.5 Diverse Attitudes Toward Risk

loves risk would actually trade expected return for additional risk. These various attitudes are depicted in Figure 2.5.

Rational Risk Taking

Rational risk taking is epitomized by successful insurance firms. This industry turns a handsome and highly predictable profit by allowing insured parties to substitute the certainty of a small loss (the insurance premium) for the uncertainty of a larger, possibly catastrophic loss, such as the loss of a home to fire or flood or a family member's incapacitation due to major illness. Insurance companies can do this successfully through astute risk management. They carefully calculate the odds of loss, against which they issue insurance policies, and they always ascertain that the premium is sufficient to compensate for the chance of loss.

Insurance firms might be characterized as *risk takers by design;* so might rational investors in real estate. Such investors will, before committing substantial resources:

1. Carefully specify investment objectives concerning return on investment, timing of return and acceptable risk levels;
2. Identify the major risks and quantify them as completely as possible;
3. Eliminate some risks, transfer others via insurance or other techniques and "constrain" the remaining risks to acceptable levels;
4. Base their decision on whether expected returns justify bearing the remaining risks in view of the contribution the venture makes toward overall investment objectives.

Of course, not all real estate investment ventures represent examples of rational risk taking. Emotional risk takers are likely to adopt an entirely different approach. Characteristic of the latter are investments made on a "hot tip" or a "hunch." Emotional risk takers are seemingly rendered blind to risk by the glare of expected return. Successful investors who have adopted emotional attitudes toward risk are prone to use their personal experiences as vindication for the approach. ("If investment analysts are so smart, why aren't they rich like me?") Those driven into bankruptcy by this approach are generally not considered newsworthy.

SUMMARY

Investment analysis follows a consistent pattern regardless of the investment vehicle or investor entity: The streams of benefits from alternative proposals are forecast and are adjusted for timing and risk differences. Alternatives are then ranked according to their desirability, in terms of the trade-off between perceived risk and anticipated return. Rankings will differ according to the discount rate used for timing adjustments and with varying investor attitudes toward risk.

Several terms are defined in Chapter 2 to avoid confusion in later discussions. These include *transaction price* (the price at which a transaction actually occurs), *most probable selling price* (a probabilistic expression of the price at which a transaction is likely to occur under prevailing market conditions), *market value* (the most probable price under carefully stipulated market conditions), *subjective value* (the value in use to a specific individual), *investment value* (subjective value of property held as an investment) and *transaction range* (the price range within which a transaction can occur between the present owner and a prospective buyer).

Investment value is the highest price a prospective buyer is justified in paying for a property or the lowest price a prospective seller is justified in accepting. Investment value is a function of available financing, the investor's income tax position, the yield available on alternative investments and the timing and amount of anticipated benefits flowing from the investment under consideration. The investment decision is subjective, and investment value will be different for each investor.

Investment value can be estimated by summing the present value of the equity position and the debt position associated with a proposed venture. Present value of the equity position is the discounted value of all anticipated future cash flows to the equity position. Present value of the debt position is the available loan or the remaining balance on an existing loan.

The investment value model can be employed to solve a wide variety of investor problems. It can be used to select a choice from among alternative assets, from among various possible ownership entities and from among differing financing proposals or to decide upon different ways to structure a proposal.

Investors differ in both their perceptions of and their attitudes toward risk. The difference among attitudes is sometimes expressed as degrees of risk aversion. The more risk-averse the investor, the greater the expected reward will have to be to induce investment in a given project.

RECOMMENDED READINGS

Barrett, G. Vincent, and John P. Blair. *How to Conduct and Analyze Real Estate Market and Feasibility Studies.* New York: Van Nostrand Reinhold Company, 1982, pp. 66–68.

Greer, Gaylon E., and Michael D. Farrell. *Contemporary Real Estate: Theory and Practice.* Hinsdale, IL: The Dryden Press, 1983, pp. 273–78.

Ratcliff, Richard U. *Modern Real Estate Valuation.* Madison, WI: Democrat Press, 1965, pp. 112–28.

———— . *Real Estate Analysis.* New York: McGraw–Hill, 1961, pp. 115–17.

Shafer, Thomas W. *Real Estate and Economics.* Reston, VA: Reston Publishing Company, Inc., pp. 157–72.

REVIEW QUESTIONS

1. What are the major steps in modern investment decision analysis?
2. Discuss the difference between the transaction price and the most probable selling price.
3. Discuss the difference between the most probable selling price and market value.
4. Explain how the transaction range for a given property is set. What is the role of investment value in arriving at the transaction range?
5. When estimating investment value, what factors are of concern to the investor?
6. What effect does the timing of cash flows have on investment value?
7. Discuss basic traits most investors have in common.
8. Discuss the steps a rational risk taker will follow in making a real estate investment decision.

DISCUSSION QUESTIONS

1. Under what circumstances would transaction price, most probable selling price and market value be essentially the same? Under what circumstances might they differ significantly?

2. To better determine just what a property is worth in the marketplace, would it make sense to ask an exorbitant price and wait for a series of offers, then accept the first subsequent offer that is higher than any received during the trial, or information-gathering, period? What problems do you see with such a procedure?

3. The text suggests that gambling is risk-loving behavior and that buying insurance is a risk avoidance measure. Yet many people who gamble also buy insurance. How can these contradictory actions be reconciled?

CHAPTER 3

Price, Value and the Concept of Market Efficiency

INTRODUCTION

Chapter 2 carefully distinguished the market price of a real estate asset from its investment value. Investment decisions depend upon the relationship between these two measures. Investors acquire real property for the anticipated future financial benefits ownership bestows. For a given expected future stream of benefits, the lower the price at which a property interest can be acquired, the greater the expected yield on the investment.

We saw in Chapter 2 that parties to a potential transaction not only may disagree about a property's investment value but also may hold different perceptions of its market value. Reliable estimates of market value are difficult and time-consuming to generate because of peculiarities surrounding the real estate market. This chapter investigates the phenomena associated with market-determined prices in general and specific market characteristics that influence the pricing of real estate assets.

DEMAND AND THE PRICE OF REAL ESTATE ASSETS

In his classic treatise, *Progress and Poverty*, Henry George urged that land-owners be deprived of what he believed to be an "unearned increment." George shrewdly observed that ownership itself is largely irrelevant. Let landlords keep title to their land, he argued, but strip them of benefits stemming from its use. George understood that ownership and occupancy rights are separable and that the former has value only to the extent it enables one to capture a portion of the benefits of the latter. Real estate students sometimes fail to grasp this important idea.

In real estate rental markets, tenants in effect buy owners' occupancy rights for a period of time. Ownership interests in rental property are valuable only because there is a market for these occupancy rights. Yet, even though the value of occupancy rights influences demand for ownership interests, the two are traded in entirely separate markets.

Land and the physical structures that constitute real estate can best be thought of as an *intermediate product*, one that derives its value from its contribution to production of another product, in contrast to a final product, which is consumed for its own sake. Its value stems in part from its contribution to the desirability of occupancy rights. Demand for real estate assets, as is the case for all intermediate products, is said to be a *derived demand*.

Demand for Real Estate Assets

Because limited resources is a universal condition, buying one item entails forgoing some other. For this reason, high prices act as a deterrent to acquisition; the higher the price, the smaller amount of a *product* buyers will purchase. (We use the term *product* to mean anything offered for sale or exchange. Economists have traditionally categorized products as *goods* or *services*. Reflecting major shifts in modern economic processes, a more meaningful classification would be goods, services and *knowledge*. Growth in the knowledge, or *information*, sector is outstripping that in either of the other two categories.) As prices rise, some potential purchasers opt instead for less expensive substitutes or are forced by limited budgets to drop out of the market altogether. Lower prices bring additional purchasers into the market and permit each purchaser to buy more. As prices fall, consumers switch from relatively more expensive substitutes, and aggregate demand for the item increases.

This relationship between price and quantity is illustrated in Table 3.1, as a *demand schedule*. The table relates demand for ownership interests in prime downtown office space to price per square foot.

A *demand curve* presents the same information in graphic form. Such a function is illustrated in Figure 3.1. Quantity of office space is shown on the horizontal axis, and price per square foot is shown on the vertical axis. The first entry in Table 3.1 indicates that at $120 per square foot investors will buy 2.3 million square feet per annum. The same information is plotted as point *A* in Figure 3.1 at $120 along the vertical axis and at 2.3 million units along the horizontal axis. In like manner, the second entry in Table 3.1 is plotted as point *B* in Figure 3.1, the third is plotted as point *C* and so on.

This specific demand schedule applies only to a defined population vying for a particular class of space during a specific time period. In many discussions of supply and demand this qualification is not made explicit. It nevertheless should be clearly understood that a demand relationship holds true only for the

TABLE 3.1　Hypothetical Demand Schedule
for Downtown Office Space

Price (per sq. ft.)	Square Feet Demanded (millions)
$120	2.3
115	2.5
110	2.8
105	3.2
100	3.7
95	4.3

FIGURE 3.1　Hypothetical Demand Curve for
Downtown Office Space

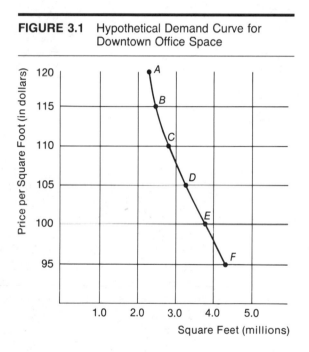

time period for which it is plotted and only for the product and market it is intended to portray.

Demand Schedules and Equilibrium Prices

Equilibrium denotes a stable, balanced or unchanging system. *Equilibrium price*, therefore, is the price at which there will be sufficient quantity of a product to satisfy desires of all consumers at that price, but with no surplus remaining on the market. With no consumer desiring to purchase additional units at the prevailing price, there will be no competitive bidding to drive the price still higher. With no unsalable inventory on hand, however, purveyors have no incentive to discount prices.

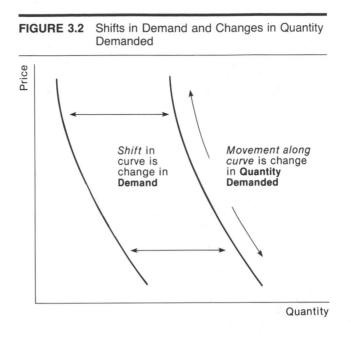

FIGURE 3.2 Shifts in Demand and Changes in Quantity Demanded

Shifts in Demand

Demand schedules such as that shown in Table 3.1 and graphed in Figure 3.1 are applicable only so long as other factors that influence buyer behavior do not change—in other words, so long as everything except price and quantity remains constant. Economists use the term *ceteris paribus* to describe this condition. As time passes, however, other things do change. In the case of our office space illustration, variation in the general level of business activity will affect rental rates, vacancy levels and operating expenses. This alters the rate of return on assets purchased at given prices. Investors therefore will revise their responses to posted prices. This represents a *shift* of the entire demand curve, as illustrated in Figure 3.2. Economists use the term *demand* to refer to the entire range of relationships between price and quantity, so such a shift in the relationship is a *change in demand*. Movement along a curve, in contrast, represents a change in *quantity demanded*. Were the altered relationships in Figure 3.2 such as to make real estate investment less attractive, the depicted shift in demand would be inward to the left, resulting in less space demanded at each possible price. Were the relationships altered in the opposite direction, the shift would be outward to the right, representing greater quantities demanded at every possible price.

Among the more significant determinants of the location and shape of demand curves for real estate assets are the following factors.

Number of Prospective Tenants. An increase in the number of people desiring to occupy space in available buildings causes rental rates to increase and vacancy rates to decline. In the absence of offsetting changes, net profits from building operations will improve, and real estate investment becomes more attractive relative to other investment opportunities. As investment resources are shifted into real estate assets, demand for real estate assets increases at every possible price level. Conversely, when a decline in the number of people desiring space causes the general level of rents to decline or vacancy rates to increase, real estate investment becomes relatively less desirable. Resources are shifted out of real estate and into other ventures, and quantity demanded declines at every possible price. Such shifts occur due to changes in population numbers and composition, income levels, employment distribution and growth and other demographic factors.

Changes in Operating Expenses. When the general level of operating expenses increases or decreases relative to rental revenue, net profits are altered accordingly. This change in profitability alters the desirability of real estate acquisition (relative to other investment ventures), and the entire demand schedule shifts.

Yields Available on Other Assets. Altered yield expectations on investments considered to be acceptable substitutes for real estate ownership will change the relative desirability of investment mediums. This causes resources to be shifted into or out of real estate assets and thereby alters the entire demand schedule.

Technology. Changes in technology can shift demand for rental space and thereby the derived demand for land and buildings. Technological changes can shift the curve in either direction, and the actual effect of a particular change is often unpredictable. Data processing technology, for example, has greatly reduced the number of employees required to produce a given volume of management information. This might reasonably have been expected to contract the size of the office work force and perhaps thereby reduce aggregate demand for office space. But this consequence generally has not occurred. Rather, reducing the time and cost of generating business information seems to have increased management's thirst for data, and a veritable flood of information is the result. In many cases, businesses have required additional office space to accommodate equipment to handle the increased quantity of reports for which they now feel a need.

Tastes. A change in consumer tastes will alter the demand for goods and services produced by tenants and thereby change the demand for productive space. As vacancy and rental rates adjust to new social and business conditions, the profitability of owning real estate in certain areas (at prevailing prices) makes ownership more or less desirable than before. Resources are shifted into or out of real property. Taste in residential rental space affects demand for apartment building ownership in the same manner and even more directly.

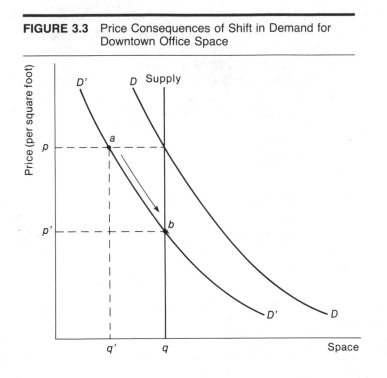

FIGURE 3.3   Price Consequences of Shift in Demand for Downtown Office Space

Demand Shifters at Work: An Illustration

To see how demand shifters actually affect demand, and thus equilibrium price, consider again the demand schedule for prime downtown office space illustrated in Table 3.1 and Figure 3.1. Remember that the schedule and related graph assume all significant factors other than price remain constant. Price changes alter the quantity of office space demanded, as indicated by a movement along the demand curve in Figure 3.1, from the old price to the new.

Among the factors assumed to remain constant in constructing Table 3.1 and Figure 3.1 was the price of substitute office space. This includes office space in the same geographical area but of a slightly different class due to age or condition or to the nature of other tenants. It also includes space embodying similar amenities but so located that its accessibility differs.

Now consider what happens when after-tax cash flow from real estate declines, due perhaps to changes in federal income tax policy or a drastic shift in the local tax burden onto property owners. Some investors who were interested in local real estate might now find other assets or other market areas relatively more desirable and thus drop out of the bidding for prime downtown property. As a consequence, less prime downtown space will be purchased by investors at each possible price per square foot. This is illustrated in Figure 3.3 as a shift from demand curve *D* to curve *D'*.

At the previously prevailing market price *p* in Figure 3.3, there will now be unsalable inventory as indicated by the distance on the quantity (horizontal)

axis from q to q'. Price concessions will eventually reduce the prevailing price for this class of downtown office space from p to p', at which approximate price current owners can sell all they wish. This represents a movement along the new demand curve D' in Figure 3.3 from point a to point b.

THE SUPPLY OF REAL ESTATE ASSETS

Relative scarcity is also a factor in the power of a product to command value in exchange. Many items from which we derive great satisfaction have little or no exchange value. An obvious example of this seeming paradox is the relationship between water and diamonds. Water, a basic requirement for life, certainly has as much want-satisfying power as can be imagined. Diamonds, on the other hand, bear no relation to the survival needs of the species. Yet lives are sacrificed and revolutions fomented in search of these precious stones.

Relative scarcity is the missing element in this apparent paradox. No matter how useful an item is, it will command no substantial value in exchange if it is relatively abundant. Water generally has very little exchange value, except in desert regions or during a period of drought. In those places and at those times, water may well become more precious than diamonds.

Supply is defined as the relationship between price and the quantity of a product suppliers place on the market during a specified time period, for all possible prices. A key phrase in this definition is *during a specified time period*. The supply function differs rather drastically as the specified time period is lengthened or shortened.

Supply and Quantity Supplied: An Important Distinction

Just as demand and quantity demanded are qualitatively different concepts, so are supply and *quantity supplied*. Whereas *quantity supplied* refers to the amount of a product that will be placed on the market per period of time at a specified price, *supply* denotes the relationship between price and quantity supplied over the entire range of possible prices.

Figure 3.4 illustrates the distinction. Supply, the entire range of relationships, is indicated by the curve labeled S. Quantity supplied is measured at the intersection of the supply and demand curves (and is read off the horizontal axis). Thus, for supply curve S and the demand curve shown on Figure 3.4, the quantity supplied at the equilibrium price p is q.

A change in the demand function results in an altered quantity supplied, as indicated by the movement along the supply curve from point a to point b in Figure 3.5a. A shift in supply, in contrast, results in movement of the entire relationship between price and quantity supplied as illustrated by the shift from curve S to curve S' in Figure 3.5b.

FIGURE 3.4 Illustration of Supply and Quantity Supplied

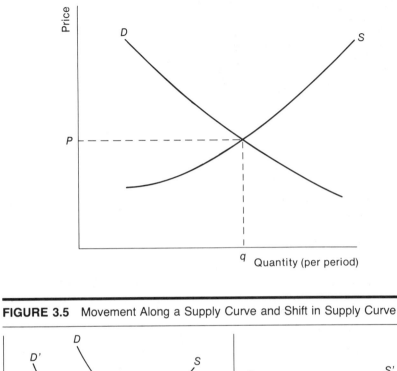

FIGURE 3.5 Movement Along a Supply Curve and Shift in Supply Curve

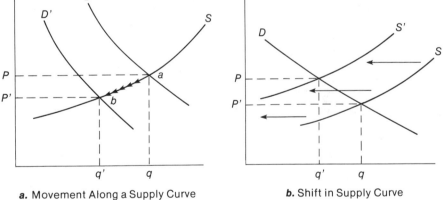

a. Movement Along a Supply Curve   *b.* Shift in Supply Curve

Shifts in Supply Curves

Supply curves may be more stable than demand curves, but they are not eternally fixed. Moreover, shifts in supply curves alter *equilibrium prices* in much the same fashion as do shifts in demand curves. Suppose, for example, that a major fire wipes out a significant portion of the prime downtown office space posited in our earlier example. If the conflagration has no impact on demand (though well it might), then the consequence will be a movement in the market clearing price for such space from *p'* to *p* in Figure 3.5b.

TABLE 3.2 Demand to Hold Rental Units

Price (per sq. ft.)	Desired Ownership Quantities (units per market participant)						
	A	B	C	D	E	F	Total
$95	3	0	2	0	0	0	5
90	4	1	3	0	1	0	9
85	5	2	4	0	1	0	12
80	5	3	4	0	1	1	14
75	5	3	4	1	1	2	16
70	6	4	5	1	1	2	19
65	6	5	5	1	2	3	22
60	6	6	6	2	2	4	26
	Current Ownership Quantities						
	A	B	C	D	E	F	Total
	2	4	4	3	3	0	16

Supply curves for real estate improvements (other than over the very short term) are determined in large part by *production costs*. If costs decline, producers will increase their output, thereby shifting the supply curve to the right. Higher costs will have exactly the opposite effect, shifting the supply curve to the left.

Prices paid for items employed in production are major determinants of production costs. Yet, even as these prices increase, technological advancements may reduce overall production costs. Producers then become willing to supply more at any particular price. This represents a shift to the right in the supply curve.

The Time Element in Supply Analysis

Over the short run, variations in the supply of real estate placed on the market are a function of individuals' perceptions of the relationship between market value and investment value. We saw in Chapter 2 that an owner's investment value (or subjective value) determines the minimum price at which a property transaction can occur. A property will be sold only if the proceeds (that is, sales price minus taxes and transactions costs) equal or exceed the property's value as an element in the owner's portfolio. Early economists made the same observation by differentiating between *value in use* and *value in exchange*.

Consider a market for rental property in which only six people participate. Assume that all rental units are completely substitutable (that is, interchangeable) and that each participant's desire to own units is as indicated in Table 3.2. Suppose only 16 rental units exist in this market and that two are held by A, four by B, four by C, three by D, three by E and none by F. At various possible prices each participant will enter the market, as either a buyer or a seller, to adjust current inventories to reflect desired holdings at that price level.

Table 3.3 expresses desired inventory adjustments of all parties at various possible prices per rental unit. The difference between the amount each partic-

TABLE 3.3   Demand to Buy and Supply to Sell Rental Units

| Price | Market Participants | | | | | | Aggregate | |
(per sq. ft.)	*A*	*B*	*C*	*D*	*E*	*F*	*Demand*	*Supply*
$95	+ 1	− 4	− 2	− 3	− 3	0	1	12
90	+ 2	− 3	− 1	− 3	− 2	0	2	9
85	+ 3	− 2	0	− 3	− 2	0	3	7
80	+ 3	− 1	0	− 3	− 2	+ 1	4	6
75	+ 3	− 1	0	− 2	− 2	+ 2	5	5
70	+ 4	· 0	+ 1	− 2	− 2	+ 2	7	4
65	+ 4	+ 1	+ 1	− 2	− 1	+ 3	9	3
60	+ 4	+ 2	+ 2	− 1	− 1	+ 4	12	2

ipant currently has (shown at the bottom of Table 3.2) and the amount each demands to own at different prices are the amounts *demanded to purchase* or *supplied to sell* at each price. The schedule for participant B in Table 3.2 indicates that at a price of $70 he or she wants to own four units, which is the number in his or her current inventory. Participant B therefore will not enter the market at that price. At a higher price, say $90, B wants to own only one unit and will therefore offer to sell three from his or her inventory. At a lower price, say $65, he or she wants to own five and hence will enter the market to purchase one unit. These desired inventory adjustments are shown in Table 3.3 as B's demand to buy or supply to sell. In like manner, Table 3.3 shows the desired inventory adjustments at various prices for all participants to adjust their current holdings to the amount shown in Table 3.2 as their desired inventories at those prices.

If at each price we add all the negative amounts in Table 3.3, we obtain the aggregate quantity supplied at that price. Adding the positive amounts yields the aggregate quantity demanded for purchase at each price. These quantities are shown in the last two columns of Table 3.3. The price at which aggregate demand and aggregate supply are equal ($75 per unit) is the price that will permit all mutually advantageous exchanges to occur. This represents the short-term equilibrium price of rental units in this particular market. Figure 3.6 shows these relationships in graphic form.

Over a longer period, the supply curve of real estate is influenced by the cost of construction. As prices of existing improved property move above the cost of new construction, entrepreneurs have an incentive to contract for construction of new buildings. The higher the market price, the greater the incentive to increase the rate of construction. The result is a long-term supply curve that is considerably more responsive to changes in price than is the curve depicted in Figure 3.6. (The supply of *improvements* can be expanded virtually without limit, but the question of a fixed supply of *land* must be addressed. Since much of the land surface of the earth has no ready market value, we must conclude there is no current shortage of land as such. What is in short supply is land

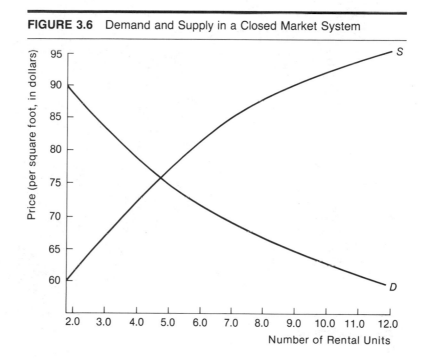

FIGURE 3.6 Demand and Supply in a Closed Market System

suitably located for specific economic enterprises. Because desirable land cannot be readily expanded through purposeful entrepreneurial action, the available supply goes to the highest bidder. Moreover, because each parcel is unique with respect to its location, land is a *differentiated product*. This introduces market inefficiencies that distort the working of supply and demand as we have just reviewed it.)

This brings us to another basic supply and demand concept. The longer a price persists, the more responsive the supply function will be to that price, because the longer the period of adjustment, the more fully the market can accommodate a new set of supply and demand relationships. Over the very long term, not only can additional structures be built on available land, but additional land can be cleared or converted from alternative uses. This relationship between the length of the time period involved and the responsiveness of supply to price changes is depicted in Figure 3.7.

Price as a Consensus

Individual efforts to adjust portfolios will result in an equilibrium price for property of a particular type within a specific market. This represents a *consensus* of value. At lower prices individuals desiring to augment their portfolios will outnumber those desiring partial liquidation. Upward pressure on prices results. At any higher price, however, individuals wishing to shift out of this category of assets will place downward pressure on prices.

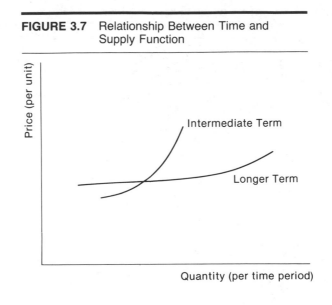

FIGURE 3.7   Relationship Between Time and Supply Function

MARKET FUNCTIONS

Markets are a valuable economic mechanism primarily because the prices they generate provide information and incentives. Changes in relative market prices signal producers when less of one product and more of another should be produced. Geographical price disparities (beyond those caused by transportation costs) signal distributors to channel fewer goods or services to the low-price area and more to the high-price area. Profit opportunities embodied in the relatively high-priced alternatives provide incentives to respond to price signals.

Market-determined prices tend to be efficient rationers of scarce goods and services. By selling to high bidders, those who control scarce resources assure that they go to buyers who place the highest value on them. (Critics of the market mechanism argue that wealth discrepancies channel resources away from the poor toward the rich, who may actually place very little relative value on them. This appears to be a criticism more of income distribution than of the market mechanism.) By placing higher prices on resources that are in short supply, the market provides incentives to shift consumption away from scarce resources and toward those that are more plentiful.

DEFINING THE MARKET

Before considering factors at work in a particular real estate market, the market itself must be delineated. This is no simple task. The unadorned concept of a market is not ambiguous, but its application to real estate is complicated both by the nature of the product and by the characteristics of market participants.

FIGURE 3.8 Markets Within Markets

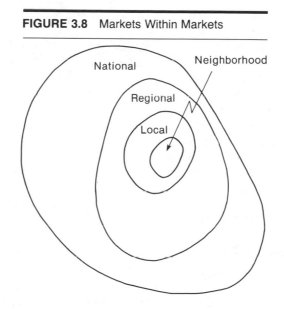

In general, a *market* is an institutional arrangement or mechanism whereby buyers and sellers are brought into contact with each other. It is not necessarily a physical entity or a geographical location. There is, for example, a market for national currencies that is comprised of an informal worldwide network of dealers connected by telephone and telex.

A market might be defined in terms of commonality of product. This leads to a description of a real estate market for industrial property, another for farmland, another for commercial sites and so on. With notable exceptions for large industrial and commercial sites, the market in each of these segments is fragmented geographically, because of the tendency of participants to concentrate in the locale with which they are most familiar. For most real estate, therefore, there is no truly national market.

Illustrating the nature of the problem, the following categories of real estate markets are described by one author:[1]

- The owner-occupant market;
- The renter-occupant market;
- Multifamily investment;
- Nonresidential market.

Within each of these broad categories, it is necessary to define submarkets within which determinable market forces work more or less uniformly. William Kinnard has described these submarkets as *neighborhoods*.[2] A neighborhood, as defined by Kinnard, is a geographical area within which change has a "direct and immediate effect" on the property under analysis. Delineating neighborhoods in this manner permits direct investigation of market forces affecting prices of real estate services and real estate assets. The relationship between broader and more localized markets is illustrated in Figure 3.8. Of course the "neighborhood" for some types of property, such as large industrial sites, might in fact be national in scope.

The issue is further complicated by the tendency of submarkets to overlap. To clarify, consider the market area from which regional shopping centers draw customers. Such centers are generally widely separated, and each tends to capture almost all customers from the immediate vicinity. Even though a center's attractive power declines geometrically with required travel time, it occasionally pulls in some customers who frequent other relatively nearby centers. Consequently, two or more regional centers may draw substantial clientele from one large geographic area.

MARKET STRUCTURES

Perhaps nowhere has economic modeling been more useful than in studying the structure of markets. Having propounded a market model in which price competition results in the most efficient allocation of resources, and another in which price competition does not exist, economists classify all other market arrangements in terms of where they fall on the spectrum between these extremes. (*Allocative efficiency* relates to the net resource cost of operating the market mechanism. The significance to the real estate analyst of degrees of market efficiency is developed later in this chapter.)

Atomistic Markets

In an atomistic market, each participant is so insignificant relative to the size of the total market that he or she has no perceptible effect on price. Every buyer can purchase as much as desired, and every seller can sell as much as desired. There are never shortages or market gluts; there is no need for special "discount" prices to clear away unwanted inventory or for any governmentally mandated rationing schemes. Sellers do not need to advertise the special virtues of their merchandise or to maintain an inventory to meet future needs. Economic literature more frequently uses the term *pure competition* or *perfect competition* to describe the *atomistic market* because these names are meaningful to economists. However, they are misleading to everyone else, since competition in atomistic markets is neither more nor less intense than in other markets.

Such a market can exist only where there is a sufficient number of participants so that no one person or group can measurably affect market prices. Reducing the quantity brought to market does not enable a seller to command a higher price. No buyer will respond to above-market price quotes. Buyers are in a similar position of not being able to bargain for better prices. Market participants are simply price takers, in that they have a choice of accepting prevailing prices or of not participating in the market at all.

Perhaps most nearly atomistic are markets for unprocessed agricultural commodities or for ownership shares in large publicly held corporations. In each case, the units of product are completely undifferentiated, and a host of market participants act with roughly equal knowledge of market conditions. These products are sold in auction markets, where each bidder instantly knows the bids of competitors.

Complete Monopoly

In markets characterized by *absolute monopoly*, there is only one supplier of a good or service for which there are no reasonably acceptable substitutes. The lower the price per unit, the greater will be the sales volume per time period. The monopolist selects the price; buyers decide how much of the good they are willing to take off the market at the posted price.

A monopolist's choice of price, and thus of quantity sold, depends upon the *marginal cost of production* (that is, the cost of adding one more unit per period to the rate of production). Monopolists seek to determine what price will yield the maximum amount of revenue in excess of costs and to produce the quantity the market will buy at that price.

Markets most nearly characterized by absolute monopoly are those so designated by government fiat. Even here there are substitutes, however flawed. What if a country has only one telephone company? If telephone rates are set too high, hiring messengers, sending telegrams or writing letters becomes economical. Some state governments operate a monopoly in the sale of packaged alcoholic beverages, but their freedom to set prices is circumscribed by actual or potential competition in a black market. Even in the coinage of money, government is unsuccessful in maintaining an absolute monopoly. Entrepreneurs have created a number of financial instruments that are such good substitutes that they are popularly known as "near money" and are included in the money supply equations economists use to measure monetary aggregates.

Price Searcher's Markets

Between these positions lie a host of markets where participants recognize that they cannot completely control the price at which goods are exchanged but also understand that they do affect market prices. Each participant must be constantly aware of the impact pricing decisions will have on the decisions of competitors. Participants in such markets might best be described as *price searchers*.

In an effort to make finer distinctions, economists have classified price searchers' markets into subcategories that reflect the ease with which new producers can enter the market. *Monopolistic competition* exists when any number of competitors produce goods or services that are sufficiently differentiated that consumers will not be entirely indifferent about which they choose. *Oligopoly* implies only a few producers and market conditions that render entry extremely difficult. Economic policymakers consider these to be important distinctions. We need only note that real estate markets fall within the range characterized as either monopolistic competition or oligopoly and that in both categories buyers and sellers exhibit price-searching behavior.[3]

TABLE 3.4 Fama's Description of Market Efficiency

Form of Efficiency Hypotheses	Information Reflected in Prices
Strong	All currently known
Semistrong	All publicly available
Weak	Previous transaction prices

SOURCE: Eugene Fama, "Efficient Markets: A Review of Theory and Empirical Work," *Journal of Finance,* May 1970.

PRICE SEARCHERS AND MARKET EFFICIENCY

If a price searcher had full knowledge of product supply and demand (that is, of competitors' plans and consumers' desires) and knew all the costs of alternative production programs, then profit-maximizing price and production quantity would be easy to determine. In fact, however, pricing and production decisions must be made without perfect foresight and with only sketchy information concerning current market conditions.

We have seen that an important function of markets is precisely to transmit information about products and prices so that participants can make rational, informed purchase and sales decisions. A market in which information is transmitted quickly and costlessly will rapidly eliminate any possibility of above-average profits such as those enjoyed by monopolists. Such a market is said to be *efficient*. The time required for newly available information to be reflected in market prices is, in fact, often taken as a measure of market efficiency. In an extremely efficient market all relevant information is reflected instantaneously in market prices. In less efficient markets information takes longer to be incorporated, and some information might never be reflected in market prices.

The less efficient the market, the greater will be the degree of price-searching behavior. Participants obtain intelligent perceptions of market clearing prices in inefficient markets only by expending time and effort. Information in such markets is scarce and costly.

There is a wide and bountiful literature on the issue of market efficiency. Most of the research in this area has been designed to test the efficiency of organized stock markets, yet it provides information from which we can draw valuable inferences about efficiency in real estate markets. This in turn suggests appropriate strategies for buyers and sellers of real estate assets.

Early in his academic career, Eugene Fama established himself as a leading authority on the subject of market efficiency. He categorized market efficiency according to the degree to which information is fully reflected in market prices. Fama's framework is illustrated in Table 3.4.

It may be that no market conforms completely to the *strong form* of the efficiency hypothesis. Perhaps this model most nearly describes the most actively traded segment of those stocks listed on major exchanges. Information is constantly being perused by thousands of securities analysts who make recommendations on which daily transactions are based. Because all available information is subjected to intense and expert scrutiny, it is likely to be fairly completely incorporated in traders' value decisions and therefore in prices. As these stocks trade in extremely high volume with a large number of frequent individual transactions, newly available information is likely to be reflected very quickly in prices.

Only slightly less efficient is the market for listed stocks below the top tier of actively traded issues. Because they are less frequently considered for inclusion in portfolios of major investors, these stocks might be subjected to less widespread or less intense analysis. Certainly, because they are less actively traded, new information is reflected less rapidly in market clearing prices. Markets for unlisted securities are still less efficient in terms of the extent to which information is incorporated into pricing decisions and the time required for new information to be fully reflected.

The market for real estate equities is far removed from even "over-the-counter" securities markets. Many real estate transactions occur at prices that reflect little more information than past prices of very similar properties. Moreover, because transactions are infrequent and information is difficult and costly to generate, there is frequently a considerable lag between the time when comparable transactions occur and the time when the informational content of the transactions is fully reflected in market prices.

Sources of Inefficiency in Real Estate Markets

The concept of a market clearing price is unambiguous when applied to a public auction where bids are immediately revealed to all participants. Everyone is immediately aware of all offers so that all currently available information is almost certain to be reflected in prices. Real estate transactions, in contrast, are typically a matter of personal negotiation between buyer and seller. The prospective buyer does not know who else might be willing to bid on the property or what offers others may be prepared to make. The seller must accept or reject bids without knowing whether other bids are forthcoming.

As a consequence, real estate markets may never "clear" in the sense of all parties being able to adjust their portfolios at a stated price. Numerous factors inhibit market adjustments from readily reflecting actual supply and demand conditions.

Information Is Costly and Difficult to Obtain. Information that is too costly to be purchased (that is, the benefits are exceeded by the cost of obtaining the information) will not be reflected in market prices. So long as information cost is the same for all market participants—where no one has monopolistic control over information—all investors will be equally affected, but the market will nonetheless be rendered less efficient. Information is generally more costly and difficult to obtain in real property than in stock and bond markets, for example, due to a virtual absence of legal financial disclosure requirements, the absence of centralized markets and the inexactness of price comparisons among properties.

Transaction Costs Are High.   Transaction costs associated with real property markets are generally considerably greater than those encountered in securities markets. These costs inhibit portfolio adjustments based upon newly acquired information and thus increase the length of time required for new information to be reflected in market prices.

The Product Is Differentiated.   Product substitutability contributes to the efficiency of markets. In agricultural markets, for example, buyers are indifferent as to specific parcels of grain of a given grade. Real estate is different. We have noted that every real estate parcel is unique in at least one respect: location. In some instances a prospective buyer may find several locations equally appealing. More frequently a buyer will have a precise preference, although several alternatives will be acceptable subtitutes. In other instances there will be few if any good substitutes for the desired site. When the quantity of acceptable substitutes is limited, prospective sellers have monopolistic control over the product, and the traditional model of market clearing price must be altered to reflect these facts. Monopolistic control over supply creates barriers to efficient functioning of markets.

The Role of Middlemen

The expense of generating information about opportunities in the marketplace further contributes to real estate market inefficiency. If each market participant had to generate the necessary information for intelligent purchase and sales decisions, *information search costs* would be prohibitively high and thereby form an absolute barrier to portfolio adjustments.

Fortunately, information generated for one transaction is reusable. If assembled market information is transmitted from one market participant to another, the average cost of information search is reduced drastically. This transmission of information is a valuable function of brokers and other real estate practitioners such as appraisers and consultants. Brokerage and appraisal fees reflect the expense of generating the information these individuals provide. As technology decreases the costs of information storage, retrieval and transmission, these fees will decline unless legislative barriers prevent people from entering middleman businesses, thereby restricting the supply of services available and keeping market prices artificially high. (Of course, self-interest dictates that people already engaged in these business activities will support the enactment of legislative barriers to new entrants. Such barriers typically take the form of increasingly difficult entrance exams, progressively higher educational requirements, longer residency requirements for licensing purposes and extended apprenticeship periods.)

SUMMARY

Real estate is merely one of a wide variety of income-generating assets available for inclusion in investors' portfolios. The lower the price at which an asset can be acquired relative to the price of competing assets of the same income and risk category, the greater the relative yield on the asset in question. Therefore, the lower-priced asset will be relatively more desirable as an investment, other things being equal.

Translated into traditional supply and demand language, this means the lower the price (and thus the higher the expected yield on the investment), the greater the quantity of an asset investors stand ready to take off the market. At progressively higher prices, investors find the asset increasingly less attractive in comparison with other assets of the same general risk category. At some sufficiently high price, investors will not only be unwilling to purchase the asset; they will become net sellers of the asset.

In conventional demand and supply analysis, the supply curve depicts the marginal cost of producing additional units of the product. Most real estate transactions, however, involve buildings already in existence. And even where land availability and institutional arrangements permit substantial additions to the stock of similar structures, the total stock can be enhanced only very slowly. Market clearing prices of real property, therefore, may depart rather drastically from the marginal cost of construction—even for substantial time periods.

This does not negate conventional demand and supply analysis; it does require a closer look at the supply component. For a given perception of the demand schedule for real estate services, each real estate investor will develop a perception of appropriate prices for real estate assets. When market prices are below this perceived value, investors will be inclined to add to their inventory. Conversely, they will be inclined to sell from inventory when market prices move above the perceived value.

Markets are institutional arrangements or mechanisms that bring buyers and sellers into contact. Markets are often defined in terms of commonality of product, such as the residential real estate market or the market for industrial buildings. They are also frequently defined in geographic terms. In this respect, *neighborhood* is a term sometimes used to describe an area in which specific phenomena have a direct and immediate influence on all real estate. Real estate market boundaries are difficult to define, because submarkets tend to overlap.

Markets serve valuable economic functions by providing information about supply and demand for a product and by providing incentives for individuals and firms to respond to market signals. Market-determined prices serve to ration available supplies. They also induce producers to shift additional productive facilities into any item for which there is increased demand and out of items for which demand diminishes.

Economists classify market structures according to the extent to which individual buyers and sellers can influence prices and according to the degree to which relevant market information is readily reflected in prices. Markets in which there is only one supplier of a good or service are called *monopolies*. Those having so many participants that no one person or firm has any discernible impact on price are called *atomistic*. In the world of business affairs, most markets fall between these two extremes.

In extremely efficient markets all relevant information is reflected instantaneously in market prices. Participants in less efficient markets are sometimes able to better their market performance by searching for the best available price. Because information in inefficient markets is scarce and expensive, participants with monopolistic access to information are frequently able to consistently outperform other participants.

There is a crucial distinction between the market for real estate occupancy rights and that for real estate assets. Assets are valued for the stream of economic benefits their ownership bestows, which is a function of the supply and demand relationships for occupancy rights.

The total quantity of real estate assets is fixed over the short run. But the supply available for exchange in the marketplace is variable even over the very short run. This is because current owners become net buyers or sellers of existing assets, depending upon whether they perceive current prices to be higher or lower than justified in view of longer-range economics of real estate ownership. Thus, over the very long run, the cost of construction influences asset market prices. Current market prices, however, may vary considerably above or below current construction costs.

NOTES

1. Thomas W. Shafer, *Real Estate and Economics* (Reston, VA: Reston, 1975), 79.

2. William N. Kinnard, Jr., *Income Property Valuation* (Lexington, MA: Lexington Books, 1971), 302.

3. For an excellent discussion of markets characterized in this fashion, see Armen A. Alchian and William R. Allen, *Exchange and Production Theory in Use* (Belmont, CA: Wadsworth, 1969).

RECOMMENDED READINGS

Alchian, Armen A. and William R. Allen. *Exchange and Production Theory in Use*. Belmont, CA: Wadsworth Publishing Company, Inc., 1969, pp. 62–97 and 124–160.

American Institute of Real Estate Appraisers. *The Appraisal of Real Estate*. 8th ed. Chicago: The American Institute of Real Estate Appraisers, 1983, pp. 59–70.

Barrett, G. Vincent, and John P. Blair. *Foundations of Real Estate Analysis*. New York: Macmillan Publishing Company, Inc., 1981, pp. 231–252.

Jaffe, Austin J., and C. F. Sirmans, *Real Estate Investment Decision Making*. Englewood Cliffs, NJ: Prentice-Hall, Inc., 1982, pp. 89–101.

Ratcliff, Richard U. *Real Estate Analysis*. New York: McGraw-Hill, 1961, pp. 13–41.
Shafer, Thomas W. *Real Estate and Economics*. Reston, VA: Reston Publishing Company, Inc., 1975, pp. 73–92.

REVIEW QUESTIONS

1. How are the price and demand for an economic good related?
2. What conditions might cause a shift in the demand for office space in a downtown area?
3. What is the relationship between price and the quantity supplied of an economic good?
4. Compare short-term and long-term supply functions in real estate markets.
5. How are real estate markets categorized and how are they defined?
6. List the economic functions of real estate markets.
7. Explain the difference between atomistic and monopolistic markets.
8. What are some of the factors inhibiting market adjustments from readily reflecting supply and demand conditions in real estate markets?

DISCUSSION QUESTIONS

1. Are price and quantity demanded always inversely related? Can you think of circumstances under which increasing the price of a good or service might cause the quantity demanded to increase; under which decreasing the price might cause quantity demanded to decrease?
2. In a dynamic, constantly changing economy, would you expect most markets ever to reach an *equilibrium* price? What about markets for various classes of real estate?
3. In highly concentrated markets competition is likely to be just as furious as in atomistic markets, but it is often in arenas other than price. What are some prominent examples of nonprice competition?
4. How might modern technology and modern management techniques be used to reduce real estate brokerage costs? What barriers might inhibit introduction of such cost-saving measures?

PART ONE: Case Problems

1. Suppose the demand curve for "class A" office space in the metropolitan area were as follows.

Rental rate (per square foot per annum)	Quantity demanded (millions of square feet)
$10	3.0
11	2.9
12	2.8
13	2.7
14	2.6
15	2.5
16	2.4

a. Suppose also the quantity of "class A" office space in the area is 2.9 million square feet. If no market participant is in a position to affect the market price, and all relevant information is readily available to all market participants, what will be the generally prevailing rental rate per square foot for office space of this class over the short term?

b. Suppose a new investor enters the market, buys several office buildings and announces that rent will be $13 per square foot for all new tenants and for all lease renewals. What will be the short-term impact on his gross rental income:
   (1) If he controls three percent of the office space in this market area?
   (2) If he controls 50 percent of the office space in this market?

2. Sterling Silverspoon purchased a parking lot ten years ago for $100,000. He has earned an average annual net operating income of $14,000 and is now considering

selling the parking lot. Millicent Mum likes the parking lot's location and initiates negotiation for its purchase.

Silverspoon points out that the city has recently increased parking fees at municipal lots and observes that fees can now be raised on this lot sufficiently to move the net operating income to about $20,000 annually. He notes that the $14,000 per year he has been earning represents a 14 percent per annum return on his investment. He thinks this is a good yield and states that Mum can do equally well, based on the anticipated $20,000 per annum net operating income, by paying $143,857 for the lot.

Mum retorts that Silverspoon will have an assured rate of return once the lot is sold but that Mum will be taking a risk that the anticipated cash flow will not materialize. Therefore, says Mum, she should earn a premium. She suggests an 18 percent yield and offers a price of $111,111.

Both parties earnestly state their desire to be fair and equitable in establishing a price for this property, but they are at odds as to how a price might best be determined. What do you suggest?

PART TWO

Market Research

A particular property's desirability, from an investment perspective, depends heavily upon its ability to command rents. Evaluating investment worth therefore involves estimating the rental value of property over the prospective holding period and the market value of the property at the end of the period. Thus, reliable investment analysis incorporates a healthy dose of market research.

The starting point in assessing the worth of an investment proposal is to study past operating results and rental and building trends. Analysts must evaluate this historical information with a healthy appreciation for how economic, social and political forces may drastically alter past trends. This appreciation flows in part from a thorough understanding of the concepts of supply and demand and the factors influencing each.

Part Two constitutes an introduction to the problem of estimating what financial benefits can be expected to flow from ownership of a specific real property interest. Chapter 4 lays the theoretical foundation for the discussion by explaining economic forces that determine the desirability of a site and market forces that determine competitive rental rates and property values. Chapter 5 gives an overview of market research tools and techniques, many of which were developed outside the real estate field but are nevertheless directly applicable to real estate investment analysis problems. Part Two concludes with a chapter dedicated to a discussion of factors influencing a property's ability to command rent and thus to command value in exchange.

CHAPTER 4

Land Utilization and the Value of Real Estate Services

INTRODUCTION

Recall from Chapter 1 that real estate investors seek ownership interests in real estate assets because this permits them to vend shelter and locational benefits to ultimate users of the assets. As a matter of semantic convenience, benefits stemming from occupancy of real estate premises are called *real estate services*. Demand for real estate assets, therefore, stems indirectly from demand for real estate services.

This chapter investigates factors affecting locational benefits, which are major determinants of the value of real estate services. It demonstrates how competitive bidding allocates the most desirable locations to activities that benefit sufficiently to be able to pay more for the locational advantages than can less productive competitors. Those who are unable to secure the most desirable locations settle for the best affordable alternative. A hierarchy of locational choices trailing off from the ideal, or "100 percent," location results. This hierarchy is characterized by a descending order of density of land utilization and of declining rents as one moves further from the 100 percent location.

As society's characteristic way of carrying on social and economic activities changes, so does the relative desirability of various locations. However, the cityscape does not readily adapt to our altered needs. Its structure yields only grudgingly to changes resulting from individual economic decisions. As a consequence, cities reflect a mélange of development patterns, some created to meet contemporary needs and some simply artifacts of a bygone era. In every city, however, individual location decisions have resulted in logical, systematic development patterns whose orderliness, to untrained eyes, may be hidden by the superficial appearance of the city's configuration.

ECONOMIC FACTORS IN LAND USE DECISIONS

Locational choice is primarily an economic decision. For this reason, the pattern of urban development reflects basic economic forces. One such force that becomes increasingly evident as cities grow and mature is *specialization of function*. As hamlets become towns and towns evolve into cities, real estate uses of like character tend increasingly to be concentrated in specific functional zones.

This tendency is not only evident among major categories of use, such as residential, industrial and commercial, but within these broad categories as well. Residential users tend to segregate themselves by social and economic class, resulting in distinct neighborhoods with highly stratified levels of housing quality. Within commercial districts there is also notable clustering of like uses.

Market-directed specialization and segregation of uses is, however, never absolute. Locational decisions are often a matter of trial and error, and mistakes are difficult to correct, due to the high cost of altering locational choices. Moreover, variations in the level of economic activity, combined with perpetual change in technology and lifestyles, constantly give birth to new economic motivations, rendering old locational choices suboptimal and creating maladjustments that lead to reassessment of previous decisions.

Subject to inconsistencies and anomalies induced by the prohibitive cost of making small adjustments, by errors in judgment and by the irrational element in human nature, land utilization in a market system is determined primarily by efforts to extract economic returns. Space is leased to those who offer the highest price. The more productive users generally can outbid their rivals. The ultimate consequence is an orderly pattern of land use that generates the greatest aggregate economic benefit for the community.

Of course, not all potential users compete directly for the same land. Although railroads and freeways detract from the desirability of adjacent locations as residential neighborhoods, for example, factories and warehouses benefit from proximity to these transportation facilities. Low-priced homes are preferably built on a flat plain to minimize construction costs, but buyers of higher-priced houses might pay a premium for the excellent view from a hillside location.

However, within broad ranges of potential uses, direct competition does take place. Where the competition is based primarily on economic considerations, the use that results in the greatest rent-paying capacity is that which wrings the greatest locational advantage from a site.

Although concentration is a natural adaptation to the need and desire to overcome the "friction" of space, decentralization is a normal and continuing counterforce necessitated by market forces. Low-intensity land users are forced out of central locations by those who benefit most from proximity to the center and can therefore afford to pay higher rental rates. Land use density thus tends to be highest at the center of development activity. Progressively lower densities are encountered toward the urban fringe. The result is economically efficient allocation of scarce urban space.

Systematic Development Patterns

Economists are fond of creating abstract models to isolate key elements in economic relationships. These simplified representations of a complex world permit uncluttered concentration on issues chosen for close examination. A classic example is Johann Heinrich Von Thunen's representation of the effects of location on land utilization. In his book *Der Isolierte Staat (The Isolated State),* written in 1826, he demonstrates the effect of transportation costs on land utilization by assuming the case of an isolated economic area comprised of an urban concentration surrounded by a flat rural plain. By assuming uniform climate, soil fertility and transportation facilities, Von Thunen frees his model from complications such as competing urban areas, aesthetic considerations and differential transportation costs per unit of distance traveled. His analysis holds constant all factors except choice of market and land use. Under these circumstances, he demonstrates that land use choices will be directly attributable to variations in transportation costs. He shows that the closer land lies to the central market, other things remaining constant, the more intensively it will be employed.[1]

Reasoning similar to Von Thunen's led early urban economists to describe idealized urban development in terms of concentric rings of relatively homogeneous uses, with progressively more intensive land use dominating the inner rings. Ernest W. Burgess attempted to fit this concentric zone model to the pattern of development existing in Chicago in the early 1920s.[2] Based upon intensity of land use, Burgess's essay argues that the central area will be dominated by financial firms and major retail stores. Outside the central zone will be found wholesaling and light manufacturing businesses, somewhat overlapping a third zone containing the homes of low-income residents. Beyond this will be a zone occupied by heavy manufacturing, which needs ready access to transportation routes to the outside world. Outer zones, he argues, will be reserved for residential use, serving progressively wealthier users as distance from the center increases.

Burgess's version of the *concentric zone model* is designed to explain urban development as it existed in the 1920s, but today's readers will be hard-pressed to find the patterns Burgess thought he detected. His fourth ring, "zone of transition," in cities such as Chicago no longer contains a significant number of factories, being comprised instead of a mixture of abandoned buildings and embryonic redevelopment into middle-class residential structures. Much of industry has moved into what Burgess categorizes as the commuter's zone, leaping over residential areas that blocked the expansion of previous manufacturing facilities.

Limitations of the concentric zone model are obvious. Topography and specialized transportation corridors distort the circular pattern. Technology and lifestyle changes alter the relative intensity of land uses among various categories, thereby varying competitors' ability to bid for highly valued sites. Inner-circle users may find their expansion needs frustrated by users in the next zone and be forced to leapfrog to areas beyond.

Business Location Decisions

Market imperfections create substantial deviation from the pattern of land uses dictated by the need for efficiency in human affairs. But a systematic pattern suggestive of Von Thunen's and Burgess's models is nonetheless discernible in every urban area, reflecting the history of rational use decisions over a period of years.

Typical development patterns place major retail stores at the center, where all transportation arteries converge. As the single most convenient spot for the greatest number of people, the *central business district* is the logical locational choice for firms drawing customers from throughout an area. Financial offices and major retail stores alike are sufficiently land-intensive activities to justify this area of highest land rents. In smaller cities, retail and financial operations intermix; in the next largest metropolitan areas they are grouped side by side within the city center.

Even a cursory examination of almost any city reveals that much of the shopping is done outside the central business district, at stores that do not aspire to draw from a citywide clientele. But major stores, those drawing from the widest possible range of customers and purveying merchandise for which customers are inclined to plan a special shopping trip, are hard-pressed to justify any other than a downtown location for their main outlet.

Outside the central business district, retail location decisions create two divergent patterns of city structure. Many businesses find it economic to locate along major traffic arteries, creating business thoroughfares at various locations throughout the city. The other major pattern involves clusters of businesses that benefit from mutual proximity and thus create multiple nuclei or miniature downtowns throughout metropolitan areas.[3]

Businesses locating along major arterial streets create what has been described as a radial or axial development pattern, as illustrated in Figure 4.1. Thus cities tend to expand first along their major transportation arteries and then to be fleshed out by residential and further commercial development in the interstices between these growth axes.

Many businesses benefit from mutual proximity. Convenience shops seek locations adjacent to stores featuring shopping goods, to capture business from customers drawn by their neighbors. Stores carrying similar lines of merchandise frequently benefit from clustering, because they then draw a larger crowd of

FIGURE 4.1   Radial and Nodal Development Extends Outward from Central Area

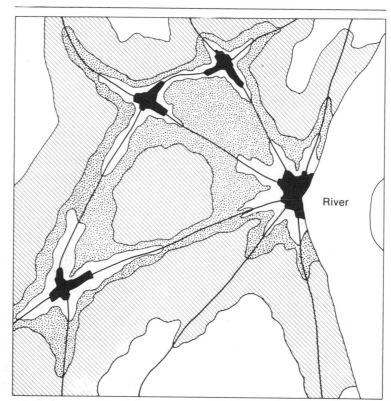

shoppers than could any one of them in isolation. Since the early 1950s, real estate entrepreneurs have catered to these special needs of merchants by developing shopping centers that, in many cases, take on the dimensions of modest central business districts.

Why clusters of stores form multiple nuclei at particular locations depends upon such diverse factors as prevailing transportation patterns, the socioeconomic status of potential customers and even the availability of sufficient space. Once formed, the nuclei create peaks in local land values and frequently spawn axial developments of their own.

BID-RENT CURVES AND "NATURAL" ZONING

In the absence of rental charges every business firm will seek a location that minimizes the costs of overcoming the "friction of space." The need to move people and things between sites creates costs that tend to reduce a location's desirability. Ideally, closely linked activities would take place at the same site, thus reducing transfer costs to zero. This, of course, is seldom possible.

Linkages and Transfer Costs

In the course of their daily lives, people must constantly travel between locations where their activities are carried on. Children travel from home to school, from home to the playground and entertainment facilities and so on. Adults travel between home and work. For many people, work itself takes place at a multitude of different sites. Entire families must travel for medical, dental and legal services, for shopping and entertainment and for a host of other activities.

Similarly, things must constantly be shuffled between various locations. Food moves from farms to processing plants to storage, thence to retail outlets and finally to homes or restaurants. Manufacturing processes start at farms or mines, from which raw materials might undergo processing at a variety of different locations before a finished product is moved to a retail location and finally to the site of consumption.

Relationships requiring such movement of people or things are called *linkages*, and the locations between which they move are *linked sites*. Costs of transportation between linked sites are sometimes referred to as *transfer costs* and may be either *explicit* or *implicit*. Explicit transfer costs get the most attention, perhaps because they are easier to determine. These are costs measurable in dollars: cost per mile of the chosen transportation medium plus the dollar value of time spent en route.

Analysts sometimes err by ignoring or underestimating the importance of implicit transfer costs. Although more subtle and difficult to identify, they are no less significant than their explicit counterparts. They include the disutility of movement between linked sites, which does not find itself registered in accounting statements. Examples of implicit transfer costs include the fear of traveling through areas considered dangerous and the aggravation and discomfort of coping with congested highways or public transportation facilities.

Linkages and Location of Industry

In addition to affecting the level of transfer costs, a firm's location decision might also affect *processing costs*. This occurs when a site has natural advantages due to soil fertility, a benign climate or some other natural endowment. Where processing costs are a major consideration, firms might accept considerable additional transfer costs to reduce their processing costs. Where processing costs are not greatly affected by locational variation, transfer costs become the prime factor in industrial location decisions. The key issue is that a wisely chosen location will minimize the sum of processing and transfer costs.

Figure 4.2 illustrates a "100 percent" location in the absence of differential rents. If revenue is unaffected by location, then the best location is the one that

FIGURE 4.2   Industrial Location Decisions with Constant Rent or No Rent

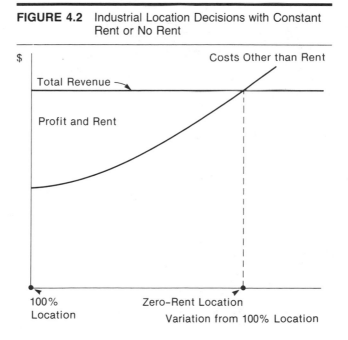

minimizes all costs. Were no rental charges levied, the best location would be at the intersection of the axes on Figure 4.2, because at that point the excess of revenue over costs other than rent is greatest.

Continuing the assumption that revenues are not affected by location, but dropping the assumption that all locations are either free or equally costly, location decisions hinge upon determining what variation from the 100 percent location will minimize the sum of rental charges and all other costs. Rent differentials are created by competition for the 100 percent location. Those firms that can benefit the most from the location are able to outbid all others, forcing their competitors out into the area of Figure 4.2 between the 100 percent location and the zero-rent location.

An industrial location decision for a given rent gradient is illustrated in Figure 4.3. The firm's total cost at each location is the sum of costs other than rent, plus the rent charged at that site. The sum of these charges is illustrated by the total cost curve at the top of the figure. The optimum location for the firm depicted in Figure 4.3 is the one that minimizes total costs, including rent.

Commercial Location Decisions

Firms whose sales are greatly affected by location decisions have more variables to consider. The qualitative difference is that such firms must factor in transfer costs borne by their customers, shoppers who consider travel time and inconvenience when deciding which stores to visit. Again, therefore, total transfer costs (regardless of who incurs them) determine the relative desirability of

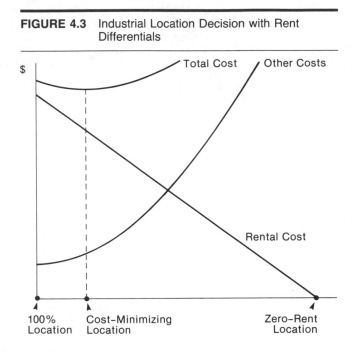

FIGURE 4.3   Industrial Location Decision with Rent Differentials

various sites. As with industrial firms, in the absence of rent (or cost of property ownership), commercial firms would all want the 100 percent location. But competition for that location drives up the rent there, and what results is a declining rent schedule as one moves farther from the location that would be most desirable in the absence of rent (the 100 percent location). This problem is illustrated in Figure 4.4, which shows both rent and profit before rent declining with distance from the 100 percent location. The optimum location is the one that maximizes total profit.

THE MARKET FOR REAL ESTATE SERVICES

We learned in Chapter 3 that all markets perform the basic function of allocating resources among various users. Thus supply and demand in the market for real estate assets result in property rights going to highest bidders. And, to the extent bid prices are based upon accurate appraisal of the stream of future benefits flowing from ownership, assets are acquired by users who can wring the greatest net benefit from their use.

Just as there is a market that allocates available ownership interests among various would-be users, so there is a market that allocates real estate services (shelter and locational benefits from occupancy). Competitive bids create the highest rents at what would otherwise be the most desirable location (the 100

FIGURE 4.4   Retail Location Decisions

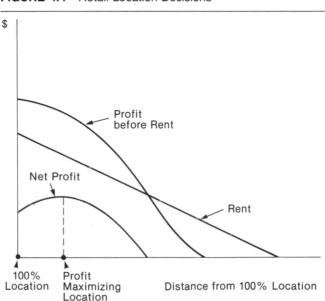

percent location), and rents tend to decline as distance from the 100 percent location increases.

Market Adjustments

Reconsider Figure 4.4. The curve labeled "Profit Before Rent" represents the absolute maximum rent a firm with such a profile can pay and still find remaining in business a worthwhile endeavor. A segment of this curve, frequently called a *bid-rent curve,* is reproduced in Figure 4.5 and labeled "Commercial Bid-Rent Curve." Were there no other bidders, commercial firms whose profit profiles are represented by this curve would occupy locations ranging from the 100 percent location outward to the point where the bid-rent curve intersects the horizontal axis.

But of course there are other contenders for available sites. Firms whose revenues are less dependent upon being near the 100 percent location will not be able to outbid commercial endeavors for nearby locations. But the other firms' bid-rent curves will decline less abruptly with distance, so they will place winning bids for more distant sites. Figure 4.5 depicts the bid-rent curve for such an industry, labeled "Industrial Bid-Rent Curve." A third economic group might have a profit profile that generates bid-rent curves such as that labeled "Agricultural Bid-Rent Curve" in Figure 4.5.

Inspection of Figure 4.5 reveals that commercial firms will outbid alternative users for space between the 100 percent location and point *a,* whereas industrial users will submit winning bids for the area between point *a* and point *b.* Beyond

FIGURE 4.5 Bid-Rent Curves and Natural Zoning

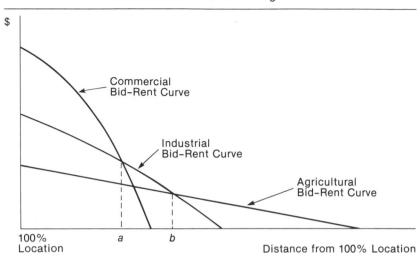

point *b,* other pursuits can afford to pay higher rents than either commercial or industrial firms. Thus, economic considerations will tend to segregate various activities even without the formal zoning regulations adopted by most municipalities.

Because the market is not a perfect allocator of resources, there will be some overlapping of uses, particularly near points *a* and *b* in Figure 4.5. These points represent the locus of zones of transition between predominant uses as dictated by firms' ability to submit winning bids for space. This is the economic rationale underlying the concentric zone and the multiple nuclei patterns of urban development discussed earlier.

Rental Rates and the Adjustment Process

Over very short time periods the supply of rentable space in any market area is relatively fixed. Shifts in the demand schedule for such space are reflected only by changes in market rents; supply over the short run is said to be *price inelastic*. It is irrational to hold available rental space off the market so long as rental rates are sufficient to cover at least the variable costs of providing the space, unless the lower rates are temporary market aberrations. Therefore, a reduction in market rent will not, under most circumstances, cause space to be taken off the market. Conversely, even large increases in rental rates will not make it possible to create additional space faster than the time required for construction.[2] (Be aware, however, that when prices become very high, some space users might be induced to sublet space they currently have under contract. At very low prices landlords might prefer to leave space vacant rather than lock in rates that they consider a temporary aberration. Thus there will always be

---

FIGURE 4.6 Short-Term Price Consequence of a
Shift in Demand

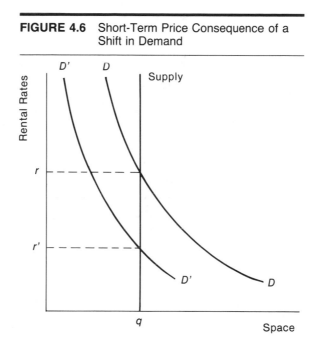

some price elasticity of supply. The aggregate impact of these sources of variation in quantity supplied, however, will generally be slight.)

Figure 4.6 depicts this relationship. If for some reason there is a decrease in the demand for office space at all possible rental rates, as depicted by the shift from demand curve *DD* to *D'D'*, note that over the short run the only impact is a decline in prevailing rental rates from *r* to *r'*. Price serves over the short run to allocate available space among competing users. Space goes to the highest bidders, who presumably can place higher bids because of the greater locational benefits they derive from the space.

Adjustments in Efficient Markets

If all rentable space within a market area were homogeneous (perfectly substitutable) and if all tenants queued daily to bid on a single day's supply, then the market mechanism would work very efficiently. All information affecting either suppliers or users of space would be reflected in market prices within 24 hours. All available space would be utilized (out to the zero-rent location), and no market research would be needed.

As we know from Chapter 3, if there were a sufficient number of participants to preclude any one person or group from inordinately affecting the outcome of the bidding process, and if market information were immediately and costlessly available, then such a market would approach the economists' definition of an atomistic (many would say perfectly competitive) market. Figure 4.7 diagrams the interaction of supply and demand factors in such a market. Each

FIGURE 4.7   Equilibrium Revenue-Cost Relationship in
              Atomistic Market

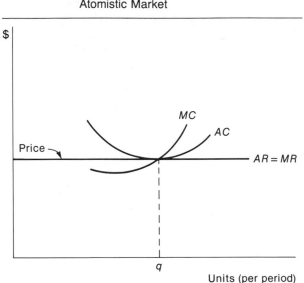

participant can buy or sell all the space desired at the market price, depicted
by the line marked *AR, average revenue*. Landlords will strive to operate at
the level where revenue received from each additional square foot rented (*MR,*
or *marginal revenue*) exactly equals the additional cost incurred (*MC,* or *mar-*
ginal cost). Marginal cost is shown as an upward sloping function because, as
capacity is approached, the additional cost of renting and maintaining each unit
will in fact increase. *Cost,* as defined by economists and as used here, includes
sufficient profit to induce business firms to operate in the rental market. Any
profit in excess of this normal profit is not included as a cost element. Such
additional profit is called *economic rent* or *pure profit. (Economic rent* is a term
that real estate practitioners have unfortunately adopted to mean something
entirely different from the meaning given the term in general economic literature.
Early real estate dictionaries used the term to refer to rental rates that property
could command on the open market, if currently vacant and available. This
definition has since been generally supplanted by the more descriptive phrase
market rent.)

In very efficient markets, production will expand quickly in search of
economic profits. Due to consequent market adjustments, the opportunity for
such profits rapidly disappears. Prices are driven downward by the increase in
the number of producers, while competitive bidding for resources drives production costs up; cost, price and production quantity move to the relationship
depicted in Figure 4.7.

Market Imperfections

But of course the rental market is not nearly so efficient as what we have described. Rental negotiations are conducted in relative secrecy and constitute a private understanding between landlord and tenant. Lease contracts are for extended periods of time so that existing rental rates seldom precisely reflect current market conditions. Indeed, because negotiators themselves do not know exactly what current conditions are, even new lease contracts might not accurately reflect them! Landlords find it prudent to maintain inventories of vacant space as a buffer against errors in judgment. If market prices drop below what landlords feel the market justifies, they prefer to let space remain vacant in anticipation of subsequent higher rents.

Each owner or manager tries to make his or her product (shelter and locational advantage) seem different from the competition's. Nevertheless, most space offered in the same market is more or less substitutable. Each landlord must therefore be alert to the actions of competitors, noting how marketing programs and rental rates affect relative positions in the marketplace. We saw in Chapter 3 that participants in such markets can conveniently be labeled *price searchers*.

Landlords in a price searchers' market operate with the same objective as do those in atomistic markets; they seek to equate marginal revenue with marginal costs, so as to maximize their profit. But because the quantity of space that can be rented by a price searcher is inversely related to rates charged, landlords do not view their marginal revenue curve as flat, as depicted in Figure 4.7. To reduce vacancy rates further, they understand they must provide some rental concessions to make their space relatively more marketable than that of their competition. This means that additional revenue generated by each additional unit of space rented per time period (marginal revenue) is a declining function of the amount of space rented per period.

Figure 4.8 depicts price and cost relationships as viewed by a price searcher. Production quantity q, measured on the horizontal axis, equates marginal revenue with marginal cost and thus generates maximum profit. Price is determined by the relationship between quantity produced and demand for the product. Quantity q can be sold at average price r and is produced at average cost c. Average profit above the "normal" profit required to induce firms to operate in the market is r minus c. This is pure profit or economic rent, resulting from the monopoly element in the marketplace.

But economic profit is destined to be relatively short-lived. Landlords do not have a long-term monopoly over the ability to satisfy tenant desires, and the presence of above-average profit will lead others to develop close substitutes for space that is found to be in unusual demand. This shifts the demand curve for the firm depicted in Figure 4.8 to the left. Profits shrink as new firms continue to enter the market with close substitute space, and eventually the abnormal profit (economic rent) disappears.

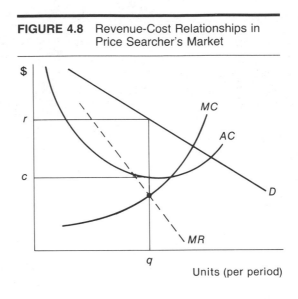

FIGURE 4.8 Revenue-Cost Relationships in
Price Searcher's Market

MARKET STRUCTURE AND THE NEED FOR MARKET RESEARCH

Those who operate in atomistic markets *(price takers)* have little need for market research. They merely deliver their homogeneous product to whatever buyer is currently in the market and sell for the established "market price." Energy is expended primarily on cost control, to attain the highest possible rate of production before diseconomies of scale render further expansion uneconomic. Price takers face continual problems with cost control, as the most efficient producers expand their output and shift the aggregate supply curve outward, thereby driving down the price that all producers must take. To the extent that market research is undertaken, it will likely concentrate on determining prevailing market standards.

Price searchers (those who operate in monopolistically competitive or oligopolistic markets) face a much more complex problem. Control over market price is closely related to the extent that their product is distinguished from closest substitutes. Considerable effort may be expended, therefore, to increase the degree of distinctiveness, whether real or imagined, between units of real estate service.

In at least one respect, all real estate might be considered a differentiated product; each piece is unique with respect to its exact location. The significance of this locational distinction, however, differs drastically from situation to situation. Parcels that are somehow unique can frequently command a considerable price premium. Product differences, whether real or spurious, desensitize buyers to price differentials. The distinction may lie in architectural aesthetics, construction quality, luxurious appointments or any other element that creates a compelling image for potential buyers.

Differences that exist only in the perception of buyers may be far more valuable than actual physical differences. Styling, quality of construction and functional features can usually be duplicated by competitors, but reputation is unique to individual properties and is often generated consciously to appeal to a specific class of tenant. Depending on the image associated with the address, a property may command premium rents or sell at a discount from prevailing rates for similarly located and outfitted space.

Price searchers who have access to better market intelligence than that available to their competitors may benefit substantially. If they can discern what locations will afford competitive advantages to tenants in the near future, they can acquire title to appropriate parcels before such information is reflected in prices. If they are able to forecast changes in locational advantage accurately over the years, they can more precisely estimate a new property's investment value. Comparing investment value with market values that do not yet reflect all pertinent information will enable astute researchers and analysts to consistently outperform the market.

SUMMARY

Real property owners who rent their space to users are in effect selling a service that is comprised of shelter and locational benefit. In many cases the rental rate a property commands is determined primarily by the locational element; the more desirable the location, the greater the rent will be per square foot. Generally, the density of land use will also be greater. At progressively more remote locations, both use density and rents tend to decline. This pattern is distorted by the fact that, once a building has been constructed on a site, the most economically advantageous use might be entirely different than if the site were still vacant.

Relationships requiring movement of people or things between sites are called *linkages*. Sites between which movement occurs are said to be *linked*. Space users strive to locate so as to minimize the total cost of rent plus aggregate transfer costs.

Because the market for real estate services is relatively inefficient, property owners or managers who are more adept at market research frequently are able to consistently differentiate their product and thereby command premium rents. They are thus able to reap above-average profits, which economists call *economic rent*. Economic rent stemming from any particular source tends to disappear as competitors become aware and rush to produce close substitutes for the real estate service noted to be in high demand. Constant market research is needed, therefore, to find new sources of product differentiation in order to perpetuate economic rent.

NOTES

1. Johann Heinrich Von Thunen, *Der Isolierte Staat,* 1826. For an English translation, see Peter Hall, ed., *Von Thunen's Isolated State* (London: Pergamon Press, 1966).

2. Ernest W. Burgess, "The Growth of the City," in Robert Park et al., *The City* (Chicago: University of Chicago Press, 1984).

3. Richard U. Ratcliff describes these patterns as string street developments and nucleation. See Richard U. Ratcliff, *Real Estate Analysis* (New York: McGraw-Hill, 1961).

RECOMMENDED READINGS

Barrett, G. Vincent and John P. Blair. *How to Conduct and Analyze Real Estate Market and Feasibility Studies.* New York: Van Nostrand Reinhold Company, 1982, pp. 138–160.

Muth, Richard F. *Urban Economic Problems.* New York: Harper and Row, 1975, pp. 28–53.

Ratcliff, Richard U. *Valuation for Real Estate Decisions.* Santa Cruz, CA: Democrat Press, 1972, pp. 15–48.

Ratcliff, Richard U. *Real Estate Analysis.* New York: McGraw-Hill, 1961, pp. 13–41.

Richardson, Harry W. *Urban Economics.* Hinsdale, IL: The Dryden Press, 1978, pp. 15–39.

Shafer, Thomas W. *Urban Growth and Economics.* Reston, VA: Reston Publishing Company, Inc., 1977, pp. 73–92.

REVIEW QUESTIONS

1. What are the limitations of the concentric ring hypothesis as developed by Von Thunen and Burgess?
2. Explain the concept of linkages.
3. How is land utilization determined in a market system?
4. Explain the axial development pattern of cities and the multiple nuclei pattern.
5. What are explicit and implicit transfer costs?
6. What should an industry consider in selecting a location?
7. How do transfer costs affect the decision for a commercial location?
8. What is the effect of shifts in demand for rentable space on the supply of space and market rents over both the short run and the long run?

DISCUSSION QUESTIONS

1. If you were designing a city to be built on virgin land, to what extent might you copy the pattern suggested by Von Thunen and Burgess? Why might you choose a different pattern and what would your alternate pattern be?

2. Think of a regional or superregional shopping mall as a central business district and try to apply what you have read to explain the pattern of adjacent development since the mall was created.

3. Since, by their influence on land values, market forces tend to create "zones" of specialized land uses, what purpose is served by legal zoning? What are some reasons citizens might prefer regulated rather than market-determined land use patterns?

4. A land acquisition specialist for a discount store chain said that when his firm decides to enter a new market it buys or leases the three best store locations in the area, uses the best one for its new store and makes certain that the other two sites are used only for noncompeting purposes. Discuss this in terms of the text's explanation of bid-rent curves and natural zoning.

CHAPTER 5

Market Research Tools and Techniques

INTRODUCTION

A random selection of real estate journals reveals a somewhat curious imbalance of subject matter. Journal articles tend to concentrate on techniques for translating cash-flow estimates into property value, but they slight the issue of collecting and verifying data. Yet the most advanced application of quantitative analytical techniques will not yield a reliable estimate of investment value unless applied to reasonably reliable cash-flow forecasts, which are derived through conscientious market research. G. Vincent Barrett and John P. Blair have called market studies both the most difficult and the most important part of the real estate development planning process.[1]

THE NEED FOR MARKET RESEARCH

Investment analysts and portfolio managers need market information at every stage in their decision-making efforts. They must, for example, estimate the most likely cash flow from each investment alternative under consideration. They need to know yields available in the marketplace so that cash-flow estimates can be adjusted intelligently for differences in the timing of expected receipts.

Market Data and Portfolio Decisions

Market information is required not only for rational acquisition decisions but also for managing the existing investment portfolio. Periodically, all assets in the portfolio should be reevaluated. Managers must decide whether to continue holding properties currently owned or to adjust the portfolio mix. If the decision is to adjust, then they must decide how to divest themselves of existing assets (whether by outright sale, sale and leaseback, an exchange of properties, etc.). If no divestiture is indicated, they must nevertheless decide whether assets should be refinanced, refurbished, converted to another use and so forth. All these decisions are based on the same basic investment criteria applied to an acquisition decision. All require extensive market intelligence.

Market Data for Better Property Management

Market research is also needed to facilitate operating management decisions. Gilbert A. Churchill, Jr., notes that research information is used by operating management for *planning,* for *problem solving* and for *control* purposes.[2]

As a planning tool, market research aids in identifying opportunities and anticipating difficulties. Property managers need to know basic trends in the economic environment within which they must market and administer rental space and must estimate how these trends will affect the market for real estate services. Market research reveals how changing income levels, consumption patterns and work practices are likely to affect demand for rental space. This may reveal needed alterations in rental rates and marketing channels. Data on competitive rents, for example, aid in deciding upon the appropriate rent structure and advertising budget.

Market research for problem solving aids in identifying needed changes in investors' property portfolios and property alterations to enhance rentability. Information about present and potential tenants' needs and preferences reveals what existing building amenities should be phased out because they do not contribute sufficient rent-generating ability to justify maintenance costs. It also suggests what amenities should be added to make buildings more competitive. Research reveals whether space is likely to be more marketable on long-term or short-term leases and which lease clauses are likely to meet with least tenant resistance. It also indicates what tenant mix will maximize the property's ability to command rents. Should a suburban office building cater to tenants in a specific profession such as law or medicine, for example, or will a heterogeneous tenant mix lead to lower vacancy rates and greater gross operating revenue?

Control-oriented market research permits early identification of existing and potential management trouble spots. It provides intelligence needed to assess the quality of current building operations and to evaluate proposed changes. Comparing building rental and vacancy rates with those of comparable properties, for example, reveals how well management is marketing existing space. Comparative tenant turnover rates highlight the degree of tenant satisfaction with a building and with building management. *Operating expense ratios* (expenses as a percent of gross rents) from comparable buildings help identify operating inefficiencies and permit early corrective action. Information relative to tenant turnover and building vacancy rates enables investors to evaluate their own management performance and indicates where adjustments are required to make actual operating outcomes conform more closely to plans. Such information might also, of course, indicate a need to revise the management plan itself.

Market Data Aid in Pricing Decisions

For profit-motivated investors there is but one arbiter of rental rates: the market. Market analysis reveals price ranges within which units can be rented. Generally, various commercial activities located in shopping centers pay different lease rates per square foot, depending upon the amount of space for which they contract. Leases usually cite a flat rental rate plus a percentage of gross sales above some base amount. A lease might specify, for example, $7 per year per square foot plus five percent of gross sales. Market research is required to determine prevailing terms in a particular market area so that the lessee can decide on the basis of that intelligence whether the proposed rental rate and flat fee are reasonable and advantageous.

HOW MUCH MARKET RESEARCH?

Suppose an investor is offered a proposition in which the seller has forecast cash flows and changes in market value for a number of years corresponding to the prospective buyer's most likely holding period. Has the market research problem been solved, or should the investor commission a separate study?

Investors and analysts with some experience in the market area and with the type of property in question might be in a position to evaluate the reasonableness of a forecast, based upon their knowledge of current market relationships. They can, if they deem it appropriate, further refine their opinion with an extensive expenditure of time and money for further data gathering and analysis. A seller's data are automatically suspect, yet there must be some limit to the amount of additional market research undertaken. The problem is in deciding how much is enough.

Figure 5.1 illustrates the problem facing investors who must decide how much market research to commission. Expected research costs and expected benefits are both measured on the vertical axis. The vertical distance between the cost and benefit functions represents the net benefit derived from research. Maximum net benefit results from the amount of research and analysis repre-

FIGURE 5.1   Cost, Benefit and Optimum Level of Research Effort

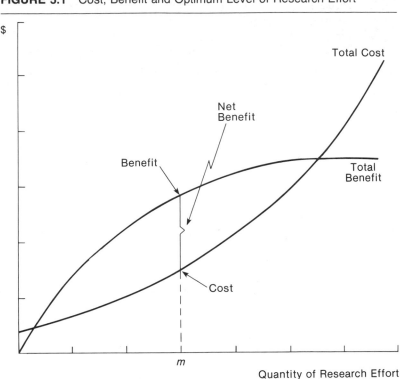

sented by point *m* on the horizontal axis. Additional increments of research and analysis beyond this point cost more than their incremental benefit, thus reducing the net benefit from such activity.

Since benefits from research are not objectively measurable, decision makers will be sorely challenged to identify the point where they reach maximum benefit. James D. Vernor has suggested that research usually proceeds in iterations with each round becoming increasingly more complex and costly.[3] Beginning with crude market data incorporated into crude financial synthesis such as first-year ratio analysis, the investigation progresses to successively more elaborate data collection efforts and financial analysis.

However the dilemma is faced, some market intelligence clearly must be gathered before substantial resources are committed to an uncertain venture. Just as clearly, there is some point beyond which research and analysis must cease and a "go or no-go" decision must be made. The problem is phrased succinctly by George Bernard Shaw: "When we have done our utmost to arrive at a reasonable conclusion, we . . . must close our minds for the moment with a snap, and act dogmatically on our own conclusion. The man who waits to make an entirely reasonable will dies intestate."

A DESIGN FOR MARKET RESEARCH

Because problems faced by investors are not uniform, research procedure must be custom-tailored. Yet, even though each project has its own special emphasis, all share a common sequence of steps. Churchill summarizes the steps of the research process neatly, and we reproduce his description in its totality.[4]

Problem Formulation. One of the more valuable roles marketing research can perform is helping to define the problem to be solved. Only when the problem is carefully and precisely defined can research be designed to provide pertinent information. Part of the process of problem definition includes specifying the objectives of the specific research project or projects that might be undertaken. Each project should have one or more objectives, and the next step in the process should not be taken until these can be explicitly stated.

Research Design. The sources of information for a study and the research design go hand in hand. They both depend on how much is known about the problem. If relatively little is known about the phenomenon to be investigated, exploratory research will be warranted. As will be seen later, exploratory research dictates a flexible data-collection strategy. Published data, interviews with knowledgeable people, and cases providing sharp contrasts can be especially productive. If, on the other hand, the problem is precisely and unambiguously formulated, descriptive or causal research is needed. In these research designs, data collection is not flexible but is rigidly specified, both with respect to the data-collection forms and the sample design.

Design of Data Collection Method and Forms. Quite often, the information needed to solve the problem cannot be found in internal or published external records. The research then must depend on primary data, which are collected specifically for the study. The research questions here are several. Should the data be collected by observation or questionnaire? Should the form be structured as a fixed set of alternative answers or should the responses be open-ended? Should the purposes be made clear to the respondent or should the study objectives be disguised? There are more questions, but these should serve to illustrate the basic concerns at this stage of the research process.

Sample Design and Data Collection. In designing the sample, the researcher must specify, among other things: (1) the sampling frame, (2) the sample selection process, and (3) the size of the sample. The sampling frame is the list of population elements from which the sample will be drawn. While we often assume the frame is implicit in the research problem and thus can take it for granted, the assumption can be dangerous.

Analysis and Interpretation of the Data. Data analysis involves the statistical tests that are applied, as well as the editing, coding, and tabulation of the data. Editing is the process by which the data collection forms are reviewed to assure that they are complete, consistent, and that the instructions were followed. Coding is the assignment of numerals to the observations so that the data can be more readily analyzed, while tabulation is the classifications and cross-classifications that result from counting the values of the observations.

The coding, editing, and tabulation functions are common to most research studies. The statistical tests applied to the data, if any, are somewhat unique to the particular sampling procedures and data collection instruments used in the research. These tests should be anticipated before data collection is begun, if possible, to assure that the data and analysis will be germane to the problem as specified.

Preparation of the Research Report. The research report is the document submitted to management that summarizes the research results and conclusion. It is all that many executives will see of the research effort, and it becomes the standard by which that research is judged. Thus it is imperative that the research report be clear and accurate, since no matter how well all previous steps have been completed, the project will be no more successful than the research report.

Churchill notes that the stages in the research process, beyond the problem formulation stage, may not proceed in the neat sequence outlined. Trying to complete a research design, for example, may reveal that the problem has not been sufficiently delineated; the researcher must return to step one and define research objectives more completely. Approaching the data collection step, the planned procedure may be revealed to be too costly. It then becomes necessary to redesign the research project to collect less data or substitute other data (or perhaps to rely on secondary sources) in order to remain within the research budget. Once data are collected, however, the researcher is probably committed to the research design, because collecting new data to satisfy requirements of an altered design is likely to be prohibitively expensive. For this reason it is imperative that the design be thought through carefully before data collection begins.

DATA SOURCES

Once a research problem is properly defined and clearly specified, researchers logically turn their attention to data collection. At this point a decision must be made to rely on primary or secondary sources for needed information. *Primary data* are statistics gathered by the researcher precisely for the problem at hand. *Secondary data,* in contrast, are those previously gathered for some other purpose. A good operating rule is to rely on primary sources only if secondary data are not available.

Secondary Data

The uninitiated are easily led to believe that primary data are necessary when in fact secondary sources may be more than adequate. Wherever available, secondary data are almost certain to be less costly and less time-consuming to generate than are primary data. Information that is readily available for free in nearby libraries or at modest cost from firms that specialize in generating such information might cost thousands of dollars and require weeks of effort for a primary researcher to gather. Because information can be reused an infinite number of times, firms that deal in its generation and dissemination can reap a tidy profit while charging a small fraction of what their customers would have to pay to generate the data themselves.

A primary disadvantage, and a major cause of researchers' frustration, is that secondary data are almost never available in precisely the desired form. Units of measure are frequently inappropriate for the intended purpose, class definitions seldom exactly fit those of the researcher, and the secondary data are frequently dated.

Secondary data are frequently available in raw form from agencies that generate it. These include government agencies, universities and private firms (real estate appraisers, brokers and counselors, market research firms, architects, accounting firms and so forth) whose research needs lead them to investigate phenomena of interest to the real estate analyst. Their data files can save many days of tedious work and costly hours of field investigation.

No primary data should be generated, therefore, until all potential commercial sources of reliable and timely secondary data have been exhausted. Large commercial data banks with computerized storage and retrieval facilities often permit information to be provided in almost any format desired and in a variety of classifications.

The U.S. Bureau of the Census, under the Department of Commerce, is the largest data-gathering agency in the nation. Census data are generally of high quality and are available in a variety of formats. Census data tapes or punched cards can be purchased from the Bureau of the Census, permitting researchers to create their own formats and classifications. There are in fact ten different censuses, all of interest to real estate analysts to greater or lesser extent.

- *Population.* Every ten years the entire population is counted. The result is a detailed breakdown of population statistics by characteristics such as age, sex, marital status, race, education, family size, occupation, income and so forth. Data are provided on a regional basis within each category. Annual Current Population Reports update the census data by incorporating the latest information on changes in population characteristics.
- *Housing.* Since 1940 the Decennial Census has reported detailed data on housing, including the size, condition and type of structures; number of occupants per household; average market value; average rents and facilities such as plumbing and major kitchen appliances. Current Housing Reports are issued annually to update this data.
- *Retail Trade.* The Census of Retail Trade, conducted every five years, reports detailed data on the number of stores of various types, total sales and number of employees. Data are reported by relatively small geographic areas such as counties, cities and standard metropolitan statistical areas. Monthly Retail Trade Reports provide the current data.
- *Service Industries.* Taken every five years, the Census of Service Industries provides data on receipts, number of firms, employment and types of business

within the service industries. Current data are published in monthly Selected Services Reports.

- *Wholesale Trade.* Wholesalers are classified into more than 150 separate business groups in the Census of Wholesale Trade. The census reports are published every five years and contain statistics on sales volume, warehouse space, expenditures, employment and so forth. Current data are reported in monthly Wholesale Trade Reports.
- *Manufacturers.* Every five years the Census of Manufacturers is authorized to report manufacturing data in about 450 different classifications of manufacturing activity. Detailed data are generated on the number of firms, their output, employment, wages, sales and value added and a number of additional measures. Supplementary data are found in the Annual Survey of Manufacturers and in Current Industrial Reports, published monthly.
- *Mineral Industries.* Also intended to be generated every five years, the Census of Mineral Industries provides information similar to the Census of Manufacturers but reports on mineral industries in approximately 50 separate categories. Annual data similar (but not directly comparable) to those contained in the Census of Mineral Industries are reported annually in the Minerals Yearbook (Bureau of Mines, Department of the Interior).
- *Transportation.* Also published at five-year intervals, the Census of Transportation provides statistics on passenger travel, truck and bus use and commodities shipped by various categories of carriers.
- *Agriculture.* The Census of Agriculture offers detailed information on land uses, employment, quantity and value of products and land use practices every five years. Data are presented by county within each state. Annual publications, Agriculture Statistics and Commodity Yearbook, provide current information.
- *Government.* General characteristics of state and local governments (employment, payroll, indebtedness, revenues and operating expenses, etc.) are reported every five years in the Census of Government.

Several private publishers provide information of special interest to real estate analysts. A number of these are included in a listing of published information sources in Appendix 5.A.

Primary Data

Secondary sources can prove completely fruitless. Data may prove outdated, unreliable, or inappropriately classified and may provide no useful intelligence. More frequently, secondary data prove useful but inadequate. It may then be necessary for real estate analysts to resort to primary data sources.

Primary data may be gathered by *communication* or by *observation,* with the choice usually dictated by the nature of the intelligence desired. Communication involves questioning respondents. Questions may be oral or written and may elicit responses in either form. Questions may be short and to the point or may involve in-depth interviews. Observation means checking and recording relevant facts or behavior. For example, a researcher might estimate the boundaries of a store's trade area by checking customers' license plates and noting their counties of origin.

Communication is a more versatile means of gathering data than is observation. It is more amenable to the collection of a variety of factual data. Whatever a person's behavior, attitude, degree of awareness or intention of interest, all one has to do is ask. There is, of course, a constant concern about the accuracy of responses.

When it is possible to use communication as the primary means of gathering data, this method usually proves to be faster and more cost-effective than mere observation. Researchers are not forced to wait for events to occur so that they can be observed.

Data collected by communication, however, are sometimes tainted by a lack of objectivity. Interviewees are sometimes inclined to say what they believe their interrogators want to hear. Responses are influenced by how questions are structured, or in many cases, merely by the demeanor of the interviewer.

Data collected by observation are more likely to be objective and factual. Data that can be collected by either method are generally more reliable if secured by observation. The subject's perceptions play less of a role when data are collected in this fashion. Observation tends to be more time-consuming, however, and therefore more expensive.

DESCRIPTIVE RESEARCH

Much of the research data needed by real estate investment analysts is descriptive in nature. Examples include:

1. Describing the profile of a typical tenant. Based on information gathered from tenants in similar buildings, one might attempt to describe the profile of a most likely tenant for a proposed structure, characterizing the tenant with respect to amenities desired, amount of space taken and special facilities required.
2. Estimating the proportion of people in a specific population who behave in a particular manner. To illustrate, one might need to estimate the proportion of residents within a certain radius of a proposed shopping center who would shop at the complex.
3. Estimating reactions to proposed alterations in rental terms, such as length of leases or the relative degree to which rent depends upon a flat fee versus a percentage lease clause. One might also wish to estimate typical reactions to separating rental rates for basic facilities and rates for special amenities, such as swimming pools and health club facilities.

Planning for Descriptive Research

No data should be gathered until the researcher has clearly determined who is to contribute information, what information is to be collected, when the information is to be solicited, where interviews are to be conducted and how collection is going to be accomplished.

Data collection should also be preceded by the preparation of a cataloging system. This aids in early identification of analytical problems that may be faced after data are collected. Many potential research design errors will be discovered before incurring the time and expense of data collection if a dummy table of cataloged variables is fully worked out in advance, leaving only the actual data to be recorded in the catalog space provided. With this precaution, researchers are less likely to overlook a crucial variable that should have been included in the data program; they are even less likely to fall into the common trap of gathering information that may be interesting in its own right but does not prove useful for solving the research problem.

Cross-Sectional and Time Series Data

Descriptive surveys may be *cross-sectional* or *time series*. Cross-sectional surveys, which involve one-time sampling from a population of research interest, are by far the most frequently encountered type of data collection assignment. All elements are measured at a single point in time. The cross-sectional survey thus provides a snapshot of the variables under observation at the time of the survey.

Time series, in contrast, measure changes over time. Sometimes called *longitudinal studies*, they involve repeated measures of the same phenomena, recording any variation through time. Time series analysis in no way implies that time itself is a causal factor in observed change. Rather, the analyst observes changes in both the phenomena of interest and other factors presumed to bear a causal relationship.

QUANTITATIVE RESEARCH TECHNIQUES

Modern statistical techniques are a powerful addition to the analyst's repertoire of analytical tools. These techniques permit rapid and inexpensive analysis and synthesis of masses of data. They also permit reliable generalizations to be drawn after examination of a limited portion of the total pool of information.

Statistical techniques have received an undeserved reputation among students as requiring a high level of mathematical skill. Deriving or proving fundamental rules (called *theorems* by mathematicians) does require recourse to calculus or higher mathematics. Applying generally accepted theory is an entirely different matter. To apply the most commonly employed statistical tools, one needs no more than perhaps an eighth-grade knowledge of arithmetic. What is required is an understanding of the statistical relationships themselves, their strengths and weaknesses, their uses and potential misuses.

This makes statistical tools particularly valuable in market research, where conclusions about consumer preferences must be drawn from questionnaires distributed to only a small proportion of the total market and where predictions about the future must be made on a basis of past occurrences.

Statistical applications divide conveniently into two broad categories. *Descriptive statistics* involve measuring characteristics that are important to a problem and bringing them together in summary form. Descriptive statistics employ quantitative expressions to describe characteristics of a sample or an underlying population. Knowledgeable and busy analysts appreciate the reduction of large masses of data to essentials. Statistical methodology permits this to be done in an inexpensive and timely manner.

Inferential statistics involve drawing conclusions from evidence contained in the data. Real estate analysts frequently use inferential statistics to make inferences about a general class of phenomena from a small sample or to estimate future occurrences by studying data from the recent past.

The Population and the Sample

Modern statistics offers a variety of analytical techniques to aid in forecasting and decision making. A common element in most of these techniques is the use of sample data to make estimates and predictions or to draw conclusions. *Samples* are drawn from a larger body of data called a *population*. The population (also sometimes referred to as a *universe*) contains all elements of interest to the researcher, but observing and measuring every element in the population is frequently impossible or impractical. A sample serves as a small-scale representation and permits the researcher to draw conclusions about the underlying population.

Selection of sample subjects and sample size is crucial in market research. Information is costly to collect, so it is important to determine the minimum sample size needed for a specific research objective. The cost of market research can be reduced greatly, and the reliability of conclusions can be substantially enhanced, through careful sampling design.

In one of the better introductory statistical textbooks currently available, William Mendenhall and James E. Reinmuth describe statistical problem solving as a five-step procedure:[5]

1. Clearly specify the question to be answered and the population from which data are pertinent. This is a statistics-slanted restatement of the time-honored axiom that a problem well-defined is half-solved.
2. Develop the sampling procedure. Data collection is extremely expensive, and it is imperative that only pertinent data are collected. Including too many observations in the sample is wasteful; including too few may be even more wasteful because sample data will not be sufficiently representative of the population.
3. Analyze the sample data. A sophisticated understanding of statistical procedures permits selection of appropriate techniques for extracting information from the data.
4. Use information extracted from sample data to draw inferences about the underlying population. A variety of inferential tools are available, and the

appropriate choice will vary with the estimate or decision to be made as well as with the form in which information is available.

5. Estimate the degree of confidence justified in inferences drawn from the sample data. Are estimates reliable enough to justify an investment commitment? Statistical estimation and prediction procedures permit quantitative expressions of confidence.

Simple Linear Regression and Correlation

Many market research problems faced by real estate investment analysts involve *forecasting,* or predicting a value from known, related data. An investor might wish to estimate the future relationship between gross rental revenue and operating expenses, between economic activity and the level of future rental vacancies or between operating income and market value. These are but a few of the ubiquitous forecasting problems that plague investment analysts.

To illustrate, consider the problem of predicting a property's market value by observing its rental value. If the investor finds a consistent relationship between market and rental values, he or she might be able quickly and inexpensively to eliminate from consideration properties whose prices appear grossly disproportionate to their abilities to generate rent. The investor would then proceed with a more extensive (and more costly) analysis of properties that met his or her preliminary criteria of reasonableness.

Of the several regression techniques available, *simple linear regression* is easiest both to understand and to employ. It involves measuring the association between observed values of two important property characteristics. One of the characteristics, the *independent variable,* is considered largely determinative of the value of the other, the *dependent variable.* There results a measure of the extent to which variation (within the sample) in the dependent variable is associated with variation in the independent variable.

Example 5.1

Three properties have the following gross rental incomes (the independent variable) and recent sales prices (the dependent variable):

	Gross Rent	**Sales Price**
Property 1	$6,000	$54,000
Property 2	$8,000	$62,000
Property 3	$9,500	$68,000

The relationship in Example 5.1 is presented graphically as Figure 5.2, with the dependent characteristic (sales price) on the vertical axis and the

FIGURE 5.2   Linear Relationship Between Gross Income and Market Value

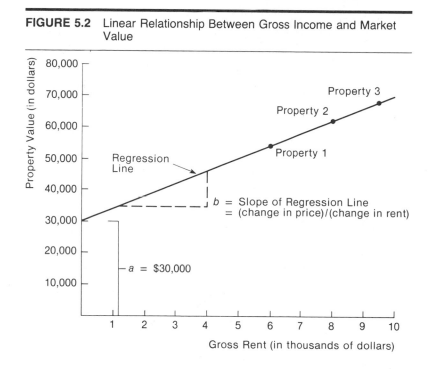

independent characteristic (gross rent) on the horizontal. The diagonal line intersecting the vertical axis indicates the linear relationship between gross income and selling prices for these properties.

This relationship is described by the equation

$$y = a + bx$$

where:

y = the dependent variable
a = a constant
b = a constant
x = the independent variable

The y value in the equation is considered dependent because its value depends upon the other values in the equation. In Figure 5.2 price is the dependent variable. The constant factor, a, in the equation is the point at which the regression line (the diagonal line in Figure 5.2) intersects the vertical axis. The other constant, b, indicates the slope of the regression line. It is a measure of the average change in the dependent variable for a given change in the independent variable.

Note that the regression relationship does not in any way imply causality. Changes in the independent variable may or may not exert influence upon the dependent variable, but nothing in the regression equation is intended to measure or test for any such influence. All the equation does is measure association

FIGURE 5.3 Price-Revenue Relationships in a Chicago Neighborhood

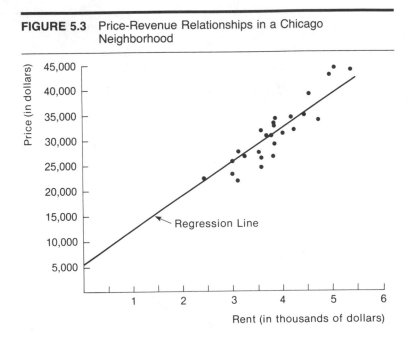

between changes in the dependent variable and changes in the independent variable.

Figure 5.2 is derived from an example deliberately contrived to result in a straight-line relationship between the independent and the dependent variables. Relationships actually observed in the marketplace are not so accommodating.

Figure 5.3 illustrates a more nearly typical set of observations. Each dot in the scatter diagram represents an observation taken from a property on Table 5.1, which records a sample of 26 three- to four-unit apartment buildings sold in Chicago. The sum of the variations (positive and negative) of all sales prices in the sample from those indicated by the regression relationship must equal zero.

The usefulness of the regression technique depends upon how exactly the regression line reflects the relationship between independent and dependent variables. A commonly employed measure of representativeness is the *coefficient of determination*. More commonly referred to as *r-square*, and denoted by the symbol r^2, the coefficient of determination measures the percent of variation in the value of the dependent variable associated with variation in the value of the independent variable. Remember that there is no implication of causation in this measure. It indicates only that the fluctuations are related in some systematic manner to the extent of the value of the coefficient of determination.

The coefficient of determination is measured on a scale from zero to one. In general, the higher the coefficient, the greater the portion of the variation in the dependent variable explained by variation in the independent variable. Note, however, that the coefficient relates only to the systematic relationship between

TABLE 5.1 Price-Revenue Relationships for Apartment Buildings Sold Within One Neighborhood

Sale Number	Gross Income	Sales Price
1	$2,440	$22,800
2	3,000	23,000
3	3,000	26,000
4	3,120	22,000
5	3,240	27,000
6	3,240	27,500
7	3,540	27,500
8	3,600	24,500
9	3,600	26,500
10	3,600	32,000
11	3,720	31,000
12	3,780	31,000
13	3,840	27,000
14	3,840	29,000
15	3,840	32,900
16	3,840	33,000
17	3,840	34,000
18	4,080	31,500
19	4,200	34,500
20	4,224	32,000
21	4,440	35,000
22	4,560	39,000
23	4,740	34,000
24	4,980	43,000
25	5,100	44,400
26	5,400	44,000

the measured values of observations in the sample. A high coefficient of determination does not in itself assure that value estimates based on the regression relationship will be reliable.

Perhaps the most useful measure of predictive ability is the *standard error of the forecast*. The smaller the standard error of the forecast, the greater the degree of confidence an analyst is justified in placing in estimates based upon the regression relationship.

For a predetermined regression relationship, the standard error of the forecast varies with the observed value of the independent variable upon which a value estimate is to be made. The further the observed value of the independent variable lies from the mean value of the independent variables in the sample upon which the regression equation is based, the larger the standard error of the forecast will be.

Figure 5.4 illustrates the concept. Because observed gross rental revenue for Property *A* lies almost directly at the mean of the values of gross rental revenues for the observations used to construct the equation, the standard error of the forecast is quite small. The analyst can have a high degree of confidence that the predicted market value is representative of the relationship found in the sample. Property *B*, in contrast, lies a considerable distance from the mean of

FIGURE 5.4   Variance from Mean and Related Standard Error of the Forecast

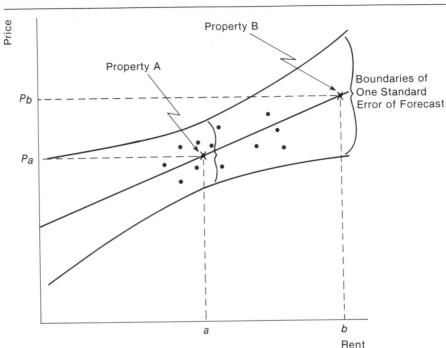

the properties in the sample. *B's* market value might vary considerably from that predicted by the equation, because *B* is not representative of properties included in the sample. Very little confidence can be placed in the market value estimate for *B* drawn from the regression equation. This is reflected in a very high standard error of the forecast.

The Example Extended.   Table 5.1 presents data from observed sales of 26 small apartment buildings of three to four units each. The sample was drawn during the period between 1984 and 1985. The observed relationship between gross rents and actual sales price can be combined in a simple linear regression equation, which can then be used to estimate the probable sales price of a similarly situated property in the same general market category. (Current data, of course, would be employed to estimate probable sales prices today.) Recall the form of the equation

$$y = a + bx$$

where *y* is the dependent variable (in this case, the sales price of the properties), *x* is the independent variable (for this example, the gross rent) and the *a* and *b* values are constants. The equation is solved for values for the constants that will minimize the variation between observed sales prices and prices predicted by the regression line. The *a* constant, you will recall, is the value of the *y*

TABLE 5.2   Computerized Linear Regression Analysis

MULTIPLE REGRESSION HP 2000F VERSION 3/19/75
YOU NEED INSTRUCTIONS (1 = YES, 0 = NO)?0
DATA ON FILE, 0 = DATA IN DATA STATEMENTS. WHICH?0
NO. OF OBSERVATIONS AND NO. OF INPUT VARIABLES?26,2
X TRANSFORMATIONS (1 = YES, 0 = NO)?0
CORRELATION MATRIX
             .934
    34   1.
DETERMINANT OF MATRIX = 1.10017E+07
              MULTIVARIATE CURVEFIT

VARIABLE	MEAN	STD. DEV.
1	31,503.8	6,087.07
2	3,896.31	663.377

VARIABLE	COEFFICIENT
CONSTANT	−1,878.99
1	8.56781

STANDARD DEVIATION OF RESIDUALS = 2,224.06
INDEX OF DETERMINATION (R−SQ) = .871842

---

variable at the point where the regression line intercepts the vertical axis. The *b* constant is the slope of the regression line.

Data from Table 5.1 are plotted on the scatter diagram in Figure 5.3, along with a regression line that minimizes the sum of absolute variation between points on the line and actual sales prices. Solving manually for the values of the constants is somewhat laborious. Computational chores have been greatly simplified, however, by the advent of sophisticated calculators that are preprogrammed to solve such problems and by recent drastic reductions in the cost of small computers.

Data from Table 5.1 were fed into a computer programmed to solve linear regression problems. A partial printout of the computer solution is presented in Table 5.2. The first boxed data at the bottom of the table are the computed values for the constants in the equation: The best fit for the intercept constant, *a*, is −1,878.99; the best fit for the slope constant, *b*, is 8.56781. Substituting these values into the generalized linear regression equation presented earlier, we have

$$\text{Sales Price} = a + b \text{ (gross rent)}$$
$$= -1,878.99 + 8.56781 \text{ (gross rent)}$$

The computer solution includes a measure of the extent to which differences in gross rents explain differences in sales prices for data in the sample. The final boxed data in Table 5.2 present the coefficient of determination as .871842.

TABLE 5.3   Computerized Regression
Analysis: Table of Residuals

Actual	Calculated	Difference	% Difference
34,000	38,732.4	4,732.4	12.2
23,000	23,824.4	824.4	3.4
32,900	31,021.4	−1,878.6	−6.0
27,500	28,451.1	951.1	3.3
22,000	24,852.6	2,852.6	11.4
26,500	28,965.1	2,465.1	8.5
26,000	23,824.4	−2,175.6	−9.1
27,000	25,880.7	−1,119.3	−4.3
44,000	44,387.2	387.2	0.8
33,000	31,021.4	−1,978.6	−6.3
27,000	31,021.4	4,021.4	12.9
32,000	28,965.1	−3,034.9	−10.4
27,500	25,880.7	−1,619.3	−6.2
29,500	28,965.1	−534.9	−1.8
22,800	23,310.4	510.4	2.1
31,000	30,507.3	−492.7	−1.6
43,000	40.788.7	−2,211.3	−5.4
31,500	33,077.7	1,577.7	4.7
31,000	29,993.3	−1,006.7	−3.3
34,000	31,021.4	−2,978.6	−9.6
44,400	41,816.9	−2,583.1	−6.1
29,000	31,021.4	2,021.4	6.5
34,500	34,105.8	−394.9	−1.1
39,000	37,190.2	−1,809.8	−4.8
32,000	34,311.4	2,311.4	6.7
35,000	36,162.1	1,162.1	3.2

This indicates that differences in gross rent account for approximately 87 percent of the variation in observed sales prices.

Differences between actual selling prices and those predicted by the equation are generated by the same computer program used to estimate the selling price. These data, presented in Table 5.3, are called a *table of residuals*. The table shows differences between predicted and actual sales prices of properties in the sample, presented as a percent of predicted values. Inspection reveals that all but two of the observed sales fell within ten percent of those predicted by the equation, indicating fairly good predictive ability for the regression equation.

Now consider how the equation can be used to estimate the probable sales price of another property, assumed to come from the same underlying population as those in the sample. If the observed gross income from such a property were, say, $3,900, the expected sales price would be $31,535.47, determined as follows:

$$\text{Expected Price} = a + b \text{ (gross rent)}$$
$$= -1,878.99 + 8.56781 (\$3,900)$$
$$= \$31,535.47$$

From the table of residuals presented in Table 5.3, the analyst can compute the standard error of the forecast. Probable sales prices can then be expressed as a range of possible outcomes, with related probabilities of occurrence.

Multiple Regression Analysis

Multiple regression differs from simple linear regression in that the analysis may incorporate any number of independent variables. The equation used to represent a linear relationship between multiple independent variables and the dependent variable is

$$y = a + b_1x_1 + b_2x_2 + \ldots + b_nx_n$$

where

y = the dependent variable
a = a constant
b = coefficients of the independent variables $x_1, x_2, \ldots, x_n$
x = values of the independent variables (ranging from 1 through n)

The constant, a, is roughly analogous to the a constant previously described with respect to simple linear regression. The coefficient b_1, b_2 and so on through b_n represent the net relationship between the independent variables x_1, x_2 and so on through x_n, when all factors incorporated in the regression equation are taken into account. Values for all the coefficients are solved simultaneously to determine the solution that produces the best fit for the sample data.

No cause-and-effect relationship is implied by the regression model. Coefficients of the independent variables are in no way related to dollar adjustments appraisers employ in the traditional market data approach. Multiple regression equations are to be judged only in terms of their overall ability to predict values for the dependent variable. Any attempt to interpret regression results in terms of the traditional market data approach is invalid.

As in the case of simple linear regression, the multiple regression equation yields a measure of the percentage of variance in the dependent variable that is explained by variation in the independent variables. This measure, called the *coefficient of multiple determination,* can range from zero to one. The closer it moves toward one, the higher the percentage of explained variance.

The degree of confidence to be placed in a forecast value for the dependent variable can be measured by the standard error of the forecast, which is conceptually similar to the measure calculated in simple linear regression. The measure can be used to estimate probabilities of occurrence associated with ranges of possible outcomes. Standard error of the forecast is affected both by the standard error of the estimate of the sample data and by the relationship between the value of independent variables within the sample and the same data for the property being evaluated.

SUMMARY

Market research is an essential element in rational investment decision making. Revenue and expense forecasts, opportunity cost of capital, and market value estimates are all derived from the market. Investors must refer to market data in order to evaluate management performance and to identify potential areas of performance improvement. Research should be pursued to the point where incremental research and analysis costs equal incremental benefits anticipated.

To a significant extent, market research programs are dictated by the nature of the research problems. Generally, however, the program will start with definition of the problem to be solved and development of the research design. Data collection methods and sample design are then developed, and data are collected. Data are then analyzed and interpreted, and the research report is prepared.

Data sources are designated as primary or secondary, depending upon whether data were collected specifically for the current research problem or for some other problem. Secondary data (collected for other uses) are generally more convenient and less costly to collect but are frequently in a format or in units other than those needed. Primary data are generally collected only after exhausting all available sources of secondary data.

Primary data are gathered by communicating with research subjects or by observing and reporting upon their actions. Communication is more versatile and, where practical, tends to be faster and more cost-effective. Subjectivity is sometimes introduced, however, by the tendency of respondents to give answers they believe researchers expect.

Most market research is descriptive in nature. Descriptive studies may involve a one-time sampling from a population of research interest (cross-sectional data) or repeated measures of the same phenomena to detect changes over time (time series data).

Inferential statistics permit conclusions to be drawn about an entire class of phenomena from observing a sample of the population. Where possible, samples from which inferences are to be drawn are collected on a random basis. Generally, however, real estate data represent judgment samples in which observations are judged to be representative of the underlying population of interest.

Linear regression measures the relationship between independent and dependent variables, permitting judgment about probable values of dependent variables based on observed values of independent variables. Simple linear regression measures the relationship between a dependent variable and one other variable. Multiple regression is similar but permits a variety of independent variables to be incorporated into the analysis.

NOTES

1. G. Vincent Barrett and John P. Blair, *How to Conduct and Analyze Real Estate Market and Feasibility Studies* (New York: Van Nostrand Reinhold, 1981), 9.

2. Gilbert A. Churchill, Jr., *Marketing Research: Methodological Foundations,* 3d ed. (Hinsdale, IL: The Dryden Press, 1983), 10.

3. Dr. James D. Vernor of Georgia State University, in private correspondence.

4. Churchill, *Marketing Research: Methodological Foundations,* 21–24.

5. William Mendenhall and James E. Reinmuth, *Statistics for Management and Economics,* 3d ed. (North Scituate, MA: Duxbury Press, 1978), 6–7.

RECOMMENDED READINGS

Kurtz, David L., and Louis E. Boone. *Marketing,* 5th ed. Hinsdale, IL: The Dryden Press, 1984, pp. 169–210.

Mendenhall, William, and James E. Reinmuth. *Statistics for Management and Economics.* 4th ed. North Scituate, MA: Duxbury Press, 1982, Chapters 11 and 12.

Urban Land Institute. *Mixed Use Development Handbook.* Washington, DC: The Urban Land Institute, 1987, pp. 225–312.

———. *Shopping Center Development Handbook.* 2d ed. Washington, DC: The Urban Land Institute, 1985, pp. 195–302.

REVIEW QUESTIONS

1. Why is there a need for market research in real estate investment decisions?
2. How much market research should be done?
3. What steps are customarily employed in research procedures?
4. Which are preferable, primary or secondary data sources?
5. Describe some methods of collecting primary data.
6. What are the major differences between cross-sectional surveys and time series studies?
7. What sort of sample is generally used in real estate analysis? Why can't entire populations be surveyed?
8. How does multiple regression compare to simple linear regression?
9. Why might multiple regression be preferred over simple linear regression in real estate analysis?
10. Results of a linear regression analysis indicate a high correlation between gross income and sales price. Can it therefore be said that changes in gross income cause changes in sales price?
11. What information does "*r*-square" provide about the relationship between dependent and independent variables?

DISCUSSION QUESTIONS

1. One of your investment clients intends to put virtually all of his or her capital into a large apartment complex. Another client is acquiring a portfolio that will eventually include more than 100 duplex apartments scattered more or less randomly over the cityscape. In what ways might your recommended market analysis for these two clients differ?

2. What are some local sources of secondary market data that might prove useful for real estate investment analysis, and how might one go about gaining access to these data?

3. Suggest some instances where *cross-sectional* and *time series data* might be combined usefully.

APPENDIX 5.A: Sources of Secondary Data

- *Dollars and Cents of Shopping Centers*. Published every two or three years by the Urban Land Institute, 1200 Eighteenth St. N.W., Washington, DC 20036. Contains statistical data on operation of superregional, regional, community and neighborhood shopping centers. Presents operating results by geographic location and shopping center age. Also contains tenant information and characteristics. Some information is provided for Canadian centers.

- *Downtown and Suburban Office Building Experience Exchange Report*. Published annually by the Building Owners and Managers Association, 1221 Massachusetts Ave. N.W., Washington, DC 20005. Provides statistical data about income and expenses for office building operations. Data are divided into downtown and suburban categories. Information is further subdivided according to building age, geographic location, size and height. The publication includes some time series data.

- *Expense Analysis: Condominiums, Co-operatives and P.U.D.s*. Published annually by the Institute of Real Estate Management, 430 N. Michigan Ave., Chicago, IL 60611. Provides expense data for condominiums, cooperatives and Planned Unit Developments. Data are classified by building age, geographic location and price range. Includes statistical series on interior and exterior common area maintenance costs, utilities expense breakdown and a summary of building amenities.

- *Income and Expense Analysis: Apartments*. Published annually by the Institute of Real Estate Management, 430 N. Michigan Ave., Chicago, IL 60611. Provides income and expense data for apartment buildings in each of the following categories:

- Unfurnished elevator buildings
- Low-rise, 12 to 24 units, unfurnished
- Low-rise, 25 or more units, unfurnished
- Garden-type, unfurnished
- Furnished units

Data are presented by region, location and building age. Separate series are provided for major metropolitan areas. Includes vacancy losses, tenant turnover, bad-debt losses and parking revenue. Some trend data are provided.

- *Income and Expense Analysis: Suburban Office Buildings.* Published annually by the Institute of Real Estate Management, 430 N. Michigan Ave., Chicago, IL 60611. Income and expense data for suburban office buildings are provided on national, regional and major metropolitan area bases. Data are divided according to building size, age, rental range and building type. Utility cost analysis and trend data are included.
- *Trends in the Hotel Industry.* Published annually by Pannell, Kerr and Forster, 420 Lexington Ave., New York, NY 10170. Provides revenue and expense data separately for hotels and motels, transient hotels, resort hotels, motels with restaurants and motels without restaurants. Includes data on occupancy rates, room rental rates, total revenues and expenses, energy costs and property taxes.
- *U.S. Lodging Industry.* Published annually by Laventhol and Horwath, Certified Public Accountants, 1845 Walnut St., Philadelphia, PA 14103. Contains descriptive information about the lodging industry around the nation. Also provides income and expense data. Facilities are listed according to location as center city, airport, suburban or highway and resort. Buildings are classified into four different size categories. Includes occupancy rate data, food and beverage sales data and ratios of sales per room.

CHAPTER 6

Measuring Demand for Real Estate Services

INTRODUCTION

Individual urban land parcels are heavily affected by economic, social and political forces operating within the metropolitan area. These forces are translated into rent-generating ability through their influence on the desirability of locational advantages afforded by each site. There is an old axiom among real estate practitioners that the three most important characteristics of a site are location, location and location. A well-located facility may exhibit impressive rent-generating ability even when poorly marketed and ineptly managed. Locations that appear substandard can often be transformed by astute development efforts, but the scale of such development typically must be relatively large and so may exceed the financial resources of many developers.

PRODUCTIVITY AND ABILITY TO COMMAND RENT

A property's ability to command rent depends upon its capacity to satisfy the needs of prospective tenants and its locational advantages relative to those of competing rental properties. It depends also, of course, upon the relative scarcity of properties that are acceptable alternatives—the supply and demand relationship discussed in Chapter 2.

A property's ability to satisfy tenant needs (to provide *utility,* economists would say) is the measure of its *productivity.* Both natural and man-made features contribute to productivity, as does location. Elements of productivity, therefore, may be classified as *physical characteristics* and *locational char-*

95

acteristics. (Some authorities include a classification called *transfer character-istics,* but these are subsumed by the more inclusive term *locational characteristics.*)

Physical Characteristics

Physical characteristics, which may be either natural or man-made, affect the efficiency with which a site can be used for its intended purpose. They include soil composition, drainage characteristics, mineral content and so forth. They also include improvements such as sewers, landscaping, buildings and roads. Almost all productive land has been improved to some extent. Sites can therefore be described accurately as a manufactured product.

The acid test of a property's *functional efficiency* is how well the structure accommodates its intended use. The very concept of functional efficiency is related to use, and that is the only context in which it can be judged. Warehouses are tested against the requirements of modern storage technology, retail facilities against the demands of contemporary merchandising techniques and so on.

As its efficiency declines, a building is said to exhibit *functional obsoles-cence,* which is inherent in all structures. It is an inevitable consequence of social, business and industrial evolution and consequent alteration in demands placed on buildings housing these activities. It reflects potential users' percep-tions of deviation from ideal layout, space, structural specifications, amenities and diminished productive capacity.

Locational Characteristics

We saw in Chapter 4 that locational advantages are of paramount importance in determining urban land values. Urban growth both creates and destroys locational advantage. We learned, moreover, that locational benefits are deter-mined primarily by the network of relationships among locations, which are described as *linkages*. The movement of goods from factory to warehouse and from warehouse to retail outlets are examples of important linkages. Other significant examples include workers who commute between home and em-ployment. Linkages, as we have seen, give rise to transfer costs, which are the explicit and implicit costs of moving people and things between linked sites. Were there no other factors to be considered, the optimal location for any activity would be the one that minimizes total transfer costs.

Attempts to minimize transfer costs explain the tendency of natural resource processing firms to locate near their source of raw material, of retail outlets to locate near their customers or on major transportation arteries, of service firms to locate next to major users of the service, of labor-intensive firms to locate near major labor pools and so on. Locational decisions in each instance represent attempts to mimimize transfer costs where they are significant in comparison with other costs affected by the location decision.

Locational choices are constrained, however, by desirable or undesirable economic and social environments and by intractable institutional arrangements.

Neighborhood Influences. Fixity of location makes any site vulnerable to social and economic influences from surrounding properties. Environmental factors that influence site value are often called *neighborhood influences*. Tenants may knowingly shoulder additional transfer costs to escape undesirable neighborhood influences or to locate in desirable neighborhoods. Economists refer to neighborhood influences as *externalities*. Desirable influences are called *external economies;* undesirable ones are referred to as *external diseconomies*. Externalities stem from situations where decision makers escape bearing all the costs (external diseconomies) or are unable to capture all the benefits (external economies).[1]

Special value often attaches to sites in a neighborhood considered to reflect favorably on the character of residents, for example. For many residential users, and for certain types of businesses, prestige is a powerful influence on locational choice. Thus, in Chicago a Gold Coast residential address implies a certain socioeconomic status, as does a Park Avenue address in Manhattan. For similar reasons, law firms often want to locate near other law firms that have achieved a high level of professional recognition, financial firms tend to seek the favorable aura of a location in established financial districts and so on.

Favorable neighborhood influences also include aesthetic considerations. For residential users, and for many commercial purposes, a pleasing view is considered particularly important. Locations adjacent to golf courses, near attractive parks or with an impressive view of a large body of water or of the cityscape often command premium rents unrelated to the issue of transfer costs.

Just as residences and business establishments are attracted by desirable neighborhood factors, so are they repelled by undesirable or incompatible conditions or activities. Objectionable influences include noise, smoke, odors and unsavory neighbors. A favorable location shields one from these objectionable influences, whether by physical barriers, by distance or by law.

The influence of neighborhood factors stems from real estate's long life and physical immobility. Since a firm or a family, once established, cannot easily move to escape undesirable external factors or to capture desirable ones, neighborhood influences are a powerful factor in initial locational choice. Such influences may be favorable and thus attract people or firms, or they may be unfavorable and thereby act as repellents.

Physical barriers such as rivers, unbuildable terrain or the existence of intervening compatible structures and uses are frequently valued as protection from unfavorable neighborhood influences. In urban areas, people often rely on private or public land use control provisions to afford this protection.

Special provisions in a deed of conveyance may create restrictions on land utilization. Deeds of conveyance delivered by a subdivision developer, for example, might contain a restriction against usage thought to be incompatible with the intended purpose of the subdivision. Such provisions, called *restrictive covenants,* may enhance site value by assuring potential residents freedom from neighborhood influences they might consider objectionable.

Public land use restrictions and other land use control ordinances have also become increasingly important as protection from inharmonious or incompatible uses. *Zoning regulations, subdivision controls* and *building codes* are all designed to regulate the nature, density and quality of structures erected at a locality as well as the nature of activities conducted there. Public land use controls exert a pervasive influence on the type and intensity of property use and thus on the power to command rent.

DEMAND ANALYSIS FOR RESIDENTIAL RENTAL PROPERTY

Overall demand for residential rental space in a given market area is a function of the interrelationship among householder locational preferences, householder purchasing power and the quality and availability of the housing inventory. The type of housing desired and locational preferences depend upon household characteristics such as age composition, family size, incomes and lifestyle preferences. Locational preferences are further influenced by density and zoning patterns, transportation systems, nature and quality of educational and health care facilities, environmental characteristics and a host of other factors that vary with the socioeconomic characteristics of householders themselves.

Establishing the Market Area

An early step in analyzing rental demand at a specific site is to establish approximate limits of the geographic area from which tenants will be drawn. The market area for housing has been defined as the area "within which all dwelling units are linked together in a chain of substitution."[2] Within such an area most housing of a particular type and price will be mutually substitutable by prospective renters.

Precise market area boundaries are impossible to define. To approximate the boundaries, however, one need only establish the most probable linkages between potential tenants and the housing units being analyzed. A major linkage, for example, is place of employment. The range of possible employment from any given residential site is determined by the time, expense and difficulty of the journey to work. Whether this is measured in terms of automobile driving time and distance or of accessibility and cost of public transportation depends upon the characteristic transportation mode of the socioeconomic tenant most likely to find the residential facility desirable and affordable. If recourse to primary data gathering is required, the analyst might distribute questionnaires at employment centers to establish current places of residence. Results should enable the analyst to establish existing commuting patterns. Based on conclusions drawn about tolerable commuting time and expense, a map can be drawn indicating the approximate geographic area of employment of potential tenants.

Major employment centers within these boundaries constitute the employment base for prospective tenants who might find the housing units desirable. Other residential areas that are equally accessible to these employment centers

FIGURE 6.1 Estimating the Market Area

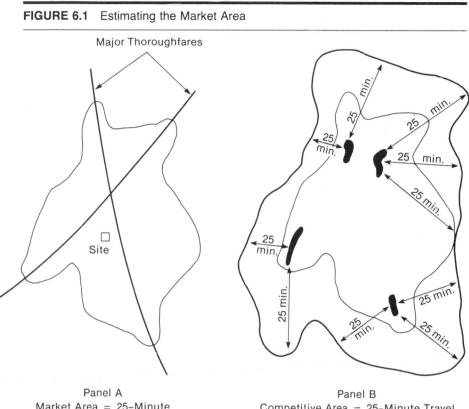

Major Thoroughfares

Panel A
Market Area = 25-Minute
Travel Time from Site

Panel B
Competitive Area = 25-Minute Travel
Time from Major Employment Nodes

form competitive market areas. Figure 6.1 shows maps of market area and area of competitive rental units.

Surveying the Competition

Data on rental and vacancy rates for competitive housing can now be collected to determine likely rental rates that the market will support. These data will be meaningful only if they relate to rental units that are truly comparable. This means surveyed units must be of the type and approximate rent level anticipated for the site under analysis. Factors in the survey should include:

- Location of competitive project;
- Number of units;
- Unit mix (two-bedroom, one-bedroom, etc.);
- Size of units;
- Unit amenities (appliances, carpets, drapes, etc.);
- Project amenities (pool, party room, etc.);

- Rental range for each unit size;
- Rental terms;
- Marketing strategies employed;
- Vacancy rates;
- Overall competitiveness (judgmental evaluation).

Data on competitive properties serve as the basis for estimating probable rents for a planned rental project. The data also serve as a gauge of the reasonableness of data collected from an existing project whose investment value is being estimated. When market information conflicts with that drawn from an existing project under analysis, greater weight should be given to data from competitive units in drawing final conclusions, unless data from the units under analysis can be verified from unbiased sources. Data from competitive units may reveal shortcomings in existing projects—unmet tenant needs that represent voids in the local apartment market. Planned rental housing projects are thereby afforded an opportunity to establish a competitive edge. Chapter 9 contains an extensive illustration of conclusions about rental rates drawn from analysis of competitive data.

DEMAND ANALYSIS FOR RETAIL COMMERCIAL RENTAL PROPERTY

The ability of a retail facility to command rent is primarily a function of locational desirability for the intended retail activity. Rents on retail facilities are usually expressed as a flat fee plus a percentage of gross sales. The better the sales of the tenant, the greater the yield to the landlord. Estimating the ability of a site to command rents, therefore, is primarily an exercise in forecasting retail sales.

An early step in the analysis is to determine what type of retail establishment is most likely to be attracted to the site. If the site appears appropriate for a number of alternative types of retail or service activity, the analysis might be replicated under several different assumptions. This will reveal which of the possible tenants can be expected to generate the largest annual rental revenue.

Site-specific factors influencing retail sales include the number and location of competitive retail locations in the same trade area and purchasing power and expenditure patterns of trade area residents. Factors that are not site-specific (and usually not amenable to analysis without reference to a specific retail tenant) include management and marketing ability, prices and the availability of credit.

Establishing the Trade Area

A store's *trade area* is the geographic area from which the major portion of patronage is drawn. Within the trade area, the strongest drawing power is felt close to the site itself, with influence diminishing gradually with distance. In most actual analytical problems, travel time is more important than geographic distance.

A number of techniques have been suggested for estimating trade area boundaries for various types of retail and service establishments, and analysts dealing in these types of properties will need specialized study to appreciate the strengths and weaknesses of each. John McMahan suggests basing estimates of trade area boundaries on the length of time required for potential customers to reach the facility. He further suggests the following rough rules of thumb:[3]

- Neighborhood shopping centers: five to ten minutes;
- Community shopping centers: ten to 15 minutes;
- Regional centers: 15 to 30 minutes.

McMahan's rules of thumb correspond closely to the suggestions of the Urban Land Institute, which characterizes trade areas as primary, secondary and tertiary. The primary trade area is viewed as that requiring not more than about five minutes of travel to reach stores offering convenience items and about ten minutes of travel time to regional shopping centers. The Urban Land Institute estimates that about 60 to 70 percent of ultimate sales volume will come from the population within this area. The balance will be drawn from the secondary and tertiary areas, which are farther away and for which the store or shopping center is less readily accessible. The institute characterizes the tertiary trade area as the farthest from which even major regional shopping centers can expect to draw customers. They set the outer distance in travel time at about 25 to 30 minutes.[4]

Trade area boundaries that result from applying these estimates must be adjusted to reflect any physical barriers to the flow of customer traffic. The resulting trade area boundaries are then adjusted to conform to boundaries encompassing available data, such as census tracts or retail sales reports.

Retail Expenditures Within Trade Area Boundaries

Appendix 5.A lists a source for data on population, average income and retail expenditures by trade area residents. To estimate the percentage of sales likely to flow to the facility under consideration, the analyst must first survey competitive facilities. Identifying the location and size of merchant facilities that deal in substitutable goods or services, noting the quality of facilities and available parking and judging the merchandising ability of management are necessary steps preparatory to estimating the market penetration potential of a prospective retail tenant.

Sales in competing stores must be estimated. This information may be available from sales tax data on file with the state government. Alternatively, sales can be estimated by referring to data available in *Dollars and Cents of Shopping Centers*, published by the Urban Land Institute, or other data-reporting agencies.

Consumer surveys may be necessary to collect data from which to estimate potential market penetration. Such surveys involve information collected from a random sample of consumers living within the trade area. The survey is typically made by telephone. Deriving reliable data from surveys requires much more technical market research competence than most real estate analysts possess. The surveying, therefore, should be done by professionals in that field. This is an expensive procedure, and the value of data must always be weighed against the cost.

Average sales per square foot of retail area for stores within the trade area are estimated by calculating retail demand within the area for merchandise of the type offered by the facility under analysis and dividing that figure by the estimated gross area devoted to the merchandise. This estimate, adjusted for any reasonable expectations about differences in potential market penetration by the facility being analyzed, is translated into an estimate of probable gross sales by the facility.

DEMAND FOR OFFICE SPACE

Approximately two-thirds of all office space since 1950 has been developed on a speculative basis, with no specific tenant identified as the ultimate user of the space.[5] Economic growth since World War II has created relatively steady expansion in demand for rental office space nationwide. Demand growth has varied widely among regions due to differentials in rates of economic growth.

Estimating demand for commercial office space has been called the most difficult and least accurate of all land use determinations.[6] Statistical data are spotty and unreliable at best; in many cases information is not available at all. Office building construction tends to occur in broad cycles of overbuilding and underbuilding which cause vacancy rates to swing widely.

Surveying the Competition

The size and nature of a proposed office project determine the scope of the competitive survey. Office buildings tend to be developed in clusters or local nodes within a metropolitan area.[7] Figure 6.2 illustrates a typical nodal development pattern. Relatively small- to medium-sized office buildings intended for general office space usage compete primarily with other buildings in the same node. Larger buildings or those catering to specialized users may compete with buildings throughout the entire metropolitan area. In each instance the competitive survey will encompass the area within which major competitive buildings are located.

Information gathered on competitive buildings should include:

- Location;
- Gross building area;
- Net rentable area within the building;
- Net rented area;
- Scheduled rent per square foot;

FIGURE 6.2   Nodal Pattern of Office Building Development

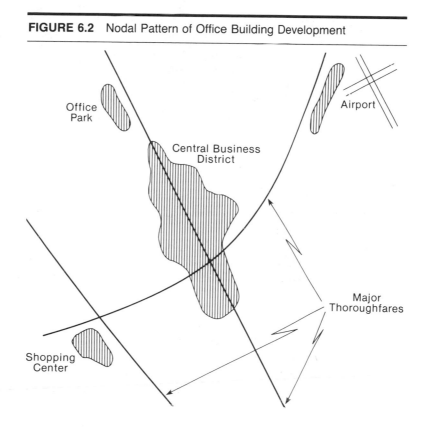

- Minimum lease term;
- Building services provided;
- Parking facilities and tenant cost;
- Building amenities (conference facilities, restaurants, etc.);
- Judgment regarding comparative quality of building.

Information is gathered through discussion with leasing agents and tenants, on-site inspections and review of building plans on file with the county. The information is used to judge the reliability of information provided concerning a building under analysis or to estimate rent-generating ability for a building whose construction is being contemplated.

Estimating Future Trends

Growth in demand for office space depends upon the general rate of growth of business activity in the metropolitan area. Estimation involves projecting economic trends in the area, a business forecasting problem that requires a sophisticated understanding of economic analysis. Such data as neighborhood change, crime rates and traffic congestion must be analyzed to estimate the degree to which general demand growth will be shared by the office node in which the target site is located. Within the node itself, ability to compete will be affected by the relative desirability of specific locations—their accessibility, view, exposure to sunlight, the availability of close-in parking and so forth.

Future trends in supply are at best difficult to estimate. Because construction runs in spurts, long-term trends are difficult to discern. The availability of appropriately zoned (or rezonable) sites with soil and elevation characteristics amenable to office construction suggests that supply will expand along with demand, though perhaps not directly apace.

PATTERNS OF DEMAND GROWTH: A NATIONAL PERSPECTIVE

Demand for shelter and locational advantages provided by real estate does not exist in a vacuum. Whether a real estate parcel is located in the middle of Manhattan Island or on the fringe of Dry Prong, Louisiana, its ability to command rents is affected by national economic events and social and demographic trends. Fundamental relationships between national and local phenomena must never be ignored when attempting to forecast the pattern of change in a property's rent-generating ability.

Economic, social and political changes do not impact on all regions of the nation with equal force. In fact, the directions of the consequences are frequently exactly opposite; changes that create growth and prosperity in one region may wreak economic havoc elsewhere. To see this, consider the economic consequences of the shift in industrial growth from the smokestack industrial states of the upper Midwest to the South and Southwest.

Local economic phenomena are not divorced from national events, but widespread phenomena are translated into local consequences in ways that may be unique within each urban area. Moreover, the relationship between specific national economic phenomena and local economic activity may be sufficiently tenuous to merit little or no consideration in a specific market analysis assignment. Cash-flow estimation for a 12-unit apartment in an area with a well-diversified economic base will not require analysis of national monetary and fiscal policy over the projection period. Yet a building located in an area whose economy is heavily dependent upon defense-related industries will justify consideration of defense spending patterns and a forecast of future trends.

Relationships between national economic events and local economic phenomena are not always so self-evident. Nor are cause and effect necessarily direct or immediate. Long-term national economic, social or political change does eventually impact on local real estate economics, however, and analysts must be alert to discern broad patterns that are relevant to specific research and analysis problems.

Charting Demographic Trends

Demand for real estate services at the national level is affected both by the rate of growth in the population and by changes in its age distribution. There are few abrupt changes in either of these factors. Alert analysts can easily extrapolate recent data into a reasonably accurate near-term projection at the national level.

Population growth is influenced both by the relationship between birth and death rates and by the rate of net migration. In brief, forecasts of population growth are simply the difference between forecasted births and deaths, plus forecasted gains or losses from net migration.

In the United States, immigration has long been a major source of net population growth. Immigrants' origins influence where they settle in the United States and what they do after arrival. This in turn affects the impact their immigration has on demand for real estate services. And countries of origin have changed radically over the years.

For analysts trying to forecast changes in demand for specific categories of real estate, changing age composition of the population may be more important than the absolute rate of increase. An aging population alters both its working and its leisure habits. Significant changes in age levels alter the demand for nursery, educational and health care facilities, to cite rather obvious examples. Population groups beyond childbearing age demand smaller residential units, to cite another.

Changing patterns in marriage and household formations are closely related to the changing age distribution of the population and also greatly influence the pattern of demand for real estate services. Both average age of the citizenry and average household size may differ drastically from one region to another.

SUMMARY

A property's productivity, and hence its ability to command rent, is determined primarily by physical and locational characteristics. Physical characteristics relate to natural endowments such as drainage and soil composition, as well as to site improvements. The nature of the improvements affects rent-generating ability because it determines the nature of the tenants. Beyond the type and size of structure, however, productivity is influenced by functional efficiency, how well the structure is designed to accomplish its intended function.

Buildings may be poorly designed and, as a consequence, functionally inefficient from their inception. More typically, changes in technology and lifestyle eventually render even well-designed structures functionally obsolete. Deviation from ideal design, layout and amenities in keeping with modern production methods results in diminished productive capacity and thereby detracts from the property's ability to command rent.

Locational factors can diminish the productivity of even functionally efficient properties. Conversely, fortunate locational choices can enhance the rent-generating ability of even poorly designed buildings. Ideal locations are those that minimize transfer costs and also enjoy desirable environmental influences.

Transfer costs result from the need to move people and things between linked sites. If all other factors were equal, tenants would choose sites that minimize the sum of all transfer costs, both implicit and explicit. Tenants may knowingly incur additional transfer costs, however, to capture benefits of desirable environmental factors or to avoid undesirable environmental influences.

Social and economic influences from surrounding properties are called *neighborhood influences* and may have a substantial impact on a property's ability to command rent. Many tenants will pay premium rents to be adjacent to certain locations or facilities. Others will accept undesirable neighbors or neighborhood conditions only if the site is available at bargain rates. Many will not occupy such premises at any price.

Analysis of demand for residential rental property starts with an estimate of the extent of the market area. This is the geographic area within which potential tenants will be willing to commute from the proposed site to places of employment. Competitive rental locations are then surveyed to determine their quantity, quality and marketing strategies. Data on competitive properties serve as a basis for estimating the rent-generating prospects for a proposed project.

Demand analysis for retail rental property requires that the probable trade area of most likely tenants be estimated. Estimating the sales of similar establishments within the trade area permits projection of likely gross sales for prospective tenants. From these estimates gross rent projections are derived.

Estimating the demand for office space requires a survey of competing space. Information on rental and vacancy rates, size, location, amenities and other factors influencing desirability to present and prospective tenants should be gathered. Data are projected into the future by estimating the rate of growth of aggregate demand for office space within the metropolitan area.

National data should be gathered and analyzed only if they offer some usable intelligence for the research problem at hand. National data will almost always come from secondary sources, usually from published statistics.

NOTES

1. For a more complete discussion of externalities and their consequences in real estate decision making, see Gaylon E. Greer and Michael D. Farrell, *Contemporary Real Estate Theory and Practice* (Hinsdale, IL: The Dryden Press, 1983), Chapter 5.

2. The Institute for Urban Land Use and Housing Studies, Columbia University, *Housing Market Analysis: A Study of Theory and Methods* (Washington, DC: Housing and Home Finance Agency, 1953), Chapter 2.

3. John McMahan, *Property Development: Effective Decision Making in Uncertain Times* (New York: McGraw-Hill, 1976), 161.

4. The Urban Land Institute, *Shopping Center Development Handbook*, 2nd Edition (Washington, DC: The Urban Land Institute, 1985), 22–23.

5. McMahan, *Property Development*, 178.

6. Ibid., 183.

7. Ibid., 182.

RECOMMENDED READINGS

Barrett, G. Vincent, and John P. Blair. *How to Conduct and Analyze Real Estate Market and Feasibility Studies*. New York: Van Nostrand Reinhold, 1982, pp. 44–51.

Canestano, James C. *Real Estate Financial Feasibility Analysis Handbook: A Guide to Project Cost-Benefit Evaluation*. Chicago: National Association of Realtors, 1982.

Clifton, David S., Jr., and David E. Fyffe. *Project Feasibility Analysis: A Guide to Profitable New Ventures*. New York: Wiley-Interscience, 1977.

Graaskamp, James A. *A Guide to Feasibility Analysis*. Chicago: Society of Real Estate Appraisers, 1970.

Hanford, Lloyd D., Sr. *Feasibility Study Guidelines*. Chicago: Institute of Real Estate Management, 1972.

Lukens, Reaves C., Jr. *The Appraiser and Real Estate Feasibility Studies*. Chicago: American Institute of Real Estate Appraisers, 1972.

Urban Land Institute. *Mixed Use Development Handbook*. Washington, DC: The Urban Land Institute, 1987, pp. 54–90.

———. *Shopping Center Development Handbook*. 2nd ed. Washington, DC: The Urban Land Institute, 1985, pp. 20–27.

REVIEW QUESTIONS

1. What factors affect a property's ability to command rent?
2. What are the concepts of functional efficiency and functional obsolescence?
3. How do factors outside a property affect its ability to command rent?
4. What major factors should be considered in establishing boundaries of a residential market area?
5. What comparisons should be made when surveying the competition in a selected residential market? Of what value is this information in determining the investment value of a specific property?
6. What factors should be considered in estimating demand for commercial rental property?
7. What determines the trade areas of various commercial enterprises and what are their importance to the enterprises?
8. How do national economic events and social and demographic trends affect the rent-generating ability of a property?

DISCUSSION QUESTIONS

1. Relate the concept of functional efficiency to the trend toward redeveloping older neighborhoods and converting old buildings to new uses.
2. How might a store's trade area be influenced by:
   a. alterations in transportation routes and transportation technology?
   b. external factors such as the Middle Eastern oil embargo of the 1970s?
   c. increasing intensity of land use in surrounding areas?

PART TWO: Case Problems

You are approached by a group of local physicians who want to invest in real estate. After discussing their goals, needs and resources, you jointly agree that the ideal investment would be an apartment complex in the $1 million range. You are aware of several apartment buildings of the appropriate value that are currently available. You also know of several available and appropriately zoned sites on which a new apartment of this size could be constructed. The metropolitan area in which the investment will be made has a population of about three million.

1. What information will you need to make a rational choice between buying an existing building and constructing a building on newly acquired land? What are some possible sources of such information, and how will you go about collecting it?

2. In what ways, if any, would your research program differ if this investor group were contemplating a $10 million apartment project? In what ways would your program differ if the group were considering a $100,000 investment?

PART THREE

Forecasting Cash Flows

Rational investment decisions must incorporate consideration of all anticipated future benefits from ownership. This implies a careful estimate of probable cash inflows and outflows during the investment period and an assessment of likely forecasting error. Extra effort to develop carefully considered cash-flow forecasts pays dividends not only in terms of more accurate analysis; the attempt enhances appreciation for the degree of risk and uncertainty associated with any attempt to foretell the future. Healthy skepticism is frequently a valuable by-product.

Chapter 7 explains how a typical real estate cash-flow statement is developed. Chapter 8 adds the impact of using borrowed funds by showing how mortgage financing influences expected future cash flows to the equity investor. Chapter 9 discusses how analysts move from reconstructing a property's operating history to extending the analysis over the anticipated holding period.

CHAPTER 7

Developing the Operating Statement

INTRODUCTION

Astute real estate investors are interested in the physical property in which they acquire an ownership interest only to the extent that it affects the anticipated stream of economic benefits. The real property interest is only a means to the ultimate end of financial gain. The economic desirability of an investment proposition is strictly a function of the *amount, timing* and *certainty* of after-tax cash flows.

This is not to argue that nonfinancial aspects of real estate are unimportant. Aesthetics may well be valued as an end in themselves, apart from the question of their economic worth. Such issues transcend the investment decision, however. After making a dispassionate economic evaluation of a proposal an investor may elect to incorporate other considerations into the decision; such ventures then become in part consumption expenditures rather than purely investment proposals.

The starting point for forecasting future benefits from a proposed venture is the property's immediate past operating history or the recent history of comparable properties. This is incorporated into a forecast by considering how anticipated changes in the economic, social and political environment will affect the property's ability to generate rents and how they will affect the cost of maintaining and operating the property. Rational analysis must also include a forecast of the likely change in a property's market value over the anticipated holding period.

TABLE 7.1 Apartment Building Annual Operating Statement

Potential Gross Rent		$1,500,000
Less: Allowance for Vacancies and Rent Loss		45,000
		1,455,000
Plus: Other Income (Parking)		9,000
Effective Gross Income		1,464,000
Less: Operating Expenses		
Management Fee	$ 72,750	
Salary Expense	133,900	
Utilities	157,700	
Insurance	74,400	
Supplies	19,000	
Advertising	9,000	
Maintenance and Repairs	116,000	
Property Tax	183,000	765,750
Net Operating Income		$698,250
Less: Debt Service		625,000
Before-Tax Cash Flow		$73,250
Less: Income Tax Liability		52,000
After-Tax Cash Flow		$21,250

OVERVIEW OF THE OPERATING STATEMENT

Whereas traditional income statements seek to show operating revenues "when earned" and operating expenses "when incurred," whether or not these represent actual cash receipts and disbursements, real estate investment analysts are concerned with actual cash flows into and out of the investor's coffers. Operating statements therefore usually present cash inflows and outflows from operations and extend the presentation to include nonoperating cash flows such as those from debt service, income tax and capital expenditures. A typical income property operating statement is illustrated in Table 7.1.

Potential gross rent is the amount of rental revenue a property would generate with no vacancies. Adjusting potential gross rent to reflect losses from vacancies and uncollectible accounts and to include income from sources other than rents results in *effective gross income*. On a historical basis, this is the gross revenue a building has actually produced.

Operating expenses, shown in the next section of the operating statement in Table 7.1, include all cash expenditures required to maintain and operate the property so as to generate the gross rent. *Net operating income* is simply the difference between effective gross income and operating expenses. Were there no income taxes and no nonoperating expenditures, this would also be the net cash flow to the investor.

All entries on the statement in Table 7.1, below net operating income, reflect cash flows arising from property ownership but not directly attributable to its operation. *Debt service,* for example, is a consequence of using borrowed money to acquire a property. Likewise, the final item affecting cash flow, *income taxes,* is determined in large measure by the investor's individual income tax position rather than specifically by the operating results of property on which the report is based. The bottom line, *after-tax cash flow,* is the amount of cash remaining at the end of the reporting period, after all operating expenses have been paid, all obligations to borrowers satisfied and all income tax obligations met.

ESTIMATING CURRENT OPERATING RESULTS

The usual starting point for estimating the results of current operations is the history of recent operations, as reflected by the property's records. But unless prepared by a reliable and disinterested party from original source documents, such records must be considered suspect. Analysts seek to verify all records by reference to original source documents and by comparing reported operating results with known or determinable outcomes from comparable properties.

To estimate recent gross income, inspect the property's *rent roll* and leases to determine contract rental rates, vacancies and *concessions* (agreements between landlords and tenants that result in making effective rents less than those reflected on leases). Verify indicated rental rates, if possible, by conversing with the building manager and tenants. Check conclusions for reasonableness by comparing them with estimates of effective rents in comparable properties in the same market area.

As with gross income, the most appropriate starting point for estimating operating expenses is the immediate past experience of the property. If possible, reconstruct several years of operating history in order to detect trends. Adjust information provided by the current owner to allow for inconsistencies with data from other sources. Compare results with published averages where possible and further investigate any seeming inconsistencies or anomalies.

Identifying Comparable Properties

Reference to the experience of comparable properties is frequently the most valuable source of data for estimating a property's recent operating history. The challenge is to find properties that are truly comparable. For purposes of estimating ability to command rents, a comparable property must function as a close substitute for the property under analysis. This means that it must not only offer approximately the same amenities but also be comparable with respect to locational desirability. It is the latter criterion that presents a particular challenge and frequently renders impossible the task of collecting a sizable sample of comparable observations.

Comparable properties will closely replicate the physical and locational characteristics of the property under analysis, to the extent that these characteristics affect the ability of the property to command rent.

Key Physical Characteristics. *Functional efficiency and physical durability* are major physical characteristics affecting a property's ability to remain competitive. Functional efficiency is a measure of how well a property is designed to do the job it is intended to perform. Physical durability is a measure of a structure's remaining physical life and is a function of soundness of design plus the extent to which routine maintenance has forestalled structural deterioration.

Functional efficiency is related to specific property uses and can be evaluated only in that context. Houses are compared with design needs for modern family lifestyles; warehouse design is evaluated in terms of compatibility with modern storage and transportation technology; office buildings are judged according to modern business needs. Well-designed structures may be functionally very efficient when first put into service but may be rendered less appropriate for their tasks as lifestyles, taste and technology alter use patterns. Less well-designed buildings may be functionally inefficient from the outset. Loss of efficiency due to defective or dated design is called *functional obsolescence*. It reduces a building's competitive position relative to more functionally efficient structures and may eventually lead to abandonment or succession of use.

Key Locational Characteristics. The economic specialization characteristic of modern urban life creates interdependence among sites. Activity at one location generates movement of people and things, the expense of which is called *transfer costs*. Relationships that create such movement are called *linkages,* and properties between which the movement occurs are said to be *linked*. Examples include movement between place of residence and work, school or shopping; movement of goods between wholesaler and retailer; movement of raw material to manufacturing locations and of finished goods to points of consumption. The desire to minimize transfer costs is an important factor in many location decisions. Sites that offer greater transfer cost economies have a competitive advantage that enhances their ability to command rents.

Tenants are frequently enticed to locations that actually increase their transfer costs, because the desirable neighborhood factors such sites offer more than compensate. Desirable neighborhood factors are those environmental influences that increase a site's value due to their attractiveness. These include such considerations as a prestigious address or aesthetic surroundings, a desirable view or neighbors whose activities somehow complement those of a tenant.

Using Published Data

Published sources of valuable information on operating expenses for various types and sizes of properties are readily available. These data are generally not sufficiently precise to serve reliably as a sole source of information for re-creating the most probable recent operating history of a property, since they are simply averages of a group of properties and provide no measure of dispersion about the mean of the sample. They do, however, serve as valuable benchmarks against which to compare other data for reasonableness. The most freuqently used sources are listed below.

- *Income/Expense Analysis: Apartments* (Chicago: Institute of Real Estate Management), published annually.
- *Income/Expense Analysis: Condominiums, Cooperatives and P.U.D.s* (Chicago: Institute of Real Estate Management), published annually.
- *Income/Expense Analysis: Suburban Office Buildings* (Chicago: Institute of Real Estate Management), published annually.
- *Dollars and Cents of Shopping Centers* (Washington, DC: The Urban Land Institute), published periodically.
- *Downtown and Suburban Office Building Exchange Report* (Washington, DC: Building Owners and Managers Association International), published annually.
- *Trends in the Hotel Industry* (Pannell, Kerr, Forster and Company), published annually.

RECONSTRUCTING THE OPERATING HISTORY

To illustrate procedures for estimating the results of current operations where reliable accounting data are not readily available, consider Example 7.1, which provides data on a 280-unit apartment complex called *Noname Apartments*.

Example 7.1

Noname Apartments is a 280-unit complex consisting of 50 two-bedroom units, each having 1,000 square feet of living area; 150 one-bedroom units, each containing 700 square feet of living area; and 80 studio-type units, each with 500 square feet of living space. The owner provides a statement of the property's most recent annual operating results, which is presented in Table 7.2.

Estimating Effective Gross Income

Inspecting the rent roll of the property in Example 7.1 reveals that some tenants are on 24-month leases, some are on 12-month leases and some are renting on a month-to-month basis. Contract rental rates, as reported on the rent roll and verified by inspection of the leases, are deemed unreliable indicators of actual market experience, because tenants report having received a number of conces-

TABLE 7.2   Noname Apartments Prior Owner's Operating Statement for Year Ended December 31, 19XX

Gross Revenue:		
Rent Receipts		$1,512,000
Parking Fees		97,000
Total		$1,609,000
Expenses:		
Management Fees (5% of gross)	$ 80,000	
Salaries	133,900	
Utilities	157,700	
Insurance	74,400	
Supplies	19,000	
Advertising	9,000	
Maintenance and Repairs	142,000	
Property Taxes	90,000	706,000
Net Income for the Year		$ 903,000

sions from the landlord. Some received special decorating allowances as an inducement to sign their leases. Others received substantial discounts on parking fees at a nearby garage operated by the same company that owns the apartment building. Concessions seem to be related to periods when vacancies were particularly high, but this is impossible to verify because both the owner and the management firm refuse to confirm concessions reported by tenants.

Fortunately, a number of apartment buildings in the immediate neighborhood offer very similar accommodations. Services provided by these other properties are essentially the same as those of the property being analyzed. All the units chosen as sources of comparable market data offer single baths and kitchen-dining room combinations, which conforms to the profile of units in the property under analysis. The data on comparable properties are:

- *Property A* contains a total of 250 units: 175 two-bedroom units with 890 square feet of living area rent for $540 per month, 50 single-bedroom units with 625 square feet rent for $405 per month and 25 studios with 500 square feet rent for $325 per month. Currently, five two-bedroom units and seven studios are vacant. All the one-bedroom units are under lease.
- *Property B* is a 185-unit building with 75 two-bedroom, 75 one-bedroom and 35 studio units. The two-bedroom units have 925 square feet of living area and rent for $575 per month. The single-bedroom apartments have 650 square feet of living area and rent for $415. The studios contain 510 square feet and command rents of $330. Currently, ten one-bedroom and five studio units are vacant. All the two-bedroom units are occupied.
- *Property C* has 360 units, of which 225 are two-bedroom and 75 are one-bedroom apartments. The remaining 60 units are all studios. Two-bedroom units contain 870 square feet of living area and rent for $535. One-bedroom units have 630 square feet of living area and rent for $405. Studios, which

---

TABLE 7.3 Derivation of Market Rental Rates on Properties Deemed Comparable to Noname Apartments

| | *Comparable Property* | | | |
	A	B	C	D
Two-Bedroom Units				
Monthly Rental	$540	$575	$535	$545
Square Feet	890	925	870	895
Rent per Square Foot	$.61	$.62	$.61	$.61
One-Bedroom Units				
Monthly Rental	$405	$415	$405	$412
Square Feet	625	650	630	655
Rent per Square Foot	$.65	$.64	$.64	$.63
Studio Units				
Monthly Rental	$325	$330	$315	$350
Square Feet	500	510	495	550
Rent per Square Foot	$.65	$.65	$.64	$.64

---

have 495 square feet of living area, rent for $315. This complex currently has two vacant two-bedroom units and 15 vacant studios. All one-bedroom units are rented.

- *Property D* is a 300-unit building containing 100 two-bedroom, 125 one-bedroom and 75 studio apartments. Two-bedroom units each have 895 square feet of living area and rent for $545. The one-bedroom units have 655 square feet of living area and rent for $412. Studios rent for $350 and have 550 square feet of living area. There are ten vacant one-bedroom and ten vacant studio apartments.

Table 7.3 consolidates and arrays gross rental data from the sample of comparable properties. Expressing gross rents on a per-square-foot basis for each type of rental unit eliminates minor differences due to variation in the size of units and thus facilitates comparison. The data suggest that the single best estimate of market rental value for two-bedroom units is 61 cents per square foot. Sixty-four cents per square foot appears the best estimate of rental values both for one-bedroom units and for studios. Studio apartments renting for no more per square foot than one-bedroom units is cause for reflection, but this conclusion is reinforced by the higher vacancy rate for studios found in comparable units as well as in the Noname Apartments.

Vacancy data from the market sample are consolidated and arrayed on Table 7.4, along with inferences drawn about appropriate market vacancy rates. Because the data are drawn from such a small sample, there is a large probable error. Ideally, a much larger sample would be employed, perhaps permitting application of formal statistical sampling techniques. But that kind of sample is frequently either impossible or prohibitively expensive to collect.

Because the sample is so small, the unusually high vacancy rate in one of the comparable properties has a disproportionate impact on the average for the

TABLE 7.4   Derivation of Market Vacancy Factors Applicable to Noname Apartments

	Comparable Property				Total (Weighted Average)
	A	*B*	*C*	*D*	
Two-Bedroom Units					
Number of Units	175	75	225	100	575
Vacancies	5	0	2	0	7
Percent Vacant	2.9	0	0.9	0	(1.2)
One-Bedroom Units					
Number of Units	50	75	75	125	325
Vacancies	0	10	0	10	20
Percent Vacant	0	13.3	0	8.0	(6.2)
Studios					
Number of Units	25	35	60	75	195
Vacancies	7	5	15	10	37
Percent Vacant	28.0	14.3	25.0	13.3	(19.0)

sample. The rate on the nonconforming comparable property may be an aberration caused by some temporary problem with the property, by incompetent management or by some other factor that should not be attributed to the property being analyzed. For these reasons, the analyst's judgment is an important factor in drawing inferences from sample data. For the Noname Apartments, we conclude that market estimates in fact reflect most likely experience under typically competent management.

Data concerning market rental rates and most probable vacancy experience, drawn from the comparable properties and exhibited in Tables 7.3 and 7.4, are employed to arrive at estimates of potential gross rent and allowance for vacancy losses for the Noname Apartments. Final conclusions are computed in Table 7.5 and are incorporated into the first-year operating forecast, which is shown in Table 7.6.

Estimating Current Operating Expenses

Recall that operating expenses are cash expenditures required to maintain properties in condition to generate the effective gross revenue. A first step toward estimating a property's current operating expense is to convert the current owner's statement to a more useful format.

The present owner's reported operating results are shown in Table 7.2. Questioning the owner about his or her reported maintenance and repair charges reveals that the owner included expenditures to replace outmoded bathroom fixtures. Further inquiry reveals that the owner held other expenses down by doing considerable maintenance work himself or herself. Comparison with similar buildings in the area reveals that a proper maintenance and repair program,

TABLE 7.5 Estimated Gross Revenue and Vacancy Rates for Noname Apartments

	Two-Bedroom	*One-Bedroom*	*Studio*
Estimated Potential Gross Monthly			
Market Value per Square Foot	$ .61	.64	.64
Square Feet per Unit	×1000	×700	×500
Rent per Unit	$ 610	448	320
Number of Units	×50	×150	×80
Total Potential Monthly Rent	$ 30,500	67,200	25,600
Annual (Monthly × 12)	$366,000	806,400	307,200
Estimated Vacancy Factor			
Annual Potential Gross	$366,000	$806,400	$307,200
Vacancy Factor (from Table 7.4)	×.012	×.062	×.190
Vacancy Loss Estimate	$ 4,392	49,997	58,368

Total Annual Potential Gross Revenue (rounded to nearest $1,000) = $1,480,000
Total Annual Vacancy Loss Estimate (rounded to nearest $1,000) = $113,000

TABLE 7.6 First-Year Operating Forecast for Noname Apartments

Potential Gross Rent	$1,480,000
Less: Allowance for Vacancies	113,000
	1,367,000
Plus: Other Income (Parking)	97,000
Effective Gross Income	1,464,000
Less: Operating Expenses	
Management Fee	$ 72,750
Salary Expense	133,900
Utilities	157,700
Insurance	74,400
Supplies	19,000
Advertising	9,000
Maintenance and Repairs	117,000
Property Tax	182,000 765,750
Net Operating Income (Annual)	$ 698,250

including all routine costs but excluding items properly attributable to capital expenditures, is approximately eight percent of effective gross rent. The owner also excluded property taxes from the operating statement. Inquiry reveals that taxes for the ensuing year will probably be $182,000. All other reported maintenance items appear reasonable for a building of this size and age, based upon the analyst's experience with comparable properties and upon reference to published standards.

Revised Operating Forecast

Effective gross income estimated for the ensuing year, after including revised estimates of vacancy losses and parking income, is $1,464,000. Revised operating expenses, adjusted for expected changes during the ensuing year, total $765,750. These computations yield an estimated first-year net operating income of $698,250. These revised revenue and expense estimates are presented in the operating forecast in Table 7.6.

FACTORS AFFECTING FUTURE OPERATING CASH FLOWS

Estimating current operating results is but a first step toward analyzing an investment proposal. Data from the past are employed to develop a forecast for every year in the anticipated holding period. Without systematic forecasting procedures, uncertainty concerning future eventualities will overwhelm the analyst and lead to reliance on rules of thumb, which have gained widespread popularity as substitutes for hard analysis. Shortcuts may serve tolerably well so long as major causal factors affecting cash flows remain unaltered. But they can lead to disastrous investment outcomes by blinding analysts and investors to significant trends that careful investigation would reveal.

Forecasting effective gross revenue over an anticipated holding period requires anticipation of changes in major factors affecting a property's ability to command rents. These may conveniently be categorized as physical and locational characteristics and must be compared with anticipated changes in the same characteristics affecting the properties against which the subject property will compete for tenants. Revenue forecasting is largely an exercise in estimating how these factors will change over the forecasting period and how such changes will affect the subject property's ability to command rent. This topic is addressed in greater detail in Chapter 9.

SUMMARY

Real estate value stems from the stream of future benefits that ownership or use bestows. Estimating the value of real estate to individual investors therefore entails forecasting the stream of benefits that will flow from the investment. The starting point for such a forecast is to re-create the operating history of the property. Past trends are projected into the future, with revisions to reflect perceived changes in the economic, political and social environment that are likely to affect the property's ability to generate future benefits.

All benefits are expressed on an after-tax cash flow basis. A typical operating statement starts with an expression of the gross rent the property would generate if fully rented. This amount is adjusted for vacancies and rent losses, plus revenue from sources other than rent, to arrive at effective gross revenue. Subtracting operating expenses from the effective gross revenue yields net operating income. This amount is adjusted for financing costs and income taxes to arrive at an estimate of net cash flow to the equity investor.

Sources of information regarding rental revenue and operating expenses include the past operating history of the property itself, the operating records of comparable properties and data from published sources. The last source supplies primarily benchmark information against which to gauge the reasonableness of data from other sources.

RECOMMENDED READINGS

Friedman, Jack P., and Nicholas Ordway. *Income Property Appraisal and Analysis*. Reston, VA: Reston Publishing Company, Inc., 1981, pp. 133–150.

Greer, Gaylon E. *The Real Estate Investment Decision*. Lexington, MA: Heath, 1979, pp. 27–62.

Greer, Gaylon E., and Michael D. Farrell. *Contemporary Real Estate: Theory and Practice*. Hinsdale, IL: The Dryden Press, 1983.

Jaffee, Austin J., and C.F. Sirmans. *Real Estate Investment Decision Making*. Englewood Cliffs, NJ: Prentice-Hall, 1982, pp. 192–215.

Neels, Kevin. *Revenue and Expense Accounts for Rental Properties*. Santa Monica, CA: Rand Corporation, 1982.

Ring, Alfred A., and James H. Boykin. *The Valuation of Real Estate*. 3d ed. Englewood Cliffs, NJ: Prentice-Hall, 1986, pp. 248–282.

REVIEW QUESTIONS

1. How do income and expense statements prepared by accountants differ from operating statements used by real estate investment analysts?
2. What items should be considered when forecasting income and expenses over an investor's anticipated holding period?
3. Carefully inspect the prior owner's operating statement for Noname Apartments (Table 7.2). Do you see any problems with the owner's presentation of income and expenses?
4. Describe the process used to estimate rentals for the Noname Apartments.
5. List some of the considerations inherent in the expense items as presented by the current owner of the Noname Apartments.
6. What is the value of published data in developing an estimate of the operating history of a property?
7. Describe some of the forces affecting the ability of a property to generate rents.

DISCUSSION QUESTIONS

1. Offering brochures for rental property frequently state that current rental rates can be raised. Comment on such claims.
2. How does our concept of gross income and operating expenses differ from those you studied in accounting? Which is the correct definition?
3. You are analyzing a new apartment complex (the only one of its kind) recently constructed on the fringe of an urban area. Because of its access to open areas and freedom from congestion, noise and so forth, the units are in great demand. In fact, net operating income per rental unit is almost 50 percent above that of slightly older but otherwise comparable units that are clustered in an area closer to the central city. Because of the high rents and virtual zero vacancies that yield a 50 percent premium in net operating income, the owner argues that his property is worth 50 percent more than the other units. Comment on this assertion.

CHAPTER 8

Financial Leverage and Investment Analysis

INTRODUCTION

Real estate investors often rely on debt financing for a major portion of project funds. In many cases, this is the only way the investor can gain control of a large real estate project. Even where it is not absolutely necessary, however, investors frequently use borrowed money to enhance the expected yield on equity resources.

Income tax laws create a major incentive to use borrowed money. Interest payments are generally deductible from taxable income on a dollar-for-dollar basis, yet investors are allowed a deduction from taxable income for an estimate of the wearing away of buildings and other improvements to real estate, whether or not any actual reduction in market value is evident. This allowance—called a *depreciation* or *cost recovery allowance*—is based on the total purchase price of a property, without reference to whether borrowed funds are employed. Thus, buying with borrowed money greatly enhances the tax savings that frequently make real estate investments so attractive.

FINANCIAL LEVERAGE: THE CONCEPT AND THE CONSEQUENCES

Using borrowed funds to amplify the outcome of equity investment is called *financial leverage*. The greater the ratio of borrowed funds to equity, the greater

TABLE 8.1   Cash-Flow Consequences of Financing Alternatives
in Example 8.1

	No Loan	$1,000,000 Loan	$1,200,000 Loan
Net Operating Income	$ 240,000	$ 240,000	$ 240,000
Less: Debt Service (Annual)	0	144,456	173,352
Before-Tax Cash Flow	$ 240,000	$ 95,544	$ 66,648
Purchase Price	$1,500,000	$1,500,000	$1,500,000
Less: Loan Amount	0	1,000,000	1,200,000
Equity Invested	$1,500,000	$ 500,000	$ 300,000
Before-Tax Cash Flow/Equity	16.0%	19.1%	22.2%

the degree of financial leverage employed. Leverage is said to be favorable so long as the rate of return on assets exceeds the cost of borrowing. When the cost of borrowing exceeds the rate of return on assets, leverage is said to be unfavorable.

The difference between the rate of return on assets and the cost of borrowing is often called the *spread*. Even a small *favorable spread* greatly magnifies return on equity on a highly leveraged investment. A small *negative spread* (unfavorable leverage) on such a project, however, can result in a negative rate of return to the equity position.

Example 8.1

A property that has a market value of $1.5 million is expected to generate annual net operating income of $240,000. A $1 million mortgage loan that will be repaid in equal monthly installments over 25 years, with interest at 14 percent per annum, is available. The monthly payments of approximately $12,038 include both interest and principal. Annual debt service is simply 12 times this amount, or approximately $144,456.

Example 8.1 illustrates the potential impact of financial leverage. In the example, cash flow before debt service and income taxes is 16 percent of the market value of the property. This total amount flows through to the equity investors if they elect to use no financial leverage. In that case, their equity investment will be $1.5 million, and they will expect to receive $240,000 per annum before income taxes. The first column of Table 8.1 summarizes this information.

As a consequence of the decision to borrow $1,000,000, however, not all of the net operating income accrues to the equity position. Instead, $144,456 is remitted to the mortgage lender, and only the $95,544 balance is avail-

TABLE 8.2   Outcomes from Example 8.1 with Less Than Expected Net Operating Income

	No Loan	$1,000,000 Loan	$1,200,000 Loan
Actual Net Operating Income	$ 190,000	$ 190,000	$ 190,000
Less: Debt Service (Annual)	0	144,456	173,352
Actual Before-Tax Cash Flow	$ 190,000	$ 45,544	$ 16,648
Purchase Price	$1,500,000	$1,500,000	$1,500,000
Less: Loan	0	1,000,000	1,200,000
Equity	$1,500,000	$ 500,000	$ 300,000
Before-Tax Cash Flow Equity	12.7%	9.1%	5.5%

able to equity investors. The impact on before-tax cash flow and current before-tax yield on the equity investment is shown in the second column of Table 8.1.

Now see what happens when even greater financial leverage is employed. Assume that an 80 percent loan ($1,200,000) is also available on the investment in Example 8.1. This loan will be for the same period and at the same interest rate as the lesser loan set forth in the example. The monthly payments required by the second loan will be approximately $14,446, and the annual debt service will be 12 times this amount, or approximately $173,352. Thus the cash flow to the equity position will be reduced to $66,648, while the equity investment will be reduced to $300,000. This reduces both the required equity investment and cash flow to the equity position. The impact on cash flow to the equity position, expressed as a percentage of the initial equity investment, is summarized in the third column of Table 8.1.

The fundamental principle illustrated by Table 8.1 is that, so long as the *debt service constant* (the annual debt service expressed as a percentage of the amount borrowed) is less than the rate of return on total assets, additional financial leverage increases cash flow to the equity position, expressed as a percentage rate on the equity investment. In Table 8.1, the rate of return on total assets is seen to be 16 percent; the annual debt service constant is only 14.45 percent.

But the salutary effects of financial leverage are easy to overemphasize. Remember that the operating results in Example 8.1 are mere expectations. The actual outcome might be much less attractive. If net operating income, as a percent rate of return on assets, drops below the debt service constant, then using financial leverage will reduce the current return on equity.

To illustrate, consider again the data in Example 8.1. The expected net operating income of $240,000 notwithstanding, assume the actual net operating income is just $190,000. The consequences of having used financial leverage based on an overoptimistic cash-flow forecast are illustrated in Table 8.2. The possible outcomes dramatize the adverse consequences of unfavorable financial leverage.

THE COST OF BORROWED MONEY

Many loans require monthly payments designed to pay all interest currently and to retire the principal over a specified period. Such a loan is said to be fully *amortizing*. Each payment will include interest accrued since the last preceding payment, as well as a portion of the remaining principal balance.

Partly amortizing loans and term loans are sometimes employed. A term loan generally calls for payments comprised wholly of accrued interest (no principal) during the term of the loan, with the entire principal amount becoming due and payable when the loan matures. A partly amortizing loan will include some repayment of principal during the loan period, with a remaining balance due at the end. This remaining balance is called a *balloon payment*.

Determining the Debt Service

The size of the required mortgage loan payments (debt service) depends on the loan amount, the interest rate and repayment provisions. Consider, for example, a $100,000 loan with interest at 12 percent per annum that requires monthly debt service payments. To find the monthly debt service, look at the amortization factors in Table 8.3 (a more complete set of factors is provided in Appendix A at the end of the text). Move down the left-hand column of the table to the row for 25 years. Read across to the column headed by an interest rate of 12 percent. The number found at the intersection of the 25-year row and the 12-percent column is the monthly payment required to fully amortize a $1 loan over 25 years with interest at 12 percent: .010532. The monthly payment on the $100,000 loan will simply be 100,000 times this amount, which will be approximately $1,053.

The Annual Constant

Debt service requirements are often expressed as a debt service constant. The most common way of expressing the constant is as a percent of the face amount of a loan. The annual constant associated with a $100,000, eight percent, 25-year loan with monthly payments is:

$$12 \times (\$771.80/\$100,000) = .0926, \text{ or } 9.26 \text{ percent}$$

Alternatively, the constant may be expressed as the debt service obligation per $100 of indebtedness. This is nothing more than the percentage calculation expressed in dollar terms. The 9.26 percent in the preceding calculation therefore becomes $9.26.

Debt service may be expressed as an *annual constant* or a *monthly constant*, depending on the use to be made of the information. Since an annual constant (assuming monthly payment) is simply 12 times the monthly constant, the distinction between them is trivial. Tables are readily available that provide monthly and annual constants for various interest rates and loan periods. More-

TABLE 8.3   Monthly Payment to Amortize a One-Dollar Debt

Number of Years	Annual Interest Rate						
	6.0%	*7.0%*	*8.0%*	*9.0%*	*10.0%*	*12.0%*	*14.0%*
1	.086066	.086527	.086988	.087451	.087916	.088849	.089787
2	.044321	.044773	.045227	.045685	.046145	.047073	.048013
3	.030422	.030877	.031336	.031800	.032267	.033214	.034178
4	.023485	.023946	.024413	.024885	.025363	.026334	.027326
5	.019333	.019801	.020276	.020758	.021247	.022244	.023268
6	.016573	.017049	.017533	.018026	.018526	.019550	.020606
7	.014609	.015093	.015586	.016089	.016601	.017653	.018740
8	.013141	.013634	.014137	.014650	.015174	.016253	.017372
9	.012006	.012506	.013019	.013543	.014079	.015184	.016334
10	.011102	.011611	.012133	.012668	.013215	.014347	.015527
11	.010367	.010884	.011415	.011961	.012520	.013678	.014887
12	.009759	.010284	.010825	.011380	.011951	.013134	.014371
13	.009247	.009781	.010331	.010897	.011478	.012687	.013951
14	.008812	.009354	.009913	.010489	.011082	.012314	.013605
15	.008439	.008988	.009557	.010143	.010746	.012002	.013317
16	.008114	.008672	.009249	.009845	.010459	.011737	.013077
17	.007831	.008397	.008983	.009588	.010212	.011512	.012875
18	.007582	.008155	.008750	.009364	.009998	.011320	.012704
19	.007361	.007942	.008545	.009169	.009813	.011154	.012559
20	.007164	.007753	.008364	.008997	.009650	.011011	.012435
25	.006443	.007068	.007718	.008392	.009087	.010532	.012038
30	.005996	.006653	.007338	.008046	.008776	.010286	.011849

over, relatively inexpensive hand-held calculators now are able to compute debt service automatically and provide a breakdown of the interest and principal portions of each payment.

OTHER BENEFITS OF FINANCIAL LEVERAGE

Rational investors, it is frequently assumed, will not knowingly accept unfavorable financial leverage. Yet during periods of very high interest rates and rapid inflation, financial leverage as traditionally measured is almost certain to be unfavorable. Many astute investors nevertheless do enter into highly leveraged deals during such periods.

This seeming paradox stems from the conventional practice of computing rates of return on a before-tax basis and ignoring anticipated price appreciation during the holding period. Yet during periods of rapid inflation, appreciation may constitute a significant portion of expected return on such an investment.

Moreover, income tax effects are so pervasive that any investment calculation that ignores them is virtually useless.

Amplifying the Tax Shelter

Part Four of the text is devoted to an extended discussion of income tax aspects of real estate investment. Briefly, federal income tax rules provide for an allowance (a depreciation or cost recovery allowance, depending upon which set of tax rules applies) to be offset against real estate gross income each year, to account for gradual decline in value over the years.

Rules for calculating depreciation or cost recovery allowances vary, but in all instances the initial basis for the calculation is that portion of property cost attributable to buildings and other improvements. It does not include the cost of land. Cost, however, and thus the initial basis, includes borrowed funds as well as the taxpayer's equity investment in the property. Thus, any new mortgage note, or the remaining balance of any note to which the newly acquired property remains subject, is included in the taxpayer's initial basis.

As a consequence, financial leverage can magnify tax savings generated by depreciation or cost recovery allowances. These savings may, in a matter of only a few years, exceed an investor's entire initial equity investment.

Example 8.2

An investor purchases a residential rental property that has a market value of $185,000. Of this amount, $20,000 is attributable to the land and the balance to the improvements. The property generates annual gross rental income of $46,000 and requires an annual cash outlay for tax-deductible operating expenses of $22,000. The investor is in the 28 percent marginal tax bracket.

Consider the transaction outlined in Example 8.2. The annual cost recovery allowance, other than for the first and last years of ownership, is $6,000, calculated as follows:

Total Cost of Property	$185,000
Less: Portion Attributable to Land	20,000
Basis for Cost Recovery Allowance	165,000
Annual Allowance ($165,000/27.5 years)	$ 6,000

Adjusting before-tax cash flow from this investment to account for income tax consequences yields after-tax cash flow. If no funds are borrowed, the income tax consequences during the first full year of the venture will be:

Gross Rental Income	$46,000
Less: Operating Expenses	22,000
Net Operating Income	24,000
Less: Cost Recovery Allowance	6,000
Taxable income	18,000
Times: Marginal Income Tax Rate	.28
Income Tax Consequences	$ 5,040

Since we have assumed no mortgage indebtedness, there will be no debt service requirement. Consequently, after-tax cash flow from the investment is simply the before-tax cash flow (net operating income) minus the income tax consequences. This amounts to $18,960, calculated as follows:

Net Operating Income	$24,000
Less: Income Tax Consequences	5,040
After-Tax Cash Flow	$18,960

Since no borrowed funds have been employed in the transaction, the investor's initial equity investment is the market value of the property, $185,000. The first year's after-tax cash flow, expressed as a rate of return on initial cash outlay, is $18,960 divided by $185,000, or approximately 10.25 percent.

To illustrate the potential impact on income tax consequences of employing financial leverage, assume that a mortgage loan is available in the amount of $148,000, with interest at nine percent, and monthly payments sufficient to completely retire (that is, amortize) the loan over 29 years. Monthly payments on such a loan will be approximately $1,199, including both principal and interest. Total annual debt service is therefore approximately $14,388. Of this amount, approximately $13,266 represents interest on the debt during the first full year, with the balance representing repayment of principal. (Over the life of the loan, the portion of the payments representing interest regularly declines as the loan balance is reduced by periodic payments. Computations necessary to verify the numbers above are explained in Chapter 10.)

If our investor borrows the $148,000, net cash flow from the investment during the first year of ownership will be reduced by the amount of the annual debt service. The revised cash flow before taxes is:

Gross Rental Income		$46,000
Less:		
Operating Expenses	$22,000	
Debt Service	14,388	36,388
Before-Tax Cash Flow from Investment		$ 9,612

Income tax consequences of the investment are also altered by mortgage borrowing. The portion of debt service attributable to interest payments is tax-deductible. The first year's income tax consequence of the investment, with the $148,000 mortgage loan, is a tax of $1,326. Here are the computations:

TABLE 8.4   After-Tax Cash Flow from Example 8.2

	With Leverage	*Without Leverage*
Income Tax Consequences		
Gross Rental Income	$ 46,000	$ 46,000
Less:		
Operating Expenses	22,000	22,000
Cost Recovery Allowance	6,000	6,000
Interest Expense	13,266	0
Taxable Income	4,734	18,000
Times: Tax Rate	.28	.28
Income Tax	$ 1,326	$ 5,040
After-Tax Cash Flow		
Net Operating Income	$ 24,000	$ 24,000
Less: Debt Service	14,388	0
Before-Tax Cash Flow	9,612	24,000
Less: Income Tax	1,326	5,040
After-Tax Cash Flow	$ 8,286	$ 18,960
Equity Investment		
Market Value	$185,000	$185,000
Less: Mortgage Loan	148,000	0
Equity Invested	$ 37,000	$185,000
After-Tax Cash Flow/Equity	22.4%	10.25%

Net Operating Income		$24,000
Less:		
Recovery Allowance	$ 6,000	
Interest Expense	13,266	19,266
Taxable Income		4,734
Times: Marginal Income Tax Rate		.28
Tax from Investment, First Year		$ 1,326

As we have seen, after-tax cash flow is simply the before-tax cash flow adjusted for income tax consequences. The first full year's after-tax cash flow is $8,286 (the income tax consequences will change during later years, as the portion of debt service comprised of interest expense declines), calculated as follows:

Net Operating Income	$24,000
Less: Debt Service	14,388
Before-Tax Cash Flow	9,612
Less: Income Tax	1,326
After-Tax Cash Flow	$ 8,286

Financial leverage reduces after-tax cash flow in our example, from $18,960 to $8,286. Initial cash outlay also decreases, however, from $185,000 to $37,000.

The first year's after-tax cash flow, expressed as a percentage rate of return on the initial cash outlay, is now $8,286 divided by $37,000, or 22.4 percent. Financial leverage has more than doubled the first year's percentage return. Computations with and without financial leverage are summarized in Table 8.4.

Amplifying the Gain on Disposal

Pressure of population growth and urban sprawl has made land in most parts of the United States experience a more or less continuous increase in value during the post–World War II period. This has been particularly true during periods of rapid monetary inflation such as that experienced without significant relief throughout the decades of the 1960s and 1970s. (Of course, this has not been a universal experience. Speculative buying may drive prices above all reasonable indices of value. The thinking of participants in these speculative binges seems to be based on the "bigger fool" theory: Buyers knowingly pay more for a property in the expectation that they can subsequently sell at a profit to "an even bigger fool." Such speculative bubbles eventually burst. They leave the unlucky holder of the property in a sadder but wiser financial position and provide writers and lecturers with rich anecdotal material.) Financial leverage can multiply the potential gain from such appreciation. Consider the land investment opportunity outlined in Example 8.3.

Example 8.3

A parcel of land well situated to benefit from rapid urban growth can be acquired for $60,000. A prospective investor expects that the land will double in value during the next five years, at which time he plans to sell. During the interim, the land can be leased to a turnip farmer for an annual rental that just covers the property tax liability, so there will be zero annual cash flow before debt service and income taxes.

The land can be purchased for $60,000 cash, or the present owner will agree to accept a $15,000 down payment accompanied by a note and purchase-money mortgage for $45,000. Both the principal and the accumulated interest on the note will be due and payable at the end of the fifth year, with interest accumulating at a compound annual rate of ten percent.

The expected rate of return on the land in Example 8.3 will differ significantly with the choice of available financing terms. Because the interest rate on the purchase-money mortgage is less than the expected rate of increase in the market value of the property, leverage is expected to be favorable. The expected annual rate of return on equity, calculated on a pretax basis under both of the available financing alternatives, is presented below.

	With Leverage	Without Leverage
Proceeds from Sale after 5 Years	$120,000	$120,000
Less: Balance Due on Note	72,473	0
Net Proceeds, Before Tax	$ 47,527	$120,000
Initial Cash Outlay	$ 15,000	$ 60,000
Approximate Annual Pretax Rate of Return	25.9%	14.9%

The $72,473 balance due on the purchase-money note in the preceding calculation represents the value, after five years, of a $45,000 deposit (the face amount of the note) drawing interest at a compound rate of ten percent per annum. The annual rates of return (14.9 and 25.9 percent) represent compound annual growth rates that will make the initial cash outlays under each alternative financing arrangement approximately equal to the net proceeds from sales after five years.

These types of calculations are explained in detail in Part Five.

MEASURING FINANCIAL LEVERAGE

Financial leverage can be measured as the relationship between equity investment and total market value of assets acquired. Corporate financial analysts frequently express this relationship as a *debt-equity ratio,* the ratio between borrowed funds and equity funds. For reasons having to do more with its origin than with its usefulness, the ratio between borrowed funds and the market value of the asset being financed (the *loan-to-value ratio)* is more commonly employed in real estate circles.

The loan-to-value ratio provides mortgage lenders with a tool for estimating the margin of safety associated with mortgage-secured loans, and it is for this purpose that the measure was initially devised. Should a borrower default on an obligation to repay a mortgage loan, the lender expects to recoup the loss from the proceeds of a sale of the mortgaged property. In most states sale is by public auction with the property going to the highest bidder. Should the winning bid be less than the amount of the outstanding loan (plus administrative costs associated with the foreclosure sale), the lender is almost certain to suffer financial loss. Expressing loans as a percentage of the value of the mortgaged property provides some indication of the risk of such a loss. The loan-to-value ratio associated with the property in Example 8.1 ($1 million ÷ 1.5 million, or 67 percent) expresses the fact that, in the event of immediate default, the property could sell for as much as one-third below its current value before the lender would suffer a significant loss.

Loan-to-value ratios serve an entirely different function for the investment analyst. They provide a measure of the dollar amount of real estate that can be controlled with a given amount of equity funds. If, for example, the available loan-to-value ratio is 0.67, then the investor can control $1 ÷ (1 − 0.67), or $3 of real estate for every $1 of equity funds invested. This is the case in Example 8.1, where $500,000 of equity investment confers control of a $1.5 million asset. The loan-to-value ratio, therefore, serves as a measure of available financial leverage.

The debt-equity ratio expresses the degree of leverage available in a slightly different fashion. In Example 8.1 the debt-equity ratio is $1 million to $500,000, or two to one. This indicates that the investor can borrow $2 for every $1 of equity funds employed.

Greater leverage increases the risk that cash flow from the investment will be insufficient to meet the debt service obligation. The greater the amount of financial leverage employed (and therefore the greater the required debt service), the greater is the risk that equity investors will either have to invest additional funds or have to default on a mortgage note. Risk that cash flow from investments will be insufficient to service mortgage debt is called *financial risk*. It is a direct consequence of employing financial leverage. This and other elements of risk associated with real estate investment decisions are discussed at length in Part Six.

The degree to which actual net operating income can fall below expectations and still be sufficient to meet the debt service obligation is expressed as a *debt coverage ratio*. This is simply the ratio between net operating income and the debt service obligation, or, in equation form:

$$\text{Debt coverage ratio} = \frac{\text{Annual net operating income}}{\text{Annual debt service}}$$

The debt coverage ratio in Example 8.1 is 1.66, calculated by dividing the net operating income ($240,000) by the annual debt service requirement (12 × $12,038, or $144,456). This expresses an expectation that annual cash flow before debt service will be approximately 1.67 times the amount required to service the debt. It indicates a substantial cushion for underestimated expenses or overestimated revenues before actual net operating income falls below that required to service the mortgage indebtedness.

DEBT COVERAGE RATIOS AND AVAILABLE FINANCING

On all except very small investment properties, lenders can expect that investors will honor their debt service obligations only if the properties generate sufficient cash flow for this purpose. Moreover, since a mortgaged property's value depends upon its ability to generate income, the value of the property will decline if the anticipated income does not materialize. An important measure of a lender's security, therefore, is the relationship between annual net operating income from real property and the debt service obligations associated with mortgage loans.

We have previously seen that the ratio that expresses this relationship is called the *debt coverage ratio*. Recognizing the relationship between cash flow and the likelihood that mortgagors will honor their debt service obligations, lenders often specify minimum acceptable debt coverage ratios for properties. In such cases it is possible to estimate the available mortgage financing by using what has been described as a "back door" approach. Dividing the estimated annual net operating income by the minimum acceptable debt coverage ratio yields the maximum amount of annual debt service the property will support. Dividing this amount by the annual loan constant for the most likely loan terms results in an estimate of the loan that the property will support. Example 8.4 illustrates.

Example 8.4

Conversation with lenders results in an estimation that they will insist on a debt coverage ratio of not less than 1.20 in connection with a loan on a specified property and will lend at 14 percent per annum, amortized over 20 years with monthly payments. The property is expected to yield first-year net operating income of $50,000.

The expected $50,000 income from the property in Example 8.4 must be at least 1.2 times as great as the annual debt service obligation. The debt service obligation, therefore, cannot exceed $50,000/1.2, or $41,667. The amortization table in Appendix A at the end of the text (and the excerpt in Table 8.3) reveals that a 14 percent, 20-year, fully amortizing loan requires monthly payments of $.012435 per dollar borrowed. The annual debt service per dollar borrowed is simply 12 times this amount, or $.149220. Since the maximum debt service the net operating income will support is $41,667, the property will support a maximum loan of $41,667/.149220 = $279,232.

SUMMARY

Financial leverage, the use of borrowed money, enables an investor to acquire a much more expensive property than would otherwise be possible. It also permits acquiring more separate properties and thus may reduce aggregate risk.

Risk that cash flow from an investment will be insufficient to meet associated mortgage-debt payments is called *financial risk*. Increasing financial leverage also increases financial risk. The borrowing decision involves weighing off-setting elements of enhanced earnings potential and increased financial risk.

Interest expense may be deducted from taxable income, thereby decreasing the after-tax cost of borrowing. Borrowing enables investors to control a much larger financial investment, with the consequent possibility of claiming greatly increased income tax deductions for cost recovery allowances. An increased probability of ultimately realizing a substantial gain on disposal of the property also results.

RECOMMENDED READINGS

Axelrod, Allan, Curtis J. Berger, and Quintin Johnstone. *Land Transfer and Finance*. Boston: Little, Brown and Company, 1971, pp. 877–986.

Bagby, Joseph R. *Real Estate Financing Desk Book*. 2d ed. Englewood Cliffs, NJ: Institute for Business Planning, 1981.

Beaton, William R. *Real Estate Finance*. 2d ed. Englewood Cliffs, NJ: Prentice-Hall, 1982, pp. 233–36.

Britton, James A., Jr., and Lewis O. Kerwood, eds. *Financing Income-Producing Real Estate: A Theory and Casebook*. NY: McGraw-Hill, 1977.

Greer, Gaylon E., and Michael D. Farrell. *Contemporary Real Estate: Theory and Practice*. Hinsdale, IL: The Dryden Press, 1983, pp. 173–185.

Wiedemer, John P. *Real Estate Finance*. 3d ed. Reston, VA: Reston Publishing Company, Inc., 1980, pp. 13–32.

REVIEW QUESTIONS

1. How do income tax laws create an incentive to borrow money?
2. When financial leverage is used, what is the potential impact on before-tax cash flow and the current before-tax yield to the equity position?
3. How do fully amortizing loans differ from partly amortizing loans?
4. Explain the meaning of the loan-to-value ratio from a mortgage lender's perspective and from the viewpoint of an investor.
5. Describe financial risk in real estate investment and explain a useful method of measuring financial risk.
6. How can the debt coverage ratio be used to determine the amount of available financing for a project?
7. Financial leverage can amplify the gain realized on the disposal of a property. Explain how this occurs.
8. Why might an astute investor knowingly enter into a financing arrangement that appears nominally unfavorable?

DISCUSSION QUESTIONS

1. The initial interest rate charged on variable-rate mortgage loans is usually lower than that charged on fixed-rate loans of equal length.
   a. Why is this so?
   b. As a borrower, what are some factors you should consider in deciding whether to accept a variable-rate or a fixed-rate loan, when the variable-rate is somewhat lower than the fixed-rate?

2. William Zeckendorf, a legendary real estate developer and promoter, is said to have commented during a real estate negotiation, "You can name the price if I can name the terms." What was the logic (if any) of Zeckendorf's position?

3. Two loans are negotiated for the same amount of money, at the same annual interest rate. They require equal periodic payments to fully amortize the loans over 20 years. One loan calls for level monthly payments, the other for level annual payments.
   a. Will the annual payment loan require a payment of exactly 12 times the monthly payment on the other loan? Explain.
   b. Over the full 20-year repayment period, will the cumulative total interest paid on the two loans be the same? Explain.

CHAPTER 9

Forecasting Income in an Uncertain Future

INTRODUCTION

Estimating current operating expenses, as explained in previous chapters, is the starting point for developing information critical to all investment decisions: the ability of a property to generate net cash flows over the prospective holding period. The task of calculating a property's present ability to generate cash flows, albeit complicated, pales in comparison with the difficulty of forecasting this ability for future years.

This chapter addresses major factors affecting a property's competitive position and thus its ability to generate rental revenue. Because locational factors dominate other considerations, they are the primary locus of our attention. Important locational elements include site desirability as perceived by potential space users and the degree and strength of monopoly elements. Other determinants include the extent and condition of physical amenities both in the property under analysis and in competitive locations. This chapter addresses the problem of anticipating future changes in these key variables.[1]

FORECASTING GROSS INCOME

Both the desirability of space being offered for lease and the attractiveness and price of competing space are key elements influencing a property's ability to command rent. Prospects for continued income-generating ability over the projection period depend upon relative changes in the same factors. Gross rent forecasts, therefore, are in reality estimates of future locational advantages that incorporate a specific set of physical amenities. The rent a property can command depends upon its capacity to satisfy user needs and the relative scarcity of competitive properties—the supply and demand relationship discussed in Chapter 3.

Both natural and man-made features contribute to a property's desirability, as does its location. For this reason, elements of productivity were classified in Chapter 6 as physical characteristics and locational characteristics. Estimating future productivity is an exercise in forecasting changes in these characteristics, and in their desirability, over the projection period.

Influence of Physical Characteristics

Physical characteristics by their very nature have limited useful lives. As their usefulness wanes, the property becomes less desirable relative to newer properties or those that are better maintained. Estimates of the extent of this inexorable decline in competitive posture are a crucial element in accurate projection of a property's future earning capacity. The impact of physical characteristics is often considered in the separate categories of functional efficiency and physical durability.

Changes in Functional Efficiency.   Declining conformity with current standards of acceptabilty and diminished ability to render intended services inevitably means increasing vacancy rates and inability to command previous levels of rent. This decline in competitive position due to defective or dated design or engineering characteristics is called *functional obsolescence*. For many structures it eventually results in abandonment or recycling into alternative uses.

Examples abound. Changes in manufacturing procedures, transportation and storage technology have injected obsolescence into structures designed to house these activities. Modern industrial technology favoring single-story manufacturing plants has rendered older, multistoried facilities obsolescent. Ceilings with insufficient clearance, floors with inadequate load-bearing capacity, and unacceptably narrow spans between load-bearing walls all represent examples of functional obsolescence.

Altered Physical Durability.   Physical durability is the measure of how long a structure will continue to be productive. Design integrity and current condition form a basis for evaluating a structure's durability.

Some clues to inherent defects can be noted by comparing a building's physical appearance with that of other structures of approximately the same age. Past abuse to which the structure has been subjected leaves traces that suggest whether future deterioration is likely to proceed more or less rapidly compared with other properties of approximately the same age. Knowledge of structural design and building techniques is required to evaluate physical durability adequately. Analysts who lack this knowledge frequently seek competent outside counsel.

Analyzing Locational Influences

Locational factors have a pervasive influence on land value. A prime factor determining a property's ability to command rent is its location relative to the desires of prospective tenants. Cities, after all, exist in response to the economic and social needs of inhabitants. Changes in locational preferences cause alterations in the structure of urban space and in the value of urban locations.

Unlike physical features, which can be altered more or less at will, locational elements are not generally amenable to manipulation and control. Neighborhood economic and social trends have a strong impact on a property's marketability as rental space. As a consequence, gross rent forecasts must incorporate estimates of the neighborhood's ability to retain its attractiveness over the projection period.

Important locational factors include the economic and social status of the immediate neighborhood, ease of access to closely linked activities and the desirability of the specific site relative to close substitutes. Revenue forecasts must include estimates of the direction and rate of change in these key locational variables.

Locational analysis is always important. It is even more so when a venture's success hinges on anticipated changes in locational factors. Examples include acquiring vacant land in the path of expected urban expansion, rehabilitating property in older neighborhoods in the expectation of imminent urban economic revival and major rehabilitation expenditures intended to spark renewed economic growth in a stagnant downtown business district.

Identifying the linkages resulting from existing or intended land use is the first step in locational analysis. This involves studying present or planned economic activity at the site to determine major geographic points to or from which there will be movement of people or products.

The analyst then judges the relative importance of each linkage and estimates transfer costs associated with the proposed usage. Comparing these costs with those incurred by people engaged in the same economic activity at competing locations yields an estimate of the contribution the location makes to the site's ability to command rent.

Total transfer costs include both explicit and implicit costs of getting from one location to another. The frustration and bother of such movement generate disutility, which constitutes an implicit cost. Total cost is the product of the cost per trip, both implicit and explicit, and the number of trips made per period of time.

FUTURITY IN PRODUCTIVITY ANALYSIS

Relative locational desirability is the dominant factor in a site's ability to command rent. Accurate forecasts of rent-generating ability, therefore, depend heavily on the analyst's ability to assess the future desirability of the site. The analysis occurs today, but its focus is on the future. Yet locational factors are subject to change over time. Moreover, the importance of the factors themselves may vary during the projection period. Estimating the probable direction and rate of these changes is an essential step in productivity analysis.

Properties embodying questionable physical or locational characteristics may be particularly vulnerable to shifts in demand for rental space. Total demand in the relevant market might change only minutely during a projection period, yet the impact of the change is felt disproportionately by the least desirable facilities in any market classification. As a consequence, such properties are likely to experience much wider swings in vacancy rates than is suggested by aggregate data.

Site value may be created, destroyed or drastically altered by social, technological and economic change. Because contributing factors are diverse and interrelated, analysis of probable change in locational benefits must take into account likely future trends, not only in the factors themselves but also in relationships among them.

New Linkages May Emerge

Altered lifestyles, changing business patterns or shifts in technology can sever existing linkages and create new ones. The shift from urban to suburban living, for example, combined with the advent of the automobile to create linkages between communities and regional shopping centers while reducing the significance of old linkages between residential neighborhoods and the central business district.

A drastic decline in public transport facilities has reduced the locational value of housing and retail stores along major public transportation arteries such as commuter railways and major bus routes. During the same period, mass ownership of automobiles has greatly increased the locational value of residential sites convenient to major highways. Shifting transportation patterns have reduced the relative value of access to railroad sidings for industrial sites. Concomitantly, increasing congestion in urban areas has added value to industrial sites that are outside yet convenient to major urban concentrations.

Existing Linkages May Become Less Significant

Changes in lifestyles or production techniques may reduce the value of ready access to linked sites, thereby making old linkages less important in location decisions. The importance of existing linkages to community entertainment centers, for example, has been greatly decreased by almost universal ownership of televisions. Home refrigerators and frozen food facilities have reduced the frequency of shopping trips and thereby weakened the need for quick and convenient access to grocery stores and restaurants.

Relative Transfer Costs May Be Altered

As major transportation systems are modified or supplanted, transfer costs may be altered drastically. Contemporary examples include rerouting of major highways, closing of railway spurs and alterations in the cost and availability of parking facilities. Such changes may sever ready access to linked sites and thereby destroy the locational value of proximity to places of work or shopping. A bridge over a previously impassable river or a new limited-access highway can destroy the locational advantage of a site by providing ready access to competing sites. Freeway construction in many areas has altered traffic patterns and shifted the relative advantages of locations that share common linkages.

Neighborhood Influences Are Subject to Change

Changing the location of support facilities such as schools or churches may significantly alter neighborhood influences. Consolidating school districts or simply destroying the traditional linkage between place of residence and location of school attendance can result in massive and often unforeseen shifts in the relative desirability of residential neighborhoods.

Destroying physical barriers or creating new ones can have the same effect. Removing a railroad bed or public building complex that previously separated a highly desirable residential area from an area of decay or slum housing, for example, might spark a decline in a neighborhood that has a long reputation for stability. Altering barriers that are more psychological than physical might generate a similar outcome. A small park or neighborhood shopping area, for example, might be a symbol of neighborhood solidarity and uniqueness, setting the residents apart from those in surrounding areas. Destroying such a symbol, however well-meaning the action might be, can rend neighborhood cohesiveness and set the previously stable community on a path of decay and desolation.

Institutional Arrangements

Institutional influences can also have a profound effect on site desirability. These include contractual agreements between private parties to the effect that certain activities will or will not be conducted at the site. They also include government regulations such as zoning ordinances, building codes and fire regulations, as well as other federal, state and local ordinances impinging upon an owner's freedom to determine how property will be used.

Inharmonious or incompatible land usage can quickly destroy a neighborhood's unique character and reduce its locational value. Zoning and building codes are designed to protect against such an eventuality. Private contractual agreements are often intended to accomplish the same objective. Recent successful court challenges of existing arrangements deemed to be unfairly exclusionary cast serious doubt on the future usefulness of these institutional arrangements as a major element in preserving locational value.

THE SUPPLY FACTOR

A good's or service's desirability and the relative scarcity and price of close substitutes affect its exchange value. A forecast of changes in the supply of comparable rental space is therefore an essential element in the analysis of a property's ability to command rents over the projection period.

Availability and cost of substitute space are strong influences on rental value. The nature of both present and potential competition must, therefore, be thoroughly analyzed. This implies consideration of existing properties catering to the same clientele as well as the potential for additions to the existing stock. Factors that must be studied include building sites that are properly zoned and currently available and the likelihood of significant zoning changes during the forecast period. The analyst will also consider the probable cost and availability of construction loan funds.

The supply of land is demonstrably far in excess of current needs. The 1980 census reports that approximately 16 percent of the land in the United States accommodates about 76 percent of the total population. Moreover, more than 60 percent of nonurban space is uncultivated and available for uses other than agriculture.[2] As urban boundaries expand arithmetically, urban space expands geometrically. Clearly, there is abundant room for urban expansion.

Land ideally located for specific uses, however, is an altogether different proposition. The urban fringe is not the optimum location for many activities. Yet that is where most undeveloped urban land is located.

We saw in Chapter 3 that there is one "best" location for many economic activities because of the site's location relative to other urban economic and social activities or due to the site's unique physical characteristics. Yet it is equally true that there are almost always a number of other sites that are nearly as good. These substitute sites may yield slightly less total productivity, but several may adequately fulfill the basic requirements of most prospective tenants.

Beyond the questions of the availability and price of competing space, future rental revenue depends on the relative degree of prestige associated with a property. The physical amenities and locational convenience of Chicago's Water Tower Place are not appreciably greater than those of surrounding properties, yet Water Tower Place commands premium rents. The distinction lies solely in the perception of tenants who desire identification with this specific address. Economists refer to this as a *monopoly element*. Marketing specialists prefer the more neutral term *product differentiation*.

To summarize the supply issue: Sites are what economists call *differentiated products*. They are all different in at least some aspects, but the distinction generally is not so great that several slightly different locations will not serve almost equally well. Potential users will base choices among ideal sites and close substitutes on relative occupancy costs and relative benefits flowing from their use.

FORECASTING SUPPLY CHANGES

When aggregate vacancy rates within any market segment drop significantly below the generally prevailing level, it is safe to infer that there is "excess demand" at currently prevailing prices. General rental rates in the market area can then be expected to move upward until a new equilibrium is reached over the short run.

When vacancy rates are significantly above historical levels, demand is likely to be insufficient to maintain past rates of increase in rental rates. As the general price level moves upward faster than do prevailing rental rates, "real" (that is, price-adjusted) rates decline. Because landlords are loath to actually reduce rental rates, any decline in excess of the rate of increase in general prices is likely to be reflected in concessions granted to tenants. Classical demand and supply analysis leads to the expectation of a drop in prices (rents) under these circumstances. In real life, prices tend to be "sticky" on the downside. Landlords resist reductions in rents in the expectation of better opportunities in the future. Reductions that do occur are often hidden in the form of rent concessions, which are not apparent to the casual observer. Close investigation is necessary to determine whether market rents are actually less than current contract rates because of the existence of widespread rent concessions. Such concessions may take the form of additional decorating allowances, free parking or a reduction in the tenant's share of common-area expenses.

To estimate whether significant upward or downward movement in prevailing rents is likely over the forecasting period, analysts must estimate probable alterations in demand and supply relationships. The task of estimating likely supply changes during the projection period is simplified by viewing the long-term supply curve as a series of points on a succession of short-run curves.

Remember that the supply of rental units is relatively fixed over the short run. Thus the short-run supply function will always be essentially unresponsive to changes in price. This is depicted as a vertical line on a supply graph. Between short-run time periods, however, construction continues so that at a later time the short-term supply function will be fixed at a greater total supply. A series of point estimates of the short-run supply function through time results in an estimate of the location of the long-term supply curve.

Over the longer term, the supply of rental units will be continuously augmented so long as production cost is less than the present value of expected future rents. Long-term supply changes, therefore, are dependent on future rates of change in construction cost, on the cost and availability of appropriately zoned land and on developers' perceptions of the direction and rate of changes in demand.

PRODUCT DIFFERENTIATION AND SUPPLY ANALYSIS

Real estate that has unique features can command a premium price. In marketing terms, product differences—whether real or spurious—desensitize buyers to price differentials. The distinction may lie in unique architecture, high-quality construction, luxurious appointments or other elements that create a compelling image for potential tenants.

Physical differences may be significantly less valuable than those that exist only in the perception of tenants. Styling, quality and functional features can be duplicated by competitors. Image, in contrast, is unique to individual properties and is often generated consciously to appeal to a specific market segment. Due solely to its reputation, a property may consistently command a premium price or sell at a discount from prevailing rates for similarly located and outfitted competitors. Successfully cultivating and protecting a uniquely desirable property image captures some of the monopoly advantages associated with unique location. Such a property is far less vulnerable to competition from otherwise comparable rental space.

FORECASTING OPERATING EXPENSES

Current and past operating expense information provides a basis for projections. These data may not be available for a specific property, or reported data may be considered unreliable. But data for comparable properties are usually readily obtainable from real estate practitioners in the market area. These data can be rendered directly comparable by expressing them either in dollars per standardized unit (such as per square foot or per room) or in ratio terms (such as an operating expense ratio).

Analysis of recent trend data will usually show a reassuringly stable relationship between expenses and income or in expense per standard unit of space. Note that we have not predicted a constant relationship, merely a stable one. Factors affecting these relationships tend to be long-term influences, and the trends are likely to shift only slowly over time.

Examples of this stability are presented in Table 9.1, which presents annual operating expenses for garden-type apartment buildings in the Chicago area over an eleven-year period. Table 9.2 shows similar data for low-rise apartment buildings during the same period. Each table presents data both in dollars per room per annum and as a percent of gross income.

Using techniques discussed in Chapter 5, we can express this relationship in terms of simple linear regression. Recall that the equation is:

$$y = a + bx$$

where y is the dependent variable, x is the independent variable and a and b are constants expressing the relationship between the two variables.

TABLE 9.1   Average Income and Operating Costs for Garden Buildings (Chicago)

Year	Gross Possible Total Income (a)*	(b)**	Vacancy (a)	(b)	Total Expenses (a)	(b)	Net Operating Income (a)	(b)
1	$400.10	100%	$18.25	4.6%	$206.86	51.7%	$174.99	43.7%
2	405.64	100	5.27	1.3	208.63	51.4	191.74	47.3
3	400.33	100	2.61	.7	215.59	53.9	182.19	45.5
4	558.98	100	58.00	10.4	278.01	49.7	202.97	39.9
5	579.02	100	50.75	8.6	305.50	52.8	212.77	36.8
6	591.92	100	66.30	11.2	291.51	49.3	234.11	39.6
7	657.48	100	27.03	4.1	344.30	52.4	286.14	43.5
8	660.82	100	45.26	6.9	350.23	53.0	265.33	40.2
9	713.82	100	80.02	11.2	380.79	53.4	256.31	35.9
10	675.33	100	———		345.97	53.7	286.86	41.5
11	722.62	100	———		409.45	53.2	318.27	43.4

*Dollars per Room per Annum
**Percent of Gross Possible Total Income per Room per Annum
SOURCE: Institute of Real Estate Management, *Income and Expense Analysis: Apartments, Condominiums and Cooperatives* (various years).

TABLE 9.2   Average Income and Operating Costs for Low-Rise Buildings of 25 or More Units (Chicago)

Year	Gross Possible Total Income (a)*	(b)**	Vacancy (a)	(b)	Total Expenses (a)	(b)	Net Operating Income (a)	(b)
1	$370.94	100%	$ 7.33	2.0%	$227.90	61.4%	$135.83	36.6%
2	412.37	100	10.87	2.6	255.61	62.0	145.89	35.4
3	448.24	100	12.62	2.8	227.60	61.9	158.36	35.3
4	506.02	100	47.21	9.3	292.05	57.7	170.64	33.7
5	499.32	100	12.34	2.5	315.22	63.1	175.33	35.1
6	523.94	100	13.77	2.6	310.44	59.3	199.74	38.1
7	570.92	100	19.11	3.4	323.75	56.7	227.89	39.9
8	626.39	100	32.97	5.3	363.30	58.0	230.91	36.9
9	645.78	100	19.97	3.1	365.97	56.7	260.07	40.3
10	629.28	100	———		408.52	63.8	193.10	33.5
11	702.63	100	———		415.21	62.8	233.94	33.0

*Dollars per Room per Annum
**Percent of Gross Possible Total Income per Room per Annum
SOURCE: Institute of Real Estate Management, *Income and Expense Analysis: Apartments, Condominiums and Cooperatives* (various years).

Keying data from Table 9.1 into a calculator or a computer with a simple linear regression program reveals that the relationship generates a line with slope and intercept as follows:

$$y = a + bx$$
$$= -12.68 + .557x$$

These measures can be used to estimate operating expenses for ensuing years. If, for example, we were expecting gross revenue per room during Year 12 to be $800, then we would project operating expenses to be:

$$y = a + bx$$
$$= -12.68 + .557(\$800)$$
$$= \$432.92$$

Having developed a forecast of gross rents by projecting past experience into the future (with appropriate adjustments for anticipated changes in the economic, political and social environment), we can estimate operating expenses by extrapolating in this fashion over the entire projection period.

Just as alterations in the economic, political and social environment can alter gross revenue trends, however, so can they change trends in operating expenses. Legislation drastically increasing the legal minimum wage, for example, could cause operating expenses to escalate faster than gross rents. New union contracts among organizations servicing a property (garbage collectors, security firms, maintenance firms and so forth) might have a similar impact. Such contingencies can be anticipated only by keeping a sharp eye for current conditions, applying common sense and being a shrewd judge of the shifting nuances of political winds.

SUMMARY

Revenue forecasting is essentially a marketing research problem. Demand for rental space at a specific location depends primarily upon the desirability of amenities and locational factors the site confers and upon the price and availability of competing sites that offer approximately the same level of want-satisfying power. Thus, both physical and locational characteristics affect a property's ability to command rents. Physical characteristics include both geological features and man-made improvements. Locational characteristics relate to how well a location is suited for its intended use.

The contribution that physical characteristics make to a property's competitive position changes over time. These changes are attributable both to physical deterioration and to altered needs or tastes on the part of prospective tenants. Improvements become less suitable with age, as a result of decline in their attractiveness and due to increased maintenance costs. Technological innovation or variation in style and tastes may render existing physical structures less desirable than before, even without the factor of physical deterioration.

Linkages, neighborhood influences and institutional factors all contribute to relative locational desirability. Linkages require movement of goods or people between properties, the costs of which are called *transfer costs*. The importance of locations that minimize transfer costs increases with the relative importance of these costs to the total cost of producing and delivering a good or service. Both explicit and implicit transfer costs must be factored into location decisions. Implicit costs include such things as the value of time spent in transit and the bother and frustration of providing for transportation.

Linkages, relationships that require movement of people or things between linked sites, are almost certain to change over time. Altered lifestyles, new technology, shifts in consumer tastes—these and a host of other phenomena may promote the emergence of important new linkages as well as a decline in the significance of old ones. Because linkages play such a dominant role in determining a property's ability to command rent, accurate perception of emerging trends that will alter key linkages are a major factor in reliable income forecasting.

Even if linkage relationships remain virtually constant over the forecast period, their impact on a property's income-generating capacity might shift importantly due to changes in relative transfer costs. As the cost of moving people or goods between linked sites is increased or decreased by modification of transportation facilities or other economic shifts, the linkage's impact on a site's ability to command rent may be altered.

Sites are subject to both desirable and undesirable neighborhood influences. Such influences are particularly important in real estate decisions because site immobility prohibits moving to escape the influence of neighborhood factors.

Building and zoning ordinances, fire codes and federal, state and local land use laws are frequently designed to protect against the encroachment of neighborhood factors deemed to be undesirable. Private agreements are often designed with the same objective.

Both demand and supply considerations must be factored into revenue forecasts. This involves estimating probable changes in site linkages, in neighborhood influences and in institutional factors that may influence demand or supply. Supply is a less troublesome consideration when significant monopoly elements are present. Monopoly elements may result from unique physical or locational factors, or they may exist only in the perception of potential tenants. Regardless of their origin, they reduce the property's vulnerability to competitive inroads from comparable property.

NOTES

1. This entire chapter, including the terminology, is based on our interpretation of the writings of Richard U. Ratcliff. We most emphatically acknowledge our intellectual debt. Both custom and fact dictate that we bear responsibility for our interpretation of Ratcliff's ideas, including both errors and heresies. For a more lengthy exposition of these ideas, and for an introduction to a most rewarding and innovative original source, read Ratcliff's work, with special attention to *Real Estate Analysis* (New York: McGraw-Hill, 1961).

2. U.S. Bureau of the Census, *Statistical Abstract of the United States* (Washington, DC: U.S. Government Printing Office, 1984).

RECOMMENDED READINGS

American Institute of Real Estate Appraisers. *The Appraisal of Real Estate*. 8th ed. Chicago: The American Institute of Real Estate Appraisers, 1983, pp. 351–385.

Barrett, G. Vincent, and John P. Blair. *How to Conduct and Analyze Real Estate Market and Feasibility Studies*. NY: Van Nostrand Reinhold Company, 1982, pp. 99–105.

Friedman, Jack P., and Nicholas Ordway. *Income Property Appraisal and Analysis*. Reston, VA: Reston Publishing Company, Inc., 1981, pp. 133–149.

Greer, Gaylon E. *The Real Estate Investment Decision*. Lexington, MA: Lexington Books, 1979, pp. 47–62.

Greer, Gaylon E., and Michael D. Farrell. *Contemporary Real Estate: Theory and Practice*. Hinsdale, IL: The Dryden Press, 1983, pp. 262–264.

REVIEW QUESTIONS

1. List some of the key physical characteristics that influence a property's income-producing capability.
2. List some of the locational factors that will influence a property's ability to command rents.
3. What future trends must be considered in forecasting the rent-generating ability of a property?
4. How does supply affect the rent-generating capability of property?
5. List the relationship between price and supply of rental property.
6. Operating expenses cannot be estimated based on past experience and are totally unrelated to revenue projections. Do you agree? Discuss.
7. What is functional obsolescence and how does it affect a property's ability to command rent?
8. What are linkages and how do they influence tenants' location decisions?
9. How do explicit and implicit transfer costs differ? Give some examples of both.
10. Give at least two examples of institutional arrangements that can either enhance or detract from a property's ability to command rent.

DISCUSSION QUESTIONS

1. In an inflationary environment, cash flows in future years will have less purchasing power than those in earlier years. Thus, a multiple-year cash-flow forecast is not a consistent measure of a property's performance. How might this difficulty be addressed?

2. What examples (other than those in the text) can you think of where significant new linkages have emerged or the importance of existing linkages has shifted significantly to alter the relative value of properties that are imperfect substitutes?

3. Give some examples from your community where relative transfer costs have been altered enough to shift the competitive positions of properties in the area.

4. Give examples from your community where a site has been differentiated from the competition through imaginative marketing or by controlling a unique site.

5. Technological changes that will have a significant impact on functional efficiency often have long lead times. Give some examples of such changes and the clues that might have alerted analysts of their impending impacts.

6. Discuss the relationship among inflation, interest rates and increases in the supply of rental property.

7. The text distinguishes between the responsiveness of short-run and long-run supply curves to changes in rental rates. What determines the length of time that comprises the "long" rather than the "short" run?

PART THREE: Case Problem

Arnold Benedict is thinking of buying an apartment complex that is offered for sale (asking price, $1.7 million) by the firm of Gettabinder and Flee. The following statement of income and expense is presented for Benedict's consideration:

The Sated Satyr Apartments
Prior Year's Operating Results
Presented by Gettabinder and Flee, Brokers

78 units, all two-bedroom apartments, $250 per month		$234,000
Laundry room and soda machines		10,000
Gross annual income		$244,000
Less Operating Expenses:		
Manager's salary	$10,000	
Maintenance man ($150 per week)	$ 7,800	
Seedy landscapers	1,300	
Property taxes	9,000	28,100
Net Operating Income		$215,900

By checking the electric meters during an inspection tour of the property, Benedict determines the occupancy rate to be about 80 percent. He learns by talking to tenants that most have been offered inducements such as one month's free rent or special decorating allowances. A check with competing apartment houses reveals that similar apartment units rent for about $230 per month and that vacancies average about five percent. Moreover, these other apartments have pools and recreation areas that make their units worth about $10 per month more than those of the Sated Satyr, which has neither.

A check with the tax assessor's office reveals that apartments are reassessed immediately after they are sold and that the tax rate is $35 per $1,000 of assessed value; the assessment rate is 80 percent of market value.

Benedict learns that the resident manager at Sated Satyr, in addition to a $10,000 salary, gets a free apartment for her services. Benedict also discovered other possible expenses: Insurance will cost $6.50 per $1,000 of coverage, based on estimated replacement cost of $1.5 million; workers' compensation ($95 per annum) must be paid to the state; utilities for hallways and other common areas for similar properties cost about $65 per month; supplies and miscellaneous expenses typically run about one-fourth of a percent of effective gross rental income.

Informed opinions in the area are that rental rates and operating expenses will remain fairly constant for the immediate future.

1. Restate the operating statement for the Sated Satyr Apartments, presenting all information in good form.
2. If Benedict can get a $1.2 million mortgage loan for 30 years at ten percent (level monthly payments), how much can he pay for the Sated Satyr if he wants the annual cash flow, net of debt service payments but before considering income taxes, to equal ten percent of his equity investment?
3. Develop an amortization schedule for the $1.2 million loan, showing interest expense, principal payments and total debt service on an annual basis for the first seven years.

Important! Save all your work for use with case problems in Parts Four through Six.

PART FOUR

Income Tax Considerations

A multitude of income tax savings opportunities become available when one joins the property-owning class. With these opportunities comes a host of potential income tax difficulties to beset the unwary or imprudent. This section of the book outlines major income tax issues facing real estate investors. Readers should understand that income tax rules regarding real estate held for personal use are often radically different from those for real estate held for use in a trade or business or for production of income. Material presented here relates solely to the latter types of real property.

Federal income tax law is found in a bulky document known as the *Internal Revenue Code,* frequently referred to merely as the *Code.* Approximately 18 pages of the Code are devoted to explaining what income is taxable. This is followed by more than 3,000 pages of exceptions, amplifications and attempts at clarification. The Treasury Department has supplemented the Code with over 5,000 pages of regulations in a generally vain attempt to make its provisions more comprehensible. The Internal Revenue Service has published voluminous material devoted to clarifying the Treasury Department regulations. All this is overshadowed by a massive library of court decisions in settlement of disputes between tax collector and taxpayers.

In the next three chapters we can cover only a minute portion of the tax issues addressed by this massive outpouring of authoritative proclamations. Nor do we wish to do more. Our concern is with the minor portion of the Code and implementing regulations that directly influences income tax consequences of real estate investment decisions. Even here we must limit ourselves to an overview of many issues, in order to discuss in greater detail the matters of overriding importance. No prudent investor will make a financial commitment without a detailed investigation of its income tax implications. Specialized income tax counsel is readily available and should be consulted wherever tax issues surpass the analyst's understanding.

CHAPTER 10

Basic Income Tax Issues

INTRODUCTION

Income taxes constitute a claim superior to that of equity investors, whose interest is a mere residual. The relevant measure of investment outcomes, therefore, is the value of after-tax cash flows. Rational analysis must always incorporate estimates of income tax consequences of investor actions.

In general, cash receipts generated from a property constitute taxable income. Likewise, expenditures incurred to generate the revenues generally are tax deductible, either when incurred or at a later date. This chapter focuses on the most significant exceptions to these general rules.

From the time of acquisition, property has a *tax basis* in the hands of the owner. This basis, as adjusted during the holding period, is a fundamental concept in tax planning. It is a primary determinant of tax consequences during the holding period and of the taxable gain or loss from property disposal. Determinants of the initial tax basis and major events causing upward or downward adjustments thereto are the first issues addressed in this chapter.

Gains or losses from property disposal may affect taxable income in different ways, depending upon how the transaction is structured. Varying circumstances surrounding property disposal may cause gains or losses to have immediate income tax implications or may result in the taxpayer's being permitted (in some cases, required) to defer recognition of tax consequences until a later date. Major examples of such circumstances and the resulting income tax alternatives available to investors are treated at length in the chapter.

Because tax law is extensive and complex, only abbreviated and oversimplified explanations of relevant issues can be presented here. Moreover, all issues are presented from the perspective of individual noncorporate taxpayers. Tax law applicable to corporations frequently differs significantly from noncorporate tax law.

NATURE AND SIGNIFICANCE OF THE TAX BASIS

A newly acquired property's *initial tax basis* is the starting point in determining income tax consequences of operating the property and, ultimately, the tax consequences of disposal. During the holding period, the tax basis is adjusted to reflect additional capital investment as well as disinvestment. Selling or exchanging a property generates a gain or loss equal to the difference between the sales price and the *adjusted basis* of the property at the time of disposal.

Example 10.1

An apartment building is purchased on the following terms: $50,000 in cash at closing, with the purchaser taking title subject to an existing mortgage note, which has a remaining balance of $400,000, and signing a note and second mortgage for $50,000. The buyer also pays $2,000 into a tax and insurance escrow account (*escrow* involves the holding by a third party, an escrow agent, of something of value that is the subject of a contract between two other parties, until that contract has been consummated), $240 for the seller's prepaid water bill, $250 for heating oil remaining in the building's tanks, $25 for document recording and $90 for state documentary stamps. Other expenditures include $1,500 for legal representation, $210 for an owner's title insurance policy, $450 for a lender's title insurance policy and $180 for a credit report.

The purchaser's initial tax basis is $501,825, determined as follows:

Purchase Price		
Cash Down Payment	$ 50,000	
Second Mortgage Note	50,000	
First Mortgage Note	400,000	$500,000
Attorney's Fee		1,500
Owner's Title Policy		210
Recording Fee		25
Documentary Stamps		90
Initial Tax Basis		$501,825

All other outlays represent costs of obtaining financing or are incidental to the purchase and therefore are not properly includable in the initial basis.

When property is acquired by purchase, its cost forms the buyer's initial tax basis. This includes everything of value given in exchange. It also includes all costs incurred in obtaining and defending title. Thus cost includes purchase commissions, legal fees, title insurance and other items that are incurred in connection with acquisition and are not deductible as current operating expenses.

The initial basis of buildings and other improvements constructed by the investor is the cost of construction.

ALLOCATING THE TAX BASIS

If land and improvements (buildings and so forth) are acquired together, the initial tax basis must be allocated between them. That portion properly attributable to the improvements results in an annual tax-deductible expense to account for the inevitable decline in value and usefulness of the asset due to wear and tear, obsolescence and destructive exposure to the elements. This deduction, called a *depreciation* or *cost recovery allowance*, is discussed later in the chapter. The land itself is considered to be virtually indestructible and therefore is not subject to such adjustments. (Of course, every investor knows that even though land may be indestructible, its value as a site is created by external factors and can disappear with social and economic change in the surrounding area. Such a decline in land value represents a real loss to the investor but is not considered in the nature of cost recovery and is therefore not deductible concurrently with its occurrence. When the land is ultimately sold, the loss can be charged off as a capital item. In this manner the loss, when actually realized [as opposed to its mere anticipation], reduces the investor's tax liability.)

Tax law states that allocation of the tax basis among two or more assets must reflect their relative market values. But market value is necessarily an estimate, and taxpayers who carefully document the rationale for their estimates may be able to justify allocating a substantial portion of total cost to those assets that generate tax deductions for depreciation or cost recovery allowances. As we shall see shortly, significant tax benefits flow from such a strategy.

Perhaps the simplest approach to allocating the initial tax basis between land and improvements is to specify the price of each in the original purchase contract. If the purchase is an arm's-length transaction, such contractual determination forms a defensible cost allocation basis.

A more commonly employed allocation method is to use the ratio of land value to building value estimated by the tax assessor, who usually assesses land and improvements separately. Example 10.2 illustrates.

Example 10.2

An investor buys a property for $80,000. No mention is made in the purchase agreement regarding the portions of the purchase price that apply to land and to improvements. The county assesses the property for tax purposes at $8,000, of which $2,000 is specified by the assessor as applying to the land and the balance to improvements. Using the assessor's ratio, property value is divided between land and improvements as follows:

Land ($2,000/$8,000)	25%
Improvements ($6,000/$8,000)	75
Total ($8,000/$8,000)	100%

The investor's initial tax basis for the property is therefore:

Land (25% of $80,000)	$20,000
Improvements (75% of $80,000)	60,000
Land and Improvements	$80,000

A third generally acceptable allocation approach is to have an independent appraiser estimate the relative values of land and buildings. Although values determined by the appraiser might differ considerably from the investor's tax basis, they nevertheless provide necessary data for allocating the basis in accordance with relative market values.

ADJUSTING THE BASIS FOR COST RECOVERY

From the time of its fabrication, every human-made object embarks upon an irreversible trek to the salvage yard. Wear and tear, obsolescence and destructive exposure to the elements can be arrested briefly through careful maintenance and periodic rehabilitation, but there inevitably comes a day when further efforts to lengthen an asset's life span are not economically justifiable.

Income taxes are intended to be levied only upon *income* from such assets, rather than upon their conversion into more liquid form. Toward this end the Internal Revenue Code permits taxpayers to deduct from otherwise taxable real estate revenue an allowance for recovery of invested capital. The allowance, appropriately called a *cost recovery allowance,* is sufficient to recover completely the cost of property improvements (buildings and improvements to the land) over the recovery period. (Cost recovery allowances apply only to improvements to real property put into use in 1981 or later and not acquired in a "churning" transaction as discussed in Appendix 10.A. Property put into service before 1981, or after that date but acquired in a churning transaction, qualifies instead for depreciation deductions designed to recover cost over the property's useful economic life. Depreciation allowances are discussed in Appendix 10.A. Property put into use after 1980 but before the effective date of the 1986 Tax Act qualifies as recovery property but with slightly different rules.)

Only assets held for business or income purposes qualify for the cost recovery allowance. Note that the determining factor is *intent* to produce income, rather than actual success in doing so. Thus an owner of rental property may claim a cost recovery allowance regardless of whether a tenant actually occupies the premises. But the Internal Revenue Service may insist upon evidence of intent. For example, a house previously occupied by the owner will not qualify for a deduction when vacated and offered for sale simply because it suffers a loss in value during the period of vacancy. It will be considered income property, and thus will qualify for a cost recovery allowance, only if the owner actively seeks to rent it after moving out.

Allowable Cost Recovery Periods

Prior to 1981 the Internal Revenue Code required recovery of costs to be spread over a property's useful economic life in the taxpayer's trade or business. This approach never worked very well, and it was abandoned in 1981 in favor of specific statutory recovery periods.

Since 1981 the allowable recovery periods have been altered repeatedly in response to political expediency and in pursuit of transitory economic objectives. Currently, the cost of residential income property, excluding land costs, is recovered over 27.5 years. Recoverable nonresidential property costs must be spread over 31.5 years. A property is considered residential in nature only if at least 80 percent of building gross rents stem from residential tenants.

Computing the Cost Recovery Allowance

Costs are recovered in equal annual increments over the recovery period. If property is owned for less than a full year, the annual allowance is spread ratably over the number of months that it is owned. Half a month's allowance is claimed during the month in which a taxpayer first puts a property into service, regardless of how many days during that month the property is actually in service. Another half month's allowance is claimed in the month of disposition, again without regard to the actual number of days the property is owned that month.

Example 10.3

During March 1988, a taxpayer who files tax returns on a calendar-year basis acquires a residential income property that she operates until November 1990, the month in which she sells. The portion of the purchase price (including applicable transactions costs) properly attributable to the building is $240,000.

To see how the allowance is computed, consider Example 10.3. Since the property is residential in nature, the $240,000 initial tax basis of the building will be recovered over 27.5 years. The monthly allowance, therefore, will be $727.27:

$$\text{Recoverable Amount}/(12 \times \text{Recovery Period}) = \$240,000/330$$
$$= \$727.27$$

Allowable cost recovery allowance during the year of acquisition is $727.27 times the number of months held, including a half month's allowance for March. Hence our investor's first-year allowance, rounded to the nearest whole dollar, is $6,909:

$$\text{Months in Use} \times \text{Monthly Allowance} = 9.5 \times \$727.27$$
$$= \$6,909$$

The allowance during each whole year of this investor's ownership will be 12 times $727.27, or $8,727. During the year of disposal the taxpayer will claim the allowance for only 10.5 months. Thus, the final year's allowance will be 10.5 times $727.27, or $7,636.

Had the property in Example 10.3 been nonresidential—perhaps an office or a store building—the allowance would have been somewhat smaller. Since the recovery period for nonresidential properties is 31.5 years, the monthly allowance for this property would have been $634.92:

$$\text{Recoverable Amount}/(12 \times \text{Recovery Period}) = \$240,000/378$$
$$= \$634.92$$

Under the revised assumption that the property in Example 10.3 is non-residential, therefore, the first year's allowance will be 9.5 times $634.92, or $6,032. The annual allowance until the year of disposal will be 12 times $634.92, or $7,619. In the year of disposal the taxpayer will claim an allowance of 10.5 times $634.92, or $6,667.

OTHER ADJUSTMENTS TO THE TAX BASIS

A number of factors other than cost recovery allowances result in adjustments to the initial tax basis. Some of these, such as capital improvements by the investor or by a tenant, may increase the basis. Others decrease it.

Adjustments Decreasing the Basis

Examples of capital recovery other than via the cost recovery allowance include sale of a portion of the property or its destruction by fire, flood, storm or other casualty. A partial sale requires the tax basis to be reduced by the portion of the total basis properly attributable to the part sold. In the case of casualty losses, the basis of the property must be reduced to reflect allowable loss deductions in the year of the casualty, plus any loss for which compensation is received. Example 10.4 illustrates a series of adjustments.

Example 10.4

An investor acquired 20,000 square feet of land at a price of $4 per square foot. Land cost is properly allocable proportionately to each square foot acquired. The investor constructs a building on the easternmost 10,000 square feet, incurring material and construction costs totaling $250,000. After claiming cost recovery allowances of $25,000, the investor sells the westernmost 10,000 square feet of land for $100,000. The adjusted basis of the investor's property after consummating these transactions is $265,000, determined as follows:

Initial Basis		
Land (20,000 Square Feet at $4)		$ 80,000
Building (Cost of Construction)		250,000
Total		$330,000
Adjustments		
Cost Recovery Allowance	$25,000	
Land Sale (10,000 Square Feet with Basis		
of $4 per Square Feet)	40,000	65,000
Adjusted Basis of Building and		
Remaining Land		$265,000

Adjustments Increasing the Basis

An owner's tax basis is increased by all expenditures that are required to be *capitalized*. Generally these include any expenditure connected with the property that is not deductible as a current expense. Of course, a taxpayer usually prefers to deduct expenditures as current operating expenses where permissible. This causes an immediate reduction in tax liability, whereas capitalizing the expenditure results in a reduction of tax liabilities in future years as the capitalized expenditure is reflected in cost recovery allowances.

The distinction between capital expenditures and currently deductible repairs and maintenance is set forth in Treasury Regulation 1.162-4. That regulation specifies that owners of income and investment property may currently deduct those expenditures for repairs that materially add to neither the value nor the life span of the improvements but only maintain it in ordinarily efficient operating condition. Expenditures that arrest deterioration and appreciably prolong useful life must, according to the regulation, be capitalized and charged off over the appropriate recovery period.

The theoretical difference between currently deductible expenditures and those that increase a property's tax basis is unequivocal. Appropriate treatment of expenditures falling at polar ends of the distinction is easily determined. Patching a leaky roof is clearly a currently deductible item, for example, whereas the cost of completely replacing a roof is unequivocally a capital item. It is unclear, however, how large a patch may be before it is characterized as a partial replacement.

In some instances, whether an expenditure is currently deductible or must be added to the basis depends upon how the expenditure transpired. For example, a general plan of property improvement often requires a series of separate repair operations. Taken individually, these repairs may be currently deductible. But because they are a part of a general plan, they would probably be considered capital expenditures and therefore added to the owner's basis.

Conversely, expenditures that are generally considered to be capital outlays, if made piecemeal over an extended period, might be treated as repair or maintenance items, and therefore be currently deductible. The cost of improvements, alterations or additions that must be capitalized (that is, added to the tax basis) will be written off via cost recovery allowances in the same manner as the initial recoverable cost but on an entirely separate schedule beginning with the month that the improvements, alterations or additions are first placed in service.

Tenant Improvements.   A tenant may be required under the terms of a lease — or may elect — to make property improvements. The landlord usually acquires ownership of such improvements on termination of the lease. Whether tenant improvements have been made in lieu of rent and so constitute income to the landlord depends upon agreement between the parties. Evidence of agreement might be based upon the terms of the lease or upon surrounding circumstances. Procedures for making such a determination are set forth in Treasury Regulation 1.61-8(c).

Reference to "surrounding circumstances" in determining intent with respect to tenant-installed improvements gives the parties considerable control over the tax consequences of such expenditures. Explicit provisions in a lease generally are acceptable evidence of intent. In the absence of an explicit statement of intent, determination may hinge on the relationship between the cost of improvements and the amount of rent concession granted by the landlord or upon the degree of control exercised by the landlord as to the nature and timing of improvements.

If the cost of an improvement made by a tenant is treated as rent, it is taxable as rental income to the landlord. The tax liability is generally incurred in the year the improvement is made. But where this results in a disproportionately high initial rent, the cost may be treated as advance rent and be amortized over the life of the lease. The landlord's basis is increased accordingly, and improvement costs are reflected in cost recovery allowances just as if the landlord had directly incurred the expenditure.

Carrying Charges on Unproductive Property.   Real estate taxes paid or accrued on vacant or unproductive property are deductible currently or may be capitalized at the option of the taxpayer. A current deduction is generally preferred. There may be circumstances, however, under which current income is insufficient to warrant this treatment. A property owner may then wish to defer recognition. In such a case the expenditure increases the tax basis of the property.

TAX CONSEQUENCES OF FINANCIAL LEVERAGE

Borrowing or repaying money is not a taxable event—it neither increases nor decreases tax liability. Expenditures for *interest* on borrowed money, in contrast, are usually deductible in the taxable year of the expenditure. *Prepaid interest,* however, is generally not deductible by the borrower until the interest is actually earned by the lender. There are exceptions, of course (there always seem to be exceptions).

There is a dollar limit on the amount of investment interest that can be deducted in any one taxable year on loans used to finance passive investments (that is, those that do not take on characteristics of operating a business). Any investment interest in excess of currently permissible deductions is carried forward and claimed as investment interest in subsequent years.

There are also overall limits on the amount of net losses from real estate that can be offset against income from specific other sources, and these limits may prevent some business-related interest expenses from being deducted concurrently with their payment.

Any interest expense that cannot be deducted for either of these reasons is carried forward and treated as interest expense incurred in the next year. There are no limits on the number of years that interest expense can be carried forward in this manner.

Construction-period Interest

Interest incurred during construction of real estate improvements is considered a part of the construction cost. Thus, it is a part of the initial tax basis of the improvements and figures into the cost recovery allowance.

TAX CONSEQUENCES OF PROPERTY SALES

Recall that the adjusted tax basis is the cost of property acquisition, adjusted for cost recovery allowances and property improvements, plus certain other adjustments that may sometimes apply. The gain or loss on disposal is simply the difference between the amount realized from sale or exchange and the adjusted basis at the time of the transaction.

The Sales Price

Everything of economic value received in exchange for a property comprises the *consideration*. This includes the balance due on any mortgage to which the property remains subject, whether or not the purchaser assumes personal liability. If the seller receives other property or services as a part of the transaction, these must be included at their fair market value. The principle is illustrated in Example 10.5.

Example 10.5

A taxpayer transfers title to a store building (which is owned free and clear) in exchange for $50,000 in cash at the time of the transaction and a note for $100,000 due in 12 months. The purchaser also transfers title to a vacant lot (market value $70,000) and a pickup truck (market value $8,000). In addition, the purchaser, who is an attorney, agrees to prepare the seller's income tax return for the year and to represent the seller without cost in divorce proceedings that are scheduled in the near future. The usual fee for these legal services is $3,000. The buyer takes title subject to an existing mortgage-secured note, which has a remaining balance of $300,000. Total consideration involved in the transaction is $531,000.

Computing the Gain or Loss

If a property is sold at a price (net of all selling costs) that exceeds the seller's adjusted basis, the gain is usually subject to some amount of income tax. Example 10.6 illustrates.

Example 10.6

Suppose the seller in the preceding example incurred transaction costs of $3,000 and had an adjusted basis (just prior to the sale) of $42,000. The gain on disposal is $486,000, computed as follows:

Sales Price (from Example 10.5)		$531,000
Less:		
Basis Prior to Sale	$42,000	
Selling Costs	3,000	45,000
Gain on Disposal		$486,000

Tax Treatment of Gains

Gains on disposal may be treated as ordinary income or as a capital item, depending upon whether the property was held for resale in the ordinary course of business and upon whether the seller has used an accelerated method of claiming depreciation or cost recovery allowances. The difference in characterization is significant primarily when a seller recognizes capital losses during the year the gains are to be recognized.

When gains or losses are treated as ordinary income items, they are simply merged with net income from other sources to figure tax liability for the year. There are special limitations, however, on the degree to which net losses from passive sources can be offset against active revenue.

Recapturing Depreciation or Cost Recovery Allowances. Investors who put their properties into use before the effective date of the 1986 tax bill had the option of computing depreciation or cost recovery allowances using an accelerated method. This permitted much larger annual deductions in the early years of ownership, offset by proportionally smaller ones later. Gains on disposal of property written off on an accelerated schedule will often be characterized as recapture. To the extent they are so characterized, they will be recognized as ordinary income rather than capital gains. Recapture rules are explained further in Appendix 10.B.

Property Held Primarily for Resale. Real estate and other property held primarily for resale in the ordinary course of business is called *inventory,* and taxpayers who hold property for this purpose are called *dealers*. The sale of dealer property generally results in ordinary income rather than capital gains. The only exception to this rule involves large-block sales of inventory for liquidation purposes—such sales may give rise to capital gains or losses.

When Capital Gain Rules Apply. Gains realized from the sale or taxable exchange of long-lived assets held for use in a trade or business or for production of income and not intended primarily for resale in the ordinary course of business are treated as capital gains unless characterized as recapture of depreciation or cost recovery allowances.

Long-lived assets (that is, those that ordinarily last more than one year) intended for personal use are also considered capital items when there is a gain on disposal. Examples include one's personal residence, household furnishings, autos and so forth. Losses on the sale of personal assets, however, have no income tax consequences whatsoever.

Capital gains are first merged with other capital gains for the taxable year and offset against capital losses. Any remaining capital gains are treated much the same as ordinary income. If what remains are capital losses, there are severe limitations on their deductibility.

Tax Consequences of Losses on Disposal

When property is sold (or disposed of in a taxable exchange) for less than the seller's adjusted tax basis, the resulting loss offsets either ordinary income or capital gains, depending upon how the loss is characterized. This is an important issue, because there are strict limits on the amount of capital losses that can be offset against ordinary income—and thus reduce income tax liability—during any one tax year.

Section 1231 Losses. A special rule applies to assets used in a trade or business, as opposed to those held for investment purposes or for personal use. Reflecting the section of the Internal Revenue Code that contains the special provision, these are generally called *Section 1231 assets*. Gains on the sale of Section 1231 assets are treated as capital gains; losses are treated as offsets against ordinary income.

This rule applies only to assets that are not a part of one's inventory and that have been held for more than 12 months before disposal. Rental real estate with respect to which the owner is actively engaged in management is considered a Section 1231 asset.

Computing Net Capital Gains or Losses. Transactions involving capital assets or Section 1231 assets must be cataloged according to whether they resulted in gains or losses. Example 10.7 illustrates the procedure.

Section 1231 gains and losses are then offset against each other. If this yields net Section 1231 losses, these are offset against ordinary income for the year. If it results in net Section 1231 gains, they are added to capital gains for the year.

Capital gains, including net Section 1231 gains, are then offset against capital losses. If gains exceed losses, the remainder is added to ordinary income. If there are more losses than gains, however, the Internal Revenue Code imposes strict limits on the extent to which the net losses can be offset against other taxable income. Net capital losses offset ordinary income (on a dollar-for-dollar basis) only to the extent of $3,000 during any one tax year. Any remaining capital losses must be carried over and lumped with capital transactions in the succeeding year. There is no limit on the number of years such losses may be carried forward.

To see the significance of these rules, consider Examples 10.7 and 10.8.

Example 10.7

In a series of transactions during the year, a taxpayer experienced both gains and losses. The results are summarized below:

Transactions Resulting in Gains	
Capital Assets	$24,000
Section 1231 Assets	8,000
Transactions Resulting in Losses	
Capital Assets	$10,000
Section 1231 Assets	6,000

The taxpayer in Example 10.7 has net Section 1231 gains, which must be added to capital gains for the year. Taxable income stemming from the transactions summarized in Example 10.7 is $16,000, determined as follows:

Step One: Net Section 1231 Transactions

Section 1231 Gains	$ 8,000
Less: Section 1231 Losses	6,000
Net Section 1231 Gains	$ 2,000

Step Two: Net Capital Transactions

Capital Gains	$24,000
Plus: Net Section 1231 Gains	2,000
	$26,000
Less: Capital Losses	10,000
Net Capital Gains (included in ordinary income)	$16,000

To see what happens when losses exceed gains, and the significance under those circumstances of the special treatment accorded Section 1231 assets, consider Example 10.8.

Example 10.8

In a series of transactions during the year, a taxpayer experienced both gains and losses. The results are summarized below:

Transactions Resulting in Gains

Capital Transactions	$10,000
Section 1231 Transactions	2,000

Transactions Resulting in Losses

Capital Transactions	$24,000
Section 1231 Transactions	8,000

Here losses exceed gains in both capital transactions and Section 1231 transactions. Net Section 1231 gains offset ordinary income for the year without limit. Of the $14,000 of net capital losses, however, only $3,000 can be offset against ordinary income for the year. The remaining $11,000 of losses must be carried over to the next tax year. Here are the computations:

Step One: Net Section 1231 Transactions

Section 1231 Losses	$ 8,000
Less: Section 1231 Gains	2,000
Net Section 1231 Losses (offset against ordinary income)	$ 6,000

Step Two: Net Capital Transactions

Capital Losses	$24,000
Less: Capital Gains	10,000
Net Capital Losses	$14,000
Offset Against Ordinary Income This Year	3,000
Losses Carried Over to Next Year	$11,000

USING THE INSTALLMENT SALES METHOD

When a seller receives only partial payment for real property during the year of sale, reporting the transaction under the *installment sales method* permits a portion of the income tax liability to be deferred until the balance of the cash is collected. Tax liability is incurred only on a pro-rata basis with each year's collection of sales proceeds.

Advantages of Installment Sales Reporting

When third-party mortgage loans are expensive or difficult to obtain, sellers who provide a substantial portion of the necessary financing can greatly facilitate property disposal. Installment sales provisions in the Internal Revenue Code are intended to make this possible without the unfortunate side effect of having income tax liability exceed cash collections in the year of the transaction.

A possible by-product of the installment method, of great potential benefit, is that taxes on the gain may be deferred until the seller is in a lower tax bracket. A sale might be arranged during peak income-earning years, for example, with payment spread over the seller's retirement years. The amount of taxable gain and the nature of the gain (ordinary income and/or capital gain) are determined at the time of the transaction. But the applicable tax rate is that in effect when taxes become due.

What Gain Qualifies

Owners who have used an accelerated method to compute depreciation or cost recovery allowances may find a portion—sometimes all—of their gain characterized as ordinary income due to recapture of these allowances, as explained in Appendix 10.B. The portion of a gain that represents recapture does not qualify for reporting under the installment method. The *installment method gain*, therefore, is the total gain on a transaction minus the portion that represents recapture. This is illustrated in Example 10.9.

> ### *Example 10.9*
>
> Residential income property that has an adjusted tax basis of $160,000 is sold for $200,000. The buyer taxes title subject to the $150,000 balance of an existing mortgage-secured promissory note, pays $5,000 in cash at the closing and agrees to pay the $45,000 balance of the purchase price in ten equal annual installments payable at the end of each succeeding year, with interest at eight percent on the unpaid balance. The seller pays

a broker's commission of $6,000. Other closing costs incurred by the seller total $2,500.

As a consequence of his having used an accelerated cost recovery method, $10,000 of the seller's gain on disposal is characterized as ordinary income due to recapture. The gain on the sale is $31,500, of which only $21,500 qualifies for reporting under the installment method:

Selling Price		$200,000
Less:		
Adjusted Basis Prior to Sale	$160,000	
Broker's Commission	6,000	
Other Transaction Costs	2,500	168,500
Gain on Sale		$ 31,500
Less: Recapture		10,000
Installment Method Gain		$ 21,500

The Contract Price

The *contract price* is the total selling price (that is, the market value of all consideration tendered by the buyer) less the balance of any mortgage note payable by the purchaser to a third party. Note, however, that if the property is sold subject to such a mortgage (and whether or not the buyer assumes personal liability for the balance to which the transfer is subject), then the contract price is reduced by only that portion of the mortgage note that does not exceed the seller's adjusted tax basis in the property. Example 10.10 shows how to compute the contract price.

Example 10.10

Although the selling price of the property in Example 10.9 is $200,000, the buyer will pay only $50,000 directly to the seller. The remaining $150,000 represents the balance of an old mortgage-secured note that the buyer will pay to a third party. The contract price, therefore, is only $50,000:

Selling Price (from Example 10.9)	$200,000
Less: Balance of Old Note, to Be Paid by Buyer	150,000
Contract Price	$ 50,000

If the existing mortgage note in Example 10.10 had exceeded $168,500 (the seller's adjusted tax basis after adjusting for transactions costs incurred in the sale), then the excess would have to be included in the contract price.

The Recognized Gain

The relationship between the installment method gain and the contract price determines the portion of each year's collections on the contract that must be recognized as a taxable gain. Divide the installment method gain by the contract price to derive this percentage figure. Then multiply the year's collections on the principal amount of the contract by this ratio. The product is the currently taxable installment method gain. The balance of the year's collections (other than the interest, which is taxable as ordinary income in the year received) represents recovery of capital and has no tax consequences.

These instructions can be reduced to a six-step procedure:

1. Compute the realized gain just as if the installment sales method were not to be used.
2. Divide the realized gain into two portions: *recapture* and *installment method gain*.
3. Compute the *contract price* by subtracting from the total selling price the balance of any mortgage note that calls for payments by the purchaser to a third party and adding back any amount by which any preexisting note (to which the property remains subject) exceeds adjusted tax basis of the seller.
4. Divide the installment method gain (from step 2) by the contract price (from step 3) to determine the portion of annual collections on the principal amount of the contract that represents collection of the installment method gain.
5. Determine the amount of the principal collected during the year. Be careful to exclude from this calculation any amount collected that represents payment by the purchaser of interest indebtedness. Only the principal portion is included.
6. Multiply the collections (from step 5) by the percentage representing the gain (from step 4). This is the amount of the collections that is to be recognized as installment method gain for the year. The balance of the principal collected represents a return of the taxpayer's investment and is not taxable.

Example 10.11

Continuing calculations from Example 10.10, the seller's taxable gain in the year of the sale will be $12,150, determined as follows:

Initial Payments

Down Payment	$ 5,000
Additional Principal Payments During Year	0
Amount of Mortgage Assumed by Buyer in Excess of Seller's Adjusted Tax Basis	0
Total Initial Payments	$ 5,000

Gross Profit Ratio

Installment Method Gain (from Example 10.9)	$21,500
Total Contract Price (from Example 10.10)	50,000
Ratio ($21,500/$50,000)	.43

Taxable Gain for Year	
Installment Method Gain to Be Recognized	
($5,000 × 0.43)	$ 2,150
Plus: Recapture (from Example 10.9)	10,000
Recognized Gain in Year of Transaction	$12,150

The Imputed Interest Problem

A buyer usually signs a note as evidence of his or her obligation for the unpaid portion of the purchase price. Credit terms ordinarily provide for periodic payments to retire the note, plus interest payments on the unpaid balance. The principal portion of these payments is considered a part of the purchase price. The interest payments, in contrast, are simply additional income taxable to the seller and generally have no impact on recognition of the gain on sale.

The Internal Revenue Service insists that any installment sales contract or mortgage note include a provision for a reasonable rate of interest. If no such provision exists, the IRS imputes interest by reducing the total selling price to an amount representing the value of the down payment plus the present value of the obligation to make future payments, when the future payments are discounted at a minimum rate of interest as stipulated by the Commissioner of the Internal Revenue Service.

The Outstanding Indebtedness Problem

Sellers who employ the installment method of reporting their gains but who themselves owe substantial sums will find the benefits of the installment method greatly reduced. The Internal Revenue Code of 1986 incorporates complex (and, quite possibly, transitory) rules requiring sellers to recognize progressively greater portions of their installment method gains as the total amounts of their own indebtedness grows.

SUMMARY

Because income taxes are so pervasive, they must be factored into all real estate investment analysis. As a general rule, operating expenses that require cash outlays are also tax-deductible expenses, and revenues that result in cash inflows are taxable income. Additionally, owners of real property held for use in a trade or business or for production of income are allowed to deduct an allowance for recovery of their capital investment in buildings and other improvements.

All cost recovery allowances represent downward adjustments to the taxpayer's tax basis for the property. When the property is sold, the gain on disposal is computed by deducting the adjusted basis from the selling price (net of the seller's transactions costs).

When sellers take back promissory notes in part payment for property, they may defer recognition of taxable gains until they collect proceeds from the notes. The gain is recognized on a pro-rata basis as the principal portion of the note is collected. Deferral does not affect the nature of the recognized gain (that is, its status as ordinary income or a capital gain).

RECOMMENDED READINGS

Commerce Clearing House. *U.S. Master Tax Guide*. Chicago: Commerce Clearing House. Published annually.

Journal of Real Estate Taxation. A quarterly periodical published by Warren, Gorham & Lamont, 210 South St., Boston, MA 02111.

Grossman, Harold A., ed. *Prentice-Hall's Explanation of the Tax Reform Act of 1986*. Englewood Cliffs, NJ: Prentice-Hall, 1986, pp. 201–304.

REVIEW QUESTIONS

1. How is the initial tax basis of a property determined?
2. Describe three common methods of allocating the tax basis between land and other assets.
3. List the reasons for cost recovery allowances. Under what conditions are cost recovery allowances permitted?
4. List several adjustments that decrease the basis of a property and several that increase the basis.
5. What is the principal advantage of using the installment sales method of reporting property sales?

DISCUSSION QUESTIONS

1. In view of the increasing frequency of major income tax legislation in recent years, discuss the wisdom of relying on special income tax considerations as a major element in the flow of benefits from property ownership.
2. Explain why a corporation whose shares are traded publicly might wish to show one measure for depreciation or cost recovery when reporting taxable income to the Internal Revenue Service and an entirely different measure when reporting the results of operations to shareholders.
3. Why do you suppose the Congress has provided shorter cost recovery periods for residential than for nonresidential property?
4. Can you suggest reasons why the Internal Revenue Service might resist setting forth precise rules for determining whether an expenditure will be treated as a repair or an improvement?

APPENDIX 10.A: Accelerated Depreciation or Cost Recovery Allowances

Taxpayers who put their properties into use before the effective date of the 1986 Tax Reform Act had the option of using an accelerated method for computing their depreciation or cost recovery allowances. Precisely how they were permitted to do this differs depending upon the subperiod in which they put their properties into use.

PROPERTY PLACED IN SERVICE BEFORE 1981

Assets put into service by their owners before January 1, 1981, are written off over their useful lives in the taxpayers' trades or businesses. As a matter of terminological convenience we characterize these as *depreciable assets* and distinguish them from assets that qualify for different rules by having been put into service after December 31, 1980. This latter category we will call *cost recovery assets*.

Assets put into use on or after January 1, 1981, will also be treated for tax purposes as if they were put into use before that date (that is, they will be treated as depreciable rather than cost recovery property) if acquired in what the Internal Revenue Code calls a "churning" transaction. This includes property that was:

1. Owned during 1980 by the taxpayer or a related person;
2. Leased back to a person who owned the property during 1980 or to a related person;

3. Acquired in a tax-deferred transaction (such as those discussed in Chapter 12) in return for property owned in 1980 by the taxpayer or a related person;

4. Acquired in a transaction with a principal purpose of circumventing rules 1 through 3.

In applying the "anti-churning" rules, the Code interprets *related person* rather broadly. It includes not only blood relatives, but also certain entities that are partly owned by the taxpayer, depending primarily upon the extent of such ownership.

The IRS views the depreciation allowance as providing an opportunity for investors to recover capital investments over their assets' productive lives. But the amount of the allowance bears no necessary relationship to actual change in an asset's value. Rather, in a period of consistent inflation like that experienced in the United States since the Second World War, much real property actually increases in market value while being depreciated for income tax purposes.

Annual depreciation deductions are sufficient to permit recovery of the tax basis of depreciable improvements, net of their salvage value, over their useful economic lives. The initial tax basis is determined and allocated between land and improvements as described in Chapter 10 for recovery property.

Estimating Useful Life

Whichever permissible depreciation allowance method is adopted, the depreciation rate depends upon a property's estimated useful life as well as upon its initial basis. *Useful life* is the period over which a property may reasonably be expected to yield economic benefit to its owner. Useful life is limited by both physical and socioeconomic factors; therefore, it is not necessarily synonymous with physical life.

Physical factors that are considered in estimating useful life include wear, tear and action of the elements. This recognizes the immutable fact that all man-made articles share the mortality of their makers. Any conceivable program of maintenance and repair can only retard the rate of decline, which can never be reversed.

Social, technical and economic change can destroy a property's usefulness as surely as can physical decay. Obsolescence is accordingly given due recognition in estimating useful life.

Example 10.A.1

A strip shopping center was built in a mixed residential and industrial area in 1969. The area's rapid transition away from residential use coincident with its being rezoned to industrial usage, combined with the drawing power of a new regional shopping center erected a short distance away, has since made it obvious the anchor tenant in the strip center will not renew its lease, which expires in 1989. Without the anchor tenant the center is not economically viable and will be razed and replaced with warehouses. Though the physical life of the building is approximately 60 years, the economic life is only 20.

Allowable Depreciation Methods

Three methods of computing the depreciation allowance are specified in the Code. Any other consistent method may be used so long as it does not, during the first two-thirds of the asset's useful life, result in cumulative depreciation deductions in excess of those allowable under the specified method for that class of asset. This section describes the two most common methods of computing depreciation allowances and gives examples of where each is applicable. The third method (called *sum of the year's digits*) is omitted, since it has become increasingly irrelevant with the passage of time.

Straight-Line Method.   The simplest and most straightforward of all depreciation methods, the straight-line method provides for recovery of a constant dollar amount in each year of a depreciable asset's useful life. To calculate the amount to be recovered over the useful life, subtract the estimated salvage value from the portion of the initial basis that is applicable to the improvements. The annual allowance can then be determined by dividing the remainder by the number of years in the estimated useful life.

The investor in Example 10.A.2 below may continue to deduct depreciation of $1,375 annually until the remaining undepreciated balance equals salvage value. Under no circumstances may the improvements be depreciated below their estimated salvage value (although estimated salvage value may change over the holding period). To determine salvage value, estimate the market value of salvageable materials and deduct the estimated cost of demolition and removal. In most cases, estimated salvage value is zero.

Example 10.A.2

A property is purchased for $80,000, of which $20,000 represents the value of the land and $60,000 represents the value of improvements that have an estimated useful life of 40 years and estimated net salvage value of $5,000. Annual depreciation deductions, using the straight-line method, are determined as follows:

Depreciable Base	
Improvements	$60,000
Less: Salvage Value	5,000
Depreciable Base	$55,000

Annual Depreciation Allowance	
Depreciable Base	$55,000
Times: Straight-Line Rate (1/40)	0.025
Annual Deduction	$ 1,375

The straight-line method may be used with all depreciable real property, since it does not result in a depreciation deduction in excess of other allowable methods during the early years of an asset's useful life. Moreover, this is the *only* method permitted for depreciation of real estate used for purposes other than generating residential income, if the taxpayer is not a "first user" of the property.

Declining-Balance Method.   The *declining-balance method* provides the greatest allowance during the first year of useful life. A progressively smaller allowance is afforded for each successive year. Taxpayers utilizing this method apply a constant percentage rate each year to the remaining unrecovered basis of depreciable property. Since there is always a remaining undepreciated balance, no adjustment need be made for salvage value. But an asset may not be depreciated below its estimated salvage value.

The constant rate to be applied to the declining balance is 200 percent, 150 percent or 125 percent, depending upon the nature of the real estate being depreciated. The 200 percent rate applies only to new residential income property. The 150 percent rate applies only to new nonresidential income property, and the 125 percent rate applies to used residential income property.

In Example 10.A.3 the declining-balance method is illustrated using each of the three rates. The example assumes a building with a 20-year useful life. In each case the allowable rate is calculated by multiplying the straight-line rate (in this case, 1/20) by the appropriate multiple (200 percent, 150 percent or 125 percent). This product is then multiplied by the remaining balance (cost minus accumulated depreciation) for each year.

Example 10.A.3

Assuming a $60,000 cost applicable to the improvements and a useful life of 20 years, the annual depreciation allowance for the first five years of ownership is:

Year	Declining Balance*	×	Rate**	=	Depreciation Allowance***
(Using the 200% declining-balance method)					
1	$60,000		10%		$6,000
2	54,000		10		5,400
3	48,600		10		4,860
4	43,740		10		4,374
5	39,366		10		3,937

(Using the 150% declining-balance method)

1	$60,000	7.5%	$4,500
2	55,500	7.5	4,163
3	51,337	7.5	3,850
4	47,487	7.5	3,562
5	43,925	7.5	3,294

(Using the 125% declining-balance method)

1	$60,000	6.25%	$3,750
2	56,250	6.25	3,516
3	52,734	6.25	3,296
4	49,438	6.25	3,090
5	46,348	6.25	2,897

*The declining balance is simply the balance from the preceding year minus last year's depreciation allowance. The beginning depreciable balance of $60,000 is thus reduced by the first year's depreciation allowance of $6,000 in the 200 percent declining-balance illustration, for a second-year balance of $60,000–$6,000, or $54,000.

**The straight-line rate of depreciation is (1/useful life). In the present example this is 1/20, or five percent per annum. The 200 percent declining-balance rate then is 200 percent of the straight-line rate, or ten percent. Likewise the 150 percent declining-balance rate is 150 percent of the straight-line rate, or 7.5 percent, and the 125 percent declining-balance rate is 125 percent of five percent, or 6.25 percent.

***The depreciation allowance is calculated by multiplying the declining balance by the appropriate accelerated rate.

PROPERTY PLACED IN SERVICE AFTER 1980 BUT BEFORE 1986

Cost recovery allowances are permitted on the man-made portion (generally called the *improvements*) of all real property held for use in a trade or business or for production of income, provided that the property was put into use by the taxpayer after December 31, 1980, and was not acquired in a "churning" transaction as previously described. Cost recovery rules have been revised repeatedly, however, and their investment consequences differ radically depending upon which set of rules applies.

Cost recovery rules for property put into use after the effective date of the 1986 Tax Reform Act are described in Chapter 10. There are two other subperiods with which we must be concerned.

The Early Period: January 1, 1981, Through March 14, 1984

Taxpayers who placed their property into service during this period had the option of recovering their capital costs in equal annual increments (the *straight-line method*) or claiming large annual allowances during early years, offset by correspondingly smaller allowances later (the *accelerated method*). An exception existed for those who elected the optional 35- or 45-year recovery period rather than the standard 15-year period. Those making this election had to use the straight-line cost recovery method.

The straight-line method is simple and straightforward. Annual recovery allowances are determined by dividing the amount to be recovered by the recovery period. Thus, if the individual in Example 10.2 used the straight-line method to recover building costs over 15 years, the annual allowance would be $60,000/15, or $4,000.

Taxpayers using the accelerated method claim their largest annual allowance during the first year of the recovery period. A progressively smaller allowance is afforded for each successive year. The Internal Revenue Service has prepared a table of allowable percentages of the recoverable basis that can be recovered each year. The table, which is based on the 175 percent declining-balance method, incorporates a 15-year recovery period and an automatic switch to the straight-line method when such a switch will maximize the annual recovery allowance.

Capital expenditures for qualifying residential income property intended for low-income tenants may be recovered at an even more accelerated pace. Recovery allowance tables for such properties are based on the 200 percent declining-balance approach.

Choosing Between Accelerated and Straight-Line Recovery

Cumulative recovery allowances over the entire 15-year recovery period are not affected by choice between straight-line and accelerated recovery methods. In any one instance the total cost of the asset is recovered over the course of the recovery period. What is affected by this decision is the timing of tax deductions for the recovery allowance.

Accelerated cost recovery bunches tax-deductible allowances in the early years, offset by correspondingly smaller allowances later. If there were no related disadvantages, most investors would prefer tax savings sooner rather than later and would therefore opt for the accelerated cost recovery method. Unfortunately, there are costs associated with such a choice. In many cases the costs outweigh benefits from accelerated cost recovery, prompting property owners to elect the straight-line recovery method.

Potential costs of using the accelerated method include liability for an *alternative minimum tax*. The excess of deductions taken by using the accelerated method over what would have resulted from using the straight-line method is called a *tax preference item* and is potentially subject to additional taxes under the alternative minimum tax rules. Preference items and the alternative minumum tax are treated at length in Appendix 10.C.

A second potential disadvantage of the accelerated method arises when the property is sold. Because cost recovery allowances reduce the property's adjusted basis, they increase the potential gain on disposal (sales price minus adjusted basis and transactions costs equals the gain on sale).

Potential liability for the alternative minimum tax in the year accelerated cost recovery allowances are claimed, combined with additional taxes upon disposal, led many investors to elect the straight-line recovery method even when doing so increased current income tax liability. This decision should be made using the same analytical methods as employed for the investment decision itself: Forecast net benefits (in this case, tax savings) from each method and discount at the appropriate rate. Choose the recovery method that yields tax savings with the greatest present value.

Switching Recovery Methods

People who use the accelerated cost recovery method will switch to the straight-line method when doing so increases annual recovery allowances. After switching to the straight-line method, annual allowances will be sufficient to recover the remaining capital investment over the remainder of the recovery period. The Internal Revenue Service tables incorporate a switch to the straight-line method at the appropriate point.

The Middle Period: March 15, 1984, Through December 31, 1986

Even before the Treasury Department could write implementing regulations, the Congress reneged on the compact with taxpayers written into Internal Revenue Code Section 168. For property placed in service after March 14, 1984, but before January 1, 1987, recovery periods are stretched to 18 years for all cost recovery real estate except that intended for low-income residential tenants. Recapture rules for taxpayers who use the accelerated method were also rendered more punitive, as explained in Appendix 10.B.

APPENDIX 10.B: Recapture Rules

Appendix 10.A, which explains depreciation rules that affect property put into use before 1981, describes how accelerated depreciation allowances benefit taxpayers by permitting them to claim larger tax deductions in the early years of ownership. Taxpayers who put their properties into use after 1980 but before 1987 qualify for even more rapid write-offs. They may use accelerated methods to recover their property costs over statutorily specified periods that are generally substantially shorter than the properties' economic lives.

The large tax deductions that these accelerated methods generate during the early years of ownership are followed by correspondingly smaller allowances later, but accelerating benefits (tax savings) and deferring costs (additional tax liability) is a strategy much to be desired if there are no offsetting costs.

WHEN RECAPTURE RULES MATTER

Unfortunately, there almost always are offsetting costs. Taxpayers who use the accelerated method will find that a portion—sometimes all—of their gains on disposal are characterized as ordinary income due to recapture of depreciation or cost recovery allowances. There are two circumstances under which this will prove particularly onerous.

When Using the Installment Sales Method

As Chapter 10 explains, the installment sales method of reporting transactions permits sellers who take back promissory notes in part payment to defer taxes on their gains until they collect related sales proceeds. But the portion of a gain that represents recapture of depreciation or cost recovery allowances does not qualify for recognition under the installment sales method. Thus, a transaction involving substantial seller financing may, if there is potential recapture, generate tax liability in excess of the seller's cash receipts in the year of the transaction.

When the Seller Has Capital Losses

Recall from Chapter 10 that capital losses can be offset against capital gains without limit but that only $3,000 of capital losses can be offset against ordinary income during any one tax year. A substantial gain from real estate sales will be particularly beneficial if it occurs in the same year that a taxpayer incurs extensive capital losses from unrelated transactions, but only if the gain is treated as a capital item. Having a portion of the gain characterized as ordinary income due to recapture reduces the extent to which it can be used to offset capital losses.

HOW RECAPTURE RULES WORK

Recapture rules differ depending on the law in effect during the years in which accelerated depreciation or cost recovery methods were applied.

Recapturing Depreciation Allowances

For property put into use before January 1, 1981, capital costs are recovered via a depreciation allowance as explained in Appendix 10.A. When these properties are sold for more than the seller's adjusted tax basis, the degree to which the gain is characterized as ordinary income due to recapture depends upon the relationship between the accumulated allowances actually claimed and those that would have been claimed had the taxpayer used the straight-line depreciation method. It also depends on when the property was first put into use by the taxpayer, on how long it was held and on the type of depreciable property involved.

For these properties, only *excess* depreciation allowances are subject to recapture. This is the cumulative allowance actually claimed, minus what the cumulative allowance would have been had the taxpayer used the straight-line depreciation method from the beginning. Thus, only taxpayers who elect an accelerated depreciation method need be concerned with the recapture rules.

All excess depreciation claimed on real property during and subsequent to 1976 is subject to 100 percent recapture without regard to the character of the property or the length of time it has been held, except for certain rental housing intended for low-income tenants. For each subperiod prior to 1976, depreciation recapture rules differ for residential and nonresidential property held for the same period of time.

For nonresidential real property all excess depreciation taken in 1970 or later is 100 percent subject to recapture (to the extent of the gain on disposal). Applicable recapture rates for each subperiod before 1970 are as follows:

1. For excess depreciation taken after 1963 but before 1970: 100 percent minus one percent for each month the property was held in excess of 20 months.
2. For excess depreciation taken prior to 1964, recapture rules do not apply.

Recapture rules for depreciable residential property are somewhat more permissive. Applicable recapture rates for each of the subperiods affected by periodic revisions to the tax code are:

1. Excess depreciation taken in 1976 or later: 100 percent.
2. Excess depreciation taken before 1976 but after 1969: 100 percent minus one percent for each month the property was held over 100 months.
3. Excess depreciation taken before 1970 but after 1963: 100 percent minus one percent for each month the property was held over 20 months.
4. No recapture provisions apply to excess depreciation taken before 1964.

Recapture is determined on a "last-in, first-out" basis. Excess depreciation taken since 1975 is recaptured first. If any gain on disposal remains after subtracting the post-1975 recapture, proceed to calculate the recapture applicable to the period after 1969 but before 1976. If any gain not accounted for by this recapture remains, go back to the next earlier subperiod and so on. Of course, the total recapture cannot be greater than the total gain on disposal. If the gain exceeds the total amount of excess depreciation subject to recapture, the balance is taxed as a capital gain.

Recapturing Cost Recovery Allowances

We have seen that a property's adjusted basis is a major determinant of the amount of gain or loss on disposal. The lower the basis, the greater the amount of the gain. Yet the adjusted basis reflects all cost recovery allowances claimed during the period of ownership. Since accelerated cost recovery allowances result in a lower adjusted basis than do allowances computed with the straight-line method, they also generate a greater gain on disposal.

To counter this consequence, the Internal Revenue Code provides that all or a portion of the gain may be taxed more heavily when a property owner has used an accelerated recovery method. To the extent that the gain is attributed to recapture, it is taxed as ordinary income. Any remaining gain after accounting for recapture is accorded capital gains treatment.

Rules for recapture of recovery allowances differ, depending upon whether the property is used for residential or nonresidential purposes. In no case, however, can recapture exceed the amount of the gain on disposal.

Example 10.B.1

During the first month of the taxable year, an investor acquires a recovery property for $100,000. Eighty percent of the cost is appropriately attributable to the improvements. After five years the investor sells the property, realizing $150,000 net of transaction costs. The adjusted basis, and therefore the gain on disposal, depends upon whether the 175 percent declining-balance or the straight-line recovery method has been employed. The adjusted basis at the time of sale, under each recovery method, is shown below:

	Straight-line	175% Declining-balance
Cost	$100,000	$100,000
Less: Total Recovery Allowances	26,667	36,800
Adjusted Basis	$ 73,333	$ 63,200

If accelerated cost recovery is employed, the investor's basis will have been reduced by $36,800 over the five-year holding period. The adjusted basis at time of sale, therefore, will be $100,000 minus $36,800, or $63,200. If the straight-line method of cost recovery is employed, accumulated recovery allowances will have totaled only $26,667, and the adjusted basis will be $100,000 minus $26,667, or $73,333.

The gain on disposal is the difference between the net sales price and the adjusted basis. The gain, under each recovery allowance method, is shown below:

	Straight-line	175% Declining-balance
Sales Price (Net)	$150,000	$150,000
Less: Adjusted Basis	73,333	63,200
Gain on Disposal	$ 76,667	$ 86,800

Consider Example 10.B.1. Cumulative *excess cost recovery allowances* equal the difference between allowances the investor claims using the 175% declining-balance method and the cumulative total that would have resulted from using the straight-line method. If the property is residential in nature, the gain is ordinary income to the extent it represents recapture of excess recovery allowances. Only the balance is a capital gain.

In contrast, if accelerated cost recovery is employed with *nonresidential* recovery property, then the total accumulated recovery allowance (rather than just the excess over straight-line) is subject to recapture as ordinary income, to the extent of the gain on disposal. Only the portion of the gain that exceeds total cumulative recovery allowances will be accorded capital gains treatment. The portion of the gain in Example 10.B.1 that represents recapture, and therefore is taxed as ordinary income, differs solely on the basis of being characterized as residential or nonresidential property. Example 10.B.2 extends the illustration from Example 10.B.1 and demonstrates apportionment of the gain between recapture (ordinary income) and capital gain.

Example 10.B.2

If the investor in Example 10.B.1 does use the 175 percent declining-balance cost recovery method, the nature of the gain will depend upon whether the property is residential or nonresidential in nature.

	Residential	*Nonresidential*
Gain on Sale (from Example 10.B.1)	$86,800	$86,800
Less: Recapture (ordinary income)	10,133	36,800
Capital Gain	$76,667	$50,000

APPENDIX 10.C: *Alternative Minimum Tax*

After determining taxable income and income tax obligation using the regular computational procedure, taxpayers must compute an alternative minimum taxable income and alternative minimum tax. If the alternative computation results in a greater income tax obligation than does the regular computation, the alternative tax is paid instead of the regular tax.

Appendix 10.C explains the alternative minimum tax rules for in viduals. The rules for corporations differ significantly and are beyond the intenc ed scope of the text.

HOW REGULAR TAXABLE INCOME IS DETERMINED

To appreciate the import of alternative minimum taxable income and the alternative minimum tax, one must first understand the procedure for computing taxes under the regular method. Be aware, however, that the Internal Revenue Code is riddled with exceptions and special rules to accommodate every conceivable taxpayer circumstance. Our objective is to provide general background sufficient for students to understand the impact of the alternative minimum tax on real estate investment decisions. This limited objective permits us to ignore the exceptions and concentrate on general rules.

The starting point for the regular computation is *gross income*. From this amount certain items are deducted to derive *adjusted gross income. Dependency exemptions* and *itemized deductions* in excess of a deduction incorporated into the tax schedules (called the *zero-bracket amount*) are subtracted from adjusted gross income to arrive at *tax schedule income*. Income tax liability is then determined through direct reference to tax schedules provided by the Internal Revenue Service.

Gross Income

Gross income includes all revenue from whatever source derived, unless specifically excluded by Sections 101 through 130 of the Internal Revenue Code. These sections contain a catalog of items, none of which is related specifically to real estate investment decisions.

Adjusted Gross Income

Code Section 62 defines *adjusted gross income* as gross income minus a set of specific deductions itemized in that section. In general, adjustments to gross income represent expenses associated with generating business income (including rental income).

Dependency Exemptions

A specified portion of adjusted gross income is exempted from taxable income for the taxpayer and each qualified dependent of the taxpayer.

Itemized Deductions

Part VI of the Internal Revenue Code details a list of expenditures that can be itemized and deducted from adjusted gross to arrive at taxable income. Those who compute their income tax liability by referring to tax schedules contained in the Code may deduct these itemized deductions only to the extent they exceed the maximum amount of taxable income for which no income tax is imposed. This amount, called the *zero-bracket amount* by Code Section 6(d), varies with the taxpayer's filing status.

Tax Liability Before Tax Credits

Subtracting dependency exemptions and itemized deductions (in excess of the zero-bracket amount) from adjusted gross income yields tax schedule income. Reference to the schedules in Section 1 of the Code reveals the associated tax liability. This amount is compared with the alternative minimum tax, and the taxpayer incurs liability for the greater of the two.

COMPUTING ALTERNATIVE MINIMUM TAXABLE INCOME

Adjusted gross income is the starting point for computing alternative minimum taxable income. Subtract any allowable losses carried over from prior years and allowable itemized deductions from the adjusted gross income. Then add all tax preference items.

Allowable Itemized Deductions

No standard deduction is allowed in the alternative computation, and itemized deductions are much less generous than those allowed in the regular computation. The only allowable deductions are:

1. Medical expenses, to the extent they exceed ten percent of adjusted gross income.
2. Interest expense incurred to acquire or carry investments, but only to the extent of net investment income.
3. Interest on "qualified indebtedness" secured by a lien on one's personal residence, to the extent the debt does not exceed the taxpayer's adjusted tax basis in the residence. Code Section 163(h) defines *qualified indebtedness* as that incurred to pay for medical care for immediate family members (provided the cost is not covered by medical insurance) and tuition and related expenses for immediate family members at a legitimate educational institution.
4. Interest on loans to purchase, construct or rehabilitate the taxpayer's personal residence.

Tax Preferences

Tax preferences are items that represent adjustments (that is, reductions) to gross income in the regular tax computation but are not permitted in the alternative computation. These items, which must be added back to adjusted gross to determine alternative minimum taxable income, are:

1. The difference between real estate depreciation or cost recovery allowances computed in the regular computation and that resulting from using the straight-line method over a 40-year recovery period;
2. The difference between depreciation or cost recovery allowances actually taken on personalty and the allowance that results from considerably less lenient rules applicable to the alternative minimum computation;
3. The difference between gains on disposal recognized in the regular tax computation and what those gains would have been had the taxpayer's adjusted tax basis reflected the less lenient cost recovery rules employed in the alternative minimum tax computation;

4. Gains on disposal of property held primarily for resale in the ordinary course of business, which, in the regular tax computation, were deferred by using the installment sales method of reporting transactions;
5. A host of other items that are permitted as adjustments to gross income under the regular method and are considered to have been accorded preferential treatment. Because these items are not related directly to real estate, we will not address specifics. Yet an investor might incur additional tax liability from a real estate transaction due to having made deductions for one or more of these items. Thus, accurate investment analysis requires that all such preference items be incorporated in estimating the alternative minimum tax consequences of a proposed real estate transaction. Real estate analysts must work closely with their clients' tax advisors in estimating the income tax consequences of any proposed real estate portfolio adjustment.

The Statutory Exemption

Taxpayers are permitted to subtract a *statutory exemption* from alternative minimum taxable income before applying the 21 percent alternative minimum tax rate. The amount of the exemption differs with the taxpayer's filing status:

Filing Status	Statutory Exemption
Married, filing jointly	$40,000
Unmarried	30,000
Married, filing separately	20,000

The statutory exemptions are phased out, however, as alternative minimum taxable income moves above a "trigger" amount. For married taxpayers filing joint returns the trigger amount is $150,000. It is $112,500 for single taxpayers and $75,000 for married taxpayers filing separate returns.

Above the trigger amounts the exemption is reduced by 25 cents for every additional dollar of alternative minimum taxable income. To illustrate, suppose a married couple who file a joint return have alternative minimum taxable income of $200,000. Instead of the usual $40,000, their statutory exemption will be reduced to $27,500:

Basic exemption		$40,000
Less: Reduction due to alternative minimum taxable income (AMTI):		
Actual AMTI	$200,000	
"Trigger" amount of AMTI	150,000	
Difference	$ 50,000	
Times: 25 percent	.25	
Reduction in basic exemption		12,500
Allowable exemption		$27,500

When alternative minimum taxable income exceeds the trigger amount by four times the statutory exemption, the entire exemption will have been phased out.

Beyond that point, the entire alternative minimum taxable income will be subject to the 21 percent alternative minimum tax.

INVESTMENT PLANNING IMPLICATIONS

Chapters 10–12 repeatedly make the point that all calculations must be made on an after-tax basis if they are to lead to rational investment decisions. Examples illustrating this point always assume the tax is to be computed using the regular method. This is generally a valid assumption, since taxpayers will rarely incur liability for the alternative minimum tax.

Investors and analysts must be alert, however, for circumstances where an investment decision will generate an alternative minimum tax liability. In many such situations, a different investment strategy might prove more desirable.

CHAPTER 11

Tax Consequences of Ownership Form

INTRODUCTION

Investors undertaking real estate investment ventures face a bewildering array of ownership entity choices. Legal and financial distinctions among alternatives may appear inconsequential; the reality is that the choice of titleholding entity is often crucial to a venture's outcome.

A decision to involve other investors in some form of pooling-of-equity arrangement vests the entity question with particular urgency. Outside investors generally insist upon an arrangement that limits their personal liability for financial obligations of the venture.

Asset liquidity is interrelated with the issue of financial liability and is significantly affected by choice of ownership entity. The ability to liquidate a position at the investor's own volition is often a powerful determinant of willingness to enter into cooperative ventures. To enhance liquidity, cooperative ventures generally employ an entity that enables investment shares to be transferred in relatively small increments.

A continuous thread running through all deliberations concerning the entity question is the importance of maintaining decision-making control over operational matters. Sacrificing control to induce associates to contribute additional funds to a venture is self-defeating if the associates prove to be inept managers. The entity decision should be made only after careful consideration of its impact on operational control.

In most instances, it is the income tax advantages afforded real estate over alternative forms of investment that make it particularly attractive. Financial benefits of the tax shelter provided by real estate are of limited value if they accrue directly to a taxable ownership entity rather than to investors as individuals. Yet, injudicious choice of an ownership entity can cause investors to be denied these income tax advantages.

TITLE MAY VEST IN OWNERS AS INDIVIDUALS

Investors' initial impulses are generally to have title vest solely in themselves as individuals or as cotenants where a pooling of interests is involved. The cotenancy arrangements most commonly encountered are *tenancy in common* and *joint tenancy*. When property is held as a tenancy in common, each investor's name appears on the deed, and each holds an undivided interest in the whole property. Unless there has been a specific agreement to the contrary, each common tenant has the use of the whole property. Substantial alterations or improvements require agreement among the owners, thereby effectively reducing the operational control of any one owner. The usual arrangement is to provide that one owner operates the property under a power of attorney from the others.

Joint tenancy has essentially the same characteristics as tenancy in common, with one overpowering exception. In the event of a joint tenant's death, the deceased person's interest in the property may go to the other joint tenant or tenants rather than to the deceased tenant's heirs. This provision of joint tenancy is called *right of survivorship*.

Cotenancy has the attraction of ease in legal arrangements. No special provisions are required other than appropriate wording on the deed of conveyance; the exact wording needed to assure creation of joint tenancy as opposed to tenancy in common differs among the states. Agreement among cotenants regarding operational matters can be arranged as they please but should be in writing and signed by all parties to avoid misunderstanding and to serve as a guide in case of future disputes. To ensure enforceability and access to legal remedies, any such agreement should be made under the guidance of legal counsel.

A cotenancy is not a tax-paying entity. All profits and losses accrue to the investors as individual taxpayers and are reported on their personal tax returns. Profits and losses are divided among the owners in accordance with their relative ownership interests in the property. With respect to a personal interest in the property, therefore, each investor is in the same tax position as if the investor held title to a part of the property as a sole owner.

Individual ownership and cotenancy arrangements have the seemingly compelling attraction of simplicity. But simplicity is one of the less significant of a myriad of considerations. Further analysis is justified before making a final decision.

TITLE MAY VEST IN A CORPORATION

In every state, statutes permit creation of a corporate entity. *Corporations* are empowered to hold property in their own names and to buy, sell and otherwise enter into contracts. They can sue and be sued and transact all manner of business in the same manner as corporal individuals. As legal entities, corporations have an identity separate and distinct from that of their owners.

Corporations are also taxable entities. They must file corporate income tax returns and pay taxes on their net earnings. For this reason, flow-through accounting treatment (as discussed later with respect to limited partnerships) is not available to corporate shareholders.

Any distribution of corporate earnings in the form of cash dividends is taxable to corporate stockholders as regular income (with the exception of a relatively minor dividend exclusion). This, in effect, results in double taxation of distributed earnings. Moreover, refusal to declare a cash dividend may result in an even higher tax on accumulated earnings in excess of the needs of the corporation. This *excess accumulated earnings tax*, when added to the regular tax, is essentially confiscatory.

For many investors, therefore, a corporation is not the best entity choice. But the corporate entity does have certain advantages that should not be dismissed out of hand. The one most often cited is limited shareholder liability. As a legal entity, the corporation is empowered to own property and to contract for debt in its own name. Corporate liabilities are separate and distinct from those of the owners of the corporation. Unless they voluntarily enter into a contrary arrangement, stockholders are not liable for any debt contracted by the corporation. Thus they are personally exposed to risk only to the extent of their investments in the corporation.

Another advantage that may accrue to the corporate form of ownership is added *liquidity*. Fractional interests in the form of one or more shares of stock can be issued as a means of transferring small portions of the ownership—a procedure that might be awkward or impossible in the case of real property held in the name of a corporal investor.

INVESTORS MAY FORM A GENERAL PARTNERSHIP

From an income tax standpoint, the essential feature distinguishing partnerships from corporations or other entities is that partnerships are not taxable. They function instead as *conduits* for passing income and loss items directly to the tax returns of individual partners. Moreover, income and loss items incurred by the partnership retain their characters on the partners' returns. Income that would be a tax preference item if the partnership were a taxable entity, for example, is reported as a tax preference item on the personal tax returns of individual partners.

Partnerships are required to file tax returns, but the purpose is purely informational. They must show the amount and nature of income, expenses and deductions and indicate how each item is allocated among the partners. Partners must in turn report these individual items on their personal income tax returns. Tax consequences of partnership business transactions thus accrue directly to the partners rather than to the business entity itself.

Partners in a *general partnership* share all profits and losses equally, unless they jointly agree upon an alternative arrangement. In the absence of special wording in the partnership agreement, they also have equal authority over the activities of the partnership business. In any event, the partners are jointly and severally liable for all partnership obligations, even if the obligation is created as a consequence of one partner having exceeded the authority granted under the partnership agreement.

Shared management authority, combined with unlimited joint and several liability, places severe limitations upon the usefulness of general partnerships as real estate ownership entities. As a practical matter, general partnerships tend to be limited to a few business associates who are well acquainted and share a high degree of mutual confidence.

A LIMITED PARTNERSHIP MAY HOLD TITLE

When a substantial number of investors wish to merge resources in a real estate venture but want to avoid income tax difficulties associated with using a corporate entity, they usually seek an alternative to both the general partnership and the corporate entity. Investors who contribute capital but do not participate in management will wish to be exculpated from personal liability for financial obligations resulting from the venture. For many real estate investment projects, the solution is a limited partnership. There will be one or more general partners, who are charged with conducting partnership business affairs and who have unlimited personal liability for partnership obligations. There will also be one or more limited partners, who have no personal liability but who share in partnership profits and losses in the same way partners do in a general partnership.

Limited partnerships enable investors to enjoy the same limitation of personal liability that they could attain with a corporation, while avoiding the double taxation that makes the corporate form less than desirable for many purposes. This propitious merging of corporate and proprietorship characteristics alone would probably assure considerable utilization of the limited partnership entity as a form of business organization.

Several traditional problems of real estate as an investment medium are also alleviated by limited partnership arrangements. Chief among these are lack of liquidity, a low disaster threshold, need for specialized knowledge of the market, and professional investment management skills.

Instead of committing all resources to one venture, as might be necessary in an individual real estate investment, participants in limited partnerships can spread resources over several such ventures and so gain the benefits of diversification, both geographically and across types of real estate. Diversification is an important method of reducing risk—investors need not put all their eggs in one basket. Having misjudged the market with respect to one investment venture, they are not faced with financial disaster as would have been the case if all available resources had been committed to that one project.

Investors frequently cite as a reason for avoiding real estate ventures the time required to manage such investments. Professional management is often too expensive for a small-scale apartment or office complex to be practical. Pooling funds via a limited partnership enables investment in a large enough project that professional management is both practical and economical.

The General Partners

Every limited partnership arrangement must have one or more general partners. It is they who conduct the affairs of the partnership. Any claims against the partnership that exceed the assets of the entity can be collected only from the general partner or partners. The dual functions of general partners are to exercise decision-making control (within the parameters of the partnership agreement) and to assume unlimited liability for the general financial obligations of the partnership. Any attempt to catalog benefits from acting as a general partner is hampered by the almost endless variations these benefits can take. They are limited only by the promoter's ingenuity.

Perhaps the most frequent promoters of limited partnership deals are real estate brokers. Their place in the center of real estate activity uniquely positions them for this role. They know which properties are ready for development, where mortgage funds can be procured, the condition of the market and the names of people interested in real estate investment opportunities. And, depending upon the laws of the state in which they are licensed, they may be able to collect a commission or fee at every step in the process of forming the partnership and carrying out its intended functions.

Lawyers and accountants are probably the next two groups most active in promoting limited partnerships. They are in positions to know people who need tax-sheltered investments, they are frequently asked for advice concerning such matters and they generally appear knowledgeable in the legal and tax intricacies of partnership formation.

The Limited Partners

Partners who supply the bulk of investment capital are usually passive investors. They are attracted to a limited partnership for the same reasons they might be attracted to any other investment opportunity: the prospect of substantial yields on funds placed at risk. But real estate limited partnerships offer an additional attraction not always available elsewhere. By remaining passive with respect to operation of the venture, investors limit their liability for partnership debt to the amount of funds actually invested in the venture, plus any additional assessments to which they may voluntarily commit themselves.

Yet this limitation of liability is not different from that afforded a corporation. What, then, is the special attraction of limited partnerships? The answer lies in the special tax status of the partnership itself and of the partners. Tax benefits that make real estate investment so attractive to individuals holding property in their own names are not generally available to corporate shareholders. But property held by a limited partnership is treated as if it were owned directly by the individual partners.

This special blending of the limited liability of the corporate form of organization with the tax benefits of sole proprietorship explains why limited partnership shares are especially enticing to investors who earn substantial income from other sources but who are not particularly knowledgeable in the field of real estate. Real estate tax shelter reduces taxes on other passive income. And limitation of personal liability reduces fear of the unknown.

While tax benefits are less alluring for investors in lower tax brackets, they are by no means inconsequential. Of particular appeal to those of modest means are ventures designed for capital appreciation. The more inviting real estate investment opportunities are generally beyond the means of such investors as sole owners. The initial cash investment is simply greater than they can personally generate. Limited partnership arrangements can be tailored to solve this dilemma. They provide the means for a group of investors of limited means to pool financial resources with experienced and skillful management to benefit from large projects that would otherwise be available only to wealthy individuals or to institutional investors.

TAX CONSEQUENCES OF PARTNERSHIP ENTITIES

Limited and general partnerships generally have identical income tax consequences for the partners. They differ primarily with respect to the personal liability of partners. Consequently, we need discuss partnership tax consequences only in general terms, with the understanding that the principles apply to general and limited partnerships alike.

Tax Basis of Partnership Shares

All assets have a tax basis in the hands of their owners. Income tax consequences during the holding period, as well as the tax consequences of disposing of the assets, are determined in large part by the owner's tax basis.

Initial Basis. The general rule is that a partner's initial tax basis is equal to the amount paid into the partnership, plus any partnership liabilities for which the partner assumes personal liability. If noncash assets are contributed, the partner's basis is increased by the amount of his or her basis in these assets (rather than by their market value).

Example 11.1

Jones purchases shares in a limited partnership. He pays $25,000 in cash and transfers title to property with a market value of $100,000. His adjusted basis for the transferred property, however, was only $20,000. Although the value of cash and other assets contributed by Jones totals $125,000, his initial tax basis in the partnership shares is only $45,000:

Cash Contributed	$25,000
Property Transferred, Adjusted Basis	20,000
Tax Basis of All Property Transferred to Partner-ship and of Partnership Shares Received	$45,000

In Example 11.1, the tax basis of partnership shares is the substitute basis of property given in exchange. In the example, no gain or loss is recognized on the transfer. The only exception to this rule is when a partner performs a service in exchange for a partnership interest. In that case, the partner performing the service is deemed to have received compensation in the amount of the fair market value of shares received and then to have invested this amount in the partnership. The market value of the interest received is therefore taxable as ordinary income to the partner. Market value, in this case, also forms the initial basis of the partnership interest. Example 11.2 illustrates.

Example 11.2

An attorney forms a limited partnership and takes a ten-percent interest in exchange for her services in completing the legal work. The market value of partnership assets in excess of partnership liabilities is $200,000. The attorney is deemed to have received ten percent of this amount, or $20,000, taxable as ordinary income from personal services. If the shares are for services already performed, the entire $20,000 is taxable in the taxable year in which the interest is transferred. If only a portion of the services have been performed, with the balance to be performed in the future (perhaps upon sale of assets and dissolution of the partnership), then only the market value of that portion of the interest representing compensation for services actually performed is taxable when the interest is transferred. The balance is taxable as income from services when the rest of the services are performed, provided there are restrictions upon disposition of the interest in advance of completion of the services.

At-Risk Rule

If an investor transfers to a partnership property subject to an existing mortgage, the investor's basis in the partnership is increased by the amount of the adjusted basis of property transferred and decreased by the amount of debt relief resulting from the transfer. This rule holds whether the partnership assumes the existing debt or merely takes the property subject to the debt. Consider Example 11.3.

Example 11.3

An investor exchanges property (adjusted basis = $24,000) for newly issued shares in a limited partnership. The property transferred is subject to a note and first mortgage that has a remaining principal balance of $14,000. The investor becomes a limited partner and assumes no personal liability for partnership debts. The general partners do assume full liability for all debts of the partnership, including any mortgages on partnership property. The investor's basis in the partnership is a substitute basis and is computed as follows:

Adjusted Basis of Property Contributed	$24,000
Less: Debts Assumed by Other Partners	14,000
Basis of Partnership Interest	$10,000

If a real estate partnership incurs debts for which no partner has personal liability, then each partner's interest is determined by his or her ratio for sharing profits under the partnership agreement, providing the debt stems from an arm's-length third-party loan secured solely by a mortgage on the real estate. "Commercially reasonable" loans that are not arm's-length transactions may be treated as arm's-length in applying the at-risk rule if loan terms are substantially the same as those available from arm's-length sources. (This constitutes a specific exception to the general Internal Revenue Code provision that a partner's tax basis does not include any portion financed by partnership borrowing unless the partner is personally liable for the indebtedness. The exception applies only to partnerships whose principal business is real estate ownership. See Code Section 465.) This rule has particular significance because it applies to any mortgage on partnership realty where the general partners are exculpated from personal liability for the mortgage debt.

Example 11.4

Three investors form a limited partnership for purposes of investing in an apartment complex. Partner Able is the general partner and assumes general liability for the debts of the partnership. For her role as general partner,

> Able receives a 20 percent interest in all profits and asset distributions and bears 20 percent of all partnership losses. Partners Baker and Charles contribute cash but assume the role of limited partners. The partners agree that Baker and Charles, each of whom contributes $20,000, will each receive 40 percent of all profits or assets distributed and bear 40 percent of all losses up to the amount of their interests in the partnership. It is agreed that Baker and Charles assume no personal liability beyond their initial $20,000 investments. The partnership buys an apartment complex having a total market price of $150,000, paying $40,000 down and signing a note and mortgage for the balance of $110,000.

Consider the facts in Example 11.4. If the active partner assumes personal liability for any balance on the note that cannot be satisfied from partnership assets, then the limited partners' initial basis is $20,000 each (the amount invested in the partnership). Their cumulative losses from the partnership to be reported on their personal tax returns cannot exceed their tax bases. As a result of depreciation or cost recovery allowances and financial leverage, they might reasonably expect to have large tax losses in the early years, perhaps coupled with substantial cash distributions by the partnership. When their cumulative tax losses and cash distributions equal the amount of their initial tax bases, their adjusted bases will have been reduced to zero, and additional operating losses cannot be passed through to their personal tax returns (additional cash distributions will be taxed as realized gains). Losses in excess of their bases may be carried forward indefinitely, however, and charged off in future years when partnership profits result in an increase in their total bases equal to the charges so deferred.

But consequences are altered dramatically if the mortgage-secured loan in Example 11.4 contains a clause relieving the general partner of personal liability for the balance on the note (even though he or she remains liable for all other partnership obligations). If no partner has personal liability for the mortgage debt and if it stems from arm's-length financing, each partner's basis is increased in the same proportion as he or she shares in the profits. Each of the limited partners, therefore, has his or her basis increased by 40 percent of the mortgage debt, or $44,000. The adjusted basis of each limited partner's interest is now $64,000: the initial $20,000 of cash contributions and the $44,000 increase due to assumption by the partnership of debt for which no partner has personal liability. Each limited partner may now claim cumulative basis reductions of $64,000 before losses must be carried over.

Adjustments to the Partner's Basis.   A partner's basis in a partnership is adjusted to reflect the tax effect of subsequent transactions. Additional capital contributions increase the basis, as does the partner's share of undistributed partnership income. A partner's basis may also be increased to reflect a pro-rata share of newly acquired partnership liabilities. This would be the case, however, only if the partner assumes personal liability for a portion of the debt or if no partner has personal liability.

The tax bases of partnership interests are decreased by the partners' distributive shares of partnership losses (without regard to whether the losses can be currently offset against other income), by their shares of partnership expenditures that are not chargeable either to expenses or to capital (for example, charitable contributions) and by the amount of cash or the adjusted basis of noncash assets distributed to them. Example 11.5 illustrates the impact of a series of partnership transactions.

Example 11.5

At the end of the prior year's operations, a limited partner's investment, representing a ten percent interest in the partnership, had an adjusted basis of $110,000. During the current year, the partnership earns taxable income of $100,000 before accounting for cost recovery and makes a charitable contribution of $1,000. Cost recovery allowances for the year are $140,000. The partnership distributes a total of $10,000 in cash to the partners.

At the end of the taxable year the partner's adjusted basis is $104,900, determined as follows:

Adjusted Basis at Beginning of Year			$110,000
Less: Distributive Share of Net Loss			
Cost Recovery Allowance	$140,000		
Less: Income Before Recovery Allowance	100,000		
Net Loss for Year	40,000		
Times: Partner's Distributive Interest	.10		
Partner's Distributive Share of Loss		$4,000	
Distributive Share of Contributions (10% of $1,000)		100	
Cash Distributed to Partner (10% of $10,000)		1,000	
Total Deductions and Adjustments			5,100
Adjusted Basis at End of Year			$104,900

Termination of a Partnership Interest

If the partnership agreement and applicable state laws permit, a partner may sell or otherwise dispose of a partnership interest at will. Doing so does not affect the tax status or position of the partnership itself unless the partnership is terminated as a consequence.

Disposal of a partner's interest is viewed for tax purposes as taking place solely between the partner and persons acquiring the interest. A partner's gain or loss on such a transaction is simply the difference between value received and the adjusted basis of shares transferred. The gain or loss is generally treated as a capital item.

Perpetual life is not a characteristic generally associated with the partnership form of organization. The day comes when a limited partnership's business is complete, and it is time to distribute remaining assets and close the books.

If the asset distribution involves only cash, the difference between a partner's adjusted basis and cash received represents a taxable gain or loss in the year of distribution. If the distribution involves only assets other than cash, uncollected accounts receivable or substantially appreciated inventory, no gain or loss is recognized as a consequence of their distribution. The partner's basis for assets received is the adjusted basis of the partner's interest just prior to liquidation, less any cash or cash-equivalent assets received in liquidation. If a partner receives more than one noncash asset upon liquidation, the basis of the partnership interest (less cash or cash-equivalent assets received on liquidation) must be allocated among the assets received.

Partnership Tax Pitfalls

A number of serious income tax problems can befall the unwary or unfortunate partnership investor. Every step in partnership operations must be taken with one eye on the Internal Revenue Code and Treasury Department rulings.

Assuring Conduit Treatment. Tax conduit treatment is an essential element in the desirability of most partnerships. Partnership revenue and expense items are passed through to the partners' individual tax returns without losing their identities. Since this is such a valuable aspect of the partnership entity, it is imperative that the partnership agreement be structured to avoid loss of conduit status.

An organization is treated as a partnership for tax purposes if it does not have more corporate than partnership characteristics. Internal Revenue Service regulations spell out six characteristics, two of which—the existence of associates and the objective to carry on a business and divide the profits—are common to both partnerships and corporations. The remaining four, therefore, determine whether the entity is treated as an association or a partnership. The four critical corporate characteristics are:

- Continuity of life;
- Centralized management;
- Limited liability for all partners;
- Free transferability of interests.

Treasury Regulation 301.7701-2 contains rules for determining whether these corporate characteristics exist. It states that continuity of life does not exist if an organization is not continued in the event of death, insanity, bankruptcy, retirement, resignation or expulsion of any member, without the express agreement of all remaining members. Since such a provision is included in the *Uniform Limited Partnership Act,* continuity of life does not exist for limited partnerships in states having statutes that correspond to the uniform act. In other states, an article in the partnership agreement to the effect that unanimous agreement is required to continue the partnership under these circumstances should assure that the partnership lacks continuity of life.

Centralized management is deemed to exist under Regulation 301.7701-2 when a general partner resembles "in powers and functions the directors of a statutory corporation." This implies that management is empowered to make independent business decisions on behalf of the organization without need for ratification. The regulation goes on to state that limited partnerships generally do not have centralized management unless ". . . substantially all the interests in the partnership are owned by the limited partners."

The corporate characteristic of limited liability exists if partnership creditors may look only to the assets of the organization for satisfaction. In a limited partnership, of course, debtors may look to the general partner or partners for satisfaction when debts exceed the assets of the partnership. If general partners are not possessed of "substantial assets" from which to satisfy such claims, however, their personal liability may be ruled a sham by the Internal Revenue Service. The partnership would then be considered to provide limited liability for all partners. Just what constitutes substantial assets is not specified by the Internal Revenue Service. The IRS has, however, specified net worth requirements for general partners before it provides an advance ruling on the question.

Free transferability of interests is the final corporate characteristic not always present in partnerships. If a member's interest can be transferred to an outsider without the consent of other members, conferring on the outsider all rights and privileges of the transferor, then free transferability exists. A mere assignment of rights to share in profits does not constitute free transferability as contemplated by the regulation. It is generally relatively simple to avoid the free transferability of interests characterization by making the transfer to outsiders subject to a consent requirement, though the consent requirement may be ruled a sham if it is routinely given.

Remember that to be treated as a taxable association the partnership must have *more* corporate than partnership characteristics. This means that three of the four characteristics must be present. A carefully drawn agreement should circumvent this eventuality without sacrificing the flexibility needed by general partners to assure successful pursuit of investment goals. Treasury Regulation 301.7701-3(b)(2) contains two examples of real estate organizations that qualify for treatment as partnerships. These examples are reproduced here as Examples 11.6 and 11.7.

Example 11.6

Three individuals form an organization that qualifies as a limited partnership under the laws of the state in which the organization was formed. The purpose of the organization is to acquire and operate various pieces of commercial and other investment property for profit. Each of the three individuals who are general partners invests $100,000 in the enterprise. Five million dollars of additional capital is raised through contributions of $100,000 or more by each of 30 limited partners. The three general partners are personally capable of assuming a substantial part of the obligations to be incurred by the organization. While a limited partner may assign his or her right to receive a share of the profits and a return of his or her contribution, his or her assignee does not become a substituted limited partner except with the unanimous consent of the general partners. The life of the organization as stated in the certificate is 20 years, but the death, insanity or retirement of a general partner prior to the expiration of the 20-year period will dissolve the organization. The general partners have exclusive authority to manage the affairs of the organization but can act only upon the unanimous consent of all of them. The organization has associates and an objective to carry on business and divide the gains therefrom, which characterize both partnerships and corporations. While the organization has the corporate characteristic of centralized management since substantially all of the interests in the organization are owned by the limited partners, it does not have the characteristics of continuity of life, free transferability of interests or limited liability. The organization will be classified as a partnership for all purposes of the Internal Revenue Code.

Example 11.7

Three individuals form an organization that qualifies as a limited partnership under the laws of the state in which the organization was formed. The purpose of the organization is to acquire and operate various pieces of commercial and other investment property for profit. The certificate provides that the life of the organization is to be 40 years, unless a general partner dies, becomes insane or retires during such period. On the occurrence of such death, insanity or retirement, the remaining general partners may continue the business of the partnership for the balance of the 40-year period under a right so to do stated in the certificate. Each of the three individuals who is a general partner invests $50,000 in the enterprise and has means to satisfy the business obligations of the organization to a substantial extent. Five million dollars of additional capital is raised through the sale of freely transferable interests in amounts of $10,000 or less to limited partners. Nine hundred such interests are sold. The interests of the 900 limited partners are fully transferable; that is, a transferee acquires all the attributes of the transferor's interest in the organization. The general partners have exclusive control over management of the business, their interests are not transferable and their liability for debts of the organization is not limited to their capital contributions. The organization has associates and an objective to carry on business and divide the gains therefrom. It does not have the corporate characteristics of limited liability and continuity of life. It has centralized management, however, since the three general partners exercise exclusive control over the management of the business and since substantially all of the interests in the organization are owned by the limited partners. While the interests of the general partners are not transferable, the transferability test of an association is met since substantially all of the interests in the organization are represented by transferable interests. The organization will be classified as a partnership for all purposes of the Internal Revenue Code.

Limitations on Deductibility of Losses

Limited partners must pay income taxes on their shares of partnership profits yet often find they cannot deduct net losses. This is a consequence of the *passive activity* rules of Code Section 469, which are explained in more detail in Chapter 10 and apply to all limited partnership interests. For investments made before the effective date of the Internal Revenue Code of 1986 (January 1, 1987) there is a five-year phase-in period during which successively smaller percentages of net losses from passive activities may be used to offset income from nonpassive sources. Even more liberal transitional rules apply to ownership of qualifying low-income housing projects acquired before enactment of the new law. These special transitional rules comprise one of the most complex portions of the tax law applicable to real estate and, in any event, are applicable in only very limited circumstances.

Income and losses from activities the Code characterizes as *passive* must be segregated from income generated by portfolio-type investments such as stocks and bonds and from general income sources such as wages, salary and profit from a trade or business. With only very limited special exceptions, net losses from these passive activities cannot be offset against income from other sources.

Instead, net losses must be carried over and offset against passive income in future years. Any passive losses carried over and not yet offset against passive income become deductible when the related asset is sold or otherwise disposed of in a taxable transaction.

Passive activities include all trade or business activity in which a taxpayer has an ownership interest but does not *materially* participate. Limited partnership interests are specifically included by the wording of Code Section 469(h)(2), which says, "Except as provided in regulations, no interest in a limited partnership as a limited partner shall be treated as an interest with respect to which a taxpayer materially participates."

Special provisions permit up to $25,000 of losses (and loss-equivalent tax credits) from operating rental real estate to be offset against otherwise taxable income from general (that is, nonpassive) sources such as wages and profits from business activities each year, without requiring that real estate investors meet the Code's definition of material participation in the rental activity. However, this special exception is denied to taxpayers with high adjusted gross income. It is phased out ratably as adjusted gross income (computed before adjusting for net passive losses) moves through "trigger" amounts set out in the Code. The amount of adjusted gross income that triggers the phaseout varies, depending upon the taxpayer's filing status.

To qualify for this exception, a taxpayer who holds at least a ten percent ownership interest need only be an *active* participant in the rental operation. Active participation is defined far more leniently than is *material* participation. Code Section 469(i)(6)(C) excludes limited partnership interests from the special provision, however, by stating that "No interest as a limited partner in a limited partnership shall be treated as an interest with respect to which the taxpayer *actively* participates."

TAX OPTION CORPORATIONS

Owners of certain corporations may elect to have income from the corporation (other than certain specified capital gains) taxable directly to shareholders rather than to the corporation. Losses are also passed through to shareholders, but only to the extent of the shareholders' adjusted bases in the stock. Additional losses must be carried forward until the stockholder makes further contributions to the corporation. Unlike real estate partnership interests, the basis of stock is not increased by a pro-rata share of mortgage debt. Corporations that qualify for and make this election are called *S* or *tax option* corporations.

Until late in 1982 the Internal Revenue Code stipulated that no more than 20 percent of a tax option corporation's gross receipts in any one taxable year could consist of passive investment income. Rental income (other than from the operation of a hotel or motel facility) and interest income were included in the definition of passive investment income. These being the primary sources of gross receipts for most real estate investment ventures, the limitation generally precluded the use of tax option corporations as ownership entities.

Code revisions in 1982 drastically reduced restraints on qualifying for tax option status. Previous limitations on the number of allowable shareholders were liberalized, and the Code now permits issuance of nonvoting stock. Most importantly, restrictions on income from passive sources were eliminated.

Technicalities surrounding the election can still be quite complex, and success requires an intimate knowledge of the mechanics of the statute and implementing regulations. Moreover, an unfavorable ruling that terminates the election could have catastrophic financial consequences for investors.

SUMMARY

Real estate investors may choose from a wide array of ownership entity alternatives. Rational choices must incorporate business, legal, financial and income tax considerations. Frequently selected alternatives include individual ownership or cotenancy, partnerships and corporations.

Individual or joint ownership in the investors' own names has the compelling attraction of legal simplicity. No special arrangements need be made prior to acquiring title. The deed is merely conveyed to the investors by name. If title is to be held jointly by two or more people, the wording in the deed of conveyance is a major determinant of the exact nature of the cotenancy.

Corporations are legal persons and thus may hold title to property in their own names. Ownership of a corporation does not entail ownership of corporate assets, although as a practical matter it frequently provides control thereof. Corporations are also taxable entities and must file income tax returns in much the same fashion as individuals. Income is first taxable to the corporation, and then any earnings distributed to shareholders in the form of dividends are taxable to those individuals. This possibility of double taxation reduces the attractiveness of the corporate entity to many investors. Moreover, any tax-deductible losses on corporate-owned real estate accrue to the corporation rather than to the corporate shareholders; corporations (other than those qualifying for and electing S corporation status) are not tax conduits.

Partnership offers an attractive ownership entity alternative. Title may be recorded in the partnership name, but the individual partners report income and losses from partnership operations on their personal income tax returns. If properly documented and reported, income is not taxable to the partnership. Each item of partnership income and expense retains its character when reported on the tax returns of the individual partners. For this reason partnerships are said to be tax conduits.

RECOMMENDED READINGS

Commerce Clearing House. *U.S. Master Tax Guide*. Chicago: Commerce Clearing House. Published annually.

Grossman, Harold A., ed. *Prentice-Hall's Explanation of the Tax Reform Act of 1986*. Englewood Cliffs, NJ: Prentice-Hall, Inc., 1986, pp. 217–223 and 501–515.

Kratovil, Robert, and Raymond J. Werner. *Real Estate Law*. 7th ed. Englewood Cliffs, NJ: Prentice-Hall, 1967, Chapter 6.

Lynn, Theodore S., Harry F. Goldberg and Daniel S. Abrams. *Real Estate Limited Partnerships*. 2d ed. NY: Wiley-Interscience, 1983, pp. 1–66 and 133–214.

Parisse, Alan. *Real Estate Review Portfolio No. 11: How to Syndicate Real Estate*. Boston, MA: Warren, Gorham & Lamont, 1977.

REVIEW QUESTIONS

1. Describe the differences between joint tenancy and tenancy in common.
2. List the major advantages and disadvantages of the corporation as an ownership form.
3. List the major characteristics of a limited partnership.
4. What are the major functions of the general partners in a limited partnership?
5. How is the initial tax basis of partnership shares determined?
6. How are profits and losses treated in a limited partnership?
7. Under what conditions might a partnership be treated for tax purposes as an association to be taxed as a corporation?
8. Describe the major advantages of an S corporation.

DISCUSSION QUESTIONS

1. Why would you expect property ownership in joint tenancy to be more common with married couples than with otherwise unrelated business partners?
2. Should government policy be designed to influence the choice between partnership and corporate ownership forms? Explain your reasoning.
3. Master limited partnerships are a limited partnership form where the limited partnership interests are traded much like shares of stock. The Internal Revenue Service is publicly opposed to proliferation of master limited partnerships. Evaluate this issue from a public policy perspective.

CHAPTER 12

Other Taxing Issues

INTRODUCTION

Framers of the Internal Revenue Code deliberately incorporated a number of special tax-saving opportunities either as a break for special interest groups or as encouragement for certain types of economic activity considered to be in the public interest. A goodly portion of these special opportunities involves investment in real estate. But failure to fully understand the tax implications can result in additional income tax liabilities—in many cases, long after the intended income tax benefit has been fully dissipated.

Insufficient attention to the Code's often complex details causes many investors to miss tax avoidance opportunities or to encounter tax planning problems needlessly. Careful planning will enable prudent and knowledgeable taxpayers to avoid the anguish of realizing too late that thousands of dollars in tax liabilities have been incurred unnecessarily.

INCOME TAX CONSIDERATIONS IN PROPERTY REHABILITATION DECISIONS

Tax shelter benefits, eroded elsewhere by the pernicious combination of preference tax and recapture rules, are still available to investors involved in renovation and rehabilitation. But not all opportunities are created equal. Qualifying expenditures to renovate low-income housing or selected nonresidential properties generate special benefits in the form of tax credits. More generous tax benefits are provided for rehabilitation of certified historic structures.

Tax Credits for Rehabilitating Nonresidential Structures

Provided they meet carefully specified criteria, expenditures to rehabilitate certain nonresidential buildings qualify for a rehabilitation tax credit. *Tax credits* differ from *tax deductions;* deductions are offset against taxable income, whereas credits are offset directly against tax liability. A taxpayer in the 28 percent marginal income tax bracket, for example, will find his or her tax liability reduced by $1 for every dollar of tax credit, but by only 28 cents for each dollar of tax deductions.

At least 75 percent of a rehabilitated building's existing external walls must continue to function as external walls after rehabilitation. Rehabilitation expenditures must have totaled more than $5,000 and must have exceeded the taxpayer's adjusted basis in the property before rehabilitation.

There are special rules for claiming a rehabilitation tax credit in connection with work on *certified historic structures*. These rules, and the associated tax credit, are discussed in the next section. Expenditures on a certified historic structure, if they do not meet the criteria for the special credit associated with such rehabilitations, will not qualify for any tax credit.

A taxpayer seeking the credit for rehabilitating a nonhistoric structure, therefore, must carefully ascertain that the building is not a certified historic structure. If it is not, but is nevertheless located in a *registered historic district*, then the Secretary of the Interior must certify that the building is not of historical significance to the district. Both *certified historic structure* and *registered historic district* are defined in the next section.

If qualifying rehabilitation expenditures are associated with a building that was first placed in service before 1936, the tax credit equals ten percent of the qualifying rehabilitation outlay. (Qualified rehabilitations of historically significant structures yield larger credits, as discussed in the next section.)

The tax basis of a rehabilitated property must be adjusted to reflect the amount of the tax credit. This, of course, reduces the amount of the annual cost recovery allowance and increases the taxable gain on property disposal.

If a taxpayer sells property within five years of the date of rehabilitation, a portion of the tax credit will be subject to recapture and will become a tax liability in the year of sale. The portion of a tax credit that is subject to recapture depends upon how long the property is held after rehabilitation:

Years Held After Rehabilitation	*Percent of Tax Credit Subject to Recapture*
Less than 1	100%
1, Less than 2	80
2, Less than 3	60
3, Less than 4	40
4, Less than 5	20
5 or more	0

If a taxpayer's basis in a property is reduced by the amount of the tax credit, the basis will be increased by the amount of any credit recaptured. A capital gain or loss is then computed on the adjusted basis, which includes the portion of the credit that has been recaptured, and the gain or loss will be the same as it would have been had the recaptured tax credit never been claimed.

Tax Credits for Rehabilitating Historic Structures

Rehabilitation of properties that federal functionaries deem of historical significance is heavily subsidized via credits against the rehabilitator's federal income tax liability. Whereas the maximum allowable tax credit for other projects is ten percent of the rehabilitation outlay, qualifying historic property rehabilitations earn a credit equaling 20 percent of the amount expended.

A certified historic structure is any structure that is either listed in the National Registry of Historic Places or located in a registered historic district. In the case of a noncertified structure listed in a registered historic district, however, the Secretary of the Interior must certify that the structure is of historic significance to the district.

A registered historic district is any district listed as such in the National Registry of Historic Places. The designation also includes any district so identified by appropriate state or local statute, provided that the Secretary of the Interior certifies that the statute will substantially achieve its purpose of preservation and rehabilitation and that the district meets substantially all the requirements for listing in the National Registry.

The same recapture rules that apply to other rehabilitation credits (discussed earlier) apply also to credits for rehabilitating certified historic structures.

Annual Limit on Tax Credit Benefits

There is no limit on the dollar amount of tax credit that can be earned, but the maximum amount of earned credit that can be used to offset income tax liability in any one year is $25,000 plus 85 percent of tax liability in excess of $25,000. Thus a taxpayer whose liability is $40,000 before credits and who has $50,000 of credits will pay only $2,250 in taxes for the year. The computation is:

Liability Before Tax Credits		$40,000
Less:		
Credit on first $25,000	$25,000	
Credit on balance (.85 × $15,000)	12,750	37,750
Liability After Net Allowable Credits		$ 2,250

Earned tax credit in excess of the amount allowable in the current year can be carried back and offset against tax liability in each of the three preceding taxable years (resulting in tax refunds). Any remaining credit is carried forward for as many as 15 years.

LIKE-KIND EXCHANGES

An otherwise taxable gain realized on an exchange of like-kind assets need not be recognized in the year of the transaction. Rather, the tax liability is postponed until a future, taxable transaction occurs with respect to the newly acquired property. A series of such exchanges can pyramid one's real estate holdings by retaining wealth that would otherwise be chipped away in tax liability with each transaction. The government in effect extends an interest-free loan in the amount of taxes so deferred.

Enabling legislation for like-kind exchanges, sometimes (erroneously) called *tax-free exchanges,* is contained in Section 1031 of the Internal Revenue Code. Reflecting this, they are sometimes referred to simply as *Section 1031 exchanges.* From their inception, potential benefits of exchange rules became evident to astute real estate investors. These rules became even more attractive with the tightening of recapture rules (explained in Chapter 10) in 1976 and again in 1981.

Example 12.1

An investor has been investing all his available savings in small parcels of real estate such as single-family dwellings, duplexes and small stores. Over the years, he has built up a substantial equity in those properties and now is considering moving into a large property that can be managed professionally, will yield economies of scale and will free him from time-consuming chores associated with his present holdings.

Assume that his equity in his present holdings has a market value of $500,000 and an adjusted basis of $200,000. The investor, who is in the 28 percent marginal income tax bracket, has no other tax preference items. The cash available for reinvestment if he sells his equity at the indicated market value will be $416,000, calculated as follows:

Taxable Gain on Transaction	
Selling Price of Equity	$500,000
Less: Adjusted Basis	200,000
Taxable Gain	$300,000
Income Tax Liability at 28%	$ 84,000
Cash Flow (Available for Reinvestment)	
Selling Price of Equity	$500,000
Less: Income Tax Liability	84,000
Net Cash Flow	$416,000

In Example 12.1, the investor pays a heavy price for moving into an alternative investment opportunity: His $500,000 equity is reduced to $416,000 due to the income tax. If, instead of selling his current holdings and reinvesting the net proceeds, he can involve himself in a tax-free exchange of present assets for the desired investment opportunity, he will be able to invest his entire $500,000 equity in the new property. The financial advantage of this alternative is obvious.

Given the versatility and potential profitability of this tax-planning tool, it is not surprising that like-kind exchanges have gained widespread popularity. The remainder of this chapter details basic requirements for an exchange to be tax-free under Code Section 1031.

Exchange Versus Sale and Purchase

To qualify under Section 1031, there must have been a bona fide *exchange* of the assets involved. It appears that the question of whether a transaction is treated as an exchange or as a sale and purchase is more a matter of form than of intent. Cautious investors ascertain that proper steps are taken by all parties to document transactions as bona fide exchanges. The other parties may not be in a position to have their tax liability deferred under Section 1031, regardless of the form of the transaction. They may therefore be considerably less motivated to structure the transaction appropriately.

Purpose for Which Property Is Held

To qualify as a like-kind exchange, property conveyed must have been held for productive use in a trade or business or as an investment and must be exchanged for like-kind property that is also to be used in a trade or business or held as an investment. Properties may qualify if they fall into either of these categories; that is, property held for use in a trade or business may be exchanged for investment property and vice versa. As a general rule these two categories of property may be considered together in like-kind exchange transactions.

Certain types of property, however, are specifically excluded by statute. These include securities or evidence of indebtedness (stocks, bonds, notes and so forth), beneficial interest in a trust and <u>inventory</u>. For real estate investors the last type of property is likely to prove the most troublesome, since inventory includes one's stock in trade or other property (including real estate) held primarily for resale.

What Is Like-Kind Property?

Only like-kind property qualifies for tax-deferred exchange treatment. The like-kind concept relates to the nature of the property, but not to its quality or grade. While this distinction may be somewhat less than clear, its main implication for real estate investors is that real estate may be exchanged for other real estate without regard for the type of realty involved, so long as it is held as an investment or for use in a trade or business. Examples issued by the Treasury to amplify this point[1] include:

1. Property held for use in trade or business, together with cash, for other property intended for use in a trade or business;
2. Urban real estate for a farm or ranch;
3. Improved or unimproved real estate held for investment purposes;
4. A leasehold (with not less than 30 years to run) for a freehold;
5. Mineral interest in land (not merely an assignment of payments) for a fee title in real estate.

Tax Consequence of Like-Kind Exchanges

If all property involved in an exchange qualifies as like-kind and all parties qualify, then no party to the exchange may recognize any gain or loss on the transaction. Note that this is mandatory, not elective. Any gain or loss realized in an exchange but not recognized for income tax purposes is reflected in the tax basis of the newly acquired property.

Should some of the property involved in an exchange fail the like-kind test, then some portion of a gain (but not of a loss) must be recognized in the year of the transaction. The balance of the realized gain is deferred as before and is reflected in the adjusted basis of acquired property.

Not All Parties Need Qualify.   The test of whether a transaction qualifies as a tax-deferred exchange is applied separately to each party to the trade. To qualify, individuals must not have held their properties for resale or for personal use. A property must have been held either as an investment or for use in a trade or business (but not as inventory). If one party's motive for ownership was inappropriate under Section 1031, the other party to the transaction may nevertheless qualify.

Example 12.2

Alice B. Accumulator wants to acquire Larry D. Liquidator's property in an exchange. Liquidator is willing to sell outright but has no interest in Accumulator's property. The broker involved in the deal finds a third party who is willing to buy Accumulator's property. The deal is completed by an exchange of property interests between Accumulator and Liquidator and a purchase by the third party of the property acquired by Liquidator from Accumulator. Accumulator has a tax-deferred exchange; Liquidator does not.

In Example 12.2 Accumulator may defer any gain on the transaction because she acquired like-kind property to be held as an investment. Liquidator, however, does not qualify under Section 1031 and so must recognize any realized gain. Liquidator is disqualified because the property acquired from Accumulator is held for resale.

Even if Liquidator had not found an immediate buyer for property acquired from Accumulator in Example 12.2, it is possible that recognition of gains could not be deferred under Section 1031. Had the property traded to Accumulator been listed for sale for a period of time immediately before the exchange, this would have established that it was held primarily for sale. The important point here is that the tax consequences to Accumulator are independent of those to Liquidator.

Effect of Receiving Unlike Property.   Receipt of property that does not meet the like-kind definition has the effect of partially disqualifying a gain from deferral under Section 1031. The person receiving unlike property, or *boot*, must recognize any gain realized on the transaction to the extent of the boot received.

Boot includes anything of economic value other than like-kind assets involved in the transaction. Examples include cash, services rendered or an obligation to render services, debt forgiveness and a promise to convey something of value in the future.

A special rule applies to one category of unlike property: the acceptance of an obligation to pay mortgage debt encumbering like-kind property being received from the other party, thus relieving that party of his or her obligation to pay. When each party takes title subject to an outstanding mortgage, receipt of unlike property is computed on the basis of net debt relief. (The net debt relief rule applies when properties are exchanged subject to existing mortgages, whether or not the parties assume and agree to pay the obligations.) Example 12.3 illustrates.

Example 12.3

Smith and Jones agree that their respective equities are equal in value. They agree to trade equities, each party taking title subject to the mortgage note on the property received. Their positions before the exchange were as follows:

	Smith	*Jones*
Market Value of Property	$75,000	$140,000
Less: Balance of Mortgage	25,000	90,000
Value of Equity	$50,000	$ 50,000

Jones has received boot of $65,000 in the form of net debt relief (old debt of $90,000 minus new debt of $25,000). She incurs an income tax liability for any gain realized on the transaction, to the extent of the $65,000 of net debt relief.

An investor may receive net debt relief and yet have to pay cash to balance the market value of assets exchanged. In that case, subtract the cash paid from net debt relief received. Only the balance must be reported as boot received. However, receipt of cash or other unlike assets is not offset against net mortgage liability assumed. Example 12.4 illustrates.

Example 12.4

Farrell and Greer agree to exchange properties. Each party is to assume the balance of the outstanding mortgage note on realty received in the exchange, and Greer agrees to pay cash to Farrell to "balance the equities." Their positions before the exchange were as follows:

	Farrell	*Greer*
Market Value of Realty	$110,000	$110,000
Less: Balance of Mortgage	60,000	70,000
Market Value of Equity	$ 50,000	$ 40,000

Based on this analysis, Greer agrees to pay Farrell $10,000. Even though he receives net debt relief in the exchange, Greer has not received boot as defined in Section 1031 and need not report a taxable gain. This is because the net debt relief is offset by payment of cash boot. The effect is the same as if the $10,000 cash had been applied instead to reduce the mortgage balance prior to the trade. Offsetting the $10,000 of net debt relief against the $10,000 cash paid by Greer results in an even trade from Greer's point of view.

When cash is received, however, it is not offset by mortgage liability assumed. Farrell, therefore, has received $10,000 boot in the form of cash, notwithstanding the fact that he has assumed $10,000 of additional mortgage liability.

A party who receives unlike property in an exchange must recognize any gain to the extent of the value of boot received. Note that this applies only to gains. Losses realized in a transaction may not be recognized if the exchange qualifies even partly as like-kind.

Treatment of Transaction Costs.   Transaction costs include such items as brokerage commissions, recording fees, transfer taxes and attorney's fees. Transaction costs may be thought of as a reduction in proceeds from the old property or an addition to the purchase price of the new. In either case, they reduce the realized gain and thereby become a part of the tax basis of newly acquired property. Transaction costs may also be offset against any unlike property (boot) received and thereby reduce the portion of the realized gain that must be recognized.[2]

Tax Basis of Acquired Property

While we frequently speak of Section 1031 exchanges as tax-free, it is more accurate to use the term *tax-deferred*. There may be no tax liability at the time of the transaction, but the day of reckoning is merely delayed rather than totally avoided. The basis of the new property is a *substitute basis* reflecting any deferred gain. It consists of the adjusted basis of the property conveyed, with further adjustments reflecting the circumstances of the exchange.

Example 12.5

Mr. Investor exchanges property having an adjusted basis of $90,000 for like-kind property with a market value of $150,000. He pays transactions costs of $150 but neither receives nor pays any boot. Both properties are exchanged on a free and clear basis.

Mr. Investor has a realized gain of $59,850, computed as follows:

Market Value of Property Received		$150,000
Less:		
Transaction Costs	$ 150	
Adjusted Basis of Old Property	90,000	90,150
Realized Gain on Transaction		$ 59,850

Mr. Investor's basis for the new property at the time of the exchange is $90,150, computed in the following manner:

Basis of Old Property		$ 90,000
Plus:		
Additional Consideration Paid	0	
Transaction Costs	$150	150
Less: Additional Consideration		
Received		0
Basis of New Property		$ 90,150

The same result can be reached by subtracting from the fair market value of the property received the amount of any gain realized but not recognized:

Market Value of New Property		$150,000
Less: Unrecognized Gain		
Amount Realized	$59,850	
Minus: Amount Recognized	0	59,850
Basis of New Property		$ 90,150

When Mr. Investor sells the substitute property acquired in Example 13, his taxable gain is computed on the difference between the net proceeds and adjusted basis at that time. And since the basis of the substitute property reflects the deferred gain, selling the substitute property triggers recognition of the gain.

We have deliberately kept examples simple to better illustrate how the basis of a newly acquired property is computed. Example 12.6 is a more complex exercise designed to demonstrate how the same rules can carry an analyst through the computational thicket.

Example 12.6

Ms. Ima Gottsome owns income property with a market value of $2,000,000 and a mortgage of $750,000. Her adjusted basis before the transaction is $1,200,000. She exchanges this for another income property with a market value of $3,500,000 that is subject to a mortgage of $1,500,000. Gottsome pays $750,000 cash for the difference in equities, and each party takes title subject to existing mortgages. Gottsome pays transaction costs of $20,000.

Gottsome's realized gain is the difference between the market value and the adjusted basis of her original property, minus transaction costs. Having received only like-kind property in the exchange, however, she defers recognition of the entire gain. The initial basis of the new property is determined as follows:

Basis of Old Property		$1,200,000
Plus:		
Transaction Costs	$ 20,000	
Mortgage Assumed	1,500,000	
Cash Paid	750,000	2,270,000
		$3,470,000
Less: Old Mortgage		750,000
Basis of New Property		$2,720,000

Note that the basis of the substitute property in Example 12.6 is simply its fair market value less any unrecognized gain ($3,500,000 minus $780,000 equals $2,720,000).

If, due to receiving unlike property, some portion of a realized gain must be recognized, the basis of substitute property is increased by the amount of the recognized gain. This is illustrated in Example 12.7.

Example 12.7

Dr. Dudly Dullbit exchanges his dental office building (market value of $152,800) for another office and a used dental drill (market value estimated to be $2,800). Dr. Dullbit owes a mortgage balance of $80,000 on his building, which has an adjusted basis of $100,000. Each party agrees to assume the existing mortgage on property received in the exchange. The building received by Dr. Dullbit has an outstanding mortgage balance of $70,000 and a fair market value of $140,000. Transaction costs to Dr. Dullbit are $5,000.

Dr. Dullbit has a realized gain, part of which must be recognized since he receives unlike property in exchange. The realized gain is $47,800, computed as follows:

Market Value of Assets Received		
Real Estate		$140,000
Personalty		2,800
Net Debt Relief		10,000
Total		$152,800
Less: Basis of Property Conveyed		
Real Estate	$100,000	
Transaction Costs	5,000	105,000
Realized Gain on Exchange		$ 47,800

The realized gain generates tax liability to the extent of any unlike property received in the exchange, net of transaction costs. Dr. Dullbit must therefore recognize $7,800 of the realized gain as currently taxable.

Mortgage on Old Property	$ 80,000
Less: Mortgage Assumed	70,000
Net Debt Relief	$ 10,000
Value of Other Unlike Property Received	2,800
Total Value of Unlike Property Received	$ 12,800
Less: Transaction Costs	5,000
Net Boot Received	$ 7,800

The tax basis of the new property received by Dr. Dullbit is the adjusted basis of his old property, increased by any additional payments made and any recognized gain and reduced by any other value received:

Adjusted Basis of Old Property		$100,000
Plus:		
Transaction Costs	$ 5,000	
Debt Assumed	70,000	
Recognized Gain	7,800	82,800
		$182,800
Less:		
Old Mortgage	$ 80,000	
Personalty Received	2,800	82,800
Basis of New Property		$100,000

The substitute tax basis in Example 12.7 can be proved by reducing the market value of the new property by the amount of the unrecognized gain. The results should be the same as in the example. The calculations are:

Market Value of Property Received		$140,000
Less: Unrecognized Gain		
Realized Gain (from Example 12.7)	$47,800	
Minus: Recognized Gain	7,800	
Unrecognized Portion of Gain		40,000
Basis of New Property		$100,000

Effect of Losses in Section 1031 Exchanges.   So far all examples have assumed a gain on the exchange, with the discussion centering on whether a portion of the gain must be recognized and on the resulting tax basis of substitute property. But what happens if there is a loss on an exchange?

If a transaction qualifies fully under Section 1031 as like-kind, then neither a gain nor a loss may be recognized. We have seen, however, that if the party experiencing a gain receives any unlike property (including net debt relief), then a portion of his or her gain must be recognized. This partial recognition relates only to gains; receipt of some unlike property in an otherwise like-kind exchange never triggers partial recognition of a loss.

Example 12.8

Silvia Smart trades income-producing real estate for like-kind property. The property received by Smart has a fair market value of $80,000 and is subject to a mortgage of $55,000. Smart's old property has an adjusted basis of $95,000 and is subject to a mortgage of $60,000. The parties exchange equities, each assuming the mortgage on the property received. Transaction costs are zero.

The transaction in Example 12.8 qualifies under Section 1031 as a like-kind exchange, but Ms. Smart has received unlike property in the form of net debt relief. Had there been a gain, it would be recognized to the extent of Smart's net debt relief ($5,000). In this example, though, Smart has experienced a loss rather than a gain:

Market Value of Property Received	$80,000	
Mortgage Assumed by Other Party	60,000	$ 140,000
Less:		
Mortgage Assumed by Smart	55,000	
Adjusted Basis of Old Property	95,000	150,000
Gain (Loss) on the Exchange		$ (10,000)

Although Smart may not recognize her loss in the year of the transaction, it is reflected in her tax basis for the new property. Thus, its recognition is merely deferred until the new property is sold. Smart's basis for the new property is her old basis, adjusted for the other property involved in the transaction. (In this illustration, we have simplified by assuming there are no transaction costs. Were such costs incurred, they would be added to the new basis.) Smart's new basis is:

Basis of Old Property	$ 95,000
Plus: Mortgage Assumed	55,000
	$150,000
Less: Mortgage Assumed by Other Party	60,000
Basis of New Property	$ 90,000

Note that the basis of Smart's new property is simply its market value adjusted by adding any additional value given by Smart and subtracting any value received plus any unrecognized loss or less any unrecognized gain:

Market Value of Property Received	$80,000
Plus: Unrecognized Loss	10,000
Basis of New Property	$90,000

Note also that the substitute basis of Smart's new property exceeds its fair market value by the amount of the unrecognized loss. It would also include any transaction costs incurred by Smart. If she subsequently sells the property, her recognized loss on the sale will reflect this substitute basis in excess of fair market value. The deferred loss will be recognized at that time.

Allocating the Substitute Basis

Just as the initial basis of purchased property must be allocated between land and improvements to determine cost recovery allowances, so must the substitute basis of property acquired in a Section 1031 exchange be allocated. The basic rule remains invariant: allocate on the basis of relative market values.

Example 12.9

Geltloss and Smith trade like-kind properties. Both parties own their properties on a free and clear basis. Relative values before the exchange are agreed to be as follows:

	Adjusted Basis	Market Value Dollar Amount	Percentage of Total
Geltloss			
Land	$20,000	$20,000	40%
Improvements	10,000	30,000	60
	$30,000	$50,000	100%
Smith			
Land	$ 5,000	$ 5,000	10%
Improvements	20,000	45,000	90
	$25,000	$50,000	100%

Consider Example 12.9. To keep the illustration simple, assume there are no transaction costs. Since no boot is involved, Geltloss will have a substitute basis equaling the adjusted basis of his or her old property: $30,000. This basis is allocated to the acquired land and improvements in the ratio of their relative market values: ten percent to the land and 90 percent to the improvements. Geltloss's basis after the exchange is:

Land (10%)	$ 3,000
Improvements (90%)	27,000
Total Basis	$30,000

Our illustration assumes relative market values are known. In a real situation, these values must be determined. This may be accomplished by agreement between the parties in an arm's-length transaction, by an independent appraisal or by using relative values as determined by the property-tax assessor. These do not exhaust the potential means of arriving at an estimate of relative market values, but they are all approaches that have been accepted in the past.

If more than one property is received in an exchange, the substitute basis is allocated among acquired properties in the ratio of their relative market values as of the date of the exchange. The allocated substitute basis of each property is in turn allocated between land and improvements on the basis of relative values. To illustrate, assume the property received from Smith in Example 12.9 consists of a store building on one small plot of land and an adjoining vacant lot. Assume further that each of the lots is worth $2,500 if unimproved, and the store building alone is worth $45,000 before considering the value of the site. Geltloss's $30,000 substitute basis is first allocated to the two separate properties in the ratio of their relative values: five percent to the vacant lot and 95 percent to the store and site. The substitute basis of the store and site (.95 × $30,000 = $28,500) is then allocated to site and improvements based on their relative values. The resulting substitute basis is:

	Market Value	Percentage of Total Value	Substitute Basis
Vacant Lot	$ 2,500	5%	$ 1,500
Store			
Site	2,500	5	1,500
Improvements	45,000	90	27,000
Total	$50,000	100%	$30,000

Nonsimultaneous Exchanges

In 1979, the Ninth Circuit Court of Appeals issued a precedent-setting opinion that an exchange in which a taxpayer did not receive title to the substitute property at the time he transferred title to his property nevertheless qualified for tax deferment under Code Section 1031.[3]

The plaintiff had exchanged timberland for properties of equal value, with the provision that substitute properties were to be acquired by the other party and transferred to the plaintiff within five years of the date of the agreement. The Internal Revenue Service disallowed like-kind exchange treatment. The plaintiff, T. J. Starker, had paid the resultant tax deficiency and sued for a refund in federal district court.

The trial court ruled in favor of the Internal Revenue Service, but the plaintiff won on appeal. Because the case involved rulings in earlier litigation that became issues in this case also, and because a number of properties and legal issues were involved, the Ninth Circuit's decision covered a great amount of legal territory.

The Internal Revenue Code was subsequently revised to seal the hole that the Starker decision punched in Section 1031. For nonsimultaneous exchanges to qualify for tax deferment the substitute property must be identified within 44 days following the day of the initial property transfer, and the final transfer must be completed by the earlier of (a) 179 days following the day of the initial property transfer or (b) the due date for the taxes that would be imposed if the transaction did not qualify for tax deferment.

Limitations on Deductibility of Losses

The Internal Revenue Code of 1986 requires taxpayers to report separately their income and losses from activities characterized as "passive" under the special provisions of the Code. With only very limited special exceptions, net losses from these passive activities cannot be offset against income from other sources. Instead, the net losses must be carried forward and offset against passive income in future years. Any remaining passive loss carryovers become deductible when the passive activity asset to which they apply is sold or otherwise disposed of in a taxable transaction. For passive investments made before the effective date of the new tax law (January 1, 1987) there is a five-year phase-in period during which successively smaller percentages of net losses from passive activities may be used to offset income from nonpassive sources.

Passive activities include ownership interests in most rental property and in any trade or business activity in which the taxpayer does not "materially" participate in management. Material participation in business operations is said to be lacking if the owner is not actively involved, year-round, on a "regular, continuous, and substantial basis." The tax-writing committee listed the following "signposts" as indicative of whether a taxpayer's participation is material:

- Is the activity the taxpayer's principal trade or business?
- How close (geographically) is the taxpayer to the activity?
- Does the taxpayer have knowledge and experience in the enterprise?

Real estate held for rental purposes is defined as a passive activity by the wording of code Section 469(c)(2), which states, "The term 'passive activity' includes any rental activity." Elsewhere, however, the Code contains special provisions that permit up to $25,000 of losses (and loss-equivalent tax credits) from operating rental real estate to be offset against otherwise taxable income from such activities as wages and profits from business activities each year. But this special exception is phased out ratably as adjusted gross income (computed before adjusting for net passive losses) moves from $100,000 to $150,000.

To qualify for this exception a taxpayer must have at least a ten percent ownership interest in the property and must be an *active* participant in the real estate rental operation. The requirement of active participation is less strenuous than the *material participation* requirement described earlier. The Senate Finance Committee, in reporting on the enabling legislation, described *active participation* as making management decisions or arranging for others to provide services such as repairs and maintenance. Moreover, services performed by a taxpayer's spouse are attributed to the taxpayer in determining whether the active participation test is met.

Special rules apply to low-income housing placed in service before 1990 (or before 1991 if at least ten percent of project costs are incurred before 1989). For these projects the "active participation" requirement for passing through the first $25,000 of losses or loss-equivalent tax credits each year does not apply where a taxpayer claims the special exception with respect to losses or loss-equivalent tax credits for rehabilitating low-income housing or depreciation expense based on writing off rehabilitation costs (but not purchase or construction costs) of low-income housing. Moreover, the phase-out of the special exception does not begin until the taxpayer's adjusted gross income (before accounting for passive losses) reaches $200,000. The exception is then phased out ratably as the adjusted gross income moves from $200,000 to $250,000.

Limited partnership interests are specifically included in the passive activities category by the statute. Code Section 469(h)(2) says, "Except as provided in regulations, no interest in a limited partnership as a limited partner shall be treated as an interest with respect to which a taxpayer *materially* participates." Section 469(i)(6)(C) says, "No interest as a limited partner in a limited partnership shall be treated as an interest with respect to which the taxpayer *actively* participates." Taken together, these two provisions effectively foreclose any possibility that limited partnership interests might escape being characterized as passive activities.

The Code incorporates special relief provisions for taxpayers who acquired assets that fit the passive activities category where ownership was effective (or a binding contract leading to ownership was in effect) prior to enactment of the new law. A portion of losses from these activities may be offset against income from other sources until 1991, but the portion eligible for this treatment declines each year between 1987 and the final cutoff year of 1991.

Even more liberal transitional rules apply to ownership of qualifying low-income housing projects acquired before enactment of the new law. These special transitional rules comprise one of the most complex portions of the tax applicable to real estate and, in any event, are applicable in only very limited circumstances.

SUMMARY

Numerous tax-saving opportunities are incorporated into the Internal Revenue Code as deliberate attempts to induce actions considered socially desirable. Careful planning may enable taxpayers to exploit these opportunities and thereby avoid unnecessary income tax liability. Significant opportunities available to real estate investors include tax credits for rehabilitating certain properties and tax deferral associated with exchanging like-kind properties.

Tax credits, direct offsets against income tax liability, are available for qualifying expenditures to rehabilitate certified historic structures. These are structures listed in the National Registry of Historic Places or located in a registered historic district and certified by the Secretary of the Interior as being of significance to the district. A registered historic district is any district listed in the National Registry or any district so designated by appropriate state or local statute that has been certified by the Secretary of the Interior as substantially achieving its purpose of historic preservation, provided the district also meets "substantially all" the requirements for listing in the National Registry. Tax credits for rehabilitating qualifying historic structures equal 20 percent of the qualifying rehabilitation expenditures.

Structures that do not qualify as being historically significant may nevertheless qualify for rehabilitation tax credits, albeit at a reduced rate. Expenditures to rehabilitate qualifying structures may earn the investor a tax credit equaling ten percent of the expenditure.

Otherwise taxable gains on disposal of real estate are deferred if the property is exchanged for other property in a qualifying like-kind exchange. The tax liability is deferred until the property received in the trade is itself disposed of in a transaction that does not qualify as like-kind. To qualify as a like-kind exchange, both the property disposed of and that received in exchange must be held by the taxpayer for use in a trade or business or for production of income. Certain types of property are specifically excluded from like-kind exchange treatment. These include securities and evidence of indebtedness, beneficial interests in a trust and inventory.

If some unlike property (boot) is received in an otherwise qualifying like-kind exchange, then any realized gain must be recognized for tax purposes, to the extent of the value of the unlike property received. The balance of the gain is deferred until the new (substitute) property is sold. No part of a realized loss may be recognized, however, if the transaction qualifies even in part as a like-kind exchange.

Real estate's appeal as a tax shelter mechanism was drastically curtailed in 1986 by legislation that, with limited exceptions, prohibits using losses to offset otherwise taxable income from salaries, wages or profit from business or portfolio operations.

NOTES

1. Treas. Reg. 1.1031(a)–1.1031(b).
2. Rev. Rul. 72-456.
3. *T. J. Starker v. United States*, 2 Tax Ct. Rep. (CCH) §9541 (9th Cir. 1979).

RECOMMENDED READINGS

Grossman, Harold A., ed. *Prentice-Hall's Explanation of the Tax Reform Act of 1986.* Englewood Cliffs, NJ: Prentice-Hall, Inc., 1986, pp. 229–232.
Institute for Business Planning. *Tax-Free and Tax-Sheltered Investments for the 1980s.* Englewood Cliffs, NJ, 1981.

REVIEW QUESTIONS

1. Explain the difference between tax credits and tax deductions.
2. What qualifications permit rehabilitation expenditures on nonresidential structures to qualify for tax credits?
3. What are the qualifications and advantages of rapid amortization of rehabilitation expenses?
4. Under what circumstances will all or a portion of the rehabilitation tax credit be recaptured?
5. List the qualifications necessary for an exchange of property to be considered a like-kind exchange for tax purposes.
6. How are gains and losses in a like-kind exchange treated?
7. How is the tax basis of property acquired in a like-kind exchange determined?
8. Describe the allocation of the basis of property acquired in a like-kind exchange.

DISCUSSION QUESTIONS

1. Are tax credits for property rehabilitation the best way to subsidize these activities?

2. Should property rehabilitation be subsidized at all, either through investment tax credits as is now done or in any other way?

3. From a public policy perspective, is there any reason to accord like-kind exchanges different income tax treatment from that associated with selling the old property and buying the substitute? In either instance, are there compelling public policy reasons to permit income taxes to be deferred?

PART FOUR: Case Problem

For the following problems, refer to the Sated Satyr Apartments in the case problems for Part Three. Assume Benedict buys the Sated Satyr for $1.3 million and incurs transaction costs (not including costs associated with financing) equal to two percent of the purchase price. Assume also that he secures a mortgage loan for $1.2 million at ten percent interest, to be amortized over 30 years with level monthly payments. Assume further that the purchase occurs during the first month of Benedict's taxable year and that he sells the property for $1.7 million toward the end of the twelfth month of his seventh year of ownership. Benedict's selling costs (we will assume) equal eight percent of the sales price.

1. Develop a cost recovery (depreciation allowance) schedule for each year of Benedict's holding period, using a 27.5-year cost recovery period and assuming that 80 percent of the purchase price is properly attributable to the improvements—the balance is attributable to the land.
2. Assuming Benedict to be in the 28 percent marginal income tax bracket, and assuming he incurs no liability for the alternative minimum tax, what will be his income tax liability attributable to the sale of the Sated Satyr?
3. What will be Benedict's after-tax cash flow from selling the Sated Satyr?
4. Assuming that net operating income grows at a steady rate of three percent per annum, develop a schedule of after-tax cash flows from the Sated Satyr during the entire period of Benedict's investment, including the year of disposal.

Important! Save all your work for use with the case problem in Part Five.

PART FIVE

Measuring Investment Performance

Forecasting after-tax cash flows from investment projects, as discussed in Parts One through Four, is a necessary step in rational investment decision making. In itself, however, forecasting is not sufficient. Efforts to translate forecasts into criteria for evaluating investment alternatives have generated a host of approaches that vary widely in the extent to which they accomplish their intended purposes.

Chapter 13 provides background needed for evaluating investment performance by surveying traditional approaches to the task. It explains the virtues and weaknesses of the most commonly encountered traditional techniques, which range from simple ratios between price and expected revenue to more complex attempts to incorporate considerations such as income tax consequences and cash flow from disposal.

Intelligent consideration of more contemporary evaluation techniques requires a basic understanding of the mathematics of compounding and discounting. Chapter 14 and its appendix provide this understanding. Chapters 15 and 16 incorporate principles from Chapter 14 into a presentation of state-of-the-art investment decision criteria. Chapter 17 shows how computer-assisted analysis can eliminate the arithmetical tediousness of the techniques.

CHAPTER 13

Traditional Measures of Investment Worth

INTRODUCTION

Investment analysts must sift through a veritable mountain of informational chaff to glean the intelligence needed for rational decision making. Traditional approaches to this formidable chore have ranged from snap judgments based on little more than "hot tips" to careful and time-consuming analysis of reams of financial and economic data. Many investors compromise by using rules of thumb, which provide quick reference to past experience or benchmark measures of profitability based on market observation.

This chapter introduces the most commonly encountered traditional techniques. It proceeds from popular ratios measuring profit/price relationships and operating results to more complex evaluation techniques employed extensively by those educated in traditional real estate investment analysis. It then introduces more advanced techniques that are explored further in subsequent chapters.

RATIO ANALYSIS

Ratios are widely employed to gauge the reasonableness of relationships between various measures of value and performance. *Income multipliers* express the relationship between market value and either gross or net income from operations. The *operating ratio* highlights the relationship between gross income and operating expenses. The *breakeven ratio* shows the percent of gross income required to meet cash expenditure requirements. The *debt coverage ratio* shows the relationship between net operating income and the debt service obligation.

Income Multipliers

Income multiplier analysis is a simple technique whose contemporary usefulness belies its antiquity. Income multipliers express the relationship between price and either gross or net income. They do not serve as ample tools of analysis in isolation but can play a valuable role as preliminary filters. Multiplier analysis permits obviously unacceptable opportunities to be weeded out swiftly and inexpensively. More extensive (and more costly) analysis can then be concentrated on properties that show promise of meeting predetermined investor criteria.

To use multiplier analysis as a filter, first determine the relationship prevailing in the market area of interest for properties comparable to that being investigated. Then automatically reject all opportunities whose multipliers exceed this benchmark figure. Opportunities passing the preliminary screening test are subjected to further analysis.

Example 13.1

An investment opportunity having a market price of $100,000 and requiring a 25 percent down payment is expected to yield the following operating results during the first year:

Effective Gross Income	$25,000
Less: Operating Expenses	13,000
Net Operating Income	$12,000

Other relevant information includes:

1. There is available a $75,000, 25-year mortgage loan requiring equal monthly payments with interest at nine percent per annum.
2. Best estimates indicate that the property will increase in market value at a compound rate of about five percent per annum during the immediate future.
3. The investor is subject to a marginal income tax rate of 40 percent.

Gross income multipliers, also often referred to as *gross rent multipliers,* reflect the relationship between a property's price and its effective gross income. Using data from Example 13.1, the gross income multiplier is:

$$\text{Gross Income Multiplier} = \text{Market Price}/\text{Effective Gross Income}$$
$$= \$100,000/\$25,000$$
$$= 4$$

When using gross income multiplier analysis for initial evaluation of prospective property acquisitions, the analyst must decide whether to use potential or effective gross income estimates. The determining factor is likely to be the form in which data are available. Data regarding vacancy rates and credit losses will often be unreliable and difficult to verify. For this reason the most appropriate measure will most likely be potential gross income.

Net income multipliers are calculated in the same fashion. They differ only in that net income instead of effective gross income is employed as a divisor. Because substantial research may be necessary to determine the appropriate measure of net operating income, gross income multiplier analysis is generally the more useful profitability measure.

For Example 13.1, the net income multiplier is:

$$\text{Net Income Multiplier} = \text{Market Price}/\text{Net Operating Income}$$
$$= \$100,000/\$12,000$$
$$= 8.33$$

Financial Ratios

Ratio analysis is frequently employed to facilitate interproperty comparisons. Commonly encountered examples include the operating ratio, the breakeven ratio and the debt coverage ratio.

The operating ratio is the percentage of gross income consumed by operating expenses. It will be lower for relatively more efficient properties. However, the operating ratio can be misleading because it reflects in part the efficiency of management as well as of the property itself. Some investors, in fact, look for properties with high operating ratios, intending to reduce the ratios through efficient management and thereby increase indicated property values. The operating ratio for Example 13.1 is:

$$\text{Operating Ratio} = \text{Operating Expenses}/\text{Gross Income}$$
$$= \$13,000/\$25,000$$
$$= 52\%$$

Breakeven ratio analysis as traditionally employed in real estate tends to be less useful than its counterpart in corporate finance. Corporate financial analysts express the relationship as it exists between gross revenues and variable costs, while real estate analysts relate gross revenues to total costs. In real estate, a substantial portion of operating costs are essentially fixed. As real estate occupancy levels change, the operating ratio as traditionally expressed may be altered drastically. The ratio between gross revenue and variable expenses, in contrast, tends to remain relatively more constant and so provides a more reliable indicator. Chapter 18 presents breakeven analysis employing the relationship between gross revenue and variable costs.

Breakeven ratios (frequently called *default ratios*) are most useful when employed on a before-tax cash-flow basis. They indicate the relationship between cash inflows and outflows from all sources. The lower the breakeven cash-flow ratio, the greater the decline in gross revenue (or the increase in operating expenses) can be before investors experience negative cash flow from a project. Applying the formula to the project in Example 13.1, the ratio is:

$$\text{Breakeven Ratio} = \frac{(\text{Operating Expenses} + \text{Debt Service})}{\text{Gross Income}}$$
$$= (\$13,000 + \$7,553)/\$25,000$$
$$= 82.2\%$$

The debt coverage ratio expresses the extent to which net operating income can decline before becoming insufficient to meet the debt service obligation. It thereby provides an indication of safety associated with the use of borrowed funds. The debt coverage ratio in Example 13.1 is:

$$\text{Debt Coverage Ratio} = \frac{\text{Net Operating Income}}{\text{Annual Debt Service}}$$
$$= \$12,000/\$7,553$$
$$= 1.59$$

Traditional Profitability Measures

A shared characteristic of all traditional profitability measures is an attempt to relate cash investment to expected cash returns in some systematic fashion. They have not been equally successful in those attempts. Traditional techniques differ in the degree to which they incorporate available data into the analysis. They differ also in that some ignore the issue of risk, while others make rudimentary attempts to adjust for risk differentials.

Overall Capitalization Rate

Also known as the *free-and-clear rate of return*, the *overall capitalization rate* expresses the first year's expected net operating income as a percentage of market price. The rate in Example 13.1 is:

$$\text{Overall Capitalization Rate} = \text{Net Operating Income}/\text{Market Price}$$
$$= \$12,000/\$100,000$$
$$= 12\%$$

Recall that the net income multiplier is market price divided by net operating income. The overall capitalization rate, therefore, is simply the reciprocal of the net income multiplier. Thus, in Example 13.1, 1/0.12 equals 8.33, which is the net income multiplier for the example.

Usefulness of overall capitalization rates is limited by the nature of financing arrangements and by the approach most investors take to arrive at an acceptable sales price. In a typical negotiating session there is an acknowledged trade-off between price and financing terms. Since this trade-off is not reflected in the overall capitalization rate, comparison of rates between properties with significantly different financing arrangements can be very misleading.

Equity Dividend Rate

Because most property transactions involve borrowed funds, and because availability and cost of mortgage financing differs among investment opportunities, the overall capitalization rate is not a very useful measure either for an accept/reject decision or for choosing among investment alternatives. A more helpful measure compares cash flow to the equity investor with the equity investment.

This measure is often called an *equity dividend rate*. As generally calculated, it expresses before-tax cash flow (net operating income minus debt service) as a percentage of the required initial equity cash outlay (purchase price minus borrowed funds). The equation is:

$$\text{Equity Dividend Rate} = \frac{\text{Before-Tax Cash Flow}}{\text{Initial Cash Outlay}}$$

Calculating the equity dividend rate for the property in Example 13.1 requires prior determination of the equity dividend (net operating income minus debt service) and the initial equity (price minus mortgage). These calculations are:

Equity Dividend (Before-Tax Cash Flow)	
Net Operating Income	$ 12,000
Less: Debt Service	7,553
Equity Dividend	$ 4,447
Initial Cash Outlay	
Purchase Price	$100,000
Less: Available Mortgage	75,000
Initial Equity	$ 25,000

Therefore, the equity dividend rate applicable to Example 13.1 is 17.79 percent, determined as follows:

$$\text{Equity Dividend Rate} = \$4,447/\$25,000$$
$$= 17.79\%$$

The equity dividend rate is useful in distinguishing among properties offering different financing structures, but it suffers from failure to incorporate income tax considerations. Cash flow to the equity position (before-tax cash flow) becomes meaningful as a measure of return on investment only after deducting the applicable income tax liability or adding back income tax savings. Where properties (and financing arrangements) involve significantly different income tax implications, the equity dividend rate will have limited usefulness as an analytical tool. Moreover, the equity dividend rate considers only the first year's consequence of ownership, whereas rational analysis demands that all consequences for the projection period be incorporated into the analysis.

Cash-on-Cash Return

To render it more useful for investment analysis, the relationship embodied in the equity dividend rate must be expressed on an after-tax basis. The modified equation is called the *cash-on-cash rate of return*. It expresses the first year's expected net spendable cash (after all financing costs and income taxes) as a percentage of the initial cash investment. To determine the expected cash-on-cash rate of return, the first year's expected income tax effect must be known. This in turn requires estimates of interest expense (a technique for splitting debt service payments into interest and principal components is described in Chapter 8; see Chapter 14 for a more detailed explanation) and depreciation or cost recovery allowances.

If the property in Example 13.1 is acquired on the first day of the year, interest expense for the year will be $6,713. Here is the computation:

Principal Paid in First Year	
Beginning Balance	$75,000
Less: Ending Balance ($629.40 × 1/0.008487)	74,160
Principal Paid During the Year	$ 840
Interest Paid in First Year	
Annual Debt Service Obligation	$ 7,553
Less: Principal Paid During the Year	840
Interest Expense, First Year	$ 6,713

The cost recovery allowance depends upon the ratio of land value to building value and upon whether the tenants use the property as their residence. Computational details are presented in Chapter 10. For this illustration, simply assume the allowance to be $2,700.

These data, combined with projected net operating income from Example 13.1, permit an estimate of the first year's income tax obligation:

Net Operating Income		$12,000
Less:		
Interest Expense	$6,713	
Cost Recovery Allowance	2,700	9,413
Taxable Income		$ 2,587

After-tax cash flow to the equity position is the net operating income minus debt service and income tax payments:

Net Operating Income	$12,000
Less: Debt Service Obligation	7,553
Before-Tax Cash Flow	4,447
Less: Income Tax at 28%	724
After-Tax Cash Flow	$ 3,723

With the preceding information, the cash-on-cash return can be calculated. For Example 13.1, the computation is:

$$\text{Cash-on-Cash Return} = \text{After-Tax Cash Flow} / \text{Equity Investment}$$
$$= \$3,723 / \$25,000$$
$$= 14.9\%$$

Broker's Rate of Return

Seeking to cast the best possible image of a property for sale, brokers are inclined to argue that any measure of return that ignores the buildup of an investor's equity is misleading. The *broker's rate of return* adjusts the cash-on-cash rate to include equity buildup resulting from amortization of mortgage debt. This, of course, increases the indicated return to the equity position and thereby makes the property appear more attractive.

For the property in Example 13.1, the broker's indicated rate of return is 18.3 percent, determined as follows:

$$\text{Broker's Return} = \frac{(\text{After-Tax Cash Flow} + \text{Equity Buildup})}{\text{Initial Equity}}$$
$$= (\$3,723 + \$840) / \$25,000$$
$$= 18.3\%$$

To after-tax cash flow plus equity buildup, some analysts add the anticipated rate of increase in property value. By making the broker's rate of return even higher, this makes the investment proposition look still more attractive to the uninitiated.

Though widely used, the broker's rate of return is misleading. The important measure of potential cash flow from disposal is the difference between market value and remaining balance on mortgage indebtedness, less estimated brokerage commission and other transaction costs. Since this cash flow is not realized on an annual basis, but only upon property sale, it is inconsistent to include equity buildup in the measure of annual cash flow.

Payback Period

One of the simplest and perhaps most common rules of thumb is to estimate the number of years required to recoup one's initial cash investment in a project. In *payback period* analysis, alternative opportunities are ranked in accordance with the length of time required for the anticipated stream of cash proceeds to equal the initial cash investment. For projects with different risk factors, the maximum acceptable payback period will be inversely related to perceived risk.

When anticipated cash flow from an investment is the same amount each year, the payback period can be calculated by simply dividing initial cash outlay by the expected annual cash flow. Thus, for a project requiring an initial cash outlay of $10,000 and expected to yield an annual cash flow of $2,500, the payback period is four years:

$$\text{Payback Period} = \text{Cash Outlay} / \text{Annual Cash Flow}$$
$$= \$10,000 / \$2,500$$
$$= 4$$

Of course, expected cash flow from a real estate investment opportunity is seldom the same from year to year. The focus of the analysis is after-tax cash flow, and variations in an investor's income tax position alone will almost certainly keep annual after-tax cash-flow estimates from being equal. Consequently, payback period calculation is seldom as straightforward as the preceding example suggests. In most instances, the payback period must be determined by summing expected proceeds from year to year until the total equals initial outlay.

Example 13.2 illustrates the procedure. The third column is simply the summation of all after-tax cash-flow estimates from the second column. With required equity investment of $48,330, the initial equity expenditure is expected to have been fully recovered at some point during the sixth year. Therefore, the payback period (expressed in whole years) is six years.

Example 13.2

A property can be acquired with an initial equity expenditure (that is, a down payment) of $48,330. Annual after-tax cash flows are expected to be as indicated in the second column below. Anticipated cumulative cash flows are indicated in the third column.

Year	After-Tax Cash Flow	Cumulative After-Tax Cash Flow
1	$ 7,145	$ 7,145
2	8,185	15,330
3	9,222	24,552
4	10,171	34,723
5	11,115	45,838
6	12,054	57,892
7	12,895	70,787

The appeal of payback period analysis is its apparent simplicity and its adaptability as a policy tool. Investors can specify some maximum payback period for real estate of a specific type or in a given location based on their perceptions of associated risks.

The major shortcoming of this method is that it ignores all cash flows beyond the payback period. This failure will cause assets with little appreciation potential to be chosen over those with almost certain large returns because of an increase in value over the holding period.

A second problem is that the method fails to discriminate among cash flows with different timing, even during the payback period. A project with all the benefits "up front" (tax benefits from accelerated depreciation or recovery allowances, for example) would not be chosen over one offering the same total benefit spread evenly over the entire payback period. The time value of money is thus ignored, and the project with the greatest potential return may not be chosen.

Failure to consider cash flows beyond the payback date and to discriminate among cash flows with different timing within the payback period makes the payback period approach unacceptable as a primary method of choosing among investment alternatives.

TOWARD MORE RATIONAL ANALYSIS

To understand the shortcomings of traditional measures of investment performance, it is helpful to review the major components of expected return. There is, of course, an initial equity cash commitment for which the investor expects to receive cash flow from operations during the holding period and cash from disposal upon termination of the investment position. Under rare circumstances, astute use of leverage techniques may enable an investor to "cash out," that is, to acquire an equity interest with no initial equity cash outlay. Traditional approaches ignore cash-flow expectations during the holding period, concentrating instead on the first year or, at best, the first few years of operation. They also completely ignore cash-flow expectations from disposal, even though this component may in some instances be the greater portion of the expected return from an investment.

There are five major factors governing the relative attractiveness of a real estate investment:

- The anticipated stream of net cash flow to the investor;
- The expected timing of cash receipts;
- The degree of certainty with which expectations are held;
- Yields available from alternative investment opportunities;
- The investor's attitude toward risk.

Regardless of particular investor predispositions, anticipated investment benefits must be adjusted for quantity, quality and timing. *Quantity* refers to the amount of expected net cash flows, after incorporating all income tax consequences and after adjusting for debt service obligations arising from use of financial leverage. *Quality* refers to the certainty with which expectations are held regarding forecasted net cash flows. *Timing* refers to when the forecasted net cash flows are expected to be received. The amount of the adjustment depends upon yields available from other investments (the opportunity cost of capital) and upon the investor's attitude toward bearing risk. An ideal measure of profitability will incorporate all these elements.

A common weakness of traditional measures of profitability is that they ignore the question of timing of net cash inflows. Time-adjusted measures have been introduced in recent years and are being consistently extended and refined by both theoreticians and practitioners.

TIME-ADJUSTED MEASURES OF RETURN

Since the timing of anticipated cash flows is at least as important as their amount, techniques that ignore the time value of money are universally inadequate. They serve at best as quick and inexpensive filters to eliminate obviously unacceptable proposals. Projects surviving a "rough-and-ready" test must be subjected to additional analysis to evaluate the significance of differently timed anticipated cash flows and to distinguish among different levels of attendant risk.

Time-adjusted techniques discount expected future cash flows to make them more nearly comparable to those receivable in the present. Some techniques adjust purely for the time value of money, while others include an adjustment for risk. One popular version takes the adjustment factor as a variable that equates future and present cash flows. All these measures are considered in greater detail in Chapter 15, after the mathematical tools necessary for their comprehension have been introduced.

Present Value

The *present value* technique adjusts all anticipated future receipts at a predetermined rate per time period. There results a present value equivalence of anticipated future cash flows. If the required initial cash outlay exceeds the present value of the future net cash inflows, the project is rejected. If present value exceeds the required cash outlay, the project is considered further.

Net Present Value

Real estate acquisition involves giving up current funds for the right to receive cash receipts from property in the future. If the present value of these future benefits exceeds the amount of current funds expended in their acquisition, the investor's wealth increases. If, on the other hand, the initial cash outlay exceeds the present value of expected future cash receipts, then the investor's wealth is diminished as a consequence. This is the concept underlying the *net present value* measure of investment performance.

After discounting anticipated future receipts at the appropriate discount rate to arrive at their present value, subtract the required immediate cash expenditure. What remains is the net present value. A net present value greater than zero represents an increase in the investor's wealth. If the cash outlay exceeds the present value of future receipts, net present value is a negative figure. This represents a net decrease in the investor's wealth.

Internal Rate of Return

Techniques for determining the appropriate rate at which anticipated cash flows should be discounted are a matter of some controversy. Some analysts avoid the issue altogether by taking the discount rate as a variable to be determined in solving the arithmetic of the discounting equation.

This approach involves taking the known initial cash outlay and the expected future cash flows as constants and seeking the discount rate that will make the present value of future cash flows exactly equal to the amount of the initial cash outlay. The net present value is set at zero, and a discount rate is found to make the equation solvable. This rate is called the *internal rate of return*.

Modifications to the Internal Rate of Return.   Critics of the internal rate of return point to a number of difficulties associated with it. Attempts to overcome these problems and salvage the technique have generated a number of variations of differing complexity. The most commonly encountered variations are the modified internal rate of return and the financial manager's rate of return. Both are discussed in Chapter 15.

SUMMARY

Investors and analysts have developed a variety of investment evaluation techniques. These include ratios for comparing income to market price and ratios for evaluating profitability and financial risk. They also include several measures of profitability designed to compare anticipated cash flows with required initial cash expenditures.

Traditional profitability measures generally fail to account properly for the time value of money. This is a serious failing because the timing of cash inflows and outflows is a major element in the comparative desirability of investment alternatives. Time-adjusted measures of return are an essential tool of rational investment analysis. Methods include present value and net present value computations and the internal rate of return.

RECOMMENDED READINGS

American Institute of Real Estate Appraisers. *The Appraisal of Real Estate*. 8th ed. Chicago: The American Institute of Real Estate Appraisers, 1983, pp. 626–629.

Brigham, Eugene F. *Fundamentals of Financial Management*. 4th ed. Hinsdale, IL: The Dryden Press, 1986, pp. 216–233.

Greer, Gaylon E. *The Real Estate Investment Decision*. Lexington, MA: Lexington Books, 1979, pp. 109–114.

Greer, Gaylon E., and Michael D. Farrell. *Contemporary Real Estate: Theory and Practice*. Hinsdale, IL: The Dryden Press, 1983, pp. 267–270.

Phyrr, Stephen A. and James R. Cooper, *Real Estate Investment Strategy, Analysis, Decisions*. Boston: Warren, Gorham and Lamont, 1982, pp. 309–316.

REVIEW QUESTIONS

1. How are income multipliers used in measuring investment worth?
2. Why might some investors search out properties with high operating ratios?
3. What is a characteristic common to all traditional profitability measures? What are the weaknesses in these forms of measurement?
4. Compare the concept of the overall capitalization rate with the equity dividend rate.
5. How is the broker's rate of return calculated? What is its major drawback?
6. List major factors governing the relative attractiveness of a real estate investment.
7. What is the difference between present value and net present value?
8. List the advantages and disadvantages of using the payback period as a measure of investment worth.

DISCUSSION QUESTIONS

1. Which of the traditional ratios employed in real estate analysis are most closely related to the following concepts employed in stock market analysis?

   a. Dividend yield
   b. Price earnings ratio

2. What impact might the inflation rate have on the usefulness of traditional profitability measures such as the cash-on-cash return, payback period and equity dividend rate?
3. What is the relationship among present value, net present value and internal rate of return? Is there a consistent relationship at all possible values for these measures?

CHAPTER 14

Mathematics of Compounding and Discounting

INTRODUCTION

Since real estate decisions generate benefits and costs that are spread differentially through time, it is necessary to adjust for timing differences to make them directly comparable. This chapter explains how such adjustments are made under a variety of circumstances.

Economic rationale for time adjustments is the first topic. The chapter then addresses how to measure growth of money through the compounding of interest income. Present value of a future sum is closely related to how a present amount grows and is logically the next topic of exploration. The chapter then moves a step further in complexity by considering the present value of a series of future amounts. Since payments to retire a loan are reciprocal to the present value of a series of future receipts, these topics are presented back to back. A final topic addressed in the chapter is techniques for extending the usefulness of compound interest and discount tables.

CONCEPTUAL BASIS FOR COMPOUNDING
AND DISCOUNTING

Compound interest and *discount* are based upon two fundamental propositions: More is better than less, and sooner is better than later. From these propositions

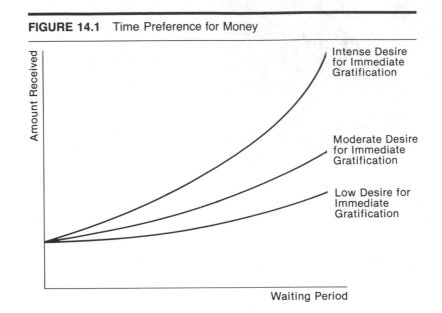

FIGURE 14.1   Time Preference for Money

it follows that people will insist upon being compensated for waiting and that there will be a trade-off between the amount received and timeliness of receipt.

That more of a good thing is better than less is not a matter for serious dispute. Economists have considered this a self-evident proposition since the dawn of their discipline. If one bottle of champagne is gratifying, two will be even more so; three are even more desirable than two and so forth. Fundamental to this concept (and certainly to our example) is that one need not consume the greater quantity if one does not wish to do so. Increased gratification stems from certain knowledge that more is readily available if desired. Two bottles thus provide the same option as one, plus the intoxicating choice of still more refreshment.

A preference for present over future receipt is only a small step further into abstraction. Who would not (other things being equal) prefer $500 today to the certain promise of $500 next month? Choosing the promise of future receipt reduces one's option for present consumption without offering anything in return. Current receipt, in contrast, provides the option of consumption now, next month or at any time in the distant future. Clearly, the want-satisfying power of a good is generally enhanced by current receipt.

The more intense the desire for immediate gratification, the greater will be the rate of trade-off, as illustrated in Figure 14.1. This relationship is sometimes called *time preference for money*, or the *time value of money*. The topmost line in Figure 14.1 represents an individual who has a very high time preference. The individual's strong preference for immediate receipt indicates that he or she will insist upon handsome compensation for waiting. The lower line in the figure represents the trade-off function of someone who has relatively low time

TABLE 14.1 How a Debt Accumulates at Compound Interest

Year	Amount Owed at Start of Current Year	Plus Interest at 7%	Amount Owed at Year End
1	$1,000.00	0.07 × $1,000.00	$1,070.00
2	$1,070.00	0.07 × $1,070.00	$1,144.90
3	$1,144.90	0.07 × $1,144.90	$1,225.04

preference and can therefore be induced to wait with very little compensation. The middle line represents the trade-off function of one with only a moderate time preference.

Growth in the amount available for consumption, as a consequence of waiting, is called *compound interest*. Reducing the amount available, as a consequence of opting for more immediate receipt, is called *discounting*. The greater the rate of compound interest or discount, the steeper will be the slope of the trade-off functions in Figure 14.1.

HOW MONEY PLACED ON DEPOSIT WILL GROW

If $1,000 placed on deposit for one year earns seven percent interest, the amount of interest will be .07 times $1,000, or $70. The amount on deposit at the end of the year (assuming no withdrawals of either principal or interest) will be $1,000 plus $70, or $1,070. This simple example incorporates all the elements of compound interest. The general relationship can be expressed as:

Final Amount = Original Amount + Interest Earned

Since annual interest is usually expressed as a rate or percentage of the amount on deposit (the *principal*), the same relationship can be expressed as:

Final Amount = Original Amount + (Original Amount × Interest Rate)

Rearranging terms on the right-hand side of the equation yields:

Final Amount = Original Amount × (1 + *i*)

where *i* is the interest rate. In the illustration of $1,000 placed on deposit for one year at seven percent interest, this becomes:

$1,070 = $1,000 × 1.07

Suppose now that the $1,000 principal amount is left on deposit for three years, with interest at seven percent per year compounding annually. Annual compounding means that accumulated interest itself earns interest in all subsequent periods. Table 14.1 illustrates how compound interest accumulates so that the final amount after three years (hereafter called the *compound value*)

TABLE 14.2   Compound Value of $1 Left on Deposit (CVIF)

Year	6%	7%	8%	9%	10%	12%	14%
1	1.0600	1.0700	1.0800	1.0900	1.1000	1.1200	1.1400
2	1.1236	1.1449	1.1664	1.1881	1.2100	1.2544	1.2996
3	1.1910	1.2250	1.2597	1.2950	1.3310	1.4049	1.4815
4	1.2625	1.3108	1.3605	1.4116	1.4641	1.5735	1.6890
5	1.3382	1.4026	1.4693	1.5386	1.6105	1.7623	1.9254
6	1.4185	1.5007	1.5869	1.6771	1.7716	1.9738	2.1950
7	1.5036	1.6058	1.7138	1.8280	1.9487	2.2107	2.5023
8	1.5938	1.7182	1.8509	1.9926	2.1436	2.4760	2.8526
9	1.6895	1.8385	1.9990	2.1719	2.3579	2.7731	3.2519
10	1.7908	1.9672	2.1589	2.3674	2.5937	3.1058	3.7072
15	2.3966	2.7590	3.1722	3.6425	4.1772	5.4736	7.1379
20	3.2071	3.8697	4.6610	5.6044	6.7275	9.6463	13.7435
25	4.2919	5.4274	6.8485	8.6231	10.8347	17.0001	26.4619

totals $1,225.04. Expressed in terms of the preceding equation, the compound value at the end of three years is:

> After 1 year: $1,000 × 1.07
> After 2 years: ($1,000 × 1.07) (1.07)
> After 3 years: ($1,000 × 1.07) (1.07) (1.07)
> $\qquad$ = ($1,000) $(1.07)^3$
> $\qquad$ = $1,000 × 1.22504
> $\qquad$ = $1,225.04

This relationship among principal, compound interest and time is summarized in more general fashion as: *future value FV*

$$V_n = PV(1 + i)^n$$

where V_n is the compound value, PV is the initial amount deposited (or borrowed), i is the interest rate and n is the number of time periods involved.

The only laborious arithmetic in the formula is raising $(1 + i)$ to the nth power. For the problem illustrated, there are only three periods over which to calculate the compound value. But suppose there had been 75 periods! In the absence of a good calculator or a set of tables, the calculation of $(1 + i)^n$ would be tedious in the extreme.

Fortunately, tables are readily available that give solutions to $(1 + i)^n$ for various values of both i and n. An excerpt from such a table, showing representative values of i and n, is reproduced here as Table 14.2. A more complete table appears in Appendix A as Table A.2. Time periods in the table are expressed as years, but they could just as well be days, months, quarters or any other period appropriate to the problems being considered.

The solution shown above can be derived quickly by referring to Table 14.2. Letting the compound value interest factor, or CVIF, equal $(1 + i)^n$, our basic equation can be restated as $V_n = PV(\text{CVIF})$. Simply extract the value for CVIF by reading down the column in Table 14.2 under the seven percent rate and across the row indicating value after three years. That factor (1.2250) is the compound amount of $1 left on deposit for three years at seven percent. Multiplying this factor by the $1,000 initial payment yields the value for V.

Now consider a real estate application of compound interest. Suppose a vacant residential building lot, currently worth $5,000, is expected to increase in value at a compound annual rate of ten percent for at least the next six years. The lot's expected value after six years is expressed by the equation:

$$V_6 = PV \times (1.10)^6$$
$$= \$5,000 \times \text{CVIF}$$
$$= \$5,000 \times 1.7716$$
$$= \$8,858$$

where V_6 is expected value at the end of the sixth year. The CVIF is read from Table 14.2, at the intersection of the ten percent column and the six-year row. This factor (1.7716) multiplied by the initial $5,000 market value of the property gives its expected value of $8,858.

PRESENT VALUE OF A FUTURE AMOUNT

The equation for the future value of an initial amount can easily be altered to solve for the present value of a known future amount. The restructured equation is:

$$PV = V_n/(1 + i)^n$$

where the symbols have the same meaning as before, but the initial amount PV is the unknown. In this form, the equation is used to solve problems involving the present value of known or estimated future amounts or the interest (discount) rate required to equate known present values with known or estimated future amounts.

Example 14.1

A parcel of land is expected to be worth $1,500 per acre when water mains are extended five years hence. How much can an investor pay for the land today and still expect to earn 12 percent per annum on his investment before considering transaction costs and income taxes, assuming carrying costs (the cost to maintain the land) exactly equal rental revenue from the property?

TABLE 14.3   Present Value of $1 Due at a Future Date (PVIF)

Year	6%	7%	8%	9%	10%	12%	14%
			Annual Discount Rate				
1	0.9434	0.9346	0.9259	0.9174	0.9091	0.8929	0.8772
2	0.8900	0.8734	0.8573	0.8417	0.8264	0.7972	0.7695
3	0.8396	0.8163	0.7938	0.7722	0.7513	0.7118	0.6750
4	0.7921	0.7629	0.7350	0.7084	0.6830	0.6355	0.5921
5	0.7473	0.7130	0.6806	0.6499	0.6209	0.5674	0.5194
6	0.7050	0.6663	0.6302	0.5963	0.5645	0.5066	0.4556
7	0.6651	0.6227	0.5835	0.5470	0.5132	0.4523	0.3996
8	0.6274	0.5820	0.5403	0.5019	0.4665	0.4039	0.3506
9	0.5919	0.5439	0.5002	0.4604	0.4241	0.3606	0.3075
10	0.5584	0.5083	0.4632	0.4224	0.3855	0.3220	0.2697
15	0.4173	0.3624	0.3152	0.2745	0.2394	0.1827	0.1401
20	0.3118	0.2584	0.2145	0.1784	0.1486	0.1037	0.0728
25	0.2330	0.1842	0.1460	0.1160	0.0923	0.0588	0.0378

Example 14.1 illustrates. To solve the problem, substitute the CVIF at 12 percent and five years from Table 14.2 for $(1 + i)$ and use $1,500 as the future amount. Substituting these values into the present value equation:

$$PV = V_5/\text{CVIF}$$
$$= \$1,500/1.7623$$
$$= \$851$$

With simple algebraic sleight of hand we can reconfigure $PV = V_n/\text{CVIF}$ to read $PV = V_n \times (1/\text{CVIF})$. Note that performing the multiplication in our restructured equation (that is, multiplying V_n by 1) takes us right back to the original formulation. With this restructured format we are able to consistently multiply by factors in compound interest or discount tables. Table A.1 in Appendix A provides values for $1/\text{CVIF}$, which we use when solving for present values of single sums due in the future. Table 14.3 is an excerpt from Table A.1.

To employ Table 14.3 to answer the question posed in Example 14.1, we restate the equation as:

$$PV = V_5 \times \text{PVIF}$$

where PVIF (that is, present value interest factor) is the value of a factor taken from Table 14.3. Read down the 12 percent column and across the five-year row. The factor at the intersection of the column and row is 0.5674. Multiplying this factor by the $1,500 expected future value of the land gives the present value per acre (rounded to the nearest dollar) of $851 when the future value is discounted at 12 percent.

Note the distinction between Tables 14.2 and 14.3. The first gives values for $(1 + i)^n$, while the latter gives values for $1/(1 + i)^n$. Because these are reciprocals of each other, separate tables are not really needed. All the values for either table can be derived by dividing the corresponding values from the

FIGURE 14.2 Relationship Between Present Value and Future Value When Compounding and Discounting at 12 Percent

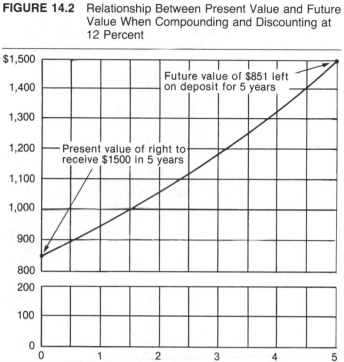

other table into 1. This reciprocal relationship is illustrated in Figure 14.2, with reference to Example 14.1. The future value of the land ($1,500) is the compound amount of $851 growing at 12 percent per annum for five years. Conversely, the value to the investor ($851) is the present value of $1,500 to be received in five years, when discounted at 12 percent per annum.

A by-product of the convenience of separate tables for present and future values is the problem of determining which to use. One way to keep this straight is to remember that the solution to factors on the future-value table is always greater than that for the present value at the same interest rate (so long as the rate is greater than zero). This reflects the basic idea that an amount received in the present is always more valuable than the promise of receiving the same amount at a future date. The future amount must be larger to induce one to wait.

HOW A SERIES OF DEPOSITS WILL GROW

Our discussion so far has focused on the present and the future value of a single sum: how a deposit grows or the present value of a single amount due in the future. But suppose a series of amounts is to be left on deposit or the present value of a series of payments or receipts must be determined?

Consider first the case of a series of fixed payments left on deposit. Any series of equal periodic amounts is called an *annuity*. Conventionally, annuity payments are assumed to be made at the end of each period, though this is not a necessary assumption. Tables can be designed with any desired assumption about the timing of periodic cash flows. As a matter of convention, however, most annuity tables are designed with the assumption that all cash flow occurs instantaneously at the end of each period. For example, payments of $500 per annum made at the end of each year for five years constitute a five-year annuity. If these payments were deposited into an account paying seven percent per annum, how much would be in the account at the time the last payment is made?

The first payment draws interest for four years, the second for three years, the third for two years, the fourth for one year and the final payment draws no interest at all. If the compound values of all these payments are summed, the total is the compound value of the annuity. The problem is expressed algebraically as:

$$S = R_1 (1 + i)^{n-1} + R_2 (1 + i)^{n-2} + R_3 (1 + i)^{n-3} + \ldots +$$
$$R_{n-1} (1 + i) + R_n$$
$$= R_k [(1 + i)^{n-1} + (1 + i)^{n-2} + (1 + i)^{n-3} + \ldots +$$
$$(1 + i) + 1]$$

where S is the compound value of the series of payments, R is the amount of the level annual payment, i is the compound annual interest rate and n is the number of payments to be made. For convenience, the above expression is frequently condensed as follows:

$$S = R_k \left[\sum_{t=1}^{n-1} (1 + i)^t + 1 \right]$$

where $\sum_{t=1}^{n-1}$ simply means add together the values of $(1 + i)^t$ for n minus one periods, and t indicates the time periods from one through n minus one.

Substituting $500 for R_k, seven percent for i, and five years for n, we solve for the compound value of $500 per year for five years:

$$S = \$500 \left[\sum_{t=1}^{4} (1.07)^t + 1 \right]$$

$$= \$500 [(1.07) + (1.07)^2 + (1.07)^3 + (1.07)^4 + 1]$$
$$= \$500 \times 5.75074$$
$$= \$2,875.37$$

The solution can be reached much more conveniently by referring to tables that give the value of the bracketed term in the above equation. Values for the compound value interest factor, annuity (CVIFa), can be found in Table A.5 of Appendix A and in the excerpt from that table presented here as Table 14.4. Read across the top of the table to the seven percent column and down the left margin to the five-year row. The value found at the intersection of the column

FIGURE 14.3   How $500 Deposited at the End of Each Year
for Five Years Will Grow

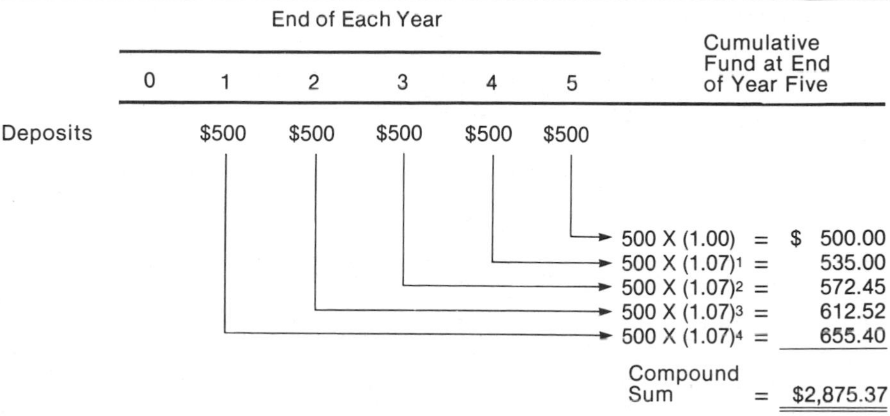

	End of Each Year						Cumulative Fund at End of Year Five
	0	1	2	3	4	5	
Deposits		$500	$500	$500	$500	$500	

$$500 \times (1.00) = \$\ 500.00$$
$$500 \times (1.07)^1 = 535.00$$
$$500 \times (1.07)^2 = 572.45$$
$$500 \times (1.07)^3 = 612.52$$
$$500 \times (1.07)^4 = 655.40$$

Compound
Sum $= \$2,875.37$

TABLE 14.4   How $1 Deposited at the End of Each Year Will Grow (CVIFa)

	Annual Interest Rate						
Year	*6%*	*7%*	*8%*	*9%*	*10%*	*12%*	*14%*
1	1.00000	1.00000	1.00000	1.00000	1.00000	1.00000	1.00000
2	2.06000	2.07000	2.08000	2.09000	2.10000	2.12000	2.14000
3	3.18360	3.21490	3.24640	3.27810	3.31000	3.37440	3.43960
4	4.37462	4.43994	4.50611	4.57313	4.64100	4.77933	4.92114
5	5.63709	5.75074	5.86660	5.98471	6.10510	6.35285	6.61010
6	6.97532	7.15329	7.33593	7.52333	7.71561	8.11519	8.53552
7	8.39384	8.65402	8.92280	9.20043	9.48717	10.08901	10.73049
8	9.89747	10.25980	10.63663	11.02847	11.43589	12.29969	13.23276
9	11.49132	11.97799	12.48756	13.02104	13.57948	14.77566	16.08535
10	13.18079	13.81645	14.48656	15.19293	15.93742	17.54874	19.33730
15	23.27597	25.12902	27.15211	29.36092	31.77248	37.27971	43.84241
20	36.78559	40.99549	45.76196	51.16012	57.27500	72.05244	91.02493
25	54.86451	63.24904	73.10594	84.70090	98.34706	133.33387	181.87083

and row is 5.75074. Substituting this value for the bracketed term in the equation above, we determine the compound amount to be $500 × 5.75074 = $2,875.37. This solution is diagramed in Figure 14.3.

PRESENT VALUE OF AN ANNUITY

We have seen that any series of periodic payments received or paid at regular intervals may be called an annuity. Examples include pension checks from a retirement fund or payments on a fully amortized installment note. While all such regular periodic streams of cash technically qualify as annuities, not all are popularly known as such. The present value of an annuity is best thought of as the amount that, if invested today at a given interest rate, will provide the known periodic payments for the prescribed period.

To illustrate, suppose funds are to be placed on deposit with interest at six percent per annum, sufficient to permit withdrawals in $1,000 increments at the end of each year for three years. To determine the amount of the required initial deposit (assuming there is to be a balance of exactly zero after the third annual withdrawal), the problem might be broken into three separate sub-questions:

- *Subquestion 1:* How much must be deposited today to accumulate $1,000 in one year? To solve this question, first restructure the basic equation to solve for the present value of a single future amount:

$$PV = R_1 \times 1/(1 + i)$$
$$= R_1 \times \text{PVIF}$$

where R_1 is the first periodic withdrawal, i is the interest rate and there is just one compounding period. PVIF is the value for $(1 + i)$ taken from Table 14.3. Substituting the appropriate numerical values into the equation, we have:

$$PV = \$1,000 \times 1/(1.06)$$
$$= \$1,000 \times \text{PVIF}$$
$$= \$1,000 \times .9434$$

- *Subquestion 2:* How much must be deposited today to accumulate $1,000 in two years? Again, substituting the appropriate numbers into the basic equation, we have:

$$PV = \$1,000 \times 1/(1.06)^2$$
$$= \$1,000 \times \text{PVIF}$$
$$= \$1,000 \times .8900$$

- *Subquestion 3:* How much must be deposited today to provide $1,000 in three years? Numerical substitution results in the following equation:

$$PV = \$1,000 \times 1/(1.06)^3$$
$$= \$1,000 \times \text{PVIF}$$
$$= \$1,000 \times .8396$$

The total amount to be deposited to provide for the three annual withdrawals is the sum of the three values just calculated. Therefore, the total present value *PV*, the amount to be placed on deposit, is:

$$PV = [\$1,000 \times 1/(1.06)] + [\$1,000 \times 1/(1.06)^2] + [\$1,000 \times 1/(1.06)^3]$$
$$= \$1,000 [1/(1.06) + 1/(1.06)^2 + 1/(1.06)^3]$$

TABLE 14.5 Present Value of an Annuity of $1 Per Year (PVIFa)

Year	6%	7%	8%	9%	10%	12%	14%
			Annual Discount Rate				
1	0.9434	0.9346	0.9259	0.9174	0.9091	0.8929	0.8772
2	1.8334	1.8080	1.7833	1.7591	1.7355	1.6901	1.6467
3	2.6730	2.6243	2.5771	2.5313	2.4869	2.4018	2.3216
4	3.4651	3.3872	3.3121	3.2397	3.1699	3.0373	2.9137
5	4.2124	4.1002	3.9927	3.8897	3.7908	3.6048	3.4331
6	4.9173	4.7665	4.6229	4.4859	4.3553	4.1114	3.8887
7	5.5824	5.3893	5.2064	5.0330	4.8684	4.5638	4.2883
8	6.2098	5.9713	5.7466	5.5348	5.3349	4.9676	4.6389
9	6.8017	6.5152	6.2469	5.9952	5.7590	5.3282	4.9464
10	7.3601	7.0236	6.7101	6.4177	6.1446	5.6502	5.2161
15	9.7122	9.1079	8.5595	8.0607	7.6061	6.8109	6.1422
20	11.4699	10.5940	9.8181	9.1285	8.5136	7.4694	6.6231
25	12.7834	11.6536	10.6748	9.8226	9.0770	7.8431	6.8729
30	13.7648	12.4090	11.2578	10.2737	9.4269	8.0552	7.0027

Values for $(1/1.06)^t$, where t ranges from one through three, are found in the six percent column in Table 14.3. Summing these three factors, we get:

$$PV = \$1,000 \times (0.9434 + 0.8900 + 0.8396)$$
$$= \$1,000 \times 2.6730$$
$$= \$2,673$$

The general form of the preceding computation can be expressed as:

$$PV = R_k \times \left[1/(1 + i) + 1/(1 + i)^2 + \ldots + 1/(1 + i)^n \right]$$

where R_k is the amount of a level periodic receipt, PV is the initial deposit and i is the discount (interest) rate.

Alternatively, the same concept can be expressed as:

$$PV = R_k \left[\sum_{t=1}^{n} 1/(1 + i)^t \right]$$

The practical problem in solving these calculations is the time required to do the computations when the number of compounding periods and thus the number of values summed from the PVIF table is very large. Precomputed tables for the cumulative PVIF again simplify the problem. These cumulative values, which we will designate PVIFa (for present value interest factor, annuity), are presented in Table A.3 in Appendix A. An excerpt is presented here as Table 14.5

Returning to the problem of a three-year annuity of $1,000 per year with a six percent per annum discount (interest) rate, determining the present value (that is, the required initial deposit) involves finding the annuity factor in Table 14.5, which lies at the intersection of the six percent column and the three-year row. This factor (2.6730) multiplied by the $1,000 annual annuity payment equals the amount of the initial deposit ($2,673):

$$PV = R_k \times \text{PVIFa}$$
$$= \$1,000 \times 2.6730$$
$$= \$2,673$$

PRESENT VALUE OF A PERPETUAL ANNUITY

A *perpetuity* is a never-ending stream of payments or receipts. For such a cash flow pattern to exist, it must necessarily be the case that each installment represents only accrued interest. If some principal were retired with each payment, then the principal would eventually be exhausted and the stream would end; there would not be a perpetual flow. This being the case, it follows that each payment is simply the interest rate per period multiplied by the principal amount of the annuity:

$$R_k = PV \times i$$

where R_k is the periodic payment or receipt, P is the present value (principal amount) of the annuity and i is the rate of interest per period. To solve for the present value, simply transpose the symbols in the equation:

$$PV = R_k / i$$

To illustrate, consider a perpetual annuity of $10,000 per annum, with interest at eight percent per annum. The present value of the perpetuity is:

$$PV = R_k / i$$
$$= \$10,000 / .08$$
$$= \$125,000$$

Suppose the appropriate discount rate associated with the above annuity moves to, say, ten percent per annum. This reduces the present value of the perpetuity to $100,000:

$$PV = R_k / i$$
$$= \$10,000 / .10$$
$$= \$100,000$$

This result leads to the generalized observation that there is an inverse relationship between the discount rate and the present value of any future series of payments or receipts.

PAYMENTS TO AMORTIZE A LOAN

Suppose you were to receive a lump-sum educational grant of $10,000 to be spent during four years of university study. How much could you withdraw at the end of each year, in four equal installments, to exactly exhaust the fund with the last annual withdrawal if the balance in the fund draws interest at six percent? This is an annuity problem not unlike those investigated earlier. Recall the general expression for a level annuity, which is:

$$PV = R_k \left[\sum_{t=1}^{n} 1/(1 + i)^t \right]$$
$$= R_k \times \text{PVIFa}$$

The essential difference here is that the initial payment *PV* is known and the periodic receipt R_k is the unknown quantity. The problem can be solved using factors from Table 14.5. First, find the value from the table for the summation of $1/(1 + i)^t$, where the interest rate, *i*, is six percent, and the time periods range from one through four years. The factor is 3.4651. The problem can thus be expressed as:

$$PV = R_k \times \text{PVIFa}$$
$$= R_k \times 3.4651$$

and, since the value of *PV* is known to be $10,000:

$$\$10,000 = R_k \times \text{PVIFa}$$
$$= R_k \times 3.4651$$

Solving for R_k yields:

$$R_k = \$10,000/\text{PVIFa}$$
$$= \$10,000/3.4651$$
$$= \$2,885.92$$

Note that the final solution involves dividing by a factor from the annuity present value table. Recall that division is the same as multiplying by a reciprocal (that is, $a/b = a \times 1/b$). Tables can easily be generated that incorporate reciprocals of values from PVIFa tables. Such a table (incorporating monthly, rather than annual, payments) is included here as Table 14.6. A more complete table appears as Table A.4 in Appendix A.

The factors in Table 14.6 are often called *loan-amortization factors*, or *debt constants*. The table itself is then referred to as an *amortization table*. It gives the equal periodic payment necessary to repay a $1 loan, with interest, over a specified number of payment periods. (A table showing the distribution of a specific payment schedule between principal and interest is frequently called an *amortization schedule*.) Because Table 14.6 gives repayment factors based on monthly payments, it is not reciprocal to Table 14.5. A table of annual payments, however, would be.

To see how an amortization table works, consider a $100,000 loan that calls for interest at eight percent per annum on the unpaid balance. If the loan is to be repaid in equal monthly installments (including both interest and principal) over, say, five years, monthly payment obligations can be determined by multiplying the $100,000 face amount by the amortization factor from Table 14.6, which lies at the intersection of the eight percent column and the five-year row. The product, $2,027.60, is the amount the lender must receive each

TABLE 14.6 Monthly Payment to Amortize a $1 Debt

Year	Annual Interest Rate						
	6%	7%	8%	9%	10%	12%	14%
1	0.086066	0.086527	0.086988	0.087451	0.087916	0.088849	0.089787
2	0.044321	0.044773	0.045227	0.045685	0.046145	0.047073	0.048013
3	0.030422	0.030877	0.031336	0.031800	0.032267	0.033214	0.034178
4	0.023485	0.023946	0.024413	0.024885	0.025363	0.026334	0.027326
5	0.019333	0.019801	0.020276	0.020758	0.021247	0.022244	0.023268
6	0.016573	0.017049	0.017533	0.018026	0.018526	0.019550	0.020606
7	0.014609	0.015093	0.015586	0.016089	0.016601	0.017653	0.018740
8	0.013141	0.013634	0.014137	0.014650	0.015174	0.016253	0.017372
9	0.012006	0.012506	0.013019	0.013543	0.014079	0.015184	0.016334
10	0.011102	0.011611	0.012133	0.012668	0.013215	0.014347	0.015527
15	0.008439	0.008988	0.009557	0.010143	0.010746	0.012002	0.013317
20	0.007164	0.007753	0.008364	0.008997	0.009650	0.011011	0.012435
25	0.006443	0.007068	0.007718	0.008392	0.009087	0.010532	0.012038
30	0.005996	0.006653	0.007338	0.008046	0.008776	0.010286	0.011849

month for five years to recover the initial $100,000 outlay and receive eight percent per annum interest on the outstanding balance of the loan.

Had the $100,000 loan in the preceding example called for annual payments, Table 14.6 would not have been usable. No table of annual amortization payments is given, because loans seldom provide for this repayment pattern. But an amortization factor can be derived easily by calculating the reciprocal of the factor for an eight percent, five-year annuity. Divide the annuity factor, 3.9927 from Table 14.5, into one. The quotient, 0.25046, is the annual payment to retire a five-year, eight percent loan of $1, with annual payments. Multiplying this factor by a $100,000 loan amount gives the annual payment necessary to retire the loan in five years: $25,046. The problem also can be solved without reference to tables. With annual payments, the equation is:

$$\text{Payment} = \text{Loan Amount} \times \left[i/(1 - [1/(1 + i)^n]) \right]$$

If payments are made monthly, the equation is revised accordingly:

$$\text{Payment} = \text{Loan Amount} \times \left[(i/12)/(1 - [1/(1 + i/12)^{12 \times n}]) \right]$$

Note that an annual payment is somewhat more than the sum of 12 monthly payments on a loan of the same size with the same amortization period and interest rate ($25,046 vs. $24,331.20 in the preceding example). This is because interest on the outstanding balance is greater for the annual payment note as a result of the balance not having been "paid down" at monthly intervals during the year. In general, the more frequently payments are made, the less the total interest obligation will be and thus the less the total debt service payment.

EXTENDING THE USEFULNESS OF FINANCIAL TABLES

Tables can help solve a wide variety of real estate investment and financial problems. Several applications are illustrated here to provide additional exercise in using the tables, as well as to demonstrate their versatility. These extended uses are by no means exhaustive. They are intended rather to demonstrate the flexibility of compound interest and discount concepts, the total usefulness of which is limited only by imagination and inventiveness.

Finding Values Not in the Tables

Interest and discount tables give factors for values at intervals over a wide range. Sometimes, however, the rate under consideration falls at an intermediate point between those in a table. When this happens, estimate the actual value by *interpolating* between table values most nearly approximating the rate being sought.

Interpolation involves assuming a linear relationship between tabular values. This introduces a degree of error, since the actual relationship is quadratic rather than linear. The convenient assumption greatly simplifies calculations, however, and the error will generally be insignificant if interpolation is between those tabular values closest to the unknown factor.

The problem is illustrated in Figure 14.4. The curved line shows the relationship between values from the PVIFa table (Table 14.5) for discount rates of seven and eight percent and for all intermediate discount rates. Interpolation results in estimates of values not in the table, as indicated by the straight line in the illustration. Distance between the curved (actual) function and the straight (estimated) line represents error introduced by interpolation. Obviously, the wider apart the known values from which an unknown factor is estimated, the greater the error introduced by the assumption of linearity.

Figure 14.4 depicts the consequence of using straight-line interpolation to estimate the appropriate present value factor for a five-year annuity when the discount rate is 7.25 percent. The PVIFa table (Table 14.5) gives annuity present value factors for discount rates of seven and eight percent but for no intermediate rates. Since 7.25 percent falls one-fourth of the way between these given factors, approximate an appropriate factor by moving one-fourth of the distance between the factor for seven percent and that for eight percent. The seven percent factor is 4.1002, and that for eight percent is 3.9927. Multiply the difference by 0.25 and subtract this amount from the factor for seven percent. The result is a factor of 4.0733, determined as follows:

$$4.1002 - 0.25 (4.1002 - 3.9927) = 4.0733$$

Figure 14.5 diagrams the preceding calculations. The total number of percentage points between seven and eight percent is eight minus seven, or one

FIGURE 14.4   Interpolating Between Known Present Value Factors

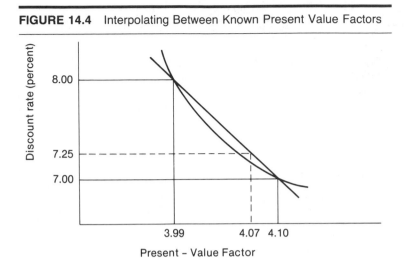

FIGURE 14.5   Interpolating to Find Values Not on the Tables

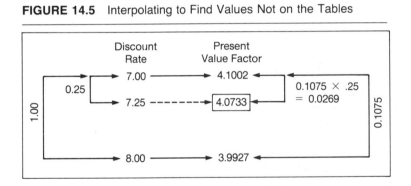

point. The distance between discount rates of seven and 7.25 percent is 7.25 minus seven, or 0.25 point. Since 0.25 point is 25 percent of one point, the "target" discount rate lies 25 percent of the distance between the known values. Assume a linear relationship and estimate the discount factor for the 7.25 percent rate by moving 25 percent of the distance between the discount factor for seven percent and that for eight percent.

The total distance between the factor for seven percent, 4.1002, and that for eight percent, 3.9927, is 0.1075. Twenty-five percent of this distance is 0.25×0.1075, or 0.0269. Moving this far from the 4.1002 value associated with the seven percent discount rate results in an estimate of 4.0733 for the factor associated with a discount rate of 7.25 percent.

Effective Interest Rates

Effective interest rates are those actually paid for the use of borrowed funds. They often differ strikingly from rates quoted by lenders. Effective rates are a function of the amount borrowed and the amount and timing of the required repayment.

Common instances of differences between *nominal interest rates* (rates quoted by a lender) and effective rates on term loans occur when the lender charges a *loan origination fee,* sometimes called *discount points,* and disburses only the remaining balance. Alternatively, the lender may disburse the full face amount of the note but require the borrower to immediately remit a specified percentage of the face amount as an origination fee. The net effect is the same in either case: The borrower has the use of only a fraction of the funds stipulated in the promissory note. Interest and principal payments, however, are based on the full face amount of the note. Because the borrower is paying interest (and making amortization payments) on funds he or she never receives, the effective interest rate exceeds the stated, or nominal, rate.

Example 14.2

A borrower signs a $10,000 promissory note payable in equal monthly installments over five years, with interest at eight percent per annum on the unpaid balance. The lender charges a loan origination fee (points) equal to two percent of the face amount of the loan. Monthly payments are determined with reference to the amortization factors in Table 14.6:

$$
\begin{aligned}
\text{Payments} &= \text{Face Amount of Loan} \times \text{Amortization Factor} \\
&= \$10,000 \times 0.020276 \\
&= \$202.76
\end{aligned}
$$

The borrower has the use of only $9,800, however. This amount, called the *net loan proceeds,* is determined by subtracting the loan origination fee from the face amount of the loan:

$$
\begin{aligned}
\text{Net Loan Proceeds} &= \text{Face Amount of Loan} - \text{Origination Fee} \\
&= \$10,000 - .02(\$10,000) \\
&= \$10,000 - \$200 \\
&= \$9,800
\end{aligned}
$$

The effective interest rate is the rate that would require monthly payments of $202.76 to amortize the net loan proceeds. This rate is 8.9 percent, determined as follows:

$$
\text{Payments} = \text{Net Loan Proceeds} \times \text{Amortization Factor}
$$

Since the payments and the net loan proceeds are known:

$$
\$202.76 = \$9,800 \times \text{Amortization Factor}
$$

we can solve for the unknown factor:

$$\text{Amortization Factor} = \$202.76/\$9,800$$
$$= 0.02069$$

Reference to the five-year row of Table 14.6 reveals that this amortization factor lies between eight and nine percent. Interpolation in the manner explained earlier reveals that the effective rate is approximately 8.9 percent.

Remaining Balance of a Note

Understanding the reciprocity of annuity tables and amortization tables (with the same time period between payments) sets the stage for easily determining the remaining balance on a fully amortizing note. The face amount of a note can be thought of as the present value of an annuity whose periodic receipts are the debt service payments. But amortization tables are used because the present value is known and the future payments are unknown, whereas with conventional annuity problems the known factors are the future payments, and the present value is unknown.

To see this relationship clearly, consider a $100,000 loan calling for level monthly payments to fully amortize the loan over 25 years, with interest at nine percent. Referring to the amortization table (Table 14.6), multiply the factor found at the intersection of the nine percent column and the 25-year row by the $100,000 face amount of the loan. The monthly payment is found to be $839.20.

Now, remembering the reciprocal relationship between annuity and amortization tables, use the amortization table to determine the present value of a monthly annuity of $839.20 that extends for 25 years, when discounted at nine percent. To derive the present value factor for the monthly annuity, go back to the intersection of the nine percent column and 25-year row of the amortization table and divide the factor into one. The result, $1/.008392 = 119.16$, when multiplied by the monthly payment, yields a present value of approximately $100,000. We, of course, already knew this to be the present value, since that is the amount of the original loan. The approach, however, can be used to determine the remaining balance at any future date.

When the loan has been outstanding for, say, five years, a portion of the principal will have been retired. To determine the remaining balance, simply recall that the balance is the amount that the (known) remaining debt service payments will retire over the remaining period. The relationship can be expressed as:

$$\text{Monthly Payment} = \text{Remaining Balance} \times \text{Amortization Factor}$$

Therefore (with 20 years remaining):

$$\text{Remaining Balance} = \text{Payment} \times 1/\text{Amortization Factor}$$
$$= \$839.20 \times 1/.008997$$
$$= \$93,275.54$$

The amortization factor in the above calculation is found in Table 14.6 at the intersection of the nine percent column and the 20-year row, which is the number of years remaining on the loan.

Present Value of a Deferred Annuity

To find the present value of an annuity that does not start until some time in the future, find the value of the annuity at the beginning of the first year of payments or receipts and then discount this amount to the present as a single sum. Alternatively, solve for an annuity that extends over both the annuity payment period and the period of the deferral and subtract the present value of the annuity for the period of the deferral; the remainder is the present value of the deferred annuity.

Example 14.3

Determine the present value, when discounting at six percent per annum, of a five-year annuity of $1,000 per annum (paid at the end of each year), with the first annuity payment due four years hence.

Example 14.3 illustrates the problem. The first annuity payment or receipt is due in four years. Since payments are made at the end of each year, the annuity period actually starts at the beginning of the year in which the first payment is made. There is, therefore, a three-year lapse before the annuity period starts.

Solution Alternative A.   The first step is to solve for the value of the annuity at the beginning of the annuity period (three years hence). At that point there is a straightforward five-year annuity of $1,000 per annum. The value at that point (which we will call V_3) is $4,212.40, determined as follows:

$$V_3 = R_k \times \text{PVIFa}$$
$$= \$1,000 \times 4.2124$$
$$= \$4,212.40$$

The second step is to discount V_3 as a single sum due three years hence. The present value is $3,537. Here is the calculation:

$$PV = V_3 \times \text{PVIF}$$
$$= \$4,212.40 \times .8396$$
$$= \$3,536.73$$

These two steps can of course be combined into a single mathematical operation, with the same results. Here is the combined computation:

$$PV = R_k \, (\text{PVIFa} \times \text{PVIF})$$
$$= \$1{,}000 \, (4.2124 \times .8396)$$
$$= \$1{,}000 \times 3.53673$$
$$= \$3{,}536.73$$

Solution Alternative B.   Determine what the present value would be if the annuity extended over both the deferral period and the payment period (three years + five years = eight years). From this value subtract the value of the annuity for the first three years (the period of the deferral). The remainder is the present value of the annuity for the period in which it is actually to be received.

For the annuity in Example 14.3, the present value would be $6,209.80 if payments extended over the entire eight-year period:

$$PV = R_k \times \text{PVIFa}$$
$$= \$1{,}000 \times 6.2098$$
$$= \$6{,}209.80$$

From this amount subtract the value of the annuity for the period of the deferral. This is three years, and the value to be subtracted is $2,673, determined as follows:

$$PV = R_k \times \text{PVIFa}$$
$$= \$1{,}000 \times 2.6730$$
$$= \$2{,}673$$

The present value of the five-year annuity that will be received, starting after three years, is simply the present value of the last five years of the eight-year annuity. To find this amount, subtract the present value of the three-year annuity (the portion of the eight-year annuity that will not be received) from the present value of the eight-year annuity. The computation yields the same solution as before, except for a small rounding error. Here are the numbers:

$$PV = \$6{,}209.80 - \$2{,}673$$
$$= \$3{,}536.80$$

These computations can also be consolidated into a single equation, with the same results:

$$PV = R_k(\text{PVIFa}_8) - R_k(\text{PVIFa}_3)$$
$$= R_k(\text{PVIFa}_8 - \text{PVIFa}_3)$$
$$= \$1{,}000 \, (6.2098 - 2.6730)$$
$$= \$1{,}000 \times 3.5368$$
$$= \$3{,}536.80$$

Annuities in Advance

Our earlier statement that annuity payments or receipts are treated as if the transaction occurred at the end of each period needs further elaboration. This is not a necessary assumption for using discounting and compounding; it is merely a convention adopted when constructing annuity tables. A table incorporating the assumption that cash flow occurs at the beginning of each period, or at any intermediate point within the periods, could easily be developed.

Such tables are not frequently available. Existing tables must therefore be modified when working with cash flows that occur at the beginning of each period. Annuities with this sort of schedule are conventionally called *annuities in advance*.

To find the present value of annuities in advance, simply multiply the annual amount by the PVIFa (from the annuity table) for the number of payments minus one and add one additional payment. Example 14.4 illustrates.

Example 14.4

Determine the present value of an annuity of $1,000 per annum for five years when the appropriate discount rate is six percent per annum and when the annuity payment is made at the beginning of each year. Round all values to nearest whole dollar.

$$PV = (R_k \times \text{PVIFa}_4) + R$$
$$= (\$1,000 \times 3.4651) + \$1,000$$
$$= \$3,465 + \$1,000$$
$$= \$4,465$$

To find the compound value of an annuity wherein payments are made at the beginning rather than the end of each period, multiply the amount of the annual annuity payment by the factor from the table for the compound value interest factor, annuity (Table 14.4), for one year more than the actual number of payments and subtract the amount of one payment. Example 14.5 demonstrates these calculations.

Example 14.5

Determine the compound (future) value of an annuity of $1,000 per annum for five years when the compound interest rate is six percent per annum and when payments are made at the beginning of each year. Round all amounts to nearest whole dollar.

$$S = R_k (\text{CVIFa}_6) - R$$
$$= \$1,000 (6.9753) - \$1,000$$
$$= \$6,975 - \$1,000$$
$$= \$5,975$$

SUMMARY

Several interest factor tables are explained in this chapter. Basic explanations of their use are summarized below.

Single Payment or Receipt. To find the future value of a single sum received or deposited, use the compound amount factor from Table 14.2:

$$V_n = PV \times \text{CVIF}$$

where V_n is the future value, PV is the initial deposit or receipt and CVIF is the factor for $(1 + i)^n$ taken from Table 14.2.

To find the present value of a single sum to be received or paid in the future, use the present value factor from Table 14.3. The formula is:

$$PV = V_n \times \text{PVIF}$$

where PV is the present value, V_n is the amount to be paid or received at the end of year n and PVIF is the factor for $1/(1 + i)^n$ taken from Table 14.3.

Value of an Annuity. Use the annuity present value factors from Table 14.5 to find the present value of a level series of receipts or payments. Use the factors to solve the equation:

$$PV = R_k \times \text{PVIFa}$$

where PV is the present value of the annuity, R_k is the level periodic payment or receipt and PVIFa is the factor for the summation of:

$$(1 + i) + (1 + i)^2 + (1 + i)^3 + \ldots + (1 + i)^n$$

Installment to Amortize a Note. Amortization tables are simply the reciprocal of those for the present value of an annuity. However, annuity problems generally involve annual cash flows, whereas most promissory notes require monthly payments. Using annual tables to solve problems involving monthly debt service payments overstates both the annual interest expense and total debt service obligations. For these reasons, a separate table of monthly amortization factors is provided in Table 14.6.

Use amortization tables to solve the equation:

$$R_k = PV \times \text{monthly constant}$$

where R_k is the monthly payment required on a note, PV is the face amount of the note and the monthly constant is the factor taken from the amortization table for a specified contract rate of interest.

RECOMMENDED READINGS

Brigham, Eugene F. *Fundamentals of Financial Management*, 4th ed. Hinsdale, IL: The Dryden Press, 1986. pp. 78–110.

Eply, Donald R., and James H. Boykin. *Basic Income Property Appraisal*. Reading, MA: Addison-Wesley, 1983, pp. 140–156.

Friedman, Jack P., and Nicholas Ordway. *Income Property Appraisal and Analysis*. Reston, VA: Reston, 1981, pp. 77–96.

Goebel, Paul R., and Norman G. Miller. *Handbook of Mortgage Mathematics and Financial Tables*. Englewood Cliffs, NJ: Prentice-Hall, 1981.

Greer, Gaylon E. *The Real Estate Investment Decision*. Lexington, MA: Heath, 1979, pp. 119–174.

Greer, Gaylon E., and Michael D. Farrell. *Contemporary Real Estate: Theory and Practice*. Hinsdale, IL: The Dryden Press, 1983, pp. 281–298.

Hoaglund, Henry E., Leo D. Stone, and William B. Bruggerman. *Real Estate Finance*. 7th ed. Homewood, IL: Richard D. Irwin, 1982, pp. 157–179.

REVIEW QUESTIONS

1. What happens to the relationship between present value and annual annuity payments as the annuity gets progressively longer? What happens to the present value at the extreme as the length of the annuity approaches infinity?

2. How can a table of present value factors for single sums to be received in the future be derived from a table of present value factors of an annuity?

3. Explain why the error introduced by interpolating between present value factors found on a table of such factors increases as the distance between the known factors increases.

4. What is the relationship between present value factors for an annuity and factors from an amortization table? Can one such table be derived from another?

5. Assuming the interest rates and terms of two debts are identical, will the amortization factor for a mortgage debt that calls for annual payments be equal to, more than or less than 12 times the monthly factor for a debt that calls for monthly payments?

6. What is the relationship between present value of a discounted series of cash flows and the internal rate of return?

DISCUSSION QUESTIONS

1. In what way might one's desire for present rather than future receipt of funds be related to one's attitude toward risk?

2. Over how many years must a level annuity stretch before, for practical purposes, one might just as well treat it as a perpetual annuity? Why might such treatment ever be justified?

3. The present value of an annuity always continues to grow as the length of the annuity gets longer. Why, then, isn't the present value of a perpetual annuity infinitely great?
4. Explain why each payment on an otherwise identical monthly amortizing loan would not be exactly one-twelfth that of an annual payment loan.

APPENDIX 14.A: Compounding and Discounting with Financial Calculators

Financial tables such as those discussed in Chapter 14 and presented in Appendix A at the end of the text have for many years been a major labor-saving device for analysts by greatly simplifying computational chores. The tables themselves are well on their way to being outmoded, however, by the ready availability of low-cost electronic calculators programmed to do financial computations. Many of these calculators are not much larger than a standard business card (some are even incorporated into wristwatches) and many of them cost less than a book of financial tables.

This appendix is intended to demonstrate the use of financial calculators to solve problems such as those explained in Chapter 14. To show comparability of calculator solutions with those derived from tables, each example demonstrates how table values themselves may be derived by using calculators. Illustrations then show how calculators can be utilized to find other values that are not found in the tables.

FUTURE VALUE OF A DOLLAR

The CVIF factor (Table A.2 of Appendix A) is used to calculate how a sum left on deposit at a compound rate of interest will grow. The compound interest formula is:

$$FV = PV (1 + i)^n$$

where:

$$FV = \text{Future Value}$$
$$PV = \text{Present Value (amount invested today)}$$
$$i = \text{Rate}$$
$$n = \text{Number of Periods}$$

Example 14.A.1

The CVIF for three years at eight percent (shown on Table A.2 in Appendix A) is calculated as follows:

$$FV = 1 (1 + .08)^3$$
$$= 1.2597$$

The CVIF factor in Example 14.A.1 can be determined using a calculator with the keys $\boxed{n}$, $\boxed{i}$, $\boxed{PV}$, $\boxed{PMT}$ and $\boxed{FV}$ by entering $\boxed{n} = 3$, $\boxed{i} = 8$, $\boxed{PV} = 1$ and solving for $\boxed{FV}$. To calculate the factors for Example 14.A.1 and all following examples in this appendix, use the following substitutions:

1. *Monthly Factors*
   $n = \text{Number of Months}$
   $i = \text{Annual Rate}/12$

2. *Quarterly Factors*
   $n = \text{Number of Quarters}$
   $i = \text{Annual Rate}/4$

3. *Semiannual Factors*
   $n = \text{Number of Half Years}$
   $i = \text{Annual Rate}/2$

Example 14.A.2

1. *FV* of one for three years at eight percent per annum, compounded monthly.

   $$FV = 1 (1 + .006667)^{36}$$
   $$= 1.27025$$

   Calculator solution:

   $\boxed{n} = 36 \quad \boxed{i} = 8/12$
   $\boxed{PV} = 1 \quad \boxed{FV} = ?$

2. *FV* of one for three years at eight percent, compounded quarterly.

$$FV = 1 (1 + .02)^{12}$$
$$= 1.26824$$

Calculator solution:

$\boxed{n} = 12 \quad \boxed{i} = 8/4$
$\boxed{PV} = 1 \quad \boxed{FV} = ?$

3. *FV* of one for three years at eight percent, compounded semiannually.

$$FV = 1 (1 + .04)^6$$
$$= 1.26532$$

Calculator solution:

$\boxed{n} = 6 \quad \boxed{i} = 8/2$
$\boxed{PV} = 1 \quad \boxed{FV} = ?$

COMPOUND VALUE OF AN ANNUITY

The CVIFa factor, Table A.5 of Appendix A, is used to calculate how much an amount invested periodically will be worth at some future date if it earns interest at a compound rate. The compound value formula is:

$$FV = PMT \times \left([(1 + i)^n - 1]/i \right)$$

where:

FV = Future Value
PMT = Payment (amount invested periodically)
i = Rate
n = Number of Periods

Example 14.A.3

The future worth of an annuity factor for three years at eight percent is calculated as follows:

$$FV = 1 \times \left([(1 + .08)^3 - 1]/.08 \right)$$
$$= 3.2464$$

The factor in Example 14.A.3 can be determined with a financial calculator by entering $\boxed{n}$ = 3, $\boxed{i}$ = 8, $\boxed{PMT}$ = 1 and solving for $\boxed{FV}$.

Example 14.A.4

1. *FV* of $1 per month for three years at eight percent per annum, compounded monthly.

$$FV = \$1 \times \left([(1 + .00667)^{36} - 1]/.00667 \right)$$
$$= \$40.54$$

Calculator solution:

$\boxed{n}$ = 36 $\boxed{i}$ = 8/12
$\boxed{PMT}$ = 1 $\boxed{FV}$ = ?

2. *FV* of $1 per quarter for three years at eight percent per annum, compounded quarterly.

$$FV = \$1 \times \left([(1 + .02)^{12} - 1]/.02 \right)$$
$$= \$13.41$$

Calculator solution:

$\boxed{n}$ = 12 $\boxed{i}$ = 8/4
$\boxed{PMT}$ = 1 $\boxed{FV}$ = ?

3. *FV* of $1 semiannually for three years at eight percent per annum, compounded semiannually.

$$FV = \$1 \times \left([(1 + .04)^{6} - 1]/.04 \right)$$
$$= \$6.63$$

Calculator solution:

$\boxed{n}$ = 6 $\boxed{i}$ = 8/2
$\boxed{PMT}$ = 1 $\boxed{FV}$ = ?

PRESENT VALUE OF A DOLLAR

The present value of a dollar factor is used to calculate how much some amount to be received in the future is worth today considering compound interest. The formula is:

$$PV = FV/(1 + i)^n$$

where:

$$PV = \text{Present Value}$$
$$FV = \text{Future Value}$$
$$i \ \ = \text{Rate}$$
$$n \ \ = \text{Number of Periods}$$

Example 14.A.5

The present value interest factor (PVIF) for three years at eight percent (found in Table A.1 in Appendix A) is calculated as follows:

$$PV = 1/(1 + .08)^3$$
$$PV = .7938$$

The present value interest factor in Example 14.A.5 can be determined using a calculator by entering $\boxed{n}$ = 3, $\boxed{i}$ = 8, $\boxed{FV}$ = 1 and solving for $\boxed{PV}$.

Example 14.A.6

1. *PV* of $1 at the end of three years at eight percent per annum, compounded monthly.

   $$PV = 1/(1 + .00667)^{36}$$
   $$\ \ \ \ = .7873$$

   Calculator solution:

   $\boxed{n}$ = 36 $\boxed{i}$ = 8/12
   $\boxed{FV}$ = 1 $\boxed{PV}$ = ?

2. *PV* of $1 at the end of three years at eight percent per annum, compounded quarterly.

   $$PV = 1/(1 + .02)^{12}$$
   $$\ \ \ \ = .7885$$

   Calculator solution:

   $\boxed{n}$ = 12 $\boxed{i}$ = 8/4
   $\boxed{FV}$ = 1 $\boxed{PV}$ = ?

3. *PV* of $1 at the end of three years at eight percent per annum, compounded semiannually.

$$PV = 1/(1 + .04)^6$$
$$= .7903$$

Calculator solution:

$\boxed{n} = 6 \quad \boxed{i} = 8/2$
$\boxed{FV} = 1 \quad \boxed{PV} = ?$

PRESENT VALUE OF A LEVEL ANNUITY

The present value interest factor for an annuity (PVIFa) is used to calculate how much an amount to be received periodically in the future is worth today, for a given rate of interest or discount. The formula is:

$$PV = PMT \times \left[\left(1 - [1/(1 + i)^n]\right)/i\right]$$

where:

PV = Present Value
PMT = Payment per Period
i = Rate
n = Number of Periods

Example 14.A.7

The present value interest factor of an annuity for three years at eight percent (found in Table A.3 in Appendix A) is calculated as follows:

$$PV = 1 \times \left[\left(1 - [1/(1 + .08)^3]\right)/.08\right]$$
$$= 2.5771$$

The factor in Example 14.A.7 can be determined using a calculator by entering $\boxed{n} = 3$, $\boxed{i} = 8$, $\boxed{PMT} = 1$ and solving for $\boxed{PV}$.

Example 14.A.8

1. PV of \$1 per month for three years at eight percent per annum.

$$PV = 1 \times \left[\left(1 - [1/(1 + .0066667)^{36}]\right)/.0066667\right]$$
$$= 31.9118$$

Calculator solution:

$$\boxed{n} = 36 \quad \boxed{i} = 8/12$$
$$\boxed{PMT} = 1 \quad \boxed{PV} = ?$$

2. *PV* of \$1 per quarter for three years at eight percent per annum.

$$PV = 1 \times \left[\left(1 - [1/(1 + .02)^{12}] \right)/.02 \right]$$
$$= 10.5753$$

Calculator solution:

$$\boxed{n} = 12 \quad \boxed{i} = 8/4$$
$$\boxed{PMT} = 1 \quad \boxed{PV} = ?$$

3. *PV* of \$1 per period semiannually for three years at eight percent per annum.

$$PV = 1 \times \left[\left(1 - [1/(1 + .04)^{6}] \right)/.04 \right]$$
$$= 5.2421$$

Calculator solution:

$$\boxed{n} = 6 \quad \boxed{i} = 8/2$$
$$\boxed{PMT} = 1 \quad \boxed{PV} = ?$$

AMOUNT TO AMORTIZE \$1 (MORTGAGE CONSTANT)

The *mortgage constant* is used to calculate the payment on a fully amortizing loan. It is the percentage of the original loan that must be paid periodically in order to fully repay principal and interest over the term of the loan. The formula is:

$$MC = i/\left(1 - [1/(1 + i)^{n}] \right)$$

where:

$$MC = \text{Mortgage Constant}$$
$$i = \text{Rate}$$
$$n = \text{Number of Periods}$$

Example 14.A.9

The mortgage constant for a three-year loan at eight percent interest, with annual payments, is calculated as follows:

$$MC = (.08)/\left(1 - [1/(1 + .08)^5]\right)$$
$$= .3880$$

The constant in Example 14.A.9 can be derived using a financial calculator by entering $\boxed{n} = 3$, $\boxed{i} = 8$, $\boxed{PV} = 1$ and solving for $\boxed{PMT}$.

Example 14.A.10

1. Payment *(PMT)* per period to amortize $1 over three years at eight percent per annum, with monthly payments.

$$PMT = .006667/\left(1 - [1/(1 + .006667)^{36}]\right)$$
$$= .0313$$

Calculator solution:

$\boxed{n} = 36$ $\boxed{i} = 8/12$
$\boxed{PV} = 1$ $\boxed{PMT} = ?$

2. Payment *(PMT)* per period to amortize $1 over three years at eight percent per annum, with quarterly payments.

$$PMT = .02/\left(1 - [1/(1 + .02)^{12}]\right)$$
$$= .0946$$

Calculator solution:

$\boxed{n} = 12$ $\boxed{i} = 8/4$
$\boxed{PV} = 1$ $\boxed{PMT} = ?$

3. Payment *(PMT)* per period to amortize $1 over three years at eight percent per annum, with semiannual payments.

$$PMT = .04/\left(1 - [1/(1 + .04)^6]\right)$$
$$= .1908$$

Calculator solution:

$\boxed{n} = 6$ $\boxed{i} = 8/2$
$\boxed{PV} = 1$ $\boxed{PMT} = ?$

CHAPTER 15

Discounted Cash-Flow Analysis

INTRODUCTION

Modern investment analysis is a practical application of the economic theory of the firm, which states that one should operate at the point where marginal revenue equals marginal cost. Translated into the language of investment analysis, this means ventures are acceptable as long as the rate of return on investment at least equals the cost of investable funds.

This chapter considers at length two common applications of the basic decision criterion, both of which were introduced in Chapter 13. Both methods have merit as investment analysis techniques, both can be supported with compelling logical arguments and several variations of each technique have been developed in the literature. Equipped with the theory and analytical tools presented here, students can evaluate all such variants and indeed can develop their own variations to meet needs peculiar to their immediate circumstances.

REVIEW OF PRESENT VALUE

Present value is the value today of benefits that are expected to accrue in the future. A present value in excess of the required initial equity cash outlay means a project is expected to yield a rate of return in excess of the discount rate employed. If the discount rate is the minimum acceptable rate of return, this

RRR

275

implies that the project is worthy of further consideration. A present value totaling less than the required initial equity expenditure results in automatic rejection.

To use this approach, discount all anticipated future cash flows at the minimum acceptable rate of return. The result is the present value of expected cash flows:

$$PV = CF_1/(1 + i) + CF_2/(1 + i)^2 + CF_3/(1 + i)^3 + \ldots + CF_n/(1 + i)^n$$

where i is the minimum acceptable rate of return, n is the number of years in the projection period and CF_1 is the cash flow expected in the first year, CF_2 that for the second year and so on through the cash-flow expectation for year n.

Example 15.1

An investment proposal is expected to generate $15,000 of after-tax cash flow each year for eight years and $40,000 of after-tax cash flow from disposal at the end of the eighth year. The required equity cash outlay to acquire the asset is $90,000. The minimum acceptable rate of return is ten percent.

The present value of anticipated cash flows from the investment opportunity described in Example 15.1 is $98,684, when discounted at ten percent. Since this exceeds the required initial equity expenditure of $90,000, the expected rate of return exceeds the minimum acceptable rate of ten percent, and the project merits further consideration.

Subtracting the required initial equity expenditure from the present value yields net present value. A positive net present value means a project is expected to yield a rate of return in excess of the discount rate and therefore merits further consideration. A net present value of less than zero means the project is expected to yield a rate of return less than the minimum acceptable rate and therefore should be rejected.

INTERNAL RATE OF RETURN

Since (as we saw in Chapter 14) there is an inverse relationship between discount rates and present value, there must be some rate that will exactly equate the present value of a projected stream of cash flows with any positive initial cash investment. This rate is known as the *internal rate of return*. It has also been called *investment yield*. Yield, however, is an ambiguous term and is often used in other contexts. Internal rate of return, the more precisely definable and more generally used term, is therefore preferable. The equation for the internal rate of return is:

$$\text{Cost} = \sum_{t=1}^{n} \left(CF_t / (1 + k)^t \right)$$

where CF_t is the cash flow projected for year t, cost is defined as the initial cash outlay and k is the discount rate that makes the present value of the expected future cash flows exactly equal to the initial cash outlay. All the terms in the equation are taken as known except k, for which the appropriate value is determined to satisfy the equation.

Consider a project expected to yield a cash-flow stream, $CF_1, CF_2, \ldots CF_n$ over n future periods. The internal rate of return is simply a rate k such that if the initial cash outlay were deposited at an interest rate equaling the discount rate k for each period, the amount CF_1 could be withdrawn at the end of period 1, CF_2 at the end of period 2 and so on through CF_n at the end of period n, to exactly exhaust the fund at the end of the nth period.

If the internal rate of return is equal to or greater than an investor's required rate of return, a project is considered further. If the internal rate of return is less than the minimum acceptable rate of return, the project is rejected.

In Example 15.1, the internal rate of return is approximately 12.2 percent. This is determined by trial and error, using successive approximations of the appropriate discount rate. Cash flows are discounted using factors from Appendix A. Since annual cash flow from operations represents a level annuity, the PVIFa table (Table A.3) is employed. The PVIF table (Table A.1) is used to calculate the present value of the final sum expected in year eight. Discounting at 13 percent, the present value of all expected cash flows equals approximately $87,028. This being somewhat less than the initial cash outlay required, the internal rate of return must be slightly less than 13 percent. Discounting again at the next lower rate for which the tables provide factors, the present value at 12 percent is seen to be approximately $90,670. Interpolating between 12 and 13 percent, as described in Chapter 14, reveals that the rate that equates the present value of expected future cash flows with the required initial outlay is approximately 12.2 percent. (Some error is introduced in the interpolation process.)

Having calculated the internal rate of return based on expected cash flows in Example 15.1, the investor compares the result with the required rate of return. Since the internal rate of return exceeds the required rate (12.2 versus ten percent), the project is considered further. Ultimate acceptance or rejection depends on estimates of relative riskiness and on the relative attractiveness of alternative investment opportunities.

Popularity of the Internal Rate of Return

That the internal rate of return approach has wide appeal is unequivocally evident from the literature. A case in point is a volume of readings compiled by the

American Institute of Real Estate Appraisers and the National Association of Realtors that contains no less than five articles recommending or commenting favorably on internal rate of return as a measure of investment worth.[1] Interestingly, more than half the articles attempt to modify the basic technique to overcome generally acknowledged weaknesses.

The major distinction between the internal rate of return approach and the present value approach is that the latter requires a predetermined discount rate to be introduced early in the analysis. This difference, however, is more illusory than substantive as an argument for one method over the other. Those who use the internal rate of return technique must specify some minimal *threshold rate* against which the internal rate of return is measured to determine its acceptability. Internal rate of return users, therefore, delay but do not escape the obligation to determine an investor's required rate of return.

Decision criteria based on internal rate of return analysis can easily be expressed in present value or net present value terms. Internal rate of return thus appears to have little to recommend it over alternative techniques based on the same discounting concept, other than perhaps practicing analysts' familiarity with the technique and their avoidance of unfamiliar alternatives.

Problems with the Internal Rate of Return

While the internal rate of return has little substantive advantage over alternative methods of applying discount rates to projected cash flows, it does have serious weaknesses not found in the alternatives. Persistent support of a flawed technique might be admirable were there no substitutes that possess equal power to discriminate between acceptable and unacceptable opportunities. Such is not the case, however, with the internal rate of return approach. Its continued advocacy is therefore somewhat curious. Austin Jaffe has suggested a possible explanation. He notes that research and debate in the real estate literature tend to lag behind general financial analysis literature by a number of years. Real estate analysts are perhaps now debating an issue that has long been resolved by those in the financial and economics mainstream.[2]

Problems associated with the internal rate of return can result in conflicting decision signals from this and other discounted cash-flow approaches. Generally, such a conflict arises because the internal rate of return signal is distorted. If heeded, it might result in serious investment error. Potential dissonance stems from peculiarities of the internal rate of return equation, which can yield more than one solution, and from problems associated with the reinvestment assumption inherent in choices among alternative investments that exhibit different patterns of anticipated after-tax cash flows.

The Reinvestment-Rate Problem.   Interproject comparison using internal rate of return analysis involves an implicit assumption that funds are reinvested at the internal rate of return. The internal rate of return method reliably discriminates among alternatives only if other acceptable opportunities expected to yield an equally high rate are available. This, of course, is an unlikely prospect when the internal rate of return is considerably above the opportunity cost of capital.

Example 15.2

An investor must select from two alternatives that require equal initial cash outlays and have identical time horizons. Expected cash flows from the alternatives are as follows:

	Investment Alternative	
	A	*B*
Initial Equity Expenditure	$10,694	$10,694
Net Cash Inflow, Year 1	7,000	0
Net Cash Inflow, Year 2	7,000	14,890

Consider the investment alternatives in Example 15.2. Internal rate of return analysis will lead to selection of alternative *A* over *B*. This is because *A* has an internal rate of return of approximately 20 percent, whereas *B*'s internal rate of return approximates only 18 percent. To satisfy yourself that this is so, discount the cash flows from each project at these rates and note that the present value of anticipated future cash flows in each case approximates the required $10,694 initial equity expenditure.

If cash flows during the holding period can be reinvested at 20 percent, then investment alternative *A* will indeed result in yields of 20 percent per annum over the two-year period. To see this, consider the cumulative cash that results if the first year's $7,000 cash flow is in fact reinvested at 20 percent. It will grow to $8,400 in one year. When this is added to the $7,000 to be received at the end of the second year, the cumulative total is $15,400. Discounting this amount over a two-year period at 20 percent yields a present value equal to the $10,694 initial equity expenditure. Here are the computations (terminal value is the future value of all intermediate cash flows when compounded forward, at a designated rate, to the end of the investment holding period):

Terminal Value of Cash Inflow with 20% Reinvestment Rate	
Year 1 (Cash Inflow $7,000)	$ 8,400
Year 2 (Cash Inflow $7,000)	7,000
Cumulative Terminal Value at 20%	$15,400
Times: Present Value Factor at 20%	.6944
Present Value of $15,400 Due in Two Years	$10,694
Less: Initial Cash Outlay	10,694
Net Present Value at 20%	$ 0

If the first year's net cash flow from alternative *A* is reinvested at any rate less than 12.7 percent, the yield on invested funds over the two-year period will be less than the internal rate of return on investment alternative *B*. Suppose, for example, that the best yield available on funds reinvested at the end of the first year is ten percent. The yield on alternative *A* for the two-year period will then be only 17.24 percent. Here is the arithmetic:

Terminal Value of Net Cash Flow with 10% Reinvestment Rate	
Year 1 (Net Cash Flow $7,000)	$ 7,700
Year 2 (Net Cash Flow $7,000)	7,000
Cumulative Terminal Value at 10%	$14,700
Times: Present Value Factor at 17.24%	.7275
Present Value of $14,700 Due in Two Years	$10,694
Less: Initial Equity Outlay	10,694
Net Present Value at 17.24%	$ 0

The reinvestment problem also limits the usefulness of the internal rate of return technique when choosing among investments having different useful lives or different holding periods. If the indicated internal rate of return is unrealistically high, so that reinvestment at that rate is not a reasonable assumption, the internal rate of return will give an ambiguous decision signal.

Example 15.3

An investor must select from alternatives having the following cash-flow characteristics:

	Investment Alternative	
	A	*B*
Required Initial Cash Outlay	$22,832	$33,522
Annual Cash Inflow		
First Three Years	10,000	10,000
Annual Cash Inflow		
Years 4 and 5	0	10,000

Example 15.3 demonstrates the problem. Both investment alternatives promise a 15 percent internal rate of return, but they are equally desirable only if the reinvestment rate is also 15 percent. In that case the yield over the five-year investment horizon will be exactly 15 percent with either alternative, as the following computations indicate:

	A	B
Terminal Value of Cash Flow with 15% Reinvestment Rate		
Year 1 (Reinvested for Four Years)	$17,490	$17,490
2 (Reinvested for Three Years)	15,209	15,209
3 (Reinvested for Two Years)	13,225	13,225
4 (Reinvested for One Year)	0	11,500
5 (Reinvested for Zero Years)	0	10,000

Terminal Value of All Cash Flows	$45,924	$67,424
Times: Present Value Factor at 15%	.49718	.49718
Present Value of Terminal Value at 15%	$22,832	$33,522
Less: Initial Cash Outlay	22,832	33,522
Net Present Value at 15%	$ 0	$ 0

But if the reinvestment rate is less than 15 percent, then alternative *A* will not offer an equally high yield over the five-year investment horizon. At a reinvestment rate of ten percent per annum, for example, yields over the entire five-year period will be approximately 11.9 percent per annum for alternative *A* and approximately 12.7 percent for *B*. These computations are shown below:

	A	B
Terminal Value of Cash Flow with 10% Reinvestment Rate		
Year 1 (Reinvested for Four Years)	$14,641	$14,641
2 (Reinvested for Three Years)	13,310	13,310
3 (Reinvested for Two Years)	12,100	12,100
4 (Reinvested for One Year)	0	11,000
5 (Reinvested for Zero Years)	0	10,000
Terminal Value of All Cash Flows	$40,051	$61,051
Approximate Discount Rate to Equate Terminal Value with Initial Cash Outlay	11.9%	12.7%

The Multiple-Solutions Problem.   Generally, a project's net present value is a decreasing function of the discount rate employed. Thus, with successively higher discount rates, a point is reached where the net present value is zero. This is the internal rate of return, and any greater discount rate will result in a negative net present value. When the discounting equation is well behaved in this fashion, there is but one internal rate of return equating all cash inflows with all cash outflows.

Unfortunately, not all cash-flow forecasts are this accommodating. Investment proposals may have any number of internal rates of return, depending on the cash-flow pattern. It is possible to have as many internal rates of return as the number of reversals in sign (positive to negative or vice versa) of the cash-flow stream. Yet sign reversals are a common characteristic of cash-flow streams from real estate projects. There is often junior mortgage financing in which the second mortgage note balloons (that is, the remaining balance becomes due and payable) in a specific number of years. In the year the second mortgage note matures, negative net cash flow is a frequent consequence. (Reversal of sign of the cash-flow pattern is a necessary, but not a sufficient, condition for multiple solutions to the internal rate of return equation. For many cases of sign reversal there will be only one solution within the realm of real numbers. For most projects, all but one of the multiple roots are imaginary numbers, and there is but one internal rate of return solution.)

Eugene F. Brigham presents a simple illustration by citing a coal-mining firm's analysis of an open-pit mining operation that requires an initial cash outlay of \$4.4 million and for which positive cash flow during the first year of operations is expected to be \$27.7 million. During the second year, in accordance with state and federal regulations, land will be returned to its "natural" state—at a cost of \$25 million. This cash-flow pattern generates two internal rate of return solutions: 9.2 percent and 420 percent.[3]

COMPARISON OF NET PRESENT VALUE AND INTERNAL RATE OF RETURN

Under most circumstances, the internal rate of return and net present value approaches will give the same decision signals. When this occurs, there is little significance in the choice of one over the other. The rules are:

1. When using internal rate of return, reject all projects whose internal rate of return is less than the minimum required rate of return. Projects with an internal rate of return equal to or greater than the minimum acceptable rate (the *hurdle rate*) are considered further. (Having solved for the internal rate of return, analysts still face the problem of comparing this rate with some benchmark to determine acceptability. This predetermined minimum acceptable rate, or hurdle rate, could have been used to derive a net present value in the first place. Thus nothing is gained by choosing the internal rate of return over the net present value criterion.)
2. When using net present value, discount at the minimum acceptable rate of return and reject all projects with a net present value of less than zero. Projects with a net present value of zero or greater are considered further.

The essential similarity of these decision criteria is reflected in their mathematical formulation. The only structural difference is the discount rate. Remember that the discount rate employed in the internal rate of return is the effective yield; the net present value will be exactly zero when the internal rate of return equals the minimum required rate of return.

There are, however, some conditions under which contradictory signals emerge. The two techniques may, for example, rank alternatives in different order. Since investors must often choose among alternative proposals rather than make a simple choice to accept or reject one investment, this can be a serious problem. Limited equity funds frequently dictate choice from among several opportunities, all of which may meet minimum acceptance criteria. Inconsistent rank ordering can occur where projects differ in the size of the initial investment or in the timing of cash receipts and disbursements.

Discrepancies with Projects of Different Size

Consider two mutually exclusive projects of greatly different size (say, the use of a given site for a hotel or a service station). The initial cash outlays and the cash flows upon completion and sale are as follows:

	Cash Flows	
Year	Project A	Project B
0	($100,000)	($1,500,000)
1	150,000	1,900,000

Project *A*, requiring an initial outlay of $100,000 and returning $150,000 after one year, has an internal rate of return of 50 percent. Project *B*, with an initial cost of $1,500,000 and a return of $1,900,000 after one year, has an internal rate of return of only 27 percent. The internal rate of return criterion, therefore, ranks project *A* ahead of project *B*.

But consider the net present value of the two projects, assuming a 12 percent minimum acceptable rate of return. Project *A* has a net present value of approximately $34,000, compared with project *B*'s net present value of approximately $196,000. This criterion thus ranks project *B* ahead of project *A*.

Discrepancies Due to Differences In the Timing of Cash Flows

Consider the following mutually exclusive investment proposals:

	Cash Flows	
Year	Proposal C	Proposal D
0 (Initial Cash Outlay)	($10,000)	($10,000)
1	2,000	4,000
2	3,000	4,000
3	5,000	4,000
4	6,000	4,500
5	7,000	5,000

Proposal *C* has an internal rate of return of approximately 28.2 percent, whereas the internal rate of return for proposal *D* is approximately 30.9 percent. If the investor's minimum acceptable rate of return is below 28.2 percent, both proposals are acceptable. Assuming they are mutually exclusive, investors using the internal rate of return as a decision criterion will choose proposal *D* over proposal *C*.

Suppose, however, that the investor's opportunity cost of capital is 12 percent. Discounting at this rate yields a net present value of $5,521.29 for proposal *C* and a net present value of only $5,304.29 for proposal *D*. When evaluating mutually exclusive investment proposals using net present value technique, the (equally risky) investment having the higher net present value is accepted, assuming both have positive net present values. In this instance, net present value analysis and the internal rate of return produce conflicting signals. Using internal rate of return, proposal *D* would be preferred over proposal *C*. Using net present value, proposal *C* would be preferred over proposal *D*.

Figure 15.1 illustrates the relationship between discount rate and net present value for proposals *C* and *D*. It reveals that at any discount rate above 15 percent, proposal *C* has the highest net present value and is therefore the more desirable project. At any discount rate below 15 percent, proposal *D* is the more desirable. At a 15 percent rate, the projects are equally desirable. If the appropriate discount rate is below 15 percent, the internal rate of return and net present value will provide conflicting decision signals for choosing between these two projects.

Where internal rate of return and net present value analysis give different decision signals, results of net present value analysis are usually preferred. This follows from most financial analysts having accepted the idea that investors should strive to maximize their wealth. Doubters are referred to an extensive discussion of the relative merits of these approaches by authors generally acknowledged as eminent authorities as well as pioneers in the theoretical aspects of capital budgeting methodology.[4]

SHORING UP THE INTERNAL RATE OF RETURN

Numerous attempts have been made to modify the internal rate of return to eradicate the multiple solutions and reinvestment-rate dilemmas. Three approaches are particularly worth noting for their ingenuity, if not for their usefulness. Each is presented here in outline form. None eliminates the serious problem of failure to consistently give solutions consonant with the objective of maximizing investor wealth.

Modified Internal Rate of Return

One approach, called a *modified internal rate of return*, solves the multiple root problem by discounting all negative cash flows back to the time at which the investment is acquired and compounding all positive cash flows forward to the end of the final year of the holding period. This process eliminates all sign changes and generally allows a unique solution.

> ### *Example 15.4*
>
> An investment proposition requires an initial cash expenditure of $1,600 and is expected to generate a net cash flow of $10,000 at the end of one year. Due to income tax and mortgage financing factors, the venture is expected to yield a negative $10,000 when terminated at the end of the second year.

Example 15.4 incorporates a numerical illustration developed by James H. Lorie and Leonard J. Savage to demonstrate the problem.[5] Discounting future cash flows at either 25 or 400 percent yields a net present value of exactly zero; both are indicated internal rates of return. Since there is no unique solution, there is no "correct" internal rate of return.

FIGURE 15.1 Discount Rates and Net Present Value

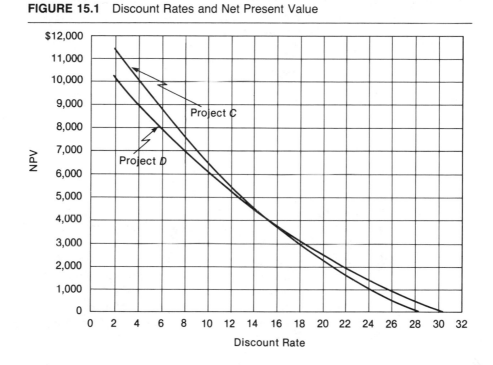

Proponents of the modified internal rate of return would eliminate the double solution problem by discounting negative cash flows back to year zero and compounding positive cash flows forward to the end of the investment holding period. For Example 15.4, if we assume an opportunity cost of capital (the presumed appropriate rate for the discounting and compounding operation) of 20 percent, there results an 18.51 percent discount rate, which equates the positive terminal value with the negative initial amount. First, discount the second year's anticipated negative cash flow back to the time of the initial cash outlay and sum its (negative) present value with the $1,600 expenditure actually encountered at that time:

Cash Expected in Year 2	($10,000)
Times: Present Value Factor for Two Years at 20%	.69444
Present Value of Second Year's Cash Flow	($ 6,944)
Plus: Initial Cash Flow	(1,600)
Initial Value	($ 8,544)

Now compound the first year's anticipated positive cash flow forward to the end of year two, again at the presumed 20 percent opportunity cost of capital. This yields a terminal value of $12,000:

Cash Flow Expected in Year 1	$10,000
Times: Compound Value Factor for One Year at 20%	1.200
Terminal Value	$12,000

There remains only to find a discount rate that will make $12,000 due in two years have a present value of $8,544. Either the present value or the compound value table from Appendix A will yield a solution. Using the compound value table, we have:

$$\text{Present Value} \times \text{CVIF} = \text{Future Value}$$

Substituting the present and terminal values from the above problem gives:

$$\$8,544 \times \text{CVIF} = \$12,000$$

Therefore:

$$\$12,000/\$8544 = \text{CVIF}$$
$$= 1.40449$$

Reference to the two-year row of the compound value interest factors in Table A.2 of Appendix A (and interpolating, as explained in Chapter 14) yields a modified internal rate of return of approximately 18.5 percent.

In addition to its intimidating complexity, this technique is extremely sensitive to variations in the rate chosen for preliminary discounting and compounding. To see this for yourself, repeat the exercise related to Example 15.4, using ten percent as the appropriate rate. Now try 15 percent. You will find the modified internal rates of return to be approximately 5.6 percent and 12 percent, respectively.

Adjusted Rate of Return

Adjusted rates of return are particularly well explained by Donald Valachi.[6] Assuming cash flows as described in Example 15.4, Valachi's article suggests that an investor has in essence "borrowed" $10,000 from the project at the end of year one and repaid the "loan" at the end of year two. Assuming a reinvestment rate of 20 percent, the first year's $10,000 cash flow will have grown to $12,000 by the end of the second year. Offsetting this against the $10,000 net outflow at the end of the second year yields a net terminal value of $2,000. The discount rate that gives this $2,000 terminal value a present value equal to the $1,600 initial cash expenditure is approximately 11.8 percent (there are actually two roots; the other is −2.1 percent).

This technique works well for the cash flows illustrated in Example 15.4, but consider the following series:[7]

Initial Cash Outlay	$ 1,000
Cash Flow in Year 1	6,000
Cash Flow in Year 2	(11,000)
Cash Flow in Year 3	6,000

This cash-flow pattern produces internal rate of return solutions of zero percent, 100 percent and 200 percent. Since it is unlikely that year one's cash flow will be compounded at a rate high enough to allow it to cover year two's negative cash flow, some other course of action is necessary. One might "borrow" from year three by discounting part of that cash flow back to year two. Or one might discount all of year three's cash flow back to year two and compound only part of year one's cash flow forward. The result of these alternatives are two drastically different adjusted internal rates of return. As *renegotiable rate mortgages* become increasingly popular, causing cash flows to alternate between negative and positive, rules needed to apply the adjusted rate of return will become increasingly complex.

There are numerous variations of the modified and adjusted internal rates of return. The number is expanding almost as fast as people can develop rules specifying discounting and compounding rates and techniques for using positive cash flows to cover negative ones. A tongue-in-cheek explanation from an unremembered source is that progress does not consist of replacing a theory that is wrong with one that is right, but rather of replacing a theory that is wrong with one that is more subtly wrong.

Financial Management Rate of Return

M. Chapman Findley and Stephen D. Messner have developed a widely publicized variation on the internal rate of return, called the *financial management rate of return*. Their version incorporates two intermediate rates, one a cost of capital rate employed to discount negative cash flows back to year zero and the other a specified reinvestment rate for compounding positive cash flows to the end of the projection period. Interested readers will do well to start their research with a study of articles by Michael Young and H. S. Kerr, both of whom provide definitive critiques of the model.[8]

SUMMARY

Modern investment evaluation techniques generally involve some variation of a discounted cash-flow model expressing the present value of all anticipated future cash flows. Most common are the internal rate of return and the present value/net present value models. The internal rate of return model is conceptually appealing to many, but it contains flaws that make it less desirable than the present value/net present value approach.

NOTES

1. American Institute of Real Estate Appraisers and National Association of Realtors, *Readings in Real Estate Investment Analysis* (Cambridge, MA: Ballinger, 1977).

2. Austin Jaffe, "Is There a 'New' Internal Rate of Return Literature?" *AREUEA Journal* 4 (Winter 1977): 483.

3. Eugene F. Brigham, *Financial Management: Theory and Practice,* 3d ed. (Hinsdale, IL: The Dryden Press, 1982), 411.

4. See, for example, Harold Bierman, Jr., and Seymour Smidt, *The Capital Budgeting Decision* (New York: Macmillan, 1971), 38–54.

5. James H. Lorie and Leonard J. Savage, "Three Problems in Rationing Capital," *Journal of Business* (October 1955): 229–39.

6. Donald J. Valachi, "More on the Arithmetic of Multiple and Imaginary Rates of Return," *Real Estate Appraiser and Analyst* (September–October 1980), 19–20.

7. These numbers are taken from an example propounded by James C. Van Horne in *Financial Management and Policy,* 4th ed. (Englewood Cliffs, NJ: Prentice-Hall, 1977), 105.

8. Michael Young, "FMRR: A Clever Hoax?" *Appraisal Journal* 47 (July 1979): 359–69; H. S. Kerr, "A Final Word on FMRR," *Appraisal Journal* 48 (January 1980): 95–103. Armed with the analytical tools these authors provide, the reader is better prepared to critically evaluate the FMRR model. Review Stephen D. Messner, Irving Schreiber and Victor L. Lyon, *Marketing Investment Real Estate* (Chicago: National Association of Realtors, 1979), 49–52.

RECOMMENDED READINGS

Brigham, Eugene F. *Fundamentals of Financial Management.* 4th ed. Hinsdale, IL: The Dryden Press, 1986, pp. 278–306.

Eply, Donald R., and James H. Boykin. *Basic Income Property Appraisal.* Reading, MA: Addison-Wesley, 1983, pp. 140–157.

Friedman, Jack P., and Nicholas Ordway. *Income Property Appraisal and Analysis.* Reston, VA: Reston, 1981, pp. 37–116.

Greer, Gaylon E. *The Real Estate Investment Decision.* Lexington, MA: Heath, 1979, pp. 153–172.

Hoaglund, Henry E., Leo D. Stone, and William B. Bruggeman. *Real Estate Finance.* 6th ed. Homewood, IL: Richard D. Irwin, 1977, pp. 180–207.

REVIEW QUESTIONS

1. Under what conditions will a project be rejected when using present value in investment decision making?
2. Describe the internal rate of return.
3. What assumption is made about reinvestment of cash flows in net present value calculations? In internal rate of return calculations?
4. What is the major difference between the internal rate of return approach and the present value approach?
5. Under what conditions might the internal rate of return yield multiple solutions?

6. List some conditions under which the present value and the internal rate of return might yield conflicting decision signals. When this occurs, which should be selected?

7. What are the advantages and disadvantages of the modified internal rate of return, the adjusted rate of return and the financial management rate of return?

DISCUSSION QUESTIONS

1. If you were appraising the extent to which a financial consultant exercised due diligence in evaluating an investment proposal, would you be influenced by the consultant's choice between internal rate of return and present value as an evaluation methodology?

2. Since cash-flow projections and cost of capital estimates are, at best, inexact in most cases, does it really make a practical difference whether an analyst uses present value or internal rate of return as a decision criterion?

CHAPTER 16

Investment Goals and Decision Criteria

INTRODUCTION

Major issues explored in this chapter include choosing a discount rate, applying discounted cash flow to various categories of investment decisions and developing an investment negotiating strategy that uses the investment value concept first introduced in Chapter 3.

CHOOSING A DISCOUNT RATE

Choice of discount rate is critical to selecting among alternative opportunities as well as to deciding what opportunities merit additional consideration. (Advocates of the internal rate of return often argue that the method avoids the need to choose a discount rate. While this argument is specious, it does dramatize the issue of appropriate selection of the rate of discount to be factored into the present value equation.)

Minor adjustments in the discount rate can result in rather dramatic changes in net present value. The further into the future cash-flow projections are made, the greater the influence of discount rate variations. Moreover, relative ranking of opportunities can be changed by altering the discount rate when opportunities differ in the timing of anticipated cash flows.

Example 16.1

An investor must choose between two projects, both of which require an initial equity expenditure of $100,000. Project *A* is expected to generate $25,000 of after-tax cash flow each year for ten years, after which the assets will be worthless. Project *B* offers a projected $500,000 of after-tax cash flow, all of which is expected to be received at the end of the tenth year of ownership.

Example 16.1 illustrates the point. Relative desirability of the projects depends on the choice of a discount rate. At a rate of 15 percent, project *A* is preferable to project *B,* with respective net present values of $25,469 and $23,592. But at a rate of 14 percent, the relative rankings are switched, with project *B*'s revised net present value of $34,872 being preferable to project *A*'s new net present value of $30,403. Thus with a discount rate of 14 percent or less, project *B* appears more desirable, while project *A* is more desirable with discount rates of 15 percent or more.

Summation Technique

One of the earliest methods proposed for developing discount rates, the *summation technique* is based upon the proposition that investors seek compensation for deferring consumption in order to invest their wealth. Moreover, additional remuneration is required for bearing risk and for losing liquidity. Portfolio management is viewed as still another burden for which recompense is expected. The sum of these compensation rates is held to comprise the appropriate discount rate.

In the summation technique the appropriate rate of compensation for investing (that is, for deferring consumption) is assumed to be the rate available on investments that are highly liquid and essentially free of default risk. Typically, the yield on short-term federal government securities is taken as the best indication of this safe rate.

Appropriate reward for illiquidity is frequently assumed to equal the difference between short-term and long-term rates applicable to government securities (on occasion, this may be a negative rate). Compensation for bearing risk and for the burden of investment management (not property management) is more troublesome, because there are no ready proxies for these rates. Table 16.1 illustrates how the summation technique might be used to derive an estimate of a discount rate.

Risk-Adjusted Discount Rate

Practical problems associated with estimating appropriate compensation for various components renders the summation technique impractical. A frequently

TABLE 16.1   The Summation Technique

Safe Rate	0.120
Compensation for Risk	0.020
Compensation for Illiquidity	0.015
Compensation for Burden of Management	0.001
Discount Rate (Summation of Above)	0.156

advocated alternative lumps compensation for all elements other than waiting (the safe, or risk-free, rate) into one "reduced form" rate, called a *risk premium*. The sum of the risk-free rate and the risk premium is held to be the appropriate discount rate.

Risk-Free Rate.   The *risk-free rate* is assumed to be the reward solely for waiting, with no premium for associated risk. The idea is to take the time value of money into account by the discounting process and then as a separate operation to incorporate considerations associated with existence of risk.

Reference to a risk-free rate generally means a rate devoid of risk of *default*. To understand the distinction, consider a loan made to the federal government. Such loans are generally considered the safest possible use of funds, but investors recognize that even here there are risks involved. While the risk of default is virtually zero, the risk of loss of purchasing power because of inflation remains. Also remaining is the risk that an unfavorable change in the current market rate of interest will either reduce the value of the investment or cost the investor the opportunity to earn a return at the new higher rate.

Risk Premium.   The *risk premium* differs according to the analyst's conception of the risk inherent in a project. The riskier the project, the higher the discount rate employed. Thus the discount rate is composed of two elements: a time adjustment and a risk adjustment.

Marginal Cost of Capital

Textbooks in corporate finance generally advocate using *marginal cost of capital* as the appropriate discount rate.[1] Marginal cost of anything is the cost of one additional unit of the item. The marginal cost of capital, therefore, is the cost of an additional dollar of new funds. A problem arises in trying to apply the marginal cost concept when funds are raised from several sources, for marginal cost differs with each source employed. Under such circumstances, some authorities recommend using several different discount rates, depending on the circumstances surrounding the decision.[2] Perhaps the most common solution is to apply a weighted average rate incorporating the marginal cost from each source employed, with the cost from each source weighted in accordance with the percent of total new capital to be generated from that source.

For most real estate projects, the cost of debt is easily identifiable, and this cost (expressed as annual debt service) is in fact subtracted from gross income to arrive at an estimate of after-tax cash flow from the project. When the cost of borrowed capital is treated in this manner, it must not also be incorporated into the discount rate; marginal cost of *equity* capital becomes a more appropriate determinant of the discount rate.

Marginal cost of equity capital for corporations whose shares are traded actively is estimated by comparing earnings per share with the market price of the shares. For privately held corporations or noncorporate investors, no such market index is available, and marginal cost of capital is a difficult concept to apply. Opportunity cost of equity capital is usually a more meaningful basis for determining the appropriate discount rate.

Opportunity Cost of Capital

The question facing an analyst is: What rate of return can be earned on the best available alternative use of funds that does not appreciably increase an investor's exposure to risk? This is the investor's opportunity cost of capital. It serves admirably as a minimum acceptable rate of return, or hurdle rate, since investors are unlikely to accept any project promising a rate of return below that available elsewhere with the same degree of risk.

Using opportunity cost as a common discount rate permits direct comparison among projects of the same general risk category. This eliminates difficulties that might otherwise arise when cash-flow projections from alternative proposals differ drastically in amount or timing.

Finally, a common discount rate for all competing projects greatly facilitates risk analysis of the type discussed in Part Six. It permits risk analysis to be incorporated into policy guidelines, which enables subordinates or analysts to screen investment proposals in much greater detail than is otherwise possible.

INVESTMENT DECISIONS AND DECISION RULES

Precise rules for making investment decisions necessarily depend upon the nature of the problem an investor faces. While general principles are universally applicable, their specific application depends upon situational factors. This section examines a number of situations and the appropriate application of general principles for each.

Comparing Projects of Different Size

Net present value does not give an unambiguous decision signal when projects require different levels of initial cash outlay. But the measure can be converted to a cost/benefit ratio, which does this task admirably. The ratio, called a *profitability index* (PI), is calculated by dividing the present value of expected future cash flows by the amount of the initial cash outlay. The quotient represents present value per dollar of initial cash expenditure. The general decision rule, then, is to accept the project with the greatest profitability index (assuming, of course, that there is no difference in the risk profile of competing opportunities).

Example 16.2

The present value of expected cash flows from an investment is $74,340, when discounted at the opportunity cost of capital. The required equity cash outlay to acquire the asset is $60,000.

Applying the profitability index technique to Example 16.2 results in a decision to accept the project tentatively since there is $1.24 of present value for every $1 of initial cash investment. The calculation:

$$PI = \text{Present value/cost}$$
$$= \$74,340/\$60,000$$
$$= \$1.24$$

When using the profitability index as an initial screening device, reject all projects with an index of less than one. This is, of course, a simple variant of the rule of rejecting any project whose net present value is less than zero. Only projects with a profitability index equal to or greater than one are subjected to additional analysis.

The profitability index is simply an alternate way of expressing net present value data, since instead of subtracting initial cash outlay from present value, we divide by that amount. Therefore, when present value minus initial cash outlay equals zero, the profitability index will equal one. It follows that when net present value is less than zero the profitability index will be less than one, and when net present value is more than zero the profitability index will be more than one.

Choosing Among Mutually Exclusive Opportunities

Investors often must select among investment alternatives, all of which are considered desirable. The most common situation of this sort springs from limited capital resources; accepting one proposition exhausts available capital and renders acceptance of other ventures impossible. A second frequently encountered choice among mutually exclusive alternatives occurs when a prospective owner-user must select a building. Acquisition of one eliminates the need for the other.

Investors constantly face mutually exclusive investment decisions. They must, for example, decide among alternative allowable capital recovery methods (depreciation). Financing alternatives, lease or buy choices, decisions to accept or reject offers to buy or sell, selection from among alternate lease terms or tenants and alternate forms of ownership all constitute examples of mutually exclusive choices.

Investors deciding among mutually exclusive alternatives accept the one producing greater (positive) net present value. When using the internal rate of return, accept the mutually exclusive proposal having the higher internal rate of return, provided it is greater than the predetermined rate.

Mutually Dependent Investment Decisions

Investment proposals are mutually dependent if acceptance of one forces the investor to accept the other. Acquisition of more than one property at a time, or a portfolio of properties, requires consideration of results from alternative combinations.

If investment decisions are related in this fashion, group the mutually dependent ventures into consolidated units and treat each unit as a single investment venture. Accept the mutually dependent combination having the highest net present value, provided it is greater than zero. If the "packages" differ in the amount of initial equity cash expenditure, compare the profitability indexes of the combinations. If the internal rate of return method is being used, accept the combination having the highest calculated return—if it is greater than the predetermined cutoff rate.

INVESTMENT VALUE AND INVESTMENT STRATEGY

Investment value was defined in Chapter 3 as the value of an income-producing property to a particular investor. Prospective investors will be motivated to buy if they believe their subjective investment values are greater than the amounts they will have to pay for the properties. Owners will be motivated to sell if they believe they will receive more than their properties are worth to them as elements in their personal investment portfolios.

Example 16.3

An investor estimates that a property has a present value of anticipated future equity cash flows of $250,000. He suspects he can acquire the property for about $725,000, paying $225,000 in cash and financing the balance via a first mortgage loan. The present owner believes she can sell for about $725,000 and that the present value of future after-tax cash flows if she continues to hold the property in her portfolio is about $400,000. An existing mortgage loan on the property has a remaining balance of $200,000. If the owner in fact sells for $725,000, she estimates that her taxes and transaction costs will total about $100,000.

TABLE 16.2   Summary of Buyer's Position

Present Value of Equity	$250,000
Available Financing	500,000
Buyer's Investment Value	$750,000
Expected Purchase Price	$725,000
Less: Available Debt Financing	500,000
Expected Equity Investment	$225,000
Present Value of Equity Position	$250,000
Less: Expected Equity Investment	225,000
Net Present Value	$ 25,000

Consider the position of the prospective buyer in Example 16.3. Summing the $250,000 present value of anticipated after-tax cash flows (the value of the expected equity cash expenditure) and the expected $500,000 mortgage loan (the cost of which is incorporated into the present value computations) yields an investment value of $750,000 to the prospective purchaser. If, as the investor suspects, the property can be acquired for $725,000, only $225,000 of equity cash will be required. Present value of future cash receipts less required equity (the cost to acquire the future cash flows) yields a net present value of $25,000. Purchase of this property is expected to increase the investor's net worth by $25,000. These relationships are summarized in Table 16.2.

Now consider the current owner's position. Summing the $400,000 present value of anticipated future after-tax cash flows if she continues her ownership and the $200,000 remaining balance of the existing mortgage produces an investment value of $600,000. Selling the property for the expected $725,000 will net her $425,000 of after-tax cash flow (sales price minus loan balance, transaction costs and income taxes).

The seller in effect exchanges the present value of future cash flows for cash proceeds of sale. Net present value of a decision to sell the property is therefore estimated to be $25,000. These relationships are summarized in Table 16.3 on page 298.

Marked differences in investment value, like those for the prospective buyer and seller in Example 16.3, might easily occur when a current owner has exhausted the property's ability to produce tax shelter and a prospective purchaser has the opportunity to exploit attractive capital recovery allowance rules. The relationship between subjective investment values in Example 16.3 is diagramed in Figure 16.1.

The greater the spread between investment value and transaction price for both buyer and seller, the greater the possible increase in both investors' net wealth. Keep in mind that neither party will know the other's subjective investment value. Because the buyer does not know the minimum amount the seller will take, and the seller does not know the maximum amount the buyer

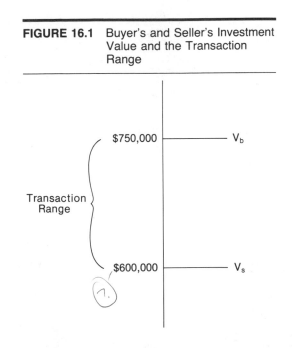

FIGURE 16.1 Buyer's and Seller's Investment Value and the Transaction Range

TABLE 16.3 Summary of Seller's Position

Present Value of Equity	$400,000
Mortgage Loan Balance	200,000
Seller's Investment Value	$600,000
Expected Sales Price	$725,000
Less: Mortgage Loan Balance	200,000
Less: Taxes and Transaction Costs	100,000
Expected After-Tax Cash Flow from Sale	$425,000
Expected After-Tax Cash Flow from Sale	$425,000
Less: Present Value of Equity	400,000
Net Present Value of Selling	$ 25,000

will pay, both bargain with incomplete information. This uncertainty increases the importance of good bargaining strategy.

APPLYING THE DISCOUNTED CASH-FLOW TECHNIQUE

This final section applies previously discussed procedures for developing after-tax cash-flow projections and discounts them at the minimum acceptable rate of return. Space limitations require that several assumptions be made about key variables that, in a realistic situation, would be subject to debate and judgmental variation. We make these assumptions to expedite the illustration of the mechanical process of developing net present value estimates. Now examine Example 16.4.

Example 16.4

An investor is considering purchase of a 48-unit apartment complex, expected to be available for $1.3 million. The investor expects to be able to arrange an $840,000, 12 percent, 25-year, fully amortizing first mortgage loan, which will require monthly payments.

Whether or not the investor makes this commitment, he or she will be in the 28 percent marginal income tax bracket throughout the contemplated investment period.

If the investment is made, it is expected that the property will be held for approximately six years, at which time it will be sold for cash to fund a retirement plan.

The investor's minimum expected rate of return on investments of this type is ten percent per annum.

The first step in analyzing the opportunity in Example 16.4 is to forecast revenue and expenses for the property over the expected holding period. The analyst notes that the area is fully developed, with no land available for significant new, competing buildings, and that the area evidences no discernible trend of either rapid growth or decline. He or she concludes that both rents and expenses should be fairly stable over the next few years, moving approximately in concert with the general movement in consumer prices. The analyst expects the consumer price index to increase at about six percent per annum (compounded) over the next few years and takes this as the expected rate of increase in both rents and operating expenses. Starting with the owner's operating statement, adjusting as explained in Part Three, results in a forecast of first-year operating figures shown in Table 16.4.

Having determined that operating results are most likely to increase at an average rate of six percent per annum over the holding period, the forecast becomes a mechanical projection at that rate. The forecast must be made on an after-tax cash-flow basis, however. This requires that taxable income or tax-deductible losses also be forecast for each year of the prospective holding period. To calculate interest expense for this purpose, an amortization table for available financing must be developed. This information is shown in Table 16.5.

The investor's expected taxable income from the real estate investment for each year consists of the expected net operating income minus interest expense and cost recovery allowances. Since the investor is assumed to be in the 28

TABLE 16.4   First-Year Operating Forecast

Potential Gross Rent		$262,000
Less: Allowance for Vacancies		17,500
		$244,500
Plus: Other Income (Parking)		1,600
Effective Gross Income		$246,100
Less: Operating Expenses		
Management Fee	$12,300	
Salary Expense	22,500	
Utilities	26,500	
Insurance	12,500	
Supplies	3,200	
Advertising	1,500	
Maintenance and Repairs	20,000	
Property Tax	30,700	129,200
Net Operating Income (Annual)		$116,900

TABLE 16.5   Mortgage Amortization Schedule*

Year	Interest	Principal	Total Debt Service**	Ending Balance
1	$100,494	$ 5,670	$106,164	$834,330
2	99,775	6,389	106,164	827,941
3	98,965	7,200	106,164	820,741
4	98,052	8,113	106,164	812,628
5	97,024	9,142	106,164	803,487
6	95,864	10,301	106,164	793,186

*Computed with a financial calculator. Computations using tables will differ slightly due to rounding.

**Computations assume a mortgage loan of $840,000, to be repaid in equal monthly installments over 25 years, with interest at 12 percent per annum.
   Monthly payment = $8,847
   Annual debt service = 12 × $8,847 = $106,164

percent marginal income tax bracket with or without this investment, the tax (or tax savings) for each year will be computed at the 28 percent rate. These calculations are presented in the upper half of Table 16.6.

Cost recovery allowances reduce taxable income, but they do not affect before-tax cash flow from an investment. Conversely, reduction of the principal amount of mortgage indebtedness reduces cash flow without affecting taxable income. The lower half of Table 16.6 contains after-tax cash-flow forecasts, which start with net operating income and are adjusted for debt service and income tax effects. Discounting forecast cash flows at the minimum acceptable

TABLE 16.6   After-Tax Cash-Flow Forecast

	Year					
	1	*2*	*3*	*4*	*5*	*6*
Effective Gross Income*	$246,000	$261,000	$277,000	$293,000	$311,000	$329,000
Less: Operating Expenses*	129,000	137,000	145,000	154,000	163,000	173,000
Net Operating Income	$117,000	$124,000	$132,000	$139,000	$148,000	$156,000
Less: Debt Service	106,164	106,164	106,164	106,164	106,164	106,164
Before-Tax Cash Flow	$ 10,836	$ 17,836	$ 25,836	$ 32,836	$ 41,836	$ 49,836
Plus: Principal Paid	5,670	6,389	7,200	8,113	9,142	10,301
Less: Cost Recovery Allowance**	36,242	37,818	37,818	37,818	37,818	36,242
Taxable Income (Loss)	$(19,736)	$(13,593)	$ (4,782)	$ 3,131	$ 13,160	$ 23,895
Times: Marginal Tax Rate	.28	.28	.28	.28	.28	.28
Income Tax (Tax Saving)	$ (5,526)	$ (3,806)	$ (1,339)	$ 877	$ 3,685	$ 6,691
Before-Tax Cash Flow	$ 10,836	$ 17,836	$ 25,836	$ 32,836	$ 41,836	$ 49,836
Income Tax Consequences	5,526	3,806	1,339	(877)	(3,685)	(6,691)
After-Tax Cash Flow	$ 16,362	$ 21,642	$ 27,175	$ 31,959	$ 38,151	$ 43,145

*Rounded to nearest $1,000.

**Assumes that 80 percent of the $1,300,000 purchase price is properly attributable to the building; that purchase closes during the first month and sale during the last month of the taxable year. See Chapter 10 for details of computation.

TABLE 16.7   Income Tax Consequences from Disposal

Sales Price		$1,800,000
Less:		
Transaction Costs (at 5%)	$ 90,000	
Adjusted Basis (Cost Minus Recovery)	1,076,244	1,166,244
Gain on Sale		$ 633,756
Tax on Sale, at 28%		$ 177,452

rate of return (ten percent) yields the present value of each year's cash flow forecast.

If the current gross rent multiplier continues to apply, this property will have a market value of approximately $1.8 million when sold at the end of the sixth year of ownership. Subtracting estimated transaction costs (five percent of the sales price) and the owner's adjusted basis before the sale (cost minus accumulated cost recovery allowances) yields the anticipated gain on disposal. Multiplying this by the investor's estimated 28 percent marginal income tax rate results in an anticipated income tax liability of $177,452. Table 16.7 summarizes these calculations.

TABLE 16.8   Forecast of After-Tax Cash Flow
from Disposal

Sales Price		$1,800,000
Less:		
Transaction Costs (from Table 16.7)	$ 90,000	
Income Tax (from Table 16.7)	177,452	
Mortgage Balance (from Table 16.5)	793,186	1,060,638
Net Cash Flow		$ 739,362

TABLE 16.9   Present Value of Anticipated After-Tax
Cash Flows

Year	After-Tax Cash-Flow	Present Value Factor at 10%	Present Value
1	$ 16,362	.9091	$ 14,875
2	21,642	.8264	17,885
3	27,175	.7513	20,417
4	31,959	.6830	21,828
5	38,151	.6209	23,688
6	43,145	.5645	24,355
6 (from Disposal)	739,362	.5645	417,370
Present Value of All Anticipated Cash Flows			$ 540,418
Plus: Available Mortgage Loan			840,000
Investment Value			$1,380,418

Table 16.8 converts the expected selling price and income tax consequences into a forecast of after-tax cash flow from disposal. This involves subtracting the estimated transaction costs, income tax liability and mortgage balance from the forecasted selling price of the property.

Anticipated after-tax cash flows are discounted in Table 16.9, to adjust for differences in timing of the expected receipts. Since the present value of all anticipated future cash flows exceeds the required initial equity investment ($540,418 present value compared to an investment of only $460,000), we conclude that the venture is expected to generate a yield in excess of the investor's ten percent minimum acceptable rate.

Estimating Investment Value

An alternative presentation of the data from Example 16.4 involves estimating the maximum purchase price to yield the lowest acceptable rate of return. This approach is a particularly valuable source of intelligence for improved negotiating. With the mortgage financing assumed to be available for the property in Example 16.4, an investor can pay the present value of cash flow to the equity position plus the amount of the available mortgage and still expect to receive a ten percent return on equity funds. Investment value for this individual is therefore equal to the $540,418 present value plus the $840,000 mortgage, which gives a total of $1,380,418. This computation is shown at the bottom of Table 16.9.

The effect of mortgage-financing assumptions on investment value serves to emphasize the most valuable use of this computation—its contribution to negotiating position. Since present value differs with the amount and cost of available financing, investment value will also vary. There is, therefore, a different investment value for every possible set of financing arrangements. When a seller finds a prospective purchaser's investment value unacceptably low, there is the possibility of a trade-off between price and credit terms.

Preparatory to negotiating price and terms, an investor should compute investment value under a variety of potential prices with attendant terms for partial seller financing. These alternatives give the investor a basis for making counteroffers, as well as a basis for quick evaluation of proposals made by the other side.

SUMMARY

Decision signals generated by discounted cash-flow models are extremely sensitive to differences in the discount rates employed. A minor shift in the choice of rate can alter the rankings of investment alternatives. For this reason, choosing a discount rate is a vital element in the usefulness of an analytical model.

An early approach employed to derive a discount rate was the summation technique. This involves choosing a risk-free rate, a risk premium, and rates to compensate for illiquidity and for the burden of investment management. The sum of these separate rates is held to be the appropriate discount rate. Difficulty in determining the appropriate rates for each of these elements renders the summation technique more a historical curiosity than a helpful tool for analysis.

Many analysts do employ a risk-adjusted discount rate, usually derived from observation of rates available in the marketplace. Conceptually, the rate is the sum of a risk-free rate and a risk premium. The most commonly used proxy for a risk-free rate is the rate available on short-term government securities. To this must be added a premium that will vary depending upon the amount of risk perceived to be associated with a particular investment venture.

Marginal cost of capital is the cost of procuring one more unit of capital. This is held by many analysts to be the appropriate rate to employ when considering the advisability of an investment venture. Since cash-flow forecasting generally yields a forecast of the cash flow to the equity investor, the marginal cost of equity capital is the most appropriate measure. Opportunity cost is frequently taken as the best estimate of the marginal cost of equity capital. Opportunity cost is the benefit forgone by not accepting the best available alternative investment proposition.

Investment decision rules that employ discounted cash-flow analysis must be adjusted to accommodate varying circumstances facing an investor or an analyst. When projects require different amounts of initial equity cash expenditure, the present value can be expressed as a profitability index. This measure indicates the present value per dollar of equity investment.

When comparing mutually exclusive projects, choose the one with the largest net present value (present value minus equity cash expenditure). When evaluating mutually dependent projects, group them into "packages" of mutually dependent alternatives. Evaluate each package as if it were a single investment venture.

Investment value is the greatest amount an investor is justified in paying for an asset, given the anticipated after-tax cash flows the asset will generate and the investor's minimum acceptable rate of return. To estimate investment value, add the available mortgage loan to the present value of anticipated after-tax cash flows to the equity position.

NOTES

1. See, for example, J. Fred Weston and Eugene F. Brigham, *Managerial Finance,* 5th ed. (Hinsdale, IL: The Dryden Press, 1975), Chapter 19.

2. Harold Bierman, Jr., and Seymour Smidt, *The Capital Budgeting Decision,* 3d ed. (New York: The Macmillan Company, 1971), v.

RECOMMENDED READINGS

Brigham, Eugene F. *Fundamentals of Financial Management.* 4th ed. Hinsdale, IL: The Dryden Press, 1986, pp. 278–292.

Greer, Gaylon E. *The Real Estate Investment Decision.* Lexington, MA: Lexington Books, 1979, pp. 153–174.

Phyrr, Stephen A., and James R. Cooper. *Real Estate Investment Strategy, Analysis, Decisions.* Boston: Warren, Gorham and Lamont, 1982, pp. 284–316.

REVIEW QUESTIONS

1. What is the importance of the discount rate chosen when evaluating investment opportunities?
2. What is the basis for the summation technique? What is assumed to be the appropriate rate of return in this technique?

3. What is a risk-free rate of return? What are the risks associated with an investment yielding the risk-free rate?
4. When is the opportunity cost of capital an appropriate discount rate?
5. How is the profitability index calculated, and when is it most useful?
6. Describe mutually dependent investment decisions. How should mutually dependent investments be treated?
7. What are mutually exclusive investment opportunities? Give some examples. When is a choice between mutually exclusive alternatives likely to occur?
8. What role does investment value play in the investment strategies of a buyer and seller?
9. What effect do the amount and cost of mortgage financing have on the present value and investment value of a property? How might this relationship be used in the negotiation process?

DISCUSSION QUESTIONS

1. Since the opportunity cost of equity capital changes over time, should long-term commitments be evaluated using a different opportunity cost than are short-term commitments?
2. When discounting long-term cash-flow forecasts using the opportunity cost of capital, should the rate employed reflect costs at the time the commitment is to be made, or should it reflect anticipated average capital costs over the forecast period?

CHAPTER 17

Computer-Assisted Analysis

INTRODUCTION

Though commonplace today, the discounted cash-flow techniques explained in Chapters 13 through 16 are a relatively recent real estate investment analysis innovation. They have been widely used only since the advent of inexpensive and easily operated microcomputers. Manually computing discounted cash flows was overly time-consuming for most analysts' tastes, and early computers were too costly and too difficult to operate. Recent wholesale adoption of these techniques after years of virtual neglect is attributable primarily to advances in electronic data processing.

COMPUTATIONAL COMPLEXITIES

University researchers and teachers incorporated discounted cash-flow analysis into their teaching and writing during the 1960s, and by the early 1970s they had developed computer programs that eliminated most of the computational tedium that had for so long rendered the technique impractical. Transplanting the new methodology from classrooms and researchers' desks to the cost-conscious world of real estate decision makers, however, proved difficult and slow.

Business school graduates employed by real estate firms during those years often found that their new employers did not have computers capable of running the recently assembled discounted cash-flow programs. Ambitious analysts who performed discounted cash-flow routines on hand-held calculators were forced to introduce numerous simplifying assumptions, some of which greatly limited the usefulness of the technique.

Early computerized discounted cash-flow programs were designed to run on university mainframe computers, the cost of which put them far beyond the capabilities of all but the largest and most prosperous real estate analysis firms. Computer time-sharing, introduced as a way to solve the dilemma, greatly reduced the cost but still proved too expensive for widespread adoption.

ADVENT OF THE MICROCOMPUTER

Widespread adoption of discounted cash-flow analysis awaited the availability of inexpensive computers and simplified software. Practical and affordable microcomputers, often called *personal computers* or *PCs*, were not generally available before 1980. Those few models introduced earlier were fairly expensive and, by today's standards, had limited capabilities.

Affordable microcomputers, however, were widely available by the mid-1980s. These newer machines often cost less than their primitive forebears yet had greater computational power than the mainframe behemoths that, just a few years earlier, cost hundreds of thousands of dollars.

Technical innovation, moreover, has not slowed. Every year computational power grows while costs decline. Operating programs, called *software,* are also steadily improving. Today, computers are affordable by every firm in the industry, and they can be used with little or no special training. Virtually everyone uses them to some degree. In many companies, each employee's desk sports a computer.

ELECTRONIC SPREADSHEETS

Microcomputers owe their prominence in no small part to one simple idea. Before computers, the analyst's primary tool was an accountant's analysis pad, and enterprising computer programmers simply transferred an image of this pad to the computer screen. They then programmed the computer to do the computational chores that analysts once did with pen and hand-held calculator. The result has come to be known as an *electronic spreadsheet.*

Accountants' analysis pads, as most readers already know, are simply multicolumn worksheets with space for a descriptive heading on each line. The intersections of the lines and columns form "cells" into which the user enters numbers. Income, expenses or other financial information is recorded using a different column for each month or year and a different row for each category of data. These pads have been perennially popular because of their flexibility of use. They simplify both the arrangement of data and the application of mathematical computations.

At their simplest, electronic spreadsheets are nothing more than computerized analysis pads. They are, however, extremely large. One of the more widely adopted spreadsheet programs incorporates 256 columns and 8,192 rows, for a total of 2,097,152 cells, or data entry points.

Spreadsheet programs vastly simplify computational chores. Instead of adding, subtracting, multiplying and dividing, the analyst "instructs" the program by entering the appropriate formula and lets the machine do the work. Recomputation is automatic (and almost instantaneous) when the analyst changes or rearranges data or alters the relationship among cells.

Electronic spreadsheets are preprogrammed to perform many common but complex computations, such as determining compound interest, present value or loan amortization. Many widely used statistical functions (such as mean, variance and standard deviation) are also preprogrammed.

Versatility is the characteristic that most distinguishes spreadsheets from other types of computer programs. Accountants use them as aids to bookkeeping, auditing and tax preparation chores. Businesspeople use them for such diverse tasks as sales forecasting, inventory control and financial analysis. Individuals use them to track their stock portfolios, to maintain household budgets, to do their income taxes and so on.

To many real estate analysts, electronic spreadsheets have become indispensable. They use the programs in virtually every phase of their analytical chores, from comparatively simple problems such as preparing depreciation or loan amortization schedules to more ambitious tasks, including constructing extensive and complex discounted cash flow models.

Depreciation Schedules

Table 17.1 shows a representative spreadsheet-generated depreciation schedule for a residential rental property. After specifying an equation that determines the rate at which depreciation will be computed, the analyst has only to enter values for three input variables to generate this schedule. Altering any one of these three variables will result in a new, totally altered depreciation schedule the program will generate automatically.

Key words appear near the top of the depreciation schedule in Table 17.1, indicating the three input variables. *Amount?* refers to the cumulative amount of depreciation to be taken over the entire depreciation period. In this example the building cost $260,000, so that amount is entered in response to the query. *Life?* refers to the number of years over which depreciation is claimed; 27.5 in the example illustrated on Table 17.1. *Month?* refers to the month in the investor's taxable year in which the asset is to be put into service; in our example, the sixth. The operator simply enters answers to these three queries, and the electronic spreadsheet routine produces the depreciation schedule.

TABLE 17.1   Residential Depreciation Schedule

AMOUNT	$260,000
LIFE	27.5
MONTH ACQUIRED?	6

Year	Beginning Balance	Depreciation	Ending Balance
Year 1	$260,000	$ 5,121	$254,879
Year 2	254,879	9,455	245,424
Year 3	245,424	9,455	235,970
Year 4	235,970	9,455	226,515
Year 5	226,515	9,455	217,061
Year 6	217,061	9,455	207,606
Year 7	207,606	9,455	198,152
Year 8	198,152	9,455	188,697
Year 9	188,697	9,455	179,242
Year 10	179,242	9,455	169,788
Year 11	169,788	9,455	160,333
Year 12	160,333	9,455	150,879
Year 13	150,879	9,455	141,424
Year 14	141,424	9,455	131,970
Year 15	131,970	9,455	122,515
Year 16	122,515	9,455	113,061
Year 17	113,061	9,455	103,606
Year 18	103,606	9,455	94,152
Year 19	94,152	9,455	84,697
Year 20	84,697	9,455	75,242
Year 21	75,242	9,455	65,788
Year 22	65,788	9,455	56,333
Year 23	56,333	9,455	46,879
Year 24	46,879	9,455	37,424
Year 25	37,424	9,455	27,970
Year 26	27,970	9,455	18,515
Year 27	18,515	9,455	9,061
Year 28	9,061	9,061	0
Year 29	0	0	0
Total		$260,000	

All the arithmetic to generate the numbers in Table 17.1 is performed by the spreadsheet program once the analyst enters values for the three input variables. But a formula—sometimes called an *algorithm*—must first be entered to instruct the program.

In this example the spreadsheet is told to divide the first input variable (the cumulative amount of depreciation to be claimed) by the second (the number of years over which the depreciation will be claimed). This quotient, the annual allowance, is divided by 12 to generate a monthly allowance figure. The program is then instructed to multiply the monthly amount by the third variable, minus one-half month, to determine the first year's allowance (the half month is subtracted to account for the half-month convention explained in Chapter 10). Twelve times the monthly allowance is the annual amount for years two through 27. For the final year's allowance, all prior allowances are simply subtracted from the original input variable, *Amount?*

Loan Amortization Schedules

Producing loan amortization schedules is another relatively simple application of electronic spreadsheets. Table 17.2 shows a typical product of a loan amortization algorithm. This program, like that for developing a depreciation schedule, requires just three input variables. The program generates the annual loan constant, annual debt service and a loan amortization schedule.

Input variables are shown at the top of the schedule in Table 17.2, denoted by key words, or queries. *Amount?* refers to the dollar amount of the loan. *Term?* refers to the number of years over which the loan is to be repaid. *Rate?* refers to the annual interest rate. *Constant:* refers to the annual debt service as a decimal fraction of the amount borrowed. *Annual Payment:* refers to the dollar amount of the annual service.

The program that produced the schedule in Table 17.2 is designed to handle loan terms of up to 30 years, but no such limitation is inherent in spreadsheet analysis. The particulars of any amortization program are controlled by the analyst who specifies the algorithm and designs the spreadsheet layout.

Discounted Cash-Flow Analysis

Depreciation and amortization schedules are elementary applications of electronic spreadsheet capabilities, because each involves only a single function. Spreadsheets, however, are very powerful tools, capable of handling extremely complex analytical chores. Many analysts claim that they do all their work on electronic spreadsheets.

Table 17.3 shows the input variables (indicated by key words followed by question marks) for a discounted cash-flow routine designed to run on an electronic spreadsheet. As with most well-designed spreadsheet programs of any complexity, this one separates input variables into a separate schedule from the primary output. The alternative of entering input variables directly onto the main spreadsheet schedule, though not uncommon, is an invitation to confusion and error. Segregating input variables as illustrated in Table 17.3 eliminates a major source of potential confusion and highlights all assumptions incorporated in the analysis.

Spreadsheet-generated cash-flow projections, based on the input data in Table 17.3, are illustrated in Tables 17.4 and 17.5. Projected cash flows from operations are shown in Table 17.4. Table 17.5 gives indicated cash flows from the sale under two assumptions: that the sale occurs in year seven and that it occurs in year eight. The spreadsheet program automatically generates these projections when an analyst enters the input variables shown in Table 17.3.

TABLE 17.2 Loan Amortization Schedule

AMOUNT?	$750,000.00
TERM?	25
RATE?	12.50%
CONSTANT:	0.13194344
ANNUAL PAYMENT:	$98,957.58

Year	Loan Balance	Interest	Principal
1	$ 750,000.00	$ 93,750.00	$ 5,207.58
2	744,792.42	93,099.05	5,858.53
3	738,933.89	92,366.74	6,590.84
4	732,343.05	91,542.88	7,414.70
5	724,928.35	90,616.04	8,341.54
6	716,586.81	89,573.35	9,384.23
7	707,202.58	88,400.32	10,557.26
8	696,645.32	87,080.67	11,876.92
9	684,768.41	85,596.05	13,361.53
10	671,406.88	83,925.86	15,031.72
11	656,375.16	82,046.89	16,910.69
12	639,464.47	79,933.06	19,024.52
13	620,439.95	77,554.99	21,402.59
14	599,037.36	74,879.67	24,077.91
15	574,959.45	71,869.93	27,087.65
16	547,871.80	68,483.97	30,473.61
17	517,398.19	64,674.77	34,282.81
18	483,115.39	60,389.42	38,568.16
19	444,547.23	55,568.40	43,389.18
20	401,158.05	50,144.76	48,812.82
21	352,345.23	44,043.15	54,914.43
22	297,430.80	37,178.85	61,778.73
23	235,652.07	29,456.51	69,501.07
24	166,151.00	20,768.87	78,188.71
25	87,962.29	10,995.29	87,962.29
26	0.00	0.00	0.00
27	0.00	0.00	0.00
28	0.00	0.00	0.00
29	0.00	0.00	0.00
30	0.00	0.00	0.00
Totals	$13,791,516.14	$1,723,939.52	$750,000.00

Changing any of the input variables results in revised projections for Tables 17.4 and 17.5, which are automatically recomputed.

Note that the schedules shown here are not significantly different from those developed in Chapter 16. Whereas all numbers were entered and calculated manually in the earlier examples, everything in these schedules is generated and printed automatically by the program once the input variables are keyed into the computer.

TABLE 17.3 Input for Discounted Cash-Flow Analysis

Purchase Price?	$325,000
Land Percentage?	20%
Land Value:	$65,000
Building Value:	$260,000
Depreciable Life?	27.5
Month Acquired?	6
Gross Income?	$75,180
Growth Rate?	5%
Vacancy Rate?	5%
Operating Expenses?	$40,060
Growth Rate?	5%
Loan Number One?	$176,670
Points?	0
Rate?	14%
Term?	29
Constant:	0.1432042
Total Cost of Points:	$0
Annual Loan Payment:	$25,300
Loan Number Two?	$0
Points?	0
Rate?	14%
Term?	29
Constant:	0.1432042
Total Cost of Points:	$0
Annual Loan Payment:	$0
Debt Coverage Ratio:	1.2396
Required Equity:	$148,330
Income Tax Rate?	28%
Rate of Change?	0%
Discount Rate?	10%
Growth Rate in Value?	5%
Selling Expenses?	3%

Note the lower section of Table 17.5. Here the spreadsheet program summarizes key investment criteria. Data are shown first under the assumption that the property is sold in the seventh year. The second column shows the anticipated results if the sale occurs in the eighth year.

The first row of this bottom section indicates the present value of anticipated cash flows to the equity investor, using the discount rate specified in the input variables in Table 17.3. The second row adds the amount of the purchase price provided by mortgage lenders, again as indicated by the input variables in Table 17.3. The sum of these values, shown in the third row, is the amount an investor could pay for this property and still anticipate earning a yield equal to the rate used in the discounting operation. This is called the *investment value* and is discussed in Chapter 2.

TABLE 17.4 Cash-Flow Projections

					CASH-FLOW FORECAST			
	Year 1	Year 2	Year 3	Year 4	Year 5	Year 6	Year 7	Year 8
Gross Income	$75,180	$78,939	$82,886	$87,030	$91,382	$95,951	$100,749	$105,786
Less: Vacancy	3,759	3,947	4,144	4,352	$ 569	4,798	5,037	5,289
Effective Gross	$71,421	$74,992	$78,742	$82,678	$86,813	$91,153	$95,712	$100,497
Operating Expenses	40,060	42,063	44,166	46,374	48,693	51,128	53,684	56,368
Net Operating Income	$31,361	$32,929	$34,576	$36,304	$38,120	$40,025	$ 42,028	$ 44,129
Less: Debt Service								
Loan One	25,300	25,300	25,300	25,300	25,300	25,300	25,300	25,300
Loan Two	0	0	0	0	0	0	0	0
Before-Tax Cash Flow	$ 6,061	$ 7,629	$ 9,276	$11,004	$12,820	$14,725	$ 16,728	$ 18,829
Plus: Principal								
Loan One	566	645	735	838	955	1,089	1,241	1,415
Loan Two	0	0	0	0	0	0	0	0
Less: Depreciation	5,121	9,455	9,455	9,455	9,455	9,455	9,455	9,455
Less: Points								
Loan One	0	0	0	0	0	0	0	0
Loan Two	0	0	0	0	0	0	0	0
Taxable Income	$ 1,506	($ 1,181)	$ 556	$ 2,387	$ 4,320	$ 6,359	$ 8,514	$ 10,789
Times: Tax Rate	28%	28%	28%	28%	28%	28%	28%	28%
Taxes	$ 422	($ 331)	$ 156	$ 668	$ 1,210	$ 1,781	$ 2,384	$ 3,021
Before-Tax Cash Flow	$ 6,061	$ 7,629	$ 9,276	$11,004	$12,820	$14,725	$ 16,728	$ 18,829
Tax Consequences	(422)	331	(156)	(668)	(1,210)	(1,781)	(2,384)	(3,021)
After-Tax Cash Flow	$ 5,639	$ 7,960	$ 9,120	$10,336	$11,610	$12,944	$ 14,344	$ 15,808

TABLE 17.5 Proceeds of Sale, Investment Value and Net Present Value

PROCEEDS OF SALE		
	Year 7	*Year 8*
Sales Price	$457,308	$480,173
Transaction Costs	$13,719	$14,405
Net Sales Price	$443,589	$465,768
Less: Book Value		
Land	65,000	65,000
Building	198,149	188,694
Gain on Sale	$180,440	$212,074
Less: Unamortized Points	0	0
Taxable Income Due to Sale	$180,440	$212,074
Times: Tax Rate	28%	28%
Tax Due to Sale	$50,523	$59,381
Net Sales Price	$443,589	$465,768
Less:		
Tax Due to Sale	50,523	59,381
Mortgage Balance	170,601	169,186
After-Tax Cash Flow from Sale	$222,465	$237,201

INVESTMENT VALUE & NET PRESENT VALUE		
	Year 7	*Year 8*
Present Value of the Equity	$161,652	$165,523
Plus: Available Financing	176,670	176,670
Investment Value	$338,300	$342,200
Present Value of the Equity	$161,652	$165,523
Less: Required Equity	148,330	148,330
Net Present Value	$13,322	$17,193

The final set of computations at the bottom of Table 17.5 shows the net present value of anticipated cash flows to the equity investor. Using the discount rate specified by the input variables, the program discounts the equity investor's expected cash flows. These amounts, under the assumptions of a seventh-year sale and again assuming a sale in the eighth year, are shown in the third row from the bottom in Table 17.5. In the second row from the bottom the required down payment, taken from the input variables in Table 17.3, is shown. The last row indicates the difference between the present value of the expected cash flows to the equity investor and the amount of immediate equity funds that must be invested. As explained in Chapter 13, this is the expected net present value of the investment.

Chapter 19 discusses partitioning present value as a risk analysis technique. Partitioning is an extremely efficacious way to gauge sensitivity to variance between anticipated and actual values for such factors as vacancy rates, income tax rates and rates of change in property values and market rents. The technique's major limitation is the extensive and laborious computations involved. Electronic spreadsheets eliminate this limitation.

Spreadsheet Templates

Of course, electronic spreadsheet programs require instructions. Someone must enter equations to tell the program what computations to perform.

Most spreadsheet programs have two formats: one for formulas and one for numbers. In the formula format the analyst expresses the intended relationship between the various cells in the spreadsheet (the squares formed by the intersection of rows and columns) and the input variables. In the number format the analyst enters the input variables. Based on the input variables and the formulas, the spreadsheet program calculates all other values and automatically fills in the worksheet.

Entering formulas onto the spreadsheet requires no computer programming knowledge. All are simply arithmetic or algebraic expressions that would be employed even if the analysis pad were being completed in pencil and all numbers were being determined with a hand-held calculator or by manual computation.

Even so, considerable thought and planning are needed to correctly specify the relationships and the formulas. The job is rendered less tedious by the knowledge that it need be done only once. The completed spreadsheet can be reused an infinite number of times by simply altering the input variables.

Analysts who lack the time, talent or patience to design their electronic spreadsheet formats and specify the equations need not abandon this valuable tool. Enterprising computer enthusiasts have developed "generic" spreadsheet programs for virtually every conceivable use. These preformatted spreadsheets, called *templates*, are widely available and generally command modest prices.

DEDICATED PROGRAMS

For many people, the need to understand what happens between the keying in of information and the printing out of computer-generated data is a serious drawback of electronic spreadsheets. Either they haven't the time or they lack the patience or will to master the intricacies of spreadsheet formatting and formula writing.

Even commercially available templates are, for some analysts, an inadequate simplification. They feel their time is better spent reviewing investment proposals or negotiating business transactions than mastering spreadsheet routines. For these people, specialized computer programs designed solely for analyzing real estate ventures have considerable appeal.

Such programs, often called *dedicated programs* to denote their specialized nature, perform a limited range of functions—often only one specific task. In abundant supply and of awe-inspiring variety, dedicated real estate programs have been designed for virtually every conceivable filing, data storage and retrieval, information display, analytic or computational chore.

Some dedicated programs are intended for a narrow range of uses. They might be designed solely to analyze office buildings, for example, or only for shopping center analysis. Others are touted as being almost as flexible as spreadsheets; their developers claim they can be used for everything from analyzing a condominium conversion project to tracking a superregional shopping center's development. Choosing between narrowly specialized and more flexible programs is a decision that prospective users of dedicated programs must make.

Generally, the more flexible a dedicated program is designed to be, the more difficult it is to master. Users must initially tailor their copies of the program for their particular needs, and these "setup" steps can be exasperating and time-consuming. Programs designed specifically for the user's intended purpose do not require these initial routines and usually require much less tutorial time for the user to become proficient.

Dedicated Programs for Complex Projects

Choice between spreadsheets and dedicated programs should be determined in part by the complexity of an analyst's task. Shopping center analysis is a particularly compelling example. A small neighborhood center can be analyzed using an electronic spreadsheet, but efficient and accurate analysis of a superregional center containing as many as 200 tenants and a wide range of lease provisions can best be completed with the help of a dedicated program.

Shopping center leases contain a variety of clauses unique to commercial space. Chapter 23 explains several of these, such as expense stops, escalator provisions and percentage rents. Market conditions and recent experience determine the exact nature of these clauses, and, because leases in a large shopping center may have been negotiated during different periods, they will have widely varying provisions.

For example, shopping center leases often include a fixed, periodic base rent plus additional rent predicated on the tenant's retail sales volume. More recently, many leases have substituted a provision for periodic increases in the base rent plus additional rent based on increases in the consumer price index. Others incorporate elements of both these provisions. Each variation requires a different approach to estimating rental income over the lease period, yet all may be in effect among different tenants in the same center. Such complexity is best handled with a dedicated program.

Dedicated programs also facilitate accounting for provisions that pass operating expenses through to tenants, that allocate common area maintenance costs and that incorporate special concessions made by landlords to induce tenants to occupy space in the project.

Inflexibility: The Cost of Power

Offsetting the special advantages of dedicated programs is their relative inflexibility. Compared with electronic spreadsheets, dedicated programs—even those that purport to be all-purpose—put the user in an analytical straitjacket. The program can do only what its designer intended it to do and is therefore subject to the designer's conceptual limitations.

Approaches that are unique to the analyst may not be compatible with the program, and most users lack the knowledge required to revise dedicated programs to fit their special needs. Yet "custom-tailored" programs are likely to be prohibitively expensive for all except those users who are regularly engaged to analyze complex and costly projects.

SUMMARY

Comparatively powerful microcomputers, affordable by even a low-volume, one-person real estate consulting operation, have greatly expanded the application of discounted cash-flow analysis. They have made it possible to incorporate complex risk analysis, a step that is gaining increasing vogue among real estate analysts. As the processing speed, internal memory and disk storage capacity of these machines continues to multiply, even more sophisticated analysis will become commonplace.

Electronic spreadsheets are an all-purpose analytical tool that can be employed to perform most real estate investment analysis chores. Their special virtues are that they are exceedingly flexible and that they require no special programming knowledge. As the complexity of the analytical task grows, however, spreadsheet analysis becomes more cumbersome, time-consuming and error-prone.

Dedicated programs fall into two general categories. Some are designed to analyze all types of real estate ventures and require users to perform an initial "setup" based on their particular needs. Others are designed to examine only one type of property or to perform a narrow range of analytic functions. Many analysts claim they find dedicated programs easier to use and more efficient than electronic spreadsheets.

RECOMMENDED READINGS

Bayer, Barry D., and Joseph J. Sobel, *Dynamics of Visicalc*. Homewood, IL: Dow Jones-Irwin, 1983.

Jaffe, Austin J. *Analyzing Real Estate Decisions Using Lotus 1-2-3*. Reston, VA: Reston Publishing Company, Inc., 1985.

Jaffe, Austin J. *Analyzing Real Estate Decisions Using Visicalc*. Reston, VA: Reston Publishing Company, Inc., 1985.

Klitzner, Carol, and Matthew J. Plociak, Jr., *Using Visicalc: Getting Down to Business*. Somerset, NJ: John Wiley & Sons, Inc., 1983.

Person, Ron, *1-2-3 Business Formula Handbook*. Indianapolis, IN: Que Corporation, 1986.

Simpson, Alan, *The Best Book of: Lotus 1-2-3, 2nd ed*. Indianapolis, IN: Howard W. Sams & Co., 1986.

REVIEW QUESTIONS

1. Why did it take so long for analytical programs, written on university computers during the 1960s, to find their way into general use among real estate practitioners?
2. Distinguish between computer hardware and software.
3. What are the principal advantages of electronic spreadsheets over columnar pads, often called *accountants' analysis pads?*
4. Does the use of electronic spreadsheet routines relieve the analyst of the need to understand the mechanics of cash-flow forecasting and discounting?
5. What is a spreadsheet template, and why have they gained such popularity?
6. Describe the principal difference between spreadsheets and dedicated computer programs.

DISCUSSION QUESTIONS

1. Dedicated analytical programs and electronic spreadsheets both contain the seed of investment disaster: Errors in the programming may go undetected by investors who make decisions based on the computer output. Discuss the relative difficulty of verifying the accuracy of software instructions embedded in electronic spreadsheets and dedicated programs.
2. Dedicated programs are sometimes preferred because they require less user knowledge of the process involved in generating the output. Discuss the wisdom of making investment decisions based on investment criteria wherein the investor does not understand the underlying analytical mechanics.

PART FIVE: Case Problem

For the following problems, refer to your worksheets from the case problem for Part Four.

1. Compute the following ratios for the Sated Satyr, based on your calculations from the case problem for Part Four and assuming that Benedict paid $1.3 million for the property and secured a $1.2 million mortgage loan payable in monthly payments over 30 years with interest at ten percent:

   Gross income multiplier
   Net income multiplier
   Operating ratio
   Breakeven, or default, ratio
   Debt coverage ratio
   Overall capitalization rate
   Equity dividend rate
   Cash-on-cash return
   Payback period

2. Discount the anticipated after-tax cash flows from the project and determine:

   Present value
   Net present value
   Investment value

3. Determine the project's anticipated internal rate of return.

Important! Save all your work relating to the Sated Satyr apartments for use in solving the case problem for Part Six.

PART SIX

The Risk Element

Traditional real estate investment literature has fallen behind related fields such as corporate capital budgeting and portfolio analysis, by not systematically incorporating risk elements into the investment decision. This section of the text summarizes traditional approaches to risk in real estate investment analysis and introduces recent efforts to incorporate more advanced risk analysis techniques from related fields of financial and investment analysis.

The intention of Part Six is to demonstrate that specific investment objectives can be related to probabilistic estimates of possible investment outcomes. Investors can compare expected outcomes with the probability that a particular venture will produce a yield equal to or greater than some predetermined minimum acceptable outcome. Faced with quantified risk and return trade-offs, investors will be well positioned to make rational investment decisions.

Chapter 18 discusses risk in general terms, with the objective of acquainting readers with the issues involved in comparing risk-return combinations of alternative investment opportunities. Chapter 19 reviews traditional approaches to dealing with the problem of risk in real estate investment analysis. Chapter 20 then introduces some contemporary alternatives and demonstrates the application of one increasingly utilized contemporary approach.

CHAPTER 18

Risk in Real Estate Investment

INTRODUCTION

Earlier chapters discuss investment evaluation based on a single best estimate of net cash flows over the projection period. The illusion of precision in these point estimates is seductive. Yet failing to appreciate the significance of possible forecasting errors can lead to grievous investment miscalculation.

Because the future is unknowable, the only certainty is that actual investment outcomes will differ from expectations. All forecasts are probabilistic in nature, and the implication of precision found in statements with values rounded to the nearest whole dollar should be rejected.

This chapter introduces risk as an issue in investment analysis. It distinguishes among major risk elements and discusses methods for controlling risk. It considers the relationship among risk, risk taker and profit expectations. The chapter concludes with an introduction to problems in measuring risk and incorporating risk perception into the investment decision.

MAJOR RISK ELEMENTS

Risk elements can be usefully characterized according to their origins. Risk inherent in the use of borrowed funds, and thus determined by choice of financial arrangements, is called *financial risk*. Risk of loss from natural hazards (fire, flood, storm and so forth) can be transferred to insurance companies and so is characterized as *insurable risk*. Risk stemming from the possibility of making inappropriate business decisions or of misjudging the economic consequences of one's actions is labeled *business risk*.

Financial Risk

We saw in Part Three that financial leverage (using borrowed funds) broadens the range of possible returns on an investment. Since variability is a measure of risk, it follows that greater financial leverage generally increases the level of risk associated with the leveraged venture. Recall from Chapter 8 that leverage increases the yield on an equity investment (and is therefore considered positive, or favorable) so long as the cost of borrowed funds is less than the yield on assets. *Unfavorable leverage*, in contrast, decreases the yield on an investor's equity funds. Financial leverage also amplifies the variability of possible returns to equity investors. Increased variability represents additional risk due to the financing decision and so is part of the financial risk associated with the investment.

Consider a property with an expected net income (revenue minus all expenditures other than debt service) of $150,000 and a market value of $1 million. Assume the range of possible net operating income is $125,000 to $175,000. If an investor purchases this asset without using borrowed funds, the expected annual yield (before income taxes) is $150,000 divided by $1,000,000, or 15 percent. Possible annual pretax yields range from $125,000 divided by $1,000,000, or 12.5 percent, through $175,000 divided by $1,000,000, or 17.5 percent.

Suppose our investor finances $700,000 of the purchase price via a mortgage loan requiring repayment in equal monthly payments over 25 years, with interest at 13 percent. Monthly payments on such a loan will be approximately $7,895, and the annual debt service obligation will be 12 times this amount, or approximately $94,740. Before-tax cash flow to the equity investor is, of course, reduced by the amount of the annual debt service obligation. With the loan, the range of possible before-tax cash flows is $125,000 minus $94,740, or $30,260, at the low end, and $175,000 minus $94,740, or $80,260, at the high end. The expected cash flow becomes $150,000 minus $94,740, or $55,260. These computations are presented in Table 18.1.

Of course, the mortgage loan also reduces the size of the required equity investment from $1 million to only $300,000. The expected annual pretax yield therefore becomes the expected before-tax cash flow of $55,260 divided by the $300,000 equity investment, or 18.4 percent. The range of possible annual pretax yields with the mortgage loan is from 10.1 percent to 26.8 percent, as shown in Table 18.1.

Alterations in the range of possible outcomes due to financial leverage are illustrated in Figure 18.1. Leverage raises the expected annual pretax yield (depicted by the small vertical bars) from 15 percent to 18.4 percent, but it also increases the range of possible annual yields rather impressively. As depicted

FIGURE 18.1   Most Likely Current Yield and Range of Possible Variation

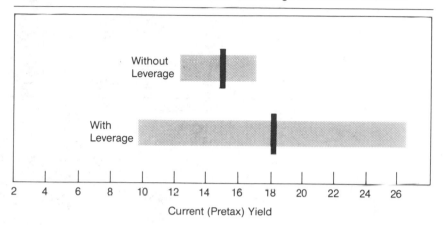

Current (Pretax) Yield

TABLE 18.1   Range of Possible Outcomes with Financial Leverage

	Lower Bound	*Expected*	*Upper Bound*
Net Operating Income	$125,000	$150,000	$175,000
Less: Debt Service	94,740	94,740	94,740
Pretax Cash Flow	$ 30,260	$ 55,260	$ 80,260
Current Yield	$30,260/$300,000	$55,260/$300,000	$80,260/$300,000
Pretax Cash Flow/			
Equity Investment	= 10.1%	= 18.4%	= 26.8%

by the horizontal bars in Figure 18.1, annual yields with leverage can fall significantly below the least possible yield without leverage. The graph also illustrates that the upper end of the range of possible yields is greatly increased by the leverage. This possibility is usually referred to as *upside risk* and is a much desired consequence. Whether the enhanced yield expectation and the greater upside risk justify the amplified downside risk attendant to financial leverage depends upon investor risk preferences, as discussed later in this chapter.

Since mortgage lenders have a prior claim on net operating income, with the investor's before-tax cash flow being a residual, increasing the amount of borrowed funds (and thus the debt service obligation) also increases the probability that net operating income will be insufficient to meet the debt service obligation. This is an additional dimension of financial risk.

To illustrate, consider a 28-unit apartment project expected to generate $10,000 per unit of gross income. Assume the units require annual expenditures of approximately $5,000 per unit for variable operating expenses. An expected $5,000 per unit remains to cover fixed expenditures—including debt service—and to provide a return to the investor. If all the units are rented for the entire year at the expected rental rate, an annual cash flow of $140,000 before ex-

FIGURE 18.2   Breakeven Occupancy Levels With and Without Financial Leverage

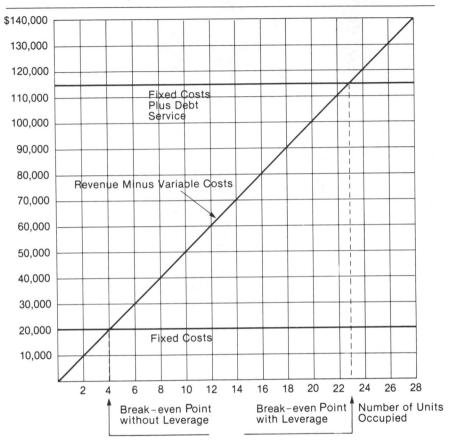

penditures for debt service and other fixed costs will result. Further assume that fixed charges other than debt service total $20,000 (these usually are comprised of insurance and property taxes). Expected rental revenues net of variable costs, at various occupancy levels, are depicted in Figure 18.2.

Occupancy levels are measured on the horizontal axis of Figure 18.2. Fixed costs are by definition the same regardless of occupancy level. Revenue varies directly with occupancy. Since, as we have seen, each unit generates $5,000 above its variable costs of operation, 100 percent occupancy will generate $140,000 to cover fixed costs and profit. Of this amount, $20,000 is applied to cover fixed costs, with the balance accruing to the investor. Therefore, with 100 percent occupancy the investor will earn before-tax cash flow of $140,000 minus $20,000, or $120,000.

Reductions in occupancy level diminish revenue available for fixed costs and profit without affecting the fixed cost element. The entire reduction, therefore, is reflected in reduced profits. At a 14 percent occupancy level (four of

FIGURE 18.3 Breakeven Rental Rates With and Without Financial Leverage

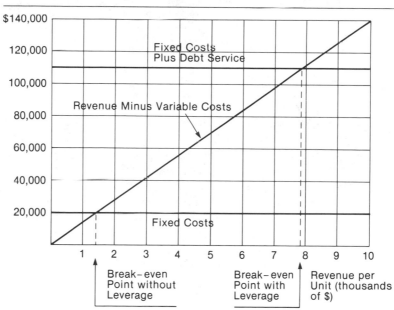

the 28 units rented for the entire year) revenue minus variable costs exactly equals the $20,000 of fixed costs; pretax profits are zero. The before-tax break-even occupancy level with no debt financing is therefore 14 percent.

Now see what happens when debt financing is used. Assume our investor borrows $750,000 at 12 percent interest, with the debt to be paid in equal monthly installments of principal and interest over 25 years. The monthly payment will be approximately $7,900, and the annual debt service obligation will be 12 times this amount, or $94,800. As with other fixed costs, the debt service obligation remains invariant regardless of occupancy levels.

Figure 18.2 also illustrates this revised financial picture. As before, the project will generate $140,000 above variable costs when fully occupied. Every vacant unit (if it remains vacant for a full year) will reduce this amount by $5,000. Since fixed costs and debt service are prior obligations, the entire reduction in revenue represents diminished before-tax cash flow to the investor. A full year's revenue from 23 units is required to meet fixed costs plus debt service. This represents an 82 percent occupancy level just to break even on the project (before taxes).

Using financial leverage in this instance has increased the occupancy level necessary to maintain solvency from 14 percent to 82 percent and has thereby greatly increased the probability (that is, risk) of insolvency.

Figure 18.3 illustrates the same point but assumes rents are varied to maintain a target occupancy level. This alternative presentation places per-unit rental rates on the horizontal axis.

Inept or misguided scheduling of debt service obligations also increases financial risk, which is a phenomenon specific to the financial arrangements surrounding an individual investment decision. The amount of financial risk associated with a particular investment venture is in this sense controlled by the investor.

Insurable Risk

Accurate prediction of loss due to fire, flood and other natural hazards is virtually impossible for any particular building or property. It is possible, of course, to calculate the odds of such a loss based on statistical sampling techniques. But to an investor who has just been wiped out by a major fire or flood, how significant is the fact that the likelihood of such an occurrence was, say, one in 10,000?

Predictability based on statistical averages is the foundation of the insurance industry. Because their dollar losses are relatively predictable, insurers can develop fee schedules that compensate for all projected losses plus a premium for expenses and profits and a reserve for the unexpected. For large firms, the degree of uncertainty involved in the insurance function is very small. Investors can transfer many risk elements to insurance firms that specialize in bearing statistically predictable risk.

Fire and extended-coverage insurance shifts the risk of property damage by fire, smoke, wind, hail, lightning, flood, etc., from the property owner to an insurance company. Liability insurance protects against claims resulting from injuries sustained on the property. Damage to plate glass can be covered, as can damage due to malfunction in sprinkler systems. Other types of insurance that property owners frequently obtain include protection against loss or damage to building contents and coverage on mechanical equipment such as boilers, hot water heaters and air-conditioning units. *Dram shop insurance* protects against liabilities arising from incidents related to liquor consumption. If building owners have employees working on the premises, workers' compensation insurance may also be necessary.

Business Risk

Even the most precisely calibrated operating projections are subject to gross errors. The likelihood that actual operating results will vary from expectations is sometimes called *business risk*.

Business risk stems both from factors internal to the investment equation and from circumstances attributable to the economic environment surrounding a project. Management inefficiencies may cause operating expenses to exceed expectations, for example, or may result in an inordinately high vacancy rate. Credit investigation and rent collection practices may result in an unexpectedly high level of credit losses. Any of these events, all internal to the investment equation, will cause net operating income to fall below the forecast.

The economic environment may be less propitious than anticipated, with consequences including an unexpectedly low level of demand for real estate services. This means either a higher-than-expected vacancy rate or reduced rental rates. In either event, an unfortunate by-product will be gross rental revenue below that anticipated at the time an investment commitment was made. This, in turn, means that net operating income will fall below expectations.

CONTROLLING RISK

Risk analysis, after years of virtual neglect, is now a popular topic in real estate literature. Chapter 20 synthesizes much of current writing on the subject and consolidates generally accepted contemporary techniques into a comprehensive approach. These sophisticated techniques, however, are inappropriate when the additional cost of analysis more than offsets the benefit from avoiding selection error. For relatively inexpensive projects, or where outcomes are highly predictable, less complex analysis might be in order. Moreover, risk can often be greatly reduced with relatively simple risk management procedures.

Reducing Risk Through Judicious Investment Selection

One way to decrease risk is simply to invest in less risky projects. Accepting only those opportunities whose outcomes are fairly well ascertained in advance reduces default risk essentially to zero and virtually eliminates uncertainty associated with the outcome of the investment itself (though not the uncertainty and risk of purchasing power loss through an inflation rate that exceeds the rate of return on the investment).

An unfortunate by-product of this strategy is that opportunities for extraordinary profits are also eliminated. The tendency for expected return to increase or decrease along with associated risk is an inescapable characteristic of free markets. Should opportunities for anticipated gains unaccompanied by commensurate risk appear, investors will quickly enter the market and drive expected returns down to a level approximating those available in other investment opportunities of the same general risk category.

There is, of course, a whole spectrum of risky investment opportunities in the economy. Financial markets allow investors to interact in competitive bidding so that an appropriate level of return is assigned by the market to each opportunity, commensurate with the level of risk perceived by market participants. Figure 18.4 depicts the trade-off between risk and expected return necessary to attract a potential investor into a project or projects. As risk increases, the investor requires a higher expected return to compensate for the additional risk exposure. Keep in mind that this diagram reflects investor *expectations* only. Expected profits may never materialize—the investor may in fact suffer substantial losses. But for the investor to accept a project in the first place, potential reward must be sufficiently high to justify bearing the perceived risk.

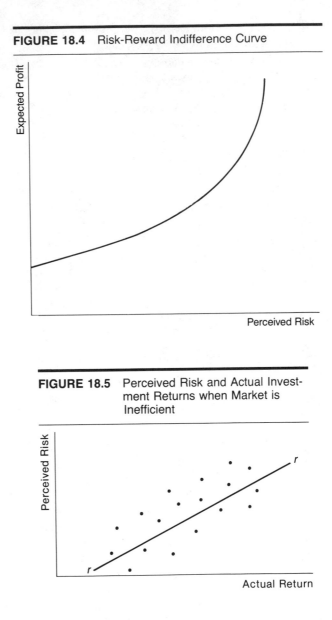

FIGURE 18.4   Risk-Reward Indifference Curve

FIGURE 18.5   Perceived Risk and Actual Investment Returns when Market is Inefficient

Whereas Figure 18.4 depicts expectations of an individual market participant, actual outcomes are more likely to be as illustrated in Figure 18.5. The dots in the diagram depict actual outcomes of market ventures as they relate to expectations of participants (depicted by the solid line *rr*). If the market is efficient, then actual outcomes will vary randomly about expected outcomes reflected by the market line (market efficiency is discussed in Chapter 3). Unusually high or low gains relative to expectations will occur randomly and will tend to cancel each other out. Since all participants in an efficient market have approximately the same information and draw approximately the same conclusions from that information, outcomes for individual participants will also vary randomly in approximately the same proportion as do outcomes for the entire market.

The significance of all this is that in an efficient market the only way to reduce risk associated with single investment ventures is to choose a venture with a lower expected return. We noted in Chapter 3, however, that real estate markets tend to be somewhat less efficient than are organized securities markets. As a consequence, real estate investors who can exploit market inefficiencies are able to reap extraordinary profits without shouldering commensurately greater risk. To do this, they must consistently identify opportunities whose outcomes lie to the right of line *rr* in Figure 18.5. They might accomplish this by attaining a monopoly position within certain locations or with respect to significant market information.

Diversification as a Risk Management Tool

Investors can further control risk exposure by considering the relationship between assets already held and potential new acquisitions. Since factors influencing profitability and market value do not uniformly impact all properties, holders of diversified portfolios can expect a more stable (and predictable) pattern of earnings than would result from concentrating all wealth in a single project.

Diversification does not ensure risk reduction, however, unless properties are chosen to avoid high correlation between investment performance of the various assets. Mortgage real estate investment trusts during the early 1970s *REITs* provide an instructive example of misguided attempts to gain risk reduction through diversification. Although they diversified their holdings geographically and by physical design, the trusts followed a uniform selection rule of employing substantial financial leverage. These portfolios proved to have higher risk than other portfolios diversified by both location and asset type, such as those held by most insurance companies.

Portfolio diversification is a relatively simple proposition for multimillion-dollar real estate investment corporations. They can diversify geographically to reduce the impact of regional shifts in economic activity. Likewise, they can easily acquire any desired mix of apartment complexes, office towers, suburban office parks and so on.

But most investors face budget constraints that complicate diversification efforts. If it means sacrificing economies of scale by investing in smaller properties, diversification may entail forgoing some expected return.

One solution is to pool equity funds with other investors facing the same dilemma. This rather popular approach to the problem is often called *syndication*. A frequent arrangement involves a promoter who organizes the syndicate and manages the venture for a fee plus a percentage ownership, while passive investors contribute all or most of the equity funds. Most syndicates are organized as limited partnerships.[1]

Real estate syndication may be viewed as a procedure for fractionalizing the ownership interest in property into individual shares in much the same fashion as common stock represents fractionalized ownership interest in a corporation. Investors contribute money with no expectation of management control and under an arrangement that strictly limits their financial and legal liability. The promoter of the syndicate, who assumes management responsibilities, also assumes full liability for the general obligations of the syndicate. Chapter 11 explored legal and income tax aspects of syndicating real estate ventures. Syndications are discussed in greater detail in Chapter 24.

Market Research as a Risk Control Tool

Real estate investors are forced to make assumptions about a venture's ability to generate income over an extended period. Risk is often viewed as the possibility of variance between assumptions and actual outcomes. One of the best methods of reducing that variance is to make more accurate assumptions.

Part Two, "Market Research," discussed techniques for generating better information upon which to base assumptions. The more information an investor has about the environment in which investments exist, the more accurate investment assumptions are likely to be. Meticulous study of market information permits better estimates of current operating results. Diligent analysis of trend data yields more reliable forecasts.

It is no easy task to decide when investment analysis should cease and a final decision be made. Obviously, there is such a point—the problem is in deciding when it has been reached. As with so many issues, this one is conceptually simple but nigh impossible in application.

That analysis costs increase with degree of refinement is obvious. Less obvious is that cost is an increasing function of the degree of refinement. Much information can be gleaned at little cost. Additional information may be available at modest cost. But past some point, further refinement of analytical data becomes very costly while adding little to a decision maker's knowledge of the risk-return relationship.

A little knowledge goes a long way when the starting point is total ignorance. But as the investor becomes more informed about a proposed investment, he or she benefits progressively less from additional (and increasingly expensive) increments of knowledge. Consequently, there must be a point where the incremental cost of knowledge exceeds its value to the investor.

✳ Property Management to Control Risk

Professional property managers are uniquely positioned to enhance accuracy of cash-flow projections. Their access to market data and their knowledge and experience regarding the economics of property operations are valuable forecasting ingredients. Capable property managers can greatly reduce the probability of variance between projections and actual outcomes.

Competent management also plays a vital role in making outcomes conform to assumptions. Resident managers are a critical element, for they control day-to-day property operations. They may be able to enhance revenue by controlling vacancy and rent loss and reducing tenant turnover. They can hold expenses down by monitoring all operations and through astute preventative maintenance.

Shifting Risk to Tenants

Lease agreements often permit landlords to shift some risk to tenants. Examples of such arrangements include *tax stops* and *rent escalator* clauses. Tax stops commit tenants to pay all property taxes above some specified level. Escalator clauses require tenants to pay all operating expenses above amounts specified in their leases.

Net leases, which make tenants responsible for all expenses, shift virtually all operating risks from property owners to tenants. Tenants are usually responsible for all operating expenses, repairs, maintenance, real estate taxes and so forth. The landlord's risk is that the tenant will become financially incapable of meeting these responsibilities.

An additional strategy frequently employed with long-term leases pegs rental rates to changes in a price-level index such as the consumer price index or the wholesale price index. This effectively shifts purchasing power risk (the risk that future receipts will have less purchasing power due to general price inflation) to tenants.

Hedging to Control Risk

Hedging, a common practice in securities and commodities markets, may also reduce risk for real estate investors. *Purchase options* are a common form of hedging used in real estate. When contemplating a development project, for example, a developer might purchase an option to buy a selected site. This provides time to plan, to obtain required governmental approvals and to secure needed financing. Soil and engineering studies may also be completed while property is under option. Purchase options thus provide time to eliminate some of the uncertainty associated with the development process.

Real estate syndicators also frequently hedge by obtaining options to buy properties. Options are exercised only after syndication shares are fully subscribed.

Interim or "standby" financing commitments are another hedging mechanism used by investor-developers. To avoid being committed to an unfavorably high interest rate, a developer who believes rates will decline during the construction period may purchase a loan commitment that is binding on the lender but is an option to the developer. This commitment will be exercised only if better terms cannot be obtained.

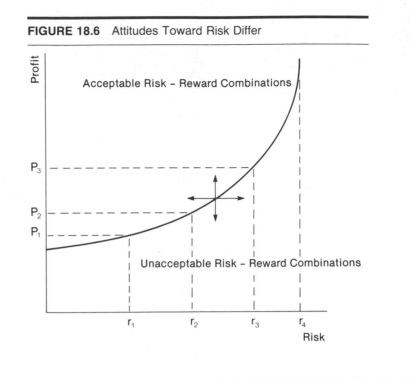

FIGURE 18.6 Attitudes Toward Risk Differ

RISK PREFERENCES AND PROFIT EXPECTATIONS

After all risk control techniques are fully exploited, a core of unavoidable risk remains. Attitudes toward this residual risk will vary with the personalities of investors and with their capacities to absorb financial reverses, as well as with personal investment objectives.

Typical investor attitudes toward risk are illustrated again in Figure 18.6. Rational investors prefer a higher to a lower return for a given level of risk; for a specified level of return they prefer less risk to more risk. They accept additional risk only if accompanied by additional expected investment rewards.

Figure 18.6 also demonstrates increasing aversion to risk as total risk exposure increases. To induce the investor whose attitude is depicted in Figure 18.6 to accept an increase in risk exposure from r_1 to r_2, there must be the expectation that returns will increase from P_1 to P_2. To persuade the same investor to accept another increment of risk (from r_2 to r_3), expected rewards must be increased by a substantially larger amount. The investor becomes so risk-averse when total risk exposure reaches r_4 that no amount of expected additional reward can induce further movement into the realm of risk. Because the investor will be equally satisfied by all risk-reward combinations depicted by the line in Figure 18.6, it is sometimes called a *risk-reward indifference curve.*

Recall the earlier observation that rational investors prefer less risk for a given level of expected return. This behavioral trait is depicted in Figure 18.6 by the arrow extending to the left from the risk-reward indifference curve, indicating that the investor will prefer any combination of risk and return that can be plotted on the figure in that direction. Since rational investors also prefer a greater return with a given level of risk, the arrow extending upward from the curve also indicates a direction in which risk and reward combinations will leave our investor feeling better off than will any combination found on the curve. In fact, a whole set of indifference curves could be plotted, filling the entire plane upon which values from the two axes of Figure 18.6 intersect. Any curve above that shown in Figure 18.6 will represent a series of risk-reward combinations that will leave the investor more satisfied than the combinations on the illustrated curve. Since we have posited that the depicted curve illustrates minimum acceptable risk-reward combinations, it follows that all combinations above the one illustrated are even more acceptable. For this reason the area above the curve in Figure 18.6 is labeled "acceptable risk-reward combinations."

Similarly, it can be demonstrated that the investor will be less satisfied with more risk for a given level of return (depicted by the right-facing arrow in Figure 18.6) or less expected return for a given level of risk (depicted in Figure 18.6 by the arrow extending downward from the curve). No combination of risk and expected return below the curve depicting minimum acceptable combinations will satisfy the investor whose attitude is reflected in Figure 18.6. The area below the minimum acceptable set of combinations is therefore labeled "unacceptable risk-reward combinations."

Degrees of Risk Aversion

Of course the precise configuration of risk-reward indifference curves will depend upon the individual investor's personal attitude toward risk. Functions depicting various investors' attitudes will not necessarily have the same shape. The more risk-averse the individual, the more steeply sloped the indifference curve showing that person's preference. The indifference curve of an investor who is indifferent toward risk will have no curvature at all; some investors may even be willing to trade expected return for the opportunity to bear greater risk and will therefore have a downward-sloping risk-reward indifference curve. These diverse attitudes are illustrated in Figure 18.7.

Rational Risk Taking

Rational risk taking is epitomized by successful insurance firms. This industry turns a handsome and highly predictable profit by allowing insured parties to substitute the certainty of a small loss (the insurance premium) for the uncertainty of a larger, possibly catastrophic loss, such as a fire, flood or major illness. Insurance companies can do this successfully through astute risk management.

FIGURE 18.7   The Trade-off Between Perceived Risk and Expected Reward

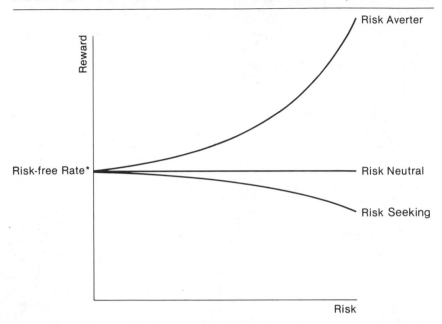

They carefully calculate the odds involved in loss, against which they issue insurance policies, and always ascertain that the premium is sufficient to compensate for the chance of loss.

Insurance firms might be characterized as risk takers by design—so might rational and knowledgeable real estate investors. Before committing substantial resources, such investors will:

1. Carefully specify investment objectives concerning return on investment, timing of return and acceptable risk levels.
2. Identify major risks involved and quantify them as completely as possible.
3. Eliminate some risks, transfer others via insurance or other techniques and constrain remaining risks to acceptable levels.
4. Make a decision to accept or reject the investment, based on whether expected returns justify bearing the remaining risks in view of the contribution the venture makes toward overall investment objectives.

Of course, not all real estate investment ventures represent examples of rational and informed risk taking. Emotional risk takers are likely to adopt an entirely different approach. They characteristically make investments on a "hot tip" or a "hunch." Emotional risk takers are seemingly rendered blind to risk by the glare of expected return. Successful investors who have adopted an emotional attitude toward risk are prone to use their personal experiences as vindication for the approach. ("If investment analysts are so smart, why aren't they rich like me?") Those driven to bankruptcy by this approach are not generally considered newsworthy.

MEASURING RISK

Instead of quantifying risk perceptions, real estate analysts and investors have traditionally developed a subjective impression and attached a return premium in addition to that required in the absence of "above normal" risk.

Traditional approaches to incorporating a risk premium have included using a shorter payback period, a higher required rate of return or a downward adjustment to projected cash flows. All these techniques result in a smaller investment value—the amount the investor is willing to pay for a project.

Traditional risk-adjustment techniques share a serious shortcoming: They do not permit quantification of the risk element. This makes interproject comparisons difficult even for the analyst doing the risk estimation. It renders completely impossible the task of communicating risk perception to a second party.

This is a particularly serious problem when analysts are working with client investors. Of what avail is the analyst's excellent grasp of the risk element if it cannot be communicated to the client?

Techniques are available for communicating risk assessment to a client without incorporating the analyst's personal risk-bearing proclivities. Such techniques are discussed in Chapter 20. They are offered as alternatives to traditional methods, which are explored more fully in Chapter 19.

SUMMARY

Risk has been skirted in earlier chapters. It is a ubiquitous problem in real estate analysis, however, and must be faced by rational investors. Some risks can be shifted to other parties or minimized through astute investment-management techniques. But risk avoidance has a price. Many investors purposely shoulder risks because the expected rewards for so doing outweigh potential costs.

Risk must be made amenable to measurement and quantification before it can be properly incorporated into real estate investment analysis. Only then can trained analysts communicate their perceptions to clients, enabling the latter to make more fully informed investment decisions.

Traditional means of adjusting for risk inextricably intertwine the analyst's risk perception and personal risk preference. These techniques are appropriate only on the rare occasions when analysts and their clients share a common attitude toward risk. Because risk preference is influenced not only by wealth and pre-existing risk exposure, but also by subtle psychological factors, common attitudes toward risk are about as likely as identical fingerprint patterns.

NOTES

1. For an extended discussion of real estate limited partnerships, see Gaylon E. Greer, *The Real Estate Investor and the Federal Income Tax,* 2d ed. (New York: John Wiley, 1982), Chapter 11.

RECOMMENDED READINGS

Brigham, Eugene F. *Fundamentals of Financial Management.* 4th ed. Hinsdale, IL: The Dryden Press, 1986, pp. 155–187.

Greer, Gaylon E. *The Real Estate Investment Decision.* Lexington, MA: Lexington Books, 1979, pp. 177–186.

Greer, Gaylon E., and Michael D. Farrell. *Contemporary Real Estate: Theory and Practice.* Hinsdale, IL: The Dryden Press, 1983, pp. 273–280.

Jaffe, Austin J., and C. F. Sirmans. *Real Estate Investment Decision Making.* Englewood Cliffs, NJ: Prentice-Hall, 1982, pp. 57–62.

Phyrr, Stephen A., and James R. Cooper. *Real Estate Investment: Strategy, Analysis, Decisions.* Boston: Warren, Gorham and Lamont, 1987, pp. 317–340.

REVIEW QUESTIONS

1. What is the effect of using financial leverage on the pretax yield of a property? What is its effect on the level of risk associated with the venture?
2. What is insurable risk?
3. What is business risk, and how can it be reduced for the investor?
4. Are real estate markets efficient?
5. How is diversification used as a risk management tool?
6. How do landlords shift risk to tenants?
7. What steps are involved in rational risk taking?
8. List some of the traditional risk-adjustment techniques and their common shortcoming.

DISCUSSION QUESTIONS

1. Risk can be characterized as diversifiable or nondiversifiable, depending upon whether it is possible to eliminate the risk by holding a sufficiently diversified portfolio. Insurable risk is diversifiable. Why, then, don't real estate investors simply eliminate such risks by diversifying rather than paying an insurance company to handle the risk?

2. Since diversification, appropriately pursued, reduces risk, should investors extend their diversification until all diversifiable risk has been eliminated in this way?

3. Diversification has been described as "not putting all of one's eggs in one basket," with the connotation that this is a good policy. Mark Twain's response is "Put all of your eggs in one basket and —watch that basket." Comment.

4. How might risk be:

   a. shifted by the wording of tenant leases?
   b. avoided by choice of organizational entity?

CHAPTER 19

Traditional Risk-Adjustment Methods

INTRODUCTION

This chapter reviews traditional risk-adjustment and analysis practices with a view toward demonstrating their major strengths and shortcomings. Adjustments to the payback period, adjustments to the discount rate and adjustments to projected cash flow are discussed. In each case both theoretical and practical objections to the techniques are presented. Partitioning and sensitivity analysis are then introduced as useful tools of analysis that have more recently found their way into common practice.

THE PAYBACK-PERIOD APPROACH

Recall from Chapter 12 that the payback period is the time required for cash inflows from an investment to equal the original cash outlay. If, for example, an investment requires a down payment of $16,000 and is expected to yield $2,000 per annum, the payback period is eight years. This is determined by dividing the down payment by the annual net cash inflow:

$$\$16,000/\$2,000 = 8$$

Where annual cash-flow projections vary from year to year, the payback period is estimated by accumulating the annual expected net cash flows until they equal the initial cash outlay.

Proponents of this technique adjust for risk by varying the minimum acceptable payback period. Risky investments are expected to have a shorter payback period than less risky investments. The precise amount of the adjustment is necessarily subjective, since risk itself is generally not measured. Analysts simply state how much shorter a particular investment's payback period must be than the "normal" acceptable payback period, based on an impression of inherent risk.

Payback-period analysis is an inadequate method of evaluation even in the absence of risk, and adding risk renders it even less useful. Desirability of real estate opportunities often depends heavily upon expected gain from disposal. Risk, in those cases, is primarily a function of the certainty associated with the anticipated sales price. But if the disposal point extends beyond the payback period, neither anticipated benefit nor attendant risk will be included in the analysis.

Consider Example 19.1. The payback period of four years is accompanied by virtual certainty that the annual cash flow from operations in fact will be realized. But how can the required payback period be adjusted for the uncertainty associated with anticipated cash flow from sale of the property five years hence?

Example 19.1

A warehouse, available for a down payment of $80,000, is almost certain to yield a net annual cash flow of $20,000 for the next five years, after which it is expected to have a market value such that the net cash flow from disposal will be $100,000. The annual cash flow during the holding period is secured by a tenant with an impeccable credit rating, who has five years remaining on his or her lease. The forecast selling price after five years is predicated upon the tenant renewing the lease—an eventuality that is far from certain. If the tenant does not renew, then the selling price will depend on the investor's ability to find a comparable tenant at the same rental rate.

RISK-ADJUSTED DISCOUNT RATE

Discounted cash-flow analysis techniques were discussed in Chapter 14, using a discount rate assumed to be appropriate. Given the appropriate rate, discounting anticipated cash flows to arrive at the present value of an opportunity is a mere arithmetical exercise. Left unanswered in that discussion was the question of what discount rate is appropriate. This deliberate omission was necessary because the answer depends on how the risk-adjustment problem is treated.

Traditionally, the discounted cash-flow model has incorporated a *risk-adjusted* discount rate. A risk-free rate is proposed to represent the pure time value of money. To this a premium is added for risk associated with a specific venture. The risk-free rate is (presumably) the same regardless of the nature of the proposal under consideration, changing only to reflect variance in the disutility of waiting. *Risk premiums,* in contrast, vary with each proposal. The amount of the premium depends on attendant risk and the investor's attitude toward risk.

The Risk-Free Discount Rate

Choosing an appropriate risk-free discount rate is more a theoretical than a practical problem. Most analysts simply select a risk-adjusted rate without bothering to stipulate values for the risk-free and risk premium components.

Analysts who wish to demonstrate derivation of their risk adjustments do, of course, have this problem. Their difficulty is rooted in the inaccuracy of the term *risk-free*. Financial commitments always carry certain risks that can neither be eliminated nor transferred. In the context of security analysis, *risk-free* implies not absolute absence of risk, but virtual absence of default risk. The risk-free rate is the one that would apply if lenders viewed a borrower's credit and collateral so favorably that they were absolutely certain of repayment at the scheduled time.

But default is not the only risk lenders face. The general level of prices may move up during the term of a loan so that lenders will be repaid in substantially depreciated dollars. The market rate of interest might increase after a loan is tendered, causing market values of existing securities to decline. Even if held to maturity, such loans will yield less than a lender could have earned by waiting to make the loan until after the movement in market interest rates.

The difficulties in specifying a riskless rate of discount lead most analysts to accept the expedient of using the rate available on short-term federal securities as a proxy. Because they are short-term and highly secure, the interest rates on Treasury bills are nearly devoid of premiums for default risk and interest rate risk.

The Risk Premium

Adjustments for perceived risk should be based on an investor's risk-return trade-off function, as discussed in Chapter 18. In practice, real estate analysts who use this approach have generally chosen a risk premium that embodies their perceptions of the risk and their personal risk-return trade-off functions. But since the trade-off function reflects personal attitude toward risk, this will be appropriate only if the analyst's attitude corresponds exactly to that of the client-investor. Because attitude toward risk is determined by such factors as financial ability to sustain loss, the extent of existing risk exposure and personal psychological preferences, there is no reason to suppose that the analyst's attitude will ever exactly match the client's. Indeed, even the analyst's attitude will likely differ when applied to an investment analyzed for a client rather than when personally placing money at risk. Making this approach operational by determining the appropriate risk premium presents a seemingly insurmountable hurdle.

Practical and Theoretical Problems

In spite of its problems, the risk-adjusted discount rate is probably the most commonly used approach among analysts. The approach is, nevertheless, fatally flawed. There are both theoretical and practical difficulties.[1]

In separating riskless and risk premium portions of the discount rate, the risk-free rate is intended to represent the time value of money, with no associated risk. But when an additional discount factor is introduced for risk, it also incorporates an adjustment for time.

As a consequence, future risk is discounted more heavily than near-term risk. Yet near-term risk is often greater than far distant risk. Consider, for example, an apartment building project. The risk of construction cost overruns and of an unexpectedly lengthy rent-up period is generally far greater than the risk of misestimation during the subsequent operating period. Yet the risk premium during the latter period is far greater than that of the former. Each subsequent year of operation is discounted more heavily than the preceding, in spite of the fact that as neighborhoods mature, operating outcomes generally become more predictable.

Example 19.2

A ten-year project is under consideration, for which the appropriate risk premium is six percent and the risk-free discount rate is estimated to be five percent. The overall discount rate, the sum of the risk-free rate and the risk premium, is therefore 11 percent. Discounting involves dividing each year's cash-flow projection by a number derived by raising the discount rate plus one to a power equaling the number of years before the cash is expected to be received.

Example 19.2 illustrates the problem. Discount factors for the first three years (discounting at 11 percent) are, respectively, 1.11, $(1.11)^2$ and $(1.11)^3$. Were there no risk involved, the discount rate would be simply one plus the riskless rate, or 1.05. The factors for the first three years would be 1.05, $(1.05)^2$ and $(1.05)^3$. The factor by which the anticipated cash flows are divided to account for perceived risk is the difference among the preceding quantities. For the first three years, the risk adjustments are:

Year	Risk-Adjusted Discount Factor	Riskless Discount Factor	Risk Factor
1	1.1100	1.0500	0.0600
2	1.2321	1.1025	0.1296
3	1.3676	1.1576	0.2100

Investment desirability, using this technique, is more greatly impaired the further in the future anticipated risk lies. This holds true in spite of the fact that the riskless discount rate has already accounted for timing differences. A problem of double accounting for time is clearly evident. For some investment ventures, risk might appropriately be viewed as increasing with the length of time involved in the forecast. H. Y. Chen and others have shown that when risk is viewed as an increasing function of time, the risk-adjusted discount rate is theoretically sound.[2]

An equally serious shortcoming is the impracticality of expressing risk-adjusted discount rates as policy statements. A policy specifying minimum risk-return combinations permits subordinates to screen out obviously unacceptable investment projects. Only opportunities that meet these minimum standards are passed for review by a final decision maker. Because risk premiums must be determined individually for each project, they are not well suited to a policy of delegating preliminary investment decisions.

THE CERTAINTY-EQUIVALENT TECHNIQUE

Double accounting for risk in the risk-adjusted discount rate can be resolved by adjusting projected cash flows instead of discount rates. The risk-adjusted cash flow projections are then discounted at the risk-free rate. This approach, called the *certainty-equivalent technique,* also neatly sidesteps the need to quantify risk perception. It does introduce other practical problems, however. These include the cost of determining appropriate certainty-equivalent adjustments and the increased risk of client alienation. When final decisions are made by a committee instead of by an individual, these new problems become almost insurmountable.

Deriving Certainty-Equivalent Amounts

Instead of a "best estimate" of future cash flows, the certainty-equivalent cash-flow technique substitutes an amount that leaves the client indifferent between expected receipt of the best estimate (with associated risk of variation from expectations) and absolute certainty of receiving the substitute amount. This substitute amount, or *certainty equivalent,* is discounted at the risk-free rate.

An early step in determining certainty equivalents is to explain carefully to the investor the expected future business environment. After being acquainted with major risk factors, the client is asked to indicate a preference for forecasted cash flows or specified riskless cash-flow alternatives. Various riskless alternatives are postulated until an amount is specified that leaves the investor indifferent between the risky and the riskless flows. This procedure might result in a set of certainty equivalents for a project such as those in Example 19.3.

Example 19.3

A project offers an anticipated net cash flow of $10,000 per annum for three years, followed at the end of the third year by an anticipated net cash receipt of $80,000 from sale of the project. Realization of the cash from disposal is contingent upon drastic alteration of current prevailing economic conditions. If anticipated changes do not materialize, the proceeds will be much less. Perceived risk and the investor's attitude toward risk are reflected in the following certainty-equivalent cash-flow transformation:

Year	Expected Cash Flow	Risk-Free Amount Equivalent to Risky Cash Flow	Certainty-Equivalent Factor
1	$10,000	$ 9,600	0.960
2	10,000	9,600	0.960
3	10,000	9,600	0.960
3	80,000	68,800	0.860

The certainty-equivalent factors in Example 19.3 are derived by dividing the risk-free equivalent cash flow by the expected cash flow for each year. The risk-free, or certainty-equivalent, cash flow is the amount of money, receivable with certainty, that is just as satisfactory to the investor as the risky expectation of receiving the forecast cash flow for that year. Thus the investor in Example 19.3 is indifferent between 96 cents received for certain in years one through three and the risky expectation of receiving $1 from operations in each of those years.

The riskier an expected cash flow is perceived to be, the smaller the certainty-equivalent factor. In Example 19.3, expected sales proceeds at the end of the projection period are assumed to be more problematic than are annual cash flows from operations. Hence a smaller certainty-equivalent factor is associated with the $80,000 expected cash flow from that source.

Implied in the preceding discussion is that the present value (PV) of an anticipated series of annual cash flows (CF_t) can be expressed as:

$$PV = \sum_{t=1}^{n} \frac{CF_t}{(1+k)^t} = \sum_{t=1}^{n} \frac{\alpha\, CF_t}{(1+i)^t}$$

where k is a risk-adjusted discount rate, i is the risk-free rate and α represents a certainty-equivalent factor such as illustrated in Example 19.3.

If, for example, the appropriate risk-free rate of return in Example 19.3 is 5.25 percent, then the present value of the certainty-equivalent cash flows is approximately $85,000. Expected cash flows have a present value of approximately $85,000 when discounted at ten percent. This implies a risk premium in the risk-adjusted discount rate of approximately ten minus 5.25, or 4.75 percent. Here are the computations:

Year	Expected Cash Flow	Present Value at 10%	Certainty-Equivalent Cash Flow	Present Value at 5.25%
1	$10,000	$ 9,091	$ 9,600	$ 9,121
2	10,000	8,264	9,600	8,666
3	10,000	7,513	9,600	8,234
3	80,000	60,105	68,800	59,010
Totals		$84,973		$85,031

Problems with the Certainty-Equivalent Approach

Certainty equivalents, in effect, translate risk-preference functions such as discussed in Chapter 18 into risk-indifference functions. Determining numerical values for these certainty-equivalent factors is the principal difficulty associated with applying the approach. Values can be determined by presenting an investor with a series of combinations of risky and risk-free cash flows and asking for a stated preference between each set of alternatives. An extended series of such experiments will result in a preference map representing the investor's attitude toward risk. From this map, certainty-equivalent factors can be extracted.

Getting an investor to state preferences in this fashion, however, is a difficult and time-consuming task. The time required and the attendant cost might well cause the investor to rebel. Success depends on the analyst's powers of persuasion. These powers will be sorely taxed as the necessity of making ever finer distinctions between risky and risk-free cash flows becomes increasingly frustrating to a client who is both paying for the exercise and doing the bulk of the mental work.

Where preliminary investment decisions are delegated, this method is particularly unsatisfactory. Because a new preference map must be drawn for each investment opportunity (reflecting the risk elements peculiar to that venture) and for each decision maker (reflecting personal attitudes toward risk), the certainty-equivalent method cannot be grafted onto a policy statement without major modification in the way certainty-equivalent factors are generated.

One such modification, suggested by Steven E. Bolten,[3] is to first quantify the risk element by using standard deviation as a risk measure. Cash-flow estimates are then reduced by a number of standard deviations to ensure virtual certainty that actual cash flow will prove to equal or exceed the certainty-equivalent cash flow. This eliminates the subjective attitude toward risk associated with an individual decision maker and permits discounting at the risk-free discount rate.

PARTITIONING PRESENT VALUE OF THE EQUITY POSITION

We have seen that real estate is valued solely for the anticipated future stream of benefits ownership bestows. Investment value depends, among other things, upon the expected quantity of these benefits and the anticipated timing of their receipt. Real estate investment, therefore, can be seen as the purchase of a set of assumptions about a property's ability to produce a benefit stream. The generally accepted measure of benefits is after-tax cash flow. Factors contributing to this flow include annual before-tax cash flows, income tax consequences, loan amortization, change in property value over the projected holding period and so forth.

In Part One, investment value was divided into present value of equity and present value of debt. Similarly, the present value of the equity position can be partitioned into its component parts. Expressing each component as a percentage of the total permits the relative importance of each to be assessed. Components that comprise major segments of the total present value of the equity position will merit extended analysis.

Example 19.4

Maegen's Magic Manor Apartments can be purchased for $2,300,000, inclusive of transaction costs. The venture requires an equity investment of $500,000, with the $1,800,000 balance of the purchase price to be financed via a fully amortizing, 30-year mortgage note. Interest on the borrowed funds will be at 12 percent per annum. Payments on the mortgage note will be made monthly. Cost recovery allowances are based on a building value of $2,000,000, employing the straight-line method over 27.5 years. The property is expected to be worth $2,900,000, net of transaction costs, at the end of an expected six-year holding period. The investor is in the 28 percent marginal income tax bracket and expects to remain in that bracket throughout the investment period. If the property is acquired, it is expected that the closing will occur early in the first month of the tax year and that the subsequent sale will close late in the last month of the sixth year of the investment period. This information is incorporated with estimates of rental revenue and operating expenses to generate the six-year cash-flow forecast presented in Table 19.1.

TABLE 19.1   Maegen's Magic Manor: Six-Year Cash-Flow Projection

	Year					
	1	*2*	*3*	*4*	*5*	*6*
Effective Gross Income	$393,000	$405,000	$417,000	$429,000	$442,000	$455,000
Less: Operating Expense	177,000	194,000	200,000	205,000	212,000	220,000
Net Operating Income	$216,000	$211,000	$217,000	$224,000	$230,000	$235,000
Less: Debt Service	222,180	222,180	222,180	222,180	222,180	222,180
Before-Tax Cash Flow	$ (6,180)	$ (11,180)	$ (5,180)	$ 1,820	$ 7,820	$ 12,820
Plus: Principal	6,532	7,360	8,294	9,346	10,531	11,866
Less: Depreciation	69,697	72,727	72,727	72,727	72,727	69,697
Taxable Gain (Loss)	$(69,345)	$(76,547)	$(69,613)	$(61,561)	$(54,376)	$(45,011)
Tax (Tax Saving)	$(19,417)	$(21,433)	$(19,492)	$(17,237)	$(15,225)	$(12,603)
Before-Tax Cash Flow	$ (6,180)	$ (11,180)	$ (5,180)	$ 1,820	$ 7,820	$ 12,820
Tax Consequences	19,417	21,433	19,492	17,237	15,225	12,603
After-Tax Cash Flow	$ 13,237	$ 10,253	$ 14,312	$ 19,057	$ 23,045	$ 25,423

Consider the investment proposal in Example 19.4. Table 19.1 contains after-tax cash-flow projections based on the data in the example, using procedures discussed in Part Three. Table 19.2 details the after-tax cash flow forecast from disposal at the end of the anticipated holding period. Tax due on sale is calculated as illustrated in Chapter 10.

Table 19.3 illustrates the technique of discounting to express expected after-tax cash flows in terms of present value equivalents. To estimate the importance of each element in the analysis in Table 19.3, discount each element separately. For example, note in Table 19.3 that the first year's expected after-tax cash flow of $13,237 has a present value equivalent of $12,034 when discounted at ten percent and rounded to the nearest whole dollar. Reference to Table 19.1 reveals that the first year's after-tax cash-flow estimate is comprised of the following elements:

Effective Gross Income	$393,000
Less: Operating Expenses	177,000
Net Operating Income	$216,000
Less: Annual Debt Service	222,180
Before-Tax Cash Flow	$ (6,180)
Plus: Income Tax Savings	19,417
After-Tax Cash-Flow Forecast	$ 13,237

Discounting each of the above elements separately (that is, multiplying each by the appropriate present value factor from Table A.1 in Appendix A) and summing the present value equivalents yields the same present value estimate

TABLE 19.2 Maegen's Magic Manor: After-Tax Cash Flow from Sale

Sales Price (Net)		$2,900,000
Less:		
Mortgage Balance	$1,746,071	
Tax Due on Sale	288,484	2,034,555
After-Tax Cash from Sale		$ 865,445

TABLE 19.3 Maegen's Magic Manor: Measures of Investment Performance

Year	After-Tax Cash Flow	Present Value Factor @ 10%	Discounted Cash Flow
1	$ 13,237	.9091	$ 12,034
2	10,253	.8264	8,473
3	14,312	.7513	10,753
4	19,057	.6830	13,016
5	23,045	.6209	14,309
6	25,423	.5645	14,351
Sales Proceeds	865,445	.5645	488,544
Present Value of Equity			$ 561,480
Available Financing			1,800,000
Investment Value			$2,361,480

(except for a $1 rounding error) shown in Table 19.3. The alternative computations are shown below:

	Amount ×	Present Value Factor =	Present Value
Gross Income	$ 393,000	.9091	$ 357,276
Less:			
Operating Expenses	(177,000)	.9091	(160,911)
Debt Service	(222,180)	.9091	(201,984)
Plus: Tax Savings	19,417	.9091	17,652
Present Value of After-Tax Cash Flow			$ 12,033

Constituent parts of the after-tax cash-flow forecast for each year can be discounted separately in this manner. Table 19.4 shows present value equivalents in this fashion. Note that the final column of Table 19.4 is the same as the present value estimates computed in Table 19.3, except for a $4 difference due to cumulative rounding error.

TABLE 19.4 Maegen's Magic Manor: Present Value of Partitioned Cash Flows*

Year	Gross Rent × PVIF	− Operating Expense × PVIF	− Debt Service × PVIF	+ Tax Consequence × PVIF	= After-Tax Cash Flow × PVIF
1	$ 357,276	$160,911	$201,984	$17,652	$ 12,033
2	334,692	160,322	183,610	17,712	8,472
3	313,292	150,260	166,924	14,644	10,752
4	293,007	140,015	151,749	11,773	13,016
5	274,438	131,631	137,952	9,453	14,308
6	256,848	124,190	125,421	7,114	14,351
Totals	$1,829,553	$867,329	$967,640	$78,348	$ 72,932

Add Present Value of Cash Flow From Disposal:
Loan Amortization × PFIV = $53,929 × .5645   = $ 30,443
Appreciation × PVIF = $600,000 × .5645   =   338,700
Taxes × PVIF = $(288,484) × .5645   =   (162,849)
Capital Recovery** × PVIF = $500,000 × .5645 =   282,250   488,544
Present Value of Equity Position $561,476

* Present value factors at ten percent.
** Original equity investment (down payment).

TABLE 19.5 Maegen's Magic Manor: Sources of Present Value

Source of Present Value	Amount of Present Value	Percent of Total
Effective Gross Income	$1,829,553	325.8
Operating Expenses	(867,329)	(154.5) (1.0)
Debt Service	(967,640)	(172.3)
Tax Consequences of Operations	78,348	14.0
Loan Amortization	30,443	5.4
Increase in Market Value	338,700	60.3
Tax Liability on Sale	(162,849)	(29.0)
Capital Recovery on Sale	282,250	50.3
Totals	$ 561,476	100.0

The present value of each constituent part of the expected after-tax cash flow, as computed in Table 19.4, is presented in summary form in Table 19.5. The final column of Table 19.5 presents each element as a percent of the total present value estimate. These measures give the analyst valuable clues concerning the seriousness of errors in the forecast.

Note, for example, that the anticipated outcome is almost totally dependent upon cash flows from tax savings and appreciation during the holding period. Approximately 14 percent and 60 percent of the present value, respectively, is expected to be generated from these sources. Consequently, results will be disproportionately dependent upon appreciation, placing a premium upon accurate forecasting of increases in market value during the holding period.

TABLE 19.6   Maegen's Magic Manor: Impact of ± 10% Variation in Sales Price on After-Tax Cash Flow from Disposal

	After-Tax Cash Flow from Disposal		
	With – 10% Variation	*Expected*	*With + 10% Variation*
Sales Price	$2,610,000	$2,900,000	$3,190,000
Less:	1,746,071	1,746,071	1,746,071
Loan Balance			
Tax on Sale	207,284	288,484	369,684
After-Tax Cash Flow	$ 656,645	$ 865,445	$1,074,245

SENSITIVITY ANALYSIS

Sensitivity analysis is a logical extension of partitioning to determine what portions of the forecast merit further refinement. Whereas partitioning emphasizes the relative importance of various sources of cash flow, sensitivity analysis reveals how possible forecasting error will affect the present value of actual after-tax cash flows. The technique consists of altering components of the forecast one at a time and studying the impact on investment value or present value of the equity position.

To see how sensitivity analysis works, consider again the venture in Example 19.4. Suppose we wanted to appraise the impact of a plus-or-minus ten percent error in the forecast selling price at the end of the anticipated holding period. The after-tax cash flow under each of these alternatives is computed in Table 19.6. Substituting these alternative after-tax cash proceeds in Table 19.3 alters the expected present value and the investment value of the venture rather significantly, as shown below:

Change in Selling Price	Present Value of Equity	Investment Value
No Change (See Table 19.3)	$561,480	$2,361,480
10% Decrease	443,612	2,243,612
10% Increase	679,347	2,479,347

There is, of course, an alternative expected present value and investment value for every possible assumption about the rate of appreciation (and thus the sales price) of the property. Figure 19.1 illustrates the relationship between percentage changes in the sales price and percentage changes in the investment value. A ten percent change in expected selling price, either plus or minus, produces a corresponding five percent change in the venture's investment value.

Now suppose the appreciation rate had been forecast correctly, but the annual net operating income had been overstated by ten percent. What impact will this have on investment value?

FIGURE 19.1   Relationship Between Changes in Forecast Variables and Changes in Investment Value

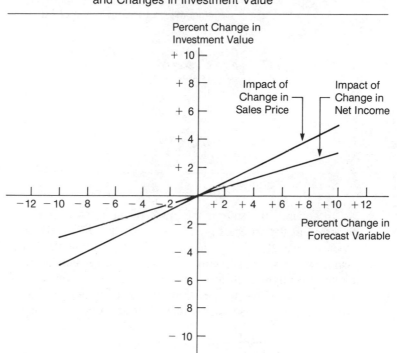

Since the taxpayer in our example is assumed to be in the 28 percent marginal income tax bracket, after-tax cash flow will be changed by 72 percent of the amount of the change in taxable income. Multiplying the remainder by the appropriate present value interest factor from the tables in Appendix A yields the dollar change in present value that results from this forecasting error. These calculations are shown in Table 19.7.

The present value and investment value of the venture after incorporating this change are shown below:

Change in Gross Revenue	Present Value	Investment Value
No Change (See Table 18.3)	$561,480	$2,361,480
10% Decrease	492,201	2,292,201
10% Increase	630,759	2,430,759

The relationship between percentage changes in annual net operating income and percentage changes in investment value is also illustrated in Figure 19.1. That the investment outcome is less sensitive to errors in the operating income forecast than in the appreciation forecast is reflected in the steeper slope of the line depicting the latter relationship. A similar graph could be constructed to show the relative impact of error in each segment of the forecast.

TABLE 19.7   Maegen's Magic Manor: Impact of ± 10% Variation in Net Operating Income on Present Value of Future Cash Flows

Year	Change in Annual After-Tax Cash Flow	× Present Value Interest Factor =	Present Value of Change
1	$15,552	.9091	$14,138
2	15,192	.8264	12,555
3	15,624	.7513	11,738
4	16,128	.6830	11,015
5	16,560	.6209	10,282
6	16,920	.5645	9,551
Total			$69,279

In general, the steeper the graph of the relationship, the more significant the error in the forecast—and therefore the greater the amount of time and expense the analyst is justified in expending to refine the forecast. If anticipated cash flows prove sensitive to variations in the vacancy allowance, for example, the analyst might wish to generate a more refined analysis of marketability; if results are sensitive to variations in the operating expense ratio, one might experiment with lease clauses that shift any upward variations to the tenants.

SUMMARY

A number of techniques have traditionally been employed to adjust for perceived risk associated with real estate investment. These techniques generally have proven inadequate. They fail to produce a risk measure separate from the analyst's personal attitude toward risk and thus are not amenable to precise communication of risk perception. In addition, they cannot readily be incorporated into a policy statement enabling delegation of preliminary decision-making tasks.

The payback-period method of analysis is not, strictly speaking, a risk-adjustment technique. But risk perception, interfaced with attitude toward risk, can be expressed in terms of the maximum acceptable payback period for a particular venture.

A technique that does explicitly consider risk, and is widely employed within the industry, is the risk-adjusted discount rate. Users add to the risk-free rates of return premiums based on their perceptions of attendant risk. Thus the appropriate discount rate increases directly with perceived risk. The technique fails, however, to divorce risk perception from the analyst's personal attitude toward risk. It also contains a technical flaw in that it discounts risk more heavily the further into the future the risk lies.

Risk-adjusted discount rates adjust for increased risk by increasing the size of the divisor in the discounting equation. The certainty-equivalent technique accomplishes the same goal by decreasing the size of the dividend. Both approaches result in a lower present value for a given expected future cash flow as perceived risk increases.

The certainty-equivalent technique avoids some of the objections associated with the risk-adjusted discount rate but introduces new problems. Principal among these are difficulty in determining the appropriate adjustment factor and need to remake the determination for each project and each decision maker. Time and expense make this approach generally impractical as a continuing risk-adjustment technique.

Partitioning and sensitivity analysis, although not methods of adjusting for risk, are useful means of sharpening risk perception. They do this by illustrating how varying degrees of error in different elements of a forecast result in discrepancies between estimated and actual cash flows.

Partitioning reveals the relative significance of each source of after-tax cash flow. Sensitivity analysis takes a speculative approach by postulating variance at different points in the analysis and recomputing outcomes with revised estimates.

NOTES

1. For an extended discussion of these difficulties, see A. A. Robichek and S. C. Myers, "Conceptual Problems in the Use of Risk-Adjusted Discount Rates," *Journal of Finance* 21 (December 1966): 727–30.

2. H. Y. Chen, "Valuation Under Uncertainty," *Journal of Financial and Quantitative Analysis* 2 (September 1967): 313–26.

3. Steven E. Bolten, *Managerial Finance* (Boston: Houghton Mifflin, 1976), 263–65.

RECOMMENDED READINGS

Brigham, Eugene F. *Fundamentals of Financial Management.* 4th ed. Hinsdale, IL: The Dryden Press, 1986, pp. 154–187.

Greer, Gaylon E. *The Real Estate Investment Decision.* Lexington, MA: Lexington Books, 1979, pp. 187–198.

Jaffe, Austin J., and C. F. Sirmans. *Real Estate Investment Decision Making.* Englewood Cliffs, NJ: Prentice-Hall, 1982, pp. 77–82.

Wendt, Paul F., and Alan R. Cerf. *Real Estate Investment Analysis and Taxation.* NY: McGraw-Hill, 1979, pp. 331–347.

REVIEW QUESTIONS

1. How do users of the payback-period approach adjust for risk? Why is the payback-period approach inadequate for evaluating real estate opportunities?
2. What does the "risk-free" rate mean? Is it really risk free?
3. What problems does the risk-adjusted discount rate have?
4. Outline the relative advantages and disadvantages of the certainty-equivalent technique.
5. What is meant by partitioning the present value of the equity position?
6. Describe how sensitivity analysis works and how it is used in evaluating a real estate investment opportunity.

DISCUSSION QUESTIONS

1. Partitioning the present value of the equity position is described as a risk evaluation measure. Discuss the probable role of electronic spreadsheets in the growth of this procedure. Will dedicated computer programs that do not include this procedure nevertheless lend themselves to using partitioning?
2. How do partitioning and sensitivity analysis complement each other as risk measurement tools?

CHAPTER 20

Contemporary Risk Measures

INTRODUCTION

Cash-flow forecasting techniques, as discussed in Part Three, generate point estimates of revenue and expenditures that are, in effect, single best estimates of most probable outcomes. They are, nevertheless, only estimates; actual outcomes will almost certainly differ from forecasts. Risk associated with cash-flow forecasting can conveniently be defined as the probability of variation between actual and expected outcomes. More formally, risk is the *measurable likelihood of variance from the most probable outcome*.

This operational definition forms the takeoff point for modern risk analysis. It permits risk estimates to be expressed quantitatively and enables analysts to rank investment opportunities in terms of investor risk-return preferences.

Probabilistic risk estimates are commonplace in corporate finance and capital budgeting literature. Real estate analysts have adopted the techniques somewhat more cautiously.

Defenders of the traditional risk measures discussed in Chapter 19 object that modern techniques require a level of quantification that is simply not practical in real estate analysis. They argue that inefficient, localized markets, spotty statistical data and high information costs make real estate a special case in which generally accepted capital budgeting and risk analysis techniques are inappropriate.

Their objections miss the point. Data are frequently even more sparse and less reliable in corporate capital budgeting situations than in real estate. Yet modern risk analysis is an integral part of the capital budgeting process in most corporations. Techniques employed there are directly applicable to real estate investment decisions.

Real estate analysts do develop some subjective "feel" for the risk inherent in investment opportunities. This is the basis for the traditional risk adjustments discussed in Chapter 19. All that is needed to accommodate modern risk analysis is a language that will permit analysts to express their perceptions in numerical form and articulate a set of decision criteria against which to weigh the outcome of analysis.

This chapter provides these additional tools. After distinguishing between risk and uncertainty, the chapter reviews basic probability concepts and demonstrates how point estimates of possible outcomes might be converted into probability distributions. It then applies traditional statistical decision rules in a real estate investment context.

PROBABILITY AS A RISK MEASURE

Probability is the chance of occurrence associated with any possible outcome. If, for example, a six-sided die is tossed onto a flat surface, there is an equal chance that any side might face up when the die comes to rest. The probability of any given side facing up is, therefore, one in six, or one-sixth. Expressed as a percentage, this is 16.67 percent.

Probabilities associated with any possible occurrence range from zero to one. If the probability of occurrence equals zero, the event certainly will not occur. A probability of one indicates certainty of occurrence. In our die-tossing example, one of the six sides must certainly face up. The sum of all associated probabilities must therefore equal one.

Formally, this is expressed as:

$$\sum_{i=1}^{n} P_{xi} = 1$$

where P_{xi} is the probability of occurrences of outcome x and the i includes all possibilities. When all possible outcomes are arrayed over their associated probabilities, the result is a probability distribution.

Risk Differs from Uncertainty

Decision situations are conveniently divisible into *certainty, risk* and *uncertainty*. With certainty there can be only one possible outcome, and decisions are based solely on the decision maker's preference among the certain alternatives. Few decision makers, however, face such clear-cut choices. More typically, they must choose among alternatives whose outcomes incorporate elements of risk, elements of uncertainty or both.

Uncertainty implies an unknown number of possible outcomes, with no significant information about their relative chances of occurrence. The distinction between risk and uncertainty is that with uncertainty, probabilities are neither known nor estimable, whereas with risk, the probabilities associated with various possible outcomes are either known or estimable. Authorities do differ, however, regarding the importance of distinguishing between risk and uncertainty.[1] Since it is by definition unmeasurable, there is no way to communicate degrees of uncertainty. Under such conditions, almost anything can happen.

Uncertainty is often a factor of time or economics. Much uncertainty may be resolved with either additional research or the passage of time. As better information becomes available, many uncertain elements can be converted to risk factors by incorporating into the analysis their associated probability distributions.

Risky events also have a number of possible outcomes, but the analyst is able to generate information upon which to estimate the probability of occurrence of each. Some risk elements are susceptible to more or less precise measure, based on sampling techniques and statistical inference. Others are subject only to educated guesses about the range of possible outcomes from one extreme possibility to the other. Formal risk analysis shapes these measures, estimates and guesses into a concrete, standardized format, incorporating probability as the measure of risk.

Estimating Probabilities

When the influence of all factors bearing on an outcome can be held relatively constant, past experience provides a reliable indication of future events. In such circumstances, experimentation or observation of sample data permits reliable inferences about future outcomes.

This is illustrated by the earlier example of a (presumed fair) six-sided die. The intuitive deduction that each side has an equal chance of facing up can be verified by observing the outcome of repeated tosses. Various sides may face up with unequal frequency during early tosses, but (if the die is fair) these are mere chance variations. The greater the number of tosses, the smaller is the role played by chance and so the greater the tendency for each side to be equally represented.

Weight one side of the die, or shave one corner, and the probability of each side facing up will no longer be equal. A new set of probabilities can be estimated quickly, however, by recording the outcome of repeated tosses. A sizable sample of such tosses yields a highly reliable indication of the average outcome of any future series of tosses, so long as major determinants of the outcome (such as the playing surface and the degree to which the die is weighted or shaved) remain constant. Varying any factor, however, produces a whole new set of probabilities.

Investment analysts are not blessed with such reliable probability estimating techniques. Estimating future cash flows from real estate ventures might best be described as part art and part science. It involves studying all factors that significantly influence outcomes, making estimates of or assumptions about the level of each factor and relating these to a specific investment forecast and its associated probability.

Point estimates of cash flow, such as those discussed in Part Three, necessarily assume some specific economic environment. Were the analyst to anticipate a different environment, a revised forecast would be required. A series of such revisions will generate a whole spectrum of net cash-flow forecasts, each reflecting a slightly modified set of assumptions about economic and social conditions during the projection period.

There is, of course, no way to determine precisely what the future portends. Yet we can develop informed estimates, which enable us to say with relative confidence that various possible outcomes will in fact materialize. In some instances estimates can be derived objectively by applying statistical techniques to accumulated data. In other instances lack of objective data might force reliance on the distilled wisdom of an analyst's past study and experience as a basis for estimating which of the alternative economic environments is most likely.

Regardless of how estimates are generated, relative confidence in various potential outcomes can be expressed by coupling each with a probability estimate. This procedure produces a probability distribution of possible cash flows. If estimates are derived objectively with statistical techniques, risk is said to be measured by objective probability distributions.

When statistical measuring techniques cannot be applied, estimates will represent a quantification of the analyst's subjective impression of the risky nature of anticipated cash flows. Such risk estimates are expressed as subjective probability distributions. They represent the quantified perception of a trained analyst and are only as reliable as the judgment of the person whose opinion they incorporate. Subjective probability measures do not simplify the analyst's task in any way; they do add precision to the communication of conclusions.

Opinions expressed in precise, readily understandable terms permit investment decisions consistent with the analyst's assessment of the situation, yet reflecting the decision maker's personal investment philosophy and risk preference. This is the special virtue of using subjective probability distributions to reflect risk. The adjective *subjective* is appended to indicate that probability estimates are statements of opinion or beliefs held by an individual analyst.

Example 20.1

A shopping center analyst develops estimates of annual net cash flow from percentage leases under economic conditions ranging from good to poor, both with and without the existence of a competing center. The analyst's estimates are as follows:

Competing Center Built?	Cash Flow Under General Business Conditions		
	Good	Fair	Poor
No	$250,000	$200,000	$150,000
Yes	225,000	175,000	125,000

Consider Example 20.1. Multiple cash-flow projections in the example reflect an analyst's estimate of the influence of general business conditions and of the presence or absence of a competing shopping center. Regardless of general business conditions, construction of a competing center will have an adverse impact on cash flows and thus on the profitability of the investment. The better the general economic environment during the lease period, the more cash a net lease will generate, whether or not the competing center is built.

Example 20.1 could be extended to incorporate as many additional possibilities as circumstances warrant. A different set of cash-flow possibilities could be developed to reflect the expected impact of labor strife or major change in the general level of employment. Additional sets of possibilities might be shown, depending upon what happens to tax laws, whether a proposed highway interchange is actually built and so on.

Expansion possibilities are virtually endless. The analyst's task is to identify those possible events that have a significant likelihood of actually transpiring and that will have a measurable impact on investment outcome. Separate forecasts are then made to reflect possible outcomes for all particularly crucial eventualities.

Conventional Probability Rules

By convention, the probability assigned to the likelihood of an event's occurrence must be a positive number between zero and one, where zero represents impossibility of occurrence and one represents absolute certainty. If a set of eventualities is mutually exclusive (only one of them can occur) and exhaustive (includes all possible outcomes), then the sum of the probabilities associated with events in the set must equal one. To illustrate the point, on any given day it will either rain or not rain. Therefore, the sum of the probabilities associated with these two possibilities must be one. If the probability of rain is 0.4 (four chances out of ten), then the probability that it will not rain must be 0.6 (six chances out of ten).

A very important probability rule is sometimes called the *multiplicative law of probability*. It is used to determine the probability of occurrence of an event whose outcome depends in turn on the outcome of some prior event. If we call these events A and B, then the probability of B is the product of the probability of occurrence of A times the probability of occurrence B, given that A occurs. This is an example of *joint probabilities*.

TABLE 20.1 Probabilistic Forecast of Various Economic States

Economic Environment	Associated Probability
Good	.20
Fair	.60
Poor	.20
Total	1.00

TABLE 20.2 Probability That Competing Shopping Center Will Be Built, Under Various Economic Conditions

Probability that Competing Center Will Be	Economic Environment		
	Good	Fair	Poor
Built	.80	.50	.20
Not Built	.20	.50	.80
	Total 1.00	Total 1.00	Total 1.00

Application of Joint Probabilities

To apply the preceding concepts to real estate investment, consider again the illustration in Example 20.1. The analyst assigns subjective probabilities to the likelihood of each specific eventuality. (Accept, for the present, the convenient fiction that these are the only possible outcomes.)

Assessing the economic environment, the analyst arrives at the probabilistic estimates of most likely general economic conditions during the forecast period, as indicated in Table 20.1.

Table 20.2 further expands Example 20.1 by relating various economic environments and the probability that a competing shopping center will be constructed. Note that the probabilities in Table 20.2 are conditional, depending on various economic conditions. For each possible set of economic conditions a competitive center either will or will not be built. Therefore, the sum of the mutually exclusive probabilities under each set of possible conditions must equal one.

Combining probabilistic estimates from Tables 20.1 and 20.2 generates joint probabilities concerning various possible economic environments and competitive conditions. For example, Table 20.1 indicates a probability of 0.20 that economic conditions will be good, and Table 20.2 reflects a probability of 0.80 that a competitive center will be built if economic conditions are good. The

TABLE 20.3 Probability Estimates of
                Economic Conditions and
                Related Competitive
                Environments

Competing Center Built?	*Economic Conditions*			
	Good	*Fair*	*Poor*	*Σ*
Yes	0.16	0.30	0.04	0.50
No	0.04	0.30	0.16	0.50
	0.20 +	0.60 +	0.20 =	1.00

probability that economic conditions will be good and that a competitive center will be built is the product of these two underlying probabilities, or 0.16. This, and all other joint probabilities generated from Tables 20.1 and 20.2, are shown in Table 20.3.

Since Table 20.3 exhausts all possible combinations of general economic conditions and competitive environments, the sum of the probabilities in the table must equal one. Moreover, the probability of various general economic conditions can be determined by summing the factors in the table vertically. Comparing the footings from Table 20.3 with the probabilities in Table 20.1 confirms that the probability of good economic conditions is 0.20; of fair conditions, 0.60; and of poor conditions, 0.20. Summing Table 20.3 horizontally gives the probability of competition. Finally, since there either will or will not be competition, and some general economic condition must prevail, both vertical sums and horizontal crossfootings in Table 20.3 must sum to one.

INTERPRETING RISK MEASURES

Probabilistic estimates of possible investment outcomes provide valuable intelligence about relative risk. Projections can be made even more useful with additional manipulation of data to provide estimates of most likely outcomes and associated probability distributions of all possible alternatives.

Probability Distributions

An array of all possible outcomes and their related probabilities of occurrence is called a *probability distribution*. The probability distribution of possible net cash flows from the venture described in Example 20.1 is presented in Table

TABLE 20.4   Expected Annual Cash Flow from Proposed Shopping Center Project

(1) Possible Economic Environment	(2) Related Cash-Flow Forecast (from Ex. 20.1)	(3) Probability of Occurrence (from Table 20.3)	(4) Weighted Average (2) × (3)
Competing center built, and economic environment is:			
Poor	$125,000	0.04	$ 5,000
Fair	175,000	0.30	52,500
Good	225,000	0.16	36,000
No competing center, and economic environment is:			
Poor	150,000	0.16	24,000
Fair	200,000	0.30	60,000
Good	250,000	0.04	10,000
		Total = 1.00	$\overline{CF}$ = $187,500

20.4. The possible net cash flows from Example 20.1 are multiplied by their related probabilities as generated in Table 20.3. The products are summed in column four of Table 20.4 to generate an expected (that is, most probable) cash flow from the shopping center project.

Distributions such as that shown in Table 20.4 are called *discrete* probability distributions, to reflect the assumption that possible outcomes are limited to specific point estimates presented in the computation. The bar graph in Figure 20.1 shows the same data.

Table 20.4 incorporates an assumption that the six cash-flow alternatives from Example 20.1 exhaust all possibilities associated with the venture. This is, of course, merely a convenient fiction. Since net cash flow from percentage leases is a function of leaseholders' sales revenue, the actual distribution must encompass all intermediate values as well. This is descriptive of a continuous probability distribution.

The discrete probability distribution of Figure 20.1 can be converted to a continuous distribution by explicit recognition of values between and beyond the point estimates of Table 20.4 as being in the realm of probabilities. This is illustrated in Figure 20.1 by the solid line tracing the outer range of the discrete estimates of possible outcomes.

Expected Value *or Mean*

The *expected value* of a probability distribution of possible cash flows is the weighted average of the possible cash flows making up the distribution, with each value weighted by its attendant probability of occurrence. The relationship can be expressed as:

$$\overline{CF} = \sum_{i=1}^{n} CF_i P_i$$

FIGURE 20.1   Probability Distribution of Cash Flows

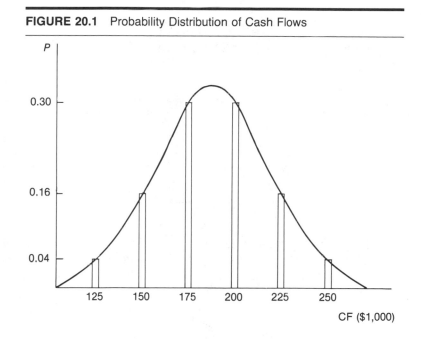

where $\overline{CF}$ is the expected value of the cash-flow distribution, CF_i is the value associated with the ith probability and P_i is the probability associated with that value.

Table 20.4 applies this formulation to compute the expected value of the cash-flow projections from Example 20.1. Column two of the table gives the various possible values of the CF_i, and column three expresses the values of the P_i. The product of $CF_i P_i$ is shown in column four. The summation of column four, and the solution to the above equation, is the expected cash flow from Example 20.1: $187,500.

Measuring Dispersion

Recall that risk is defined as the possibility of variation of actual outcomes from expectations. Expressing the expected outcome as a probability-weighted average permits using variance or standard deviation as a measure of risk.

Variance.   *Variance* is the weighted average of the squared differences between each possible outcome and the expected outcome. Expressed algebraically, this relationship is:

$$V = \sum_{i=1}^{n} (CF_i - \overline{CF})^2 P_i$$

where V is the variance, CF_i is the value of the ith possible outcome, $\overline{CF}$ is the expected value and P_i is the related probability. Applying this formula to

TABLE 20.5   Variance of the Probability Distribution of Possible Cash Flows from Shopping Center in Example 20.1

Possible Cash Flow	Expected Cash Flow	$CF_i - \overline{CF}$	Probability (P_i)	$(CF_i - \overline{CF})^2 P_i$
$125,000	$187,500	$(62,500)	0.04	$156,250,000
150,000	187,500	(37,500)	0.16	225,000,000
175,000	187,500	(12,500)	0.30	46,875,000
200,000	187,500	12,500	0.30	46,875,000
225,000	187,500	37,500	0.16	225,000,000
250,000	187,500	62,500	0.04	156,250,000
			$\Sigma = 1.00$	$V = \$856,250,000$

the possible nth-year cash flow in Example 20.1 and combining the previously calculated expected value of $187,500 with probability measures from Table 20.4 yields a variance estimate of $856,250,000. Computations are shown in Table 20.5.

Standard Deviation.   Because variance employs squared differences between observed values and the mean of a distribution, the relationship is nonlinear. The square root of the variance provides a much more usable measure of dispersion, particularly when it is used to compare alternative investment opportunities with significantly different expected values. This eliminates the distorting effect of squaring differences that vary greatly in magnitude.

The formula for the standard deviation is:

$$\sigma = \sqrt{\sum_{i=1}^{n} (X_i - \overline{X})^2 P_i}$$

where σ is the standard deviation, the X_i are the various possible values of the variable being considered, $\overline{X}$ is the mean of the distribution of possible values of x and P_i is the probability of occurrence of each possible value.

The square root of the variance, called *standard deviation*, also has other mathematical properties that make it particularly useful as a measure of risk. So long as the underlying probabilities are symmetrically distributed about the mean of the distribution, approximately 68.3 percent of all possible values will lie within one standard deviation of the expected value. Two standard deviations encompass approximately 95 percent of all possible outcomes, and three standard deviations to either side of the expected values include virtually all possible outcomes. Figure 20.2 illustrates this relationship.

Once the mean and the standard deviation are established, it is possible to determine the probability of occurrence of values over any desired interval

FIGURE 20.2   Percent of Area Under Normal Curve
Encompassed by *X* Standard Deviations
from the Mean

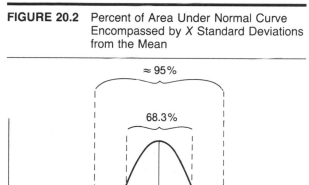

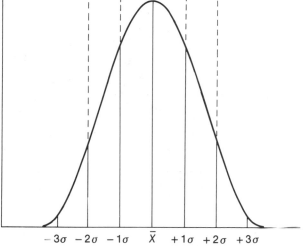

$$-3\sigma \quad -2\sigma \quad -1\sigma \quad \bar{X} \quad +1\sigma \quad +2\sigma \quad +3\sigma$$

within the distribution. This is accomplished by reference to a table of standardized values expressing the relationship. Such a table, sometimes called a
table of *Z-values,* is given in Appendix B. It shows the portion of the area
under the normal distribution lying to the left or right of various specified values.
The Z-value from the table is simply the number of standard deviations from
the mean to the value in question. The relationship is frequently expressed
algebraically as:

$$Z = \frac{X - \bar{X}}{\sigma_x}$$

where *X* is some specified value under a symmetric distribution (often called a
normal curve), $\bar{X}$ is the midpoint of the distribution (the expected value) and
σ_x is the value of one standard deviation.   *+ mean*

Having earlier determined variance of the distribution of possible net cash
flows in Example 20.1 to be $856,250,000 (see Table 20.5), the standard
deviation can be computed by simply deriving the square root of this amount.
The standard deviation is, therefore, $\sqrt{\$856,250,000}$ or approximately $29,262.
The expected value (that is, the midpoint) of the distribution was previously

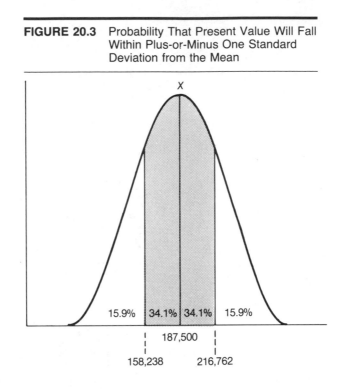

FIGURE 20.3 Probability That Present Value Will Fall Within Plus-or-Minus One Standard Deviation from the Mean

determined to be $187,500 (see Table 20.4). These two parameters, the expected value and the standard deviation, effectively determine the entire distribution of any normally distributed variable. (Standard deviation serves well as the sole measure of risk only when the probability distribution is relatively symmetrical [forms a bell-shaped curve]. If it is significantly skewed to either side, a measure of skewness may need to be incorporated into the model. This is possible, but it vastly complicates the mathematics. Our analysis considers only the symmetric distribution.)[2]

Figure 20.3 illustrates the relationship calculated for Example 20.1. The expected value of $187,500 is the midpoint of the distribution. One standard deviation is plus-or-minus $29,262, which we know (from the earlier discussion) to encompass approximately 68.3 percent of all possible values. The probability of the actual value falling within any range corresponds to the percent of the total area under the curve that falls within that range. Therefore, the probability is approximately 68.3 percent that the actual cash flow will prove to be within plus-or-minus $29,262 of $187,500, which is to say between $158,238 and $216,762.

To determine this by reference to the table in Appendix B, first calculate the percent of the total area not falling within one standard deviation of the midpoint (the unshaded area in Figure 20.3). Since this is a *symmetric* distribution (that is, the sides of the probability distribution of possible cash flows are mirror images of each other, with 50 percent of the area under the curve lying on either side of the mean), we need to solve the problem for only one side of the curve. The same value will also apply to the other side. Refer to the Z-value table in Appendix B to find the percent of the total area under the curve to the left of point X. The area is 0.1587, or 15.87 percent. Now since 50 percent of the total area under the curve lies to the left of the midpoint, it follows that the area from point X to the midpoint must be 50 percent minus 15.87 percent, or 34.13 percent. The total portion of the area under the curve that lies between one standard deviation and the midpoint, therefore, is 2(34.13%), or approximately 68.3 percent.

As an exercise, use the table of Z-values to determine the probability that cash flow in Example 20.1 will actually prove to equal or exceed $170,000. The first step is to determine how many standard deviations this variable, CF_x, lies from the mean, $\overline{CF}$:

$$Z = (CF_x - \overline{CF})/\sigma_{CF}$$
$$= (\$170,000 - \$187,500)/\$29,262$$
$$= -0.60$$

From the table in Appendix B, we can determine that approximately 0.2743 of the total area lies to the left of the point associated with −0.60 standard deviations. We can, therefore, be 0.50 minus 0.2743 equals 0.2257, or 22.57 percent confident that the cash flow will actually be between $170,000 and $187,500, provided we have correctly specified the parameters of the problem. Moreover, we know that 50 percent of the possible outcomes are above $187,500. It follows that the probability of cash flow equal to or more than $170,000 is 50 percent plus 22.57 percent, or about 73 percent.

Coefficient of Variation. Standard deviation serves admirably as a comparative measure of risk when evaluating alternatives involving approximately the same level of annual cash flow. When dissimilar cash flows must be compared, it is sometimes useful to go one step further and to calculate the *coefficient of variation,* which is standard deviation of the cash flow divided by the expected cash flow. For the project in Example 20.1 the coefficient of variation is:

/ mean

standard deviation/expected cash flow
$29,262/$187,500
= 0.156

When alternatives are being compared with respect to expected outcomes and relative riskiness, rather than for derivation of a bid price, the coefficient of variation offers the advantage of permitting direct comparisons when the mean values of the cash-flow distributions vary.

STANDARD DEVIATION AND THE DISCOUNTED CASH-FLOW MODEL

Several methods of incorporating risk into the investment decision have been utilized, the most appropriate being in part determined by the nature of the analysis. A second major factor is the pattern of the anticipated stream of investor benefits and the relationship between year-to-year forecasts.

Mean/Standard Deviation Approach

Perhaps the most useful approach to incorporating risk into an investment decision is to use the *mean/standard deviation* model. It involves developing both an expected cash flow and a standard deviation measure for each year of the projection period. The technique is best illustrated by using a single-period cash-flow forecast. This avoids complications introduced when annual cash flows are influenced by outcomes from previous years. After demonstrating the principle with this simplifying assumption concerning cash-flow patterns, we will examine more complex situations.

Example 20.2

A proposal requires an initial equity investment of $25,000. After three years it is expected that the investment position will be liquidated with a net cash inflow of $50,000. The standard deviation of the cash flow in the third year is estimated to be $7,000, and the range of possible cash flows are assumed to be distributed symmetrically about the expected amount. Cash flow during the first two years is virtually certain to be zero. The investor's opportunity cost of equity capital (the appropriate discount rate) is ten percent.

Consider Example 20.2. Though the forecast includes a point estimate of cash flow for the third year, there is in fact a whole spectrum of possible cash flows for that year. This is evidenced by the estimated $7,000 standard deviation of the cash flows. The standard deviation estimate, you will recall, is derived by comparing the range of possible outcomes with the expected outcome.

There is a present value associated with each possible cash-flow outcome in Example 20.2. Were it possible to discount every possible outcome, a probability distribution of possible present values would result. This distribution of present values also, of course, will have an expected value (the midpoint of the distribution) and a standard deviation.

Since the distribution of cash flows in Example 20.2 is assumed to be distributed symmetrically about its mean, the distribution of present values also will be symmetrically distributed. Moreover, the midpoint of the distribution of present values will be the discounted value of the midpoint of the distribution of cash flows. This amount, the expected present value, is $37,566, calculated as follows:

$$\overline{PV} = \overline{CF}/(1 + i)^3$$
$$= \$50,000/(1.10)^3$$
$$= \$37,566$$

Where there is only one anticipated future cash flow (rather than a series of forecasted outcomes), computing the standard deviation of the present value distribution is equally uncomplicated. Simply discount the standard deviation of the cash-flow distribution at the same discount rate employed in determining the midpoint of the distribution of possible present values. For Example 20.2, the computation is:

$$\sigma_{PV} = \sigma_{CF}/(1 + i)^3$$
$$= \$7,000/(1.10)^3$$
$$= \$5,259$$

Recall that when the yield rate equals the discount rate, the present value of future cash flows will equal the amount of the initial cash outlay. Should the actual cash flow from the project in Example 20.2 be such that its present value (discounting at ten percent) proves to be $25,000 more, it follows that the actual yield on the project will have been ten percent or better. The probability that this will occur equals the percent of the total area under the probability distribution of possible present values lying to the right of the point where the actual outcome is $25,000.

Figure 20.4 depicts the probability distribution of possible present values of the cash flows from Example 20.2. The probability that the actual present value will be $25,000 or better (and thus, the yield will be ten percent or more) is represented by the unshaded area under the curve. We can determine what percent of the total area this represents by using the equation discussed earlier in the chapter:

$$Z = (PV_x - \overline{PV})/\sigma_{PV}$$

where:

Z = the standardized value from Appendix B
PV_x = minimum acceptable present value
$\overline{PV}$ = the expected present value (that is, the arithmetic mean)
σ_{PV} = the standard deviation of the present value

Substituting values from Example 20.2 in the above equation yields:

$$Z = (\$25,000 - \$37,566)/\$5,259$$
$$= -2.39$$

Reference to the table of Z-values in Appendix B reveals that the area to the left of $PV = \$25,000$ is just slightly more than 0.8 percent of the total area

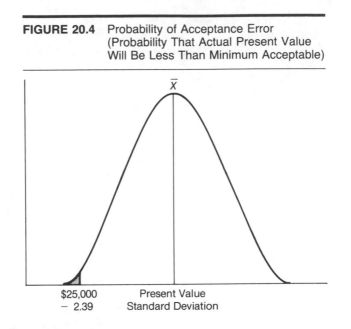

FIGURE 20.4 Probability of Acceptance Error
(Probability That Actual Present Value
Will Be Less Than Minimum Acceptable)

| $25,000 | Present Value |
| − 2.39 | Standard Deviation |

under the distribution. The probability that this project will yield at least a ten percent rate of return, therefore, is estimated to be more than 0.99. Expressed another way, the investor can be more than 99 percent confident of earning a yield equal to or more than the opportunity cost of capital.

Establishing Acceptable Risk Profiles

The probability that a venture will yield less than the minimum acceptable yield and thus its acceptance will prove to have been a mistake is called the *probability of acceptance error*. Having specified an absolute maximum probability of acceptance error beyond which no investment opportunity will be accepted, there remains the problem of discriminating between acceptable and unacceptable risk-reward combinations lying within the range of provisional acceptability. Certainly not all opportunities falling within the acceptabililty threshold are equally desirable. Within the range of tolerable probability of acceptance error, there are gradients of risk. Investors expect compensation for all incremental risk assumed.

To facilitate choosing among risky opportunities, and to ensure consistency over time, investors may specify the maximum acceptable probability of acceptance error associated with various levels of present values per dollar of invested cash or with various expected yields. This permits a more refined preliminary screening by subordinates, further reducing the time spent by final decision makers on projects destined for ultimate rejection.

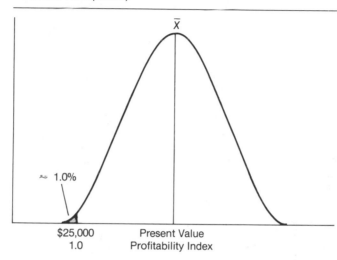

FIGURE 20.5 Probability of Acceptance Error (Probability That Actual Profitability Index Will Be Less Than Minimum Acceptable)

Before such risk profiles can be constructed, expected outcomes must be expressed in terms permitting interproject comparison of costs and benefits. Profitability indices (discussed in Chapter 13) have this characteristic, inasmuch as they represent the ratio of present value to initial cash outlay. They convert absolute present value estimates to measures of relative present value per dollar of required initial cash expenditure. To illustrate, consider again the investment in Example 20.2. The expected value of the distribution of possible outcomes, expressed in terms of present value, is $37,566, and the initial cash outlay is $25,000. The expected value of the probability distribution of possible profitability indices, $\overline{PI}$, is:

$$\overline{PI} = \$37,566/\$25,000$$
$$= 1.50$$

Recall from Chapter 13 that when present value just equals initial cash outlay, the profitability index is exactly one, and the net present value is zero. Also, recall that this means the internal rate of return exactly equals the discount rate used to determine present value. Present value, net present value and the profitability index, therefore, all measure the same relationship. An advantage of the profitability index is that it permits comparison among projects of different magnitudes.

Figure 20.5 replicates Figure 20.4, with a second scale measured in terms of the profitability index. Note that at the point where the present value of future net cash flows equals the initial cash outlay of $25,000, the profitability index

TABLE 20.6   Risk-Return Profiles for Two Investors Who Express Risk in Terms of Probability of Earning Less Than a Specified Minimum Acceptable Rate of Return

Expected Profitability Index	*Maximum Acceptable Probability That Profitability Index Will Be Equal to or Less Than One*	
	Investor A	*Investor B*
0.0	0.0000	0.0000
1.2	0.0150	0.0150
1.4	0.0230	0.0260
1.6	0.0290	0.0345
1.8	0.0330	0.0430
2.0	0.0350	0.0460
2.2	0.0350	0.0490
2.4	0.0350	0.0500

is one, indicating that this corresponds to an internal rate of return (yield rate) just equal to the ten percent minimum acceptable rate.

Specifying maximum levels of risk for various values of profitability indices (expected benefits) permits project evaluation by reference to a risk profile for an expected profitability index of the level computed for that proposal. If the dispersion of possible outcomes indicates the project is too risky for the benefit it is expected to generate, the proposal is automatically rejected. If not, it is passed to the investor for a final decision. All projects passing this preliminary filtering process are considered, and final decisions are made according to portfolio risk-return considerations, with available cash acting as a constraint.

A tabulation of acceptable combinations of risk and expected benefits will reflect a positive relationship between expected profitability and dispersion of possible returns (risk). The exact trade-off depends upon the investor's personal attitude toward risk. This permits interface of the investor's risk preferences with the analyst's informed opinion regarding the risk implicit in a particular project.

Risk profiles for two investors are presented in Table 20.6 and illustrated in Figure 20.6. The table presumes that anticipated after-tax cash flows have been discounted at a rate representing the minimum acceptable yield on the investor's equity investment. If the actual yield falls below this minimum rate, the profitability index will be less than one (that is, the present value of the cash flows will be less than $1 for each $1 of equity investment). Should this occur, the investment venture will prove to have been a mistake.

If the expected profitability index is above one, indicating an expected yield in excess of the minimum acceptable rate, the investor is willing to accept some risk (measured as probability) that the actual yield will fall below the minimum

FIGURE 20.6 Risk-Return Profiles Expressed in Terms of Profitability Index

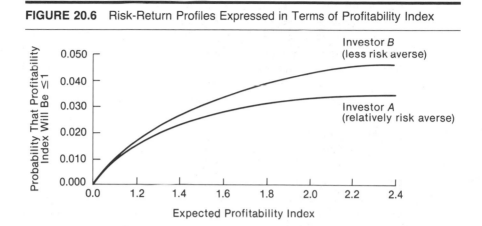

acceptable level. Thus, with an expected profitability index of 1.2 ($1.20 of present value for each $1 of equity cash invested), investor *A* in Table 20.6 will accept a probability of as much as 0.0150 that the actual profitability index will be one or less and therefore that the yield will be equal to or less than the minimum acceptable rate. The higher the expected profitability index (and thus the expected yield), the greater the acceptable risk (probability) that the actual yield will fall below acceptable levels and the venture will prove to be a mistake.

Figure 20.6 graphically portrays the relationship between expected present value per dollar invested (profitability indices) and acceptable levels of risk for the investors whose risk-return preferences are charted in Table 20.6. For each investor the area below the lines in Figure 20.6 represents acceptable combinations of risk and expected profitability indices; the area above the lines represents unacceptable combinations.

DEALING WITH MORE COMPLEX CASH-FLOW PATTERNS

To avoid premature complications, our discussion thus far has assumed a single-period cash-flow pattern. This simplifies the dialogue but, for most real estate ventures, is highly unrealistic. Cash flows (both positive and negative) usually occur periodically over a number of years. It becomes necessary, therefore, to estimate the mean and standard deviation of the cash flows for each year in the projection period, including the cash flow from disposing of the project at the end of the holding period.

With multiple-year cash-flow patterns, flow in subsequent periods will depend at least in part upon what happens in earlier periods. If projections prove overly optimistic in earlier years, chances are that the same will hold for the entire life of the project. Likewise, if cash flows in early years are greater than anticipated, favorable deviations are likely to occur in future years as well—so long as the same causal influences are present. The extent to which causal factors influence cash flows over two or more periods is called *serial correlation*. Serial correlation is measured by the *coefficient of correlation*, which can range from zero to plus-or-minus one. When the correlation coefficient equals zero, serial cash flows are completely independent of each other. A coefficient of plus-or-minus one indicates perfect correlation of the cash flows.

Serial correlation (or its absence) does not affect the expected present value of a series of cash-flow projections. It will, however, drastically alter the standard deviation of the probability distribution of possible present values. In general, the greater the degree of serial correlation of annual cash flows, the wider the dispersion of possible outcomes about the mean and the greater the standard deviation of the probability distribution of possible present values.

Perfectly Correlated Cash Flows

When serial cash flows are perfectly correlated, deviation from the expected outcome in one period will result in deviations in all future periods in the same relation. If actual cash flows in one period are exactly (say) one-half standard deviation to the right or left of the mean value of the probability distribution of possible cash flows for the period, then actual cash flows for all future periods will be exactly one-half standard deviation to the right or left of the probability distributions of all possible cash flows.

The standard deviation of the present value of a perfectly correlated stream of cash flows is:

$$\sigma_{PV} = \sum_{t=1}^{n} \sigma_{CF_t}/(1 + i)^t$$

where σ_{PV} is the standard deviation of the present value distribution, σ_{CF} is the standard deviation of the cash-flow distribution for time period t, and i is the discount rate used to derive the expected present value. For perfectly serially correlated cash flows, therefore, simply discount the standard deviation of the cash-flow distributions to derive the standard deviation of the present value distribution.

To see how the degree of serial correlation affects the standard deviation of the probability distribution of present values, consider the series of cash-flow projections in Example 20.3.

Example 20.3

A real estate project requires an initial equity outlay of $50,000. An analyst develops the following estimate of the midpoints and standard deviations for annual cash flows over the projected life of the investment venture:

Year	Mean of Cash-Flow Distribution	Standard Deviation
1	$15,000	$5,400
2	15,000	4,500
3	40,000	9,000

The probability distributions of annual cash flows are assumed to be symmetrical about the means, and the serial correlation coefficients are all assumed to be $+1$. The investor's minimum acceptable rate of return (and therefore the appropriate discount rate) is 12 percent.

Recall that the *mean* (the expected value) of the probability distribution of possible present values associated with a symmetrically distributed cash-flow distribution is simply the present value of the mean of the cash-flow distribution. Discounting the means from Example 20.3 and summing the present values yields the mean of the probability distribution of possible present values of all cash flows from the venture. These computations are shown in Table 20.7.

Recall also that the standard deviation of the probability distribution of possible present values for perfectly serially correlated cash flows is derived by simply discounting the standard deviations of the cash-flow distributions. These computations are also illustrated in Table 20.7.

Uncorrelated Cash Flows

Expected present value does not change when the possibility of serially independent (uncorrelated) cash flows is introduced, but the standard deviation of the present value distribution may be greatly altered. In general, the greater the degree of serial correlation of annual cash flows, the greater will be the dispersion, and thus the greater the standard deviation, of the probability distribution of possible present values.

To see this relationship, consider again the cash-flow projections in Example 20.3, but recompute the standard deviation of the present value under the revised assumption that the actual cash flow for each year is considered to be completely independent of that for other years. The formula for computing the standard deviation of the present value is:

$$\sigma_{PV} = \sqrt{\sum_{t=1}^{n} \frac{\sigma_{CF_t}^2}{(1 + i)^{2t}}}$$

where σ_{PV} is the standard deviation of the present value, σ_{CF_t} is the standard deviation of the cash flow for year t and i is the discount rate used to derive the present value of the cash flows. Substituting the standard deviation of the cash flows and the discount rate from Example 20.3 yields a standard deviation of the present value of $8,784. Here is the calculation:

TABLE 20.7 Mean and Standard Deviation of Probability
Distribution of Present Values from Example 20.3

Year	Expected Cash Flow	×	Present Value Factor at 12%	=	Mean of Present Value
1	$15,000		.8929		$13,394
2	15,000		.7972		11,958
3	40,000		.7118		28,472
					$53,824

Year	Standard Deviation of Cash Flow	×	Present Value Factor at 12%	=	Standard Deviation of Present Value
1	$5,400		.8929		$ 4,822
2	4,500		.7972		3,587
3	9,000		.7118		6,406
					$14,815

$$\sigma_{PV} = \sqrt{\frac{(\$5,400)^2}{(1.12)^2} + \frac{(\$4,500)^2}{(1.12)^4} + \frac{(\$9,000)^2}{(1.12)^6}}$$

$$= \$8,784$$

Comparing this with the standard deviation of the present value under the assumption of perfect serial correlation, as derived in Table 20.7, makes clear the consequence of serial correlation; moving from perfect to zero serial correlation reduced the standard deviation of the present value by $6,031, or almost 41 percent.

Partially Correlated Cash Flows

Shifting from an assumption of serial independence to one of perfect serial correlation changes the computation of standard deviation and thus the dispersion of the probability distribution of possible outcomes from an investment, but does not seriously complicate the arithmetic. Problems do arise, however, with the possibility of partial serial correlation.

In situations involving less-than-perfect serial correlation, some of the expected cash flows may be highly correlated over time, while others may be more nearly independent. This, of course, is illustrative of most real-world circumstances. When this occurs, the standard deviation problem becomes complex.

To deal with the issue, Frederick S. Hillier has developed a model that is particularly applicable to real estate investment situations.[3] His model groups annual cash flows on the basis of whether they are more nearly independent or serially correlated over time. The two groups are then treated as if they were *completely independent* and *perfectly correlated,* respectively.

The present value of the segmented income streams is unaffected by the treatment afforded in Hillier's model. The formula for the revised standard deviation of the present value, however, becomes:

$$\sigma_{PV} = \sqrt{\left[\sum_{t=1}^{n} \sigma_{CF_t} \middle/ (1 + i)^t \right]^2 + \left[\sum_{t=1}^{n} \sigma_{CF_t}^2 \middle/ (1 + i)^{2t} \right]}$$

where the first bracketed term under the radical applies to the standard deviation for the cash flows assumed to be perfectly correlated and the second bracketed term applies to the standard deviation for the stream of net cash flows assumed to be serially independent (uncorrelated).

To illustrate the use of Hillier's model, consider the data in Example 20.4, which represent a breakdown of supporting data from Example 20.3.

Example 20.4

Attempting to get a better grip on the risk element associated with the investment in Example 20.3, the analyst separates net cash-flow projections into receipt and expenditure components and develops separate standard deviation estimates for each.

Because rental revenues are so dependent on locational factors, the revenue stream is considered to be highly correlated over time. If the location is less desirable than anticipated, less-than-expected revenues will occur in each of the forecast years. The same factor will affect the selling price of the property at the end of the holding period, which is included in the expected cash flow for that year.

Operating expenses, on the other hand, are largely independent of locational influences. They are considered to be serially independent and are expected to vary from projected values only as a result of random factors.

Annual projections of revenue and expenditures, and associated standard deviation estimates, are determined to be as follows:

| | Revenue Projections | | Expenditure Projections | |
Year	Projected Revenue	Standard Deviation	Projected Expenditures	Standard Deviation
1	$27,000	$3,780	$12,000	$1,620
2	27,000	3,500	12,000	1,000
3	52,000	6,000	12,000	2,700

The expected present value of the venture in Example 20.4 remains unchanged (except for rounding differences) from that of Example 20.3:

$$PV = [(\$27,000 - \$12,000)/1.12] + [(\$27,000 - \$12,000)/(1.12)^2]$$
$$+ [(\$52,000 - \$12,000)/(1.12)^3]$$
$$= \$53,822$$

The standard deviation of the expected present value, however, is drastically altered by the assumption of serial correlation of gross revenues. Substituting standard deviation measures from Example 20.4 in the formula developed by Hillier gives:

$$\sigma_{PV} = \sqrt{\left[\frac{\$3,780}{1.12} + \frac{\$3,500}{(1.12)^2} + \frac{\$6,000}{(1.12)^3}\right]^2 + \left[\frac{(\$1,620)^2}{(1.12)^2} + \frac{(\$1,000)^2}{(1.12)^4} + \frac{(\$2,700)^2}{(1.12)^6}\right]}$$

$$= \$10,739$$

SUMMARY

Modern risk-analysis techniques have been developed in the fields of corporate finance and capital budgeting. The techniques allow risk to be expressed in terms of probability of variance from expectations. Because data are not available for statistical sampling of the type employed in the physical and biological sciences, probabilities in investment analysis are frequently subjective, reflecting the informed opinion of an analyst rather than being generated from objective information sources.

Techniques for expressing risk in probabilistic terms involve developing probability distributions of possible outcomes and estimating related standard deviations. This in turn permits expression of likely investment consequences as ranges of possible outcomes and accompanying levels of confidence. Probability distributions of possible outcomes may be expressed as present values, net present values, profitability indices or any number of other measures, as desired by an analyst or client.

NOTES

1. For contrasting approaches, compare the distinction made by Steven E. Bolten, *Managerial Finance* (Boston: Houghton Mifflin, 1976), 222–23, with that of J. Fred Weston and Eugene F. Brigham, *Managerial Finance*, 5th ed. (Hinsdale, IL: The Dryden Press, 1975), 313. For a more detailed treatment of the distinction, see R. Duncan Luce and Howard Raiffa, *Games and Decisions* (New York: John Wiley, 1957).

2. For a discussion of probability estimation involving asymmetrical distributions, see John G. Kemeny et al., *Finite Mathematical Structures* (Englewood Cliffs, NJ: Prentice-Hall, 1959), 172–78.

3. See Frederick S. Hillier, "The Derivation of Probabilistic Information for the Evaluation of Risky Investments," *Management Science* 9 (April 1963): 443–57.

RECOMMENDED READINGS

Brigham, Eugene F. *Fundamentals of Financial Management*, 4th ed. Hinsdale, IL: The Dryden Press, 1986, pp. 332–335.

Greer, Gaylon E. *The Real Estate Investment Decision*. Lexington, MA: Lexington Books, 1979, pp. 199–226.

Jaffe, Austin J., and C. F. Sirmans. *Real Estate Investment Decision Making*. Englewood Cliffs, NJ: Prentice-Hall, 1982, pp. 431–457.

Phyrr, Stephen A., and James R. Cooper. *Real Estate Investment: Strategy, Analysis, Decisions*. Boston: Warren, Gorham and Lamont, 1983, pp. 663–726.

REVIEW QUESTIONS

1. What objections to modern techniques do users of traditional risk measures have? Why are their objections off target?
2. Describe the difference between risk and uncertainty.
3. How might one estimate probabilities related to real estate investments? What role do subjective probability measures play in the analysis?
4. Explain discrete and continuous probability distributions.
5. Explain the usefulness of variance and standard deviation in risk measurement.
6. Describe the calculation for the coefficient of variation and explain its purpose in the analysis.
7. How are profitability indices used in development of risk profiles?

DISCUSSION QUESTIONS

1. Do you think the probability distribution approach to risk measurement discussed in this chapter is more likely to be adopted as microcomputer literacy becomes more widespread?
2. If probabilities cannot be measured using sample data, but must be expressed as *subjective* probabilities, is there any benefit in expressing them in quantitative terms?
3. What are some examples of events or contract provisions that could skew or attenuate the probability distribution of possible cash flows from a real estate development?

PART SIX: Case Problem

Refer again to the Sated Satyr Apartments case problem at the end of Part Three and to your solutions to problems for Parts Three, Four and Five.

1. Discounting at ten percent, what will be the present value of the project if the investor's marginal income tax rate is increased to 33 percent for the third and all subsequent years of the investment period? Will this reduce the equity yield below the investor's ten percent minimum acceptable expected rate of return?
2. Suppose the income tax rate does not change, but actual gross revenue falls five percent below expectations? How will this affect the desirability of the investment outcome?
3. Suppose the gross income is five percent above the expected level?
4. Would it be helpful to know something about the degree of confidence the fore-caster has in the cash-flow forecast?

PART SEVEN

The Investment Analysis Process Illustrated

R eaders have by now been exposed to the entire real estate investment analysis process. The road has been long and involved, however, and our final objective has at times been obscured by emphasis on detail. Part Seven is designed to bring together procedures from the preceding sections by applying the discounted cash-flow model to solve actual investment analysis problems. To demonstrate the basic model's flexibility and universal applicability, a variety of problems are introduced. Each example illustrates a separate aspect of the analysis process and none should be omitted from the serious student's reading program.

CHAPTER 21

Analyzing Subdivision Proposals

INTRODUCTION

Subdivision in the generally accepted sense consists of purchasing large tracts of land and selling off smaller parcels. From an analytical perspective, subdividing vacant land, converting large buildings into condominium or cooperative units and converting buildings into time-share units all have a great deal in common. These latter activities might profitably be thought of as vertical subdivision. All require initial cash outlays for property purchase and improvement, and all are expected to produce cash inflows as individual units are sold. Subdivision is considered an ongoing business activity, and profits are generally taxed as ordinary income from operating a business.

Proliferating land-use controls and increasingly complex regulatory provisions have transformed land development operations, commonly called *subdivision*. What was once a simple process of "buying by the acre and selling by the square foot" has become a sophisticated business operation requiring skilled legal, financial and marketing talent combined with adept community planning ability. Business operations vary in scale from part-time subdividers who control only a few acres to multimillion-dollar corporations that subdivide land tracts extending over several square miles.

OVERVIEW OF THE SUBDIVISION PROCESS

Subdivision ventures grow out of a developer's perception of unsatisfied demand for certain types of buildable sites. If the contemplated use conforms to current zoning laws and governmental land-use plans, the developer may order a feasibility study to determine the probability that subdivision operations will be successful.

Where development objectives require extensive governmental approvals the subdivider may acquire an option to purchase the land. With a secure option, the subdivider might analyze the feasibility of the project and create a detailed plan. If the intended use appears feasible and all necessary governmental permits prove obtainable, the option is exercised and the development plan is put into operation.

Title acquisition and land planning are followed by a land survey. Street locations are laid out, boundaries of individual lots are plotted and utility easements are delineated in the survey.

Physical improvements follow completion of the surveying process. Major land grading, streetbeds and utilities installation usually come first. Curbs, sidewalks and street surfacing follow. These latter improvements are often accomplished concurrently with building construction. Many subdividers are reluctant to finish streets and add curbs and sidewalks while heavy construction equipment is active in the subdivision.

Sales, the final step in subdivision development, may begin upon completion of the land plan and run concurrently with all other activities. Prospective residents, builders and investors may be willing to purchase sites prior to completion of land improvements. They may receive some discount for purchasing at this stage and will have their pick from among the choicest sites. In times of high demand, subdividers may be able to sell their entire inventory before land improvements are completed.

Subdivision is not limited to creating residential building sites. Whereas some subdividers specialize in residential projects, others create industrial parks and office parks. Apartment building sites, shopping centers, recreational parks, hospitals, cemeteries and many other projects are created through the initiative of real estate subdividers.

Significance of Location Decisions

Subdivision location decisions must be responsive to needs of ultimate users. Residential subdivisions require convenient access to schools, shopping facilities and transportation. Industrial subdivisions benefit from convenient access to materials sources and to markets. Availability of truck and rail transportation facilities, therefore, frequently plays an important role in industrial site location decisions.

Subdividers also need to consider current and potential uses of abutting sites. Large-scale subdividers frequently seek to control sufficiently large tracts of land so that they can successfully buffer their improvements from incompatible abutting uses.

Coping with Regulatory Requirements

Governmental land-use control is exercised through zoning laws and master land-use plans. Governmental agencies also exercise control through enforcement of building codes and environmental protection statutes. Many small-scale subdividers limit their land acquisition to appropriately zoned tracts. This strategy minimizes necessary interaction between developer and public agencies. Large-scale subdividers, in contrast, frequently develop plans requiring extensive rezoning and myriad government approvals. Such plans are presented for consideration by appropriate agencies and may require substantial revision before final approval.

Municipalities often seek to influence the level of subdivision activity through their control over public utilities. Subdivision may be encouraged if sewer and water are readily available. In many cases, additional capacity must be developed if these services are to be provided to a new subdivision. Some municipalities pay all costs to provide such services. Others require developers to pay all or a substantial portion. Municipalities sometimes seek, by levying special assessments, to pass these costs to ultimate purchasers.

Creating the Subdivision Plan

Contents of land plans vary with the size of developments. Large-scale plans typically divide the area by specialized use categories, provide detailed street layouts, plot individual sites and provide a utility distribution plan with appropriate easements. At the other extreme, a modest subdivision plan might entail nothing more than plotting individual sites and making provision for utility easements. In all cases, however, the plan should be detailed enough so that working drawings for streets and utilities may be developed and so that individual lots and streets may be surveyed.

Financing the Project

Subdividers generally use land acquisition and development loans to raise capital for their projects. These loans provide funds to purchase unimproved land as well as to improve it prior to resale. Lenders usually disburse loan proceeds on a piecemeal basis as improvements are completed. They regularly inspect projects to verify the existence and quality of improvements. Before disbursing any funds, lenders often require subcontractors to waive their rights to file liens against the project.

Most lenders view subdivision loans as riskier than construction loans. Lenders know that subdividers depend upon proceeds from land sales for funds to repay loans. Lenders, therefore, are vitally concerned with project marketability. For the same reason, lenders should be more interested in the subdivider's record of past successes than in his or her current net worth. Good market research and thorough investigation of subdivider credentials are essential to intelligent underwriting decisions.

INDUSTRIAL SUBDIVISION: A CASE STUDY

Subdivision encompasses a variety of projects. Some subdividers specialize in creating residential building sites; others create industrial, commercial or office sites. Apartment building sites, shopping centers, industrial parks, recreational parks, cemeteries and hospitals are all prospective uses for developable land. Subdividers must choose the most appropriate project from the spectrum of alternatives that may appear economically and legally feasible.

To illustrate major land development issues, the balance of the chapter is devoted to analyzing an industrial subdivision proposal. Property to be developed is currently owned by a railroad and was previously used as a rail switching yard. Having recently abandoned local switching operations, the railroad considers the land surplus and has offered it for sale.

Site Characteristics

Site dimensions are approximately 3,733 feet by 3,733 feet, comprising 320 acres. The property is currently zoned for heavy industrial use, and surrounding uses are primarily manufacturing. Consequently, few governmental approvals are needed for the proposed project. Desirable features of the location include good railroad and truck access. Moreover, proximity of reliable public transportation allows area businesses to draw on the surrounding labor pool.

Prior to declaring this property surplus, the railroad itself launched an industrial subdivision project. Before corporate financial difficulties led it to abandon its development plans, it had completed a site plan. The railroad also procured written assurances from appropriate sources that the site can be provided with combination sewers, water, natural gas and electricity in capacities adequate to support industrial usage. It conducted traffic studies that indicate existing public streets are adequate to handle vehicular traffic to and from buildings to be located on the site. As a consequence of predevelopment activity already completed by the railroad, a would-be developer need only purchase the property, complete necessary improvements and sell off the subdivided parcels.

Of the total 320 acres, 64 acres will be needed for streets, rail spurs, storm water retention and so forth. The remaining 256 acres will be incorporated into subdivided parcels. The site plan provides a street pattern that allows maximum flexibility regarding size of individual sites. This allows the developer to meet the needs of a wide variety of prospective industrial users.

The railroad has agreed to remove all existing improvements, which consist primarily of rail and a few small buildings. Further site preparation will be the responsibility of the purchaser or developer. A detailed survey will be required to locate streets and identify boundaries of individual parcels. Installation of underground utilities, curbs, gutters, streets and street lighting will complete site preparation activities. As a part of its own development plans, the railroad has prepared a detailed schedule, based on local contractors' estimates, of all subdivision costs. The projections include legal and survey expenses but exclude financing costs. Total estimated development costs are $3,840,000, or an average of $15,000 for each of the 256 salable acres.

Market Research

The railroad's real estate department did an excellent job of preparing the site plan and estimating development costs but undertook no research to estimate marketability of the industrial sites. To generate this essential information, the prospective purchasers hired a real estate consulting firm to estimate market demand and probable absorption rates for this project. (Absorption rates refers to the rate at which units of a product are purchased in the marketplace. The relationship between anticipated absorption rates and rates at which competitors will place new units on the market indicates the degree of balance between quantities demanded and quantities supplied.)

Interviews with local industrial brokers indicate major competition from two other large industrial parks in the area. Investigation reveals that one of these projects, the Swampy Knolls Industrial Park, has recently sold its last available parcel. The other, Tri-City Industrial Park, has an estimated five-year supply of sites. Some brokers expect sales in the Tri-City project to increase now that Swampy Knolls is sold out.

Sales information regarding the competing parks, gleaned from a search of the county recorder's files, is presented in Table 21.1. Note that 43 sales, ranging in size from 2.8 to 25 acres, occurred between 1977 and 1987 in the Swampy Knolls project. Forty-five sales ranging in size from three to 35 acres occurred in the Tri-City park between 1979 and 1987. Data from Table 21.1 are summarized in Table 21.2, which indicates that an average of 35.89 acres were sold each year in Swampy Knolls and that the Tri-City project had average annual sales of 64.57 acres. Thus, combined sales of comparable industrial land in the market area between 1979 and 1987 have totaled 893.18 acres, representing average annual absorption of 99.24 acres.

Interviews with management in local industrial firms indicate that the proposed industrial park will enjoy substantial locational advantages over major competitors. The Tri-City park appears the second most desirable and Swampy Knolls the least desirable of the three. Local industrial brokers generally agree with these conclusions. They report that parcels in Swampy Knolls have been somewhat less attractive to potential purchasers than those in the Tri-City park. They also point out, however, that Tri-City has attracted users of larger sites.

TABLE 21.1   Historic Absorption Rates: Industrial Park Properties

| | Parcels Sold | | | | | |
| | Swampy Knolls Individual Sales (Acres) | | | Tri-City Individual Sales (Acres) | | |
Year						
1977	14.00	15.60	11.10	No Sales		
	4.60	5.40				
1978	14.30	7.60	10.17	No Sales		
1979	15.04	16.30	10.05	18.70	20.00	15.30
				7.60	10.50	
1980	7.50	9.30	4.60	14.80	15.30	18.90
	15.60	4.70	5.40	7.03		
1981	16.30	8.30		18.20	15.30	10.01
1982	5.60	4.30	6.10	5.40	8.30	6.20
	5.24			3.03	3.00	
1983	12.50	8.40	5.30	30.00	25.00	9.50
	7.70			3.07	5.00	
1984	16.03	5.80	4.30	8.50	4.50	9.30
	4.60	5.40		8.20	6.40	9.40
				8.32	8.00	
1985	18.00	10.10	5.00	15.80	18.67	
1986	25.00	5.90	8.70	35.00	15.70	10.30
	3.20	7.20		11.06		
1987	14.30	7.50	2.80	25.00	17.40	14.60
				27.00	34.20	5.40
				3.20	8.50	6.53

TABLE 21.2   Sales Records of Industrial Park Properties

| | Total Sales (Acres) | |
Year	Swampy Knolls	Tri-City
1977	50.70	0
1978	32.07	0
1979	41.39	72.10
1980	47.10	56.03
1981	24.60	43.51
1982	21.24	25.93
1983	33.90	72.57
1984	36.13	62.62
1985	33.10	34.47
1986	50.00	72.06
1987	24.60	141.83
Totals	394.83	581.12

TABLE 21.3 Loan Repayment Schedule: Industrial Subdivision

Year	Beginning Balance	Principal Repaid	Interest Paid	Ending Balance
1	$10,240,000	$1,600,000	$1,382,400	$8,640,000
2	8,640,000	1,600,000	1,166,400	7,040,000
3	7,040,000	1,600,000	950,400	5,440,000
4	5,440,000	1,600,000	734,400	3,840,000
5	3,840,000	1,600,000	518,400	2,240,000
6	2,240,000	1,600,000	302,400	640,000
7	640,000	640,000	86,400	0

Sales prices in Swampy Knolls and Tri-City for the last two years are also examined. It is noted that land in both projects has sold at an average price of $2.50 per square foot during this period. Given the competitive nature of the local industrial land market, and noting that Swampy Knolls has completely sold out, the consulting firm concludes that $2.50 per square foot will make the proposed project competitive. At that price the firm estimates the proposed project can capture 40 percent of the market currently shared by Swampy Knolls and Tri-City. Therefore, it projects average annual sales for the new industrial park at 40 acres per year.

Investment Analysis

A group of ten successful dentists is considering purchase and subdivision of this property. They plan to use a general partnership, with each partner holding an equal interest in the project. Since subdivision is an ongoing business enterprise, all profits will be taxed as ordinary income.

The industrial broker who originally presented this property to the dentists is willing to supervise all phases of the subdivision project for a fee of $75,000 per year. Financial projections are based on anticipated sales of 40 acres per year for six years and sale of the remaining 16 acres in the seventh year of the marketing program.

The railroad is asking $8 million for the property. A lender is willing to provide a mortgage loan for 80 percent of the purchase price, or $6,400,000, and an additional $3,840,000 to cover the cost of planned improvements. Borrowers will be required to pay interest at 13.5 percent per annum on the outstanding loan balance and to repay $40,000 of principal for each acre of land sold. Table 21.3 shows a repayment schedule based on the assumption that 40 acres will be sold during each of the first six years of the project, with the remaining 16 acres sold in the seventh year.

As land is sold, total annual real estate taxes are expected to decrease. Taxes need not be paid on the 64 acres dedicated to streets, rail, etc. Tax liability will accrue on the 256 acres owned during year one, the 216 acres owned during year two and so forth. Tax rates for vacant land in this area produce a liability of about ten cents per square foot. Multiplying the number of square feet owned

TABLE 21.4 Calculation of Real Estate Taxes: Industrial Subdivision

	Year 1	Year 2	Year 3	Year 4	Year 5	Year 6	Year 7
Sq. Ft. Owned*	$11,151,360	$9,408,960	$7,666,560	$5,924,160	$4,181,760	$2,439,360	$696,960
Times: Property Tax Rate	.10	.10	.10	.10	.10	.10	.10
Estimated Property Taxes	$1,115,136	$940,896	$766,656	$592,416	$418,176	$243,936	$69,696

*Acres in inventory times square feet per acre

TABLE 21.5 Calculation of Before-Tax Cash Flows: Industrial Subdivision

	Year 1	Year 2	Year 3	Year 4	Year 5	Year 6	Year 7
Gross Sales Revenue	$4,356,000	$4,356,000	$4,356,000	$4,356,000	$4,356,000	$4,356,000	$1,742,400
Less: Brokerage Fees	217,800	217,800	217,800	217,800	217,800	217,800	87,120
Net Sales Revenue	$4,138,200	$4,138,200	$4,138,200	$4,138,200	$4,138,200	$4,138,200	$1,655,280
Less:							
Administrative Expenses	75,000	75,000	75,000	75,000	75,000	75,000	25,000
Advertising Expenses	50,000	25,000	25,000	25,000	25,000	25,000	8,250
Insurance Expenses	2,000	2,000	2,000	1,000	1,000	1,000	1,000
Real Estate Taxes	1,115,136	940,896	766,656	592,416	418,176	243,936	69,696
Net Operating Income	$2,896,064	$3,095,304	$3,269,544	$3,444,784	$3,619,024	$3,793,264	$1,551,334
Less:							
Interest	1,382,400	1,166,400	950,400	734,400	518,400	302,400	86,400
Loan Repayment	1,600,000	1,600,000	1,600,000	1,600,000	1,600,000	1,600,000	640,000
Before-Tax Cash Flow	$ (86,336)	$ 328,904	$ 719,144	$1,110,384	$1,500,624	$1,890,864	$ 824,934

by ten cents produces an estimate of the partners' annual property tax liability. These computations are illustrated in Table 21.4.

Annual gross revenue projections are derived by simply multiplying the expected sales price per acre by anticipated sales volume for each year. Annual expenditures for brokerage commissions are expected to total five percent of gross sales. Administrative expenses of $75,000 per year will be incurred in years one through six. The agreement with the managing broker provides that this expense will decline to $25,000 in the seventh year. Advertising expenses are expected to be $50,000 the first year, $25,000 in years two through six and $8,250 in year seven. Advertising expenses for the first year include the cost of maps, brochures and signs, which do not represent recurring expenditures. Insurance expenses are based on a quotation obtained from a local insurance broker. Table 21.5 consolidates income, expense and mortgage loan information to produce estimates of annual before-tax cash flows for each year of the project.

Table 21.6 illustrates the calculation of annual taxable income. Cost of land sold is subtracted from total sales revenue to derive gross profit. Deducting operating expenses and financing costs from this amount yields taxable income.

Cost of land sold includes the original purchase price and all expenditures to prepare the land for sale. It also includes the purchase price and site preparation costs of land dedicated for public utilities and thoroughfares. Although many of these expenditures are incurred during the first year of operations, they must be allocated to the inventory of salable land and are not deductible for tax purposes until the land is sold.

Investors are all assumed to be in the 28 percent marginal income tax bracket both before and after considering the consequence of this investment. (Our demonstration ignores state and local income taxes and sales taxes, which vary in different localities. An actual analysis would incorporate any such tax consequences.) It is also assumed that their federal income tax position will allow them to use any losses produced by this venture. Table 21.7 shows anticipated after-tax cash flow from the project. Annual taxable income (or tax-deductible loss) is simply multiplied by the investors' presumed 28 percent marginal tax rate. Before-tax cash flows are then adjusted for tax consequences to produce annual after-tax cash-flow forecasts.

After-tax cash-flow estimates are discounted at a rate of 20 percent and summed, producing a $2,094,351.50 present value of the equity position. Required equity equals land cost of $8,000,000 less available financing of $6,400,000, or $1,600,000. Net present value is equal to present value of the equity minus required equity, or $494,351.50. Positive net present value indicates a profitable venture if income and expenses occur as expected.

Investment value can also be calculated. Table 21.8 illustrates this computation. Since available financing includes the cost of subdivision improvements, funds intended for this purpose must be subtracted to isolate financing available for land. To this is added the present value of the equity position. Investment value of $8,494,351 is greater than the asking price of $8,000,000, indicating a desirable project.

TABLE 21.6 Annual Taxable Income: Industrial Subdivision

	Year 1	Year 2	Year 3	Year 4	Year 5	Year 6	Year 7
Income	$4,356,000	$4,356,000	$4,356,000	$4,356,000	$4,356,000	$4,356,000	$1,742,400
Less: Cost of Land Sold							
Purchase Price	1,000,000	1,000,000	1,000,000	1,000,000	1,000,000	1,000,000	400,000
Improvements	600,000	600,000	600,000	600,000	600,000	600,000	240,000
Dedicated Land Costs	250,000	250,000	250,000	250,000	250,000	250,000	100,000
Gross Profit	$2,506,000	$2,506,000	$2,506,000	$2,506,000	$2,506,000	$2,506,000	$1,002,400
Less: Operating Expenses							
Brokerage Commissions	217,800	217,800	217,800	217,800	217,800	217,800	87,120
Administrative	75,000	75,000	75,000	75,000	75,000	75,000	25,000
Advertising	50,000	25,000	25,000	25,000	25,000	25,000	8,250
Insurance	2,000	2,000	2,000	1,000	1,000	1,000	1,000
Real Estate Taxes	1,115,136	940,896	766,656	592,416	418,176	243,936	69,696
Interest	1,382,400	1,166,400	950,400	734,400	518,400	302,400	86,400
Taxable Income	$ (336,336)	$ 78,904	$ 469,144	$ 860,384	$1,250,624	$1,640,864	$ 724,934

TABLE 21.7 Calculation of After-Tax Cash Flows: Industrial Subdivision

	Year 1	Year 2	Year 3	Year 4	Year 5	Year 6	Year 7
Taxable Income	$(336,336.00)	$ 78,904.00	$ 469,144.00	$860,384.00	$1,250,624.00	$1,640,864.00	$724,934.00
Times: Marginal Rate	.28	.28	.28	.28	.28	.28	.28
Tax Consequences	$ (94,174.08)	$ 22,093.12	$ 131,360.32	$ 240,907.52	$ 350,174.72	$ 459,441.92	$202,981.52
Before-Tax Cash Flow	$(86,336.00)	$328,904.00	$719,144.00	$1,110,384.00	$1,500,624.00	$1,890,864.00	$824,934.00
Tax Consequences	94,174.08	(22,093.12)	(131,360.32)	(240,907.52)	(350,174.72)	(459,441.92)	(202,981.52)
After-Tax Cash Flow	$ 7,838.08	$306,810.88	$ 587,783.68	$ 869,476.48	$1,150,449.28	$1,431,422.08	$621,952.48

TABLE 21.8 Cash-Flow Analysis: Industrial Subdivision

Year	After-Tax Cash Flow	20% Discount Factor	Discounted Cash Flow
1	$ 7,838.08	0.833333	$ 6,531.73
2	306,810.88	0.694444	213,062.97
3	587,783.68	0.578704	340,152.77
4	869,476.48	0.482253	419,307.64
5	1,150,449.28	0.401878	462,340.26
6	1,431,422.08	0.334898	479,380.39
7	621,952.48	0.279082	173,575.74

Present Value of Equity	$ 2,094,351.50
Less: Initial Equity Investment	1,600,000.00
Net Present Value	$ 494,351.50
Available Financing	$10,240,000.00
Less: Cost of Improvements	3,840,000.00
Financing for Land	$ 6,400,000.00
Plus: Present Value of Equity	2,094,351.50
Investment Value of Land	$ 8,494,351.50

TABLE 21.9 Allocation of Before-Tax Cash Flows: Industrial Subdivision

Year	Before-Tax Cash Flow	Individual Partner's Share
1	$ (86,336)	$ (8,633.60)
2	328,904	32,890.40
3	719,144	71,914.40
4	1,110,384	111,038.40
5	1,500,624	150,062.40
6	1,890,864	189,086.40
7	824,934	82,493.40

TABLE 21.10 Allocation of Taxable Income: Industrial Subdivision

Year	Taxable Income	Individual Partner's Share
1	$(336,336)	$(33,633.60)
2	78,904	7,890.40
3	469,144	46,914.40
4	860,384	86,038.40
5	1,250,624	125,062.40
6	1,640,864	164,086.40
7	724,934	72,493.40

From these data each partner's individual interest can be analyzed. Tables 21.9 and 21.10 split before-tax cash flows and taxable income into an individual partner's share. This involves dividing before-tax cash flows and taxable income, shown in Tables 21.6 and 21.7 respectively, by the number of partners. Since partners have equal interests, simply divide by ten. If individual partners had unequal interests, the total would be allocated in accordance with the partnership agreement.

After-tax cash flows for a partner in the 28 percent marginal tax bracket are calculated in Table 21.11. The partners' shares of taxable income are mul-

TABLE 21.11 Partner's After-Tax Cash Flow

	Year 1	Year 2	Year 3	Year 4	Year 5	Year 6	Year 7
Taxable Income	$(33,633.60)	$ 7,890.40	$46,914.40	$ 86,038.40	$125,062.40	$164,086.40	$72,493.40
Times: Marginal Rate	.28	.28	.28	.28	.28	.28	.28
Tax Consequences	$ (9,417.41)	$ 2,209.31	$13,136.03	$ 24,090.75	$ 35,017.47	$ 45,944.19	$20,298.15
Before-Tax Cash Flow	$ (8,633.60)	$32,890.40	$71,914.40	$111,038.40	$150,062.40	$189,086.40	$82,493.40
Tax Consequences	9,417.41	(2,209.31)	(13,136.03)	(24,090.75)	(35,017.47)	(45,944.19)	(20,298.15)
After-Tax Cash Flow	$ 783.81	$30,681.09	$58,778.37	$ 86,947.65	$115,044.93	$143,142.21	$62,195.25

TABLE 21.12 Analysis of Partner's Position

Year	After-Tax Cash Flow	20% Discount Factor	Discounted Cash Flow
1	$ 783.81	0.833333	$ 653.17
2	30,681.09	0.694444	21,306.30
3	58,778.37	0.578704	34,015.28
4	86,947.65	0.482253	41,930.76
5	115,044.93	0.401878	46,234.03
6	143,142.21	0.334898	47,938.04
7	62,195.25	0.279082	17,357.57

Present Value of Equity $209,435.15
Less: Initial Equity Investment 160,000.00

Net Present Value $ 49,435.15

tiplied by their marginal tax brackets to determine annual tax consequences for each. Before-tax cash-flow forecasts are adjusted for anticipated income tax consequences to generate annual after-tax cash-flow forecasts.

Table 21.12 illustrates analysis of an individual partner's position. After-tax cash flows are discounted and summed to derive the present value of the position. The partner's required equity investment is one-tenth of the total required equity of $1,600,000, or $160,000. This amount is subtracted from the present value of the partner's position to derive net present value of $49,435.15. Analysis from the individual partner's position produces results that are consistent with that derived from analysis of the project as a whole.

SUMMARY

Subdivision is a term applied to the land development process. It consists of purchasing raw land, adding necessary improvements and selling the property in piecemeal fashion. The scale of subdivision projects may range from individuals dividing small parcels into a few building sites to large organizations dividing large tracts into areas devoted to multiple uses. Acquisition and development loans are used to finance subdivision. For a detailed examination of these issues see Gaylon E. Greer and Michael D. Farrell, *Contemporary Real Estate: Theory and Practice* (Chicago: The Dryden Press, 1981), Chapter 5.

RECOMMENDED READINGS

Barrett, G. Vincent, and John P. Blair. *How to Conduct and Analyze Real Estate Market and Feasibility Studies.* New York: Van Nostrand Reinhold Company, 1982, pp. 115–183.

Greer, Gaylon E., and Michael D. Farrell. *Contemporary Real Estate: Theory and Practice.* Hinsdale, IL: The Dryden Press, 1983, pp. 455–457.

Phyrr, Stephen A., and James R. Cooper. *Real Estate Investment: Strategy, Analysis, Decisions.* Boston, MA: Warren, Gorham and Lamont, 1982, pp. 647–662.

Rabinowitz, Alan. *The Real Estate Gamble: Lessons from 50 Years of Boom and Bust.* NY: Amacom, 1980, pp. 235–259.

Seldin, Maury. *Land Investment.* Homewood, IL: Dow Jones-Irwin, 1975.

Shafer, Thomas W. *Urban Growth and Economics.* Reston, VA: Reston Publishing Company, Inc., 1977, pp. 123–156.

REVIEW QUESTIONS

1. Explain the concept of subdivision and some of the major concerns of the subdivider.

2. Describe the process used to determine the best selling price for the subdivision of the proposed industrial park and to determine the projected annual sales.
3. Explain the considerations incorporated in the development of the revenue and expense projections over the selling period.
4. Table 21.8 illustrates the calculation of the net present value and the investment value of the project. Do both values indicate the same investment decision?
5. What does the analysis of the individual partner's shares show? Is this project worthwhile from an individual standpoint?
6. What would be the effect of the use of a lower discount factor on the cash-flow analysis shown in Table 21.8?

DISCUSSION QUESTIONS

1. In what ways are residential subdivision and condominium developments similar from the prospective of the developer, and in what important ways might they differ?
2. If you were offering individual investors an opportunity to invest in a subdivision project under your direction, would you provide them with detailed worksheets showing the reasoning behind your cash-flow projections? Why or why not?

CHAPTER 22

Development and Rehabilitation

INTRODUCTION

We saw in Chapter 21 that subdivision consists of improving and shaping land into usable parcels by grading, paving, installing utilities and so forth. In contrast, development involves placing improvements—usually buildings—on the land. Rehabilitation is the renovation and, in some cases, remodeling of existing structures.

Many developers, most particularly residential homebuilders, construct buildings primarily for resale. Others complete construction projects not for resale, but as additions to their own property portfolios. Regardless of their specific strategies, creative developers are often able to satisfy an as yet unmet demand and thereby reap the economic benefits of short-term monopoly. As other developers produce competing projects, the innovative pioneer usually moves on to exploit other unfilled market niches.

This chapter provides an overview of the development process. Concepts are illustrated with a case study of a small shopping center development project. Because rehabilitation of existing structures is a development opportunity of growing importance, this topic is also considered. The chapter concludes with a case study analyzing a proposal to rehabilitate a building that qualifies for an investment tax credit as a historic commercial structure.

OVERVIEW OF DEVELOPMENT

Real estate development projects range in size and complexity from single-family residences completed according to stock plans to entire new cities carved from decaying segments of older urban areas or from agricultural acreage or wasteland. At the lower end of the size spectrum, a developer might acquire a single-building lot and construct a house on a speculative basis. Proceeds from sale of the first house often provide necessary capital for the next single-residence venture. At the other end of the scale, developers may collaborate with major institutional leaders and with local, state or federal government agencies to complete grandiose construction schemes designed to overcome urban blight or to provide badly needed new living or working environments.

Ventures often originate with a concept for finished urban space and a perception of unmet demand. This situation has been described as "an idea in search of a site." The developer who identifies an entrepreneurial opportunity seeks out a site upon which the demand can be satisfied. In most situations, the site will be controlled through an option agreement until all details of the development can be worked out.

An equally likely impetus for a new development project is a developer or an investor seeking an appropriate use for a previously acquired site. This has been appropriately described as "a site in search of an idea." Whether development orginates with a site to be exploited or a vision to be fulfilled, the common denominator is a need for the particular blending of talent and organizational skill that characterizes successful real estate developers.

Feasibility Analysis

Once a development proposal has been matched with a prospective site, a detailed feasibility study may be commissioned. Results of the market research phase of this study are relayed to the developer's architect for incorporation into a physical design. Architects and engineers provide cost estimates that are incorporated into the financial phase of the feasibility analysis. (Large-scale developments may require a master plan, as described in the subdivision discussion. Planning efforts will be closely coordinated with the work of feasibility analysts, architects and engineers.)

Feasibility studies are generally divided into two major sections. The first consists of market research and attempts to determine the physical and locational characteristics that will have the greatest consumer appeal, as well as to determine what pricing structure the market will bear. The second section analyzes the economics of a proposed project. Construction costs are measured against project value to determine whether the proposed development is financially or economically viable.

Market research will vary with the situation. If a developer has a specific site in mind, researchers will seek to determine the type of improvements demanded at that location as well as the prices consumers are willing to pay. Consideration should be given to area demographics, to local trends and to competitive supply. Researchers might go a step further and use survey techniques to measure consumer desires for specific amenities. If a developer is not tied to a specific site, the researchers may also analyze the area in search of some unmet space demand.

Project cost is always a major feasibility consideration. Architects are frequently commissioned to provide cost estimates. Alternatively, estimates might be derived from a firm that specializes in providing such information. Many developers generate their own cost estimates based on a combination of data from these sources and from their own past experiences.

Value estimates also require detailed information. Sales price or rental rates for competitive properties are collected and analyzed. Income-producing properties require a detailed estimate of operating expenses. If projections are being made over longer time horizons, trend data will also be studied.

Economic estimates are always based on assumptions derived from market research and can be no better than the research or the assumptions they incorporate. Adequate research should result in reliable estimates, which then form the foundation for sound development decisions.

Financing Real Estate Development

In most large-scale developments, the site will be controlled through an option agreement rather than an outright purchase. After determining that a planned use is feasible, and after receiving all necessary municipal approvals, the developer is ready to exercise the option to purchase a site. At this stage, financial arrangements become a major consideration. The scarcity and cost of financing are hurdles that trip up many grandiose development schemes.

Developers generally look to construction lenders for the bulk of their development capital. Responsive lenders shoulder a substantial burden of risk. Builders may be unable to complete projects or may fall far behind schedule. Construction costs are difficult to estimate, and projects often run considerably over budget. This forces construction lenders to advance additional funds and thereby increase their risk exposure.

Lender risk can be reduced considerably by insisting that developers acquire end-loan commitments. These are agreements from other lenders to provide long-term financing upon project completion. An end-loan commitment ensures that funds with which to repay the construction loan upon completion of the project will be available.

If a developer cannot obtain an end-loan commitment prior to arranging a construction loan, standby or gap financing may be used. Under this arrangement, a lender agrees to provide funds for the gap between the time a project is completed and the time an end loan is secured. In most cases the end loan is secured before any funds are actually drawn in connection with a standby loan commitment.

The Construction Phase

Construction is one of the most important industries in our economy. It is the largest single contributor to the gross national product, it employs more people than any other industry and it uses more capital than most other industries. Construction, like other economic activity in a capitalistic economy, depends upon the relationship between supply and demand as discussed in Chapter 3.

Construction projects are carried out on either a custom or a speculative basis. Custom building takes place on land owned by the ultimate purchaser, and the structure is built to the purchaser/user's exact specifications. Speculative construction is limited primarily (but not exclusively) to single-family residences. In this situation, a developer/builder sees a demand for certain types of homes in a particular location. The builder will start construction before any homes are sold. Upon completion, the homes are sold to users.

The nature of the construction process makes the industry unique among manufacturers. Construction takes place on site—that is, where the product will be used—imposing a special set of managerial and technological problems. A successful construction company is able to expand and contract its size in response to economic conditions and differences in the scale of construction projects.

General contractors are the prime operatives on most construction projects. They look to subcontractors for excavating, cement work, brick work, plumbing, heating, electrical work, roofing and so forth. A user might enter into a contract with a general contractor for construction of a building. The general contractor then enters into agreements with subcontractors for the necessary labor and materials. General contractors coordinate the work of subcontractors and oversee construction progress.

Construction work is often put out for bid, with the job awarded to the lowest bidder. Many people, however, are more comfortable working with contractors who have proven track records, regardless of their fees. They may choose a contractor who charges for all labor and material and adds a predetermined fee to cover overhead and profit. The alternative of a fixed-price contract is much riskier for the builder. New union agreements may cause labor costs to increase, or building material prices may rise unexpectedly. The larger the job and the longer the time necessary to complete it, the greater the risk associated with a fixed-price contract.

Building contractors' modes of operation vary greatly. A small-scale homebuilder may employ only a few carpenters and own no equipment other than a small truck. On the other hand, an excavating contractor may have an enormous capital investment in such equipment as cranes, tractors and a fleet of trucks. Large-scale developers may employ artisans from all building trades and own the equipment necessary to complete massive construction projects.

Construction, unlike most other industries, is not dominated by large firms. Given the wide variety of functions involved in building construction, and the fact that general contractors and subcontractors typically do not form lasting relationships, it is unlikely that substantial economies of scale can be achieved. This implies that large firms do not gain a competitive advantage by size alone.

A DEVELOPMENT CASE STUDY

A developer recently purchased a commercially zoned site upon which to build a 108,650-square-foot community shopping center. Anchor tenants will be a

TABLE 22.1   Estimated Building Costs
for Shopping Center Project

Excavating	$ 111,000
Cement Work	240,000
Masonry	279,000
Steel and Bar Joists	142,000
Metal Door Frames	23,000
Carpentry Work	172,385
Roofing	88,000
Plumbing and Sewer Work	116,000
Electrical Work	169,000
Heating and Air-Conditioning	368,320
Insulation	2,400
Drywall	80,000
Acoustical Ceiling	42,965
Hardware	8,200
Cabinets and Mirrors	2,050
Painting	12,200
Electrical Fixtures	61,015
Tile and Carpet	50,850
Paving	150,850
Parking Lot Striping	3,500
Outdoor Lighting	8,500
Sprinkler System	110,000
Roof Paneling	30,500
Plate Glass	68,315
Gyp Roof Material	83,350
Weather Stripping	2,000
Architect Fees	93,525
Permits	40,665
Surveys	2,000
Contractor's Overhead and Profit	285,000
Estimated Total Cost	$2,846,590

food store and a drugstore, with the remainder of the space devoted to smaller specialty shops. (Shopping centers are designated as community, regional or superregional, according to the sizes of their market areas. Anchor tenants are major stores whose customer drawing power is expected to generate shopper traffic that will benefit other merchants in the center. These and other shopping center concepts are discussed in Chapter 23.) Anchor tenants have already signed leases, and approximately 20,000 square feet of the specialty shop space has been taken. A pension fund has agreed to purchase the shopping center upon completion and lease-up. The developer expects to deliver a fully occupied shopping center within 16 months.

An architectural firm has drawn plans and specifications for the building, and several general contractors submitted construction bids. The general contractor selected did not present the lowest bid but did have the most experience in shopping center construction. It is the developer's opinion that the contractor selected should be able to complete the project on time and within the budget constraints set by estimated building costs, as illustrated in Table 22.1.

TABLE 22.2 Financing Costs for Shopping Center Project

First Draw	
$948,863.33 at 13% for 12 months	$123,352.23
Second Draw	
$948,863.33 at 13% for eight months	82,234.82
Third Draw	
$948,863.33 at 13% for four months	41,117.41
Estimated Total Financing Costs	$246,704.46

TABLE 22.3 Total Project Costs for Shopping Center

Building Construction	$2,846,590
Land Cost	1,500,000
Financing Costs	246,704
Total Construction Costs	$4,593,294

Financing Arrangements

Total project costs include $1,500,000 for land purchase and $2,846,590 for construction, for a total of $4,346,590. A lender is willing to advance funds for the construction phase but requires the developer to acquire the land from equity resources. Construction funds will be advanced in three installments (draws) as work progresses. For financial planning purposes it is assumed that three equal draws of $948,863.33 will be made. The first draw will be outstanding for 12 months, the second for eight months, and the third for four months, as indicated in Table 22.2. Interest on construction loan funds will accrue at a rate of 13 percent per annum on the outstanding balance. Total interest on the construction loan is expected to be $246,704.46.

Project Cost Estimates

Table 22.3 summarizes total estimated project costs. Building costs were estimated at $2,846,590, as illustrated in Table 22.1. Total land cost equals $1,500,000, and financing costs were estimated at $246,704.46. The total of these items, or total project cost, is estimated at $4,593,294.

TABLE 22.4 Competitive Rental Survey for Shopping Center Project

Shopping Center	Anchor Tenants' Rental Rates (per sq. ft.)	Other Tenants' Rental Rates (per sq. ft.)
Marshy Valley	$4.50	$6.50–7.00
Lakemoor Commons	4.25	6.00–7.00
Floating Bogs	4.50	6.50–7.00
Swampy Basins	4.00	5.50–7.00

TABLE 22.5 Pro Forma Income and Expense Statement for Shopping Center Project

Food Store	
40,000 sq. ft. at $4.50/sq. ft.	$180,000
Drugstore	
15,000 sq. ft. at $4.50/sq. ft.	67,500
Other Space	
53,650 sq. ft. at $7.00/sq. ft.	375,550
Estimated Effective Gross Income	
	$623,050
Less: Management Fee, at (rounded) 7%	43,600
Estimated Net Operating Income	$579,450

Estimated Net Operating Income

Results of a survey of rental rates in similar shopping centers are summarized in Table 22.4. After considering this information, the developer has entered into lease agreements with a food store and a drugstore, which will serve as the center's anchor tenants and occupy 40,000 square feet and 15,000 square feet respectively. Approximately 20,000 of the remaining 53,560 square feet have been rented to smaller tenants.

Rental rates will be $4.50 per square foot occupied per year for the food store and drugstore and $7 per square foot for the smaller tenants. Rentals are on a net basis, with the tenants paying all expenses, including repairs, maintenance, insurance and real estate taxes. Tenants will also pay a pro-rata share of any common-area maintenance costs, such as parking lot repairs.

Net operating income estimates are shown in Table 22.5. Effective gross income is estimated by multiplying the amount of space devoted to a particular use by the rental rate for that type of space. The food store and drugstore leases both contain clauses calling for increased rentals based on sales (percentage leases), but neither tenant is expected to reach this sales volume within the next three years. The prospective purchaser has decided to ignore the possibility of

TABLE 22.6 Recent Shopping Center Sales

Sale	Age (Years)	Building Size (Sq. Ft.)	Sales Price	Net Operating Income	Indicated Capitalization Rate
1	2	155,000	$8,525,000	$852,500	10.00%
2	New	110,000	5,650,000	621,500	11.00
3	3	90,000	3,888,000	486,000	12.50
4	.5	115,000	6,069,000	667,500	11.00
5	New	125,000	6,060,500	666,650	11.00
6	2	85,000	4,065,000	467,500	11.50

TABLE 22.7 Estimated After-Tax Profits

Sales Price	$5,267,700.00
Less: Total Construction Costs (Table 22.3)	4,593,294.00
Before-Tax Profits	$ 674,406.00
Less: Taxes (28% Marginal Bracket)	188,833.68
After-Tax Profits	$ 485,572.32

percentage rentals and will have the property managed by a firm that charges seven percent of gross income. Based on these considerations, net operating income is estimated at $579,450.

Sales Price

Date from recent shopping center property transactions, gathered by the prospective purchaser of this project, are summarized in Table 22.6. The intended buyer notes that sales two and five in the table involved newly constructed centers and that sale number four was an almost new center. Dividing net operating income by the sales prices of these properties indicated that they were all purchased on the basis of an 11 percent overall rate of return.

Based on this information, the buyer agrees to purchase this shopping center at an overall rate of return of 11 percent. Dividing the projected net operating income of $579,450 by 0.11 (and rounding to avoid unjustified impression of accuracy) yields an expected sales price of approximately $5,267,700.

Developer's Profit

Table 22.7 illustrates calculation of the developer's total expected profit. Estimated total construction costs are subtracted from expected sales price, producing a before-tax net profit estimate of $674,406. Income tax consequences are estimated by multiplying expected profit by the developer's marginal tax rate. Adjusting expected pretax profit for tax consequences produces a developer's profit estimate of $485,572.

TABLE 22.8 Net Present Value Estimate for Shopping Center Project

Sales Price of Shopping Center		$5,267,700.00
Less: Loan Balance (Table 22.2):		
Principal Amount	$2,846,590.00	
Interest	246,704.00	3,093,294.00
Cash Flow Before Income Taxes		
Less: Income Tax Consequences		$2,174,406.00
(Table 22.7)		188,833.68
After-Tax Cash Flow		$1,985,572.32
Times: Discount Factor at 15%		0.828157
Present Value of Future Cash Flows		$1,644,365.62
Less: Initial Investment		1,500,000.00
Net Present Value		$ 144,365.62

Developer's profit is frequently expressed (on a before-tax basis) as a percentage of the initial equity investment (in this case, the cost of the land). For the project under analysis, this measure is expected to be $674,406/$1,500,000, or 44.96 percent.

Net present value of expected cash flow can also be calculated. The developer must expend $1,500,000 of equity cash resources to purchase the land. Positive cash flows consisting of return of invested funds plus after-tax profit occur at the end of construction. If the project takes 16 months to complete, and the developer uses a 15 percent discount rate, net present value is calculated as shown in Table 22.8.

REHABILITATION

Unlike new construction, where developers begin with vacant sites and create buildings, rehabilitation begins with existing structures in need of extensive renovation. The rehabilitator takes a deteriorated or functionally obsolete (that is, inappropriately designed) building and improves its physical condition or brings it up to modern design standards. Many rehabilitation projects involve both of these changes.

Gentrification, or the reclamation of residential areas containing physically deteriorated buildings, has provided much of the impetus for recent rehabilitation activity. Structurally sound buildings of interesting architectural styles are prime targets for rehabilitation. Such buildings can often be acquired at bargain prices due to their deteriorated condition or the nature of the surrounding area. As rehabilitation efforts develop in a neighborhood, property values and rental rates often soar.

Prime areas for rehabilitation seem to be older inner-city neighborhoods with convenient transportation links to places of employment. These areas should have buildings with unique or unusual architecture and should contain single-family or two- to three-unit buildings. Smaller buildings allow entry by the first wave of rehabilitators: the urban pioneers. These individuals are willing to take the risk of purchasing in older areas. They are also willing to perform many of the rehabilitation tasks themselves. As they and others build "sweat equity" in their properties, the neighborhood often gains a reputation for economic resurgence. This reputation eventually attracts professional profit-oriented rehabilitators.

Incentives for Rehabilitation

Various incentives induce people to undertake real estate rehabilitation efforts. Urban pioneers can often acquire property inexpensively. They are also able to build equity by performing many of the rehabilitation tasks themselves. The risks they bear as pioneers are often rewarded with high returns.

Real estate is a unique commodity in that it allows builders and rehabilitators the opportunity to create lasting monuments to their entrepreneurial abilities. Just as a developer might claim "that building is there because I put it there," the rehabilitator might claim "that building escaped the wrecking ball through my efforts." A rehabilitator may also enjoy the satisfaction of making a great impact on the destiny of an area or a neighborhood.

Profit expectations are, of course, among the more compelling motives for undertaking rehabilitation projects. The federal legislature has enhanced these expectations by enacting tax legislation to reward qualifying rehabilitation efforts. Investment tax credit (discussed in detail in Chapter 13) may be earned for rehabilitating older structures or structures that have been designated historically significant. Since anticipated credits generate reductions in quarterly tax payments, they are usually treated for analytical purposes as a reduction in initial cost outlays.

Judging Feasibility of Rehabilitation Proposals

During the mid- to late 1970s, tests of the feasibility of rehabilitation proposals were often omitted. Many investors purchased, rehabilitated and sold buildings profitably without the nicety of formal feasibility analysis. In many of these instances, however, much of the profit was due not so much to business acumen or value added by the rehabilitation process as to increases in general price levels in such areas. An equal or greater profit could in many such cases have been gained by simply buying and holding the buildings with no rehabilitation expenditures.

Intelligent analysis of rehabilitation proposals begins with consideration of the value or expected selling price of the completed project. Once expected value of the completed project has been estimated, rehabilitation costs must be considered. Subtracting all costs and expected profit from estimated value as completed leaves the amount available for purchase of the property. If the property can be purchased for less, the project is feasible; if the cost is greater, the project is not feasible.

Consider the two projects illustrated in Example 22.1. Estimated value after rehabilitation for both projects is $200,000. Subtracting construction costs and expected profit leaves $80,000 available for purchase. Since the asking price for project A is $60,000, this project is feasible. Project B has similar completed value and costs. However, the asking price of $100,000 is greater than the amount the rehabber can afford to pay. If $100,000 is paid, the rehabber's expected profits are reduced to zero.

Example 22.1

	Project A	Project B
Completed Value	$200,000	$200,000
Less:		
Construction Costs	100,000	100,000
Expected Profit	20,000	20,000
Available for Purchase	$ 80,000	$ 80,000
Asking Price	$ 60,000	$100,000

COMMERCIAL REHABILITATION: A CASE STUDY

Dr. R. E. Habam's office is located on a busy commercial street next to a 60-year-old frame residence. This 60-year-old structure has been vacant for two years, is in need of extensive repair and is currently available for $30,000. An architect has inspected the building and determined that it can be rehabilitated in about three months at a cost of $130,000. Two general contractors have submitted bids for the rehabilitation work; both bids were for $130,000.

Dr. Habam is aware that a ten percent investment tax credit is available if this building is rehabilitated as a commercial structure. Ten percent of estimated rehabilitation costs of $130,000 equals a credit of $13,000. Since a local financial institution is willing to make a loan covering total rehabilitation costs (see discussion of financing, below), the doctor figures his initial investment is reduced by the amount of the investment tax credit. Total equity investment (net of the investment tax credit) is therefore expected to be only $17,000. Here are the computations:

Acquisition Cost		$ 30,000
Rehabilitation Costs		130,000
Total Costs		$160,000
Less:		
Mortgage Loan	$130,000	
Tax Credit	13,000	143,000
Required Equity Investment		$ 17,000

TABLE 22.9 Loan Amortization Schedule for Commercial Rehabilitation Project

Year	Annual Payment	Annual Interest	Principal	Balance
1	$18,008	$17,550	$458	$129,542
2	18,008	17,488	520	129,022
3	18,008	17,418	590	128,432
4	18,008	17,338	670	127,762
5	18,008	17,248	760	127,002

While working with the architect, Dr. Habam has also been negotiating a lease with a medical association for the 2,400 square feet of space his rehabilitation efforts will produce. A tentative rental agreement has been reached at $8.50 per square foot for three years and $9.50 per square foot for three additional years. The lease will be on a net basis; the tenant will pay all operating costs. These costs include utilities, repairs, maintenance, insurance, real estate taxes and so forth.

Financing

A real estate appraiser has estimated the value of the completed project at $185,000. Using a 70 percent loan-to-value ratio, a financial institution is willing to make a $130,000 loan on this project. Loan terms are 13.5 percent interest for 29 years, with payments to be made annually. The lender has retained the right to renegotiate loan terms after five years. Table 22.9 splits annual payments into interest and principal components.

Cost Recovery (Depreciation) Allowances

The straight-line method of computing the cost recovery (depreciation) allowance must be used. The basis for the allowance equals rehabilitation expenditures of $130,000 plus the $10,000 of the purchase price properly allocable to the building shell, minus the amount of tax credit. (Had this building been designated a historic structure, the rehabilitation tax credit would have totaled 20 percent of qualifying rehabilitation expenditures.) This amount, $127,000, will be recovered via the cost recovery allowance over a 31.5-year period.

The annual recovery allowance is $127,000 divided by 31.5, or $4,032. The first year's allowance is reduced, as the developer plans to spend the first two-and-a-half months completing rehabilitation work. First and last year's cost recovery allowances are also adjusted for the half-month convention. Table 22.10 illustrates the capital cost recovery allowance schedule.

Calculating Annual After-Tax Cash Flows

Table 22.11 shows the calculation of annual after-tax cash-flow projections. A five percent management fee is subtracted from estimated gross income to arrive

TABLE 22.10   Capital Cost Recovery Allowances for Commercial Rehabilitation Project

Year	Beginning Balance	Capital Recovery	Ending Balance
1	$127,000	$3,024	$123,976
2	123,976	4,032	119,944
3	119,944	4,032	115,912
4	115,912	4,032	111,880
5	111,880	3,864	108,016

TABLE 22.11   Calculation of After-Tax Cash Flows for Commercial Rehabilitation Project

	Year 1	Year 2	Year 3	Year 4	Year 5
Gross Income	$15,300.00	$20,400.00	$20,400.00	$22,800.00	$22,800.00
Less: Management Fee (5%)	765.00	1,020.00	1,020.00	1,140.00	1,140.00
Net Operating Income	$14,535.00	$19,380.00	$19,380.00	$21,660.00	$21,660.00
Less: Debt Service	18,008.00	18,008.00	18,008.00	18,008.00	18,008.00
Before-Tax Cash Flow	$ (3,473.00)	$ 1,372.00	$ 1,372.00	$ 3,652.00	$ 3,652.00
Plus: Principal	458.00	520.00	590.00	670.00	760.00
Less: Depreciation	3,024.00	4,032.00	4,032.00	4,032.00	3,864.00
Taxable Income (Loss)	$ (6,039.00)	$ (2,140.00)	$ (2,070.00)	$ 290.00	$ 548.00
Times: Marginal Tax Rate	.28	.28	.28	.28	.28
Tax (Savings)	$ (1,690.92)	$ (599.20)	$ (579.60)	$ 81.20	$ 153.44
Before-Tax Cash Flow	$ (3,473.00)	$ 1,372.00	$ 1,372.00	$ 3,652.00	$ 3,652.00
Tax Consequences	1,690.92	599.20	579.60	(81.20)	(153.44)
After-Tax Cash Flow	$ (1,782.08)	$ 772.80	$ 792.40	$ 3,570.80	$ 3,498.56

at estimated net operating income. Subtracting annual debt service from net operating income yields before-tax cash-flow estimates. Principal payments are added to before-tax cash flows, and capital cost recovery allowances are subtracted, to generate estimates of annual taxable income. Tax consequences are then estimated by multiplying expected taxable income by the investor's 28 percent marginal income tax bracket. After-tax cash flows are calculated by adjusting expected before-tax cash flows for tax consequences.

Estimating the Selling Price

Dr. Habam expects to sell the property after five years. Because the initial lease is for a period of ten years, Dr. Habam thinks a purchaser will be getting a good building with a good tenant. If it is assumed that the relationship between

TABLE 22.12 Calculation of Tax on Sale for Commercial Rehabilitation Project

Estimated Sales Price (Net)		$180,000.00
Less: Adjusted Basis		
Land (Cost)	$ 20,000	
Building	108,016	128,016.00
Gain on Sale		$ 51,984.00
Times: Marginal Tax Rate		.28
Tax on Sale		$ 14,555.52

income and value remains constant, a gross income multiplier can be used to estimate selling price. The current gross income multiplier is calculated by dividing the first full year's gross income into the purchase price:

$$\$160,000/\$20,400 \; = \; 7.84$$

A sales price can then be estimated by multiplying the sixth year's expected gross income by the calculated gross income multiplier. This yields a calculated sales price of $178,752:

$$\$22,800 \; \times \; 7.84 \; = \; \$178,752$$

Calculated selling price is rounded, producing an estimated selling price of $180,000.

Estimating Income Tax and Cash Proceeds from Sale

The first step in estimating tax consequences from selling the property is to estimate the gain on sale. This is simply the estimated sales price minus the adjusted basis at time of sale and minus selling costs incurred. The gain on sale is treated as ordinary income in the year in which it occurs. Multiplying the estimated taxable income by the investor's 28 percent marginal tax rate produces estimated taxes on sale: $14,555. Subtracting transaction costs, income taxes and the mortgage balance from the estimated sales price yields the expected after-tax cash flow from the sale. These computations are illustrated in Tables 22.12 and 22.13.

Evaluating Expected After-Tax Cash Flows

Investment value is calculated by adding the present value of the equity position to the present value of available financing. In a rehabilitation project, the investor receives an additional benefit from the investment tax credit; this must also be added to the present value of the after-tax cash flows. Table 22.14 illustrates

TABLE 22.13 After-Tax Cash Flow from
Disposal for Commercial
Rehabilitation Project

Sale Price	$180,000.00
Less:	
Loan Balance	127,002.00
Tax on Sale	14,555.52
After-Tax Cash Flow from Disposal	$ 38,442.48

TABLE 22.14 Analysis of After-Tax Cash Flows
Commercial Rehabilitation Project

Year	Expected After-Tax Cash Flow	Present Value Factor at 15%	Discounted Cash Flow
1	$(1,782.08)	0.8696	$ (1,549.70)
2	772.80	0.7561	584.31
3	792.40	0.6575	521.00
4	3,570.80	0.5718	2,041.78
5	3,498.56	0.4972	1,739.48
(From Disposal)	38,442.48	0.4972	19,113.60
Present Value of Equity			$ 22,450.47
Plus:			
Tax Credit			13,000.00
Available Financing			130,000.00
Investment Value			$165,450.47
Present Value of Equity			$ 22,450.47
Less: Required Equity			17,000.00
Net Present Value			$ 5,450.47

analysis of expected after-tax cash flows for Dr. Habam's proposed project, given an appropriate discount rate (that is, target rate of return) of 15 percent.

As illustrated in Table 22.14, the present value of expected after-tax cash flows is $22,450. Adding the tax credit and available financing to this amount yields an investment value of $165,450.

Net present value can be obtained by subtracting the required equity investment from the present value of equity cash flows. Recall that the initial investment of $30,000 is reduced by a $13,000 investment tax credit to $17,000. This project is expected to produce positive net present value of $22,450 minus $17,000, or $5,450. If all assumptions hold, undertaking this project will increase Dr. Habam's net wealth by $5,450.

SUMMARY

Development involves placing improvements—usually buildings—on the land. Rehabilitation is the renovation and, in some cases, remodeling of existing structures. Many developers engage in both development and rehabilitation activities.

Development projects range in size and complexity from single-family residences built one at a time to entire cities carved from agricultural land or from decaying segments of older cities. Ventures might originate from a developer with an idea who looks for an appropriate site, from an investor with funds looking for an investment outlet or from a site owner looking for an appropriate way to utilize a property. The project might be developed on a custom basis (designed to exact specifications of a purchaser/user) or on a speculative basis (built in the expectation that a purchaser can be found after the project is completed).

Rehabilitation projects spring from existing structures in need of extensive renovation. The rehabilitator starts with a building that is physically deteriorated or functionally obsolete and improves its physical condition or brings it up to modern design standards.

RECOMMENDED READINGS

Bockle, George. *Recycling Real Estate*. Englewood Cliffs, NJ: Prentice-Hall, Inc., 1983.

Greer, Gaylon E., and Michael D. Farrell. *Contemporary Real Estate: Theory and Practice*. Hinsdale, IL: The Dryden Press, 1983, pp. 458–461.

McMahan, John. *Property Development: Effective Decision Making in Uncertain Times*. NY: McGraw-Hill, 1976, pp. 1–74.

Reiner, Laurence E. *How to Recycle Buildings*. NY: McGraw-Hill, 1979.

Warner, Raynor M., Sibyl M. Groff, and Ranne P. Warner. *New Profits From Old Buildings*. NY: McGraw-Hill, 1978.

Wendt, Paul F., and Alan R. Cerf. *Real Estate Investment Analysis and Taxation*. NY: McGraw-Hill, 1979, pp. 271–327.

REVIEW QUESTIONS

1. How does the development concept of "an idea in search of a site" relate to "a site in search of an idea?"
2. How are feasibility studies used in the development process?
3. What types of financing are generally used in new development?
4. How do custom building and speculative construction differ?
5. Who bears the greatest risk in a fixed-price contract?

6. Describe an area that would be considered prime for rehabilitation.
7. Why are people willing to take on a rehabilitation project?
8. Outline the process of judging the feasibility of a rehabilitation proposal.

DISCUSSION QUESTIONS

1. In general, would you expect cost estimates to be more precise for new development projects or for rehabilitation projects?
2. Is there a minimum size for a project (measured in dollar terms) below which a feasibility study would not be warranted prior to undertaking development efforts?
3. How does a general contractor differ from a real estate developer?

CHAPTER 23

Industrial Property, Office Building and Shopping Center Analysis

INTRODUCTION

This chapter demonstrates analysis of investment proposals involving industrial property, office buildings and small shopping centers. Examples of each are presented to illustrate differences as well as similarities. Demand factors and locational considerations are discussed for each property category. Brief case studies demonstrate differences in procedure dictated by variations in institutional arrangements or market characteristics. The industrial building case study, for example, involves a property leased on a net basis to a single tenant. The office building case study illustrates a multitenant operation with expenses paid by the property owner. Percentage leases are introduced in the shopping center case study.

INVESTING IN INDUSTRIAL BUILDINGS

Industrial buildings are perennial favorites among real estate investors. Reliable, creditworthy tenants, long-term leases, and opportunities to shift many if not all operating expenses to tenants account for the popularity of these structures among investors. For their part, business operators frequently find themselves short of operating capital and prefer to channel available resources into business expansion rather than into real estate ownership. Investors and business tenants thus find in leased industrial buildings a symbiotic relationship.

Demand for Industrial Space

Demand for industrial space is largely a function of the demand for products produced by the industrial sector. Forces that increase demand for manufactured goods also increase demand for industrial space, and, conversely, any situation that causes a decrease in demand for manufactured goods will cause a decrease in demand for industrial space; economists refer to this as a *derived demand*. Of course, changes in demand for space are not as volatile as changes in demand for industrial goods. Manufacturers generally adjust their space needs based on long-term projections of product demand.

Periodic shifts in demand for industrial space of various types and in different locations reflect alterations in composition of the industrial sector. Growth in service and technology-based industries has in recent years sparked increased demand for light assembly and research facilities. Decrease in demand for the products of heavy industry has greatly reduced the demand for structures employed in these manufacturing processes.

Locational Factors

Processing industries have a wide degree of locational discretion. They may choose sites near their raw materials sources, near markets for their finished products, near their major sources of labor supply or at some intermediate point. Their choices are usually conditioned by the economics of moving people, materials or products between various sites. Industries that process heavy or bulky raw material into light or compact products may gain significant transportation economies by locating near their raw materials sources.

Location Near Fuel or Power Supply.   For some industries, raw materials can be moved less expensively than other factors of production. Examples include processors that consume large quantities of fuel or power. The nation's first steel-making centers were located near coal mines because of the large quantities of that fuel required in early steel-making processes. High electrical power requirements favor the location of aluminum and electrometallurgical processors near sources of relatively inexpensive hydroelectric power.

Location Near Markets.   Home building, commercial baking and beverage bottling are examples of industries where transportation costs increase as the product approaches the end of the production process. Accordingly, these products are generally fabricated near the location of their final use. This tendency to choose location in order to reduce the cost of transportation to the final marketplace is sometimes offset by a desire to concentrate manufacturing to gain economies of scale in production.

Location of Footloose Industries.   Many industrial location decisions defy all the preceding classifications. Because transportation is not a major item in their production costs, some manufacturers base location decisions on other criteria. They frequently choose locations remote from both raw materials and markets, thus incurring double transfer costs, in order to gain reductions in other processing costs. These have been described as *footloose industries*.[1]

Labor is the most expensive productive factor for many footloose industries. Labor-intensive firms find it economical to seek sites that minimize labor-related costs. If they need predominantly unskilled or semiskilled labor, they are likely to choose locations where there is an abundant supply at comparatively low wage rates. If they require ready access to a pool of highly skilled workers, they will probably prefer a location near other employers who require similar skills or a locale that prospective employees will find particularly attractive.

Types of Industrial Buildings

There is no official classification system for industrial buildings. Yet a building can be characterized usefully according to the nature of its construction or the type of tenant it attracts. Approached from this perspective, most industrial structures can be classified as either heavy industrial, loft, modern single-story or incubator buildings.

Heavy Industrial Buildings.   Petroleum, steel and rubber processing facilities, as well as truck and auto manufacturing facilities, are all examples of heavy industrial buildings. Structures housing such industries are usually custom-designed to accommodate specific needs. These types of properties are typically owner-occupied and of little or no interest to investors.

Loft Buildings.   Loft buildings were one of the nation's earliest types of industrial building. They are multistory structures, usually with wood or concrete frames and masonry exterior walls. Loft buildings were designed to accommodate manufacturing processes as they existed in the early 1900s. Many loft buildings are located near central business districts, and many have been converted to uses other than manufacturing.

Modern One-Story Structures.   The most common industrial structure built today is the modern one-story facility, typically located in a suburban industrial park. These buildings are usually designed for occupancy by a single tenant and are frequently owner-occupied. Yet many are owned by investors and leased to manufacturing firms. Such buildings are attractive to institutional investors because tenants are often responsible for all upkeep and operating expenses.

Incubator Buildings.   Incubator buildings are smaller multitenant structures. New firms rent space in such buildings and, as business expands, they move to larger quarters. Incubator buildings are usually owned by investors, who collect rents and pay many operating expenses. Tenants are usually responsible for their own utility bills and may be required to compensate the owners for any operating expense increases during the period of the lease.

AN INDUSTRIAL BUILDING CASE STUDY

Single-story net-leased industrial buildings are among the simplest types of investment properties to analyze. Net leases require tenants to pay all or most of the expenses associated with operating the leased property; most of the responsibilities of real estate ownership are transferred to tenants. Investors merely collect rents and make debt service payments. This simple arrangement makes these types of buildings a favorite among institutional investors. In simplicity of operation, such investments resemble the purchase of bonds or long-term notes. Net-leased properties, however, provide income tax benefits not available with securities.

To illustrate the analytical procedures associated with net-leased industrial buildings, consider the case of a new one-story structure containing 35,000 square feet of rentable space. A developer recently signed a creditworthy tenant to a six-year lease calling for rentals of $3.50 per square foot annually for three years and $4 per square foot for the remaining three years of the lease. The tenant is to pay all operating expenses, including insurance and property taxes. The prospective purchaser of this net-leased property expects to sell after a five-year holding period.

Forecasting Income and Expenses

Net operating income is simple to forecast in this situation. Rental income will be $3.50 per square foot, or $122,500 ($3.50 times 35,000 square feet) annually for the first three years; thereafter it will be $4 times 35,000 square feet, or $140,000. Because the investor will acquire title subject to an existing lease, there will be no rental expense and no need to investigate market rental rates.

Financing

A loan of $700,000 (requiring annual payments) is available. The interest rate will be 12.5 percent per annum for the first three years and 13 percent thereafter. Table 23.1 presents a loan amortization schedule for the first five years of a 25-year amortization period. Note that the annual debt service payment increases from $92,360 to $95,337 in the fourth year. The remaining balance at the end of the anticipated five-year holding period will be approximately $669,722.

Annual Income Tax Consequences

For income tax computations the investor will use the straight-line cost recovery (depreciation) method over a 31.5-year period. (See Chapter 10 for details of

TABLE 23.1 Loan Amortization Schedule for One-Story Industrial Building

Year	Annual Payment	Annual Interest	Principal	Balance
1	$92,360	$87,500	$4,860	$695,140
2	92,360	86,893	5,467	689,673
3	92,360	86,209	6,151	683,522
4	95,337	88,858	6,479	677,043
5	95,337	88,016	7,321	669,722

TABLE 23.2 Capital Recovery Schedule for One-Story Industrial Building

Year	Beginning Balance	Capital Recovery	Ending Balance
1	$700,000	$21,296	$678,704
2	678,704	22,222	656,482
3	656,482	22,222	634,260
4	634,260	22,222	612,038
5	612,038	21,296	590,742

cost recovery rules and the income tax consequences of alternative tax strategies available to investors.) Twenty percent of the $875,000 anticipated purchase price is properly attributable to the land, with the remaining $700,000 attributable to the building. Annual cost recovery allowances, therefore, are $700,000/31.5, or $22,222. Because of the half-month convention, the depreciation allowance in the first and last years of the holding period is $21,296. Table 23.2 summarizes these computations.

Table 23.3 combines operating income, mortgage financing and cost recovery allowance data to estimate annual after-tax cash flows. Annual debt service is subtracted from net operating income to yield before-tax cash flow. Taxable income is derived by adding back the principal portion of the debt service and subtracting the capital recovery allowance. Note that this property is expected to produce positive taxable income in each year of the holding period. The prospective investor expects to be in the 28 percent marginal tax bracket both before and after considering the impact of this investment opportunity. Thus, income tax consequences are calculated by multiplying taxable income (or tax-deductible losses) by 28 percent. Adjusting expected before-tax cash flows for anticipated tax consequences produces annual after-tax cash-flow forecasts as shown at the bottom of Table 23.3.

Forecasting Sales Proceeds

The final cash flow to the supplier of equity in a real estate venture is the after-tax proceeds from disposal. Forecasting these proceeds starts with an estimate

TABLE 23.3 Annual Cash-Flow Projections for One-Story Industrial Building

	Year 1	Year 2	Year 3	Year 4	Year 5
Net Operating Income	$122,500.00	$122,500.00	$122,500.00	$140,000.00	$140,000.00
Less: Debt Service	92,360.00	92,360.00	92,360.00	95,337.00	95,337.00
Before-Tax Cash Flow	$ 30,140.00	$ 30,140.00	$ 30,140.00	$ 44,663.00	$ 44,663.00
Plus: Principal	4,860.00	5,467.00	6,151.00	6,479.00	7,321.00
Less: Cost Recovery Allowance	21,296.00	22,222.00	22,222.00	22,222.00	21,296.00
Taxable Income (Loss)	$ 13,704.00	$ 13,385.00	$ 14,069.00	$ 28,920.00	$ 30,688.00
Times: Marginal Tax Rate	.28	.28	.28	.28	.28
Income Tax (Savings)	$ 3,837.12	$ 3,747.80	$ 3,939.32	$ 8,097.60	$ 8,592.64
Before-Tax Cash Flow	$ 30,140.00	$ 30,140.00	$ 30,140.00	$ 44,663.00	$ 44,663.00
Tax Consequences	(3,837.12)	(3,747.80)	(3,939.32)	(8,097.60)	(8,592.64)
After-Tax Cash Flow	$ 26,302.88	$ 26,392.20	$ 26,200.68	$ 36,565.40	$ 36,070.36

TABLE 23.4 Tax on Sale of One-Story Industrial Building

Sales Price		$1,000,000.00
Less: Adjusted Basis		
Land (Cost)	$175,000.00	
Building	590,742.00	765,742.00
Taxable Gain		$ 234,258.00
Times: Marginal Tax Rate		.28
Tax on Sale		$ 65,592.24

of the sales price. Expected income tax consequences of disposal are computed under the assumption that current income tax laws will still be in effect.

The relationship between a property's market value and anticipated net operating income for the forthcoming year can be expressed as a ratio called a *capitalization rate*. The relationship is:

$$R = I/V$$

where R is the capitalization rate, I is the net operating income, and V is the property value. Substituting the purchase price and the first year's forecast net operating income for the property under analysis yields a capitalization rate of 14 percent:

$$0.14 = \$122,500/\$875,000$$

Assuming that this relationship still prevails when the property is sold five years hence, the value at that time can be estimated by dividing the sixth year's anticipated net operating income (which is identical to that for year five) by the capitalization rate:

$$0.14 = \$140,000/V$$

Therefore:

$$V = \$140,000/.14$$
$$\$1,000,000$$

Subtracting transaction costs and the adjusted basis at time of sale from the expected sales price yields the anticipated gain on disposal. The property's adjusted basis immediately prior to the sale will be initial cost minus cumulative cost recovery allowances. (Any additional capital expenditures during the holding period will have been added to the property's basis. Basis computations and adjustments are discussed at length in Chapter 10.) Multiplying the gain by the assumed 28 percent marginal income tax rate yields the expected income tax consequences of disposal. Detailed computations are shown in Table 23.4. (For simplicity, we assume the investor incurs no alternative minimum income tax liability. The analyst must ascertain that no such liability is likely by investigating possible interaction between this transaction and the income tax

TABLE 23.5   After-Tax Equity Reversion for One-Story Industrial Building

Sales Price		$1,000,000.00
Less:		
Tax on Sale	$ 65,592.24	
Loan Balance	669,722.00	735,314.24
After-Tax Equity Reversion		$ 264,685.76

TABLE 23.6   Investment Value of One-Story Industrial Building

Year	Annual After-Tax Cash Flow	Present Value Factor (15%)	Discounted Cash Flow
1	$ 26,302.88	0.8696	$ 22,872.98
2	26,392.20	0.7561	19,955.14
3	26,200.68	0.6575	17,226.95
4	36,565.40	0.5718	20,908.10
5	36,070.36	0.4972	17,934.18
(From Disposal)	264,685.76	0.4972	131,601.76
Present Value of Equity			$230,499.11
Available Financing			700,000.00
Investment Value			$930,499.11
Present Value of Equity			$230,499.11
Less: Required Equity			175,000.00
Net Present Value			$ 55,499.11

implications of other assets in the investor's portfolio and other transactions that may be contemplated during the same taxable year. See Appendix 10.C for a thorough discussion of the alternative minimum tax.)

Subtracting the anticipated income tax liability and the remaining balance of the mortgage loan from the net sales proceeds generates an estimate of the after-tax cash flow from disposal. As shown in Table 23.5, the expected after-tax cash flow from selling this property after five years is $264,686.

Evaluating After-Tax Cash Flows

The final step in the analysis is to estimate investment value and net present value of the equity position. Investment value is calculated by discounting expected annual after-tax cash flows and the anticipated after-tax proceeds of sale and adding the amount of the mortgage loan that was incorporated into the cash-flow forecast. Assuming the investor is seeking a 15 percent rate of return on equity funds, investment value is $930,499. Table 23.6 illustrates the computations. Since investment value is greater than the expected purchase price, equity funds expended for this project are expected to yield more than the investor's desired rate of return.

An alternative way to show expected investment consequences is to compute the net present value of the venture. Acquiring the property at the asking price involves an equity investment of $175,000. Net present value is simply the present value of expected after-tax cash flows minus the required equity investment. Since the net present value ($55,499) is greater than zero, the project is expected to yield a rate of return in excess of the 15 percent discount rate. This computation is also illustrated in Table 23.6.

INVESTING IN OFFICE BUILDINGS

Dramatic growth in the service sector of the economy has greatly increased the demand for office space in recent years. Modern high-rise structures are rapidly replacing older, smaller buildings in central business districts. Many office centers have also sprung up in suburban locations. These are usually high-rise buildings or one- and two-story structures in office parks.

Demand for office space, like that for industrial space, is a derived demand. It is related to the demand for services supplied by occupants of office buildings. Increases in the number and size of service industries such as law firms, accounting firms and financial institutions are translated into expanded demand for space to house these activities. Moreover, total demand for office space has expanded due to the trend among employers to provide more working space per employee.

Owner-occupied office buildings are often designed to project the desired image of the owner-occupant. Investor-owned buildings, in contrast, tend to be somewhat more functional and less luxurious. High-rise buildings usually have multitenant floors located near the base and single-tenant floors near the top. This minimizes space utilization problems that might otherwise be created by the need to accommodate elevator core space. Full-floor occupants usually pay for all space on their floors, including washrooms and corridors.

Office building tenants typically enter into multiyear leases. Office building owners learned long ago that if they are unable to raise their rentals annually, increases in operating expenses will greatly erode their profits. As a result, they pioneered the process of passing increases in expenses on to their tenants. Leases often contain a clause stating that the landlord will pay operating expenses up to some specified amount per square foot. Any increases above this amount are passed to the tenant. This represents a significant decrease in the risk office building ownership would otherwise impose.

Tenants often take options to renew leases on occupied space. Such lease arrangements inevitably contain a formula for computing increased rental rates for the renewal period, based upon changes in the general price level. Such a provision spares the tenant the expense and bother of finding new quarters and spares the landlord the expense of locating a new tenant.

AN OFFICE BUILDING CASE STUDY

The property to be analyzed is a two-story, multitenant office building containing 10,000 square feet of rentable space. The building is situated on a 25,000-square-foot site that is partially landscaped and contains parking for about 35 automobiles. The property is being offered for $500,000. An investor who will remain in the 28 percent marginal tax bracket after the effects of purchase is considering acquisition.

Reconstructing the Income and Expense Statement

Multitenant office buildings are generally leased on a gross rental basis. In this case, the property owner pays all operating expenses with the exception of tenants' heat and electricity. The landlord supplies heat and electricity to common areas only. All leases also contain real estate tax stops, which require tenants to pay property taxes above a stipulated base amount.

Current income from the building is $10.51 per square foot of gross rentable area, for a total of $105,100 per annum before vacancy losses. Comparable buildings in the area are generating per-square-foot rentals of between $10.25 and $10.75 for similar space. Considering competition, current rentals seem appropriate. Office buildings in the area also experience a vacancy rate equal to about seven percent of gross income. Reducing gross income by a seven percent vacancy allowance produces effective gross income of approximately $97,700.

Table 23.7 contains a reconstructed income and expense statement for the property. Expenses were estimated after studying the building's operating history and that of comparable buildings in the area. Estimates appear reasonable when compared with averages in the Building Owners and Managers Association International's current *Downtown and Suburban Office Building Experience Exchange Report* and with the Institute of Real Estate Management's current edition of *Income/Expense Analysis: Suburban Office Buildings*.[2]

Financing

A loan of $375,000 is available at 12.5 percent interest with a 30-year amortization schedule and annual payments. The rate is renegotiable after five years, which is beyond the investor's expected holding period. Table 23.8 presents an amortization schedule for this loan. Annual debt service payments are $48,285, and loan balance at the end of the expected holding period is $365,952.

TABLE 23.7 Reconstructed Income and Expense Statement for 10,000-Square-Foot Office Building

Potential Gross Income		$105,100
Less: Vacancy at 7%		7,400
Effective Gross Income		$ 97,700
Less: Operating Expenses		
Electricity	$2,000	
Water	400	
Sewer Fees	30	
Heating Fuel	3,600	
Payroll/Contract Cleaning	7,600	
Cleaning Supplies	700	
Janitorial Payroll	4,300	
Janitorial Supplies	400	
Heating/Air-Conditioning	2,100	
Electrical Repairs	400	
Plumbing Repairs	500	
Exterior Repairs	400	
Roof Repairs	400	
Parking Lot Repairs	200	
Decorating (Tenant)	1,800	
Decorating (Public)	400	
Miscellaneous Repairs	1,100	
Management Fees	4,500	
Other Administrative Fees	1,000	
Landscaping Maintenance	400	
Trash Removal	600	
Window Washing	200	
Snow Removal	2,200	
Miscellaneous Services	500	
Total Operating Expenses		35,730
Real Estate Taxes		15,800
Net Operating Income		$ 46,170

TABLE 23.8 Loan Amortization Schedule for 10,000-Square-Foot Office Building

Year	Annual Payment	Annual Interest	Principal	Balance
1	$48,285	$46,875	$1,410	$373,590
2	48,285	46,699	1,586	372,004
3	48,285	46,500	1,785	370,219
4	48,285	46,277	2,008	368,211
5	48,285	46,026	2,259	365,952

TABLE 23.9   Capital Recovery Schedule for 10,000-Square-Foot Office Building

Year	Beginning Balance	Capital Recovery	Ending Balance
1	$425,000	$12,930	$412,070
2	412,070	13,492	398,578
3	398,578	13,492	385,086
4	385,086	13,492	371,594
5	371,594	12,930	358,664

Cost Recovery (Depreciation) Allowance

The investor will use the straight-line cost recovery (depreciation) computation method over a 31.5-year period. Expected purchase price of $500,000 is allocated 85 percent, or $425,000, to building and 15 percent, or $75,000, to the land. This allocation is supported by the local tax assessor's records. Annual cost recovery allowance deductions will be $425,000/31.5, or $13,492. Because of the half-month convention, recovery allowance for the first and last years of the holding period is $12,930. Cost recovery computations are summarized in Table 23.9.

Forecasting Annual After-Tax Cash Flows

Table 23.10 contains calculations of forecasted annual after-tax cash flows. Income and expense estimates come from the reconstructed income and expense statement contained in Table 23.7. Income and expenses are expected to grow at five percent per year. This rate appears justified after analysis of data from the past five years from the Institute of Real Estate Management.[3] Note that the tax stops cause real estate taxes to remain stable over the expected five-year holding period.

Debt service is subtracted from net operating income to produce before-tax cash flows. Principal payments are added to the before-tax cash flows, and cost recovery allowances are subtracted to derive anticipated taxable income or tax-deductible losses. Taxable income or loss is multiplied by the investor's marginal tax rate to produce expected annual income tax consequences of ownership. Before-tax cash flows are adjusted for tax consequences to produce annual after-tax cash flows.

Forecasting After-Tax Cash Flow from Disposal

A capitalization rate based on the current relationship between income and market value is computed and applied to expected income from the property

TABLE 23.10 After-Tax Cash Flows for 10,000-Square-Foot Office Building

	Year 1	Year 2	Year 3	Year 4	Year 5
Total Gross Income	$105,100.00	$110,355.00	$115,873.00	$121,666.00	$127,750.00
Less: Vacancy	7,400.00	7,770.00	8,159.00	8,565.00	8,995.00
Effective Gross Income	$ 97,700.00	$102,585.00	$107,714.00	$113,100.00	$118,755.00
Less:					
Operating Expenses	35,730.00	37,516.00	39,392.00	41,362.00	43,430.00
Real Estate Taxes	15,800.00	15,800.00	15,800.00	15,800.00	15,800.00
Net Operating Income	$ 46,170.00	$ 49,269.00	$ 52,522.00	$ 55,933.00	$ 59,525.00
Less: Debt Service	48,285.00	48,285.00	48,285.00	48,285.00	48,285.00
Before-Tax Cash Flow	$ (2,115.00)	$ 984.00	$ 4,237.00	$ 7,653.00	$ 11,240.00
Plus: Principal	1,410.00	1,586.00	1,785.00	2,008.00	2,259.00
Less: Cost Recovery	12,930.00	13,492.00	13,492.00	13,492.00	12,930.00
Taxable Income (Loss)	$(13,635.00)	$(10,922.00)	$ (7,470.00)	$ (3,831.00)	$ 569.00
Times: Tax Rate	.28	.28	.28	.28	.28
Tax (Savings)	$ (3,817.80)	$ (3,058.16)	$ (2,091.60)	$ (1,072.68)	$ 159.32
Before-Tax Cash Flow	$ (2,115.00)	$ 984.00	$ 4,237.00	$ 7,653.00	$ 11,240.00
Tax Consequences	3,817.80	3,058.16	2,091.60	1,072.68	(159.32)
After-Tax Cash Flow	$ 1,702.80	$ 4,042.16	$ 6,328.60	$ 8,725.68	$ 11,080.68

TABLE 23.11   Tax Consequences of Sale of
10,000-Square-Foot Office Building

Sales Price		$685,000
Less: Selling Expenses		78,700
Net Sales Price		$606,300
Less: Adjusted Basis		
Land (Cost)	$ 75,000	
Building	358,664	433,664
Gain on Sale		$172,636
Times: Marginal Tax Rate		.28
Tax Consequences of Sale		$ 48,338

TABLE 23.12   After-Tax Cash Flow from
Disposal of 10,000-Square-Foot
Office Building

Sales Price		$685,000
Less:		
Selling Costs	$ 78,700	
Loan Balance	365,952	
Tax on Sale	48,338	492,990
After-Tax Cash Flow		$192,010

---

six years from the current date. This comprises the basis for estimated market value five years hence. The current rate is:

$$\$46,170/\$500,000 = 0.09234$$

Sales price can then be estimated by dividing the sixth year's operating income by the calculated capitalization rate:

$$\$63,291/0.09234 = \$685,413$$

This estimate is rounded to $685,000. Subtracting an estimated selling cost equaling 11.5 percent of the sales price yields an expected net sales price (rounded) of $606,300. The property's adjusted basis (initial cost minus cumulative cost recovery allowances) is subtracted from the expected net sales price to derive expected gain on disposal. This expected gain will be taxed at the investor's 28 percent marginal income tax rate. There results an anticipated $48,338 income tax liability due to the sale. These computations are presented in Table 23.11.

Subtracting the expected income tax liability and the remaining mortgage balance from the anticipated net sales price of the property yields the $192,010 forecast of after-tax cash proceeds from disposal. Table 23.12 shows the details of this arithmetic.

TABLE 23.13 Present Value Analysis for 10,000-Square-Foot Office Building

Year	Annual After-Tax Cash Flows	Present Value Factor (10%)	Discounted Cash Flows
1	$ 1,702.80	0.9091	$ 1,548.02
2	4,042.16	0.8264	3,340.44
3	6,328.60	0.7513	4,754.68
4	8,725.68	0.6830	5,959.64
5	11,080.68	0.6209	6,879.99
(From Sale)	192,010.00	0.6209	119,219.01

Present Value of Equity	$141,701.78
Less: Required Equity	125,000.00
Net Present Value	$ 16,701.78
Present Value of Equity	$141,701.78
Available Financing	375,000.00
Investment Value	$516,701.78

Analyzing After-Tax Cash-Flow Forecasts

Anticipated after-tax cash flows are discounted at the investor's required rate of return on equity capital. Subtracting the required equity investment of $125,000 from the present value of expected future net cash flows generates net present value. Since the net present value is greater than zero, we conclude that the project offers an expected yield in excess of the investor's required rate of return. These computations are shown in Table 23.13.

Alternately, we sum the present value of the anticipated future cash flows and the mortgage loan that was incorporated into the cash-flow forecast. The resulting investment value is the most the investor is justified in paying for the property (assuming, of course, that actual financing is the same as that incorporated into the forecast). Because this amount exceeds the asking price for the property, the project offers the prospect of earning more than the required yield on equity funds. Table 23.13 also summarizes these calculations.

INVESTING IN SHOPPING CENTERS

Relationships between landlords and tenants in shopping centers differ from those in freestanding stores and other structures. Major stores in shopping centers, called *anchor tenants*, attract shoppers to the center and thereby create customers for smaller specialty shops. Investors and developers have long provided favorable lease terms to anchor tenants and achieved their greatest returns on rentals received from specialty tenants. More recently, developers have allowed major tenants to construct their own buildings on sites leased from the owners or have sold sites and portions of the parking lots to the anchors. This reduces the owners' investment and often increases their return because they no longer own space subject to rental rates favoring tenants.

Lease arrangements also differ in shopping centers. A shopping center owner sets a base rental rate and often increases the rental rate as the tenant's sales volume increases. This is known as a *percentage clause* in a lease. Percentage clauses have the effect of making the shopping center owner a partner in the business of the tenants. For this reason, tenant selection as well as tenant mix is very important.

Large shopping center tenants typically lease space on a net basis; that is, they pay all expenses associated with operation of their spaces. Smaller tenants often pay their own utility expenses, while the landlord pays other operating expenses. Because these leases often extend for a number of years, landlords pay operating expenses up to some specified amount, and the tenant pays any excess costs. Shopping center tenants also often pay a common area maintenance fee. This fee reimburses the owners for maintenance of common areas such as parking lots or mall space.

Shopping centers are usually classified according to the size of the trade area from which they draw customers and according to the types of merchandise sold by their major tenants. Categories include neighborhood centers, community centers, regional centers and superregional centers.

Neighborhood Shopping Centers

Neighborhood centers serve a relatively small trade area, roughly that from which customers can commute by automobile within five to ten minutes. As anchor tenants, neighborhood centers usually have a food store and drugstore, which may occupy a combined total area of 35,000 to 50,000 square feet. The food store is expected to generate customer traffic from which other tenants—mostly purveyors of convenience goods—will benefit. Total area within neighborhood shopping centers ranges between 50,000 and 100,000 square feet.

Community Shopping Centers

In addition to a major food store, most community centers feature a junior department store or a major discount department store as an anchor tenant. The department store, typically ranging in size from 50,000 to 100,000 square feet, is usually located at the opposite end of the center from the food store, with specialty shops in between. This layout maximizes customer traffic past the specialty shops and distributes customer automobiles more evenly throughout the parking area. Having two anchor tenants increases the range of a community center's trade area, which may extend from ten to 15 minutes in driving time from the center.

Regional Shopping Centers

Considerably larger than community centers, regional shopping centers may encompass 200,000 to 400,000 square feet of retail space. They usually feature one or two major department stores as anchor tenants and provide facilities to a variety of retailers ranging from convenience goods to shopping goods such as furniture and appliances. As in community centers, anchor tenants at regional centers are considered the major attractive force for customers and are usually located at opposite ends of the center. Regional shopping centers have a trade area extending from 15 to 30 minutes in driving time from the facility.

Superregional Shopping Centers

Superregional shopping centers are a by-product of the nation's high-speed, limited-access freeway system. Ease and speed of travel have greatly expanded the trade areas of centers with good freeway access, enabling them to support much larger concentrations for retail facilities. In contrast to their regional counterparts, superregional centers may feature as many as four major department stores as anchor tenants. They tend to be very large, often encompassing from 500,000 to 750,000 or more square feet of retail space. Specialty shops within superregional centers frequently open into enclosed malls that protect shoppers from the elements.

A SHOPPING CENTER CASE STUDY

The property to be analyzed is a community shopping center containing a discount department store occupying 105,000 square feet, a food store occupying 30,000 square feet and a savings and loan association occupying 3,000 square feet. A fast-food operation has leased 30,000 square feet of the center's 435,600-square-foot site and constructed a restaurant building. All leases in the center are on a net basis, with tenants paying a pro-rata share of any common area maintenance expenses.

A group of six doctors is contemplating purchase of this center for $3,800,000. They are intrigued by real property ownership and plan to hold the center for five years. They plan to purchase through a general partnership with each physician acquiring a one-sixth interest. The group will also incur an annual management fee representing five percent of base rentals.

Financing

Title will be transferred subject to an existing first mortgage loan, which has a remaining balance of $1,640,042 and requires no assumption fee. Annual payments of approximately $160,876 include interest on the outstanding balance at a rate of 7.5 percent per annum. Sellers will take back a promissory note (to be secured by a second mortgage) for $1,511,970, leaving a balance of $647,988

TABLE 23.14 Loan Amortization Schedules for Community Shopping Center

Existing Loan

Year	Annual Payment	Annual Interest	Principal	Balance
1	$160,876	$123,003	$37,873	$1,602,169
2	160,876	120,163	40,713	1,561,456
3	160,876	117,109	43,767	1,517,689
4	160,876	113,827	47,049	1,470,640
5	160,876	110,298	50,578	1,420,062

Seller Financing

Year	Annual Payment	Annual Interest	Principal	Balance
1	$167,116	$158,757	$ 8,359	$1,503,611
2	167,116	157,879	9,237	1,494,374
3	167,116	156,909	10,207	1,484,167

Refinancing of Seller Financing

Year	Annual Payment	Annual Interest	Principal	Balance
4	$209,186	$200,363	$ 8,823	$1,475,344
5	209,186	199,171	10,015	1,465,329

be secured by a second mortgage) for $1,511,970, leaving a balance of $647,988 to be paid in cash at the closing. Terms of seller financing will be 10.5 percent interest, annual payments of approximately $167,116 (representing a 30-year amortization schedule), with the remaining balance of $1,484,167 due at the end of three years. Prospective purchasers believe that they will be able to refinance the outstanding balance of the second mortgage note when the balance becomes due. They anticipate refinancing terms to involve 13.5 percent interest with a 25-year amortization period. They realize that this new loan may have a variable interest rate or require a balloon payment, but they believe that they will have disposed of the property before any such provisions are reflected in annual cash flows.

Table 23.14 provides an amortization schedule for the existing first mortgage note, for the second mortgage note to be supplied by the sellers and for the anticipated refinancing after three years. Table 23.15 combines these amortization schedules into a consolidated debt service schedule.

Cost Recovery (Depreciation) Schedule

For income tax purposes, the investment group will use straight-line cost recovery (depreciation) over a 31.5-year period. The expected purchase price of $3,800,000 is properly allocable 80 percent to the building and 20 percent to the land. Therefore, the annual cost recovery (depreciation) allowance will be $3,040,000/31.5, or $96,508. The first and last year's allowance is $92,487

TABLE 23.15 Combined Loan Amortization Schedule for Community Shopping Center

Year	Annual Payment	Annual Interest	Principal	Balance
1	$327,992	$281,760	$46,232	$3,105,780
2	327,992	278,042	49,950	3,055,803
3	327,992	274,018	53,974	3,001,856
4	370,062	314,190	55,872	2,945,984
5	370,062	309,469	60,593	2,885,391

TABLE 23.16 Cost Recovery Schedule for Community Shopping Center

Year	Beginning Balance	Cost Recovery	Ending Balance
1	$3,040,000	$92,487	$2,947,513
2	2,947,513	96,508	2,851,005
3	2,851,005	96,508	2,754,497
4	2,754,497	96,508	2,657,989
5	2,657,989	92,487	2,565,502

due to the half-month convention. Table 23.16 contains a cost recovery schedule indicating an adjusted basis for the building of $2,565,502 at the projected time of sale.

Forecasting Income

If this property is acquired, title will be transferred subject to existing leases. Examination of these leases reveals that base rentals for the department store and the food store will be $183,750 and $50,000 respectively over the anticipated five-year holding period. Rental for the fast-food restaurant will be $30,000 annually in the first three years and $32,000 in years four and five. The savings and loan association will pay $50,000 per year.

Leases of the department and food stores also contain percentage clauses. These require the department store to pay percentage rental equal to 1.5 percent of the net sales to the extent this exceeds the $700,000 base rental. The food store must pay one percent of gross sales when the percentage exceeds its $50,000 base rental. Prospective purchasers have been supplied with audited sales figures for both stores for the past ten years. Year-to-year sales receipts have fluctuated rather widely, but both stores have experienced average annual sales growth rates of about five percent per year. Purchasers believe this rate will continue over the anticipated holding period. Table 23.17 shows projected percentage rentals based on these estimates.

TABLE 23.17 Percentage Rentals for Community Shopping Center

	Year 1	Year 2	Year 3	Year 4	Year 5
DEPARTMENT STORE					
Estimated Annual Sales	$2,200,000	$2,310,000	$2,425,500	$2,546,775	$ 2,674,11
Less: Base Sales	700,000	700,000	700,000	700,000	700,000
Percentage Sales	$1,500,000	$1,610,000	$1,725,500	$1,846,775	$1,974,113
Times: Percentage	.015	.015	.015	.015	.015
Percentage Rental	$ 22,500	$ 24,150	$ 25,883	$ 27,702	$ 29,612
FOOD STORE					
Estimated Annual Sales	$6,050,000	$6,352,500	$6,670,125	$7,003,631	$7,353,813
Times: Percentage	.01	.01	.01	.01	.01
Less: Base Rent	60,500	63,525	66,701	70,036	73,538
	50,000	50,000	50,000	50,000	50,000
Percentage Rental	$ 10,500	$ 13,525	$ 16,701	$ 20,036	$ 23,538

TABLE 23.18 Calculation of Annual After-Tax Cash Flows for Community Shopping Center

	Year 1	Year 2	Year 3	Year 4	Year 5
Base Rentals					
Department Store	$183,750	$183,750	$183,750	$183,750	$183,750
Food Store	50,000	50,000	50,000	50,000	50,000
Savings and Loan	50,000	50,000	50,000	50,000	50,000
Out-Parcel	30,000	30,000	30,000	32,000	32,000
Total Base Rentals	$313,750	$313,750	$313,750	$315,750	$315,750
Percentage Rentals					
Department Store	22,500	24,150	25,882	27,702	27,612
Food Store	10,500	13,525	16,701	20,036	23,538
Total Rentals	$346,750	$351,425	$356,333	$363,488	$366,900
Less: Management Fee	15,687	15,687	15,687	20,036	20,036
Net Operating Income	$331,063	$335,738	$340,646	$343,452	$346,864
Less: Debt Service	327,992	327,992	327,992	370,062	370,062
Before-Tax Cash Flow	$ 3,071	$ 7,746	$ 12,654	$ (26,610)	$ (23,198)
Plus: Principal	46,232	49,950	53,974	55,872	60,593
Less: Depreciation	92,487	96,508	96,508	96,508	92,487
Taxable Income (Loss)	$ (43,184)	$ (38,812)	$ (29,880)	$ (67,246)	$ (55,092)

Forecasting Annual Cash Flows and Taxable Income

Table 23.18 combines operating income, financing and cost recovery allowance data into an estimate of annual after-tax cash flows. Net operating income is simply anticipated rental revenue minus the management fee. Subtracting annual debt service from this amount yields before-tax cash flows. Adding back the principal portion for the debt service (the nondeductible part) and subtracting annual cost recovery allowances results in forecast of taxable income or tax-deductible losses for each year of the anticipated holding period.

Estimating Taxable Income and Cash Proceeds from Sale

As in previous examples, computing a capitalization rate facilitates estimating the market value of the property as of the anticipated sales date. The implied capitalization rate at the time of purchase is calculated by dividing the first year's net operating income by the purchase price:

$$\$331,063/\$3,800,000 = .087122$$

Market value at the anticipated selling date is estimated by dividing the sixth year's net operating income (which is expected to be approximately the same as that for year five) by the capitalization rate calculated for year one. Estimated sale price is:

$$\$351,113/.087122 = \$4,030,130$$

TABLE 23.19 Taxable Gain on Sale of Community Shopping Center

Estimated Sales Price		$4,030,000
Less: Selling Costs		220,180
Net Sales Price		$3,809,820
Less: Adjusted Basis		
Land Cost	$ 760,000	
Building*	2,565,502	3,325,502
Gain on Sale		$ 484,318

*Cost minus accumulated cost recovery allowances.

TABLE 23.20 Before-Tax Cash Flow from Disposal of Community Shopping Center

Estimated Sales Price		$4,030,000
Less:		
Selling Costs	$ 220,180	
Mortgage Balance	2,885,391	3,105,571
Before-Tax Cash Flow Estimate		$ 924,429

Estimated sales price, rounded to $4,030,000, is reduced by estimated selling expense of $220,180. Net sales price is then gross selling price of $4,030,000, minus $220,180, producing $3,809,820.

Table 23.19 illustrates calculation of the taxable gain on sale of the property. Adjusted basis is subtracted from net sales price, producing the gain on sale. The gain on sale is $484,318. Subtracting the outstanding loan balance at the sale date from the net sales price yields the expected before-tax cash proceeds from disposal. Table 23.20 illustrates this calculation, which produces a before-tax cash-flow estimate of $924,429. Tax consequences for partners are discussed later.

Evaluating After-Tax Cash Flows

One partner is assumed to be in the 28 percent marginal tax bracket during the first four years of the investment period. Taxable income generated from selling the property will also be taxed at the 28 percent marginal rate. Table 23.21 shows the distribution of expected before-tax cash flows and income or loss from the investment for this partner. Since the partners have not arrived at a contrary agreement, all items are distributed evenly. Table 23.22 illustrates adjustments for income tax consequences to yield after-tax cash-flow estimates for the partner.

Table 23.23 shows estimation of after-tax proceeds from sale for this partner. Table 23.24 illustrates computation of present value of the partner's equity

TABLE 23.21   Partner's Share of Cash Flows and Income or Loss on Community Shopping Center

Year	Total Before-Tax Cash Flow (Table 23.18)	Individual Partner's Share
1	$ 3,071	$ 512
2	7,746	1,291
3	12,654	2,109
4	(26,610)	(4,435)
5	(23,198)	(3,866)

	Taxable Income (Loss) (Table 23.18)	Partner's Share
1	$ (43,184)	$ (7,197)
2	(38,812)	(6,469)
3	(29,880)	(4,980)
4	(67,246)	(11,208)
5	(55,092)	(9,182)

	Before-Tax Cash Proceeds from Sale (Table 23.20)	Partner's Share
5	$924,429	$154,072

	Taxable Gain on Sale (Table 23.19)	Partner's Share
5	$484,318	$ 80,720

TABLE 23.22   Annual After-Tax Cash Flows to Partner in 28 Percent Bracket on Community Shopping Center

	Year 1	Year 2	Year 3	Year 4	Year 5
Partner's Taxable Income (Loss) (Table 23.21)	$(7,197.00)	$(6,469.00)	$(4,980.00)	$(11,208.00)	$(9,182.00)
Times: Tax Rate	.28	.28	.28	.28	.28
Tax (Savings)	$(2,015.16)	$(1,811.32)	$(1,394.40)	$(3,138.24)	$(2,570.96)
Partner's Before-Tax Cash Flow (Table 23.21)	$ 512.00	$ 1,291.00	$ 2,109.00	$ (4,435.00)	$(3,866.00)
Tax Consequences	2,015.16	1,811.32	1,394.40	3,138.24	2,570.96
Partner's After-Tax Cash Flow	$ 2,527.16	$ 3,102.32	$ 3,503.40	$(1,296.76)	$(1,295.04)

position, with a ten percent target rate of return. Since the present value of expected after-tax cash flows is less than the individual partner's share of the required equity investment ($87,433 present value versus equity investment of $107,977.88), the partner cannot expect this project to generate a yield in excess

---

TABLE 23.23   Partner's After-Tax Cash Flow from Disposal of Shopping Center

Partner's Share of Sale Proceeds (Table 23.21)		$154,072.00
Less: Taxes		
Partner's Share of Gain (Table 23.21)	$80,720.00	
Times: Partner's Marginal Tax Rate	.28	22,601.60
Partner's After-Tax Cash Flow		$131,470.40

TABLE 23.24   Present Value of Partner's After-Tax Cash Flow on Shopping Center Project

Year	Partner's After-Tax Cash Flow	Present Value Factor (10%)	Present Value of Cash Flows
1	$ 2,527.16	0.9091	$ 2,297.44
2	3,102.32	0.8264	2,563.74
3	3,503.40	0.7513	2,632.10
4	(1,296.76)	0.6830	(885.69)
5	(1,295.04)	0.6209	(804.09)
(From Disposal)	131,470.40	0.6209	81,629.97
Present Value			$87,433.47

---

of the discount rate. Remember, however, that the cash-flow projections and present value computations presuppose a specific purchase price and set of financing arrangements. The project can be made even more attractive by lowering the price or offering more favorable mortgage terms. Financing terms can be enhanced by lowering the interest rate, lengthening the repayment period or reducing the size of the down payment.

SUMMARY

Investment analytical procedures can be applied in a similar fashion to evaluate different types of real property. This has been demonstrated by applying the discounted cash-flow model to analyze an industrial building, an office building and a shopping center. In each case the procedure begins with demand analysis and proceeds to an after-tax cash-flow forecast. The anticipated cash flows, including the forecast after-tax cash flow from disposal at the end of the anticipated holding period, are discounted at the appropriate discount rate to generate a present value of the anticipated future flow of benefits.

NOTES

1. Gaylon E. Greer and Michael D. Farrell, *Contemporary Real Estate: Theory and Practice* (Hinsdale, IL: The Dryden Press, 1983), 22.

2. The *Downtown and Suburban Office Building Experience Exchange Report* (Washington DC: Building Owners and Managers Association International) is published annually, as are editions of *Income/Expense Analysis: Suburban Office Buildings* (Chicago: Institute of Real Estate Management).

3. *Income/Expense Analysis: Suburban Office Buildings* (Chicago: Institute of Real Estate Management) provides data to make this sort of comparison.

RECOMMENDED READINGS

Kinnard, William N., Stephen D. Messner, and Byrl N. Boyce. *Industrial Real Estate*. 3d ed. Washington, DC: Society of Industrial Realtors, 1979.

McMahon, John. Property Development: *Effective Decision Making in Uncertain Times*. NY: McGraw-Hill, 1976, pp. 153–202.

Phyrr, Stephen A., and James R. Cooper. *Real Estate Investment: Strategy, Analysis, Decisions*. Boston: Warren, Gorham and Lamont, 1982, pp. 585–609.

Urban Land Institute. *Industrial Development Handbook*. Washington, DC: The Urban Land Institute, 1977.

———. *Mixed-Use Development Handbook*. Washington, DC: The Urban Land Institute, 1987.

———. *Shopping Center Development Handbook*. 2d ed. Washington, DC: The Urban Land Institute, 1985.

Wendt, Paul F., and Alan R. Cerf. *Real Estate Investment Analysis and Taxation*. NY: McGraw-Hill, 1979, pp. 193–270.

REVIEW QUESTIONS

1. Why are investors attracted to industrial buildings as investment vehicles?
2. How do locational factors influence the choice of an industrial building site?
3. Consider the cash-flow projections of the industrial property illustrated in Table 23.3. In year four, the owner will have to pay taxes on income from operations. Does this mean there is no longer a tax shelter associated with the property?
4. What is the major determining factor in the demand for office space?
5. Describe the structure of most office building leases.

6. A capitalization rate was used to estimate the sales price of the office building in the case study. What other method might have been used to estimate the probable selling price?
7. Outline the lease arrangements commonly found in shopping center properties.
8. Describe the various types of shopping centers.
9. Is the community shopping center analyzed in this chapter a good investment for all the partners?

DISCUSSION QUESTIONS

1. If demand in your marketing area were about the same for rental apartments and industrial space, would you generally prefer to develop apartments or industrial buildings? What are some key factors that would affect your choice?
2. If demand factors were about equal, what would be some other considerations determining your preference for developing and owning single-tenant industrial buildings or incubator-type buildings?
3. Compare and contrast management functions in major shopping centers with those in large office buildings.
4. If demand were about equal, what are some factors that would affect your choice between developing a major regional shopping center and committing an equal amount of funds to developing a string of neighborhood or community shopping centers?

Gary Goldblest asks your advice concerning a perplexing situation. Having recently read a book about how someone turned $1,000 into $2 million in real estate in his spare time, Goldblest is anxious to participate in this bonanza. His job as an executive assistant in a major commodities brokerage firm is secure but offers no opportunity for advancement. Goldblest feels, therefore, that real estate investment is his best chance to build a personal fortune.

Goldblest talked with three real estate brokers, each of whom presented him with a different investment opportunity. Because his funds are limited to $500,000 recently presented to him by a relative, he cannot accept all of these alternatives. He therefore discussed all three ventures with each broker and became extremely confused. Although using the same financial data and operating projections, the brokers drew conflicting conclusions about probable rates of return on the investments.

THE INVESTOR

Further questioning reveals that Goldblest is employed by his father under a long-term contract at a salary that puts him solidly in the 28 percent marginal income tax bracket (his state does not have an income tax). His employment contract (which requires him to stay away from his father's place of business, to avoid public identification with the firm and to remain unmarried throughout the contract period) provides for no salary increases, so Goldblest expects that his income from sources other than real estate will remain essentially unchanged for the next ten years.

Goldblest tells you he is interested in tax shelter, cash flow, capital appreciation and security of principal. He asks you to study data concerning the three investment opportunities. He would like you to reconcile conflicting yield expectations reported by different brokers and to make a definitive recommendation concerning his best course of action.

THE PROPERTIES

Industrial Building

The first broker offered a three-year-old, 35,000-square-foot industrial building for which the owner is asking $35 per square foot, or $1,225,000. The broker feels the property can be acquired for $1 million, or $30 per square foot. The building is under lease to a Class A tenant for $3.50 per square foot, or $122,500 per year, on a net-lease basis. Based partly on the tenant's financial standing, a lender will provide a mortgage loan for 80 percent of the purchase price. The loan will be interest only (at 11 percent), payable monthly, with the principal amount due in ten years.

The tenant has seven years remaining on his or her original ten-year lease. At the end of the lease period the tenant has the option of purchasing the property for $1,200,000 and is expected to exercise the option.

Apartment Building

Broker number two recommended a 55-unit apartment building that currently generates a gross income of $297,000. The property is listed at $25,000 per unit, for a total price of $1,375,000. The owners are desperate, however, and the broker reports the property can almost certainly be acquired for $1,200,000. Of this amount, $960,000 is attributable to the improvements.

Operating expenses and vacancy losses are currently running about 50 percent of gross income. Both gross income and expenses are expected to remain constant over the (anticipated) seven-year holding period. At the end of the seventh year, the property is expected to have a market value of $1,200,000.

A 30-year, 12.5 percent mortgage loan is available for 75 percent of the purchase price. There will be no origination fee or prepayment penalty. Level payments will be made monthly.

Office Building

The final alternative is a 20,000-square-foot office building that is advertised for sale at $60 per square foot ($1,200,000 total) but can probably be bought for $1,100,000. Buildings and other improvements account for 80 percent of the property's total value.

During the first year of the prospective holding period this property should yield gross rent of $10 per square foot and incur operating expenses of about $4 per square foot. Both gross revenue and operating expenses are expected to increase thereafter at a compound annual rate of five percent. If the building is acquired, Goldblest will probably hold it for seven years. At that time he should be able to sell it for about $1,250,000.

A lender has indicated that he or she will make a 40-year, 11 percent mortgage loan for 75 percent of Goldblest's purchase price (with a ten-year call provision). There will be no origination fee and no prepayment penalty. Payments must be made monthly.

THE ANALYSIS

For each investment opportunity, develop an after-tax cash-flow projection for the anticipated seven-year holding period. Project after-tax cash proceeds from disposal at the end of the holding period. Which of these propositions, if any, seems appropriate for Goldblest? What will you advise?

PART EIGHT

Real Estate as a Security

Real estate analysts who must evaluate specific investment proposals or choose between alternative real estate ventures will find the analytical model developed in Parts One through Seven universally applicable. Many people, however, have neither the time nor the inclination to undertake extensive analysis of specific ventures. Others have inadequate equity funds to exploit the intelligence such analysis generates. Share ownership in real estate limited partnerships or real estate investment trusts represents a possible alternative for such investors. Fulfilling these investor needs enables syndicators and trusts to marshall large amounts of investor funds and thereby generate both unusual market strength and economies of scale in investment operations.

Real estate limited partnership syndications are discussed in Chapter 24. Publicly offered syndications have become a major intermediary for channeling funds from individual investors into real estate equities. The syndicates provide many of the tax-advantaged investment opportunities available to those who make direct investment in real estate ventures, plus the additional advantages of strictly limited personal financial liability and freedom from management responsibilities.

Chapter 25 explores the operation of real estate investment trusts, commonly called REITs (pronounced ''reets''). Readers with long memories may have considered REITs to be yesterday's news. Yet all indicators show that REITs have found a new lease on life. Both the number of shareholders and total assets under REIT control have increased dramatically during the 1980s. The trusts are emerging as more conservative and more stable investment entities than those (now mostly defunct) companies that so largely contributed to the REIT debacle of the mid-1970s.

Chapter 24

Real Estate Syndication

INTRODUCTION

Real estate syndicators generally use the limited partnership form of ownership to combine funds from passive investors with the real estate expertise of promoters who function as general partners. Syndicators are emerging as major intermediaries in real estate capital formation. Estimates vary, but it is generally agreed that syndicators funneled approximately $1 billion of equity funds into real estate between 1970 and 1979. In 1980 alone, they equaled the past ten years' performance by attracting another $1 billion to real estate. This record was dwarfed by their performance during 1981, when, by most estimates, they placed over $3 billion of capital into real estate ventures. In 1984, 1985 and 1986, public real estate syndications attracted $5.6 billion, $8 billion and $8.3 billion respectively. The Tax Reform Act of 1986 that greatly reduced available income tax benefits was anticipated as early as 1984. Since then, syndicators have increased the emphasis on economic yield while downplaying the importance of income tax benefits.

CHARACTERISTICS OF LIMITED PARTNERSHIPS

All limited partnerships have at least one general partner and one or more limited partners. General partners have operational control and bear unlimited liability for partnership obligations. Limited partners, in contrast, have no voice in partnership management and bear no personal liability unless they specifically agree to do so. Limited partners receive all investment benefits that typically accrue to real estate investors and may reap additional advantages from choosing this form of participation.

Investor Benefits

Potential benefits from investing in real property have been discussed at length throughout the text. These include tax shelter, equity buildup through repayment of mortgage loans, appreciation in property values, cash flows from operations and from the net proceeds of refinancing and so forth. These advantages are potentially available to anyone willing to commit funds to real estate. Limited partnerships make them available to individuals with limited capital resources and little or no real estate experience. Limited partnerships offer investors a number of benefits that would be difficult to obtain through direct real estate ownership. These include limited liability for obligations spawned by the venture and economies of scale combined with small initial equity investments. Other advantages include risk reduction through investment diversification and professional property selection and management.

Many investors rank limited liability among the premier advantages associated with real estate limited partnerships. Limited partners are at risk only to the extent of their capital contributions plus their ownership interests in undistributed profits. Liability is extended in some partnerships due to partner agreements for subsequent assessments or as a consequence of delinquent taxes or outstanding liabilities arising from premature partnership liquidation.

Investment units in limited partnership ventures sold to the general public are often priced as low as $500 each, with a minimum subscription of as few as five units. Since 1982, many partnership promoters have made shares available in units requiring an initial investment of only $2,000, where the shares are purchased by an individual retirement account. Public limited partnership offerings thus make real estate investment available to individuals with relatively small amounts of investable funds.

Investment units made available only to selected investors (private offerings) generally require larger investments due to government restrictions on the number of people to whom such units can be sold. Minimum initial investments in these ventures typically range between $10,000 and $150,000.

Investing in a limited partnership that acquires a heterogeneous real estate portfolio can accomplish diversification objectives that for individual owners might require hundreds of thousands, or even millions, of dollars. We saw in Part Six that diversification—spreading funds over a number of ventures or investing in geographically dispersed assets—has important risk-management implications. Participating as a limited partner in a real estate venture enables investors with limited financial resources to gain the same risk-reduction benefits from diversification that might otherwise be available only to the very wealthy.

Property search and negotiating skills are crucial elements in consistently favorable investment performance. Large-scale promoters of limited partnership ventures usually employ a staff of specialists who quickly gain experience and may be particularly adept at finding properties and structuring transactions on favorable terms. Of course, mere volume of transactions or size of financial resources at one's disposal does not assure that performance will be superior or even average. Large organizations do have resources, however, with which individual market participants will be hard-pressed to compete. In any event, participating as a limited partner frees the harried business or professional person from the time-consuming task of looking for good properties and arranging the myriad acquisition details.

Investment in real estate limited partnerships also provides individuals with access to professional property managers. Most large-scale promoters have their own property management divisions. Since investment performance is related directly to the quality of property management, such firms are motivated to provide the best possible service. While limited partners indirectly pay for this service, they need not spend time arranging for and monitoring management performance, as must those who invest as individual owners.

Disadvantages of Participating as Limited Partners

Offsetting the very real advantages of the limited partnership form of real estate investment are several potential difficulties. Expected income tax benefits associated with real estate ownership might not materialize for the limited partner. Limited liability, a major consideration for many investors, may prove to be illusory. Investors who find themselves facing an unexpected need for cash resources may find it impossible or prohibitively expensive to liquidate their limited partnership interests. Not least important, it is frequently difficult or impossible to assess the investment merits of limited partnership ventures.

Investment decisions based primarily on anticipated income tax advantages are always risky. Subsequent legislation may well deprive the investor of part or all of the anticipated tax benefits. The Tax Reform Act of 1986 limited the ability to use losses generated by limited partnerships to offset other income. Many individuals who invested in limited partnerships prior to 1987 saw anticipated future income tax benefits evaporate as a result of this reform act. In addition, tax law changes may reduce the attractiveness of the property to other investors and so undermine its marketability or market value.

Even without new legislation, anticipated income tax benefits may never materialize. Actions taken by the general partners, over which the limited partners have absolutely no control, may nevertheless deprive all the partners of expected favorable income tax treatment. The partnership itself may be deemed a taxable entity rather than a tax conduit. An audit by the Internal Revenue Service may result in reallocation of profits or losses among the partners, or some reported losses may be completely disallowed. Disposition of a partner's interest, or dissolution of the partnership itself, may result in unanticipated income tax liability. In extreme cases this liability may considerably exceed the partner's share of cash proceeds from disposal. These and other income tax issues associated with real estate partnership interests are discussed in detail in Chapter 11.

Limited partners wishing to dispose of their interests before the partnership itself is dissolved face dismal prospects. Due to income tax considerations discussed in Chapter 11, partnership agreements almost always require permission of the general partner or partners before limited partnership interests can be transferred. Again due to income tax considerations, such permission is not a mere formality. Moreover, securing permission for disposal does not even begin to solve the investor's dilemma; finding a buyer may prove difficult or impossible. The secondary market for most limited partnership shares is narrow (newer master limited partnerships have a broader secondary market). Unless the general partners are willing to buy back the limited partner's interest, liquidation may entail a substantial capital loss.

Limited partnership investment also entails shouldering some unique economic risks. Many ventures in which the public is invited to participate (called *public offerings*) involve raising large pools of equity that are subsequently invested in a diverse menu of properties. At the time of their commitment, investors have only a general idea of the type of properties involved. They therefore have no opportunity to evaluate the investment merits of the assets upon which investment performance depends. Investors are forced to rely on the sponsor's past performance record as their sole indication of likely investment outcome.

Investors also face the risk that the limited partnership shares may not be fully subscribed. Should this occur, invested funds may be returned with only nominal interest, or the partnership may proceed on a scaled-down basis. Either of these eventualities may result in investment yields far below those anticipated at the time of the initial commitment.

REGULATION

Real estate limited partnerships are subject to regulation from a number of sources. In states where it has been adopted, the Uniform Limited Partnership Act governs relations between general and limited partners and specifies the rights and responsibilities of each. If the partnership is to escape the burden of federal income taxation, it is subject to a number of Internal Revenue Service regulations. Limited partnership shares are securities and are therefore subject to both federal and state securities regulations. This plethora of regulations and regulators renders compliance difficult and costly.

The Uniform Limited Partnership Act

The Uniform Limited Partnership Act has been adopted in every state except Louisiana, albeit in some cases in highly modified form. It specifies rights and responsibilities of general and limited partners and defines their legal relationship with third parties. Limited partners have the right to inspect the partnership's books (courts have generally interpreted this as the right to receive audited financial statements) and to seek dissolution of the partnership. They also have the right to share in financial benefits and losses of the partnership.

A certificate of limited partnership must be filed with the appropriate state agency to create a limited partnership. If this certificate is not filed, all partners will be treated as general partners, and all become jointly and severally liable for all partnership obligations. If the certificate is filed in appropriate form, the limited partners will have no personal liability for partnership obligations.

Exercising any functions reserved for general partners by the Uniform Limited Partnership Act may cause a limited partner to lose limited liability. Section 7 of the act says, "A limited partner shall not become liable as a general partner unless in addition to the exercise of his rights as a limited partner, he takes part in control of the business." The act does not define *control*, but courts have held a limited partner liable to a third party when the limited partner's actions led the person to believe the limited partner was a general partner. In deciding whether the limited liability "shield" has been pierced, courts have also considered the ability of limited partners to initiate and determine partnership actions. In some cases potential rather than actual ability was considered when making this determination.

Some states have adopted a new Modified Uniform Limited Partnership Act. This new act removes many of the questions regarding actions that can be undertaken by limited partners without endangering their limited liability. Limited partners' powers or rights under this new act include the right to vote on dissolution of the partnership, to approve changes in partnership business, to approve amendments to partnership agreements, to remove general partners, to approve changes in partnership financing and to approve sale of partnership assets. Under this modified law, limited partners may also be employed by the partnership, and they may discuss partnership business with the general partner.

Limited Partnership Syndications and the Internal Revenue Service

Limited partnerships owe their popularity in large part to their special status under the Internal Revenue Code. Unlike corporations, partnerships are not taxable entities. Whereas corporate earnings may be taxable income to the corporation when earned, and again to shareholders when distributed, partnership income or losses are reported directly by individual partners. For this reason, partnerships are frequently called *tax conduits* and have become the favored ownership entity for investments that generate tax-deductible losses during the early years of operations. Such losses pass through the partnership conduit and are reported by partners in accordance with their individual ownership interests in the partnership. Both prospective benefits and the more notorious income tax pitfalls associated with limited partnerships are discussed at length in Chapter 11.

Limited Partnerships and the Securities and Exchange Commission

Limited partnership shares are considered securities just as are corporate stocks and bonds. As securities, they are potentially subject to both federal and state securities laws. If required to register their offerings with the Securities and Exchange Commission (SEC), syndicators must file a preliminary prospectus (known as a *red herring*) prior to any advertising. A final, approved and definitive prospectus must be provided before any shares are actually offered for sale. Sales of registered limited partnership shares may be made only through registered securities dealers.

Real estate limited partnerships may claim exemption from registration on two bases. If their partnership constitutes a private placement or an intrastate offering, they may save the time and expense associated with registration. Because exemptions are risky, securities lawyers usually advise claiming both so that a fallback position is available should one basis for exemption be denied. It should be noted that exemption from registration does not relieve the syndicator from compliance with state and federal securities laws.

Private Placement Exemption.   To qualify for a private placement exemption, promoters must refrain from general solicitation or advertising. All purchasers must acquire securities solely for their personal investment portfolios rather than for resale. SEC Rule 506 specifies sufficient compliance.

Rule 506 classifies investors as either accredited or nonaccredited purchasers. Private placements may be offered to no more than 35 nonaccredited purchasers but may also be offered to an unlimited number of accredited purchasers. Nonaccredited purchasers are those who do not qualify as accredited purchasers but who are sufficiently sophisticated to understand the risks and potential rewards associated with a securities offering.

Accredited purchasers, as defined by Rule 506, include most institutional investors and all individual investors who meet at least one of three specified criteria. An individual must either:

1. Purchase at least $150,000 of the offered securities and be sufficiently wealthy that the purchase does not exceed 20 percent of his or her net worth;
2. Have a net worth in excess of $1 million (including the net worth of his or her spouse); or
3. Have income in excess of $200,000 for each of the last two years and expect that his or her income will exceed $200,000 in the current year.

Intrastate Offering Exemption.   SEC Rule 147 clarifies the nature of an intrastate offering and thereby reduces the risk of inadvertent noncompliance. Rule 147 requires the general partner to be a resident of the state in which the offering is made. It also limits offers to sell partnership interests to residents of the same state and places responsibility for determining residency solely upon the offerer. There can be no out-of-state resales within nine months of completion of the offering. The rule also specifies that at least 80 percent of partnership assets must be within the state, and 80 percent of the revenues must originate there.

State Securities Regulation

Escaping registration at the federal level does not always ensure that an offering will not have to be registered with a state securities commission. Most states consider the size of the offering, the number of offerees, the methods of advertising and the size of fees to be received by the offeror and his or her representatives when determining whether or not to require registration.

State securities laws vary widely yet have a number of elements in common. State registration typically requires filing a preliminary prospectus prior to any advertising. Regulatory approval of this preliminary filing is required before any securities are sold. Most states also require that sales of registered securities be made through registered securities dealers. Many real estate salespeople have a special securities license that allows them to sell public real estate limited partnership shares.

Many states also have ''blue sky'' laws that allow state regulators to evaluate the investment quality of securities offerings. These states may refuse registration for an offering that is considered too risky. They may also refuse registration if promoter's fees are too large or if the distribution of profits and losses between sponsor and limited partners is deemed inequitable.

Documentation

Securities regulations require that a potential investor be supplied with a prospectus that fully discloses the nature of the offering. In addition to the prospectus, potential investors are usually given a copy of the partnership agreement. Investors also sign a subscription agreement that spells out the nature of the relationship between limited partners and the sponsoring general partner. Private placements or intrastate offerings may also require potential investors to fill out a questionnaire designed to assess their ability to qualify as limited partners.

Prospectuses or offering memoranda are designed to satisfy full disclosure requirements, which stipulate that they must contain information sufficient for investors to intelligently evaluate the offering. A summary of the contents is usually provided in the introductory section. The body of the document must include disclosure of any sponsor conflicts of interest and must specify the relationship between the general partners and any of their subsidiaries that do business with the partnership.

If the sponsors have arranged to acquire specific properties on behalf of the partnership, the prospectus or offering memorandum will contain a section providing detailed information about investment properties. Otherwise there will be a section outlining partnership investment objectives. A catalog of risks associated with the venture is also included. Accounting information such as a partnership balance sheet and a statement of sources and uses of partnership funds is typically included. A description of the general partner and the underwriters and a brief summary of the partnership agreement are also included. Other information may be included, depending on the nature of the venture.

The partnership agreement defines the relationship between limited and general partners as well as the rights and responsibilities of each. This agreement also specifies the nature of the partnership's business. Partnership agreements also often contain sections limiting transferability of partnership interests, circumstances under which the partnership may be dissolved and conditions under which limited partners may need to make additional cash contributions.

APPROACHES TO LIMITED PARTNERSHIP FORMATION

Limited partnership promoters, commonly called *syndicators*, may first acquire a property interest and seek investors. Just as frequently they start with a pool of investors and seek an appropriate property. In the first instance, called a *specific asset syndication*, the syndicator may control a property through a purchase option or outright ownership and will assemble a group of investors. In the second situation, called *blind pool syndication*, the promoter assembles a group of investors with the purpose of acquiring an undesignated asset of a specific type. Specific asset syndications were once the more popular approach. As syndicators have developed favorable reputations and as syndication has gained greater investor acceptance, blind pool offerings have become more common.

Blind Pool Syndications

Registered blind pool offerings, called *nonspecified properties programs* by the Midwest Securities Commissioners Association, are subject to a number of restrictions. In states that have adopted the commissioners' recommendations, the minimum net proceeds from blind pool offerings, net of all marketing and organizational expenses, must be $1 million. Such offerings may not extend for more than one year, and within two years all funds must be either invested or refunded. Sponsors of blind pool syndications must have had at least five years of real estate experience in an executive capacity. The commissioners also require two years of experience in management and acquisition of the type of property the prospectus indicates the pool will acquire. Finally, detailed quarterly and annual reports must be sent to all investors. It should also be pointed out that the Securities and Exchange Commission does not permit cash-flow projections in offering circulars of registered blind pool syndications.

While investors in specified asset syndications have an opportunity to evaluate the property or properties as well as the promoter, those who put funds into a blind pool have only the promoter's track record to guide them in making their investment decisions. For this reason, blind pool syndications might well be called "blind faith" ventures. Some states prohibit blind pool syndications.

REWARDS OF SPONSORSHIP

Prospective sources of financial benefits from sponsoring real estate limited partnership ventures are too numerous to catalog here. The most common sources, however, include organizational fees, property acquisition fees and reimbursement of expenses. Other sources include promotional fees, property management fees, leasing commissions, brokerage commissions and insurance commissions.

The North American Securities Administrators Association (NASAA) limits initial sponsor compensation to the greater of an amount that (a) does not exceed 80 percent of equity capital contributions reduced by .1625 percent for each one percent of borrowed capital or (b) results in not less than 67 percent of capital contributions being invested in partnership assets.

Consider a partnership that raises $10,000,000 in equity capital. If there are no borrowed funds, 80 percent or $8,000,000 must be invested, with the remaining $2,000,000 available for sponsor expenses and compensation. Subtracting the sponsor's $2,000,000 leaves 80 percent of capital contributions for investment in partnership assets; criteria (a) and (b) have both been met.

Now consider a partnership that raises $10,000,000 in equity capital and plans to finance 80 percent of asset costs with borrowed funds. NASAA specifies in criterion (a) that sponsor's fees must not exceed 80 percent of equity capital contributions reduced by .1625 percent for each one percent of borrowed funds. This limits sponsor compensation to $3,300,000. Here is the computation:

Percent of Investment to Be Financed by Borrowing	80%
Less: Sponsor Reduction per 1% Borrowed (80% of 0.1625)	13
Percent of Equity Capital that Must Be Invested	67%
Total Equity Capital Raised	$10,000,000
Times: Portion that Must Be Invested	.67
Amount that Must Be Invested in Partnership	$ 6,700,000
Total Equity Capital Raised	$10,000,000
Less: Amount that Must Be Invested	6,700,000
Maximum Sponsor Compensation	$ 3,300,000

Since these computations result in 67 percent of equity capital being invested in partnership assets, NASAA's criterion (b) is also satisfied. With 80 percent of the purchase price of partnership assets being financed with borrowed funds, the $6,700,000 of equity remaining after maximum sponsor compensation translates to $33,500,000 in assets. Sponsor compensation will have been

$3,300,000/\$33,500,000$, which equals 9.85 percent of the total value of partnership property acquired.

Sponsors are also permitted by NASAA to charge a promotional fee consisting of a percentage of annual cash flow, a percentage of proceeds of any refinancing or a percentage of proceeds of sale. They are allowed to retain as much as 25 percent of the cash generated from any of these sources after the limited partners have recouped their equity investments plus six percent cumulative interest.

Sponsors may also receive a brokerage commission for selling partnership realty. This fee is limited to the lesser of a competitive rate or six percent of the sales price of the property.

Property management fees also are allowed. For residential properties, the maximum management fee (including any rental or leasing fees) is five percent of gross income. For properties subject to long-term leases, sponsors may collect management fees of no more than three percent of gross income the first year and one percent per year thereafter. Maximum management fees for commercial and industrial properties are six percent of gross income if the sponsor is also the leasing agent; if the sponsor is not the leasing agent, the maximum management fee is three percent of gross income.

Sponsors may also charge for securing insurance. Cost of insurance plus all related fees must be less than the lowest quote from one of two outside insurance agents. Sponsors who collect insurance fees must be in the insurance business, however. Being "in the business" implies collecting at least 75 percent of total insurance revenue from noncaptive purchasers.

MASTER LIMITED PARTNERSHIPS

Master limited partnerships are the latest entry into the real estate securities sweepstakes. While master limited partnerships were pioneered by promoters of oil and gas ventures, they are gaining popularity among real estate sponsors. At the end of 1985 there were more than 45 oil and gas master limited partnerships and only seven real estate master limited partnerships. However, considering real estate's popularity, real estate master limited partnerships should become increasingly available in the near future.

Master limited partnerships are much like other limited partnerships, and their interests are often listed on major securities exchanges. Investors enjoy limited liability and may receive favorable income tax treatment while benefiting from the liquidity created by an active market for these ownership interests.

Liquidity is the greatest advantage master limited partnerships have over the more traditional limited partnership offerings. The majority of these ventures are listed on either the New York or American Stock Exchange. Those that are not listed on these exchanges are traded in the over-the-counter market. Unlike the more common traditional limited partnerships, there is no limitation on the ability to transfer one's position in a master limited partnership.

SUMMARY

Real estate limited partnerships match passive investor equity funds with sponsors who function as general partners. Real estate limited partnership sponsors have recently emerged as important intermediaries in channeling investors' funds into real estate equities.

Investors receive the benefit of limited liability for real estate ownership. Individuals are able to commit small amounts of capital to a variety of projects while taking advantage of expert acquisition and management skills. Investors also receive numerous tax-shelter benefits.

Limited partnership syndications are not without risk. Expected tax-shelter benefits and projected cash flows may never materialize. Limited partnership shares are difficult to dispose of, as no secondary market exists. Early disposal may trigger tax liability in excess of cash received.

Real estate limited partnerships are formed in one of two ways. In a specific asset offering, a sponsor gains control of a property and then finds investors. Blind pool offerings involve sponsors who raise capital before acquiring the properties.

Limited partnership offerings are regulated from a number of sources. The Uniform Limited Partnership Act specifies the legal relationship among all parties and the responsibilities and rights of each. The Internal Revenue Service sets a number of requirements that must be met to achieve expected tax conduit treatment. Limited partnership shares are securities and as such are subject to regulation by state and federal securities officials.

Fees charged by sponsors of limited partnerships are governed by the North American Securities Administrators Association. Six large public syndicators have raised more than 80 percent of all limited partnership equities. Because limited partnerships are relatively new investment vehicles, information regarding their performance is limited and contradictory.

RECOMMENDED READINGS

Bernstein, Jay B. *The Professional Syndicator: A Guide for Creating Limited Partnerships.* Dubuque, IA: Kendell/Hunt, 1981.

Hall, Craig. *Craig Hall's Book of Real Estate Investing.* NY: Holt, Rinehart, and Winston, 1982.

Lynn, Theodore S., Harry F. Goldberg, and Daniel S. Abrams. *Real Estate Limited Partnerships.* NY: John Wiley, 1977.

Real Estate Review Editorial Staff. *How Securities Laws Affect Real Estate Offerings.* Boston: Warren, Gorham, and Lamont, 1977.

———. *How To Syndicate Real Estate—Portfolio No. 11.* Boston: Warren, Gorham, and Lamont, 1977.

Stanger, Robert A. *Tax Shelters: The Bottom Line.* Fair Haven, NJ: Robert A. Stanger Co., 1982.

REVIEW QUESTIONS

1. List major differences between the positions of general and limited partners.
2. Describe the advantages of investing in a public limited partnership as opposed to direct ownership of real estate.
3. List several activities that may cause limited partners to lose their limited liability status.
4. Explain the private placement exemption.
5. What is necessary to qualify a public real estate offering for the intrastate exemption?
6. How do "blue sky" laws differ from federal securities regulations?
7. How do blind pool and specific asset real estate offerings differ?
8. Describe the relationship between the amount of financing used and the amount of front-end fees a real estate limited partnership sponsor may collect.

DISCUSSION QUESTIONS

1. What are some of the factors you would consider when choosing between investing (as a limited partner) in a *public offering* and investing in a *private placement?*
2. From an investor's perspective, does it really make any difference whether a limited partnership venture is organized as a *specific asset* or a *blind pool* offering?

CHAPTER 25

Real Estate Investment Trusts

INTRODUCTION

Real estate investment trusts (REITs) use the corporate form of ownership to channel funds from passive investor-shareholders into real estate. Section 856 of the Internal Revenue Code provides tax-free status to qualifying REITs. This permits shareholders to enjoy many of the benefits associated with direct real estate investment, while also exploiting the limited liability and enhanced liquidity of corporate ownership. Shares of REIT stock are often activity traded, making them much more liquid than shares of public real estate limited partnerships.

FAVORED REIT INVESTMENTS

Real estate investment trusts are classified as equity, mortgage or hybrid REITs, according to the type of investments they favor. Equity REITs take equity positions in real estate projects. Some mortgage REITs make primarily long-term loans; others specialize in short-term loans to finance real estate construction. "Hybrid" REITs do not fit neatly into either the equity or the mortgage category. They are active as both equity investors and mortgage lenders.

Equities accounted for 53 percent of total REIT assets in 1968. This percentage decreased steadily during subsequent years (although equities continued to grow on an absolute basis), while REITs concentrated on mortgage lending as their primary vehicle for growth. After reaching a nadir of 16 percent of total assets in 1974, equities began growing in their importance to REIT portfolios. By 1977 they comprised more than 55 percent of total REIT assets. Equity investments run the gamut of imaginable ventures, from residential rental projects through massive office towers and shopping centers to special purpose properties.

SHAREHOLDER BENEFITS

REIT shareholders are in a position somewhat analogous to that of the limited partners in real estate limited partnerships. Shareholders may incur income tax liability as a consequence of cash distributions, but they avoid the double taxation to which distributed corporate earnings are generally subject. They thereby benefit from such corporate attributes as limited liability, centralized management, continuity of life and free transferability of interests, without incurring associated tax disadvantages.

Income Tax Consequences of REIT Ownership

Since they are not taxable entities, REITs themselves do not benefit from tax-shelter benefits frequently associated with real estate equity investment. Instead, all REIT shareholders report their distributive shares of REIT taxable income on their personal income tax returns. Much of the cash distributed to shareholders, therefore, is sheltered from income tax liability by deductions for cost recovery or depreciation allowances. Net losses, however, are not passed through to shareholders as they are in real estate limited partnerships.

Diversification and Liquidity

Because REIT stock is issued at modest per-share prices, investors of limited means are able to acquire indirect interests in large-scale real estate ventures. They thereby benefit from economies that may not be available from smaller operations. Because REITs spread their investments over a large number of assets, investor risk is reduced by diversification.

REIT shares are generally more liquid than shares in real estate limited partnerships or direct ownership of real estate assets. Most REIT shares are traded either on organized stock exchanges or in the over-the-counter market and are traded reasonably actively. Their market prices are thus readily ascertainable, and they can be sold without incurring prohibitive transaction costs. In contrast, real estate limited partnership shares may not be marketable at all.

Professional Guidance

Individual investors may lack the time or the knowledge necessary to search out properties, negotiate purchases, secure financing, oversee management and supervise disposition. Investment in REIT shares provides indirect access to professionals who perform these services for the REIT. REIT advisors or managers (discussed below) engage professional property managers and monitor their performance. They also arrange financing and supervise property disposition. Investors indirectly pay for these services, but the cost per REIT share is generally modest. The same services might be prohibitively expensive for individuals committing a small amount of capital to direct ownership.

Other Benefits

Shareholders benefit from REIT investment in real estate equities in much the same manner as they would from direct real estate investment. They receive the benefits of annual cash flows, as well as equity buildup from retirement of mortgage debt and growth in property value. REITs provide a steady source of revenue, as they are required to distribute the majority of their income each year.

INVESTMENT RISK

Investors in real estate investment trusts face the same risks as owners of any other corporate common stock. Dividend distributions may vary from year to year, reflecting fluctuations in the performance of REIT assets. Share resale values are affected by general market fluctuations and by changes in performance of the REIT's asset portfolio.

Equity REITs' dividends may decline as a result of a decrease in occupancy levels or unforeseen increases in operating expenses. Rent controls may limit the ability of property managers to increase gross income and may also reduce the market value of REIT assets. Operating performance and asset values may also be affected adversely by ill-chosen or poorly timed investments or by incompetent management. All of these events will have a depressing impact on REIT share values.

Mortgage REITs face all the risks generally associated with real estate mortgage lending. Borrowers may default on loan payments, reducing trust income, which in turn reduces ability to pay dividends. Foreclosures may result in loan losses, depressing both cash distributions and net asset value of REIT shares. Any events adversely affecting REIT revenue or net worth will ultimately be reflected in the value of shares.

REIT LEGAL STATUS

A real estate investment trust is organized as a corporation or a trust. It is chartered in the state in which it is headquartered and is subject to the regulations and statutes of that state. It is also subject to provisions of the Internal Revenue Code, which specifies minimum conditions under which a REIT will be granted the special income tax status to which REITs owe their popularity with investors. Directors or trustees set REIT policy and make major management decisions; day-to-day operations are conducted by REIT employees or by outside investment advisors.

Tax-exempt Status

To qualify for tax-exempt status, REITs must meet a number of qualifications, the most significant of which are listed below.

1. Shares must be held by at least 100 persons, and five or fewer shareholders cannot own 50 percent or more of the shares during the last half of any tax year.
2. The REIT must be a passive investor rather than an active participant in property operations. However, a property manager who is an active participant may own up to 35 percent of the REIT's stock.
3. At least 75 percent of assets must consist of real estate, mortgage notes, cash, cash items or government securities. The Tax Reform Act of 1986 allows stocks and bonds purchased with the proceeds of new capital to qualify as part of this 75 percent during the first year after raising the funds.
4. At least 75 percent of gross income must come from rents, mortgage investment income and gains on the sale of real estate. The Tax Reform Act of 1986 allows income from stocks and bonds purchased with new capital to qualify as part of this 75 percent for one year.
5. At least 95 percent of ordinary income (as distinguished from capital gains) must be distributed to shareholders within one year after the end of each fiscal year. The Tax Reform Act of 1986 eases this requirement for certain types of noncash income.

Shareholder Rights

REIT shareholders have approximately the same rights as stockholders in any other corporation. Shareholders elect the trustees or directors. They also have the right to vote on proposed changes in the charter, declaration of trust or bylaws, as well as on major decisions such a new stock issues, voluntary changes in tax status or changes in investment policy.

Trustees and Directors

Shareholders elect trustees or directors who are responsible for conducting REIT investment and business activities. Guidelines enforced by the Securities and Exchange Commission dictate that the majority of trustees or directors be independent of the business activities and affiliates of the trust. Mortgage REITs usually draw trustees from the real estate lending industry; equity REITs draw from the general real estate industry.

Management

Trustees or directors hire managers to conduct the general affairs of the REIT. Some REITs have internal managers, while others use external managers, called *advisors*. The managers or advisors are responsible for property acquisition and disposition, loan arrangement or acquisition, property management or loan servicing and all other functions associated with day-to-day operations. Most REITs elect to engage outside advisors, whose operations are discussed in detail in the next section.

ADVISORS

External advisors often control day-to-day REIT operations. Table 25.1 categorizes investment advisors, shows the number of trusts employing them and shows the value of assets they control.

Outside advisors comprise a diverse group of business firms. They are frequently engaged in commercial banking, life insurance, real estate mortgage banking or a variety of related financial service activities. Many advisory companies are owned by financial conglomerates or by individual businesspeople. In almost all cases, the advisory company is a subsidiary of the individual or firm that originally sponsored the REIT.

Advisor Responsibilities

In addition to overseeing day-to-day operations, advisors frequently provide investment counsel. For this service, the advisors may engage outside professionals such as investment bankers or securities underwriters, lawyers, real estate brokers, accountants or mortgage companies to supplement their own abilities and efforts. Advisors also select property managers to oversee operation of rental property owned by the trust. Trust advisors handle property purchases and dispositions and may supervise loan origination operations or mortgage portfolio purchases and sales (in the case of REITs engaged in mortgage lending). They may also service loans on behalf of their REIT client and administer mortgage loan foreclosure or "workouts" of problem loans. REIT

TABLE 25.1   REIT Assets by Type of Advisor (year end–1985)

Category	Number of REITS	Total Assets ($ millions)
No Advisor	41	$ 5,365.3
Syndicator	23	2,425.9
Investment Banker	1	2,090.7
Individual	25	1,389.3
Mortgage Banker	7	1,197.7
Insurance Company	7	748.4
Bank	3	724.2
Developer	6	620.8
Misc. Real Estate Co.	6	580.5
Conglomerates	3	511.7
Other	6	655.2
Unknown	8	287.4
Total	136	$16,597.1

SOURCE: *REIT Fact Book 1986*

advisors also perform clerical functions and prepare quarterly and annual financial reports for REIT shareholders.

Advisor Compensation

The North American Securities Administrators Association, in a Statement of Policy on Real Estate Investment Trusts that was put into effect January 1, 1986, provides guidelines for setting advisory fees. This policy statement specifies that independent trustees shall determine at least annually that fees paid are "reasonable" for the nature and quality of services performed. In making their determination, trustees are to consider: (a) the size of advisory fees in relation to the size, composition and profitability of the REIT portfolio; (b) the advisor's success in generating opportunities that meet REIT investment objectives; (c) rates charged to other REITs and to investors other than REITs by advisors performing similar services; (d) other revenues realized by the advisor and its affiliates through their relationship with the REIT, including loan administration fees, underwriting or broker commissions, servicing, engineering, inspection and other fees, whether paid by the REIT or by others with whom the REIT does business; (e) the quality and extent of service and advice furnished by the advisor; (f) the performance of the REIT investment portfolio, including income, conservation or appreciation of capital, frequency of problem investments and competence in dealing with distressful situations; and (g) the quality of the REIT portfolio in relation to the investments generated by the advisor for its own account.

Some advisor firms are paid on a fee-for-service basis, whereby compensation depends entirely on the volume of services performed. This approach became prevalent in the mid-1970s amid widespread financial disarray among REITs. In addition to fee-for-service and expense reimbursement, some advisors recieve an annual fee computed as a percent of REIT assets. Compensation might also be a fixed fee, a percent of net income or a percent of cash flow. However computed, the Midwest Securities Commissioners' Association sets the upper limit on advisory fees at 1.5 percent of REIT net assets or 25 percent of REIT net income, whichever is greater.

SOURCES AND USES OF FUNDS

REIT financial resources come from selling shares of stock, from retaining cash generated by operations and from borrowing. Taken together, resources from selling shares and retaining earnings accounted for about half of the total in 1985. The other half came from borrowed funds; 29 percent of the total represented debt secured by mortgages on REIT assets and the balance represented miscellaneous obligations no one of which accounted for more than about five percent of the total.

Total REIT assets were $16.6 billion at the end of 1985. Approximately 46.1 percent was invested in long-term, mortgage-secured loans; another 6.2 percent was in land development and construction loans. Real estate equities accounted for about 37.5 percent of the total. The balance (net of loss reserves) was invested in miscellaneous other assets. Detailed asset and liability data for this and earlier years are presented on Table 25.2.

HISTORY OF REIT ACTIVITIES

Real estate literature of the 1970s and 1980s provides interesting insight into the history of REIT performance. Articles published in the early 1970s carried titles such as "The Real Estate Investment Trust: New Wonderchild" and "Equity Trusts: Real Estate Capitalists of the Seventies." By the mid-1970s the tune had changed somewhat: "The REITs Are Sorting Themselves Out" and "What Has Happened to REITs?" By the late 1970s REITs had lost their wonderchild status: "An Institutional Explanation of Poor REIT Performance," "What Went Wrong with REITs," and "Bank REITs: Continuing Embarrassment." Although the 1970s witnessed the demise of a number of REITs, many survived and are experiencing new prosperity. Articles during the early 1980s reflected renewed analyst enthusiasm: "Equity REITs Come Back from Debacle" and "Experts Eye REIT Market for Hidden Values in Realty."

TABLE 25-2   REIT Industry Balance Sheet (December 31, 1985*)
                  ($ millions)

ASSETS		LIABILITIES	
Mortgages:		Mortgages	2,668.4
Construction and		Mortgage-Backed	
Development	1,033.4	Bonds	2,182.4
First Mortgages	3,534.6	Convertible Debt	899.6
Junior Mortgages	1,358.7	Commercial Paper	723.0
Investment in		Bank Debt	677.5
Mortgage Pools	2,763.0	Nonconvertible Debt	616.7
	8,689.7	Other Liabilities	524.5
		Total Liabilities	8,292.1
Equity Investments:			
Property Owned	5,749.2	**Shareholders' Equity**	8,305.0
Joint Ventures	343.4		16,597.1
Investment in Other			
REITS	125.5		
	6,218.1		
Total Real Estate			
Investments	14,907.8		
Cash and Other Assets	1,771.6		
Loss Reserves	(82.3)		
Total Assets	16,597.1		

*Calculated from the most recent financial reports of 136 tax-qualified real estate investment trusts. Does not include approximately $53 million held by two new companies that have not yet published financial reports.

SOURCE: REIT Fact Book 1986

A Checkered History

After a slow start (only five new REITs were formed during the first eight years following enabling legislation in 1960), investors and promoters alike became enamored of REIT prospects. The years 1969 and 1970 witnessed the formation of over 50 new trusts. Nineteen seventy-one, 1972 and 1973 proved to be peak growth years, with more than 200 new REITs.

Annual balance sheet data shown on Table 25.3 chronicles the growth, decline and subsequent recovery of the REIT industry during the 1970s and early 1980s. Assets grew about 45 percent in 1973 and 1974, then declined by almost two-thirds over the next six years. After bottoming out in 1980, asset values began growing at an increasing pace, but by the end of 1985 they still had not recovered to their 1973 level.

Early Success

Early REITs were primarily equity trusts, acquiring ownership interest in properties. Widespread disruption of traditional saving and real estate lending channels during the late 1960s, however, created a unique opportunity for the REITs to move aggressively into mortgage lending. Interest rates available in bond

TABLE 25.3 Aggregate Balance Sheet Data for REITS ($ billions, year-end data)

Assets	1973	1974	1975	1976	1977	1978	1979	1980	1981	1982	1983	1984	1985
Land, Development and Construction Loans	$10.74	$ 9.47	$ 3.86	$1.97	$1.25	$1.04	$1.07	$0.83	$0.71	$0.72	$0.71	$ 0.74	$ 1.03
Other Loans	4.13	6.78	3.28	2.67	2.13	2.03	1.85	1.89	1.93	2.08	1.97	5.34	7.66
Property Owned	3.29	4.06	4.74	5.08	4.24	3.99	3.88	3.77	3.89	4.15	4.06	4.76	6.22
Loss Reserves	—	(0.73)	(0.76)	(0.64)	(0.37)	(0.21)	(0.14)	(0.06)	(0.05)	(0.07)	(0.04)	(0.06)	(0.08)
Other Assets	1.74	0.90	0.89	0.62	0.45	0.42	0.54	0.57	0.59	0.65	0.85	1.53	1.77
Total Assets	$19.90	$20.48	$12.01	$9.70	$7.70	$7.27	$7.20	$7.00	$ 7.07	$7.53	$7.55	$12.31	$16.60
Liabilities													
Bank Borrowings and Commercial Paper	$10.31	$10.29	$ 6.13	$3.96	$2.39	$1.79	$1.59	$1.21	$1.11	$1.01	$0.71	$ 1.03	$ 1.40
Mortgages	1.45	1.58	1.51	2.00	1.81	1.96	1.95	1.91	1.93	2.04	2.07	2.48	2.67
Mortgage-Backed Bonds		—	—	—	—	—	—	—	—		—	2.06	2.18
Other Liabilities	2.36	3.95	1.21	1.10	0.89	0.92	0.87	0.96	0.94	0.99	1.01	1.24	2.04
Total Liabilities	$14.12	$15.82	$ 8.85	$7.06	$5.09	$4.67	$4.41	$4.08	$3.98	$4.04	$3.79	$ 6.81	$ 8.29
Shareholders' Equity	5.78	4.66	3.16	2.64	2.61	2.60	2.79	2.92	3.09	3.49	3.76	5.50	8.31
Total Liabilities and Shareholders' Equity	$19.90	$20.48	$12.01	$9.70	$7.70	$7.27	$7.20	$7.00	$7.07	$7.53	$7.55	$12.31	$16.60

SOURCE: *REIT Fact Book 1986*

markets during this period moved sufficiently above the maximum rates regulated financial institutions were permitted to pay on deposits, to entice many depositors to withdraw their savings and invest directly in the bond market. This phenomenon, called *disintermediation,* severely reduced the capacities of regulated financial institutions to make real estate mortgage loans.

At the same time, life insurance policyholders found it profitable to exercise their rights to borrow at modest rates on their insurance policies and to place these funds in bond and money market instruments. Life insurance companies, therefore, found themselves equally unable to accommodate the demand for mortgage loans.

This left REITs in the enviable position of being almost the only ready source of credit for the real estate industry. With no strict limits on the interest rates they could pay, REITs were able to compete successfully with bond and money market instruments for available funds. They reloaned these funds in mortgage markets, earning a profit based upon the spread between their borrowing and lending rates. The resulting consistently good performance during the late 1960s generated high investor interest and a steady influx of equity funds for the purchase of newly issued REIT shares.

Reversals

By the early 1970s, REITs found that they could acquire all the capital they could accommodate. However, IRS regulations required that the bulk of REIT capital be invested in real estate. This put pressure on the REITs to continuously find new real estate investment outlets, and many projects funded by REITs were built at a time when there was little or no demand for the space they generated. As a result, many developers defaulted on loans from REITs. Estimates are that by 1975 almost 60 percent of all REIT mortgage loans were in default.

Default and foreclosure problems were compounded during this period by a reversal of the interest rate spread that had contributed so handsomely to REIT prosperity during the late 1960s. During much of 1973 and 1974, short-term interest rates moved above long-term rates. REITs that had previously profited by borrowing in money markets or from banks and lending in the mortgage market now found they were paying more for funds than they were earning on their mortgage loan portfolios.

Tax Code Revisions

REITs suffered particularly dismal years in 1974 and 1975. Almost all experienced net cash outflows, and many were liquidated. In 1976 the government provided some relief by easing rules governing qualification for exemption from the corporate income tax. The 1976 Tax Reform Act relaxed rules governing allowable sources of gross income and introduced an escape hatch permitting REITs to avoid the penalty for failure to distribute earnings.

REITs still must receive at least 75 percent of their gross income from real estate–related sources, but the definition of *real estate–related* is much broader.

It now includes service charges associated with real estate activities and rental revenue from personal furnishings found in apartments and transient quarters, as well as certain contingency fees. Moreover, the maximum permissible 25 percent of gross from nonrealty sources can now be exceeded without penalty if due to "reasonable" causes, provided that these do not include internal fraud and that all sources are fully disclosed.

Under the old tax law, total net income became taxable if a REIT failed to distribute at least 90 percent to shareholders. The 1976 revision permits belated dividends to meet the distribution requirement, which was increased from 90 percent to 95 percent of net income.

Minor changes in the requirements for tax-free status were enacted as a result of the Tax Reform Act of 1986. Asset and income requirements were eased during the first year of a REIT's operation. Rental income was redefined, allowing more revenue to qualify, and distribution requirements were reduced in certain cases.

REITs benefited more from the effects of this reform act on other real estate investment vehicles than changes pertaining to their own operations. This act greatly increased the desirability of real estate investment trusts relative to other types of real estate ventures. Individuals who want to invest in a real estate security will find REITs more attractive than many limited partnership ventures as a result of the Tax Reform Act of 1986.

Takeovers

Corporations whose shares are traded publicly are always susceptible to takeovers. An individual or a firm need only gain control of the majority of voting stock to replace current trustees or directors with their own people. This control might be attained by purchasing shares or by soliciting proxies that permit votes to be cast on behalf of shareholders who do not attend stockholder meetings.

Equity REITs were particularly attractive targets for takeover attempts during the late 1970s and early 1980s. Table 25.4 provides an instructive example by relating the book value of assets for two such REITs to the market value of their common stock. The market value of both trusts' stock was close to book value until 1974. In 1975, market value of both trusts' stock dropped considerably below book value. Bank America's market value moved above book value in 1979 and 1980 and has remained there since. Hubbard Real Estate Investments' market value remained below book value through 1982.

Based on book values, Bank America Realty Investors has its assets split approximately evenly between direct property ownership and mortgage loans. Hubbard Real Estate Investments has more than 90 percent of its assets in direct property ownership. Book value for equity REITs declines as depreciation allowances are claimed, but astute investors know that market values of property are often increasing even as book values decline. The spread between real stock values and value of the underlying real property portfolio might be even greater than book values indicate. For that reason, equity trusts whose share values decline close to or below book value frequently become attractive takeover targets.

TABLE 25.4   Book Value vs. Market Value of Selected REITs

| | Bank America Realty Investors | | Hubbard Real Estate Investments | |
	Book Value (per share)	Market Value (per share)	Book Value (per share)	Market Value (per share)
1970	$ —	$19.8–21.5	$23.22	$17.5–23.1
1971	18.86	23.5–30.3	23.37	20.1–25.5
1972	19.03	24.3–32.1	23.41	19.1–22.6
1973	19.07	21.0–32.9	23.42	16.3–21.6
1974	19.43	4.8–24.5	23.45	9.1–19.6
1975	14.74	4.3– 9.1	21.76	9.0–15.4
1976	14.66	5.8–10.1	21.94	11.0–16.4
1977	15.30	9.3–12.5	22.61	15.3–18.6
1978	16.92	9.8–14.6	24.76	15.9–18.0
1979	17.37	10.4–20.0	25.29	15.6–19.8
1980	17.64	12.8–27.5	25.40	13.8–18.6
1981	18.60	22.0–27.6	25.56	15.5–18.7
1982	19.01	20.5–33.0	25.50	14.5–19.9

SOURCE: Greer and Farrell

Current REIT Activity

REITs that survived the financial travails and investor disaffection of the mid-1970s have generally learned from the painful experience. As a consequence they have emerged as more viable long-term financial intermediaries. Figure 25.1 illustrates fluctuations in REIT fortunes by showing dividend distributions from 1972 through 1984 (remember, REITs must distribute at least 90 percent of their earnings to retain their tax-free status). After peaking in 1973, they declined steadily until they reached a nadir in 1976. Thereafter they experienced steady increases. Growing dividend payouts coupled with increasing share prices rekindled investor interest in real estate investment trusts in the early 1980s.

Renewed investor interest is reflected in the number of new REITs formed. Annual issues of new shares held fairly steady between 1961 and 1968. They increased dramatically during the halcyon days of the early 1970s, only to decline precipitously during the debacle of the mid-1970s. Since 1979, new share offerings have again become a growth industry. Table 25.5 illustrates these variations in new share underwriting activity. Offering activity dropped to a low of five in 1975 and increased thereafter.

SUMMARY

Real estate investment trusts (REITs) use the corporate form of ownership to channel funds from passive investor shareholders into real estate. REITs enjoy

FIGURE 25.1   Total REIT Dividends

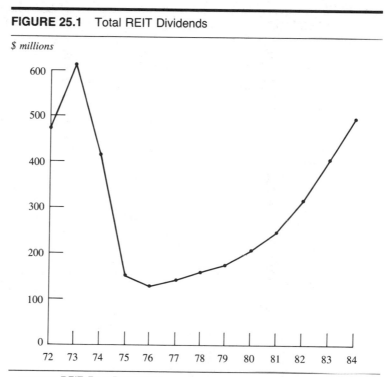

$ millions

SOURCE: *REIT Fact Book 1985*

tax-free status. Shares of real estate investment trusts are more liquid than public limited partnerships, as they are often traded in securities markets.

Investors in real estate investment trusts enjoy limited liability, centralized management, free transferability of interest and other corporate characteristics, while escaping corporate taxes. Investors also achieve a high degree of diversification, as REITs usually invest in a number of projects. REITs also provide small investors access to the expertise of real estate professionals. REIT investors face the risk of fluctuations in market price of stock as well as the possibility of variations in annual dividend distributions.

Real estate investment trusts are organized like corporations. Shareholder owners elect trustees or directors. Trustees or directors appoint managers or use outside managers known as *advisors*. Managers or advisors oversee the day-to-day operations of the trust.

Real estate investment trusts issue common stock, commercial paper and debt securities. As an intermediary, they were one of the first to tap the stock, bond and commercial paper markets for funds to invest in real estate. REITs are often split into mortgage, equity or hybrid trusts. Mortgage trusts make real estate loans and equity trusts purchase properties outright.

Real estate investment trusts have a long and varied history. Changes in tax laws in 1960 made them possible. They grew slowly at first, reached their

TABLE 25.5 Annual Summary of Public Offerings by REITS
($ millions)

	All Offerings		Initial Offerings		Secondary Offerings	
	Number	*($ millions)*	*Number*	*($ millions)*	*Number*	*($ millions)*
1961	14	$ 71.9	14	$ 71.9	0	$ 0.0
1962	16	105.9	12	81.8	4	24.1
1963	9	25.8	6	4.0	3	21.8
1964	19	36.2	11	1.4	8	34.8
1965	14	32.6	5	3.0	9	29.6
1966	3	5.8	1	0.0	2	5.8
1967	7	41.5	1	0.0	6	41.5
1968	14	122.4	4	67.6	10	54.8
1969	58	1,256.7	33	976.7	25	280.0
1970	72	1,687.4	41	1,358.4	31	329.0
1971	78	1,987.3	32	1,183.4	46	803.9
1972	67	1,223.3	29	563.2	38	660.1
1973	68	852.1	18	156.8	50	695.3
1974	17	23.7	5	1.5	12	22.2
1975	5	0.4	1	0.0	4	0.4
1976	8	19.7	0	0.0	8	19.7
1977	8	91.9	0	0.0	8	91.9
1978	12	91.5	3	8.4	9	83.1
1979	18	110.5	4	0.0	14	110.5
1980	20	264.0	4	30.0	16	234.0
1981	22	244.7	5	100.0	17	144.7
1982	12	453.6	3	315.0	9	138.6
1983	23	741.3	4	159.0	19	582.3
1984	34	2,729.9	9	378.8	25	2,351.1
1985	59	4,270.6	29	2,791.9	30	1,478.7

SOURCE: *REIT Fact Book 1986*

peak in 1973 and declined through the rest of the 1970s. By the early 1980s, REITs had started to regain favor with investors. Their market performance has been quite good, and they have increased their securities offerings.

RECOMMENDED READINGS

Brueggeman, William B., and Leo D. Stone. *Real Estate Finance*. 6th ed. Homewood, IL: Richard D. Irwin, 1977, pp. 382–472.

Campbell, Kenneth D. *The Real Estate Trusts: America's Newest Billionaires*. NY: Audit Investments Research, 1971.

Rabinowitz, Alan. *The Real Estate Gamble: Lessons from 50 Years of Boom and Bust*. NY: AMACOM, 1980, pp. 129–234.

REVIEW QUESTIONS

1. What is a real estate investment trust?
2. What are the major differences among mortgage, equity and hybrid real estate investment trusts?
3. Describe the advantages of investing in real estate investment trusts rather than limited partnerships.
4. How do investor tax benefits in a real estate investment trust differ from those of a partner in a real estate partnership?
5. Describe the functions of real estate investment trust advisors.
6. Describe the conditions that must be met for a real estate investment trust to retain its trust status under the Internal Revenue Code.
7. Describe the sources from which real estate investment trusts draw funds for investment.
8. Explain the reasons why a group of investors might want to gain control of a real estate investment trust through common stock acquisition.

DISCUSSION QUESTIONS

1. From an individual investor's perspective, contrast a publicly offered REIT with a publicly offered limited partnership in terms of:
   a. regulatory supervision;
   b. liquidity;
   c. income tax treatment.
2. From an individual investor's perspective, consider the relative merits of mortgage REITs, equity REITs and hybrids.
3. Consider the major advantages and disadvantages of *finite-life REITs* when compared with the more traditional infinite-life REITs.

PART EIGHT: Case Problem

Several friends are debating the pros and cons of various approaches to real estate investment:

Terry Talkalot (40 years old) is a vocational education specialist who teaches woodworking and blueprint reading at a local high school. Talkalot's school does not offer summer classes, so he is employed for only nine months each year. Talkalot is married and has three children, all of whom are in secondary school. The Talkalot family's annual income averages about $30,000, and their net worth is about $100,000.

Sheron Shortsell (age 40) is a very successful stockbroker. She earns more than $100,000 annually and works about 60 hours each week. She has a portfolio of common stocks worth more than $1 million and thinks real estate is an ideal way to diversify her portfolio. Shortsell is unmarried and has no dependents.

Gary Gladson (age 60) recently inherited $3 million from his father, whereupon he resigned his job as a clerk at the local library. Though he has little education beyond high school, Gladson intends to invest his inheritance and manage his own portfolio.

Formelda Hyde is a 34-year-old physician who works about 50 hours weekly and earns about $70,000 per year. Hyde is the sole source of support for three dependent children, whose ages range from three to 12. Her assets have a net value of about $200,000.

Required: These friends are arguing over the relative merits of REITs, limited partnership shares, general partnership interests, shares of stock in real estate corporations and direct investment as a sole owner of rental property.

1. To what extent might differences of opinion be attributable to personal circumstances?
2. To what extent might differences of opinion be attributable to personal education and background or professional experience?
3. To what extent might differences of opinion stem from varying attitudes toward risk?
4. Making the necessary assumptions where information is lacking, suggest possible avenues for real estate investment by each of these friends.

APPENDIX A

Financial Tables

TABLE A.1 Present Value of $1

PVIF $(r,n) = (1 + r)^{-n}$

Period	1%	2%	3%	4%	5%	6%	7%	8%	9%	10%
1	.9901	.9804	.9709	.9615	.9524	.9434	.9346	.9259	.9174	.9091
2	.9803	.9612	.9426	.9246	.9070	.8900	.8734	.8573	.8417	.8264
3	.9706	.9423	.9151	.8890	.8638	.8396	.8163	.7938	.7722	.7513
4	.9610	.9238	.8885	.8548	.8227	.7921	.7629	.7350	.7084	.6830
5	.9515	.9057	.8626	.8219	.7835	.7473	.7130	.6806	.6499	.6209
6	.9420	.8880	.8375	.7903	.7462	.7050	.6663	.6302	.5963	.5645
7	.9327	.8706	.8131	.7599	.7107	.6651	.6227	.5835	.5470	.5132
8	.9235	.8535	.7894	.7307	.6768	.6274	.5820	.5403	.5019	.4665
9	.9143	.8368	.7664	.7026	.6446	.5919	.5439	.5002	.4604	.4241
10	.9053	.8203	.7441	.6756	.6139	.5584	.5083	.4632	.4224	.3855
11	.8963	.8043	.7224	.6496	.5847	.5268	.4751	.4289	.3875	.3505
12	.8874	.7885	.7014	.6246	.5568	.4970	.4440	.3971	.3555	.3186
13	.8787	.7730	.6810	.6006	.5303	.4688	.4150	.3677	.3262	.2897
14	.8700	.7579	.6611	.5775	.5051	.4423	.3878	.3405	.2992	.2633
15	.8613	.7430	.6419	.5553	.4810	.4173	.3624	.3152	.2745	.2394
16	.8528	.7284	.6232	.5339	.4581	.3936	.3387	.2919	.2519	.2176
17	.8444	.7142	.6050	.5134	.4363	.3714	.3166	.2703	.2311	.1978
18	.8360	.7002	.5874	.4936	.4155	.3503	.2959	.2502	.2120	.1799
19	.8277	.6864	.5703	.4746	.3957	.3305	.2765	.2317	.1945	.1635
20	.8195	.6730	.5537	.4564	.3769	.3118	.2584	.2145	.1784	.1486
25	.7798	.6095	.4776	.3751	.2953	.2330	.1842	.1460	.1160	.0923
30	.7419	.5521	.4120	.3083	.2314	.1741	.1314	.0994	.0754	.0573
40	.6717	.4529	.3066	.2083	.1420	.0972	.0668	.0460	.0318	.0221
50	.6080	.3715	.2281	.1407	.0872	.0543	.0339	.0213	.0134	.0085
60	.5504	.3048	.1697	.0951	.0535	.0303	.0173	.0099	.0057	.0033

*The factor is zero to four decimal places.

12%	14%	15%	16%	18%	20%	24%	28%	32%	36%
.8929	.8772	.8696	.8621	.8475	.8333	.8065	.7813	.7576	.7353
.7972	.7695	.7561	.7432	.7182	.6944	.6504	.6104	.5739	.5407
.7118	.6750	.6575	.6407	.6086	.5787	.5245	.4768	.4348	.3975
.6355	.5921	.5718	.5523	.5158	.4823	.4230	.3725	.3294	.2923
.5674	.5194	.4972	.4761	.4371	.4019	.3411	.2910	.2495	.2149
.5066	.4556	.4323	.4104	.3704	.3349	.2751	.2274	.1890	.1580
.4523	.3996	.3759	.3538	.3139	.2791	.2218	.1776	.1432	.1162
.4039	.3506	.3269	.3050	.2660	.2326	.1789	.1388	.1085	.0854
.3606	.3075	.2843	.2630	.2255	.1938	.1443	.1084	.0822	.0628
.3220	.2697	.2472	.2267	.1911	.1615	.1164	.0847	.0623	.0462
.2875	.2366	.2149	.1954	.1619	.1346	.0938	.0662	.0472	.0340
.2567	.2076	.1869	.1685	.1372	.1122	.0757	.0517	.0357	.0250
.2292	.1821	.1625	.1452	.1163	.0935	.0610	.0404	.0271	.0184
.2046	.1597	.1413	.1252	.0985	.0779	.0492	.0316	.0205	.0135
.1827	.1401	.1229	.1079	.0835	.0649	.0397	.0247	.0155	.0099
.1631	.1229	.1069	.0930	.0708	.0541	.0320	.0193	.0118	.0073
.1456	.1078	.0929	.0802	.0600	.0451	.0258	.0150	.0089	.0054
.1300	.0946	.0808	.0691	.0508	.0376	.0208	.0118	.0068	.0039
.1161	.0829	.0703	.0596	.0431	.0313	.0168	.0092	.0051	.0029
.1037	.0728	.0611	.0514	.0365	.0261	.0135	.0072	.0039	.0021
.0588	.0378	.0304	.0245	.0160	.0105	.0046	.0021	.0010	.0005
.0334	.0196	.0151	.0116	.0070	.0042	.0016	.0006	.0002	.0001
.0107	.0053	.0037	.0026	.0013	.0007	.0002	.0001	*	*
.0035	.0014	.0009	.0006	.0003	.0001	*	*	*	*
.0011	.0004	.0002	.0001	*	*	*	*	*	*

TABLE A.2 Future Value of $1 at the End of *n* Periods

FVIF ^{k,n} = $(1 + k)^n$

Period	1%	2%	3%	4%	5%	6%	7%	8%	9%	10%
1	1.0100	1.0200	1.0300	1.0400	1.0500	1.0600	1.0700	1.0800	1.0900	1.1000
2	1.0201	1.0404	1.0609	1.0816	1.1025	1.1236	1.1449	1.1664	1.1881	1.2100
3	1.0303	1.0612	1.0927	1.1249	1.1576	1.1910	1.2250	1.2597	1.2950	1.3310
4	1.0406	1.0824	1.1255	1.1699	1.2155	1.2625	1.3108	1.3605	1.4116	1.4641
5	1.0510	1.1041	1.1593	1.2167	1.2763	1.3382	1.4026	1.4693	1.5386	1.6105
6	1.0615	1.1262	1.1941	1.2653	1.3401	1.4185	1.5007	1.5869	1.6771	1.7716
7	1.0721	1.1487	1.2299	1.3159	1.4071	1.5036	1.6058	1.7138	1.8280	1.9487
8	1.0829	1.1717	1.2668	1.3686	1.4775	1.5938	1.7182	1.8509	1.9926	2.1436
9	1.0937	1.1951	1.3048	1.4233	1.5513	1.6895	1.8385	1.9990	2.1719	2.3579
10	1.1046	1.2190	1.3439	1.4802	1.6289	1.7908	1.9672	2.1589	2.3674	2.5937
11	1.1157	1.2434	1.3842	1.5395	1.7103	1.8983	2.1049	2.3316	2.5804	2.8531
12	1.1268	1.2682	1.4258	1.6010	1.7959	2.0122	2.2522	2.5182	2.8127	3.1384
13	1.1381	1.2936	1.4685	1.6651	1.8856	2.1329	2.4098	2.7196	3.0658	3.4523
14	1.1495	1.3195	1.5126	1.7317	1.9799	2.2609	2.5785	2.9372	3.3417	3.7975
15	1.1610	1.3459	1.5580	1.8009	2.0789	2.3966	2.7590	3.1722	3.6425	4.1772
16	1.1726	1.3728	1.6047	1.8730	2.1829	2.5404	2.9522	3.4259	3.9703	4.5950
17	1.1843	1.4002	1.6528	1.9479	2.2920	2.6928	3.1588	3.7000	4.3276	5.0545
18	1.1961	1.4282	1.7024	2.0258	2.4066	2.8543	3.3799	3.9960	4.7171	5.5599
19	1.2081	1.4568	1.7535	2.1068	2.5270	3.0256	3.6165	4.3157	5.1417	6.1159
20	1.2202	1.4859	1.8061	2.1911	2.6533	3.2071	3.8697	4.6610	5.6044	6.7275
21	1.2324	1.5157	1.8603	2.2788	2.7860	3.3996	4.1406	5.0338	6.1088	7.4002
22	1.2447	1.5460	1.9161	2.3699	2.9253	3.6035	4.4304	5.4365	6.6586	8.1403
23	1.2572	1.5769	1.9736	2.4647	3.0715	3.8197	4.7405	5.8715	7.2579	8.9543
24	1.2697	1.6084	2.0328	2.5633	3.2251	4.0489	5.0724	6.3412	7.9111	9.8497
25	1.2824	1.6406	2.0938	2.6658	3.3864	4.2919	5.4274	6.8485	8.6231	10.835
26	1.2953	1.6734	2.1566	2.7725	3.5557	4.5494	5.8074	7.3964	9.3992	11.918
27	1.3082	1.7069	2.2213	2.8834	3.7335	4.8223	6.2139	7.9881	10.245	13.110
28	1.3213	1.7410	2.2879	2.9987	3.9201	5.1117	6.6488	8.6271	11.167	14.421
29	1.3345	1.7758	2.3566	3.1187	4.1161	5.4184	7.1143	9.3173	12.172	15.863
30	1.3478	1.8114	2.4273	3.2434	4.3219	5.7435	7.6123	10.063	13.268	17.449
40	1.4889	2.2080	3.2620	4.8010	7.0400	10.286	14.975	21.725	31.409	45.259
50	1.6446	2.6916	4.3839	7.1067	11.467	18.420	29.457	46.902	74.358	117.39
60	1.8167	3.2810	5.8916	10.5196	18.679	32.988	57.946	101.26	176.03	304.48

*FVIF > 99,999

12%	14%	15%	16%	18%	20%	24%	28%	32%	36%
1.1200	1.1400	1.1500	1.1600	1.1800	1.2000	1.2400	1.2800	1.3200	1.3600
1.2544	1.2996	1.3225	1.3456	1.3924	1.4400	1.5376	1.6384	1.7424	1.8496
1.4049	1.4815	1.5209	1.5609	1.6430	1.7280	1.9066	2.0972	2.3000	2.5155
1.5735	1.6890	1.7490	1.8106	1.9388	2.0736	2.3642	2.6844	3.0360	3.4210
1.7623	1.9254	2.0114	2.1003	2.2878	2.4883	2.9316	3.4360	4.0075	4.6526
1.9738	2.1950	2.3131	2.4364	2.6996	2.9860	3.6352	4.3980	5.2899	6.3275
2.2107	2.5023	2.6600	2.8262	3.1855	3.5832	4.5077	5.6295	6.9826	8.6054
2.4760	2.8526	3.0590	3.2784	3.7589	4.2998	5.5895	7.2058	9.2170	11.703
2.7731	3.2519	3.5179	3.8030	4.4355	5.1598	6.9310	9.2234	12.166	15.917
3.1058	3.7072	4.0456	4.4114	5.2338	6.1917	8.5944	11.806	16.060	21.647
3.4785	4.2262	4.6524	5.1173	6.1759	7.4301	10.657	15.112	21.199	29.439
3.8960	4.8179	5.3503	5.9360	7.2876	8.9161	13.215	19.343	27.983	40.037
4.3635	5.4924	6.1528	6.8858	8.5994	10.699	16.386	24.759	36.937	54.451
4.8871	6.2613	7.0757	7.9875	10.147	12.839	20.319	31.691	48.757	74.053
5.4736	7.1379	8.1371	9.2655	11.974	15.407	25.196	40.565	64.359	100.71
6.1304	8.1372	9.3576	10.748	14.129	18.488	31.243	51.923	84.954	136.97
6.8660	9.2765	10.761	12.468	16.672	22.186	38.741	66.461	112.14	186.28
7.6900	10.575	12.375	14.463	19.673	26.623	48.039	85.071	148.02	253.34
8.6128	12.056	14.232	16.777	23.214	31.948	59.568	108.89	195.39	344.54
9.6463	13.743	16.367	19.461	27.393	38.338	73.864	139.38	257.92	468.57
10.804	15.668	18.822	22.574	32.324	46.005	91.592	178.41	340.45	637.26
12.100	17.861	21.645	26.186	38.142	55.206	113.57	228.36	449.39	866.67
13.552	20.362	24.891	30.376	45.008	66.247	140.83	292.30	594.20	1178.7
15.179	23.212	28.625	35.236	53.109	79.497	174.63	374.14	783.02	1603.0
17.000	26.462	32.919	40.874	62.669	95.396	216.54	478.90	1033.6	2180.1
19.040	30.167	37.857	47.414	73.949	114.48	268.51	613.00	1364.3	2964.9
21.325	34.390	43.535	55.000	87.260	137.37	332.95	784.64	1800.9	4032.3
23.884	39.204	50.066	63.800	102.97	164.84	412.86	1004.3	2377.2	5483.9
26.750	44.693	57.575	74.009	121.50	197.81	511.95	1285.6	3137.9	7458.1
29.960	50.950	66.212	85.850	143.37	237.38	634.82	1645.5	4142.1	10143.
93.051	188.88	267.86	378.72	750.38	1469.8	5455.9	19427.	66521.	*
289.00	700.23	1083.7	1670.7	3927.4	9100.4	46890.	*	*	*
897.60	2595.9	4384.0	7370.2	20555.	56348.	*	*	*	ϒ

TABLE A.3 Present Value of an Annuity of $1 per Period for *n* Periods

$$PVIFa(r,t) = \sum_{i=1}^{n} \frac{1}{(1 + r)^i} = \frac{\left[1 - \dfrac{1}{(1 + r)^n}\right]}{r}$$

Number of payments	1%	2%	3%	4%	5%	6%	7%	8%	9%
1	0.9901	0.9804	0.9709	0.9615	0.9524	0.9434	0.9346	0.9259	0.9174
2	1.9704	1.9416	1.9135	1.8861	1.8594	1.8334	1.8080	1.7833	1.7591
3	2.9410	2.8839	2.8286	2.7751	2.7232	2.6730	2.6243	2.5771	2.5313
4	3.9020	3.8077	3.7171	3.6299	3.5460	3.4651	3.3872	3.3121	3.2397
5	4.8534	4.7135	4.5797	4.4518	4.3295	4.2124	4.1002	3.9927	3.8897
6	5.7955	5.6014	5.4172	5.2421	5.0757	4.9173	4.7665	4.6229	4.4859
7	6.7282	6.4720	6.2303	6.0021	5.7864	5.5824	5.3893	5.2064	5.0330
8	7.6517	7.3255	7.0197	6.7327	6.4632	6.2098	5.9713	5.7466	5.5348
9	8.5660	8.1622	7.7861	7.4353	7.1078	6.8017	6.5152	6.2469	5.9952
10	9.4713	8.9826	8.5302	8.1109	7.7217	7.3601	7.0236	6.7101	6.4177
11	10.3676	9.7868	9.2526	8.7605	8.3064	7.8869	7.4987	7.1390	6.8052
12	11.2551	10.5753	9.9540	9.3851	8.8633	8.3838	7.9427	7.5361	7.1607
13	12.1337	11.3484	10.6350	9.9856	9.3936	8.8527	8.3577	7.9038	7.4869
14	13.0037	12.1062	11.2961	10.5631	9.8986	9.2950	8.7455	8.2442	7.7862
15	13.8651	12.8493	11.9379	11.1184	10.3797	9.7122	9.1079	8.5595	8.0607
16	14.7179	13.5777	12.5611	11.6523	10.8378	10.1059	9.4466	8.8514	8.3126
17	15.5623	14.2919	13.1661	12.1657	11.2741	10.4773	9.7632	9.1216	8.5436
18	16.3983	14.9920	13.7535	12.6593	11.6896	10.8276	10.0591	9.3719	8.7556
19	17.2260	15.6785	14.3238	13.1339	12.0853	11.1581	10.3356	9.6036	8.9501
20	18.0456	16.3514	14.8775	13.5903	12.4622	11.4699	10.5940	9.8181	9.1285
25	22.0232	19.5235	17.4131	15.6221	14.0393	12.7834	11.6536	10.6748	9.8226
30	25.8077	22.3965	19.6004	17.2920	15.3725	13.7648	12.4090	11.2578	10.2737
40	32.8347	27.3555	23.1148	19.7928	17.1591	15.0463	13.3317	11.9246	10.7574
50	39.1961	31.4236	25.7298	21.4822	18.2559	15.7619	13.8007	12.2335	10.9617
60	44.9550	34.7609	27.6756	22.6235	18.9293	16.1614	14.0392	12.3766	11.0480

10%	12%	14%	15%	16%	18%	20%	24%	28%	32%
0.9091	0.8929	0.8772	0.8696	0.8621	0.8475	0.8333	0.8065	0.7813	0.7576
1.7355	1.6901	1.6467	1.6257	1.6052	1.5656	1.5278	1.4568	1.3916	1.3315
2.4869	2.4018	2.3216	2.2832	2.2459	2.1743	2.1065	1.9813	1.8684	1.7663
3.1699	3.0373	2.9137	2.8550	2.7982	2.6901	2.5887	2.4043	2.2410	2.0957
3.7908	3.6048	3.4331	3.3522	3.2743	3.1272	2.9906	2.7454	2.5320	2.3452
4.3553	4.1114	3.8887	3.7845	3.6847	3.4976	3.3255	3.0205	2.7594	2.5342
4.8684	4.5638	4.2883	4.1604	4.0386	3.8115	3.6046	3.2423	2.9370	2.6775
5.3349	4.9676	4.6389	4.4873	4.3436	4.0776	3.8372	3.4212	3.0758	2.7860
5.7590	5.3282	4.9464	4.7716	4.6065	4.3030	4.0310	3.5655	3.1842	2.8681
6.1446	5.6502	5.2161	5.0188	4.8332	4.4941	4.1925	3.6819	3.2689	2.9304
6.4951	5.9377	5.4527	5.2337	5.0286	4.6560	4.3271	3.7757	3.3351	2.9776
6.8137	6.1944	5.6603	5.4206	5.1971	4.7932	4.4392	3.8514	3.3868	3.0133
7.1034	6.4235	5.8424	5.5831	5.3423	4.9095	4.5327	3.9124	3.4272	3.0404
7.3667	6.6282	6.0021	5.7245	5.4675	5.0081	4.6106	3.9616	3.4587	3.0609
7.6061	6.8109	6.1422	5.8474	5.5755	5.0916	4.6755	4.0013	3.4834	3.0764
7.8237	6.9740	6.2651	5.9542	5.6685	5.1624	4.7296	4.0333	3.5026	3.0882
8.0216	7.1196	6.3729	6.0472	5.7487	5.2223	4.7746	4.0591	3.5177	3.0971
8.2014	7.2497	6.4674	6.1280	5.8178	5.2732	4.8122	4.0799	3.5294	3.1039
8.3649	7.3658	6.5504	6.1982	5.8775	5.3162	4.8435	4.0967	3.5386	3.1090
8.5136	7.4694	6.6231	6.2593	5.9288	5.3527	4.8696	4.1103	3.5458	3.1129
9.0770	7.8431	6.8729	6.4641	6.0971	5.4669	4.9476	4.1474	3.5640	3.1220
9.4269	8.0552	7.0027	6.5660	6.1772	5.5168	4.9789	4.1601	3.5693	3.1242
9.7791	8.2438	7.1050	6.6418	6.2335	5.5482	4.9966	4.1659	3.5712	3.1250
9.9148	8.3045	7.1327	6.6605	6.2463	5.5541	4.9995	4.1666	3.5714	3.1250
9.9672	8.3240	7.1401	6.6651	6.2492	5.5553	4.9999	4.1667	3.5714	3.1250

TABLE A.4 Monthly Installment to Amortize a $1 Loan

$$PMT = \frac{\dfrac{i}{12}}{1 - \left[\left\{ \dfrac{1}{\left(1 + \dfrac{i}{12}\right)} \right\} 12n \right]}$$

Years	6.0%	6.5%	7.0%	7.5%	8.0%	8.5%	9.0%	9.5%	10.0%
1	.086066	.086296	.086527	.086757	.086988	.087220	.087451	.087684	.087916
2	.044321	.044546	.044773	.045000	.045227	.045456	.045685	.045914	.046145
3	.030422	.030649	.030887	.031106	.031336	.031568	.031800	.032033	.032267
4	.023485	.023715	.023946	.024179	.024413	.024648	.024885	.025123	.025363
5	.019333	.019566	.019801	.020038	.020276	.020517	.020758	.021002	.021247
6	.016573	.016810	.017049	.017290	.017533	.017778	.018026	.018275	.018526
7	.014609	.014849	.015093	.015338	.015586	.015836	.016089	.016344	.016601
8	.013141	.013386	.013634	.013884	.014137	.014392	.014650	.014911	.015174
9	.012006	.012255	.012506	.012761	.013019	.013279	.013543	.013809	.014079
10	.011102	.011355	.011611	.011870	.012133	.012399	.012668	.012940	.013215
11	.010367	.010624	.010884	.011148	.011415	.011686	.011961	.012239	.012520
12	.009759	.010019	.010284	.010552	.010825	.011101	.011380	.011644	.011951
13	.009247	.009512	.009781	.010054	.010331	.010612	.010897	.011186	.011478
14	.008812	.009081	.009354	.009631	.009913	.010199	.010489	.010784	.011082
15	.008439	.008711	.008988	.009270	.009557	.009847	.010143	.010442	.010746
16	.008114	.008391	.008672	.008958	.009249	.009545	.009845	.010150	.010459
17	.007831	.008111	.008397	.008687	.008983	.009283	.009588	.009898	.010212
18	.007582	.007866	.008155	.008450	.008750	.009055	.009364	.009679	.009998
19	.007361	.007649	.007942	.008241	.008545	.008854	.009169	.009488	.009813
20	.007164	.007456	.007753	.008056	.008364	.008678	.008997	.009321	.009650
21	.006989	.007284	.007585	.007892	.008204	.008522	.008846	.009174	.009508
22	.006831	.007129	.007434	.007745	.008062	.008384	.008712	.009045	.009382
23	.006688	.006991	.007299	.007614	.007935	.008261	.008593	.008930	.009272
24	.006560	.006865	.007178	.007496	.007821	.008151	.008487	.008828	.009174
25	.006443	.006752	.007068	.007390	.007718	.008052	.008392	.008737	.009087
26	.006337	.006649	.006968	.007294	.007626	.007964	.008307	.008656	.009010
27	.006240	.006556	.006878	.007207	.007543	.007884	.008231	.008584	.008941
28	.006151	.006470	.006796	.007129	.007468	.007812	.008163	.008519	.008880
29	.006070	.006392	.006721	.007057	.007399	.007748	.008102	.008461	.008825
30	.005996	.006321	.006653	.006992	.007338	.007689	.008046	.008409	.008776

10.5%	11.0%	11.5%	12.0%	13.0%	14.0%	15.0%	16.0%	17.0%
.088149	.088382	.088615	.088849	.089317	.089787	.090258	.090731	.091205
.046376	.046608	.046840	.047073	.047542	.048013	.048487	.048963	.049442
.032502	.032739	.032976	.033214	.033694	.034178	.034665	.035157	.035653
.025603	.025846	.026089	.026334	.026827	.027326	.027831	.028340	.028855
.021494	.021742	.021993	.022244	.022753	.023268	.023790	.024318	.024853
.018779	.019034	.019291	.019550	.020074	.020606	.021145	.021692	.022246
.016861	.017122	.017386	.017653	.018192	.018740	.019297	.019862	.020436
.015440	.015708	.015979	.016253	.016807	.017372	.017945	.018529	.019121
.014351	.014626	.014904	.015184	.015754	.016334	.016924	.017525	.018136
.013494	.013775	.014060	.014347	.014931	.015527	.016133	.016751	.017380
.012804	.013092	.013384	.013678	.014276	.014887	.015509	.016143	.016788
.012241	.012536	.012833	.013134	.013746	.014371	.015009	.015658	.016319
.011775	.012075	.012379	.012687	.013312	.013951	.014603	.015267	.015943
.011384	.011691	.012001	.012314	.012953	.013605	.014270	.014948	.015638
.011054	.011366	.011682	.012002	.012652	.013317	.013996	.014687	.015390
.010772	.011090	.011412	.011737	.012400	.013077	.013768	.014471	.015186
.010531	.010854	.011181	.011512	.012186	012875	.013577	.014292	.015018
.010322	.010650	.010983	.011320	.012004	.012704	.013417	.014142	.014879
.010141	.010475	.010812	.011154	.011849	.012559	.013282	.014017	.014764
.009984	.010322	.010664	.011011	.011716	.012435	.013168	.013913	.014668
.009846	.010189	.010536	.010887	.011601	.012330	.013071	.013824	.014588
.009725	.010072	.010424	.010779	.011502	.012239	.012989	.013750	.014521
.009619	.009970	.010326	.010686	.011417	.012162	.012919	.013687	.014465
.009525	.009880	.010240	.010604	.011343	.012095	.012859	.013634	.014418
.009442	.009801	.010165	.010532	.011278	.012038	.012808	.013589	.014378
.009368	.009731	.010098	.010470	.011222	.011988	.012765	.013551	.014345
.009303	.009670	.010040	.010414	.011174	.011945	.012727	.013518	.014317
.009245	.009615	.009989	.010366	.011131	.011908	.012695	.013491	.014293
.009193	.009566	.009943	.010324	.011094	.011876	.012668	.013467	.014273
.009147	.009523	.009903	.010286	.011062	.011849	.012644	.013448	.014257

TABLE A.5 How $1 Deposited at the End of Each Year Will Grow (CFIFa)

$$CFIFa = \frac{(1 + i)^n - 1}{i}$$

Years	1%	2%	3%	4%	5%	6%	7%	8%	9%
1	1.00000	1.00000	1.00000	1.00000	1.00000	1.00000	1.00000	1.00000	1.00000
2	2.01000	2.02000	2.03000	2.04000	2.05000	2.06000	2.07000	2.08000	2.09000
3	3.03010	3.06040	3.09090	3.12160	3.15250	3.18360	3.21490	3.24640	3.27810
4	4.06040	4.12161	4.18363	4.24646	4.31013	4.37462	4.43994	4.50611	4.57313
5	5.10101	5.20404	5.30914	5.41632	5.52563	5.63709	5.75074	5.86660	5.98471
6	6.15202	6.30812	6.46841	6.63298	6.80191	6.97532	7.15329	7.33593	7.52334
7	7.21354	7.43428	7.66246	7.89829	8.14201	8.39384	8.65402	8.92280	9.20044
8	8.28567	8.58297	8.89234	9.21423	9.54911	9.89747	10.25980	10.63663	11.02847
9	9.36853	9.75463	10.15911	10.58280	11.02656	11.49132	11.97799	12.48756	13.02104
10	10.46221	10.94972	11.46388	12.00611	12.57789	13.18079	13.81645	14.48656	15.19293
11	11.56683	12.16872	12.80780	13.48635	14.20679	14.97164	15.78360	16.64549	17.56029
12	12.68250	13.41209	14.19203	15.02581	15.91713	16.86994	17.88845	18.97713	20.14072
13	13.80933	14.68033	15.61779	16.62684	17.71298	18.88214	20.14064	21.49530	22.95338
14	14.94742	15.97394	17.08632	18.29191	19.59863	21.01507	22.55049	24.21492	26.01919
15	16.09690	17.29342	18.59891	20.02359	21.57856	23.27597	25.12902	27.15211	29.36092
16	17.25786	18.63929	20.15688	21.82453	23.65749	25.67253	27.88805	30.32428	33.00340
17	18.43044	20.01207	21.76159	23.69751	25.84037	28.21288	30.84022	33.75023	36.97370
18	19.61475	21.41231	23.41444	25.64541	28.13238	30.90565	33.99903	37.45024	41.30134
19	20.81090	22.84056	25.11687	27.67123	30.53900	33.75999	37.37896	41.44626	46.01846
20	22.01900	24.29737	26.87037	29.77808	33.06595	36.78559	40.99549	45.76196	51.16012
21	23.23919	25.78332	28.67649	31.96920	35.71925	39.99273	44.86518	50.42292	56.76453
22	24.47159	27.29898	30.53678	34.24797	38.50521	43.39229	49.00574	55.45676	62.87334
23	25.71630	28.84496	32.45288	36.61789	41.43048	46.99583	53.43614	60.89330	69.53194
24	26.97346	30.42186	34.42647	39.08260	44.50200	50.81558	58.17667	66.76476	76.78981
25	28.24320	32.03030	36.45926	41.64591	47.72710	54.86451	63.24904	73.10594	84.70090
26	29.52563	33.67091	38.55304	44.31174	51.11345	59.15638	68.67647	79.95442	93.32398
27	30.82089	35.34432	40.70963	47.08421	54.66913	63.70577	74.48382	87.35077	102.72310
28	32.12910	37.05121	42.93092	49.96758	58.40258	68.52811	80.69769	95.33883	112.96820
29	33.45039	38.79223	45.21885	52.96629	62.32271	73.63980	87.34653	103.96590	124.13540
30	34.78489	40.56808	47.57542	56.08494	66.43885	79.05819	94.46079	113.28320	136.30750

10%	12%	14%	16%	18%	20%	22%	24%	26%
1.00000	1.00000	1.00000	1.00000	1.00000	1.00000	1.00000	1.00000	1.00000
2.10000	2.12000	2.14000	2.16000	2.18000	2.20000	2.22000	2.24000	2.26000
3.31000	3.37440	3.43960	3.50560	3.57240	3.64000	3.70840	3.77760	3.84760
4.64100	4.77933	4.92114	5.06650	5.21543	5.36800	5.52425	5.68422	5.84798
6.10510	6.35285	6.61010	6.87714	7.15421	7.44160	7.73958	8.04844	8.36845
7.71561	8.11519	8.53552	8.97748	9.44197	9.92992	10.44229	10.98006	11.54425
9.48717	10.08901	10.73049	11.41387	12.14152	12.91590	13.73959	14.61528	15.54575
11.43589	12.29969	13.23276	14.24009	15.32700	16.49908	17.76231	19.12294	20.58765
13.57948	14.77566	16.08535	17.51851	19.08585	20.79890	22.67001	24.71245	26.94043
15.93742	17.54874	19.33730	21.32147	23.52131	25.95868	28.65742	31.64344	34.94495
18.53117	20.65458	23.04452	25.73290	28.75514	32.15042	35.96205	40.23787	45.03063
21.38428	24.13313	27.27075	30.85017	34.93107	39.58050	44.87370	50.89495	57.73860
24.52271	28.02911	32.08865	36.78620	42.21866	48.49660	55.74591	64.10974	73.75063
27.97498	32.39260	37.58107	43.67199	50.81802	59.19592	69.01001	80.49608	93.92580
31.77248	37.27971	43.84241	51.65951	60.96527	72.03511	85.19221	100.81510	119.34650
35.94973	42.75328	50.98035	60.92503	72.93901	87.44213	104.93450	126.01080	151.37660
40.54470	48.88367	59.11760	71.67303	87.06804	105.93060	129.02010	157.25340	191.73450
45.59917	55.74971	68.39407	84.14072	103.74030	128.11670	158.40450	195.99420	242.58550
51.15909	63.43968	78.96923	98.60323	123.41350	154.74000	194.25350	244.03280	306.65770
57.27500	72.05244	91.02493	115.37970	146.62800	186.68800	237.98930	303.60060	387.38870
64.00250	81.69874	104.76840	134.84050	174.02100	225.02560	291.34690	377.46480	489.10980
71.40275	92.50258	120.43600	157.41500	206.34480	271.03070	356.44320	469.05630	617.27830
79.54302	104.60290	138.29700	183.60140	244.48680	326.23690	435.86070	582.62980	778.77070
88.49733	118.15520	158.65860	213.97760	289.49450	392.48420	532.75010	723.46100	982.25110
98.34706	133.33390	181.87080	249.21400	342.60350	471.98110	650.95510	898.09160	1238.63600
109.18180	150.33390	208.33270	290.08830	405.27210	567.37730	795.16530	1114.63400	1561.68200
121.09990	169.37400	238.49930	337.50240	479.22110	681.85280	971.10160	1383.14600	1968.71900
134.20990	190.69890	272.88920	392.50280	566.48090	819.22330	1185.74400	1716.10100	2481.58600
148.63090	214.58280	312.09370	456.30320	669.44750	984.06800	1447.60800	2128.96500	3127.79800
164.49400	241.33270	356.78680	530.31170	790.94800	1181.88200	1767.08100	2640.91600	3942.02600

APPENDIX B

Normal Distribution Table

Area of Normal Distribution that Is X Standard Deviations to the Left or Right of the Mean

Number of Standard Deviations	Area to the Left or Right	Number of Standard Deviations	Area to the Left or Right
0.00	0.5000	1.55	0.0606
0.05	0.4801	1.60	0.0548
0.10	0.4602	1.65	0.0495
0.15	0.4404	1.70	0.0446
0.20	0.4207	1.75	0.0401
0.25	0.4013	1.80	0.0359
0.30	0.3821	1.85	0.0322
0.35	0.3632	1.90	0.0287
0.40	0.3446	1.95	0.0256
0.45	0.3264	2.00	0.0228
0.50	0.3085	2.05	0.0202
0.55	0.2912	2.10	0.0179
0.60	0.2743	2.15	0.0158
0.65	0.2578	2.20	0.0139
0.70	0.2420	2.25	0.0122
0.75	0.2264	2.30	0.0107
0.80	0.2119	2.35	0.0094
0.85	0.1977	2.40	0.0082
0.90	0.1841	2.45	0.0071
0.95	0.1711	2.50	0.0062
1.00	0.1587	2.55	0.0054
1.05	0.1469	2.60	0.0047
1.10	0.1357	2.65	0.0040
1.15	0.1251	2.70	0.0035
1.20	0.1151	2.75	0.0030
1.25	0.1056	2.80	0.0026
1.30	0.0968	2.85	0.0022
1.35	0.0885	2.90	0.0019
1.40	0.0808	2.95	0.0016
1.45	0.0735	3.00	0.0013
1.50	0.0668		

APPENDIX C

Key Formulas and Frequently Used Symbols

SUMMARY OF KEY FORMULAS

Compound Interest and Discount

1. Future value (compound amount):
$$FV = PV(1 + i)^n$$

2. Present value:
$$PV = FV/(1 + i)^n$$

3. Future (compound) value of an annuity:
$$FV = PMT \times \left([(1 + i)^n - 1]/i\right)$$

4. Present value of an annuity:
$$PV = Pmt \times \left[\left(1 - [1/(1 + i)^n]\right)/i\right]$$

Investment Analysis Relationships

1. Net present value:
$$NPV = \sum_{t=1}^{n} ATCF_t/(1 + i)^t - \text{Initial equity investment}$$

2. Internal rate of return (IRR):
$$\sum_{t=1}^{n} ATCF_t/(1 + IRR)^t - \text{Initial equity investment} = 0$$

3. Profitability index:
$$PI = \text{PV of benefits}/\text{Initial equity investment}$$

Standard Deviation of the Present Value Distribution

1. With perfect serial correlation:
$$\sigma_{pv} = \sigma_\alpha/(1 + i)^t$$

2. With zero serial correlation:
$$\sigma_{pv} = \sqrt{\sigma^2_\alpha/(1 + i)^{2t}}$$

3. Hillier's model:
$$\sigma_{pv} = \sqrt{\sigma^2_{yt}/(1 + i)^{2t} + [\sigma_{xt}/(1 + i)^t]^2}$$

FREQUENTLY USED SYMBOLS

ATCF	After-tax cash flow
CF_t	Cash flow in year t
$\overline{CF}$	Mean of a probability distribution of possible cash flows
CV	Covariance
CVIF	Compound value interest factor
CVIFa	Compound value interest factor for an annuity
FV	Future value
IRR	Internal rate of return
i	Interest rate
k	Discount or capitalization factor; the cost of capital
PV	Present value
PVIF	Present value interest factor
PVIFa	Present value interest factor for an annuity
Q	Quantity produced, purchased or sold
PMT	Periodic payment or receipt
R_f	Risk-free interest rate
S_n	Compound sum
σ	Standard deviation
σ^2	Variance
t	Time period
Z	Number of standard deviations from the mean

Glossary

absolute monopoly. A market that has only one supplier of a good or service for which there are no reasonably acceptable substitutes.

absorption rates. Rates at which the market will "absorb" a product; the rate at which units will be purchased.

abstract and opinion. A summary of the chain of past title transfers for real property and an attorney's written opinion that the title contains no defects.

abstract of title. A brief summary of each recorded document pertaining to title to a specified parcel of land.

accelerated method. A method of computing depreciation or cost recovery allowances whereby large annual allowances are claimed in the early years of ownership, offset by smaller allowances in later years.

acceleration clause. A clause that permits the mortgagee to declare the full amount of a debt due and payable if the mortgagor defaults on any of the agreed-upon terms.

acceptance. The act of a party to whom a thing is offered by another, whereby he or she receives the thing with the intention of retaining it.

accredited purchasers. Investors who either (1) are sufficiently wealthy so that a contemplated securities purchase (of $150,000 or more) will not exceed 20 percent of their net worth, (2) have a net worth in excess of $1 million or (3) have a two-year earnings record of more than $200,000 per annum and expect their current earnings to exceed $200,000.

accretion. A gradual increase in land area adjacent to a body of water because of soil deposited by wave and current action.

accrued depreciation. A loss in value due to physical deterioration, functional obsolescence and economic or locational disadvantages.

acknowledgment. Certification by a notary public or other appropriate public official that the grantor has stated before the official that he or she executed the acknowledged document.

ad valorem. A Latin term used to describe the taxing of property according to value.

adjusted basis. The amount paid for property, plus all subsequent capital expenditures made to improve it, minus all tax deductions for depreciation or cost recovery allowances.

adjusted gross income. Gross taxable income minus a set of specific deductions spelled out in the Internal Revenue Code.

adjusted rate of return. Modified version of the internal rate of return, designed to eliminate problems associated with negative cash flows.

adverse possession. Wrongful occupancy of real estate in a manner and for a time period described in state statutes. Title then vests in the adverse possessor by operation of law and is independent of any previously recorded title to the property.

affirmative covenant. A mutual promise between neighbors that a property will be used in some specified manner.

after-tax cash flow. Cash flow generated from a property after accounting for all operating expenses, all debt service obligations and all income tax consequences for the current period.

agglomeration economies. An amorphous term referring to cost reductions ascribed to proximity.

all-inclusive mortgage. See wraparound mortgage.

alternative minimum tax. A provision that specifies the minimum amount of federal income tax for which all taxpayers are liable. After computing tax liability the regular way, taxpayers must perform the alternative computation. They are required to pay the greater of the regular or the alternative minimum tax.

alternative minumum taxable income. The income upon which liability for the alternative minimum tax is computed.

amortization table. A schedule of equal periodic payments necessary to repay a $1 loan, with interest, over a specified number of payment periods.

amortize. To claim an expenditure, which is incurred at the beginning of the period, as an annual expense or income tax deduction over an extended period of years.

anchor tenants. Tenants who are expected to attract customers to a shopping center and thereby generate business for other merchants in the center.

annual compounding. Accumulated interest that in and of itself earns interest in all subsequent periods.

annual mortgage constant. The percent of the original principal amount that must be paid annually in order to fully repay interest and principal over the term of the loan.

annuity. Any series of periodic payments received or paid at regular intervals.

annuity table. A schedule providing factors used to calculate the present value of a compound level annuity.

articles of agreement. See installment sales contract.

asset liquidity. See liquidity.

assignment. Transfer of contractual rights from one contracting party (the assignor) to another person (the assignee) who is not a party to the contract.

assumption clause. A clause whereby mortgagors agree not to sell mortgaged property subject to the mortgage or to have a buyer assume an existing mortgage without prior approval of the mortgagee.

assumption fee. A fee charged by a lender as a condition for permitting assumption of mortgage indebtedness by a party other than the original mortgagor. This permits mortgagees to adjust their rates of return to the current market when interest rates have risen.

atomistic markets. A market in which no one person or group can measurably affect market prices. Market participants are simply price takers, in that they have a choice of accepting prevailing prices or of not participating in the market at all.

avulsion. A sudden and perceptible shift in land boundaries due to floods or sudden alterations in the course of rivers or streams.

band of investment technique. A technique used to calculate the weighted average cost of capital for a property. The cost of each source of funds is weighted by a factor equal to the proportion of total funds that will be derived from that source.

base lines. A set of imaginary lines running east and west employed by surveyors for reference in locating and describing land under the government survey method of property description.

basic rate. The sum of the weighted average cost of capital and the equity buildup factor used in order to determine the appropriate overall capitalization rate.

bid-rent curve. A functional relationship that depicts the absolute maximum rent a firm with a specific profit profile can pay and still find remaining in business a worthwhile endeavor.

blanket mortgage. The pledge of two or more parcels of property as security for a single loan.

blind pool syndication. A form of limited partnership in which the promoter assembles a group of investors with the purpose of acquiring an undesignated asset of a specific type.

book value. The value at which assets are recorded on a firm's books of account (that is, its accounting records); usually cost minus accumulated depreciation or cost recovery allowances.

boot. (See also like-kind exchange) Assets received as consideration in what would otherwise be an exchange of entirely like-kind assets. Receipt of boot may trigger tax liability in what would otherwise be a tax-deferred transaction.

breakeven ratio. The relationship between cash expenditure requirements and gross revenue from an investment project. Sometimes called a *default ratio*.

broker's rate of return. A rate-of-return measure that adjusts the cash-on-cash return to include equity buildup from debt amortization and thereby shows a slightly more favorable return than does the cash-on-cash measure.

building codes. The set of laws that establishes minimum standards for constructing new buildings or altering existing structures. Building codes are intended to ensure minimum protection against fire damage and to safeguard against faulty design in construction.

business risk. Risk stemming from the possibility of making inappropriate business decisions or of misjudging the economic consequences of actions.

capital assets. All assets held by a taxpayer (whether or not connected with the person's trade or business) except those specifically enumerated by the Commissioner of Internal Revenue. Generally, assets of a fixed or permanent nature or those employed in carrying on a business or trade.

capital expenditure. An expenditure of funds that extends the useful life of a capital asset or adds to its value.

capital formation. The raising of debt or equity funds for real estate projects.

capital goods. Products destined to be employed in the production of other goods or services.

capitalization rate. The relationship between net income from a real estate investment and the value of the investment. This relationship is usually expressed as a percentage.

capitalize. To add an amount to the tax basis of a property.

capital recovery. The portion of an overall capitalization rate comprised of recovery of owner's capital outlay.

cash-on-cash rate of return. The first year's expected after-tax cash flow, divided by the initial cash outlay required to acquire the investment.

central business district. The focal point of urban places where goods and services are exchanged.

central place theory. The postulate that if the surrounding countryside were a flat, undifferentiated plane, central places would be located so as to minimize the distance from all points in the tributary area. It states further that the larger the city, the larger its tributary area must be.

certainty equivalents. Substitute cash flows determined by the certainty-equivalent technique.

certainty-equivalent technique. A procedure that seeks to establish substitute cash flows that leave an investor indifferent between absolutely certain receipt of the substitute amounts and the expectation of receiving the point estimates, along with attendant risk.

certificate of limited partnership. A document that must be filed with the appropriate state agency to create a limited partnership.

certified historic structure. (See also registered historic district) Any structure that is either listed in the National Registry of Historic Places or located in a registered historic district and certified as being of historic significance to the district.

ceteris paribus. A Latin term used by economists to mean that demand schedules are applicable only so long as all factors other than price that influence buyer behavior do not change.

city planning. A procedure for formulating land-use schemes, employed by municipalities in their efforts to reach specified goals in the utilization of land within the municipality.

coefficient of correlation. A measure of the extent to which the values of variables in a sample or a population are interdependent.

coefficient of determination. A measure of the percent of variation in the dependent variable associated with variation in the value of the independent variable. In regression analysis, designated by the term *r-square* (r^2).

coefficient of multiple correlation. A measure of the percentage of variance in the dependent variable that is "explained" by variation in the independent variables.

coefficient of serial correlation. A measure of the degree to which outcomes in subsequent periods are related. Possible coefficients range from zero to plus-or-minus one.

coefficient of variation. Standard deviation of the distribution of possible outcomes, divided by the expected outcome.

collective goods. See public goods.

commitment letter. A letter to a prospective borrower, wherein a lender states terms and conditions under which it will provide the requested funds. A precise period is usually specified during which the commitment remains effective. Commitment letters generally state conditions under which the lender may revoke the commitment and set forth any further provisions upon which the commitment is contingent.

community shopping center. A shopping center that typically draws most of its customers from an area extending from ten to 15 minutes in driving time. Community shopping centers usually feature a food store and a junior department store or a discount store as anchor tenants. Size may range from 50,000 to 100,000 square feet of retail space.

comparative advantage. An economic principle developed by the economist David Ricardo that provides an explanation of why some areas tend to concentrate on producing a limited number of goods and seek much of what they consume from other areas.

comparative sales approach. An appraisal procedure that analyzes recent sales data from similar properties and draws inferences about the value of the property being appraised.

comparative unit method. A valuation approach that estimates costs by comparison with similar buildings whose construction costs are known. To render buildings of slightly different size more directly comparable, costs are expressed on the basis of some standardized unit of measure, such as per square foot or per cubic foot.

complements. Goods or services whose consumption occurs in tandem with that of the item in question. A change in the price of one good or service can cause a shift in the demand curves for its complements.

compound amount. The summation of principal and compounded interest over a specified holding period.

compound interest. Interest income attributable to previously accrued interest that has been left on deposit.

concentric zone model. An urban economic model developed by Earnest W. Burgess in the 1920s. The concentric zone model was designed to explain urban development through the use of transitional zones.

concessions. See rent concessions.

condemnation proceeding. The consequence of a property owner's refusal to voluntarily convey title at a price offered by a governmental agency seeking to convert the property to public use.

condominium. An ownership arrangement whereby title to specified portions of a property vests in individual users, and title to common area vests in all users jointly.

condominium association. An association, composed of all those owning interest in a condominium, which serves as a governing and managing body, usually through an elected board of directors.

condominium declaration. The enabling document that creates a condominium. The declaration describes both individual and common areas of the premises and provides for assessment of owners for costs of maintaining and insuring common areas.

conduit. See tax conduit.

consideration. Under contract law, the impelling reason to enter into a contract. Something of value given in exchange for a promise.

constructive notice. A legal doctrine under which notice may be attributed even though a party may be completely ignorant of the facts.

Recording statutes provide that recording a document in the public record constitutes constructive notice to the world.

consumer good. The end product of the production process.

consumer price index. An index of changes in the price of a representative "market basket" of consumer goods, relating the current price to that in a designated base year.

contract for deed. See installment sales contract.

contract price. Total selling price minus any pre-existing mortgage to which a property will remain subject when sold under conditions permitting the transaction to be reported for tax computation purposes under the installment sales method. If the pre-existing mortgage exceeds the seller's adjusted basis in the property, the excess of the mortgage over the seller's basis must be added back to the contract price.

cooperative. An apartment the tenant purchases by buying stock in the corporation that owns the building rather than simply buying the apartment.

corporations. Artificial entities, created under state laws, that are empowered to own property and transact business in their own names. They may buy, sell and otherwise enter into contracts. As legal entities, corporations have an identity separate and distinct from that of their owners.

cost approach. An appraisal technique whereby an estimate of land value is added to the estimated cost of reproducing existing improvements on the land (net of accrued depreciation) to derive a value estimate for the entire property.

cost recovery allowance. An income tax rule that provides for recovery of capital expenditures on property having a finite useful life, acquired on or after January 1, 1981, and used in a trade or business or for production of income.

cost recovery assets. Assets on which tax-deductible cost recovery allowances may be claimed.

cotenancy. Real property title held in the name of two or more owners.

counseling. Providing competent, unbiased advice on diversified problems in the broad field of real estate involving any or all segments of the business, such as merchandising, leasing, management, planning, financing, appraising, court testimony and other similar services.

covenant against removal. A restriction imposed by the mortgagee prohibiting the mortgagor from removing or demolishing any part of the building without the lender's consent.

covenant against waste. A restriction imposed by a mortgagee prohibiting the mortgagor from allowing the building to deteriorate during the period of the mortgage.

covenant of insurance. A mortgage clause in which the mortgagor promises to maintain adequate insurance coverage against fire and other specified hazards.

covenant of seizin. (See also seizin) A mortgage clause whereby the mortgagor warrants that he or she is the lawful owner of the property being mortgaged.

covenant of title. A promise or assurance made by the grantor in connection with title transfer.

covenants. Promises that property will, or will not, be used in some specified manner.

covenant to pay taxes. A common mortgage clause in which the mortgagor promises to pay all property taxes and assessments levied against the property during the period of the mortgage.

cross-sectional surveys. Surveys involving one-time sampling from a population of research interest. All elements are measured at a single point in time. Cross-sectional surveys provide a "snapshot" of the variables under observation as of the time of the survey.

curtesy. A husband's interest in his wife's property.

custom construction. A construction project that takes place on land owned by the ultimate purchaser, involving a structure built to the exact specifications of the purchaser/user.

dealer. In real estate, one who is in the business of buying and selling property interests for one's own account. Gains on dealers' sales are reported as ordinary income rather than as capital gains.

debentures. Bonds secured by the borrower's income stream.

debt amortization. The process of gradually extinguishing a debt by a series of periodic payments to the creditor.

debt constant. The percentage of the original principal amount that must be paid annually in order to fully repay interest and principal over the term of the loan. The constant can be expressed as an annual percentage or monthly percentage. Sometimes called a *debt service constant*.

debt coverage ratio. The relationship between a project's annual net operating income and the obligation to make principal and interest payments on borrowed funds. Debt coverage ratios are often employed to evaluate a lender's margin of safety regarding mortgage loans.

debt service. Payments to a lender. Debt service obligations may involve payment of interest only or both principal and interest so as to fully or partially amortize a debt over a specified term.

debt service constant. See debt constant.

debt-to-equity ratio. The ratio between borrowed funds and equity funds.

decision model. A systematic process for identifying opportunities that show promise of contributing adequately to predetermined investment goals.

declining balance method. A method of computing annual depreciation or cost recovery allowances that provides the greatest allowance in the first year of ownership and progressively smaller allowances for each successive year.

decree. The judgment of a court of equity, ordering execution of the provisions of that judgment.

deed. A legal document that conveys title in real property from one party to another. The document must be signed, witnessed, delivered and accepted.

deed of trust. A deed passing title to property from an owner to a trustee, who holds that property as collateral for a mortgage loan advanced by another. Also called a *trust deed* or *trust indenture*.

default. A mortgagor's failure to fulfill any of the agreed-upon terms in a security agreement.

default ratio. See breakeven ratio.

defeasance clause. Mortgage provisions intended to render nominal conveyance void upon satisfaction of the mortgagor's obligation.

deficiency judgment. A judgment against a debtor's personal assets beyond those assets owned on a defaulted debt instrument.

delivery. The legal act of transferring ownership of real estate.

demand. An economic term that refers to the entire range of relationships between price and quantity.

demand curve. A graphic illustration of the relationship between price and the quantity of a good or service buyers will take off the market. Also called a *demand function*.

demand function. See demand curve.

demand schedule. A table that relates quantity demanded to a good's or service's price, at all relevant prices.

demand to purchase. Desired increase in a market participant's inventory of a product, at a specific price.

dependency exemption. An amount of adjusted gross income that taxpayers may exempt from taxable income for each person dependent upon them for financial support.

dependent variable. In regression or correlation analysis, a variable whose value is thought to be affected by the value of other variables (independent variables) included in the analysis.

deposit insurance. An insurance program that protects depositors from loss due to bank failures.

depreciable asset. See depreciable property.

depreciable property. Property upon which a tax-deductible depreciation allowance may be claimed.

depreciation. Decline in an asset's value or useful life, due to wear, tear, action of the elements or obsolescence.

depreciation allowance. A tax-deductible allowance to account for the decline in value or useful life of an asset due to wear, tear, obsolescence or action of the elements.

derived demand. Demand for a good or service that stems from the use of that good or service in the production of something else.

descriptive statistics. A statistical application that employs quantitative expressions to describe characteristics of a sample or an underlying population.

development. A real estate activity that involves adding improvements such as buildings.

differentiated product. Products that are sufficiently different from competitive products to reduce the degree of substitutability. Producers of differentiated products have some degree of control over price.

diminishing marginal utility. The economic principle that as additional units of a good are possessed or consumed per unit of time, the additional (marginal) utility of each successive unit is less than that of the preceding unit.

discounted cash-flow approach. An investment evaluation technique that incorporates adjustments for both volume and timing of anticipated future cash flows and is generally accepted as the most desirable approach to evaluating opportunities.

discounting. Expressing anticipated future cash flows as present-worth equivalents.

discount points. A reduction in net loan proceeds to make the effective interest rate equal the current market rate.

discount rate. A rate that measures return on investment after the recovery of invested capital.

discrete probability distribution. A probability distribution in which possible outcomes are limited in number.

disintermediation. The situation where people, seeking better yields, withdraw their savings from major institutional lenders and participate directly in financial markets.

diversification. The reduction in total risk through holding a variety of property types and spreading ownership over a wide geographic area.

dominant tenement. Land that reaps the benefit of an easement.

dower. A wife's interest in her husband's property.

dram shop insurance. Insurance against liability arising from incidents related to liquor consumption.

due process. Proceedings in accordance with legal precedent, statutes and constitutional provisions, designed to protect the rights of all parties to a dispute.

earnest money. Money paid as evidence of good faith or actual intent to complete a transaction, usually forfeited by willful failure to complete the transaction.

earnest money deposit. A good faith deposit into an escrow account (or into a broker's trust account), typically accompanied by a purchase offer.

easement. Nonpossessory interest that permits limited use of someone else's land. Conveys only a right to use the land.

easement appurtenant. An easement created on one parcel of land (the servient tenement) for the benefit of an adjacent parcel (the dominant tenement).

easement by expressed grant. Easement created by a specific agreement between the affected parties.

easement by implication. An easement created as a consequence of a landowner selling property to which access requires crossing other property that the landowner also owns. Easements by implication are created when reasonably necessary, when the need is apparent at the time property is conveyed and when the need appears to be permanent in nature.

easement by prescription. An easement acquired through the open, continuous, adverse use of real property for a specified period of time.

easement in gross. An easement that constitutes personal property, independent of any related land interest.

economic base analysis. A study that divides economic activity into domestic and export sectors and seeks to determine the degree to which activity in the domestic sector is dependent upon the level of activity in the export sector.

economic base theory. An explanation of urban growth that postulates that total economic activity in an urban area is a function of the level of activity in its export sector.

economic obsolescence. Loss in value due to inappropriate location.

Economic Recovery Tax Act of 1981. A major revision of the Internal Revenue Code, enacted into law in 1981.

economic rent. Profit generated by a good or service in excess of the profit necessary to induce firms to produce the good or service. Sometimes referred to as *pure profit.*

effective gross income. Potential gross rental revenue, minus losses for vacancies and uncollectible accounts, plus income from related sources.

effective interest rates. Rates actually paid for the use of borrowed funds. Effective rates are a function of the amount borrowed and the amount and timing of the required repayment.

efficient markets. Markets in which all relevant information is immediately and fully reflected in market prices. Participants in efficient markets are unable to consistently achieve above-average market yields. The hypothesis that a market is completely efficient is referred to as the strong form of the efficiency hypothesis.

eminent domain. Authority vested in both federal and state governments allowing them to take private property for public use without the owner's consent.

encumbrances. A lien, charge or claim against real property that diminishes the value of the property but does not prevent the passing of title.

end loan. A loan secured by a mortgage on a completed building, terminating a chain of loans to finance land acquisition and construction. Also called a *permanent loan* or a *takeout loan.*

end-loan commitment. An agreement by a lender to provide an end loan upon satisfaction of all contingencies specified by the lender.

equilibrium. In economics, a stable, balanced or unchanging system. A situation in which there is no tendency for anything to change.

equilibrium price. The price at which there will be sufficient quantity of a product to satisfy the desires of all consumers at that price but with no surplus remaining on the market; the market clearing price.

equitable right of redemption. The legal right of a borrower, or the borrower's heirs or assigns, to redeem mortgaged property for a limited period of time after default. Also called *equity of redemption.*

equity. The concept of fairness and justice applied to the portion of common law relating to the rights and duties of individuals. Also the money value of what is owned, arrived at by subtracting all that is owed from the value of the ownership to arrive at a net ownership value figure.

equity buildup. The accumulation and growth of the money value of what is owned. That is, an increase in the net financial interest in a specific property.

equity dividend rate. Before-tax cash flow expressed as a percentage of the required initial equity cash outlay.

equity of redemption. See equitable right of redemption.

equity REIT. A type of real estate investment trust that concentrates its resources on equity interests in real property.

equity yield rate. Interest earned on recovered capital.

escalator clause. Lease clause that requires tenants to pay all operating expenses above amounts specified in the lease.

escheat. The legal principle that property title reverts to the state when an intestate owner (one with no will) dies with no heirs.

escrow. The holding by a third party of something of value that is the subject of a contract between two other parties until the contract has been consummated.

escrow agent. A disinterested third party who acts as agent for parties to an escrow agreement.

escrow agreement. A contract between parties to a transaction and a third party who functions as an escrow agent. The agreement contains written escrow instructions, which govern the agent's action in performance of his or her escrow duties.

estate for years. A leasehold interest that extends for an exactly specified period, after which the interest automatically expires.

estate subject to a condition precedent. An estate created (rather than terminated) upon the happening of some specified contingency.

excess accumulated earnings tax. A penalty tax levied on corporations that accumulate earnings in excess of corporate needs.

excess cost recovery allowance. Cost recovery allowance actually claimed, minus what would have been claimed had the taxpayer used the straight-line cost recovery method from the beginning.

executory. A contract that lacks some necessary performance by one of its parties and is therefore not yet completed.

expected value. The midpoint of a symmetric probability distribution; the most likely outcome.

explicit transfer costs. (See also implicit transfer costs) Costs measurable in dollars; specifically, cost per mile of chosen transportation mode, plus the dollar value of the time spent en route.

external costs. (See also external diseconomies) Costs incurred by the public from the act or nonact of a private party.

external diseconomies. External costs where benefits accrue to the decision maker while costs are borne by others.

external economies. (See also externality) A good side effect of production or consumption, for which no payment is received or made.

externality. A good or bad side effect of production or consumption, for which no payment is received or made.

facilities management. Overseeing the physical upkeep of properties as well as keeping records of income and expenses associated with their operation.

factor of production. Goods or services that are themselves intended to be utilized in producing other goods or service.

feasibility study. Estimate of the likelihood of achieving explicit project objectives through a proposed course of action, given a specific set of constraints and limited resources.

Federal Deposit Insurance Corporation (FDIC). An independent federal agency that insures deposits up to a certain amount in all national banks and in all state banks that have been accepted as FDIC members.

fee simple absolute. The greatest real property interest recognized by law. This term expresses the idea that the interest is held with no preconditions or qualifications.

fee simple defeasible. A qualified fee estate that may be subject to a condition subsequent or determinable, depending upon the nature of the qualification. Some states also permit creation of fees subject to conditions precedent.

fee simple estate. Any real property interest.

fee splitting. Analogous to life estates and remainders whereby title passes to or reverts upon the occurrence of some event.

fee subject to a condition subsequent. A fee that extends only until the happening of some specified act or event.

fee tail. A carryover from the feudal system, requiring that title pass to lineal descendants of the property owner.

fiduciary. One who is in a position of trust or confidence with respect to another person.

financial assets. Assets such as promissory notes, bonds and commercial paper that represent financial claims rather than ownership of physical assets.

financial intermediaries. Institutions such as commercial banks, savings and loan associations, credit unions and so on that act as middlemen between savers and user-borrowers.

financial leverage. The impact of borrowed

money on investment return. That is, the use of borrowed money to amplify consequences to equity investors.

financial management rate of return. A modification of the internal rate of return, designed to eliminate problems encountered when negative cash flows are included in the forecast.

financial risk. Risk that cash flow from a project will be insufficient to meet the investor's debt service obligation.

fiscal policy. Exercise of influence on the economy by controlling government spending and taxation.

footloose industries. Industries in which firms are not restricted geographically by transportation cost considerations. Such firms frequently seek locations with a ready supply of labor or minimal labor costs.

forecasting. Predicting a future value from known, related data.

foreclosure by sale. Sale of mortgaged property at public auction as a consequence of default by the mortgagor. Foreclosure by sale extinguishes the equitable right of redemption.

foreclosure decree. A court order specifying an exact time period (a period determined by state laws) during which the equity of redemption will exist.

free and clear rate of return. See overall capitalization rate.

freehold. An estate in real property that, unless assigned or otherwise conveyed, remains in perpetuity, or for life.

fully amortized. The ultimate retirement of a mortgage debt through installment payments that include both interest and principal over the term of the loan.

functional efficiency. A measure of how well a property performs its intended function.

functional obsolescence. The loss of functional efficiency due to defective or dated design. This reduces a building's competitive position relative to more functionally efficient structures and may eventually lead to abandonment or succession of use.

fundamental analysis. An investment analysis technique that emphasizes investigation of the underlying business activity being undertaken by the firm whose securities are being considered.

gap financing. See standby financing.

general contractor. A contractor who takes full responsibility for construction of a project by formal agreement with the owner or developer and hires others as subcontractors to perform specific tasks.

general partner. See limited partnership.

general partnership. An entity in which all partners have equal rights to management and conduct of the firm; each partner is, in effect, an agent for the partnership.

gentrification. Reclamation of residential areas containing physically deteriorated buildings and restoration of a deteriorated neighborhood for the use of predominantly middle-class residents.

goods or services. (See also product) Items offered for sale in the marketplace.

graduated-payment mortgage (GPM). A mortgage that allows a borrower, in effect, to borrow additional money during the early years of the mortgage to reduce the monthly mortgage payment obligation during those early years. This additional loan is added to the mortgage and is repaid by increased debt service obligations in the later years.

grantee. A person to whom a grant is made; the purchaser.

grantor. A person who conveys real estate by deed; the seller.

gross income. For income tax computation purposes, all revenue generated from any source, unless specifically excluded by provisions of the Internal Revenue Code.

gross income multiplier. (See also income multiplier analysis and net income multiplier) Evaluation technique that describes the relationship between most probable sales price and gross revenue. Sometimes called a *gross rent multiplier.*

gross rent multiplier. See gross income multiplier.

health and safety codes. Rules and regulations

designed to promote public health and safety in the construction and/or demolition of improvements to real property.

hedging. Taking an investment position that will pay off if the investor's primary investment does not. Hedging reduces aggregate investor risk.

historic structure. See certified historic structure.

holdover tenant. A tenant who remains in possession of real estate after the expiration of the lease.

housing codes. Laws specifying minimum building standards, with the objective of promoting public health, safety or welfare.

hurdle rate. The minimum acceptable yield on investment funds. Projects that are not expected to yield at least the investor's hurdle rate are rejected.

hybrid REIT. A real estate investment trust that mixes mortgage and equity instruments in its portfolio.

implicit transfer costs. (See also explicit transfer costs) Indirect costs of moving goods or people between linked sites. Although they are often more difficult to identify than are explicit transfer costs, they may also be larger.

income. For purposes of determining federal income tax liability, all revenue generated from any source unless specifically excluded by provisions of the Internal Revenue Code.

income multiplier analysis. (See also gross income multiplier and net income multiplier) A technique for expressing the relationship between price and either gross or net income.

incubator buildings. Relatively small, multitenant structures in which new or small but growing firms rent space on an interim basis until growth generates a need for larger quarters.

independent variable. In regression or correlation analysis, a variable whose value is thought to be determined by factors other than those under analysis, but which is thought to affect the value of one or more other variables (the dependent variables) in the analysis.

indifference curve. A graphic presentation of combinations of values for two variables, representing the preferences of an individual who will be indifferent among the various combinations.

inferential statistics. The drawing of conclusions from evidence contained in statistical data.

inferior goods. Consumer goods for which demand decreases as purchasing power rises.

information search costs. The cost of generating relevant market information. High information search costs tend to reduce market efficiency.

initial tax basis. The tax basis of a property at the time of acquisition. Usually, cost plus any additional outlays required to assure good and defensible title.

installment method gain. The difference between gain on disposal of an asset that qualifies for installment method reporting and the recapture of accumulated depreciation or cost recovery allowances. Only this portion of the gain may be reported using the installment method. The remainder must be recognized in the taxable year of the transaction.

installment sales contract. Contract that sets forth terms and conditions under which a seller is obligated to render deeds of conveyance to the buyer at some future date. Also called a *land contract, contract for deed,* or *articles of agreement.*

installment sales method. A method for reporting sales to the Internal Revenue Service whereby a portion of the resulting income tax liability may be deferred when some of the proceeds from the sale are not collected during the current taxable year.

insurable risk. Risk of loss from natural hazards such as fire, flood, storm and so forth, which can be transferred to an insurance company.

interim financing. Financing used during the construction phase, to be superseded by takeout financing after construction is completed.

intermediate goods. A good combined with other goods to create consumer products.

internal rate of return. A financial analysis technique that involves setting net present value at zero and finding a discount rate to satisfy the equality condition; that is, the discount rate that makes present value exactly equal to required initial cash outlay.

Internal Revenue Code. Public Law 591— Chapter 736. This law (as subsequently revised) constitutes the statutory authority for income, employment, estate and gift taxes levied by the Internal Revenue Service. Generally referred to by tax practitioners more simply as *the Code.*

interpolation. A procedure for estimating values that fall between tabular amounts.

intrastate offering. A security issue offered for sale solely within one state by an issuer resident in or a corporation incorporated and doing business in that state. A qualifying intrastate offering is exempt from requirements for federal registration.

investment. Commitment of money or other assets in expectation of financial gain.

investment income. See portfolio income.

investment interest limitation. Provision of the Internal Revenue Code that places a dollar limit on the amount of investment interest that can be deducted in any one taxable year on loans used to finance investments.

investment tax credit. A credit against income tax liability, earned as a consequence of investing in qualifying assets.

investment value. The summation of the present value of the equity position plus the present value of the debt position. The present value of the equity position is calculated on an after-tax basis and considers the tax consequences to a specific investor.

investor. Any person or entity who takes an equity position in real estate for use in a trade or business or for production of income.

itemized deductions. Taxpayer expenditures, listed in Sections 161 through 195 of the Internal Revenue Code, that may be deducted from adjusted gross income to arrive at taxable income.

joint probabilities. The probability of joint occurrence of two or more events. The probability that both event A and event B will occur equals the probability that A will occur times the probability that B will occur, given that A occurs.

This relationship is sometimes referred to as the *multiplicative law of probability.*

joint tenancy. (See also right of survivorship) An estate held jointly by two or more persons under the same title in which each has the same degree of interest and the same right of possession. Joint tenancy usually entails the right of the surviving tenant(s) to take title to a decedent's interest (right of survivorship).

joint tenants. Parties who hold equal and undivided interests under joint tenancy.

judgment samples. A sampling technique that regards individual observations, with respect to certain characteristics, as typical of the underlying universe.

judicial partition. A court proceeding to terminate a cotenancy arrangement when the co-owners are unable to agree upon terms for sale or physical division of jointly owned real estate.

junior mortgage. A mortgage that is legally subordinate to another (senior) mortgage.

land contract. See installment sales contract.

land development. The business activity of acquiring large tracts of land, subdividing and selling off individual smaller tracts. Also frequently called *subdivision.*

land-use controls. Publicly imposed controls on land usage aimed at assuring orderly development.

lease. Legal document conveying limited right to use a property. Document generally specifies all terms of lease as well as permitted use.

leasehold. Right of a tenant in leased property.

leasehold estate. Estate of a tenant in a leased property.

leasehold interest. Interest of a tenant in a leased property.

lessee. A property owner who transfers certain rights for a limited period to a tenant. Generally referred to as a *landlord.*

lessor. The holder of a leasehold interest in a property. Generally referred to as a *tenant.*

license. Privilege to enter onto the land of a licenser in order to do certain things that would otherwise be considered trespassing.

lien. Claim against a property that allows the proceeds from a forced sale of the property to be used to satisfy the debt.

life estate. Grants a life tenant full property rights for the remainder of his or her life.

life tenant. Individual possessing full property rights in a specific property for the remainder of his or her life.

like-kind exchange. Exchanges of assets deemed under Internal Revenue Code Section 1031 to be of like kind. Gains or losses on exchanges that involve only like-kind assets must be deferred until the newly acquired (substitute) asset is disposed of. Transactions that are only partially like-kind may result in total or partial recognition of gains or losses. Also frequently called *tax-free exchanges* or *Section 1031 exchanges.*

limited partner. See limited partnership.

limited partnership. An ownership arrangement involving one or more general partners and one or more limited partners. General partners assume full liability for debts of the partnership and exercise control over operations, while a limited partner's liability is limited to the extent of actual capital contribution to the partnership or additional liability voluntarily assumed.

linkages. Relationships requiring the movement of goods or people from one location to another.

linked sites. Sites that are interrelated by linkages; that is, related by the need to move goods or people from one site to the other.

liquidation damages. Monetary award specified in a contract to be awarded to the damaged party in the event of a breach by either party.

liquidity. Ability to convert an asset to cash without incurring loss.

loanable funds. Monies held by financial intermediaries in excess of required reserves; monies available to borrowers.

loan broker. Individual who places loans with primary lenders for a fee.

loan commitment. Obligation of a lender to provide specific funds at some future date.

Terms may be specified, or they may be those prevailing on the date funds are advanced.

loan origination fee. A charge by a lender, assessed at the time a loan commitment is made or at the time funds are advanced.

loan-to-value ratio. Relationship of debt funds to total project value, stated as a percentage.

locational advantages. Advantages, garnered by an occupant, due solely to the locational desirability of a site.

locational benefits. The benefits derived from the use of real estate that are properly attributable to the desirability of the site location.

longitudinal studies. Studies of relationships among variables, measuring changes in the variables through time. They involve repeated measures of the same phenomena to record any variation through time. Also called *time series studies.*

long run. Economic term used to describe the length of time necessary for the operation of market forces to produce equilibrium.

long-term capital gains. Term used in tax accounting to refer to gains realized on disposal of assets held for more than one year.

marginal benefits. Economic term used to describe the benefits derived from an additional unit of production. In a financial sense, it might be used to describe the financial rewards of additional investment.

marginal cost. Economic term used to describe the cost associated with production of each additional unit of a good or service.

marginal cost of capital. The cost of an additional dollar of new capital funds.

marginal cost of production. The cost of adding one more unit per period to one's rate of production.

marginal revenue. Economic term used to describe revenue derived from an additional unit of a good or service sold.

marginal utility. Satisfaction derived from the consumption of an additional unit of some economic good or service.

market. Institutional arrangement that facilitates the exchange of goods and/or services.

market data approach. One of the three traditional appraisal approaches. Produces an indication of value through the analysis of recent sales of similar properties.

market demand curve. Curve showing the amount of an economic good or service that will be demanded at various price levels. Demand curves are typically downward sloping, indicating that as price increases, demand decreases.

market price. Price that occurs as a result of a transaction in the marketplace. The price at which an economic good or service actually sells in the marketplace.

market rent. The rent a property would command on the open market if it were currently vacant and available.

market research. Activity undertaken to determine consumer attitudes; attempts to determine what consumers want, where they want it and how much they are willing to pay for it.

market simulation. An attempt to replicate the actions of buyers and sellers in the marketplace. In real estate it would be an attempt to estimate the outcome of a transaction involving real property by simulating the actions of "most probable" buyers and sellers.

market value. The price at which a property can be acquired on the open market in an arm's-length transaction under all conditions requisite to a fair sale. The generally accepted definition presumes that both buyer and seller act prudently and knowledgeably and that the price is not affected by undue stimulus experienced by either party.

materialmen. Suppliers of materials in connection with construction or improvements of real property.

materialman's lien. Claim arising from having supplied materials in connection with construction or improvement of real property.

mean. In statistics, the arithmetic average.

mechanic's lien. Lien securing a claim that stems from having provided services in connection with construction or improvement of a property.

metes and bounds. A method of delineating real property boundaries by reference to enduring landmarks.

microeconomic theory. Theory of small economic units. Generally referred to as the *theory of the firm.*

modified internal rate of return. A variant of the internal rate of return, intended to eliminate the multiple root problem by discounting all negative cash flows back to the time an investment commitment must be made and by compounding all positive cash flows forward to the end of the final year of the investment holding period. The modified internal rate of return is the discount rate that equates the present value of all negative cash flows with the future value of all positive cash flows.

modified pass-throughs. Government National Mortgage Association security backed by a pool of insured mortgage loans. A pro-rata share of the repayment of interest and principal is "passed through" to holders of the pass-through securities.

Modified Uniform Limited Partnership Act. A modified version of the Uniform Limited Partnership Act, which carefully specifies actions limited partners can take without endangering their limited liability.

monetary policy. Use of control over the money supply to stimulate or dampen economic growth.

monopolistic competition. A market arrangement where any number of competitors sell goods or services sufficiently differentiated that buyers will not be entirely indifferent among them, so that selection will be affected by elements other than price alone.

monopoly elements. A characteristic of a good or service that differentiates it from other goods or services and thereby makes the others less acceptable as substitutes.

monthly constant. The monthly debt service obligation expressed as a percentage of the amount borrowed.

mortgage. A document that pledges real estate as collateral for a loan.

mortgage-backed securities. Securities backed by real estate mortgages as collateral.

mortgage bankers. Individuals or firms that originate real estate loans. They may either hold such loans in their own investment portfolios or sell them in the secondary market.

mortgage commitment. Obligation on the part of a lender to provide funds at some future date. Loan terms may be either fixed or those that prevail at the time the funds are to be advanced.

mortgage correspondents. Individual mortgage bankers or brokers representing an institutional lender in a specified geographic location.

mortgagee. Party to whom real estate is pledged under the terms of a mortgage. Typically the lender in a real estate transaction.

mortgage participation certificates. A bond backed by real estate as collateral. Bondholders participate in the proceeds of a group of mortgages that back the certificates.

mortgage REIT. A real estate investment trust that invests primarily in real estate loans secured by first mortgages.

mortgage warehousing. The process of inventorying real estate loans. Mortgage bankers or brokers sometimes inventory loans while assembling pools of loans for subsequent transfer to larger institutional real estate lenders.

mortgagor. Party pledging real estate under the terms of a mortgage. Borrower who pledges real estate as collateral for a loan.

most fitting use. Real estate use that optimally reconciles all public and private interests.

most probable selling price. A probabilistic estimate of the price at which a future property transaction will occur; a prediction of the transaction price that will emerge if a property is offered for sale under current market conditions for a reasonable length of time at terms of sale currently predominant for such properties.

most probable use. Use to which a property is most likely to be put. Recognizes that use is not certain. Most probable use is that use having the highest probability of occurrence. Recognizes the possibility of other uses while assigning lower probabilities to them.

multiple nuclei. The theory that once a metropolitan area's major central business district is completely developed, a series of miniature central business districts will spring up throughout the metropolitan area.

multiple regression. Statistical technique used to measure the association between a dependent variable and multiple independent variables.

multiplicative law of probability. See joint probabilities.

natural price. Adam Smith's concept of long-run, market-determined price. Smith held that the price of all goods and services will, over the long run, equal the cost of production.

neighborhood. Sometimes referred to as a grouping of similar buildings, residents or business enterprises.

neighborhood influences. Factors influencing the desirability of a neighborhood. These include physical, economic and locational characteristics.

neighborhood shopping centers. Shopping centers that serve a trade area from which customers can commute by automobile within roughly five to ten minutes. Anchor tenants are usually food stores and drugstores, which may occupy a combined total area between 35,000 and 50,000 square feet.

net cash flow. Net monetary benefits an individual or group of individuals receive as a reward for committing funds to an enterprise. Net cash flow before taxes ignores the tax effect of investments, and net cash flow after taxes accounts for the tax effects of investment.

net income multiplier. (See also gross income multiplier and income multiplier analysis) Property market value expressed as a multiple of its net operating income.

net lease. Lease arrangement under which tenants are required to pay all property operating costs.

net operating expenses. Total expenses associated with the operations of a real estate project.

net operating income. Effective gross revenue minus operating expenses.

net present value. Current capital value of all the benefits of an investment, minus the required initial cash outlay.

nominal interest rates. Quoted cost of borrowing. Actual or effective interest rates may be substantially higher due to charges such as loan origination fees and the cost of maintaining required compensating balances.

normalized expenses. An appraisal term for the operating expenses of a property as they would occur in a typical year.

normalized net operating income. The net income figure that would result when a typical year's operating expenses were subtracted from a typical year's effective gross income.

obligee. Individual who makes a promise to pay a specified sum under the terms of a promissory note. Typically a borrower.

obligor. Individual to whom a promise is made to pay a specified sum under the terms of a promissory note. Typically a lender.

offering memorandum. A document intended to fully disclose the nature of a private offering of a security.

oligopoly. A market arrangement characterized by few producers, into which entry by new producers is extremely difficult.

operating expense ratio. Operating expenses expressed as a percentage of gross income. Sometimes called simply *operating ratio*.

operating expenses. Cash expenditures required to maintain property in sufficient condition to generate effective gross revenue.

operating ratio. See operating expense ratio.

operative words of conveyance. Words used to indicate the intention to transfer title to real property.

opportunity cost of capital. Forgone opportunity to earn interest on funds committed to other investments.

option agreement. An agreement giving one party the right to buy or sell an asset within a specified time period at a fixed or determinable price.

overall capitalization rate. Net operating income divided by a property's market value. Also called the *free and clear rate of return*.

partial release. A mortgage clause providing for segments of a property to be released after specified lump-sum payments on the loan. Typically used in subdivision and development financing.

partnership. An association of two or more people who join together to carry on a business for profit.

partnership agreement. Document that specifies the rights and responsibilities of individuals who join together to carry on a business for profit. May be oral, but is usually written.

party wall. An exterior wall common to two contiguous structures, each under different ownership.

passive activity. Any trade or business is a passive activity for a taxpayer who is not actively involved in operations on a "regular, continuous, and substantial (year-round) basis."

passive activity income. (See also passive activity) Income from passive trade or business activities. Income from passive activities can be used to offset losses from other passive activities. Any passive activity income not offset by losses is merged with taxable income from other sources.

passive activity losses. (See also passive activity) Losses from passive trade or business activities. Passive activity losses can generally be offset against only passive activity income. Any remaining passive activity losses, with certain important exceptions, must be carried over and applied against future years' passive activity income, even though a taxpayer may have substantial taxable income from nonpassive sources during the year of the loss.

pass-through certificates. Certificates backed by a pool of insured mortgages. Interest and principal collected is used to pay interest on the certificates as well as retire them.

payback period. The amount of time required for an investor to recover the capital committed to a venture.

payee. Individual to whom a promise has been made to repay a specified sum at some future date under the provisions of a promissory note.

percentage clause. Lease provision that specifies rental based on some base rate, plus a percentage of the tenant's gross sales.

percentage lease. Lease that provides for rental payments based upon the tenant's gross sales.

permanent loan. See end loan.

perpetuity. A never-ending stream of payments or receipts.

personal consumption expenditures. Economic term used to describe individual spending on such items as food, shelter and clothing.

personal property. Ownership interests in all properties other than real property. Examples include securities, partnership interest in a business and ownership of an automobile. Also called *personalty*.

personalty. See personal property.

physical deterioration. Term used by appraisers to describe any loss in value due to physical wear.

physical durability. Ability of a building to withstand physical wear and tear.

plat. Diagram of a proposed subdivision, showing the location of all streets, sites and easements.

police power. Power of a municipality to enforce laws designed to promote health, safety, morals and general welfare. Building codes, planning objectives and zoning ordinances are all enforced through the exercise of police power.

population. In statistics, the entire universe of data from which samples are drawn.

portfolio income. Income from interest, dividends, rents, royalties, gain from disposition of investment property, passive activity income that is treated as portfolio income under the phase-in rules of the Tax Reform Act of 1986 and income from a trade or business in which the taxpayer does not materially participate (unless the activity is a "passive activity" under the passive loss rules).

portfolio risk. Overall risk associated with ownership of a group of assets. Risks associated with one investment may decline when combined with another investment having offsetting risk patterns.

possibility of a reverter. Residual interest in a property that becomes effective when a life estate terminates.

potential gross income. The maximum amount of revenue a property would produce if fully rented at market rates.

potential gross rent. The amount of rental revenue a property would generate if there were no vacancies.

preliminary prospectus. Memorandum providing full disclosure of all items pertinent to a public security offering. A preliminary prospectus must be submitted to and approved by the Securities and Exchange Commission prior to any advertising of the offering.

prepaid interest. Interest paid prior to the date on which it is due. In real estate loans, prepaid interest is often deducted from the loan amount when funds are advanced.

prepayment clause. Typically a clause in a mortgage specifying penalties to be paid by the borrower in the event a loan is prepaid.

present value. The value today of anticipated future receipts or disbursements.

present value approach. Technique used to express anticipated future cash flows in terms of their current worth by adjusting for the opportunity cost of capital.

present value of an annuity. Present worth of a series of level payments received at even intervals. Current value reflects the compounded opportunity cost of capital.

price elasticity. A measure of the responsiveness of supply (price elasticity of supply) or demand (price elasticity of demand) to changes in price of a product or service.

price inelastic. (See also price elasticity) A market condition in which price reductions cause a decline in total revenue and price increases result in increased total revenue.

price makers. Economic units operating on a large enough scale to have some control over the price of their goods or services in the marketplace.

price searchers. Economic units that recognize that they cannot completely control the price at which goods are exchanged, but also understand that they do affect market prices. Price searchers must be constantly aware of the impact their pricing decisions will have on the decisions of competitors.

price takers. Economic units operating on such a small scale that they have no control over the price of their goods or services in the marketplace.

primary data. Data gathered by researchers specifically for the problem with which they are currently grappling.

primary mortgage markets. Markets in which real estate loans originate.

principal. In finance, the amount upon which interest liability is computed.

principal meridians. Imaginary lines extending north and south between the Earth's poles, used as reference lines in property surveys.

principle of substitution. Valuation principle stating that a person is not justified in paying more for a property than the cost to construct or acquire a substitute property.

private goods. Economic goods where consumption by one individual reduces the amount available for consumption by others.

private grants. Voluntary transfer of title to real property. These include transfer for consideration, gifts and bequests.

private offering. See private placement.

private placement. Sale of a securities offering to a small group as opposed to a public offering, where sale is advertised to the general public. Sometimes called a *private offering*.

private placement memorandum. Prospectus for a private placement. Does not have to be submitted for SEC approval, but must provide full disclosure.

probability. A measure of the chance of occurrence associated with any possible outcome.

probability distribution. An array of all possible outcomes and their related probabilities of occurrence.

probability of acceptance error. The probability that accepting a proposed investment will prove to have been a mistake.

processing costs. The cost of converting unfinished goods to finished goods.

product. (See also goods and services) The end result of the production process.

productivity. The ability of a property to generate utility, or want-satisfying power. A property's ability to command rent is a measure of its productivity.

profitability index. Measure of present value per dollar of cash outlay, calculated by dividing the present value of expected future cash flows by the initial cash outlay.

promissory note. Agreement containing promise to pay a specified sum at some specific future date.

property management. Overseeing the operations of real property for others. Includes renting space, collecting rentals, supervising maintenance, budgeting, etc.

prospectus. A document that fully discloses the nature of a securities offering.

public goods. Economic goods or services for which consumption by one individual does not reduce the amount available for consumption by others. Also called *collective goods*.

public infrastructure. In real estate, the systems used to deliver public services to a site. Includes streets, sidewalks, sewer pipes, water pipes, etc.

public issue. Securities issue offered for sale to the general public. Such an issue requires registration of a prospectus with the Securities and Exchange Commission. Also referred to as a *public offering*.

public offering. See public issue.

purchase-money mortgage. Mortgage given by a buyer to a seller to secure part payment of the purchase price. A purchase-money mortgage is typically recorded when deed is passed, establishing its precedence over all other claims.

purchase option. The right to purchase a property within a specified time and at a predetermined price.

pure profit. See economic rent.

quantity demanded. Amount of an economic

good or service purchasers will buy per period of time at a specific price.

quantity survey method. A technique used to estimate the cost of new real property improvements. Costs are estimated in the same way an architect or builder figures construction costs.

quarter sections. Squares resulting from the intersection of guide meridians and standard parallels are divided into 36 sections, each containing 640 acres. Sections are then divisible into four quarter sections containing 180 acres each.

quiet title suit. Suit filed by an adverse possessor to gain title to property by adverse possession.

quitclaim deed. A deed that purports to convey only those rights in a property that are possessed by the person making the conveyance, with no warrants that any such rights in fact exist.

radial/axial development. Theory of urban development based on the idea that businesses locate along major arterial streets, creating a radial or axial pattern of growth outward from the central business district.

real assets. Physical things with economic value, such as land, buildings, machinery, gold, antiques and so forth. In contrast with financial assets such as promissory notes, bonds and commercial paper, real assets tend to hold their value during periods of price inflation.

real estate investment. Acquiring an ownership or a leasehold interest in real property, with a profit motive.

real estate investment trusts (REITs). Untaxed corporate entities organized to pool the resources of individual investors for investment in real estate. Some REITs invest in mortgages while others take ownership positions.

real estate service. Benefits of use of real property. Real estate provides shelter and location for users.

Real Property Administrator (RPA). Professional designation conferred on property managers by the Building Owners and Managers Association International. Designation is a sign of professional achievement for those who

completely fulfill prescribed educational and experiential requirements.

recording statutes. Statutory provisions for permanent records of all transactions involving real property.

recovery property. Property subject to the cost recovery allowance provisions first introduced into the tax system by the 1981 revision of the Internal Revenue Code.

rectangular survey system. Use of a grid-type arrangement to identify land in a branch area by reference to a single geographic point.

redevelopment. Process of clearing older structures in an area and replacing them with new buildings.

red herring. Term sometimes used for a preliminary securities prospectus, which must be submitted to and approved by the Securities and Exchange Commission before any advertising is undertaken for a public issue.

redlining. Term used to describe the unwillingness of certain financial institutions to provide real property financing in certain areas; derived from the practice of delineating areas with red lines on city maps.

regional planning. Setting standards for the overall development of large geographical areas. Standards apply to land use, transportation systems, infrastructure, etc.

regional shopping center. A shopping center that draws the majority of its customers from a trade area extending from 15 to 30 minutes in driving time from the center. It may encompass 200,000 to 400,000 square feet of retail space and usually features one or two major department stores as anchor tenants.

registered historic district. Any area listed in the National Registry of Historic Places. Also includes any area so designated by appropriate state or local statute, provided that the Secretary of the Interior certifies that the statute will substantially achieve its purpose of preservation and rehabilitation and that the district meets substantially all the requirements for listing in the National Registry.

regression analysis. Statistical technique used

to measure the association among two or more variables.

Regulation B. Implementing regulation of the Federal Reserve to enforce provisions of the Equal Credit Opportunity Act enacted in 1974.

Regulation Z. Implementing regulation of the Federal Reserve to enforce provisions of the Truth-in-Lending Law enacted in 1969.

rehabilitation. Process of refurbishing older or physically deteriorated buildings for current use.

reliction. Recession of the water line of a lake or river resulting in the exposure of additional dry land.

remainderman. Individual possessing a remainder interest in real property. Remainder interest becomes operative upon expiration of a life estate.

remainders. (See also reversion) Residual interests that become effective when the life estate of another ends.

renegotiable rate mortgage. Mortgage with an interest rate subject to redetermination at fixed intervals, as specified in the body of the mortgage or the accompanying promissory note.

rent concessions. Agreements between landlord and tenant that reduce actual rental payments or receipts below those specified in a lease. A landlord might, for example, give one month's free occupancy, thereby reducing the effective rental rate over the entire occupancy period. Also simply called *concessions*.

rent escalator clauses. Lease provisions that require tenants to pay all operating expenses above amounts specified in their leases.

rent roll. A record of all tenants, showing the rent paid by each.

replacement cost. Appraisal term used to describe the cost of building a structure similar in utility to the one for which value is being estimated. Replacement cost assumes construction at current standards.

reproduction cost. Appraisal term used to describe the cost of building a structure identical to the one for which value is being estimated.

reservation. Clause used in a deed to withhold some portion of the grantor's property rights.

reserve for repairs and replacements. Appraisal adjustment used in the normalization of operating expenses to account for repairs or replacements that do not occur on an annual basis.

residential member (RM). Professional designation conferred by the American Institute of Real Estate Appraisers on individuals specializing in residential valuation. Designation signifies satisfaction of prescribed educational and experiential requirements.

residential specialists. Real estate brokers who concentrate on the sale of single-family detached dwellings, townhouses, condominiums or cooperatives.

residual capitalization. Appraisal technique that splits income between land and building. If building value is known, remaining income is capitalized to estimate land value, and if land value is known, remaining income is capitalized to estimate building value.

restrictive covenant. Promise to refrain from using land or buildings for purposes specified in the clause creating the covenant.

revenue bonds. Securities used to finance revenue-generating projects where the income produced by the undertaking will be used for interest payments and retirement of securities.

reversion. Term used to describe the interest of one who will receive title if a conditional fee is extinguished.

right of survivorship. (See also joint tenancy) A right unique to joint tenancy. Should one joint tenant die, his or her interest passes to the remaining joint tenants.

right to rescind. Right of an individual to terminate an agreement, returning all parties to the legal position or relationship existing prior to the agreement.

riparian lands. Lands abutting waterways or lakes. Title may extend to the water's edge or to the center of the water, depending on whether the waterway is navigable.

risk. Measurable likelihood of variance from an expected outcome. Risk is generally measured as variance or standard deviation.

risk-adjusted discount rate. A discount rate that includes the minimum acceptable yield on a riskless investment, plus a premium to compensate the investor for perceived risk associated with the venture under consideration.

risk averters. Refers to the economic concept that individuals prefer less risk to more at a given level of return. Most individuals avoid risk and will assume additional risk only if it is accompanied by expectations of additional return.

risk-free discount rate. Opportunity cost of capital based on riskless alternative investments.

risk premium. Incremental return necessary to induce investors to assume additional risk.

risk-reward indifference curve. A graphic representation of the relationship between perceived risk and acceptable rates of expected return where the investor will be equally satisfied by all risk-reward combinations.

r-square (r²). See coefficient of determination.

S corporation. See tax option corporation.

sample. A group of observations drawn from a larger body of data (called a *population* or *universe*) and thought to be representative of the larger body.

secondary data. Data employed in a research project that were previously gathered for some other purpose.

secondary financial markets. Markets comprised of arrangements for buying and selling existing financial instruments.

secondary mortgage market. A market in which existing mortgage notes are traded.

Section 1031 exchange. See like-kind exchange.

sector theory. A theory developed by Homer Hoyt and based upon the observation that successive waves of residential development within a given socioeconomic class tend to continue outward from the urban center in a wedge-shaped pattern.

seizin. A covenant found in a warranty deed whereby the grantor warrants that he or she does in fact possess the rights or interest being transferred.

senior mortgage. A mortgage that takes priority over all other mortgages.

Senior Real Estate Analyst (SREA). A professional designation awarded by the Society of Real Estate Appraisers.

Senior Real Property Appraiser (SRPA). A professional designation awarded by the Society of Real Estate Appraisers. The SRPA designation is awarded to commercial and industrial appraisers.

Senior Residential Appraiser (SRA). A professional designation awarded by the Society of Real Estate Appraisers.

sensitivity analysis. Financial analysis in which all variables but one are held constant and the result of a change in the remaining variable on the outcome is analyzed.

serial bonds. Secured debt instruments that are retired in the sequence of their individual serial numbers.

serial correlation. A measure of the extent to which causal factors influence outcomes over two or more time periods.

servient tenement. Land bearing the burden of an easement appurtenant.

shift in demand. The result of a shift in the relationship between price and quantity.

short-term capital gains. Taxable gains on the sale of capital assets that have been owned for one year or less.

simple linear regression. A statistical technique used to measure the association between two variables.

simulation. The construction of a model intended as a simplified representation of reality, within which the impact of various factors can be isolated and quantified.

sinking fund payments. Payments drawn from a fund set aside from the income of property that, with accrued interest, will eventually pay for replacement of the improvements.

sinking fund recapture technique. A recapture computation that involves computing the recapture rate such that the sum of recovered capital and compound interest thereon will, over the useful life of the wasting asset, accumulate an amount equal to its cost.

space-time. A four-dimensional concept combining the three dimensions of space with a fourth dimension of time. Real estate services are typically sold in space-time units.

special agent. One whose authority to act is limited to a particular job or a specific task. Typically, a real estate broker acts in the capacity of a special agent.

special assessment. A legal charge against real estate by a public authority in order to pay the cost of public improvements such as streetlights, sidewalks and other street improvements.

special warranty deed. A deed in which the grantor warrants or guarantees title only against defects arising during his or her ownership of the property and not against pre-existing defects.

specific asset syndication. A type of syndication where the promoter gains control of a property and then assembles a group of investors.

speculation. Assumption of business risk in hope of gain; purchase or sale of assets in hope of benefiting from market fluctuations.

speculative construction. A business strategy where a developer/builder starts construction before any homes are sold, in anticipation of sufficient market demand to render the project profitable.

spread. The difference between interest earned on mortgage loans and interest paid to depositors by financial intermediaries.

standard deviation. A measure of dispersion about the mean of a probability distribution, frequently employed as an indication of risk associated with an investment venture. The square root of the variance.

standard error of the forecast. The degree of confidence to be placed in a forecast value for a dependent variable. Conceptually similar to the same measure as calculated in simple linear regression.

standard metropolitan statistical area. A federally designated geographically described urban area with cohesive patterns of trade, communication, employment and transportation.

standard parallels. Imaginary lines running parallel with base lines (east-west lines) at 24-mile intervals, used as reference points in surveys employing the rectangular survey method.

standby financing. An arrangement where a lender agrees to keep a certain amount of money available to a prospective borrower for a specified period of time.

standby forward commitment. An agreement for future purchase of mortgage notes at yield rates specified in advance. These commitments are sold by and binding upon the Federal National Mortgage Association but are optional for holders of the commitments.

standby loan commitment. A binding option sold for a nonreturnable standby fee by a lender to a borrower, providing that the lender will loan a specific amount on stated terms to a borrower at any time within a stated future period. The borrower may or may not exercise the option.

statistical induction. Drawing conclusions about an underlying population from data contained in a sample.

statistical inference. Drawing conclusions about the future from a measured record of the past.

statutory exemption. The portion of income that is exempt from the alternative minimum tax.

statutory right of redemption. A statutory right granting a defaulting mortgagor an additional opportunity to recover foreclosed property. Limited in time by state statute.

straight-line method. A method of computing depreciation or cost recovery allowances whereby the allowance is claimed in equal annual increments.

strict foreclosure. Foreclosure accomplished by transferring a defaulting mortgagor's title directly to the mortgagee.

strong form efficiency hypothesis. See efficient markets.

subagent. One appointed by an agent to perform some duty, in whole or in part relating to the agency.

subcontractor. A person who contracts to do work for someone who has a larger contract to do the job. For example, electrical work on a new house might be done on a subcontract for the contractor who has overall responsibility for building the house.

subdivider. One who buys undeveloped acreage wholesale, segments it into smaller parcels and sells it retail.

subdivision. See land development.

subdivision controls. Regulations imposed by various levels of government to regulate or control subdivision operations.

subjective value. The value of an asset to the present owner or to a prospective purchaser. Similar to the economic concept of value in use.

subordination agreement. A clause in a mortgage or lease stating that the right of the holder shall be secondary or subordinate to a subsequent encumbrance.

subscription agreement. A document that specifies the relationship between limited partners and the sponsoring general partner in a limited partnership arrangement.

substitute basis. The initial tax basis of property acquired in a like-kind exchange. The substitute basis reflects any deferred gain or loss on the property tendered in the exchange.

summation technique. A method used for developing capitalization rates, based upon the idea that investors must be compensated to induce them to invest their wealth and that additional compensation is required for risk bearing and for illiquidity.

superregional shopping center. A shopping center that draws customers from an extremely wide geographical area and supports very large concentrations of retail facilities. Superregional centers frequently feature as much as 500,000 to 750,000 square feet of retail space. They may have as many as four major department stores as anchor tenants.

supply. The relationship between price and the quantity of a product suppliers place on the market during a specified time period, for all possible prices.

supply to sell. Desired decrease in a market participant's inventory of a product, at a specific price.

symmetric probability distribution. A probability distribution in which each side is a mirror image of the other.

syndicate. A group of two or more people united for the purpose of making and operating an investment. A syndicate may operate as a corporation, a general partnership or a limited partnership.

table of residuals. A listing of differences between actual values for a variable and those values predicted by a regression equation.

takeout loan. See end loan.

tax auction. A procedure for selling tax-delinquent land or real property where verbal or written offers are taken and the property is sold to the highest bidder.

tax basis. See initial tax basis.

tax conduit. A partnership characteristic whereby tax-deductible losses "pass through" the partnership "conduit" and are reported by each partner in accordance with his or her individual ownership interest in the partnership.

tax credits. Direct offsets against a taxpayer's income tax liability, provided as tax incentives to induce actions thought to be in the best interests of the nation.

tax deductions. (See also itemized deductions) Reductions in taxable income.

tax deed. A deed to property taken by government for nonpayment of taxes and resold at auction pursuant to law.

tax-deferred exchange. See like-kind exchange.

tax-free exchange. See like-kind exchange.

tax lien. A lien placed on a taxpayer's property by government for nonpayment of taxes.

tax option corporation. A qualifying corporation whose shareholders have elected to be taxed directly for their shares of corporate income, rather than having the corporation itself incur income tax liability. Provisions are found in Subchapter S of the Internal Revenue Code. Sometimes called an S corporation.

tax preference item. Tax deductions or exemptions that are added back to adjusted gross income for purposes of computing the alternative minimum tax liability.

tax schedule income. The amount of taxable income used as a reference for computing income tax liability when employing tax rate schedules provided by the Internal Revenue Service.

tax stops. Lease provisions that require tenants to pay all property taxes beyond some specified level.

technical analysis. Attempting to estimate future changes in market values by investigating the past market behavior.

tenancy at sufferance. Wrongful occupancy, which can be terminated by a property owner at any time.

tenancy at will. A tenancy stating no fixed period and that either landlord or tenant may terminate at any time, or in the time specified by statute, usually 30 days.

tenancy by the entirety. A type of joint tenancy that can exist only between spouses, in which wife and husband take conveyance of the tenancy interest in common, with that interest being treated as a single, indivisible unit and with the survivor continuing to hold the tenancy as a matter of right.

tenancy from period to period. A tenancy by one who holds a leasehold interest for an unstated period and pays rent each period, each payment serving as renewal for an additional period. This often results from the holding over of a previous specified-term tenancy on which rental was paid each period.

tenancy in common. Tenancy by two or more parties holding an interest in the same property, that interest being undivided, although not necessarily equal in each holder.

the Code. See Internal Revenue Code.

theorems. Fundamental mathematical rules from which various mathematical operations are derived.

time preference for money. Preference for more immediate rather than delayed receipt of funds, so that investment benefits are more valued the sooner they are received.

time series surveys. See longitudinal studies.

time value of money. See time preference for money.

title closing. The meeting of parties to a sales contract at a designated place and time for the purpose of executing the contract.

title defect. A possible legal difficulty that may limit the marketability of the title.

title insurance. Insurance against losses resulting from the passage of legally invalid title, issued by a title insurance company after a title search by that company has established that legally valid title exists in the seller, who then is able to pass that title to the insured.

title insurance policy. A contract wherein the title insurer agrees to indemnify the insured against losses resulting from imperfect title.

title search. A circumspect review of all documents and records in the recorder's office pertaining to a property to determine if the seller has good title to the property.

title transfer. To convey or relinquish title to another party.

Torrens system. A system of registering title to real property that accurately determines the ownership of land and every lien and claim upon it. Under this system, land title is registered in much the same way as is title to an automobile.

township. A six-mile-square area containing 36 sections, each one mile square, used in the rectangular survey system of land description.

trade area. The geographic area from which a store or shopping center draws the majority of its patronage.

transaction price. The price at which a transaction actually occurred; the outcome of a bargaining process between buyer and seller.

transaction range. The range of prices at which a transaction can occur between an owner and a prospective purchaser. The owner's subjective value determines the lower level of the transactions range; the prospective buyer's subjective value determines the upper level.

transactions balances. The quantity of money required to finance general business operations and satisfy day-to-day demands of householders.

transaction costs. Items such as brokerage fees, recording fees, transfer taxes and attorney's fees, incurred in connection with a real estate transaction.

transfer costs. (See also implicit transfer costs, explicit transfer costs) Costs of transportation between linked sites.

transport breakpoints. Points along major transportation routes where the mode of transport must change.

trust account. A bank account separate and apart and physically segregated from a broker's own funds, in which a broker is required by state law to deposit all monies collected for clients. Similar to an escrow or special account.

trust agreement. A document that sets forth terms of security arrangements and instructs the trustee in the event of default.

trust deed. See deed of trust.

trustee. The person in a trust relationship who holds property for the benefit of another person (the beneficiary).

trust indenture. See deed of trust.

Truth-in-Lending Law. One of a series of modern consumer protection acts, requiring lenders to fully disclose the rates of interest, other charges and all terms and conditions of each loan, in writing and clearly stated.

uncertainty. An environment holding an unknown number of possible outcomes, where there is no significant information about the relative chance of occurrence of each.

unfavorable financial leverage. Use of borrowed funds when their cost exceeds the rate of return on assets being financed.

Uniform Limited Partnership Act. A model law to govern creation and operation of limited partnership entities that has been enacted (in some cases, in substantially revised form) by every state except Louisiana.

unit-in-place method. A means of assessing replacement costs, in which an appraiser estimates the cost of building components separately, developing a unit cost for each and including overhead and profit allocation estimates as well as direct labor and materials cost, and then adds all costs together to reach total cost and thereby replacement cost.

universal agents. Agents who are empowered to perform all legal acts for their principals.

universe. In statistics, the entire population of data from which samples are drawn.

urban growth. An increase in the intensity of use of land resources. This may or may not entail an increase in population of an urban land area. It usually includes higher capital investment per unit of land employed and increased productivity associated with urban economic processes.

useful life. The period over which a property will benefit the owner's trade or business.

utility. An economic term for the want-satisfying power embodied in a good or service.

value in exchange. The value an asset can command in the marketplace.

value in use. The value of an asset to its owner or to a prospective owner.

variable rate mortgage. A financing instrument that permits the lender to alter the interest rate, with a certain period of advanced notice, based on a specific base index.

variance. A measure of dispersion of possible values about the midpoint of a probability distribution of possible outcomes, frequently employed as a measure of risk. The square of the standard deviation.

vendee. The purchaser of real estate under articles of agreement or a contract for deed.

vendor. The seller of real estate under articles of agreement or a contract for deed.

void. To have no force or effect; that which is unenforceable.

voidable. That which is capable of being adjudged void but is not void unless action is taken to make it so.

voluntary conveyance. Voluntary transfer by a defaulting mortgagor of the mortgaged property to the mortgagee, to avoid a foreclosure suit and a possible deficiency judgment.

warranty deed. A deed that contains a clause warranting that title to real property is clear and the property is unencumbered.

weighted average cost of capital. Capital cost computed by weighting the cost of each component in accordance with the proportion of total capital it comprises.

wholesale price index. An index of changes in the wholesale price of a representative "basket" of goods, referenced to a specified base period.

workers' compensation insurance. Insurance against claims for injuries sustained by employees.

wraparound lender. (See also wraparound mortgage) Assumes responsibility for meeting debt service obligations on the mortgage note that has been "wrapped."

wraparound mortgage. A mortgage subordinate to, but still including, the balance due on a pre-existing mortgage note, in addition to any amount to be disbursed on the new note. Also called an *all-inclusive mortgage*.

zoning ordinance. The fixing by government of geographic areas in which specified kinds of buildings and businesses may be developed.

zoning regulations. See zoning ordinance.

Index